FIFTH EDITION

Sport Marketing

Windy Dees, PhD
University of Miami

Patrick Walsh, PhD
Syracuse University

Chad McEvoy, EdD
Northern Illinois University

Stephen McKelvey, JD
University of Massachusetts Amherst

Originated By

Bernard J. Mullin, PhD
The Aspire Sport Marketing Group LLC

Stephen Hardy, PhD
University of New Hampshire, Professor Emeritus

William A. Sutton, EdD
University of South Florida, Professor Emeritus
Bill Sutton & Associates

HUMAN KINETICS

Library of Congress Cataloging-in-Publication Data

Names: Dees, Windy, 1977- author. | Walsh, Patrick, 1978- author. | McEvoy,
   Chad D., 1971- author. | McKelvey, Stephen, 1959- author. | Mullin,
   Bernard James, author. | Hardy, Stephen, 1948- author. | Sutton, William
   Anthony, 1951- author.
Title: Sport marketing / Windy Dees, PhD, University of Miami, Patrick
   Walsh, PhD, Syracuse University, Chad McEvoy, EdD, Northern Illinois
   University, Stephen McKelvey, JD, University of Massachusetts Amherst ;
   Originated by Bernard J. Mullin, PhD, The Aspire Sport Marketing Group
   LLC, Stephen Hardy, PhD, University of New Hampshire, Professor
   Emeritus, William A. Sutton, EdD, University of South Florida, Professor
   Emeritus, Bill Sutton & Associates.
Description: Fifth edition. | Champaign, IL : Human Kinetics, Inc., [2022]
   | Includes bibliographical references and index.
Identifiers: LCCN 2020034180 (print) | LCCN 2020034181 (ebook) | ISBN
   9781492594628 (paperback) | ISBN 9781492594635 (epub) | ISBN
   9781492594642 (pdf)
Subjects: LCSH: Sports--Marketing.
Classification: LCC GV716 .M85 2022 (print) | LCC GV716 (ebook) | DDC
   338.4/3796--dc23
LC record available at https://lccn.loc.gov/2020034180
LC ebook record available at https://lccn.loc.gov/2020034181

ISBN: 978-1-4925-9462-8 (paperback)
ISBN: 978-1-7182-0158-3 (loose-leaf)

The web addresses cited in this text were current as of September 2020, unless otherwise noted.

Acquisitions Editor: Andrew L. Tyler; **Developmental and Managing Editor:** Amanda S. Ewing; **Copyeditor:** Amy Pavelich; **Proofreader:** Leigh Keylock; **Indexer:** Kevin Campbell; **Permissions Manager:** Dalene Reeder; **Graphic Designer:** Denise Lowry; **Cover Designer:** Keri Evans; **Cover Design Specialist:** Susan Rothermel Allen; **Photograph (cover):** Clive Brunskill/Getty Images; **Photo Asset Manager:** Laura Fitch; **Photo Production Manager:** Jason Allen; **Senior Art Manager:** Kelly Hendren; **Illustrations:** © Human Kinetics, unless otherwise noted; **Printer:** Walsworth

Printed in the United States of America   10 9 8 7 6 5 4 3

The paper in this book was manufactured using responsible forestry methods.

Human Kinetics
1607 N. Market Street
Champaign, IL 61820
USA

United States and International
Website: **US.HumanKinetics.com**
Email: info@hkusa.com
Phone: 1-800-747-4457

Canada
Website: **Canada.HumanKinetics.com**
Email: info@hkcanada.com

E7990 (paperback) / E8243 (loose-leaf)

Tell us what you think!
Human Kinetics would love to hear what we
can do to improve the customer experience.
Use this QR code to take our brief survey.

Contents

Foreword

Transition is defined as "the process or period of changing from one state or condition to another." For the three of us, this text has been in transition since its earliest days in 1978 when Bernie started teaching the world's first class in sport marketing. Finding minimal literature or research on the topic, he pulled together whatever he could find and created the original manuscript in his graduate class at UMass. Over the course of 42 years, we have transitioned from one edition to the next, reflecting societal changes and advances. The first HK edition in 1993 was the first textbook in sport marketing. That same first edition had at its core a radical theory called the Escalator and promoted internal marketing via the building of a management information system (MIS), now called a master data management (MDM) system. This data-driven marketing approach was to be executed via outbound proactive phone sales, which was called *telemarketing* at the time and is now referred to as *fan relationship management*. That inaugural text was, of course, well before the Internet and cell phones. Subsequent transition editions were heavily affected by the introduction and adoption of sophisticated ticketing technology and fan engagement applications; the advancement of social media; the emergence of new sports and new leagues; the importance of content as a vehicle for marketing expression, especially video content; and on and on.

We are very proud of how our textbook has grown and the impact our writing has had throughout the world in helping to shape young minds eager to begin their careers. When Bernie and Bill worked at the NBA in the early to mid-2000s, the information in those previous editions helped shape team marketing at the NBA. Our time and experiences at the NBA and in subsequent industry positions heavily influenced the third and fourth editions. Our goal was always to produce a first-rate textbook that would be valuable both to students and practitioners—a reference book that would follow them from their classroom days to their offices. We feel that we have achieved and surpassed that goal in the United States and globally with special thanks to the true scholar among us—Steve, who ensured that everything was placed in its true historic context and logical sequence and, of course, provided academic rigor and accurate citations.

We were an interesting mix, all having worked in the industry and taught at the university level: Bernie was the academic-turned–sports executive, Steve was the researcher and stabilizing force in our efforts, and Bill was the pragmatist—walking the tightrope between the industry and academia. We have thoroughly enjoyed these past 42 years, but like everything else, our time has come and it's time to pass the baton.

Windy, Patrick, Chad, and Steve were selected based upon our recommendations to HK. They have our utmost confidence to produce a fifth edition that not only recognizes its roots in the past editions but also innovates and brings fresh and new perspectives for a transition edition that we have anxiously awaited. The new authorship team represents the best and brightest of the sport marketing academic community while still having experience working in the industry. We are excited that they were eager to take the baton from us and continue the popularity and success of this textbook. We know this text will continue to be of great value in preparing the next generation of sport marketers.

As Bruce Hornsby sings in "Swan Song," *it's been a good long run*. It really has, but our marathon has come to a close. We have new authors who now enter the race and will take it from here.

Enjoy the text and your sport marketing class, whether it be in the classroom or online.

All the best,
Bernie, Steve, and Bill

Preface

The sport marketing industry is vast and rapidly evolving. Technology and communications are at the heart of sport marketing, and both fields experience change almost daily. The tools, technology, and platforms that sport marketers have at their disposal to disseminate information can be both a blessing and a curse. There are more ways than ever to communicate and engage with sports fans, but this explosion of communication channels means marketing professionals have to be knowledgeable, adaptable, and highly skilled more than ever. It also means that fan bases are more fragmented, and finding and interacting with your fans takes better strategy and execution. Therefore, contemporary sport marketing requires continuous education on the part of executives and professionals working in the field to keep pace with the ever-changing wants, needs, and communication styles of today's sport consumers.

Sport Marketing, Fifth Edition, is designed to help students at multiple levels prepare for careers in the fast-paced world of sport marketing, as well as provide a resource for practitioners looking for the latest information in the field. The new edition blends theory, research, and practical examples into an easy-to-read format and imparts the latest data available on a multitude of sport marketing topics. Despite the continued growth and changes of the industry since 2010, marketers have adapted. Practitioners throughout the sport world stay connected to the industry and get the latest news, information, and data through reputable trade publications and media outlets, such as the *Street & Smith's Sports Business Journal*, *Front Office Sports*, *Sport Techie*, *Sport Business*, and *IEG*, just to name a few. Many of these valuable resources are cited throughout the text. While traditional outlets and Internet-based sources are still reputable and reliable, sport marketers also employ digital and social technologies to gather and dispense information. We have incorporated many of the latest marketing methods in this edition, but new products and services are emerging daily.

The field of sport marketing has shifted dramatically since the last edition of the text, but one constant has remained: The competition for the sport and entertainment dollar is as fierce as ever. Sport marketing is a competitive business whose front office requires as much strategy, risk, discipline, and energy as that shown by the players and coaches who figure so prominently in the public's imagination. The fifth edition of *Sport Marketing* offers abundant examples of the latest issues in the competitive marketplace.

We have tried to balance theoretical models with case studies from the rinks, fields, courts, slopes, gyms, tracks, and other venues that make up the sport marketplace. If theory is the skeleton that gives structure to thinking, then case studies put meat on the bones. Most of our examples in the previous editions were from the United States, but in updating this edition we have added considerable material from sports in other countries and cultures, and we have done our best to highlight sport forms that have historically received less media and academic attention. Many industry professionals with diverse backgrounds, knowledge, and experience have contributed sidebars and other chapter content. Their job titles and affiliations are current as of the first printing of this edition. We believe the content and context from a multitude of academicians and industry professionals only enhances the value of the textbook and provides better preparation for the next generation of sport marketers.

Readers of past editions will find both continuity and change in this book. Chapters 1 through 3 provide an overview of the sport market and sport marketing as an area of study and as a process. Chapters 4 and 5 consider conceptual tools and steps of preliminary market research and market segmentation, which are critical to overcoming a tendency to equate promotions with marketing. Chapters 6 through 13 explore the nuts and bolts of marketing plans—the five Ps of sport marketing: product, price, promotion, place, and public relations. But these Ps are conceptually robust, so readers will note special chapters or chapter sections on branding, sales and service, engagement and activation, community relations, and social media. The last two chapters offer some important elements on legal issues and future projections. The book is filled with fantastic content written by prominent industry executives and academic leaders. We thank them all for their timely and significant contributions.

Sport Marketing, Fifth Edition, has undergone a complete overhaul, and the result is a contemporary resource with the latest theories, data, industry examples, and unique sidebars. The theoretical and conceptual foundations have been updated to reflect the most advanced approaches to marketing management and strategy. A greater focus on data and analytics is provided, and there are specific examples of how sport organizations use marketing research to make better informed business decisions. An expanded discussion on vital topics like branding and sponsorship with detailed sections on athlete endorsement and activation is included. The ticketing and sales topics have delved deeper into the secondary market with a focus on the consumer's desire for a unified sport and entertainment marketplace. The frequency escalator has been replaced with the frequency elevator to depict the transformation of the sales process and how sport brands build fluid relationships with fans over time. We discuss advancements in advertising and promotions and how these strategies and tactics support sport sales and influence fan loyalty. We cover the explosion of digital and social platforms in great depth with explanations on how these critical communication channels drive sport marketing strategy and execution. We also detail how the shift from more traditional forms of communication to a reliance on digital and social media has affected areas like advertising, branding, sponsorship, and public and community relations. We explore current trends in venue design, seating, and experiences, as many new and renovated facilities have changed the game of sport marketing. We examine all of the new legislation affecting the sport industry and marketing professionals, including the legalization of sports

gambling. The textbook once again concludes with a look into the crystal ball to see what the future holds for sport marketing professionals over the next 5 to 10 years.

The world of sport marketing continues to challenge and excite us. We only hope that this edition is as enjoyable to read as it was to write.

Student Resources in HK*Propel*

HK*Propel* gives students the opportunity to listen to sport industry leaders talk about how they incorporate marketing strategies into their daily work through exclusive video clips produced by David Perricone, who has experience as an academic and a practitioner. We built activities around these video clips, asking students to do what these industry experts already do: integrate core concepts and strategies from the textbook into applied situations. A fresh, sleek, and user-friendly digital platform allows students to seamlessly navigate the media pieces and study tools provided. The activities included are designed to help students think critically and creatively while immersing them in practical examples and industry-focused content.

Besides the video-based exercises, web search activities allow students to assess and compare strategies that can be found on sport organization websites, YouTube, and other digital and social platforms. These activities ensure that students will have even more opportunities to engage in the material found in these pages. Finally, flash card activities allow students to test their knowledge of the book's glossary terms.

Instructor Resources in HK*Propel*

A variety of instructor resources are available online within the instructor pack in HK*Propel*:

- *Presentation package*—The presentation package includes more than 300 slides that cover the key points from the text, including select figures and tables. Instructors can easily add new slides to the presentation package to suit their needs.

- *Image bank*—The image bank includes most of the figures and tables from the book, separated by chapter. These items can be added to the presentation package, student handouts, and so on.
- *Instructor guide*—The instructor guide includes a sample syllabus and ideas for semester-long activities and case studies. Individual chapter-by-chapter files include a chapter summary, chapter objectives, chapter outline, and classroom ideas, which include the suggestion of case studies from the online journal *Case Studies in Sport Management*.
- *Test package*—The test package includes 300 questions in true-false, multiple-choice, fill-in-the-blank, and short-answer for- mats. These questions are available in mul- tiple formats for a variety of instructor uses and can be used to create tests and quizzes to measure student understanding.
- *Chapter quizzes*—These LMS-compatible, ready-made quizzes can be used to mea- sure student learning of the most import- ant concepts for each chapter. 10 questions per chapter are included in true-false and multiple-choice formats.

Instructor ancillaries are free to adopting instructors, including an ebook version of the text that allows instructors to add highlights, annotations, and bookmarks. Please contact your Sales Manager for details about how to access instructor resources in HK*Propel*.

Chapter 1

The Special Nature of Sport Marketing

OBJECTIVES

- To understand the market forces that create the need for contemporary marketing strategies in the sport industry

- To understand marketing myopia and other obstacles to successful marketing strategy

- To recognize the components of the sport product and the sport industry

- To recognize the factors that demand a different approach to the marketing of sport

Jose Breton/NurPhoto via Getty Images

1

After dominating and winning the 2019 Women's World Cup in France, team leader and media darling Megan Rapinoe quoted lyrics from deceased rapper Nipsey Hussle's track, "Hussle & Motivate," to summarize her journey to the championship podium—the gist being that she respected the game and now her name is widely recognized.[1]

Social Media

Rapinoe and teammate Alex Morgan were the faces of the U.S. Women's National Team (USWNT), but Rapinoe and her brightly colored hair and dynamic personality, along with her performance, captivated the world. According to Hookit data provided by SportsPro, the U.S. forward used the World Cup platform to increase her social media following by more than 50 percent.[1] Her presence on social media was prominent, not only during the event but also throughout the team's celebratory tour.

Social media growth for any athlete helps sponsors achieve more recognition. For female athletes, though, who receive so little media coverage, a prominent social media presence is vitally important to attract and retain sponsors. Rapinoe not only added many more followers but also generated high levels of engagement with her promoted posts during the World Cup. Hookit also reported that she garnered the most views of any USWNT player with her video content. She racked up over 1.1 million more views than the next closest player, Alex Morgan.

Megan Rapinoe's "open arms" and Alex Morgan's "sipping tea" celebrations were main reasons why the two stars were the most mentioned athletes of the global competition. The U.S. team's battle for equality also took center stage as it began to close in on the title during the championship game. Social media posts on Twitter went viral referencing #EqualPay in support of female soccer players earning the same salaries as their male counterparts who had seen considerably less success. The individual star players, and the USWNT team as a whole, captivated fans on social media around the world for the duration of the tournament.

Attendance

In terms of attendance for the 2019 Women's World Cup, FIFA reported that 1.13 million tickets were sold and the average attendance for a match was 21,756. All games for France, the host country's team, were sellouts; so was the final match. Previous average attendance was 26,029 in Canada, 37,218 in China, and 26,430 in Germany.[1] Even with a lack of significant marketing efforts for matches in many cities around France in 2019, there was clearly demand for women's world-class soccer regardless of the teams playing.

Ticket prices for the Women's World Cup started at €9 and were priced at €84 for the championship game. In comparison, according to SportsPro, the cheapest group stage ticket at the 2018 Men's World Cup in Russia was €90.[1] Therefore, the women's event provided great value, and any matches with low attendance were likely due to lack of marketing support versus ticket pricing. For example, only the major games were broadcast on free-to-air television stations, so the lesser matchups may not have been heavily promoted. This was clearly a missed marketing opportunity for a mega sports event.

Viewership

Media numbers for the 2019 Women's World Cup were strong despite the time difference between North America and France. The final game viewership numbers were down slightly from the previous edition, but when the United States took on host country France in the quarterfinals, viewership peaked at 8.24 million. That was a 7 percent increase over the 2015 championship game when the United States triumphed over China.[1]

In 2019, France added 25 new broadcasters for the tournament for a total of 62, and the games were presented in more than 200 countries around the globe. Total viewership worldwide surpassed one billion according to FIFA. In the United Kingdom, a soccer-crazed country, fans tuned in in huge numbers (28.1 million), with the majority (62 percent) being male. When England was knocked out of the semifinals by the United States, over 11 million people watched. It was the most-watched broadcast in the nation the entire year. For the Brazil-France matchup, more than 35 million Brazilians and 10 million French fans tuned in to the game, making it the most-watched women's soccer match ever.[1] The media success of the Women's World Cup demonstrated that women's sports are desirable and profitable, and men tune in as much as or more than women.

Branding

Brands marketing during the 2019 Women's World Cup challenged each other for the attention of global soccer fans. Adidas and Nike went head-to-head on social media, but Nike came out the clear winner. Hookit data provided by SportsPro had Adidas making 535 promoted posts to Nike's 449 posts. However, the engagement rates were an average of 7,844 for Adidas compared to a whopping 36,735 for Nike. Part of the reason for Nike's success was the status of the brand as the official kit supplier for 14 out of the 24 teams.[1] Nike also sold out almost immediately of the USWNT jersey. It became Nike's most popular jersey ever, for both men and women, in one season. The success of the team and continued demand for the jersey after the championship gave Nike plenty of marketing material to build on once the tournament concluded. Other major brands that experienced social media and marketing success through engaging with women's soccer fans were Hulu and Anheuser-Busch. As a marketing platform, women's professional soccer delivered as brands generated tens of millions of total engagements throughout the tournament with fans worldwide.

While the data for the 2019 Women's World Cup would suggest that the event delivered in the way of social media, attendance, viewership, and branding, the compensation of the players tarnished the overall tournament image. It became evident over the course of the month that the women make far less money than the men despite training and competing equally. For the USWNT, its winning bonuses had to be supplemented by $31,000 per player to be in line with the men's bonuses. This money came in the form of a donation by LunaBar to help the women's equal pay cause.[1] Without sponsorship support and brands stepping up to bridge the gender pay gap, even the most decorated women's professional soccer team in the world, the USWNT, would not come close to earning what the male professional soccer team earns. This is why stars like Megan Rapinoe and Alex Morgan use their platform to speak out on the pay gap issue and push for women's sports, not just women's soccer, to get more media coverage. With more media coverage comes more marketing opportunities, and with more marketing comes more money. Everything begins and ends with exposure.

The 2019 Women's World Cup put women's sports on the big stage once again, and marketers paid handsomely to be a part of it. The female athletes delivered talent, performance, and passion, and their efforts helped brands communicate their marketing messages globally to consumers. The USWNT showed sport organizations that women's soccer can be more successful than men's and that success, no matter what gender has it, will drive more business for brands if they are willing to come along for the ride.

While sports have always had the power to bring people together, the global nature of the sport industry has exploded since 2000. Technology, and its impact on all forms of marketing communication, has created an almost endless amount of opportunity to promote sports worldwide and an equal amount of demand for consumption. The vast international support for the 2019 Women's World Cup and its athletes demonstrates just how much sport marketing has advanced and affected the industry since the 1999 World Cup in the United States. While the 1999 Women's World Cup was considered a watershed moment in terms of generating interest and participation in women's soccer in the United States, the 2019 event was historical from a digital and social standpoint. The USWNT was referred to as a "commercial behemoth" due to the massive fan engagement and merchandising opportunities that followed them.[1] The interest in the World Cup teams, the information communicated about the tournament, the increased followings on social media, the distribution of content around the world, and the revenue generated from the mega-event would not have been possible without substantial innovations in sport marketing.

Although entrepreneurs have been selling sport for centuries, strategic and integrated marketing communication systems in sport are relatively new, and they are generating growth in the industry at a rapid pace. In this chapter, we discuss the importance of learning and employing these modern marketing principles in the sport domain. We examine current industry trends in growth, competition, and revenue that heighten the need for continued scientific, professional approaches to sport marketing. We first consider examples of lingering marketing myopia, as well as significant progress. Next, we consider the components of the sport product and the sport industry. Finally, we outline the numerous features that in combination make sport marketing unique.

Sport Marketing Then and Now

If you attend any professional or even intercollegiate sports event in the United States, you will likely purchase your ticket online, sit in a state-of-the-art arena or stadium with Wi-Fi access, and enjoy an array of physical and technological amenities that create a comfortable and exciting experience. As sport has globalized and other countries have adopted the commercialized American model, large-scale sports events have become commonplace around the world. This can be seen in the capacities of stadiums like Rungrado 1st of May Stadium in Pyongyang, North Korea (114,000), Melbourne Cricket Ground in Melbourne, Australia (100,024), and Camp Nou in Barcelona, Spain (99,354).[2]

The sport industry is vast, complex, and lucrative, but that was not always the case. In the late 1800s and early 1900s, when sport only existed as a form of leisure in the United States, the idea of promoting sport as a commercial occupation was uncertain. Many questions surrounded this idea of sport as a business endeavor:

- Would recreational activities and games be of widespread interest to the public?
- Would people in their spare time pay money to watch others compete?
- Would businesses financially support local teams, and if so, could the investment be used to capture the interest of their constituents?

Over the next 100 years, sport grew from fledgling production to global enterprise, and sport continues to gain momentum, particularly as other countries see the social and economic benefits the sport industry brings to society.

Marketing has been a driving force behind the growth of commercialized sport since its inception. Advertisers sensed the value that sport could deliver based on the amount of interest it garnered and the fandom that existed even in its infancy. As early as the 1870s, tobacco cards—small inserts that featured popular baseball players—were used to sell cigarettes. This was one of the first known forms of sport marketing whereby a company used sports figures to help promote its products. The strategy was used to sell more cigarettes and increase loyalty to the brand. The tobacco cards evolved into the bubble gum baseball cards that became popular collector's items.[3]

In the early 1900s, the sport of baseball was extremely popular, and Honus Wagner was a major star. He is still considered by some to be

Bruce Bennett Studios via Getty Images Studios/Getty Images

Honus Wagner was the first known athlete endorser. He was paid by Louisville Slugger to allow the company to sell his signed baseball bats.

the best shortstop in baseball history. At the time, Louisville Slugger, a baseball bat manufacturer, engraved the name of the company and the player on each bat so players could distinguish their equipment from one another. In 1905, due to Wagner's success and popularity, Louisville Slugger requested permission to sell Wagner-signed bats in stores in return for compensation. This was the first paid athlete endorsement.[4]

Seven years after Honus Wagner helped sell the first endorsed sport product in stores, the first professional baseball stadium, Fenway Park, was constructed in 1912. The era of professional sport stadiums brought with it another unique form of sport marketing called stadium signage. As fans packed baseball stadiums to watch the best players compete, businesses harnessed fans' attention with branding and advertising in the ballparks. Advertising in and around sports stadiums today is expansive and remains an effective marketing tool for companies targeting sports fans and spectators. Stadium naming rights and corporate sponsorships also provide significant financial support for the construction of new and renovated facilities by sport organizations. In chapter 10, we go into great detail regarding how sponsorship works and discuss the value of naming rights. Table 1.1 lists the biggest naming-rights deals.[5]

TABLE 1.1   Largest Naming-Rights Deals

Facility	Total price (US$)	Deal length
Scotiabank Arena	$639 million	2017-2038
MetLife Stadium	$425-$625 million	2010-2036
Chase Center	$300-$400 million	2016-2040
Citi Field	$400 million	2006-2028
Mercedes-Benz Stadium	$324 million	2015-2043
NRG Stadium	$310 million	2000-2032
SunTrust Park	$250 million	2014-2042
Hard Rock Stadium	$250 million	2016-2034
Levi's Stadium	$220.3 million	2013-2033
US Bank Stadium	$220 million	2015-2041
FedEx Field	$205 million	1999-2025
Barclays Center	$200 million	2007-2032
American Airlines Center	$195 million	1999-2030
Philips Arena	$185 million	1999-2019
Minute Maid Park	$178 million	2002-2029
University of Phoenix Stadium	$154.5 million	2006-2025
Bank of America Stadium	$140 million	2004-2023
Lincoln Financial Field	$139.6 million	2002-2022
Little Caesars Arena	$125 million	2016-2036
Lucas Oil Stadium	$121.5 million	2006-2027

Data from "Top Naming-Rights Deals," *Sports Business Journal* (2018). www.sportsbusinessdaily.com/Journal/Issues/2018/04/30/Marketing-and-Sponsorship/Naming-rights-deals.aspx

One of the most common and comical sights at major sports events is the flying of blimps high above the action. Blimps provide panoramic views of the environment and have become staples at large-scale competitions. In 1925, Goodyear Tire and Rubber Company built the very first blimp, dubbed "The Pilgrim." It not only provided aerial shots of an event but also advertised products and provided public service announcements to attendees. Although most people still refer to the airship as the "Goodyear Blimp," other companies, like MetLife, have been providers of the aerial coverage of sports events. Branding on blimps was a major milestone in the history of sport marketing, and less than a decade later, another iconic advertisement emerged: the Wheaties Box. General Mills featured Lou Gehrig on the cereal box in January 1934 in order to sell more of the breakfast staple (better known as "the breakfast of champions"), and the most famous athletes have adorned Wheaties boxes ever since.

One of the most important dates in sports history is May 17, 1939, when the first ever game was broadcast on television. NBC aired a college baseball game between the Columbia Lions and Princeton Tigers, and the sports media industry that we have come to know today was born. Sports events have been, and continue to be, some of the most popular shows watched on television. In addition, televised sports events bring in tremendous amounts of advertising dollars due to high viewership and ratings. The sport of baseball was also responsible for giving women professional sport league opportunities for the first time. During World War II when many MLB players were serving overseas, the All-American Girls Professional Baseball League (AAGPBL) was established by Philip Wrigley, the owner of the Chicago Cubs. The league operated for 12 years and was designed to keep major league ballparks full, and interest peaked despite male players being absent from the game. Over 600 female athletes played in the AAGPBL from 1943 to 1954, and it was the inspiration for the famous sports movie *A League of Their Own*.[6]

By the 1950s, the power of sport marketing and the revenue to be gained in this area was becoming more apparent. A watershed moment came when the St. Louis Cardinals baseball franchise offered to sell the naming rights for Sportsman's Park to local brewery Anheuser-Busch. The ballpark was renamed Busch Stadium and the era of commercialized sport venues began. Although fans were dismayed at the transition of their beloved, historic ballpark names to corporate brands, the money that began to flow through professional sports and improve the games eventually quieted the crowds. Today, very few stadiums and arenas still have their original monikers because the financial upside of naming rights to teams has become too advantageous. Wrigley Field and Fenway Park are two such stadiums that still have their original names.

An entirely new era of sport marketing began in 1964 when Phil Knight and Bill Bowerman founded Blue Ribbon Sports, now known as Nike. Phil Knight went from selling track shoes out of the back of his car to running a sports apparel empire that totally transformed how sport brands do business. The sidebar How Nike Changed Sport Marketing Forever tells the story of how Phil Knight, Michael Jordan, and the Swoosh became iconic and changed sport marketing forever.

Blue Ribbon Sports rebranded as Nike in 1972. Seven years later, another historic sport brand was born: ESPN. Entertainment and Sports Programming Network (ESPN), now owned by The Walt Disney Company, launched on September 7, 1979, and became the very first station presenting "All sports, all the time." Today, "The Worldwide Leader in Sports" includes nine domestic cable networks: ESPN, ESPN2, ESPNEWS, ESPNU, ESPN Classic, ESPN Deportes, SEC Network, ACC Network, and Longhorn Network. According

How Nike Changed Sport Marketing Forever

The story of Phil Knight and Nike is one of innovation, entrepreneurship, and decades of hard work. Phil Knight was on the track team at the University of Oregon and was passionate about running, as was his track coach, Bill Bowerman. After Knight graduated from Oregon, he completed an MBA at Stanford University and had aspirations of starting his own business. Bowerman, who was fascinated with designing track shoes, joined forces with Knight and started Blue Ribbon Sports in 1964.[9] The company, in its earliest days, was buying inexpensive track shoes from a supplier in Japan, and Phil Knight was selling them out of the back of his car around Eugene, Oregon. Even while running the start-up, Bowerman continued testing new track shoe technology by stamping a waffle-like pattern on the soles of the shoes to add greater traction. The adaptation was a success. In 1971, the "Waffle Trainer" became known as the Tiger Cortez, and Blue Ribbon Sports rebranded as Nike.

Knight and Bowerman changed the company name to Nike, after the Greek goddess of victory, but they did not have a logo. With little money for marketing, they hired a graphic design student (for only US$35!) to draft logo options, and they settled on the "Swoosh." Although Knight admits he chose the design he disliked the least, the iconic Swoosh became a globally recognized symbol. In the late 1970s, Nike patented its Air sole technology that became an incredible success and led to the company going public with an IPO in 1980 that generated US$178 million. The company took another big risk that paid off tremendously in 1984 when they signed an endorsement deal with rookie NBA player Michael Jordan.

> continued

> continued

They signed Jordan for a mere US$500,000 per year for five years to promote the Air Jordan basketball shoe, and the rest, as they say, was history.[9]

The following is a time line of Nike's aggressive marketing strategy over the next 20 years, which catapulted the company into the upper echelon of global brands and cemented its status as the leading sport apparel company in the world:[9]

Michael Jordan wearing his Air Jordan signature basketball shoe in 1985.

1987. Nike drops ad for new Air Max shoes set to The Beatles' "Revolution," making it the first ad to use the band's music.

1988. First "Just Do It" campaign launches with ad featuring 80-year-old running icon Walter Stack running across the Golden Gate Bridge.

1989. "Bo Knows" ad campaign drops featuring baseball and football star Bo Jackson.

1990. First Niketown store opens in Portland, Oregon.

1991. Activist Jeff Ballinger publishes report exposing low wages and poor working conditions among Indonesian Nike factories. Nike responds by instating its first factory codes of conduct.

1996. Nike signs Tiger Woods.

1998. In the face of widespread protest, Nike raises the minimum age of its workers, increases monitoring, and adopts U.S. OSHA clean-air standards in overseas factories.

1999. Nike co-founder Bill Bowerman dies at 88.

2002. Nike acquires surf-apparel company Hurley.

2003. Nike signs LeBron James and Kobe Bryant.

2004. Nike acquires Converse for US$309 million.

2004. Phil Knight steps down as CEO and president of Nike but retains chairman role as William D. Perez becomes the company's new CEO.

2008. Nike signs Derek Jeter.

2012. Nike becomes official supplier for NFL apparel.

2015. Nike becomes official supplier for NBA apparel.

2018. Nike unveils ad campaign featuring athlete and political activist Colin Kaepernick, garnering a mix of public approval and backlash.

TABLE 1.2 North American Sport Market by Segment 2014 to 2023

	US$ millions										
	2014	2015	2016	2017	2018	2019	2020	2021	2022	2023	CAGR
Media rights	14,595	16,305	18,372	19,073	20,138	20,910	21,708	22,597	23,862	25,257	4.6%
Gate revenues	17,448	17,963	18,649	19,015	19,189	19,551	20,203	20,763	21,255	21,763	2.5%
Sponsorship	14,689	15,481	16,301	16,658	17,169	17,865	18,892	19,439	20,129	20,648	3.8%
Merchandising	13,493	13,806	13,966	14,390	14,565	14,714	14,906	15,080	15,258	15,426	1.2%
Total	60,225	63,555	67,288	69,136	71,061	73,040	75,709	77,879	80,504	83,104	3.2%

CAGR = compound annual growth rate

Reprinted by permission from PwC Outlook, *At the Gate and Beyond.* 2019. www.pwc.com/us/en/industries/tmt/assets/pwc-sports-outlook-2019.pdf

to ESPN, the company is "the leading multinational, multimedia sports entertainment entity featuring the broadest portfolio of multimedia sports assets with over 50 business entities. In 2019, ESPN will have presented 24,749 live events and 83,340 total live hours of studio and event programming—TV and digital combined."[7]

It is no wonder that in the same year, 1979, the term *sport marketing* was coined by *Advertising Age* to describe the activities of consumer and industrial product and service marketers who were increasingly using sport as a promotional vehicle. Since that time, fans have seen sport images and personalities used to sell beer, cars, insurance, and an almost unlimited range of other products.[8]

From the 1980s on, the sport industry exploded, and marketers have been at the heart of its expansion. The 1980s brought jumbotrons, the 1990s delivered the World Wide Web, and the 2000s ushered in social media. All these technological and digital advancements revolutionized how marketers promoted sports both domestically and globally. Today, the sport industry is immense, and the United States is at the forefront of marketing sports around the globe.

The Sport Industry

Economists and journalists have occasionally cobbled together estimates on the size of the U.S. sport industry. Unfortunately, each study has employed different methods and different assumptions. Consequently, we have no longitudinal data tracking sport industry growth over time, using generally agreed-upon methods. In any case, one must recognize that the sport industry, by any calculation, is a small piece of the economic pie. For instance, one report, the Sports Outlook by PwC, provides data on the size of the sport marketing industry as well as five-year projections forecasting the future of the field. Table 1.2 displays 10 years of data on the North American sport market by segment from 2014 to 2023. The report breaks down the sport marketing industry into four main revenue-generating categories:[10]

1. Media rights are fees paid to show sports events on broadcast and cable television networks, television stations, terrestrial radio, satellite radio, the Internet, and mobile devices.

2. Gate revenues are primary market ticket sales for live sports events. Nonrecurring seat premiums and license costs are not included.

3. Sponsorship is fees paid to have a brand associated with a team, league, facility, or event, including naming and category rights.

4. Merchandising is the sale of licensed products with team and league logos, player likenesses, and other intellectual property. Food concession revenues are not included.

The 2019 PwC Sports Outlook data from 2014 to 2023 reveals that the overall sport marketing industry was valued at US$60.2 billion in 2014 and is projected to grow to US$83.1 billion by 2023. What is driving that growth, and will it continue for the foreseeable future? In order to answer these questions, let's examine each category more closely.

Media Rights

In 2017, media rights became the largest category in the sport marketing industry due to the increasing fees media companies were paying to purchase sports content. During a five-year span from 2019 to 2023, four of the five U.S. professional sport leagues will renegotiate rights fees: National Football League (NFL), Major League Baseball (MLB), National Hockey League (NHL), and Major League Soccer (MLS). The National Basketball Association (NBA) is set to renegotiate its deal in 2024. Here are the professional sport leagues' media rights fees through 2022:[11]

- NFL: US$27 billion (from Fox, CBS, NBC, ESPN)
- NBA: US$24 billion (from ABC, ESPN, TNT)
- MLB: US$12.4 billion (from Fox, TBS, ESPN)
- NHL: US$5.2 billion (from Rogers in Canada) and US$2 billion (from NBC, Versus)
- MLS: US$600 million (ESPN, Fox Sports)

The escalating prices being paid for media rights will likely continue to fuel the growth of sport marketing as more content than ever is being produced for platforms such as digital, social, and mobile.

Gate Revenues

Although attendance at many live sports events is declining, gate revenues from ticket sales are expected to grow slightly from US$19.2 billion in 2018 to an estimated US$21.8 billion in 2023. Some of the growth is due to professional sport leagues like MLS adding new franchises during the five-year period. Some leagues, like MLB, have sold fewer tickets at higher prices and maintained revenue growth. According to MLB Commissioner Rob Manfred, "Given the explosion of entertainment alternatives and the growth of the secondary market, it is not surprising that season ticket sales can be challenging."[12] In 2019, *Front Office Sports* reported that overall MLB attendance had dropped for four straight seasons. However, in that same season, revenue was up US$19 million from 2018 due to an average ticket price increase of 2.1 percent. Even though fewer fans are walking through the doors, many people are paying more for the opportunity to be at the stadium, and this is one factor contributing to gate revenue growth.

Sponsorship

PwC predicts that the sponsorship category is poised to overtake gate revenues to become the second biggest category in the Sports Outlook over the next five years. Several factors are driving growth in the area of corporate partnerships:

- The legalization of gambling in the United States has opened up the sponsorship rights category to many casinos and sports betting operators that were once forbidden to buy in.
- The proliferation of digital and social mediums has increased the amount of space and content that sponsors can use to leverage and activate their brands.
- The area of naming rights has grown, as more teams and leagues are providing access to jerseys, practice and training facilities, and other unique spaces for corporate partners to place their logos.

Merchandising

The sale of licensed merchandise has long been a profitable revenue stream for sport organizations. It continues to be a focus for leagues, teams, and events as marketers search for ways to provide new product lines that youth, women, and other groups with strong purchasing power will want. While the North American market has reached a point of saturation in this area, purchases of licensed sport merchandise remain steady or even are growing slightly. PwC projects growth in this area from US$14.6 billion in 2018 to US$15.4 billion in 2023.[10]

Sport Marketing Defined

As the needs and demographic makeup of sport consumers have become more complex and as competition for the spectator and participant dollar has increased, the demand for strategic and integrated marketing has also grown. Professional teams, small colleges, high schools, sport clubs,

Legalized gambling in the United States has given sponsors like Draft Kings the ability to be present in the sport market.

and youth programs have all looked for a better way to attract and maintain consumers. Among other things, they know that they compete for time and money with a host of rivals, including concerts, festivals, and other live events; sports bars and at-home viewing; and the Internet and social media. Today's marketers clearly need a more advanced system that can match sport consumers with sport products. This is the essence of contemporary sport marketing.

This text recognizes two components in sport marketing: marketing *of* sport and marketing *through* sport. A professional team engages in the former; a brewery or an auto dealer employs the latter. Although most of this book addresses the marketing of sport, we also consider (especially in chapter 10) the corporate sponsor that markets through sport. We will also use the singular *sport marketing* rather than *sports marketing*. We do this because we see a need to conceptualize sport industry segments (e.g., pro, college, and club leagues; various media) as a homogeneous entity. In the chapters that follow, we hope first to provide a general theory of sport marketing across all segments.

Given these notions about the sport industry and marketing, we offer the following definition of sport marketing, adapted from standard definitions of general marketing:

> **Sport marketing** consists of all activities designed to meet the needs and wants of sport consumers through exchange processes. Sport marketing has developed two major thrusts: the marketing of sport products and services directly to consumers of sport and the marketing of other consumer and industrial products or services using partnerships and promotions with sport properties.

As you will see, the terms *sport consumers* and *sport consumption* entail many types of involvement with sport, including playing (both real and virtual games), officiating, watching, listening, reading, socializing, and purchasing.

Marketing Myopia in Sport

If sport marketing ideally consists of activities designed to meet the wants and needs of sport consumers, then historically the industry has been guilty of what Theodore Levitt called *marketing myopia*, or "a lack of foresight in marketing ventures."[13] We like to call it the vision thing.

Following are some of the standard symptoms of sport marketing myopia.

Lack of Research to Support Sales Strategy

Often times, teams are focused on selling tickets and getting as many butts in the seats as possible. Tickets are what the organization is in the business of selling. But what if fans don't want to even sit in seats anymore? What if they want to attend the game and have a more social and interactive experience? This has become a major trend in sport venues today. Fans want to stand, walk around, or sit in a club-like space with friends and watch the game from a comfortable seating area, not a row of plastic chairs. Sport marketers need to identify the types of experiences fans want through the collection and analysis of data and try to provide these new opportunities even if it requires updating or adjusting venue spaces.[14]

The Belief That Winning Absolves All Other Sins

Winning makes everyone in an organization happy: owners, coaches, marketers, and fans. Winning seems to make everything easier business-wise as well, because winning often stimulates demand. However, the one thing that sales and marketing teams cannot guarantee is success. They can offer fans good seats, great food and entertainment, an enjoyable experience, but they cannot sell wins. In fact, it is better to guarantee a good time than a team win because the positive fan experience is what will endear customers to the organization long-term. Bandwagon fans who attend games while the team is enjoying success will likely abandon the team when the run is over,

so marketing departments should avoid creating a strategy that overemphasizes team success or winning streaks.

The Tampa Bay Lightning has become known in the NHL and beyond as a franchise that is fan-focused whether winning or not, and the strategy has paid off. Fans voted the Tampa Bay Lightning best in sports in the Ultimate Standings. When Steven Stamkos was the Lightning captain, he stated that, "When you can't necessarily sell your product on the ice, you really have to sell the fan experience. In larger markets, you can sell out your games whether you go 82-0 or 0-82, but Tampa isn't like that. So now we give fans a lot of access to players, like at Carnival Day. Fans enjoy the huge scoreboard and the lightning inside the arena and concerts before and after the game. The staff is friendly."[15]

Confusion Between Promotions and Marketing

Promotion is a short-term tactical approach, whereas marketing is a long-term strategic endeavor. Promotions should be used occasionally, when appropriate for the target audience, timing, and objective, and to supplement the overall marketing strategy. Think of it this way: Marketing is the "meat" and promotions are the "potatoes." Promotion—including advertising and special events—is only one part of a marketing mix, or strategy.

Baseball is the most heavily promoted sport, due to having a long season and so many games. Promotions certainly help attract fans and bring them to the ballparks, but the promotions must be

- carefully thought-out,
- aimed at a specific segment,
- strategically placed on the schedule, and
- executed successfully.

The magic happens when promotions complement the overall marketing strategy. In Major League Baseball, bobbleheads are still the most coveted premium promotional item. Rather than simply giving away regular player bobblehead dolls, teams giving away entertainment-related bobbleheads (like the Chicago White Sox Iron Man bobblehead) on a weekend theme night saw up to a 31 percent increase in attendance. Knowing what types of promotions different fans prefer is also critical to success. Data suggest that avid MLB fans prefer collecting bobbleheads while casual fans want to take home a jersey.[16]

Ignorance of Competition Inside and Outside Sport

In today's digital and social world, the biggest competitors of sports events may not even be in the business of sport. Smartphones, tablets, big-screen TVs, and social media sites are combining to make the second screen experience as good as or better than the live fan experience. Many people choose to watch sports at home and not attend games so they can take advantage of all the Internet has to offer.

The Atlanta Hawks realized this and decided to create one of the most captivating promotions by combining live sports with online dating. On "Swipe Right Night," Hawks fans were encouraged to search the Tinder dating app for love connections by swiping right on potential suitors in attendance at the game. The in-arena promotion included a Tinder Suite for successful matches that was stocked with mints, roses, and more.[17] The event was such a hit that the NBA team hosted a Swipe Right Night 2.0 and offered to pay for one couple's wedding. A couple who met on Swipe Right Night were married two years later at half-court and given an all-expenses paid reception in the Courtside Club.[18]

Short-Term Focus on Pricing Versus Long-Term Focus on Relationships

This predisposition is especially true at the professional level, because escalating salaries have prompted front offices to raise prices on everything from tickets to parking to concessions, rather than finding ways to make it easier for small groups, families, and individual ticket buyers to attend. Worse yet, too many teams gouge their fans whenever teams sense that demand is greater than supply. When many NFL teams began to charge fans to see preseason practice, Robert Kraft, owner of the New England Patriots whose Super Bowl champs had enjoyed a long train of sellouts, understood that preseason fans represent future generations of Patriots

Nation. To this end, New England's preseason camp had free admission, free parking, free rosters, and players lingering to sign autographs. Special events like preseason, exhibition, and spring college football games are great opportunities for giving fans free or low-cost access and building a loyal consumer base for the future.

More recently, teams have also adjusted concessions pricing to make eating at games more affordable and attract more fans to attend. The Atlanta Falcons announced "Fans-First Pricing" on concessions when they opened Mercedes-Benz Stadium with all items on the special menu valued at US$5 or less.[19] It was so well-received that other professional sport teams followed suit, such as the Miami Marlins with their 305 Menu. Lowering some concessions prices and improving the fan experience led to the following long-term benefits for the Falcons organization:

- Fan spending on food and beverage increased by 16 percent.
- The Falcons were ranked in the NFL within the top three for overall game-day experience; second for providing family-friendly entertainment; and second in arrival experience (more fans entering the stadium one hour early).
- Merchandise sales increased 90 percent.
- Fan surveys revealed stronger intent to return to a game, particularly among families.

Poor-Quality Research

When Matt Levine, who we consider the father of modern sport marketing, broke into the NBA in 1974, the cutting-edge of market research belonged to the L.A. Lakers, which collected patron names and addresses on raffle entries available at Forum ticket gates. Levine's boss, Golden State Warriors GM Dick Vertlieb, posed a simple question to Levine: "Isn't there more we could learn than their names and addresses?" Since our first edition of *Sport Marketing* in 1993, the sport industry has come a long way with research.

In 2006, Jessica Gelman, CEO of Kraft Analytics Group (KAGR), cofounded the MIT Sloan Sports Analytics Conference, where sport industry professionals from around the country convene to share best practices in data analytics for sports. The use of data to make strategic business decisions was on the rise, and the sports world needed to catch up. Today, almost all sport teams and leagues are collecting as much data as possible and hiring teams of people to analyze those numbers and make recommendations. The information comes from ticketing and other purchases, mobile apps used by fans, shared sponsor and vendor data, as well as the in-venue experience. Data are helping marketers make more informed decisions on everything from ticket and concessions pricing to promotions to in-game entertainment. The Golden State Warriors began analyzing decibel levels within their arena to determine what promotions and entertainment aspects fans enjoyed most.[20] Clearly, they enjoyed Steph Curry hitting 3s.

Poor Sales and Service

Although many sport firms have equated sales and promotions with marketing, only recently have they invested heavily in the development of properly trained and supported sales staff. Historically, sales have been driven by quota and commissions mentalities, and little emphasis has been placed on training, tactics, data usage, or sales as part of the larger marketing strategy. We should not conflate the notion of sales with boiler room operations using untrained and exploited staff and interns. The philosophy there seems to be this: "If they don't hit the numbers we want, we'll just let them go and bring in more from the hundreds who have sent in resumes." Heavy turnover and continued hiring of new sales employees do not benefit the organization in the long run. In all this, more thought should be given to the value of sales employee development, support, and incentives, all of which might improve the interaction between the sport organization and its consumers.

Arrogance and Laziness

Since professional leagues operate much like monopolies in their respective sports, this can lead to arrogance and laziness in terms of how they run their businesses. When there are no other true professional sport alternatives, the major sport leagues can operate their businesses how they choose, often ignoring consumers' wants and needs. This freedom of competition can lead to higher prices, limiting competitive options in the marketplace, and pressuring municipalities into building or renovating new stadiums.[21]

The 1890 Sherman Antitrust Act was established to promote economic competition by preventing businesses from working together to restrict trade. However, the *Federal Baseball Club of Baltimore v. National League et al.* Supreme Court ruling made MLB exempt from the Sherman Antitrust Act. This meant collusion among clubs would not be considered illegal as of 1922. According to sports economist Andrew Zimbalist, "There is no industry like baseball in our country. It has special status as a monopoly, and it is completely unregulated. Right now, baseball exploits the hell out of the cities."

Failure to Adapt to Industry, Market, and Consumer Change

Adapting to new ideas and technologies has been a constant necessity for sport executives and their marketing and media counterparts. Something new is always shaking up the status quo, and calling an innovation a fad or a waste of time is easy. People said that about the telephone and cell phone, video games, social media, and virtual and augmented reality. But each of these innovations changed the way that many people lived their everyday lives. The business world, in and out of sport, is littered with the carcasses of firms that failed to adapt. Having a willingness to learn, experimenting with new ideas and technologies, and adapting to the evolving wants and needs of younger consumers are all hallmarks of successful sport firms and their leadership.

Uniqueness of Sport Marketing

Overcoming sport marketing myopia requires an appreciation of this particular domain of human experience. Our book, in fact, rests on a simple premise: that humans view sport as a special experience or as having a special place in their lives, and that marketers must approach sport differently than they do used cars, donuts, or tax advice. Sports are so multifaceted, and the industry cuts across many other sectors, including

Bill Veeck: Sport Marketing's Foremost Prophet

Bill Veeck (1914-1986) was bred to sport marketing. His father, William Veeck Sr., was a Chicago sportswriter who switched fields to become president of the Cubs. In the cozy confines of Wrigley Field, young Bill Jr. learned the trade of the baseball magnate, from the bottom up—working with the grounds and concessions crews or with the ticket office, like any good intern today. The short biography on his plaque in the National Baseball Hall of Fame sums up his rich and varied sports life:

> Bill Veeck, owner of Indians, Browns, and White Sox. Created heightened fan interest at every stop with ingenious promotional schemes, fan participation, exploding scoreboard, outrageous door prizes, names on uniforms. Set M.L. attendance record with pennant-winner at Cleveland in 1948; won again with "go-go" Sox in 1959. Signed A.L.'s first black player, Larry Doby, in 1947 and oldest rookie, 42-year-old Satchel Paige, in 1948. Champion of the little guy.

Veeck was a champion of the little guy not because he once used a little person as a pinch hitter, but because he believed that everyday fans were baseball's true royalty. His two classic books, *Veeck as in Wreck* and *The Hustler's Handbook,* still hold up as invaluable guides for any would-be sport marketer or executive. Veeck happily considered himself a hustler, but here was his definition: "An advertiser pays for his space. A promoter works out a quid pro quo. A hustler gets a free ride and makes it seem like he's doing you a favor."[29] For high school and small-college athletics directors or youth program administrators who need to cut deals on slim budgets, Veeck's "hustler" should be a prototype.

Bill Veeck also left a legacy of 12 commandments that capture an enduring vision for successful sport marketing:

1. Take your work very seriously. Go for broke and give it your all.
2. Never ever take yourself seriously.
3. Find yourself an alter ego and bond with him for the rest of your professional life.
4. Surround yourself with similarly dedicated soul mates, free spirits of whom you can ask why and why not. And who can ask the same thing of you.
5. In your hiring, be color blind, gender blind, age and experience blind. You never work for Bill Veeck. You work with him.
6. If you're a president, owner, or operator, attend every home game and never leave until the last out.
7. Answer all of your mail; you might learn something.
8. Listen and be available to your fans.
9. Enjoy and respect the members of the media, the stimulation, and the challenge. The "them against us" mentality should only exist between the two teams on the field.
10. Create an aura in your city. Make people understand that unless they come to the ballpark, they will miss something.
11. If you don't think a promotion is fun, don't do it. Never insult your fans.
12. Don't miss the essence of what is happening at the moment. Let it happen. Cherish the moment and commit it to your memory.

Bill Veeck's 12 commandments offer an effective antidote to marketing myopia.

12 commandments reprinted, by permission, from P. Williams, 2000, "Marketing your dreams: Business and life lessons," In *Baseball's marketing genius*, edited by Bill Veeck (Champaign, IL: Sports Publishing), xiv.

business, entertainment, fashion, culinary, and community. People who want to work in sport marketing need to have an understanding and appreciation for all the different areas in which sports intersect.

For example, the U.S. Open in New York used to be just a two-week tennis tournament, but it has morphed into a three-week festival-style event with the creation of Fan Week leading into the official matches. Fan Week is a free-to-attend week at the U.S. Open venue where there are player practice sessions, interviews, autograph signings, concerts, food vendors, tennis clinics, and other sports activities for kids and families. Previously, the week before the U.S. Open, only the qualifying matches took place. Organizers saw this time period as an opportunity to give all fans free access to learn about and grow the sport of tennis.[22] The marketing and execution of the U.S. Open now entails much more than just organizing a professional tennis tournament. It has become a three-week global entertainment event hosted in one of the biggest cities in the world.

The sport domain has distinct features, which we discuss in the following sections, and there is no simple road to mastery. This book can provide an overview, but tangible experience is also needed. Just ask any general manager (GM) or chief marketing officer (CMO) of a franchise if they treat their sports fans like regular customers, and they will likely tell you the relationship is different. Although to some extent we can argue that marketing is marketing, the field is full of failures that treated soccer, golf, and basketball as though they were the latest fashion design or tooth whitener. In the following sections, we suggest components that, collectively, make sport a unique phenomenon.

Sport Product

A product can be described generally as "any bundle or combination of qualities, processes, and capabilities (goods, services, or ideas) that a buyer expects will deliver wanted satisfaction." A peculiar bundling distinguishes the sport product, including at least the following elements:[23]

- Playful competition, typically in some game form
- A separation from normal space and time

- Regulation by special rules
- Physical prowess and physical training
- Special facilities and special equipment

Figure 1.1 illustrates the importance that this special bundling has for the sport product. At its core, the sport product offers the consumer some basic benefit such as health, entertainment, sociability, or achievement. Of course, many other products may offer the same core benefit. The sport marketer must understand why a consumer chooses to satisfy a given want or need by purchasing a sport product rather than some other type of product. Why do some people seek achievement in sport whereas others prefer to grow prize orchids? Although research on such a question is sparse, we may assume that the preference relates partially to the generic product components of sport—emphasis on physical activity that is regulated in special game forms. At the same time, the hockey players among this sport group might scorn tennis and vice versa. The tennis players may be split into groups that prefer hard courts versus those who prefer clay courts. We can recognize the complex dynamics behind each level of segmentation (considered in later chapters), but the fundamental point is that the sport product is unique.

Additional elements of the basic sport product—the game or event—make it unusual. Some of these elements reflect the nature of sport as a service.[30]

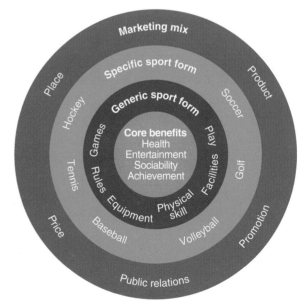

FIGURE 1.1   The bundle of characteristics of the sport product.

An Intangible, Ephemeral, Experiential, and Subjective Nature

Sport is an expression of our humanity; it can't be bottled like wine. Even tangible elements like equipment have little meaning outside the game or event. Few products are open to such a wide array of interpretations by consumers. What each consumer sees in a sport is subjective, making it extremely difficult for the sport marketer to ensure a high probability of consumer satisfaction. For example, two friends attending a Red Sox and Yankees game, who are on different sides of the rivalry, will likely experience the game in totally different ways. Even though these baseball fans watch all the same plays and view the same outcome, they will have totally different experiences. If the two friends were considering buying the same model of a new car, however, they would get exposed to the same types of options and features. Thus, selling the benefits of consuming sport (compared to those of a car) is difficult because the benefits of sport are hard to pinpoint or describe.

Strong Personal and Emotional Identification

As we discuss in chapter 3, few products or services elicit passions and commitments as sport does. Most readers will remember the first time they were bitten by a sports bug—volleyball, softball, swimming, track, or whatever. The addiction for more is striking. Fan identification with players and teams has spawned its own nomenclature. For example, there's BIRGing, or "basking in reflected glory," which can be seen in fans using the words *we*, *us*, and *our* when their favorites win or proudly displaying team gear after a victory, and CORFing ("cutting off reflected failure"), as seen when the words *them* or *they* are used to discuss a loss, and team apparel suddenly disappears. This strong identification is connected to the general feeling that "I could do that if only I had the chance." In the world of sport, it sometimes seems that everyone is a passionate expert. No wonder that fantasy games, talk radio, and sport blogs are successful.

Simultaneous Production and Consumption

Sports are perishable commodities. As events, they must be presold, and there are no inven-
tories. Sport consumers are typically also producers: They help create the game or event that they simultaneously consume by generating the electric atmosphere. Although replays, highlight videos, and media accounts extend product life in a different form, the original event is fleeting. No marketer can sell a seat for yesterday's game. Day-of-game sales alone are not sufficient, because inclement weather or some other factor may diminish gate sales. Preselling, especially of season-ticket packages or yearly memberships, guarantees minimum revenue.

Dependence on Social Facilitation

The loneliness of the long-distance runner notwithstanding, sport usually occurs in a public setting. Enjoyment of sport, as player or fan, is almost always a function of interaction with other people. Typically, less than 4 percent of those attending collegiate and professional sport events attend by themselves. Only a few sports, such as running, can be undertaken by a single person. And who watches the Super Bowl or the World Cup alone? Consequently, sport marketers need to recognize the central role of social facilitation. As mentioned earlier, we are seeing a metamorphosis in sports venues because sport marketers are starting to sell "social spaces" designed for mingling over "selling seats" where particularly Gen Z and millennials prefer the freedom of interaction. This will be particularly important in collegiate athletic venues in the future since budgets and a low number of home games, compared to professional sport venues, restrict the ability to remove seating areas and replace them with spaces. But this will definitely provide new unique inventory for sponsors whose brands speak to freedom, flexibility, and social interaction.

Inconsistency and Unpredictability

A rugby match played today will be different from next week's match even if the starting lineups are the same. Numerous factors such as weather, injuries, momentum, rivalries, and crowd response create the logic of "On any given day . . ." Who can predict a no-hitter, triple overtime, or the sudden squall on a mountain? Unpredictability is one of the lures of sport, but it makes the marketer's job more complex. For marketers selling products like shampoo, the product remains the same every day, so marketing messages are planned and predictable. Sports events are exciting because of the unexpected every time a competition begins. But how do you market what you cannot predict? Fans could watch something stale one day and witness something historic the next.

Core-Product Control Beyond Marketers' Hands

As suggested, most sport marketers have little control of their core product—the game itself. General managers make trades. Leagues make schedules and game rules. Although some core-product decisions are clearly made with an eye on marketing (in baseball, one such decision was the designated-hitter rule to create more offense), these decisions are still typically made by coaches and administrators whose agendas are often the game's "purity" or equalizing offense and defense. Sport team marketers must sell the sizzle as much as the steak. Boston Marathon managers sell T-shirts, collector's item medals, and special marathon-label wine. Only one person finishes first, but everyone can have a winning memento. That objective became doubly important in the aftermath of the 2013 Boston Marathon bombings.

Sport Market

Following are some special features of the sport market.

Many Sport Organizations Simultaneously Compete and Cooperate

Few sport organizations can exist in isolation. To have meaningful competition, professional, intercollegiate, and interscholastic sports require other franchises and schools. The same is true for private and amateur sport clubs. Unlike business rivals, such as McDonald's and Burger King or Walgreens and CVS, sports rivals do not want to see the competitor go away. When major National Collegiate Athletic Association (NCAA) conference realignments took place, some historic college rivalries were lost. Texas A&M University (TAMU) moved to the Southeastern (SEC) Conference, for example, and no longer played against the University of Texas (UT). Although both schools continued competing, the UT/TAMU rivalry game was the biggest event of the season in almost every sport, and marketers promoted those games heavily to fans. When games like these no longer exist, both sides may see diminished interest from fans and lower attendance.

Many Sport Consumers Believe They Are Experts

There is a reason the title "Monday Morning Quarterback" exists. Just read the comments on social media from fans discussing the weekend's games, and you quickly see how many people believe they could play, coach, and manage sport teams more successfully than those on the field. This goes for the boardroom as well. Students and professionals with years of training and specialized degrees in sport business may also find themselves being given advice on how to do their jobs from friends, family, or even total strangers without any expertise. Executives in sport management have decades of knowledge and experience in their respective fields; however, many of them face criticism from fans and community members telling them how to run their business. Very few people tell their doctor how to perform surgery or their accountant how to prepare their taxes, but many people provide feedback on how sport organizations should be managed.

Demand Tends to Fluctuate Widely

Each sport form tends to have an annual life cycle, and spectator sport fans are especially prone to quick changes in interest. Season openers bring high hopes and high demand; but midseason slumps, injuries, or weak competition may kill ticket sales.

There are so many factors that affect sport consumption, and any time these variables change, fan attendance can increase or decrease. Marketers need to have a clear sense of what factors most affect demand (besides performance) and be able to tap into what drives consumer interest. For example, do more fans attend weekend games or rivalry games? Do certain promotions drive greater attendance for females or families? How much does weather influence attendance? Data and analytics are key components to assist marketers in determining these drivers within each unique fan base.

Sport Has a Universal Appeal and Pervades All Elements of Life

Sport is truly a universal language. Regardless of age, culture, religious background, or economic

Nothing unifies people around the world more than watching sport.

status, athletes who take the field share a common passion and purpose that needs no words to describe it. The book *How Soccer Explains the World* examines how one sport, played all over the world, has the ability to bring countless different people together and helps them understand each other in a way no other institution can.[24] What appear to be simple games—soccer, cricket, handball, or basketball—link easily to other facets of our humanity, for better or worse.

Sport Financing

The financing of sport encompasses the following special features.

Pricing in the Sport Industry Is Difficult

It is virtually impossible for the sport marketer to allocate fixed and operating costs to the individual ticket or membership. How can one account for the possible use of an usher, an instructor, an attendant, or an intern? Further, the marginal cost of providing an additional product unit is typi-cally small. Therefore, pricing the sport product is often based on the marketer's sense of consumer demand—for certain seats, for certain times of day, for certain privileges.

Pricing the Sport Product Differs From the Sport Experience

As we will see in future chapters, marketers must recognize the hidden costs of sport. The cost of tickets to a sports event may be only one-third of a family's total costs, which include travel, parking, food, drinks, and merchandise—all perhaps controlled by someone other than the team hosting the event.

Indirect Revenues Are Frequently Greater Than Direct Operating Revenues

Because consumers are (and should be) cost sen-sitive, income from fans is often not enough to cover total expenses, especially debt service to the shiny, high-tech facilities that consumers demand.

The direct income–expense gap has focused more attention on media and sponsor revenues. The quest for television and sponsors extends to all levels and segments of the sport industry, in part because the money is there. A good example is the NCAA. Of the NCAA's total revenues for 2018 to 2019 (US$1.04 billion), 83 percent came from media and marketing rights fees. And most of this amount was from rights associated with March Madness, the men's Division I basketball tournament.[25]

Sport Promotion

Promoting sport is not as easy as it seems, despite widespread media attention. Consider the following.

The Widespread Media Exposure Is a Double-Edged Sword

Unlike a hardware store, sport teams get free promotion daily, on the Internet, radio, and television. Individual athletes on social media carefully curate their personal brands and promote themselves to tens of millions, or even hundreds of millions, of fans in an instant on their smartphones. One premier athlete alone can receive billions of engagements annually. This is an incredible amount of exposure. Many companies now turn to individual athletes to promote their brands because popular athletes often have more followers than the teams they play for and can engage fan bases more effectively. Here are the 2019 Top 10 Athletes on Social Media according to Opendorse (total followers across all platforms):[26]

1. Cristiano Ronaldo (soccer)—399.6 million followers
2. Neymar (soccer)—236 million followers
3. Lionel Messi (soccer)—230.1 million followers
4. LeBron James (basketball)—121.8 million followers
5. Virat Kohli (cricket)—117 million followers
6. David Beckham (soccer)—112 million followers
7. Ronaldinho (soccer)—103.8 million followers
8. James Rodriguez (soccer)—95.3 million followers
9. Gareth Bale (soccer)—89.2 million followers
10. Andres Iniesta (soccer)—83.8 million followers

Of course, athletes who are the most recognized and followed tend to also be the most scrutinized. Their positive and negative stories resonate throughout the media landscape making the attention a double-edged sword. Cristiano Ronaldo, for example, generated 1.7 billion engagements across his social media platforms in 2019, which topped the list for sports stars. He also has been covered extensively in the media for an alleged sexual assault in Las Vegas, Nevada. Neymar has been accused of rape and Lionel Messi of tax fraud, both of which have been documented for years by international media.[27]

Media and Sponsors Emphasize Celebrities

Sport marketers work hard to shape their organization's image, and athlete endorsers and influencers are extremely effective in cultivating the desired brand personality. Certain star athletes may become synonymous with the brands they represent, such as Serena Williams and LeBron James with Nike, or Chris Paul and Aaron Rodgers with State Farm. While this may seem like a good thing, considering all the positive publicity they bring, athletes have their own personal issues or public problems that can be transferred to sponsors or other organizations with which they do business. For example, when LeBron James spoke out against an NBA general manager's support of Hong Kong, it created a backlash that was considered the worst of his career.[28] This type of scenario, where athletes blend personal and professional beliefs, becomes problematic because the bulk of sponsor and media attention is focused on a few notable celebrities, whose egos can lead to wholesale problems both inside and outside the locker room.

Wrap-Up

Sport is a distinct enterprise. It cannot be marketed like soap or tax advice. A sport marketer is asked to market a product that is unpredictable, inconsistent, and open to subjective interpretation. The marketer must undertake this task in a highly competitive marketplace with a much lower promotional budget than those of similarly sized organizations in other industries. Finally, the sport marketer must do all this with only limited direct control over the product mix.

On the bright side, the media are eager to give wide exposure to the general product, and many opportunities exist to generate revenue through associations with business and industry.

Activities

1. List several reasons why there needs to be continued improvement of sport marketing as technology and media advances.

2. Define *marketing myopia*, give a specific example in the sport industry, and provide data that demonstrate the organization's short-sided approach to marketing.

3. On the basis of figure 1.1, discuss how two golfers (or participants of another sport) might consume different products in terms of benefits, sport forms, or marketing mix.

4. Conduct research on the major sports leagues (NFL, NBA, MLB, NHL, and NCAA) and determine their revenues from media rights and sponsorships. Why is it important to leagues that businesses market through sports rather than rely heavily on ticket sales?

5. Discuss the three elements of sport that you believe most contribute to the uniqueness of sport marketing. How might these elements affect your job once you become a sport industry executive?

6. Identify a sport or a sport organization on the rise and one on the decline. What types of evidence support the notions of either rise or decline? What impact has marketing (or lack thereof) had on the rise or decline of the business?

Your Marketing Plan

In the following chapters, you will be asked to develop your own marketing plan, step by step. This activity will allow you to apply the topics that are presented in each chapter. Take advantage of these opportunities and have fun!

 Go to HK*Propel* to complete the activities for this chapter.

Chapter 2

Strategic Marketing Management

Warren A. Whisenant

OBJECTIVES

- To understand the strategic management process
- To understand the distinctions among the five Ps of sport marketing: product, price, place, promotion, and public relations
- To become familiar with multiple marketing models used for analyzing and developing a strategic marketing plan

Michael Reaves/Getty Images

For 18 years (2002 to 2019), the Homestead-Miami Speedway hosted NASCAR's championship weekend. All three of NASCAR's national series—Cup Series, Xfinity Series, and Gander RV & Outdoors Truck Series—held their season finale at the South Florida track. In 2020, the track's race weekend was rescheduled for March, becoming one of NASCAR's early events. The schedule change meant two races in less than four months at the speedway. It also meant the track marketing team had to reposition the race and develop and execute a new strategic plan since it was no longer "championship weekend."

Marketing for the new 2020 race was framed to celebrate the 25th anniversary of the track's opening. On August 24, 1992, Hurricane Andrew moved over the city of Homestead, destroying everything in its path. A week later, a deal was made to build Homestead-Miami Speedway as an effort to revitalize the city. Construction began a year later, and the track opened on November 3, 1995, hosting the Miami 300. Since that time, the speedway has been the home for motor sports in South Florida. The annual economic impact of the track for the city of Homestead and the county was approximately US$300 million dollars.[41]

With only eight days before the 2020 race and two-thirds of its marketing budget already spent for promotion, the race's running was in doubt due to the COVID-19 pandemic. Just 10 days before the race, it was announced that the race would run without fans. The following day, the race was postponed indefinitely. Due to the uncertainty of the pandemic and unknown date NASCAR would return to racing, the marketing team had to prepare multiple scenarios. A typical marketing campaign would begin six to eight weeks out before a race. A rescheduled race would not have that much lead time.

The new revised marketing plan excluded many of the traditional activities. There would be no onsite marketing activation by sponsors. Revenue streams were eliminated due to a ban on fans attending the event—ticket sales, corporate hospitality, concessions, and NASCAR and team merchandise. Once the race was rescheduled for June 13 and 14, the theme was expanded from a 25th anniversary to emphasize a return to some level of normalcy. NASCAR announced its decision to allow a limited number of fans to attend the race. Approximately 1,000 local service members were honorary guests of NASCAR. Being the first major sports event with fans in attendance, Homestead-Miami Speedway would once again be an example of how sport can be positioned in the market as a symbol of hope. In 1995, it was a symbol of hope for the city of Homestead. In 2020, it was a symbol of a return to a new normal not only for South Florida but also the nation.

NASCAR's return to racing, while other professional sports remain on the sideline, has given the sport a distinctively competitive advantage. Replacing the on-track race with an eNASCAR race that was televised by Fox Sports, drew nearly one million viewers. The esport activity introduced NASCAR to new consumers who were not traditional fans. FS1's weekly coverage was the only sport available at the time. Once on-track racing returned, Fox's coverage remained the only live professional sport available to consumers deep into the summer.[1]

In today's competitive environment, organizations need strategically minded leaders. Developing and implementing a sound strategy will enable the organization to achieve and sustain a competitive advantage over its competitors. A good strategy requires

- a clear understanding of the competitive environment,
- a consistent commitment to following the plan, and
- an implementation of the plan.[2]

The absence of any of those three actions will result in competitive parity at best. This chapter presents the basic elements required for the development of a comprehensive, strategic, and creative marketing plan. Subsequent chapters

The Southeastern Conference (SEC) has consistently been one of the competitively leading conferences (for example, Alabama in football and Kentucky in basketball), as well as financially leading conferences. Collectively, its members in 2018 to 2019 generated over US$1.89 billion in revenues with expenses at US$1.77 billion.[42] One could argue that a key contributing factor for its financial success is the alignment of resources to support elements within the Conference mission:

> To assure proper emphasis on the funding of athletics activities; to provide leadership and a voice in the development of public attitudes toward intercollegiate sports generally; and to address the future needs of athletics in a spirit of cooperation and mutual benefit of the member institutions and their student-athletes.[43]

In 2013, the Conference began collecting data to focus on enhancing the fan experience, using data from over 26,000 fans to determine what experiences were important to them when attending games, and how satisfied they were with those experiences—an I-PA that is discussed in greater detail later in the chapter.

In 2018, Ole Miss conducted its own survey of six categories: first impressions, concessions, restrooms, band and cheers, video board, and mobile connectivity. It collected the data in a way that allowed the organization to segment the fans as general seating, premium areas, or students. Ole Miss' efforts to focus on the fan experience was another example of resources being aligned with the organization's mission:

> Operating within the principles of sound fiscal management, the Department will sponsor athletics teams which reflect the interest of the citizens of Mississippi and promote enthusiasm, financial support, cohesiveness, and loyalty within the University community.[44]

With a 2020 operating budget of US$112.5 million, in which US$9.3 million was allocated to facilities and event management and US$6.2 million to media relations, marketing, and ticket office, 13.8 percent of the operating budget was focused on the fan experience.[3-8]

present various tactical steps in the marketing management process. This chapter places each step in the broader perspective of strategy.

In addition to discussing the importance of strategic thinking, several models are introduced that may be used in developing, monitoring, and adjusting the organization's strategic initiatives. These models enable an objective assessment of product performance, market data, and consumer perceptions of the product. Models that focus on consumer data include the brand positioning map, customer lifetime value (CLV) matrix, importance-performance analysis (I-PA), loyalty ladder, and unique selling proposition (USP). Product performance and market data models include a SWOT (strengths, weaknesses, opportunities, threats) analysis, Boston Consulting Group's matrix, growth strategy matrix, Porter's five forces, and the product life cycle. Each model is discussed later in this chapter.

Marketing Planning Process

Just as an organization has to organize and align its various business functions within its strategic plan, each function can narrow its strategic initiatives to further define the strategic plan to meet its goals. The elements of a marketing strategy can be conceptualized in models. Marketing theorist Philip Kotler has called one model the marketing management process (MMP). Kotler's model has been blended with others (figure 2.1) to create a step-by-step process and a way of thinking. An effective strategic plan will be proactive in nature providing guidance for leaders as they

- make decisions to increase revenues,
- build and sustain customer loyalty, and
- outperform competitors in the marketplace to sustain a competitive advantage.

As some of the activities at the end of the chapter suggest, the MMP can be used to develop a marketing plan. However, the marketing plan must be integrated into an organization's larger strategic plan, which requires aligning all of the organization's resources, including finance, sales, marketing, and human resources, among other elements. The MMP is the backbone of marketing, emphasizing interdependencies at all stages.[9-12]

Later chapters examine the MMP steps in greater detail (e.g., research, product development, pricing, and promotion). A brief introduction is important here to emphasize that decision-making is an ongoing, circular process. The strategic management process comprises five basic steps:

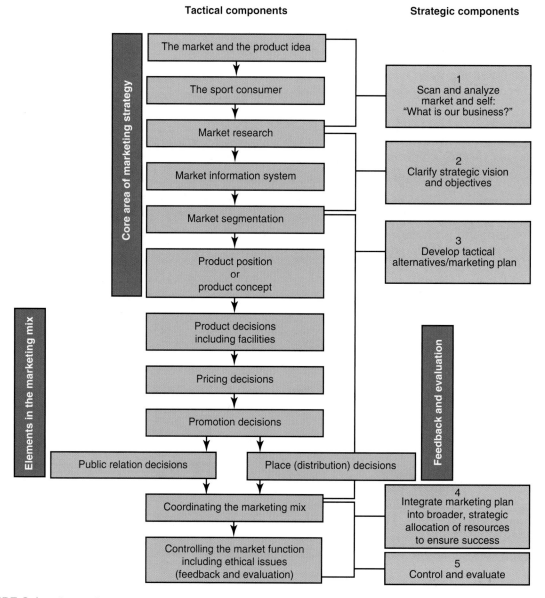

Tactical components

Strategic components

Core area of marketing strategy

- The market and the product idea
- The sport consumer
- Market research
- Market information system
- Market segmentation
- Product position or product concept

Elements in the marketing mix

- Product decisions including facilities
- Pricing decisions
- Promotion decisions
- Public relation decisions
- Place (distribution) decisions
- Coordinating the marketing mix
- Controlling the market function including ethical issues (feedback and evaluation)

Feedback and evaluation

1 Scan and analyze market and self: "What is our business?"

2 Clarify strategic vision and objectives

3 Develop tactical alternatives/marketing plan

4 Integrate marketing plan into broader, strategic allocation of resources to ensure success

5 Control and evaluate

FIGURE 2.1   The marketing management process in sport.

Adapted by permission from B. Mullin, "Characteristics of Sports Marketing," in *Successful Sport Management*, edited by H. Appenzeller and G. Lewis (Durham, NC: Carolina Academic Press, 2000), 123.

1. Develop a strategic vision, business mission, and values.
2. Set goals and objectives.
3. Craft a strategy for achieving the objectives.
4. Align resources to implement and execute the strategy.
5. Evaluate performance by monitoring developments in the market and adjusting to maintain a competitive advantage within the market.[13]

Michael Porter stated, "The job of the strategist is to understand and cope with competition."[14] As figure 2.1 suggests, a marketing plan aligns tactical details and operations (such as pricing) with broader organizational strategies (such as setting attendance goals). This chapter introduces that important blend of strategy and tactics.

The strategic steps of the MMP and their relation to the remaining book chapters are as follows:

1. Develop vision, position, and purpose (chapters 3-5, 16).
2. Develop strategic goals and objectives (chapter 5).
3. Develop a marketing mix plan (chapters 6-13).
4. Integrate the marketing plan into the broader organizational strategy (chapter 15).
5. Control and evaluate all elements of the marketing plan (chapters 14, 15).

Strategic Step 1: Develop Vision, Mission, and Values

The following sections describe the way the core vision and ideology should guide decisions and position the sport product or service. The importance of using a variety of techniques or models is discussed, which enables managers to use data-based marketing (DBM) systems and customer relationship management (CRM) systems to provide market intelligence and identify fads and trends (and determine which is which). DBM systems store fan contact data and essential information, such as purchase history. CRM systems provide a 360-degree record of all customer interactions with the organization, such as complaints about traffic, fans sitting nearby, and broken seats.

A well-defined vision clearly states the organization's aspirations. Knowing what the organization wants to accomplish allows for distinctive goals to be established and provides a purpose for employees to rally around. The mission describes how the vision will be achieved through the organization's product or service offerings. The ethical standards that guide the organization's culture are set forth in the organization's values statement.

Riot Games' League of Legends is an example of how strategic planning can lead to market dominance as a market leader in esports. The free-to-play game generated over US$1.5 billion in revenues in 2019 and had 44 million viewers of its world finals.[15] Figure 2.2 outlines the com-

---

"Building a Riot Games where everyone can thrive."

We're focused on two big work streams to make Riot a great home for people who love making games: setting a high bar for diversity and inclusion (D&I), and fostering a fair, collaborative, high-performing culture.

To get there, we're driven by a few simple beliefs. We believe:

- That when teams are both diverse and inclusive they win. Every time.
- That leveraging our strengths, knowing our weaknesses, and being honest about both is the best way to succeed, whether that's in the office or in a game.
- That we must call out sexism, racism, homophobia, transphobia, ableism, ageism, religious discrimination, and bigotry of all kinds.
- That work can be a place where you make lifelong friends, partner with clutch teammates, and embrace the joy of making games.

FIGURE 2.2 Riot Games' company vision.

Imagine an organization's strategic plan that is grounded by its primary product price point being zero dollars. The core product is free to consumers. Riot Games' League of Legends is an online free-to-play video game that does just that. Despite giving players free access, the company had over US$1.5 billion in revenues in 2019. Since its introduction in 2009, the game has awarded over US$73 million in prize money to over 6,800 players in over 2,600 tournaments. With 8 million players logging in each day, the company has access to a brand-loyal consumer base any marketing executive would cherish.[17]

The company's strategic marketing plan appears to follow an aggressive growth strategy focusing on the player experience. It engages in each of the four quadrants in the growth strategy matrix (discussed in greater detail later in the chapter):

1. *Market penetration.* By listening to its players, the company continues to enhance the game leading to greater play and viewership, which drives market penetration.

2. *Diversification.* The company's diversification into a wide range of merchandise—toys to apparel—allows it to take new products into new markets. Diversification has also led to partnerships with a variety of companies, such as Nike and Louis Vuitton.

3. *Market development.* The company's entrance into the sport world through esports is an example of its market development activities.

4. *Product development.* Product development, such as in-game currency, allows the company to bring a new service to its existing market.

Aligning its marketing activities with its vision and values has placed League of Legends at the top of the emerging esport market, with over 100 million viewers of the league's 2019 world championship.[17]

pany's vision.[16] Its values are player experience first; dare to dream; thrive together; execute with excellence; and stay hungry, stay humble.

Strategic Step 2: Develop Strategic Goals and Objectives

The development and reassessment of goals and objectives is an ongoing process through constant analysis. Although people sometimes interchange the terms *goals* and *objectives,* goals are typically broad statements, whereas objectives provide more detailed, usually quantified targets.

The 2020 NASCAR season is a prime example of how events outside the racing world can recast the goals and objectives of an entire sport and its supporting entities. First was the COVID-19 pandemic that resulted in a complete cessation of sports events globally. Many organizational goals within the NASCAR community, such as profitability, consumer satisfaction, and diversity, were modified, but not eliminated. To achieve those newly adjusted changes, new objectives were needed. The pandemic pushed eNASCAR to the forefront by creating the eNASCAR iRacing Pro Invitational Series. To fill the on-track racing void, iRacing, NASCAR, and FS1 turned to virtual racing with nearly one million viewers. The event was so successful, Fox Sports agreed to televise the events until on-track racing resumed. The death of George Floyd in 2020 and the subsequent Black Lives Matter protests resulted in NASCAR banning the Confederate battle flag from its properties, and eNASCAR hosted the George Floyd 100.

Strategic Step 3: Develop a Ticket Marketing, Sales, and Service Plan

With a mission and objectives in place, the marketer must develop a plan at both the broad (strategic) and specific (tactical) levels. A ticket marketing, sales, and service (TiMSS) plan could be used here based on the notion that ticket sales and attendance are the trunk of the sport business money tree that feeds all the other sport marketing revenue streams (marketing partnerships and sponsorships, food and beverage and hospitality, merchandise and licensing, and so on). A sales database can be created to identify targeted consumer segments. One of the most important ways for sport marketers to segment consumers is by their position on the escalator of involvement, a concept that is examined later. After identifying target segments, the marketer must develop products; prices; distribution systems; promotions; and public relations, media, and sponsorship programs that will ensure the successful attainment of objectives and mission.

These functions make up the core of this book—chapters 6 through 15.

Market Segmentation and Determination of Key Targets

Market segmentation involves dividing consumers into multiple groups based upon a range of variables. Targeting follows segmentation as the most attractive segments are identified. Marketing theorists have typically considered several bases for segmentation, which are discussed in detail in chapter 5:

- *Demographic information.* Age, sex, income, education, profession
- *Geo-market information.* Location of residence by zip code
- *Psychographic information.* Lifestyle factors, such as activities, interests, and opinions
- *Product usage rate.* Attendance or activity frequency, or size of donation
- *Product benefits.* Product attributes or benefits that are most important to consumers

The market strategy you employ affects what audience you target. If you're selling luxury seating, the typical college student isn't your target audience.

Joe Robbins/Getty Images

and consumers' perceptions regarding the major benefits of the product and its competitors

Collecting the segmentation data allows marketing databases to be created. This data allows the marketing team to establish individual marketing strategies, sometimes called *relationship marketing*. For instance, a database of information on season-ticket holders would allow a marketer to send birthday greetings along with information on special events (such as concerts) or special group deals (for children's birthdays).[18]

Market Development Using the Escalator Concept

User segments are especially important in the sport business because they constitute the sport consumer escalator (figure 2.3). The escalator is a graphic representation of consumer movement to higher levels of involvement in a sport, as a player or a fan. The escalator suggests that sport organizations should invest first and foremost in nurturing existing consumers. The second step is focusing on turning casual fans into more avid fans. The final step is trying to create new fans. Although campaigns to attract

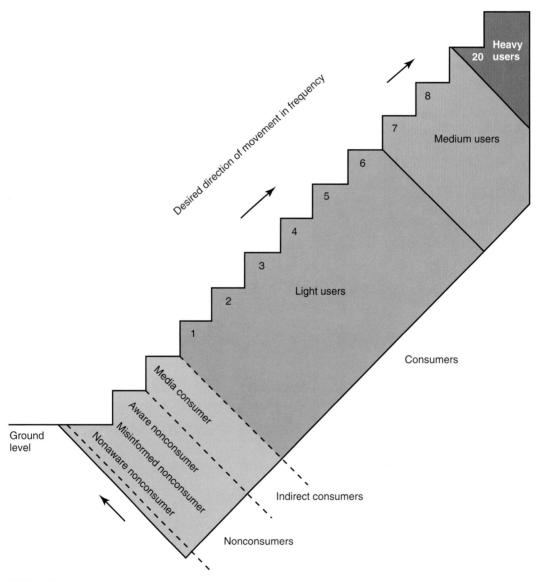

FIGURE 2.3   The frequency escalator for sport attendance and participation.

new fans are important, they cannot match for impact a strategy that moves current consumers a few steps up the escalator of involvement and commitment.

The escalator concept has been supported by consumer research among both participants and spectators. In the 1970s, for instance, Dick Lipsey began national, syndicated research on the sporting goods business. These studies, one of which is now the annual National Sporting Goods Association survey, supported some important elements of the sport escalator, including the fact that new participants represented a minor portion of total purchases (from 5 to 12 percent of dollars and from 10 to 20 percent of units sold). The conclusion was that sport participants moved up an escalator of involvement and that most equipment buyers were already playing the sport and looking for ways to improve.[19,40]

For team sport marketers, the escalator is crucial, in part because fan surveys indicate clear intentions to move up the escalator. For instance, fans who currently attend three games per year typically indicate their intention to attend five or six games the next year. The key is to create a TiMSS plan, using an array of elements and tactics, that can satisfy the needs of various consumer clusters and thereby move user groups up the escalator.

Product Development and Positioning

One way to move consumers up the escalator is to design, redesign, and promote products to capture special space in the minds of target consumers. This strategy is sometimes called positioning. Two advertising executives promoted the concept in the 1980s, and their book title

Successful sport organizations know that they must evolve their marketing position in order to gain a larger audience.
Scott Barbour/AFL Media/Getty Images

captured their argument: *Positioning: The Battle for Your Mind.* Their basic mantra was simple: "Positioning is not what you do to a product. Positioning is what you do to the mind of the prospect. That is, you position the product in the mind of the prospect."[20] Product positioning is not simply a matter of branding and advertising; it also involves research, development, and design. Some leagues use rule changes to reposition themselves. Baseball redesigned its basic product with the designated hitter, largely to reposition itself as a more exciting and offensive sport in the face of football's smashing popularity in the 1960s. Ice hockey clamped down on the worst of its street-fighting image with tough rules against the third man in and against leaving the bench during a fight.

Five Ps in the Sport Marketing Mix

The product is often referred to as one of marketing's four Ps:

1. Product (development and positioning)
2. Price
3. Place (or product distribution)
4. Promotion (personal selling, advertising, special events)

Because sport enjoys so much media attention, public relations (usually considered part of promotion) is treated as a separate P:

5. Public relations

In a service-oriented industry like sport, all the Ps are influenced by how well employees interact with consumers; this is process management, which is critical to the running of any promotion. For instance, if stadium personnel are surly to fans looking to exchange giveaway T-shirts (often for a different size), those fans, who might well be at their only game of the year, will likely fall off the escalator in the belief that the stadium is a hostile place to bring a family. In a wireless age, staying connected to consumers is possible 365/24/7. But that connection must always be positive. Nothing can replace the human touch. Great customer service will always be the major force moving fans up the escalator.

Strategic Step 4: Integrate the Marketing Plan Into a Broader, Strategic Resource Allocation

Before, while, and after developing the five Ps into a plan for action, the marketer must ensure that senior executives will support the plan. There's nothing worse for a marketer than to develop an imaginative, can't-miss plan that fails because it lacks support at a higher level. College athletics staffs often face this problem. Surefire plans for creating a bigger fan base in women's sports linger on the shelf because the limited funds go into promoting the traditional revenue sports (usually men's sports) that have historically helped fund everyone else. Although shifting money to a promotion of women's sports might result in a greater revenue yield, the risks seem too great. This scenario is almost a self-fulfilling prophecy. Successful marketers make sure that they have support as they move along, so step 4 must be ongoing.

The key to developing and executing any successful sport marketing plan is to include research and input from all the key stakeholders (ticket buyers and users, corporate marketing partners or sponsors, the media and broadcast rights holders, and the community as a whole). Additionally, the input and the buy-in of senior and middle managers and the program directors who will implement the plan are essential. For those reasons, we call it the marketing planning process—an intellectual process of creating ideas and testing them with the key constituents. Once adopted, a strategy may require some changes in personnel or in the organizational structure.

An effective marketing plan will carefully blend all the Ps into a portfolio of activities that move a range of consumer clusters up the escalator. An enlightened school, college, or professional sport program will blend several of the Ps into packages differentiated in cost and benefits, promoted with different messages, and targeted at different segments or even niches. A college program might offer special plans for students, area families, distant alums, and corporate sponsors. Careful coordination of efforts is required. The athletics director, coaches, players, sports information personnel, facilities managers, and the ticket office must all be on board. Marketing is not the work of just a few people.

Strategic Step 5: Control and Evaluate Implementation of the Plan

Step 5 is another ongoing step. Waiting for the end of the season to see whether you're in last place makes little sense. Marketers (and their bosses) are quick to analyze failures. But analysis, evaluation, and control should be everyday events. Evaluation (or control) requires not only discussion and debriefing sessions but also rigorous quantitative analysis.

Ultimately, success in marketing is determined only through consumers' eyes. It is a simple equation:

Consumer satisfaction = Product benefits - Costs

Consumers provide the answers to the equation. Do they buy the product? Do they use the product? Do they repeat the purchase, or do they try something else? Although marketers must control their own budgets and costs, their more important control function is to ensure customer satisfaction. This measure must be tempered by the long-term effect of various strategies. As the escalator concept outlines, the key to growth in customer base is actually the attendance frequency, and therefore product and service menu (PSM) design along with the promotional and marketing communications strategy of the sport property must be strategically focused on fan retention first, then repeat purchase (growing casual fans into avid fans), and then finally new fan acquisition. Indicators of satisfaction, benefits, and cost must be monitored and evaluated not just in the short-term but also the long-term, which is why we emphasize the importance of measuring lifetime asset value (LAV) in determining the effectiveness of all sport marketing strategies and evaluating true return on objectives (ROO) and return on investment (ROI). Consider a few examples of possible indicators:

- Satisfaction
  Attendance
  Ticket or member renewal rates

- Benefits
  Food quality
  Access to and speed of parking
- Total cost of the experience
  Time spent in the parking lot after the game
  Beer spilled on children by a drunken fan
  Annoyance caused by a surly usher

The marketer must consider other issues as well, including ethical principles.

Any MMP must consider social responsibility. Beyond the legal issues (see chapter 14), any marketing plan or decision includes ethical dimensions. Moreover, numerous frameworks can guide ethical decisions—in business, in marketing, in sport, or in any domain of activity.

Eight-Point Ticket Marketing, Sales, and Service Plan Model

The Aspire Sport Marketing Group LLC, a leading global outsourced ticket marketing, sales, and service consulting business, has developed an eight-point plan (figure 2.4) that speaks to the key elements in developing a comprehensive

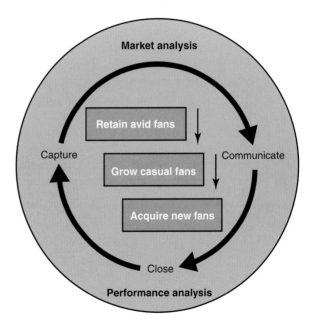

FIGURE 2.4 The Aspire Group's unique TiMSS plan structure, which drives their fan relationship management philosophy.

ticket marketing and sales plan. This plan logically starts with market research, which has the purpose of determining who the existing fans of the sport property are, whom they attend with, what they like and don't like, why they attend, and what it will take to get them to attend more games. It also provides information on those not currently attending and what it will take to get those who have interest in the sport, the team, or the university product to attend.

The essential strategies of retain, grow, and acquire are then outlined as mentioned previously in this chapter, followed by the recommended tactics for executing these strategies:

- Capture the essential fan contact data, clean it, remove the duplicates, review past purchase patterns, and segment the various fan groups by level of interest and their desired product alternatives (the appropriate offer from the ticket product ladder).
- Communicate the offer that will most likely resonate best with that fan segment through the fans' preferred communication medium (email, text, tweet, direct mail, and so on). In this manner, digitally prequalify sales leads by targeting those who respond to the offer, next to those who open, click through, and make social media postings.
- Close the offer by having staff in the fan relationship management center (FRMC) call those fans who purchased as the result of the offer to build a relationship, better identify their needs, and possibly upsell to a higher-level ticket plan. Staff members also call those who opened and clicked through the electronic communication because they have clearly qualified themselves as warm leads. Those who do not open the communication are then retargeted electronically with another offer that the marketer thinks will have the best chance of being accepted.

All ticket marketing and sales campaigns are then fully reviewed for ROO and ROI, using standard performance analysis that involves measurement and production of critical analytics on such items as open rates, click-through rates, and sales or revenue response measured against campaign costs. This review is done for every initiative using embedded promotional codes that enable sales response tracking through the ticket service vendor software (Ticketmaster, Paciolan, Veritix, Agile, and so on).

Marketing Models

At various points in the strategic planning process, an organization will need to evaluate its performance. To do so, a variety of models may provide detailed analyses evaluating the competitive nature of the market as well as assessing the organization's own performance. A well-structured and viable strategic plan will include the use of multiple models. Step 1 of the marketing plan may include a SWOT analysis or Porter's five forces to see how well the company is following its vision. Boston Consulting Group's matrix or the brand positioning map can help establish strategic goals and objectives for step 2. Step 3 may call for the use of a segment-target-position (STP) or unique selling proposition (USP) exercise. The growth strategy matrix may be useful in step 4. And the use of an I-PA would provide data needed in step 5 to evaluate how well the plan was implemented. The following sections explain these marketing models.

Boston Consulting Group's Matrix

Boston Consulting Group assists in accessing individual product performance when an organization has a diverse line of offerings. Products are plotted based upon their growth rates and market shares. The model allows for the organization to identify products in one of four categories:[28]

1. *Dogs* are low performers in low-growth markets, and often operate with a negative cash flow. These products should be considered expendable and, if they serve no strategic or competitive purpose, removed from the company's portfolio.

2. *Questionable products* require the most attention since they are in high-growth markets but have yet to secure their place in the market. While they may show potential to become stars, they may require considerable investment and shifts in marketing strategies to become established brands.

3. *Stars* are high-performing products in growth markets. Stars represent products

that generate cash but also require considerable investment. These products should continue to be supported because they may eventually become cash cows.

4. *Cash cows* are products in mature markets and are market leaders. These products have reached their growth potential and have solidified their place as market leaders. They require minimal investment and due to their high profitability, should be used to support products in the other three quadrants.

Once assigned to a category, the organization can determine to what extent it wants to allocate resources to support the product.

Figure 2.5 illustrates how products can be accessed. Products B and C are considered cash cows. Although sales declined, the products' profitability was high. The stars (D, F, and G) not only have strong profitable results but also continue to grow. The contributions by the cash cows and stars to the organization's bottom line are significant and fuel funding for the investment in the questionable products and sustain the cogs. Items E, H, and I show strong growth but have not met the profit expectations the company has set for its products. The goal for the marketing team should be to move products from the questionable category to the stars category. The only dog in the analysis (A) should be retired and have its marketing support moved to the questionable products.

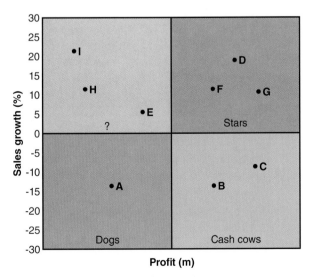

FIGURE 2.5 Example of Boston Consulting Group's matrix.

Brand Positioning Map

Brand positioning is the process of having your brand well thought of by consumers. A brand positioning map allows for comparisons to be made of the perceptions consumers have of key attributes of competing products or services. Each axis represents an attribute used by consumers that drives their purchase intent. The goal is to identify a position in the market that the organization's product can occupy. Having a clearly differentiated product in the market helps with product recall and brand identity, which should in turn lead to strong sales and profits. Types of attributes to target may include product value, perceived customer quality, differentiating qualities, and level of emotional attachment. The mapping process will involve the development of multiple maps focusing on critical attributes.[29] In figure 2.6, the company conducting the research may want to focus on the attributes that have led consumers to perceive D, E, and F as having high value.

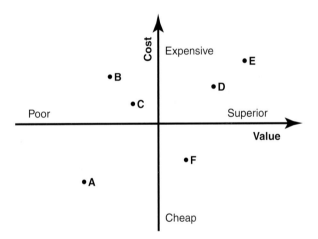

FIGURE 2.6 Brand positioning map.

Customer Lifetime Value

Customer lifetime value (CLV) encourages organizations to take a long view of its relationship with consumers (figure 2.7). It enables organizations to quantify the future value of a customer over the lifetime of the product in terms of profits. To calculate the CLV, three variables are needed:

1. Average revenue (AR) generated by each customer
2. Gross margin (GM) per customer
3. Churn rate (CR) of each customer

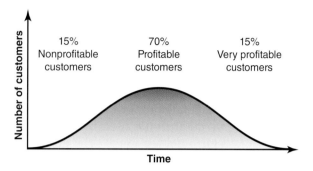

FIGURE 2.7 Customer lifetime value.

The churn rate is the percentage of customers who discontinue purchasing the product each period, and it is used to establish the average revenue generated by each customer. The formula is CLV = (AR × GM) / CR.[30,39]

Growth Strategy Matrix

A growth strategy matrix allows an organization to consider existing or new product growth strategies within existing markets or potentially new markets. The quadrants within the matrix represent market and product development strategies (figure 2.8).[31]

1. *Market penetration* centers on existing products in existing markets. A market penetration strategy focuses on increasing market share through promotional activities and price reductions.

2. *Diversification* introduces new products into new markets. Diversification may be a more risky investment because an organization is relying on a new product in a market that is new to the organization.

3. *Market development* moves existing products into new markets. A market development strategy may mean the organization is taking its current products or services and targeting either a new consumer or customer segment, a new geographical location, or a combination of both.

4. *Product development* focuses on developing new products to compete within existing markets. As consumer preferences change over time, products change as well to meet those emerging interests of consumers.

Importance-Performance Analysis

The importance-performance analysis (I-PA) is an effective means of accessing service quality. It allows the organization to see how well it is meeting customer expectations and identifies which attributes or services are important to the consumer. Consumers provide feedback on activities or offerings based upon their importance to the consumer and the consumer's level of satisfaction with the organization's performance (figure 2.9).[32]

- The items requiring the organization's immediate attention are those with low

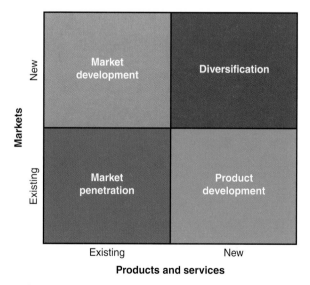

FIGURE 2.8 Growth strategy matrix.

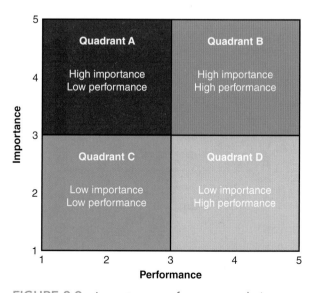

FIGURE 2.9 Importance-performance analysis.

performance and high importance scores. Consumers judge their experience on these items.

- Items with high importance and high performance scores must remain a priority and be exploited whenever possible. The customer values these items and recognizes the high level of performance by the organization.

- Items that have low importance and low performance scores should not receive a great deal of attention by the organization. These products or services might be worth eliminating.

- Items with low importance but high performance suggest the organization may be placing too much emphasis on these items. The organization may continue to support these items but also recognize they could be eliminated.

Loyalty Ladder

Loyalty ladder identifies the steps consumers take as they become brand loyal (figure 2.10).[33] The primary goal of marketing in this model is to establish a relationship with prospective customers and move them along the ladder.

1. The first step is to identify who might be a customer if exposed to the product. This potential customer is the Prospect.

2. Once convinced to purchase the product, the Prospect steps up to become a Customer.

3. Having met the Customer's initial expectations and been satisfied with the product, the Customer takes another step up the ladder with repeat purchases to become a Client. As a Client, the relationship with the product grows and so does the loyalty to the brand.

4. The Client's next step is as a Supporter of the brand, with a strong sense of loyalty to the brand. The Supporter trusts the brand to deliver a satisfying product, so other products are purchased. The Supporter tries other products the brand offers.

5. Once the Supporter promotes the brand's products to others, the Supporter reaches the top rung as an Advocate or brand champion.

Porter's Five Forces

Developed by Michel Porter in 1979 to analyze the competitive nature of the market, Porter focuses on five forces that shape competition and impact profitability (figure 2.11):

1. Industry rivalries
2. The threat of new entrants
3. Bargaining power of buyers
4. Bargaining power of suppliers
5. The threat of substitutes

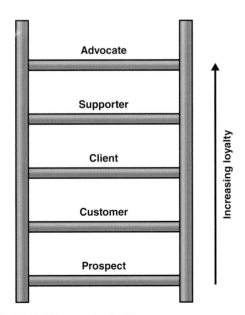

FIGURE 2.10   Loyalty ladder.

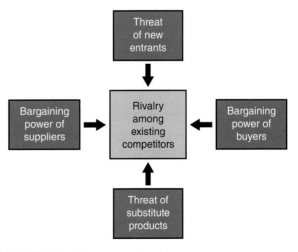

FIGURE 2.11   Porter's five forces.

Defining industry rivals in sport is not as easy as in other industries. For example, in the food industry, identifying salty snack rivals is somewhat straightforward. The market leader is Frito Lay, followed by Snyder-Lance, private labels, and multiple regional companies. For the University of Miami's football marketing team, should it only consider Florida International University and Florida Atlantic University football programs? The marketing team should also consider UM's women's teams—volleyball and soccer—as well as other local sports–related activities. The competitive environment may also include both the entertainment and tourist industries in South Florida.

The threat of new entrants appears in the market when entry costs are low and the opportunity for profits exists. The two most readily available actions UM football can take in response to the threat of new entrants are pricing and exploiting brand loyalty toward The U.

The power of buyers lies in their ability to sway price. Unlike other industries that can influence price by increasing supply of a product, sport organizations may decide to offer incentives or access to select stadium amenities to add more perceived value for their fans.

The power of suppliers stems from their control over pricing to the industry. As their prices increase, the users must react by raising prices, accepting reduced profits, or seeking out new suppliers.

The threat of substitutes is high for sport programs in large metropolitan markets with multiple sport and entertainment options as well as markets with multiple tourism options. However, a sport organization may be able to leverage itself as a substitute if competitors do not recognize the sport organization as an existing competitor.[34]

Product Life Cycle

The product life cycle depicts sales activity over the lifespan of a product. The lifespan is divided into four basic categories, each requiring its own strategic marketing plan to address changes in the market (figure 2.12):

1. *Introduction.* Early in the product's life, costs are often high with low sales and profits. The initial costs include product

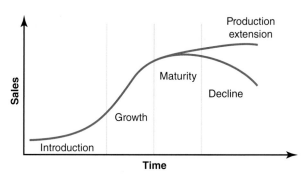

FIGURE 2.12   Product life cycle.

development, capital for production capabilities, and marketing costs to introduce the product to consumers.

2. *Growth.* Sales and profits rise as more consumers are aware of the product, and production costs decrease due to economies of scale, boosting profits.

3. *Maturity.* As the product matures, the company may see sales begin to decrease due to market saturation and/or increased competition. Profits may also begin to trend downward as sales decline, and the product's price may be reduced to defend market share.

4. *Decline.* Once the product enters stage four, decline, sales and profits accelerate to lower levels. At this point the organization may attempt to revive the product through some type of product or brand extension or prepare for its removal from the market.[35]

Segment-Target-Position Model

The segment-target-position (STP) model identifies market segments, targets the most attractive segments, and positions the product to best counter the completion and attract consumers (figure 2.13). During the segmentation process, consumers may be grouped by demographics, psychographics, behavior traits, and geographic location. Once consumers are segmented, the organization identifies the groups with the most potential interest in the product. Those groups offering the greatest sales and profit potential become the target market. During the positioning phase, the product is differentiated from the competitors, making consumers more enticed to purchase the product.[36]

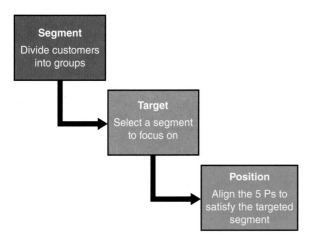

FIGURE 2.13   Segment-target-position model.

SWOT Analysis

The SWOT analysis is used to identify an organization's position in the market by listing its strengths, weaknesses, opportunities, and threats (figure 2.14). The exercise focuses the organization's attention to preexisting internal and external factors (or those with the potential to exist) that will influence the success of the organization.

The internal assessment focuses on the organization's strengths and weaknesses:

- Strengths include everything that the organization has mastered or acquired over time: financial and intellectual resources, image in the market, attributes that consumers feel differentiate the company from its competitors, etc.

- Weaknesses are the strengths of competitors, personnel turnover, financial or governmental constraints, as well as internal structural obstacles. Weaknesses often go undeclared due to individual vested interests. All risks, current and anticipated, should be identified.

External factors are divided into either opportunities or threats:

- Opportunities include product voids in the market, consumers dissatisfied with current choices in the market, and unresponsive or complacent competitors.

- Threats emerge from competitors entering the market, product substitutions, governmental regulations, or events creating a negative social image.[37]

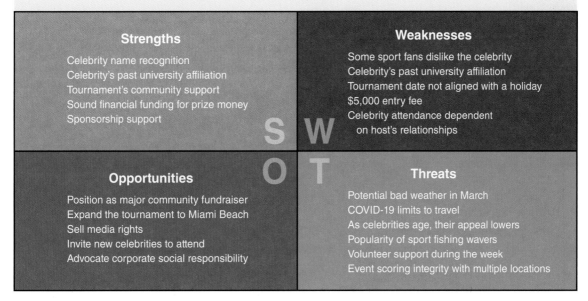

FIGURE 2.14   SWOT analysis.

Unique Selling Proposition

The unique selling proposition (USP) assists the organization in identifying those attributes that can be used to convince consumers that the product stands out from competitors and is worth switching brands. The process involves first identifying what consumers want and what the organization and its competitors each do well (figure 2.15). Then the organization must identify a unique characteristic or feature that will inspire new consumers to enter the market by purchasing and current consumers to switch brands. The unique attribute must be something the competitors cannot emulate.[38]

FIGURE 2.15   Unique selling proposition.

Wrap-Up

Sport organizations clearly face many unique challenges and demands, not all of which they can meet with frenzied marketing action. Many challenges require considerable thought and a well-planned response. Yet the majority of demands have comparatively simple solutions after all the data are put together. In the coming years, sport will continue to be unique, but it will follow one principle experienced without modification in all industries: The organizations most likely to succeed will be the ones that have the best handle on the marketplace. Such a handle comes only with a disciplined approach to research and input from all stakeholders, including the staff, followed by the development, analysis, and integration of every function of marketing. In the following chapters, we consider all these steps in detail.

Activities

1. Define the five Ps of the sport marketing mix.
2. Find evidence of a sport organization that does an excellent job of recognizing market trends and adjusting its strategy accordingly. How does the organization stay true to a core vision while also repositioning its products?
3. Describe a new product concept that you think would meet unfilled consumer needs in your favorite sport.
4. List the market or consumer segments that most clearly relate to a tennis or golf club near you.
5. From the stories or ads in any online sports outlet, try to find examples of the five Ps of the marketing mix.
6. Look closely at the list of Laura Nash's ethics questions. Discuss a recent example of an ethical issue in sport marketing and analyze the issue using those questions.

Your Marketing Plan

The first step in this project is to choose (or create) an organization for which you will develop a marketing plan, or perhaps just a TiMSS plan. Your ultimate goal is to prepare a 20- to 30-page plan that helps the organization attain strategic objectives. This plan should become an item in your personal portfolio. Do you aspire to work for a particular organization? Do you have an idea for a sport product that will fill some existing consumer needs or wants?

1. Identify the key stakeholders and a market research and data capture plan.
2. Identify resources for internal and external scanning.
3. Identify the three most important market trends affecting your firm or product.
4. Begin to define your business and your product.
5. Develop the draft of your mission statement.
6. Utilize four models to assess the competitive marketplace.
7. Conduct a SWOT analysis using the data collected from step six.
8. Set specific objectives for each element of the marketing plan.

 Go to HK*Propel* to complete the activities for this chapter.

Chapter 3
Understanding the Sport Consumer

OBJECTIVES

- To recognize the differences between socialization, involvement, and commitment for sport consumers

- To understand the various internal and external factors that shape consumer involvement and commitment in sport

- To understand the decision-making process and purchase behavior of sport consumers

Ian Hitchcock/Getty Images

In 2020, the United States began making what has been called the minority-majority shift. According to Forbes, the year 2020 marked the first time that the majority of people under the age of 17 came from nonwhite ethnic backgrounds.[1] It is also estimated that by the 2040s, the country will be populated more by minority groups than a White majority. This is a shift that has taken place slowly as the United States became more multicultural with various races from all over the world. The greatest demographic increases have been in Hispanic and Asian populations, and this continues to be the case. The minority-majority shift will impact all types of businesses over the coming decades, and the sport industry needs to be ready. Some changes and challenges have already been addressed by sport marketers, but more needs to be done to meet the wants and needs of a younger, more diverse fan base that is growing up in a demographically evolving America. Forbes provided insight into the multicultural shift and strategies for marketers to reach new fans as the minority becomes the majority:[1]

- *Invest in soccer.* Soccer is the most popular sport around the globe, and the attraction of what is truly "football" has taken hold in the United States. Soccer is the preferred sport of Hispanics in the United States and very popular with Asian fans as well. It is growing tremendously among non-Hispanic White fans, and the ability of soccer to reach so many different ethnic groups is attractive to sport marketers. Unlike professional sports with aging audiences like American football and baseball, soccer has youth and diversity on its side, which is what many brands are looking for to connect with consumers of the future. A challenge of soccer as a marketing platform for brands is the fragmentation of the sport at the professional level. There are myriad leagues around the world with incredible talent and competition, such as the English Premier League (EPL), Bundesliga, LaLiga, LIGA MX, and Major League Soccer (MLS). This means that even though soccer has the largest amount of fans around the world, fans are consuming the sport in so many different places, which could make it harder for sport marketers to reach these consumers than those watching pro leagues with only one professional division.

The sport industry is vast, and fans can choose from countless products, services, and experiences. How do consumers go about searching the endless options, narrowing down their selections, and ultimately, making a purchase? What happens after that purchase and how does it affect subsequent decision making? As we noted in chapter 1, the marketing concept begins and ends with the consumer. The marketer of any commodity—golf, grain, or gasoline—needs to understand who might be interested in buying the product. Therefore, the intelligent marketer constantly seeks to answer a series of questions, including the following:

- Who are my consumers—past, present, and future—in terms of both demographics (age, gender, income), geographics (location), and psychographics (attitudes, opinions, lifestyles)?
- Where, when, and how have my consumers been exposed to my product? What social media platforms are they on and what marketing messages did they consume?
- How and why did they become involved with my product?
- If they have been loyal to my product, why? Why have some lost that commitment?

Chapter 2 provided the big picture of how consumer research may drive effective marketing strategy. This chapter explores the literature on some of the how and why questions about sport

- *Find the influencers.* Every sport has multiple stars that transcend the sport itself. They shine brighter than the others and may have more followers and influence than the teams they are on. Many of these stars like Cristiano Ronaldo, LeBron James, Serena Williams, and Megan Rapinoe appeal to minority and multicultural consumers and wield immense influence in the marketplace. Aligning with athletes who represent what the world will look like in the future will benefit brands who are trying to send relatable marketing messages and showcase a variety of personalities, lifestyles, and preferences.
- *Address your weaknesses.* Sport professionals have made strides in multicultural marketing and promotions, but there is much work to be done. Some leagues have been more successful than others. In order to get better, executives must be willing to admit they are lacking in certain areas and address and improve upon their weaknesses. Long popular with Black and White fans, the NFL has recently tried to attract more Hispanic fans by holding games in Mexico City and to lure European fans with games in London. NASCAR has also dedicated resources to Hispanic marketing initiatives across the entire league. MLB struggles with bringing in younger fans, for whom the pace of the game seems slow in comparison to technology-driven entertainment. The league has discussed rule changes to speed up the games and make them more exciting for consumers. The NBA, which has long been the gold standard in globalization, is constantly innovating and looking for ways to penetrate new markets and grow the game internationally.

Sport has the ability to change the world because so many people play and watch sports. The sports that will grow in the future are the ones whose organizations will take the time to invest in grassroots efforts, get kids playing early, and provide a clear path to enjoy the sport into adulthood. Sports have the ability to change business because everyone still wants to watch them live. Companies that authentically connect with consumers through sports, demonstrate the ability to relate on a multicultural level, and make the brand experience welcoming for everyone will successfully navigate the minority-majority shift.

consumers. Chapter 4 examines research methods to address all the preceding questions and develop a database on consumers—the foundation for all the subsequent chapters. As we discuss here and in chapter 4, sport marketers must look beyond basic demographic research (who, what, and where) to examine the psychographic reasons (why) consumers are (or aren't) aware of, involved in, or committed to their organization or product.

Countless studies, theories, and models attempt to get into the mind of the consumer. Here are 10 of the most common consumer behavior theories:[2]

1. Pavlovian model
2. Economic model
3. Stimulus-response model
4. Psychological model
5. Howarth Sheth model
6. Sociological model
7. Family decision-making model
8. Engel-Blackwell-Kollat model
9. Industrial buying model
10. Nicosia model

Most of these theories characterize the factors that influence behavior as either external (environmental) or internal (individual). One of the most prominent theories used to explain this phenomenon, developed by marketing professor Philip Kotler, is the black box model of consumer behavior. Figure 3.1 depicts the relationship between external factors (stimuli in the environment), internal factors (the buyer's

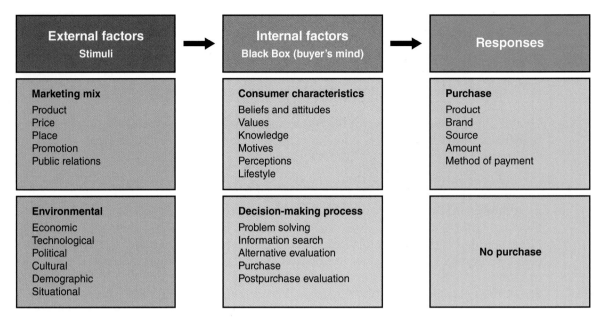

FIGURE 3.1   Black box stimulus-response model of consumer behavior.

mind, often referred to as the black box), and the buyer's responses. In the end, a host of variables influences consumer responses (purchase and no purchase) in today's global sport market.

Socialization, Involvement, and Commitment

External and internal factors influence how and how much people become involved with and committed to sport. Think about your own sports activities, whether as a child, youth, or adult. Something or somebody got you interested, somehow, in an activity. Perhaps it was a trip to watch a game, an afternoon playing with a parent or friend, a television broadcast of an exciting event or championship, or a cool new app. A trigger of interest prompted your involvement and perhaps your socialization into sport.

Sociologists typically consider socialization to be the process by which people assimilate and develop the skills, knowledge, attitudes, and other "equipment" necessary to perform various social roles. This process involves two-way interaction between the person and the environment. Socialization, in turn, demands some kind of involvement—in our case with sport. Often referred to as the ABCs of involvement, the three basic stages are affective, behavioral, and cognitive:

- **Affective involvement** is the attitudes, feelings, and emotions that a consumer has toward an activity. Pep rallies and pregame festivities are standard fare for affective involvement, but so too are the best advertisements. Just think of any Nike ad. Like them or not, these ads stir the emotions about a sport, about Nike, or about issues that extend far beyond the playing field. Nike rarely focuses on the products in its advertising. It highlights star athletes, tells an emotional story that resonates with the target audience, and ends with a poignant message and the famous tagline, Just Do It.

- **Behavioral involvement** is the actual doing. This behavior includes athletes practicing and competing; it also includes the activities of fans at a venue, at home, or on a mobile device, watching and listening and cheering. To sport marketers, behavioral involvement often means purchasing.

- **Cognitive involvement** is the acquisition of information and knowledge about a sport. Players sitting through position meetings, booster club members listening to a head coach's speech, and fans reading about their favorite team's performance on social media all exemplify cognitive involvement. Magazines, websites, apps, radio, television, and smart devices are key media for cognitive involvement by consumers eager to know more about sport. Sport industry executives

Paul Chesne/Michael Ochs Archives/Getty Images

Nike's powerful Colin Kaepernick ad supporting his fight for social justice.

have predicted a significant swing in the sport industry from heavy reliance on subscription television to an overwhelming future focused on streaming and wireless devices. Sport, more than any other category, is the most popular form of content watched by digital-only consumers, with 41 percent choosing streamed sports content over linear broadcasts. More than 60 percent of sports fans view their favorite content via an over-the-top (OTT) or premium social media service, according to a consumer behavior research study by Grabyo.[3]

Commitment refers to the frequency, duration, and intensity of involvement in a sport, or the willingness to expend money, time, and energy in a pattern of sport involvement. Movement up the frequency escalator normally indicates a deeper commitment. As you learned in chapter 2, the frequency escalator is a graphic representation of consumer movement to higher levels of involvement in sport, with the three main stages of retention, growth, and acquisition (see figure 2.3). When the escalator was created, it introduced the idea of constant motion into the original staircase model, because the sport industry is always evolving and fan attendance is a progression. Dr. Bill Sutton expounded on this important marketing theory by developing the frequency *elevator*, which differs from the escalator in that it considers fan involvement as more than a constant one-way progression (figure 3.2). Fans consciously choose to become more or less committed to sport organizations over time, and their behavior will reflect those decisions.[4] When fan commitment and behavior changes, either positively or negatively, sport organizations have to be ready to meet evolving consumer wants and needs. In the sidebar On My Elevator: A New Way to Think About Fan Consumption, Dr. Sutton introduces the frequency elevator and discusses how to service sports fans of the future.

Frequency Elevator

Based on a 44-game pro team schedule

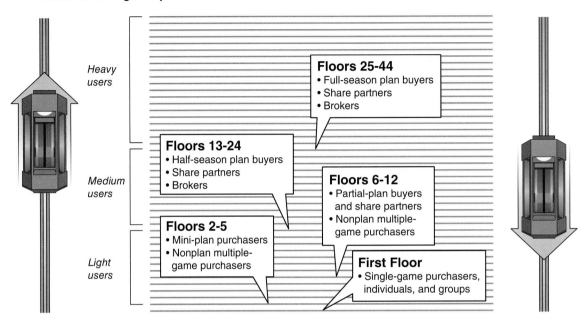

Floors 25-44
• Full-season plan buyers
• Share partners
• Brokers

Floors 13-24
• Half-season plan buyers
• Share partners
• Brokers

Floors 6-12
• Partial-plan buyers and share partners
• Nonplan multiple-game purchasers

Floors 2-5
• Mini-plan purchasers
• Nonplan multiple-game purchasers

First Floor
• Single-game purchasers, individuals, and groups

Heavy users

Medium users

Light users

Nonpurchasing product consumers remaining outside the venue: Media consumer, aware nonconsumer, misinformed consumer, and nonaware consumer
Secondary entrance: Bargain hunters, last minute shoppers, and secondary market patrons

Elevator would have the same divisions for college sports, pro football, and pro baseball. Only the number of games would vary accordingly. For example, a heavy user in college basketball might attend 12+ games while a heavy user for pro football might attend 8 or more games.

Illustration by Old Hat Creative (oldhatcreative.com)

FIGURE 3.2   Frequency elevator.

Reprinted with permission from B. Sutton, "On My Elevator: A New Way to Think About Fan Consumption," *Sports Business Daily*, April 13, 2015. https://www.sportsbusinessdaily.com/Journal/Issues/2015/04/13/Opinion/Sutton-Impact.aspx

Marketers must clearly understand the types of involvement and commitment that consumers represent. The WNBA season-ticket holder who attends every game, follows player tweets, tracks game statistics, pays for special-content websites, downloads the team app onto her cell phone, plays in a fantasy league, and roots with great emotion is obviously different from the father who takes his child to one game to satisfy a sense of parental duty. The casual spectator who attends a game with a free ticket is distinctly different from the rabid fan watching the same game at home. The act of attendance may or may not reflect or develop a deeper commitment. The committed fan thinks more, feels more, and does more.

Research conducted by SSRS/Luker on Trends looked at the relationship between a fan's connection to his or her favorite professional team and how that connection affected overall engagement in sports. The survey measured team connection on a four-point scale from "Not at all" to "Very much" connected. The survey measured the engagement for weekly hours viewing, monthly spending, and yearly attending of sports games. The research suggested that 21 percent of Americans feel "Very much" connected to their favorite professional team. This group of Americans had far more sports engagement than less-connected sports fans. Highly connected fans watched almost 10 hours of sports per week (9.6) and attended roughly eight games (7.4) annually compared to their nonconnected counterparts at four hours per week (3.6) and two games (1.8) annually. In addition, 30 percent of Americans who labeled themselves as very connected fans indicated that they spend money monthly (or more often) on sports.[5]

On My Elevator: A New Way to Think About Fan Consumption

In 1993, when the first edition of . . . "Sport Marketing" was published, the concept of the frequency escalator was introduced. The escalator was created and designed as an American sales model that employs direct and indirect sales techniques to create awareness and enhance understanding among consumers to position purchase as a need or a want and ultimately to initiate action.

The escalator evolved from the staircase, which was developed by baseball executive Bill Giles to explain how increasing frequency of attendance was a key in driving revenue by developing fan avidity through a deeper connection to the team. The escalator differed from the staircase in that it was always moving forward, showing the progression of the relationships between the fan and the organization.

When the escalator and its predecessor were conceived more than 40 years ago, the world was a much different place. The Internet, satellite television, and radio and sports subscription packages were nonexistent. Cable television was available only in limited areas and not as a source of multiple programming options.

The limited number of broadcast stations also restricted the number and variety of sports and entertainment programming options. A Sunday NFL broadcast could be limited to the national game if one did not live in an NFL market or perhaps just a local team. College football games were only on Saturdays, and televised games were regional in nature except on rare occasions or during the bowl games, which were primarily only on New Year's Day. In some markets, the NBA Finals were shown in tape-delay format, broadcast several hours after the game had been played.

There was really no initial need for the escalator because people either bought tickets to individual games, bought season tickets, were a media-only consumer, or a nonconsumer. Partial plans and mini-plans had not been created because sports marketers lacked the sophistication and the analytics to segment and understand their consumers. The approach was what we can find in a number of countries outside of the United States today—build a winning team on the field/pitch/court and consumers will come, then be prepared to suffer fewer attendees when you lose until you start winning again.

Compare that to today with the unprecedented amount of sports and entertainment options that one can not only attend but consume in a home theater, on a computer, tablet, phone, or other mobile device—the second screen. Technology and the proliferation of sports-only television channels and the competition among those channels for viewers have created a level of competition for the attention of consumers that is unprecedented.

The secondary market (which as I have mentioned in the past as the real primary market for first contact) existed only in the form of scalpers walking in front of the venue holding available tickets for sale.

Thus, the overwhelming options and choices for sports and entertainment consumption, regardless of whether that consumption comes in the form of attendance, viewership, or some other interactive experience, can be a definitive challenge not only in initially getting people on the escalator but retaining them as well. The secondary market, downturns in the economy, demands on the time of consumers, and the plethora of choices and options available to them have given me pause and led me to determine that the frequency model most appropriate for 2015 and beyond is an elevator and not an escalator.

> continued

> continued

Why an Elevator?

The elevator permits the person riding to not only ascend to higher levels but also to descend to a lower level or simply stop and get off in an area of interest to them. It is not always moving forward as the escalator. Demand influences behavior and necessitates that during the lifetime association of the consumer with the sport organization, the relationship will not always be moving forward. There could be times of decrease or times of contentment where the purchaser finds a level that fits his/her lifestyle in terms of commitment—time, financial, emotional, or a combination thereof.

Keys to the Elevator

- Promotes getting on, finding the right floor to begin shopping. Then, once they are comfortable, exploring the upper floors and other departments.
- May involve descending to lower floors to shop for bargains, more affordable options but staying in the same store. Could involve downselling.
- As with any shopper, there is always an interest in a bargain or a good deal, so consumers can elect to press "B" for basement and find a variety of sellers willing to sell at a price less than [what] the organization/team is offering.
- Conversely, customers can elect to become premier customers, frequent buyers, or members and receive preferred treatment and benefits not available to all customers in exchange for their loyalty and willingness to buy direct from the organization/team.
- The elevator has a button that corresponds to the number of games and/or the number of events. There is also an "E" button to exit the store and possibly not return.

Thus, while a full-season-ticket purchase might remain the goal, the elevator model encourages buyers to be happy and satisfied with their level of commitment, leading to a longer association with the organization.

A 10-game-plan buyer who finds she is happy with that level of time and monetary investment may elect to stay at the level for 20 years. The key is understanding that and accepting that as a possible outcome. The customer may choose to add games from time to time or may choose to decrease games because of personal situations, such as job loss, having very young children, etc.

The key to the elevator is understanding and accepting that while consumer demand might fluctuate from time to time, the most important factor is keeping them on the elevator in your building. If they leave your building or organization, it may be difficult to persuade them to return. The options of other attractions or opportunities or the convenience of viewing at home might be a strong enough siren song to keep them away.

The elevator implies that the purchaser can determine the size and scope of their commitment rather than the organization, a fact that will make some organizations uncomfortable. But as we live in a world of customization and personalization, isn't it logical that the consumer would seek those same elements in the purchase of a ticket plan?

Why Is It Here?

The elevator has been in play in the secondary market for quite some time. The secondary market (maybe a better term is the *reseller market*) has flourished in part because of the number of consumers who found that ticket plans offered by the teams contain more games than they can attend either in terms of time or cost. They then create their own elevator stop where they feel most comfortable and post the remaining tickets for sale on a reseller's website or even on the team's website. The funds generated by reselling the tickets are then used to pay for playoff tickets or are credited toward the purchase of next year's ticket plan.

In reality, season tickets are really not functioning as tickets to every game. The unintended consequence of the escalator approach of moving ticket buyers up into larger plans is when those individual games are sold to a third party, particularly tickets that have been dynamically or even variably priced, those tickets can end up in the possession of fans for the opposing team, affecting the perception and impact of home-field/court advantage.

The elevator model is not limited to tickets but is now becoming a practice for suites and other multiyear premier seating options as well.

The combination of the number of tickets in a suite, usually between 12 and 16, and the number of events to which a suite holder is entitled has caused a similar reselling market to emerge. The presence of multiple teams in the market and having contracts and obligations with multiple teams also is contributing to a suite elevator. Suite resellers have the ability to enter markets, purchase suites or premium products from each team, and create hybrid packages that include multiple games and events from each team and venue without the obligation to own every event or even to sign multiyear agreements.

Thus, the elevator is about personalization and customization for buyers, as they can establish their own level for monetary and time expenditures. As customization is available to consumers in almost every facet of their lives, why should sports be any different? The current economic times and the uncertainty of what tomorrow brings dictates the shift from the escalator to the elevator, and unlike the escalator, it is the consumer who controls the elevator and elects whether to ascend or descend, to get off and shop, or to just get off and exit the product.

The elevator encourages the organization to think about long-term or even lifetime value for each consumer account rather than the type of ticket they are buying this year and the amount of that investment. As with any advance or change, there will need to be a period of adjustment before there is widespread acceptance. A team's experience with the elevator might be bumpy and jerky before it becomes smooth and routine.

Organizations take note: The elevator isn't coming tomorrow; it's already here. Your customers are well aware of how to not only push its buttons but also yours.

Reprinted with permission from B. Sutton, "On My Elevator: A New Way to Think About Fan Consumption," *Sports Business Daily*, April 13, 2015. https://www.sportsbusinessdaily.com/Journal/Issues/2015/04/13/Opinion/Sutton-Impact.aspx

External Factors

Phase one of the black box consumer behavior model is stimuli. Consumers are surrounded by a host of factors that may influence their decisions about sport involvement. As we consider some of the most prominent (marketing mix and environmental) factors, we stress again the constant interaction between and among them.

Marketing Mix

One of the biggest external factors weighing on consumers is their daily exposure to the constant barrage of marketing messages. The marketing mix is ever-present, especially in today's 24/7 connected world. In the 1970s, the average person in the United States was exposed to roughly 500 advertisements per day. That number is now 10 times greater—an unprecedented *5,000 ads per day*.[6] Digital and social media have certainly changed the marketing game. While marketers are desperately vying for consumers' attention and trying to influence their future behavior, other factors in the external environment are shaping that behavior simultaneously. Even though consumers are exposed to thousands of marketing messages daily, they also have the technology to prevent much of that communication. According to Ryan Holmes, CEO of Hootsuite, 86 million users of ad-blocking software in the United States are able to avoid US$20

Courtesy of Modern Woodmen Park

With an abundance of games played in MiLB, promotions and entertainment are paramount to keeping fans in the stands. The Ferris wheel at Modern Woodmen Park, home of the Quad City River Bandits in Davenport, Iowa, is a unique entertainment option.

billion worth of advertisements targeted at them each year.[6] This is a great example of two very prominent external stimuli (marketing mix and technology) working against each other to affect consumer behavior.

As America's pastime, professional baseball is played all over the United States in many towns, big and small, due to the vast farm system that supports Major League Baseball (MLB). The sport of baseball at the minor league level is marketed heavily because there are so many games and so many stadiums that need to be filled. Let's examine how the marketing mix influences consumer behavior in Minor League Baseball (MiLB) from an external stimuli perspective and how it is implemented to encourage fan attendance at games.

Product

Psychologists suggest that much of fan behavior relates to the wins and losses of fans' favored teams or players. Although marketers cannot control game or match results, they can control how the product (including past or future performance) is packaged and presented to consumers. The behavior of teams, leagues, suppliers, and

distributers clearly influences consumers. MiLB is an excellent example of a league that has crafted a highly desirable product that is not wins and losses based. MiLB markets an affordable, family-friendly sport product that draws millions of fans to ballparks each year without the use of star power, luxury facilities, or elaborate entertainment. According to MiLB, 41,504,077 fans attended games in 2019, which was the 15th consecutive season that MiLB drew more than 40 million fans.[7] The 2.6 percent increase from 2018 totaled over one million additional fans and was the largest year-over-year increase since the 2006 to 2007 season.[7]

Price

Price is still a major factor that dictates whether or not fans attend sports events. Getting a great seat at the game and doing so at an affordable price is important to individuals, but especially families, as professional sports have become a luxury item. In order to fully experience a professional event, one would likely need tickets, parking, food, drink, and possibly some merchandise. The cost to attend one game could add up quickly. The Fan Cost Index (FCI) compiled by *Team Market-*

ing Report (TMR) is a measure of the cost for a family of four to attend one professional sports event when purchasing the aforementioned items related to the full fan experience (two adult and two child tickets, two small beers, four small soft drinks, four hot dogs, two programs, two adult-size ball caps, and parking).[8] In MLB, the average ticket price in 2019 was US$32.99 and the FCI was US$234.38, as compared to MiLB where the average ticket price was US$8 and a family of four could attend for US$64.[9] Clearly, price is the part of the marketing mix that MiLB focuses on to differentiate itself in the sport entertainment market and lure individuals and families to the parks.

Place

Fans having convenient access to the product is another critical component in sport marketing. Fortunately for MiLB, there are 176 teams in 15 leagues across the United States, and these teams compete in major markets as well as bedroom communities and tiny towns. Nine teams that set single-game stadium attendance records in 2019 were in the following areas:[54]

Clearwater, Florida

Durham, North Carolina

Fort Wayne, Indiana

Midland, Michigan

Greenville, South Carolina

Myrtle Beach, South Carolina

Omaha, Nebraska

Pulaski, Virginia

Richmond, Virginia

MiLB provides access to the sport for so many fans that many other professional leagues simply cannot provide. The ballpark in baseball is still a major draw for many fans as well. Although minor league parks do not have the seating, amenities, and entertainment of pro stadiums, many are newly constructed or renovated venues designed to provide a more comfortable, intimate, and exciting experience. Since 2000, 68 new ballparks were built with three additional parks under construction in 2020.[54] For baseball fans, having the product close to home in a new or renovated venue makes minor league sport entertainment highly desirable.

Promotion

If there is any league that has mastered the art of promotion, it is MiLB. When you have roughly 10,000 games to sell each season, you have to get creative.

- The Bowling Green Hot Rods held Facebook Fan Night where friends of the team could select almost every aspect of the evening's entertainment using the social media site.
- The Lowell Spinners hosted the Human Home Run where David "The Human Cannonball" Smith was shot out of a cannon over the outfield wall.
- The Memphis Grizzlies Taco Truck Throwdown offered a US$23 ticket to the game, which included a themed T-shirt and eights tacos, one from each of eight local taco trucks.[10]

Silly promotions, gameday giveaways, fun-filled theme nights, and deep discounts are at the center of MiLB's brand. Fans look forward to the ancillary activities at the park almost as much as the games themselves. Due to the long season and the lack of star power at this level, designing authentic and attractive promotions to bring people to the parks is key to increasing attendance.

Public Relations

Baseball may be a traditional sport, but good marketers understand the value of every fan who walks through the gate. The more people you market to, the more fans you bring to the sport, and the better business will be. MiLB has embraced the communities in which it operates and created public relations strategies to communicate with and market to a variety of target audiences. One Hispanic fan engagement initiative called the Copa de la Diversión consisted of 403 games where MiLB teams adopted Spanish-language identities. Copa de la Diversión brought in nearly 20 percent larger crowds than average for MiLB attendance. MiLB also established a Pride initiative that consisted of 71 event nights, and Pride crowds were 12 percent larger than average for MiLB attendance.[54] Taking an inclusive marketing approach, even in a sport with a long-standing traditional image, has been one of the reasons MiLB has seen greater fan support and increased attendance numbers over the last decade.

Environmental

Marketing does not happen in a bubble or a vacuum. It would be nice for marketers to have consumers' full attention and focus when they are communicating with them. It would be even better if there were no barriers or challenges to people purchasing products and services after being exposed to marketing communication. The reality, though, is while marketers are trying to exert their advertising influence on consumers and persuade them into making purchase decisions, a multitude of environmental factors are interacting in the same space, exerting force on the consumer. A successful sports marketer must not only understand the marketing mix but also be able to craft a marketing strategy that can overcome these barriers and challenges posed by the environment. According to the black box of consumer behavior model, the six components of environmental influence are economic, technological, political, cultural, demographic, and situational.

Economic

We will begin our discussion of environmental factors with economics, as the economy has the most obvious effect on consumer behavior and buying. Economics is a social science that promotes the study of people and societies and how they use limited resources. It examines how those societies produce, distribute, and consume various goods and services. Economics is delineated into two types:

• *Macroeconomics.* The branch of economics that studies the overall working of a national economy. It is more focused on the big picture and analyzing things such as growth, inflation, interest rates, unemployment, and taxes. When you hear the Federal Reserve is raising interest rates or that the national unemployment rate is 7.5%, you are hearing about macroeconomic topics.

• *Microeconomics.* The branch of economics that studies how households and businesses reach decisions about purchasing, savings, setting prices, competition in business, etc. It focuses at the individual level, while macroeconomics looks at the decisions that affect entire countries and society as a whole.[11]

Macroeconomics focuses on how economies are performing and what factors are influencing that performance, either positively or negatively. Two important elements of macroeconomics are the Gross Domestic Product and the business cycle. Gross Domestic Product (GDP) is the total value of all goods and services produced by a country over a period of time, and it is considered to be a broad measure of a country's economic health. The GDP affects the overall business cycle, or fluctuations in economic activity over time, which contains six stages:

1. *Expansion.* A period when employment, income, production levels, and sales increase and the economy is booming.

2. *Peak.* The highest point of the economy with maximum level of growth, and when a downturn is inevitable.

3. *Recession.* A period of increased unemployment and decreased production due to declining demand, sales, and income.

4. *Depression.* A period when unemployment and bankruptcy levels increase, production plummets, and consumer and business confidence is extremely low.

5. *Trough.* The lowest point of the economy with minimum level of growth, and when an upturn is inevitable.

6. *Recovery.* A period when low prices spur demand; production, sales, and income levels rise; and the economy starts to turn around.[12]

While macroeconomics certainly has an effect on the sport industry, most of what concerns sport marketers happens at the microeconomic level where individuals and businesses make decisions. The Great Recession in 2008 was one of the worst economies the United States has experienced since the Great Depression, and it rocked the sport industry. Sport businesses and front offices everywhere were dramatically affected, and one could argue the sport entertainment landscape has been decidedly different since that time. In 2009, *The New York Times* reported on the negative impact of the recession on U.S. sports business, leagues, and organizations, which suffered the following losses:[13]

• NFL cut 169 jobs and the commissioner cut his own salary by 20 percent.

• AFL cancelled the entire 2009 season.

• NBA released one-tenth of its staff.

• WNBA released two players per team, reducing rosters to 11.

- ESPN did not fill 200 vacant jobs.
- USOC laid off 54 workers and cut millions from its budget.
- NASCAR laid off hundreds of employees.
- LPGA Tour lost three title sponsors and dropped four tournaments.
- PGA Tour lost three title sponsors but no events.
- Honda ended Formula One sponsorship.
- IndyCar lost one race.

In addition to the lost revenue from sponsorship nonrenewals, which was widespread across much of the industry, teams also reduced ticket prices and offered refunds to season-ticket holders who became unemployed.

While the Great Recession of 2008 was much longer lasting than the COVID-19 global pandemic, the sport industry was still able to operate, even though times were tough. When COVID-19 gripped the entire world, every sport league and event essentially shut down. Large-scale sports events at all levels, from youth sports tournaments to professional leagues to the Olympic Games, were deemed dangerous gatherings in terms of escalating the spread of the virus, and they were postponed or cancelled. For months, the sport world completely stopped, and the financial ramifications were devastating. The sidebar The Day the Sport World Stopped Turning outlines the crushing economic outcomes of the COVID-19 global pandemic on many sectors of the sport industry.

The Day the Sport World Stopped Turning

On March 11, 2020, Rudy Gobert of the NBA tested positive for the coronavirus and the league suspended their season. After that night, nothing in the sport world was the same. The COVID-19 global pandemic had made its way to the United States, and now everyone, at least in the sport industry, knew it. Over the next several days and weeks, individual sports events and entire leagues postponed or cancelled operations and the sport world ground to a halt. Even the biggest sports spectacle in the world, the Olympic Games, hung in the balance, and all eyes were on Tokyo as the Olympic Organizing Committee met and tried to determine the best course of action. Ultimately, the International Olympic Committee announced that the Tokyo 2020 Olympic Games would be held in the summer of 2021 due to the pandemic. Nothing like this had ever happened in sports. EVER.

As people all over the globe were quarantined in their homes not attending or watching sports events, executives anxiously watched the calendar and began to estimate the devastating impact the work stoppage would have on the industry after the pandemic. While the duration of the virus would extend well beyond summer 2020, the greatest economic impact would hit during that time. While it was difficult, or even impossible, to put an exact number on the economic losses sustained by the sport industry due to COVID-19, the estimates of what was lost in the spring and summer of 2020 was unprecedented.

By May, it was estimated that the sport industry had lost at least US$12 billion. It was also estimated that the cancellation of the college and professional football seasons in the fall would more than double that amount, a number that was hard to even fathom, given that the sport industry in the United States was valued at US$100 billion.[14] The US$12 billion figure was broken down this way:

Professional sports: US$5.5 billion
College sports: US$3.9 billion

> continued

> continued

Youth sports: US$2.4 billion

Total: US$11.8 billion

The number was calculated under the assumption that the NBA and NHL did not finish their seasons and that MLB and MLS were only able to play 50 percent of their seasons. Any postponements and cancellations beyond that estimate only added to the financial damage. So, what types of revenues were lost that could total almost US$12 billion? Revenues included things like media rights fees (television), gate receipts (tickets), concessions, and youth sports tourism money spent by families on their kids' training, travel, and competitions. Youth sports tourism alone was estimated to be a US$19 billion industry, and the strongest driver of sports revenue in the country, with so many American children playing and competing in sports around the nation. Many families travel multiple weekends per month to tournaments and meets for their children who are serious athletes. All of these activities stopped due to COVID-19.

ESPN suggested that US$12 billion was likely a conservative number given that many professional sport leagues like tennis, golf, NASCAR, and others were not even included. Outdoor recreational activities, which are very popular in the summertime, were also not factored into the analysis of revenue loss. What this meant was the sport industry was suffering its biggest setback ever and the numbers were consistently increasing as the virus spread around the country and the rest of the world. As everyone braced for football season in the fall, it was reported that the Power-5 schools stood to lose roughly US$4 billion in revenue if the sport was not played. NFL games were worth US$24 million *each* if they were not played, and that money was just the television rights fees lost. That estimate did not include all the other ancillary monies from ticketing and concessions.

March 11, 2020, was a day everyone in sports would remember forever. It was the day the sport world stopped turning. Everything sat still for months while COVID-19 spread and the health and safety of all humankind was addressed. Sport consumption and distribution would change permanently on the other side of the pandemic, and sport marketers would be forced to tackle the tough questions brought about by the coronavirus, and find answers that would take the sport industry into a whole new era. Some of these questions were:

- How do you bring sports content to fans and engage with them consistently when games are not being played?
- How do you keep players, coaches, and staff safe as they return even without fans?
- When live sports return, how do you make stadiums and arenas cleaner and safer?
- Would fans consume live sports differently when they came back? Should the physical venue spaces look the same or be different?
- What should pricing be like and how much would people be willing to spend?
- What would the new role of sponsors be, and how should their promotions be tailored to address consumers' changing emotions and economics?

These were just some of the challenges faced by sport marketing professionals during and after the shutdown caused by the global pandemic. These questions needed answers for sport organizations to recoup the massive amounts of lost revenue. Although COVID-19 brought about one of the most devastating economies the United States had ever seen, halting the entire sport business industry and causing billions in lost revenue, the pandemic also forced sport marketers to reevaluate how they do business, meet the wants and needs of all types of consumers, and consider the ever-increasing role of technology in sport consumption and distribution.

Just as the economy has a profound impact on the business of sport, the sport industry, conversely, influences the overall economy of a country. In 2009, the North American sport market was valued at US$48.73 billion. By 2018, it had grown by 50 percent and was valued at US$71.06 billion, and is projected to hit US$83.1 billion by 2023.[15] These figures represent revenues derived from gate receipts, media rights, sponsorships, and merchandising. According to the North American Industry Classification System (NAICS), which publishes statistical data and ranks all major industries contributing to the U.S. business economy, the sport industry and its revenues are listed at 71, just behind educational and healthcare services.[16] Clearly, the business of sport is lucrative and contributes to a healthy national economy.

At the macro level, it may be hard to discern the overall financial impact of sports on our nation, but at the local level, it is easy to see how sports are at the heart of the economy. Sports events and facilities are often used as catalysts to stimulate a community's growth and economic prosperity. City and county officials bid for expansion franchises and large-scale events to bring new sports activities to their area. The belief is that teams, stadiums, and events bring new construction, jobs, growth, and pride to the region, and public administrators are willing to invest heavily in these initiatives. The city of Charlotte, North Carolina, spent US$110 million on a bid to secure the 30th MLS franchise. Carolina Panthers owner, David Tepper, purchased the team for a record US$325 million, which was US$125 million more than the cost of the previous two MLS franchises. Tepper said the following to explain why he wanted MLS: "Seven-plus million people within an hour and a half drive. The only city that has only two major sports. No major league summer sport in Charlotte. A large Hispanic population which are not served by the two other sports. It's sort of a perfect storm for what is needed in the community."[17]

Tepper, a huge soccer enthusiast, and the city of Charlotte were willing to pay top dollar to bring professional soccer to town and also plan to build a state-of-the-art retractable roof stadium to house both the Panthers and new MLS team.

Economic impact studies conducted after sports events have come to town indicate that while it takes money to make money, the long-term investment for communities can pay dividends. An economic impact study uses data to quantitatively estimate the economic benefits of a particular event or activity on a region. It tracks how money is spent by tourists visiting the area to attend the event, and the total economic impact is calculated by adding three different levels of impact:

1. *Direct.* Production changes that are associated with the immediate effects of changes in tourism expenditures (tourists spending money on hotels, restaurants, and entertainment).
2. *Indirect.* Production changes that result from various rounds of re-spending within other industries (hotels, restaurants, and other businesses having to buy more supplies to support increased tourist demand).
3. *Induced.* Changes in economic activity that result from household spending of income earned, either directly or indirectly, from increased tourism spending (hotel, restaurant, or other business employees spending money in the area after earning more due to a spike in event-related tourism).[18]

Mega events like the Super Bowl and Olympic Games bring thousands of visitors to a city to spend money for weeks at a time. The bidding process for mega events can be very competitive and takes years to complete because the estimated economic impact, both short-term and long-term, is substantial and many cities participate in the process.

When Super Bowl LIII was held in Atlanta in 2019, it was reported that the city along with the Super Bowl Host Committee spent US$46 million to attract the NFL championship game. It was also reported that Atlanta's total economic impact was US$400 million. Georgia Department of Economic Development Chief Officer Bert Brantley said, "For us, it was a complete and total win. We could not have scripted it any better in terms of having the chance to show off Atlanta to the world, but also to the folks who were here in town."[19] Atlanta hosted more than 150 parties and events during Super Bowl week, which is the biggest corporate gathering in all of professional sports.

Although economists speculate as to the accuracy of impact studies, there is certainly money to be gained by communities hosting teams and

Mercedes-Benz Stadium in Atlanta, Georgia, is home to the Atlanta Falcons, Atlanta United FC, and hosted the 2019 Super Bowl.

sports events. It is also obvious that the sport industry affects local and national economies to the tune of hundreds of millions or billions of dollars annually.

Technological

Technology has changed everything around us and will continue to be the biggest factor that shapes how the world works. The intersection of sports and technology is apparent on a daily basis. Technology has drastically changed how athletes play sports, how fans consume it, and how sport marketers distribute and communicate about the product.

Technology and the Athlete Technology is providing an edge in multiple facets of the game. Advances in clothing, equipment, training, and coaching have taken athlete performance and competition levels to an all-time high. Athletic

apparel, wearable tech, and protective gear are making athletes more comfortable, safe, and productive. The creation of compression as well as "reactive" fabrics for athletic and athleisure wear are very popular among sport participants and spectators. Compression clothing comes in varied levels of tightness and applies external pressure to the body to aid in training and recovery. Compression materials improve blood flow, delivering oxygen and nutrients to the muscles and removing waste from the same area. Reactive clothing has moisture-wicking and thermal capabilities, so the fabric senses warmth and sweat and pushes dampness away from the skin to evaporate. Apparel companies such as Nike, Adidas, Under Armour, and Lululemon market high-quality sport apparel made of these and other advanced materials. Many of these brands have research labs where human movement is analyzed and innovative new products are constantly being developed to improve the performance of athletes.[20]

Some clothing, but especially sport equipment, incorporates wearable technology. **Wearable tech** collects and analyzes participant data to provide information related to performance. The wearable tech market is projected to hit US$9 billion in revenue by 2022.[21] Many athletes already wear smart watches to track their workouts. Treadmills and stationary bikes, like those produced by Peloton, allow athletes to work out virtually with an instructor by using a Wi-Fi–enabled, 22-inch touchscreen that streams live and on-demand classes. Sport leagues are also adopting wearable tech to improve player and coaching performance, providing a more sophisticated entertainment product for their fans. The NHL became the second major professional sport league behind the NFL to institute wearable tech, tracking puck and player movement. Microchips were inserted into player pads and hockey pucks to track all types of game-related data. As Dave Lehanski, Senior Vice President of Business Development for the NHL, said, "We'll know who took the shot, where the shot was taken, how fast the puck was moving. It's going to create new opportunities for telling stories."[22] In-game data usage is still in its infancy, but it could revolutionize how professional athletes train and prepare, how coaches strategize, how sports are broadcast, and how fans watch and wager.

Athletes' equipment for training and competition has also benefitted from technological upgrades. As concussions in sports like American football and soccer become of more concern, scientists use tech to create safer balls and helmets. Lighter soccer balls have been constructed for training so players can practice headers without injury. Football helmets continue to undergo transformation to better withstand impact from tackling. The Seattle-based start-up VICIS crafted the $ZERO_1$ helmet, which combines style, safety, and functionality. The company enlisted a group of mechanical engineers and neurosurgeons who designed the $ZERO_1$ helmet "with an outer LODE shell that is 'deformable' as well as an inner layer of columnar structures designed to absorb the force of impact."[23]

Technology and the Fan   Athletes are not the only ones benefitting from technology's impact on the industry. Watching sports and cheering for your favorite team or athlete has never been easier due to the plethora of technology that delivers the fan experience to the palm of your hand. Advances in smart technology and streaming options allow sports fans to watch almost anything from anywhere. Whether you want to watch on your mobile device or tablet, subscriptions to services like Hulu, YouTube TV, Sling TV, fuboTV, Amazon Prime Video, ESPN+, CBS All Access, DAZN, and others provide access to international, national, and regional sports coverage.

Cable TV is no longer a necessity if you are a sports fan who wants to watch all your favorite programming. In fact, cord cutting has revolutionized how sports content is distributed. In a seven-year span from 2011 to 2018, ESPN lost 14 million subscribers (dropping from 100 million to 86 million) due to cord cutting, and those 14 million subscribers were generating ESPN and Disney US$1.44 billion per year.[24] Although many people still kept cable, the plummeting numbers forced "The Worldwide Leader in Sports" to reconsider its distribution strategy and delve into the streaming game, finally launching ESPN+.

As consumer preferences have changed and more and more people are streaming over mobile devices, this has led to a rapid proliferation of over-the-top (OTT) services. Tech companies and social media platforms are now competing against traditional media outlets for the rights to broadcast sports content. Twitter and Facebook were the first to join the sports streaming battle. Twitter first paid for sports media rights when it purchased Thursday Night Football (TNF) games from the NFL for US$10 million in 2016. Amazon then took over those TNF games after Twitter's deal expired, and the company paid US$65 million annually for the next two seasons. In 2020, Amazon renewed for three more years and agreed to stream one regular season game annually on Prime Video.[25] Amazon also had the rights to stream English Premier League (EPL) soccer matches. When Google-owned YouTube TV signed a contract to stream MLS LA Galaxy games, it was the first time a streaming service had signed directly with a sports team.[26] Facebook inked a deal with Disney and ESPN to provide digital sports content and shows via Facebook Watch. The partnership allowed Facebook to stream La Liga matches in India and EPL soccer matches in Cambodia, Laos, Thailand, and Vietnam through 2022. Facebook also secured broadcast rights to MLB games and partial rights to stream Copa Libertadores, South America's premier club soccer tournament.[27]

Fans who still choose to attend games live have the luxury of high-tech jumbotrons and mobile apps that give them the best of both viewing worlds. They can watch their teams compete while also enjoying replays, score updates, game stats, and other special content that helps to replicate the at-home viewing experience. Team apps also provide convenient services like preferred travel routes, parking information, game-day events, and a wealth of other offerings that make visiting the venue more enjoyable.

Technology and the Sport Marketer Ask any sport marketer and she or he will tell you that technology has made the job both easier and harder. Technology has given teams and their marketing departments so many ways to provide the product and communicate to fans, but this has also added complexity and cost. Data are at the heart of marketing today, and the means to collect consumer data takes technology, time, and even trial and error. Apps are one way that sport organizations can collect data. Profile information, purchasing history, stadium usage, and other demographic and psychographic variables can be gleaned from app users and analyzed to make marketing decisions.

Mobile ticketing is also critical to sport marketers since fans increasingly want to make convenient purchases using their cell phones. Fans can purchase and transfer tickets, scan into the game, and order food to their seats all with a few touches and swipes of their smartphones. In 2018, Ticketmaster and the NFL brought digital ticketing to all 32 teams, which allowed fans to download tickets to their smartphones and receive push notifications about the games. Mobile Marketer had this to say about the advantages of digital ticketing:

> A key advantage of digital ticketing is a marketing strategy described by Pay Pal's Braintree as "contextual commerce," meaning cross-selling products and services based on what people see or do with their smartphones. Sports teams can learn more about digital ticket holders than those who use mostly anonymous paper tickets. Digital ticketing can help to build

stronger, individualized relationships with fans around a team, while offering them additional products and services through mobile platforms, such as parking and stadium information and added convenience.[28]

Digital ticketing also allows organizations to run promotions and other value-added activities that improve the fan experience. The NFL and Ticketmaster ran a social media promotion so followers of Ticketmaster on Twitter and Instagram could post a photo supporting their favorite NFL team and hashtag #TicketmasterNFLentry to win season tickets. Some teams provide discounts if fans purchase merchandise digitally along with their tickets. SeatGeek partnered with Snapchat to allow fans to purchase event tickets directly within the app, which is becoming a very effective way for marketers to reach young consumers. The mobile device ticket-purchasing market was estimated at US$14 billion globally in 2018.

Political

Some people believe that sports and politics do not mix. Others have gone so far as to say that athletes should "shut up and dribble." Since 2016, the political climate has caused a wide variety of athletes across different sports to speak openly about their political and social beliefs, and athlete activism has been covered extensively by the media. While this may seem like a new trend, the reality is that sports and politics have been intertwined for hundreds of years. Both the ancient and modern Olympic Games have been used as a platform for political policy. Not only were the Olympic Games in ancient Greece a time for celebration and competition, they also were a meeting place for leaders to gather and discuss political and military activity. Modern Olympic Games have also seen countries try to establish political dominance over one another despite being touted as a time for the world to come together in peace. In 1936, Jesse Owens won four gold medals and made a political statement against the Hitler regime of host-country Germany. In 1968, Tommie Smith and John Carlos raised their fists on the podium of the Olympic Games in Mexico to display solidarity with the Black Power movement. In 1972, 11 Israeli athletes were kidnapped and killed in the Munich Games by a Palestinian terrorist group.[30]

Mobile Video Streaming

When *SportsBusiness Journal* launched in 1998, fans getting scores on their pagers was still common. But within the next decade, broadband Internet, smartphones, the first iPhone, and Apple's App Store all helped pave the way toward fans getting live games on their phones and exponentially growing the notion of fans being able to watch a game wherever they are. Today, every major sports programmer gets most of their digital traffic via mobile, and no rights deal of any consequence is negotiated without mobile video rights.

Apps

From checking scores to watching video to finding a particular craft beer stand at your favorite stadium, apps have revolutionized the fan experience. Fans in many markets can now even order stadium food without leaving their seat by using a mobile app and having their order brought to them. App overload, however, has now swung the other way as consumers have grown more selective about what they will download, and the battle for virtual shelf space on a fan's smartphone has grown fierce. As a result, many leagues, teams, and media networks have sought to bake more features into broad-based flagship apps.

Virtual Broadcast Enhancements

The virtual first-down line is now so pervasive in football broadcasts, it's nearly impossible to think about watching a game on TV without one. But prior to September 1998, that's how every football game was shown. That Sportvision-created enhancement, likely the most impactful change to sports broadcasting since instant replay, has led to similar developments in baseball, soccer, tennis, and other sports, allowing viewers to gain a more accurate sense of what's happening in a game.

Free Fantasy Sports

For almost 40 years, fantasy sports typically involved a tedious, manual tabulation of statistics to determine winners in a particular league. And even when the Internet began to automate that process, it was often a fee-based service appealing to only the most devoted of players. But in the mid-2000s, several leading sports websites began to offer free fantasy leagues with scoring in or near real time. The shift led to a massive increase in participation and moved fantasy sports from a niche hobby into an industry force.

High-Definition TV

HDTV broadcasts, though now long established across the sports industry, had a long and bumpy beginning. After technical specifications for the enhanced video format were first agreed upon in the early 1990s, HDTV made its domestic introduction in 1998. Astronomical HDTV set prices, sometimes exceeding $10,000 at first, and minimal available programming made for slow consumer acceptance. But the significant increase in picture quality was undeniable, and for some sports like hockey, the improved resolution and detail it offered completely transformed the at-home viewing experience. In 2003, ESPN started an HD channel, and within a few years, sports in HD was commonplace.

> continued

> continued

Scoreboards

Similar to what's happening in the home with HDTV and 4K video technology, outdoor display technology has become much larger and far more detailed in resolution. Old dot-matrix-based scoreboards, still in use in some markets in the 1990s, have given way to massive video boards capable of displaying high-end video and intricate animation. Even classic ballparks, such as Fenway Park and Wrigley Field, that still use hand-operated scoreboards have also incorporated state-of-the-art video boards. Custom shapes and more elaborate installations, such as the Colorado Rockies' new mountain-shaped board, have pushed the intricacy even further.

Player Tracking

The origins of player tracking were fairly modest. Initial questions, such as how fast or how far a certain player runs during a game, were answered using either wearable sensors or optical-based tracking systems that used cameras and mathematical coordinates to track player movement. Those simple beginnings, however, quickly gave way to much more sophisticated systems capable of tracking an array of player biometric data. Player tracking has also generated new ways to measure player performance, such as exit velocity and launch angles in baseball, that have become just as closely followed as a batting average or home run distance, in turn altering how general managers develop their rosters.

Artificial Intelligence

Nearly everything across the sports industry has now been digitized in some fashion, and computer systems continue to grow more powerful. The next step, then, is allowing those computers to take the data and yield insights, products, and content without having to be manually programmed every time. Signs of AI in sports are now cropping up everywhere, including voice-activated news and score updates on a smartphone or home speaker, video highlights automatically created by analyzing crowd noise and player gestures, or internally by a team or league analyzing fan data.

Digital Ticketing

For nearly the entire history of ticketing, access to a sporting event has involved using a paper-based ticket that yields little to no data to the team, league, or venue operator as to who is actually in their building. But just within the last several years, ticketing advancements using technologies, such as mobile barcodes, near-field communications (NFC), radio frequency identification (RFID), and beacons, have opened vast new realms of data on who is going to the games, their individual preferences, and their movements from and around a venue.

Social Media

It's now hard to imagine being a sports fan without the constant presence of Facebook, Twitter, and other social media platforms. But Twitter is only 12 years old and Facebook 14 years old. And in that time, Twitter has become how sports news is broken, how we create larger communities of fandom, and stay deeper in the moment as sports are happening. Players have been particularly active on social media, showing off their personalities and giving voice to issues, whether it's their contract status, important social causes, or just the state of their latest workout.

Online Secondary Ticketing

Online ticket resale markets took sales activity that had been occurring in stadium parking lots and back alleys into an open and much more transparent forum, allowing buyers, sellers, teams, and leagues to get a broad, real-time pulse on what markets were actually bearing. That data in turn has had all sorts of ripple effects, most notably influencing teams' decisions on how to price their tickets on the primary market. And leagues and teams that once fought such activity now embrace it and form long-term business partnerships around it.

Virtual Reality

Still a work in progress, the core idea of VR is to allow someone to have an immersive experience as if they are physically present while still being somewhere else, such as attending a game occurring thousands of miles away. In only the last few years, many leagues and broadcasters have developed both live and on-demand VR broadcasts for many sports. Not unlike the evolution of HDTV, consumer adoption has been slow, owing in part to a confusing array of bulky, often unsatisfying VR headsets. But belief in VR among its advocates remains steadfast, and many experts predict VR technology will ultimately be miniaturized and embedded into headsets much more akin to a pair of sunglasses.

Reprinted with permission from E. Fisher, "Technologies That Have Revolutionized the Sport Industry," *Sports Business Journal*, April 30, 2018. https://www.sportsbusinessdaily.com/Journal/Issues/2018/04/30/Technology/Tech-milestones.aspx

On a national level, many prominent American athletes have spoken out against the social injustices prevalent in the United States. Muhammad Ali was staunchly opposed to the Vietnam War, refused to serve in the military, and was banned from boxing due to his unwavering political stance. He became an icon as much for his beliefs as for his boxing. Colin Kaepernick kneeled during the national anthem before NFL games to take a stance against police brutality and racial injustice toward minorities. He was cut from the San Francisco 49ers and unable to find work with another football franchise after becoming a social activist. Megan Rapinoe, star of the 2019 U.S. Women's National Soccer Team, supported Kaepernick in kneeling during the anthem and has been an outspoken advocate of women's rights and LGBTQ rights.

After the killing of George Floyd by a Minneapolis police officer, the protests that erupted across the United States were supported by a plethora of athletes, teams, and leagues. Roger Goodell, Commissioner of the NFL, released a Black Lives Matter video in response to multiple high-profile NFL stars calling for action. The protests over racial and social injustice spread worldwide. Activism was seen in the Premier League when it was announced that as play resumed, all 20 clubs would replace the name plates on their kits with "Black Lives Matter." Premier League athletes collectively made a statement that,

> We, the players, stand together with the singular objective of eradicating racial prejudice wherever it exists, to bring about a global society of inclusion, respect, and equal opportunities for All, regardless of their color or creed. This symbol is a sign of unity from all players, all staff, all clubs, all match officials and the Premier League.[31]

Players were also granted permission to kneel before the start of a match to display solidarity with others in the movement.

Not all political activity within the sport world comes in the form of activism. Often politics is hidden in the guise of support and celebration. Presidents and other politicians often attend sports events to support athletes, watch major championships, or simply be present at important gatherings to gain social support. President George W. Bush was a managing general partner of the Texas Rangers. During his presidency, he also threw out the ceremonial first pitch at a New York Yankees baseball game following the 9/11 terrorist attacks to display the strength and resilience of the nation. President Barack Obama sat courtside at WNBA and NBA games and golfed with players such as Steph Curry. Championship-winning teams are invited to the White House to celebrate and be recognized for their accomplishments, and many have brought the current president a custom jersey with his name and number on the back.

Foreign leaders with ties to the United States have voiced support of American teams. For example, when the Cleveland Cavaliers advanced to the NBA Finals, Israeli Prime Minister Benjamin Netanyahu called the Cavaliers' head coach David Blatt, a U.S.-Israeli citizen, to give his well-wishes and extend the support of the Israeli people.[32] The ultimate display of the convergence of sports and politics is when a prominent athlete runs for public office. Arnold Schwarzenegger (body-builder) was Governor of California, Jesse Ventura (wrestler) was Governor of Minnesota, Bill Bradley (basketball player) was a Senator in New Jersey, and Vitali Klitschko (boxer) was a mayor in Ukraine.

Political policies can be enacted that have major consequences on the sport industry. Most recently, the changes in gambling regulations at the state level have tremendously altered how sports are marketed. The Professional and Amateur Sports Protection Act (PASPA) was overturned by the Supreme Court on May 14, 2018, allowing states to put forth bills to legalize sports gambling. One year after the ruling, 38 states representing almost 90 percent of the adult population in the United States had introduced more than 150 bills addressing the issue of sports gambling. Eight states (including Nevada) had legalized sports betting by the end of the first year post-PASPA.[33] Many other states began the process of creating similar legislation once the revenue from sports gambling proved to be profitable. In the first year of legalized sports betting, the state of New Jersey saw US$3.2 billion in wagers.[34]

Cultural

Culture is a shared set of values, conventions, or social practices associated with a particular field, activity, or social group. People tend to convey the beliefs, attitudes, and behaviors that typify their own cultural settings. In a society's broader framework, however, alternative cultures, sub-cultures, and countercultures nurture different lifestyles. This point is as true in sport as it is in all areas of living; if not for the dynamics of culture, society would not change over time. A stagnant society would greatly affect sport. Consider, for example, that as late as the 1920s, many U.S. communities outlawed organized sports on Sunday. Can you imagine being arrested for playing golf or basketball on a Sunday? That circumstance is unthinkable today, yet at the turn of the 20th century, it happened with some regularity in U.S. cities where cultural groups fought over secularism and the Sabbath.[35] And in 1980, who would have predicted that sellouts for the Minnesota high school hockey championship were for the girls? Or that the star hockey team at the 1998 Olympic Games was female?[36] As times change, people change, and the cultures surrounding groups of people are transformed.

Some aspects of culture are dictated, not as much by people, but by climate and topography. For instance, the dry sun and long coast of California spawned both surfing and skateboarding. Minnesota and Massachusetts still dominate the production of U.S. hockey players. Northern cities with long hockey traditions—Pittsburgh, Buffalo, Detroit, and Boston—tend to have higher local ratings for hockey telecasts than do Southern cities. The mountainous areas of North America and Europe produce far more world-class skiers than other parts of the globe do. Conversely, warm, southern climates like those found from Florida to Arizona are conducive for golf and generate the most rounds played in the sport.

Culture not only has an effect on sport participation but also on sport organization as well. Sport businesses are just like other companies in that they have different organizational cultures. Organizational culture refers to the consistent, observable patterns of behavior found within organizations. Organizational culture is like a "company personality" of sorts. When you listen to administrators discuss what the company stands for, or observe how employees go about their day-to-day tasks, or analyze what behaviors and processes are repeated over time, you are witnessing organizational culture. Every company will have a slightly different (or even dramatically different) personality. For instance, if you walk into the front office of one sport organization and everyone is in suits and behind a desk, you may characterize the culture as formal and serious, whereas another front office with casual dress and open work spaces may be labeled relaxed and chill. As Aristotle once said, "We are what we repeatedly do," and that is the essence of organizational culture.[37]

Demographic

When you fill out the final portion of a consumer survey, you may be asked to provide your demographic information. Demographics include, but are not limited to, a person's age, race, gender, sexual orientation, and household income. Demographic variables are often used to predict patterns in consumer behavior since people with similar characteristics may behave in similar ways. Marketers use demographic data to better serve consumer groups by providing customized products and experiences fans want.

Age is just a number, but when it comes to marketing, that number is paramount in meeting consumer wants and needs. Baby Boomers, Gen X, Gen Y, and Gen Z all have an interest in sports, but due to their age differences, those interests and activities are diverse. This means sport marketers must create new products, services, and experiences that are tailored to meet generational needs over time.

As sports fans across all leagues age, Gen Y, or millennials (born 1981 to 1996), have been the primary focus of sport marketers as they look to the future, due to the sheer numbers and immense buying power of this generation. Millennials constitute one-quarter of the U.S. population at roughly 80 million people and have demonstrated US$200 billion in purchasing power annually.[38] They were the first digital natives that grew up with the Internet and social media. Millennials dramatically changed the sport industry because online access to sports content meant these young consumers did not have to resort to traditional television broadcasts to watch and follow their favorite teams, players, or events. Not only did millennial sports fans drive the transition to streaming, they also transformed how brands marketed themselves. According to a study of over 1,300 millennial consumers, only 1 percent said that advertising makes them trust a brand more. Millennial consumers choose instead to interact and engage with brands online through social media, and this has forced brands to adopt a human voice and market to millennials on a personal level. According to *Forbes*, marketers need to know the following unique aspects about millennials:

- 33 percent will review a blog or social media post before making a purchase.
- 43 percent rank authenticity over content when consuming news.
- 62 percent will be more likely to show brand loyalty to companies that interact with them on social media.
- 42 percent are interested in helping companies create future products and services.
- 87 percent use two to three different tech devices daily.
- 60 percent are often or always loyal to brands they currently purchase.
- 75 percent feel it is fairly important or very important for brands to give back to society.

If Gen Y is a valuable group of consumers, then Gen Z could be a goldmine! Gen Z (born 1997 or later) made up 40 percent of all consumers by the end of 2020, and this generation is even more digitally and socially savvy than its millennial counterparts. Gen Z spends even more time on social media, scrolling through endless photos and videos on Instagram, Snapchat, and TikTok, and they expect brands to be there communicating with them on the most personal and authentic level. This generation has grown up with influencer marketing, in which "regular" people (not celebrities per se), with thousands or millions of followers, become "Insta-famous" and get paid handsomely to promote brands online.[39] Other characteristics of this younger generation are decidedly different from millennials, and marketers should take note. According to the Digital Marketing Institute, these are the biggest distinctions separating Gen Z from Gen Y:

- It is the most diverse generation in U.S. history, with 47 percent ethnic minorities.
- Only 48 percent identify as strictly heterosexual (65 percent for millennials).
- Their average attention span is eight seconds (12 for millennials).
- They are twice as likely to shop on mobile devices than Gen Y.
- YouTube is their favorite platform over Facebook or Instagram.

Many sports executives fear that the root cause of declining ratings and aging audiences is the disengagement of millennials from live sports. TV trends—including declining ratings, cord shaving, and cord cutting—present a long-term challenge for traditional sports, but the belief that millennials are to blame is misplaced. With so many sports options across so many screens, fans of all ages—not just millennials—are watching fewer games and quitting them faster.

From our analysis of Nielsen data, in the 2016-2017 regular season, National Football League (NFL) ratings among millennials declined 9 percent. However, the number of millennials watching the NFL actually increased from the prior season (from 65 percent to 67 percent of all millennials). The ratings decline was caused by an 8 percent drop in the number of games watched and a 6 percent decline in the minutes watched per game (down to 1 hour 12 minutes per game). The same was true for Generation X for the NFL (a 6 percent decline in ratings, no change in reach) and for millennials and Generation X for the most recent Major League Baseball (MLB), National Basketball Association (NBA), and National Hockey League (NHL) seasons. Overall reach for sports on TV hasn't declined; ratings have dropped because fans are watching fewer and shorter sessions.

In a world with so many sports options across so many screens, sports fans of all ages are clicking away from low-stakes or lopsided games.

Millennials Versus Gen X: The Wrong Way to Segment Sports Fans

As sports executives seek to build new direct-to-consumer channels, we find that age is an ineffective way to segment and target digital sports fans. Older generations (Gen Xers in particular) are adopting digital technology almost as fast as millennials, and fans' online behaviors are far better signals of purchase intent. The following are a few important findings:

- *Millennials are sports fans too.* Although more Gen Xers than millennials follow sports closely (45 percent versus 38 percent), the gap disappears for English Premier League (EPL), Major League Soccer, NBA, Ultimate Fighting Championship, and college sports, where support among millennials is as high or higher than among Generation X. Furthermore, the gender gap is closing: 45 percent of millennial sports fans are women versus 41 percent for Generation X.

- *Most millennials have cable.* As of November 2016, 78 percent of millennials had cable, satellite, or telco TV service at home, according to Nielsen. That's pretty close to the 84 percent of Gen Xers with cable.

- *It's not about getting older; it's about having kids.* It's true that on average, millennials watch less TV. They watched 28 percent fewer hours per week of TV in 2016 than people their age did in 2010, whereas Generation X viewing slipped by only 8 percent over the same period. However, when Nielsen segments millennials into those living with parents, those living on their own, and those starting their own families (at age 27, all three segments are about equal in size), big differences show up. Millennials with kids watch 3 hours and 16 minutes of live TV per day, fully 55 percent more than millennials living on their own and just 14 percent less than Gen Xers under 49. Another important finding: millennials living on their own spend 15 percent more time out of their homes and are 31 percent more likely to own a multimedia device than millennials with kids, and they watch 6 percent more live sports on TV than millennial parents do.

- *Millennials still watch live games.* Millennial sports fans watch almost as many live games per week as Generation X sports fans (3.2 games per week versus 3.4 games per week) and the same amount of highlights and other non-live sports (about 32 minutes per day). And more believe they have increased the amount of live sports they watch on TV than those who think they have decreased (30 percent versus 25 percent, similar to the rates for Generation X).

- *Everyone's digital.* Virtually everyone in Generation X owns a smartphone, as do millennials (95 percent versus 97 percent). The two groups own multimedia devices (36 percent versus 40 percent) and use streaming or subscription video on demand (68 percent versus 75 percent) at nearly the same rates. And they both spend over 5 hours per day on smartphones and PCs. Somewhat surprisingly, mobile video usage averages under 15 minutes per day, but PC video consumption is almost four times as high.

A Difference of Degree: Streaming and Social Media

For all the similarities in technology adoption and viewing behaviors, millennials differ from their parents' generation in the following two ways that matter to sports-rights holders:

- *Millennials stream sports more often.* In our research, millennial sports fans report using streaming web sites and apps (for example, NBCSports.com, Twitter, and WatchESPN) almost twice as much as Generation X (56 percent versus 29 percent). They are also more likely to admit to using unauthorized sports streaming sites, such as Reddit streams (20 percent versus 3 percent). A recent BBC survey found that 65 percent of British millennials stream EPL matches illegally at least once per month.

- *Millennials are social fans.* While millennials and Gen Xers use sports sites and apps equally, significantly more millennials follow sports on social media. For example, 60 percent of millennial sports fans check scores and sports news on social media versus only 40 percent for Generation X. Twice as many millennials use Twitter, and five times as many use Snapchat or Instagram for that purpose. Facebook is the leading social platform for both groups, but YouTube dominates sports highlights for millennials (edging out ESPN.com). Overall YouTube engagement per monthly unique viewer has reached 37 minutes per day for 18- to 24-year-olds versus just 15 minutes per day for Generation X.

Despite millennials' heavier use of streaming and social media for sports, the gap is closing. As of 2016, millennials spent 24 percent of their media time on social media compared with Generation X at 22 percent and Boomers at 20 percent, and Gen Xers and Boomers are growing their social media usage at higher rates than millennials.

Implications: Targeting Digital Sports Fans

Given the similar trends in sports viewing among millennials and Generation X, how should sports marketers target digital fans? Here are five strategies:

- *Target mobile viewers of live streams.* In predicting the number of live sports events watched per week, we found that generational difference (that is, millennials versus Gen Xers) was not statistically significant. However, those who watch live sports on mobile watch 20 percent more live sports events than those who do not.

- *Convert the pirates.* Fans who admit to watching unauthorized streams watch 22 percent more games (across all platforms) than those who do not. Although it may be impractical to target these users, they are evidently avid sports fans who could be a primary target for new direct-to-consumer streaming services.

- *Target moms.* In our sample, male sports fans with children watched 14 percent fewer live games than those without, but women with children watched 24 percent *more* sports events than those with no kids.

> *continued*

> continued

- *Promote tickets on social media.* Teams know to target fans making over US$100,000 per year (51 percent of whom attend live games versus 40 percent of those earning under US$100,000 per year), but they may not know that 56 percent of fans who follow athletes or teams on social media attend games (versus only 30 percent of fans who do not).

- *Highlights are the gateway to subscription video.* Fans who consume over 30 minutes per day of sports highlights are three times as likely to subscribe to sports over-the-top services as fans who do not. Fans who follow teams and players on social media are also more than twice as likely to subscribe as those who do not. Use of sports apps and mobile sites is a leading indicator; 52 percent of fans in our sample who check news and articles on sports sites and apps also watch live sports streams versus only 22 percent of those who do not.

Implications: Innovating the Digital Sports Experience

The problem of declining attention spans will not be solved merely by replatforming TV video for PCs and mobile devices. As sports marketers develop new digital products—including services for live-streamed events, highlights, fan commentary, news, and analysis—they should design for new, digital behaviors that cut across generations:

- Shorter viewing sessions (for example, with whip-around viewing and quick navigation to other games)
- One-click tune-in access from social media or search, prompted by alerts on high-stakes game situations (rather than appointment viewing)
- Convenient access (for example, the ability to watch any game for user's favorite team or player or fantasy player, regardless of the TV network on which they are broadcast)
- Rapid, simple sign-on (ideally using fingerprints or other biometrics) and payment
- Fast, intuitive social sharing of game highlights and fan chatter
- Quick navigation between fantasy sports rosters and live streams, especially for avid daily fantasy sports players (and sports bettors)
- Fun, quick social contests to keep casual fans engaged with live games

Generation X wanted its MTV. Millennials have fear of missing out. Both generations are consuming digital sports voraciously, at the expense of traditional TV viewing. Sports marketers who target the right digital behaviors (rather than traditional viewer segments) and develop digital products to take advantage of them will build stronger fan bases than ever before.

Dan Singer is the leader of the McKinsey Global Sports & Gaming Practice.

- They prefer messaging apps over texting or email.
- 93 percent of Gen Z say their decision to take a job is influenced by a company's impact on society.

Just as age helps guide sport marketers in making strategic decisions, other demographic groups provide direction as well. Ethnic, gender, and even sexual orientation groupings can be extremely important segments to sport brands. There are very distinct patterns in participation and fandom when you break consumers down by these traits.

According to Statista, participation in sports activities steadily increased in the United States from 1999 to 2017. In 1999, 18 percent of men participated in sports activities and so did 12.1 percent of women. By 2017, those numbers had increased to 29 percent for men and 20.2 percent for women.[40] The rise in sport participation in the United States is good news for sport brands selling equipment and apparel, as well as those organizations marketing to participants like workout facilities, sport clubs, and events and competitions.

U.S. men and women also demonstrate sports fandom at relatively high levels. Table 3.1 shows data on U.S. male and female sports fans as reported by Statista in 2020.[41] More men play and watch sports than women, but the gap is shrinking, and sport marketers always need to be concerned with participation and fan data in order to make better segmentation and targeting decisions.

Sports fandom can also be broken down by ethnicity, and the statistics in this area are revealing. Table 3.2 shows data on U.S. sports fans by ethnicity as reported by Statista in 2020.[42] People in the United States who identify racially as African American are the largest group of "Avid fans" followed by Hispanic. Conversely, people who identify as White have the lowest numbers of "Avid fans" and highest numbers of "Non-fans." The diverse makeup of the United States is reflected in the sport industry, and fandom levels are different depending on the ethnic groups with which people identify.

While age, gender, and ethnicity are more obvious demographic segments that sport organizations target, the LGBTQ community has also become an important target audience for teams and leagues. In 2014, the Women's National Basketball Association (WNBA) was the first professional sport league to create a specific marketing strategy aimed at LGBTQ fans, which make up a considerable percentage of the league's consumer base. After conducting consumer behavior research, the league found that 25 percent of lesbians watched WNBA games on television while 21 percent attended games live. A multifaceted campaign was created that included a dedicated website, participation in pride festivals and parades, grassroots diversity and inclusion efforts, and advertising with lesbian media outlets. Former WNBA President Laurel Richie stated, "For us it's a celebration of diversity and inclusion and recognition of an audience that has been with us very passionately. This is one of those moments in the 'W' where everybody comes together."[43]

The WNBA was a pioneer in this area of marketing, and other leagues soon realized the passion and power of the LGBTQ consumer. *Bloomberg Businessweek* reported that the LGBTQ community wields US$1 trillion in spending power and that financial support is sought after by leagues and teams. Creating an inclusive and welcoming environment is not only the right thing to do socially, but it has tremendous financial implications for front offices.[44] Almost all the professional sport leagues have some form of LGBTQ programming like Pride Nights, and many teams create their own local promotions, like the Orlando Magic who opened their 2016 season with a ceremony honoring the Pulse Nightclub shooting victims or the NHL who partnered with the organization You Can Play, which promotes LGBTQ participation in grassroots sports programs.[45]

Situational

Situational marketing is a strategy that targets consumers' individual wants and needs, often by communicating with them in real time versus advertising to the masses. Delivering highly personalized marketing messages in the right place at the right time is far more effective than blanketing space with ads when people no longer pay attention. According to Marketing Tech, 86 percent of consumers admit to having "banner blindness," meaning they no longer look at banner ads on the websites and apps they view.[46] This type of behavior—ignoring overt advertisements—has

TABLE 3.1   Breakdown of U.S. Male and Female Sports Fans

Gender	Avid fan	Casual fan	Not a fan
Male	36%	38%	26%
Female	12%	42%	46%

TABLE 3.2   Breakdown of U.S. Sports Fans by Ethnicity

Ethnicity	Avid fan	Casual fan	Not a fan
African American	34%	41%	25%
Hispanic	30%	41%	30%
White	22%	40%	38%
Other	23%	42%	35%

Billie Weiss/Boston Red Sox/Getty Images

Pride Night has become a popular promotion with most sport leagues after the WNBA pioneered this celebration.

been going on for years. Many people enjoy recorded television shows primarily because they can fast-forward through all the commercials. Digital, and in particular, mobile, marketing has become crucial as television ads go increasingly unseen and mobile screen time escalates. In 2019, total digital ad spending in the United States grew 19 percent to US$129 billion, roughly 54 percent of estimated total U.S. ad spending. Mobile marketing accounted for more than 67 percent of digital ad spending at US$87 billion.[47]

Digital and mobile marketing allows personalized messages to appear based on when and where a customer displays certain activity. For example, right after a sports fan browses her favorite mobile app to check scores and see if her team won, a targeted ad offering her official team gear appears on screen. This advertisement is not only offering exactly the team merchandise she may want based on her browsing patterns, but if she is checking scores during the playoffs,

this fan may be more likely to purchase official playoff gear. This type of situational marketing is often geotargeted to offer fans the right products or services based on the location and timing of their Internet activity.

Internal Factors

Phase two of the black box consumer behavior model delves into the buyer's mind and examines all the internal factors that affect consumer responses. External or environmental factors swirl constantly around the consumer, but internal or individual factors influence the way the consumer interacts and makes sense of that larger world.

Consumer Characteristics

In the black box, which represents the buyer's mind, many different consumer characteristics exist that impact purchase decisions. Every consumer has a different composition, and these individual traits will drive how that consumer acts in the marketplace and inform the purchases the consumer ultimately makes. We look now at how these may affect involvement in and commitment to sport.

Beliefs and Attitudes

Over time, people develop beliefs and attitudes based on their life experiences that help guide their decisions. Positive beliefs and attitudes toward a brand or product will certainly benefit marketers trying to make a sale. Consumers who have a predisposition toward Under Armour will usually respond favorably to the brand's marketing messages and be receptive to new products. However, negative beliefs and attitudes toward a brand or product will be extremely difficult, or even impossible, to overcome. If a consumer has had a bad experience with Under Armour products and feels they are overpriced given the level of quality he has received, that consumer's beliefs and attitudes may shift his involvement with Under Armour to another apparel brand. While it is possible to change consumer attitudes, this may require a great deal of time, effort, and resources on the part of the marketer and may not be worth the investment. It may be more beneficial to focus on groups of buyers who love and are committed to the brand. For example, if consumers hold the belief that Adidas is a strong soccer brand while Under Armour excels in basketball or American football, these companies may decide to market heavily in those respective sports and endorse star athletes who compete in those areas.

Values

Values are the guiding principles in our lives or the standards by which we behave. Values are also ideals that are important to us and shape who we are and what we become. The realm of sport is full of values that people learn from participation and that they witness through spectatorship. Some of the values often seen and developed in sports are honesty, equality, teamwork, discipline, dedication, determination, and perseverance. The values that people possess are at the core of who they are as human beings and are major drivers of behavior.

Marketers need to understand what makes people tick in order to effectively meet their wants and needs. A person who values honesty and equality will likely be attracted to brands with the same type of projected ideals. The Olympic "Thank you, Mom" and "Love Over Bias" campaigns by Proctor and Gamble demonstrated these values and targeted mothers of Olympic children who made major sacrifices to help their kids succeed. Highly determined and risk-taking people will want to use brands that help them portray those traits. Red Bull is constantly daring and innovative in the sports and activities it chooses to sponsor and in the types of new products it develops for its fans.[48] Marketers create the brand personality for their products and services, which are designed to appeal to consumers based on the ideal self that consumers want to achieve and demonstrate to others through use of the brands they select.

Knowledge

Knowledge is acquired through learning. Whether it is product knowledge or any other kind of information that marketers want to share, consumers gain this knowledge through learning, and there are various theories that explain how people learn. The definition of *learning* is "the acquisition of knowledge or skills through the process of experience, study, or instruction." This definition includes several components common to learning theories:

1. The first component encompasses drives or arousal mechanisms that cause a person to act; the desire for esteem is an example.
2. The second component includes cues or environmental stimuli that may trigger an individual drive. Advertisements for luxury cars during televised tennis tournaments are good examples of cues that attempt to trigger esteem drives.
3. The third component includes reinforcements or outcomes (usually positive rewards) that serve to reduce the drive. The tennis fan who purchases a Mercedes may (or may not) learn the connections between lifestyle and esteem.

Several areas of learning theory have special relevance to the sport marketer. For example, cognitive, affective, and behavioral types of involvement correspond to the hierarchy of effects sometimes used to describe consumer

Ezra Shaw/Getty Images

Red Bull markets itself as one of the most daring brands in sports as evidenced by the athletes and activities it chooses to represent.

purchase behavior. The basic hierarchy suggests that consumers first process information about a product (cognition), often through advertising. If additional messages succeed, consumers next develop a new feeling about the product (affect), which may in turn lead them to buy the product (behavior). This hierarchy is displayed as

Learn → Feel → Do

One way or another, product knowledge is an important variable in consumer behavior. Knowledge links to involvement and commitment in an endless loop. Anyone who has ever been bitten by the golf bug understands this. The more you play, the more you want to learn about the game and its nuances. The more you learn, the more you want to play. The same is true for sports fans. Fans who follow their favorite athletes on social media learn a lot about the athletes' personal lives, feel a deeper connection to those athletes, and then act on those feelings by making purchases (buying jerseys, team merchandise, or tickets to watch the players compete, or supporting the players' foundations).

Some researchers suggest that the standard hierarchy Learn → Feel → Do may not apply to

services, which are intangible and therefore less conducive to initial cognitive messages about product, price, and so on. This notion is certainly true for many sport products, which often involve intricate physical activities. In sport, consumers may be more responsive to information that triggers their emotions about an overall experience, even if the initial image is limited in its detail. Consumers may be willing to act on such information, try the sport product, and then learn more about it after the trial. In sport, then, the hierarchy may be more like

Feel → Do → Learn

This approach is the one used by most Nike ads, which look to stir emotions before anything else. Nike ads are viewed, consumers are consequently moved by the inspirational images and messaging, shoes and gear are then purchased, and finally consumers learn about the new products they have acquired. Many times people know little about Nike products before they purchase them because they do not go online and research the items if they are already brand loyal.

In some instances, a consumer may actually purchase first and progress through the other two stages after possessing the product. Although it seems counterintuitive for a person to act, develop emotions, and then learn at the end of the cycle, this form of learning does happen, particularly in the case of an impulse purchase. These activities reflect the following hierarchy:

Do → Feel and Learn

Special sales or promotional efforts, targeted at youth and family groups, are often packaged in a way to attract casual fans. The hope is that in coming with friends, eating together in a special area, getting group recognition on a big screen or PA announcement, smelling the aromas, hearing the unique sounds, and cheering together will, in combination, create consumers who want to return. Fan fests that offer people the chance to swing at a big-league pitch or test their slapshot ability also follow a Do → Feel and Learn approach.

Motives

Amid a constant swirl of stimuli, can we identify any individual triggers of sport involvement? According to motivation theory, environmental stimuli may activate the drive to satisfy an underlying need. Theorists such as Abraham Maslow, Henry Murray, and David McClelland have outlined elaborate models explaining how physiological, psychological, and social needs influence human behavior. In the last decade, a number of researchers have focused their efforts on explaining what makes sport consumers tick. At the same time, historians have outlined a number of long-residual factors that have motivated involvement in sport across vast extents of time and space. The research is extensive and growing, but some motivational factors have emerged rather clearly:[49]

- *Achievement and self-esteem.* The notion of winning does matter, for players and fans. For serious athletes, winning is often the number one goal of competition. Likewise, numerous studies show that fans tend to bask in reflected glory (BIRG) when their team wins. Conversely, when the team loses, fans often try to distance themselves from the poor performance, known as cutting off reflected failure (CORF).[50]

- *Craft.* Winning isn't all that counts. For many, developing or enjoying physical skill prompts sport interest. Learning a new skill typically ranks high among reasons people list for playing. And the chance to watch a star display great skill brings a crowd to any game.

- *Health and fitness.* This is an obvious motive for club membership and equipment purchase. Even golfers can argue that a "good walk spoiled" beats watching television or an afternoon at the office.

- *Fun and festival.* Humans have a long history of framing their games with circles of spectators and fun lovers, who exchange money for sight lines, food, and merchandise. Descriptions of ancient festivals sound much like those of modern events. There was and is more than the contest. What is big time football without the tailgating? For similar reasons, most new venues contain a concourse, which is the locus of fun and festival—the midway, if you like. Perhaps the most visible symbol of festival is the team mascot, now almost a necessity.

- *Eros.* Evidence is clear that many players and fans have erotic motives. Finely tuned athletic bodies are widely used in advertising and marketing to sell products and attract fans to events. Cheerleaders, dance teams, and highly sexualized forms of music and entertainment are staples at professional, and even collegiate, competitions. Look no further than the *Sports Illustrated* "Swimsuit Issue" or the now defunct *ESPN Magazine*'s "Body Issue" to see how sexual attraction to athletes and athletics is a widely accepted notion in sports. Social media platforms like Instagram have provided not only athletes but also workout enthusiasts a place to showcase their bodies to large audiences who want to view their photos, videos, and promoted products. Eros has become an increasingly evident aspect of sports for participants and spectators alike, and further examination of the effects of sex in sports is warranted.

- *Affiliation or community.* Being with friends or family is a common reason that people give for any sport involvement, as indicated in studies of tennis participation, athletics club membership, and fan motivations. Fan communities have existed for thousands of years, represented in the Roman factions of blues, greens, reds, and whites, who passionately rooted for their color in the chariot races. Their modern counterparts may wear official merchandise, but the motives are the same. Research has clearly shown that few fans (1 to 3 percent) attend games alone. Fantasy sport participation is on the rise, particularly among teenage boys. Being a fan or a participant can become of paramount importance to a person's social identity.

- *Eustress, risk, and gambling.* The emotional ride of rooting is much like that of gambling—an addictive combination of euphoria and stress. It is no wonder that sport and gambling have gone together as far back as our literary and archeological records will take us. Sport gambling is on the rise again as legalization spreads throughout the

Dwyane Wade displays the *ESPN Magazine* "Body Issue" where he graced the cover.

Paul Archuleta/FilmMagic

United States, and fans who enjoy placing wagers will increasingly experience the effects of stress and eustress.

- *Entertainment and escape.* Many fans believe (and report on surveys) that a day at the ballpark or an evening in front of the TV, cheering on their favorite team, takes their minds off their everyday troubles. Some may argue that an escape motive (relaxation) and a eustress motive (tension) may be in contradiction. After all, rooting for the Knicks may be simply trading work troubles for leisure troubles. But who's to tell a fan what is best? Regardless of fan motives for attending, sport marketers are increasingly focused on providing an exciting entertainment product that will bring everyone out to the game.

Researchers are beginning to tease out the differences between the motives of fans of men's sports and women's sports, or revenue sports and nonrevenue sports. Although motivations are elusive and difficult to quantify, they will remain essential constructs for understanding consumer behavior in sport. A better understanding of fan motives promises to help marketers develop better communications with their consumer base and provide more customized sport experiences.

Perceptions

Learning requires the consumer to use *perception*, which may be defined as "the process of scanning, gathering, assessing, and interpreting information in the environment." Perception depends on the characteristics of the person, situation, or thing perceived (stimulus factors) and on the characteristics of the perceiver (individual factors). A roaring crowd may be an exhilarating and uplifting experience for a knowledgeable fan but a threatening mob to someone else. Our perceptions, then, are something of a filter, influenced by our values, attitudes, needs, and expectations. This filter contributes to selective exposure, selective distortion, and selective retention of the innumerable stimuli that confront us daily.

Consumers and prospective consumers are constantly filtering and interpreting cues about sport products in relation to their self-concepts. Failure to provide congruent and consonant images to consumers will typically reduce involvement. For example, luxury brands keep their high-priced products out of discount stores because the place of purchase enhances the perception of quality.

Lifestyle

Lifestyle marketing is a strategy in which a brand or product is marketed so that it is perceived to possess certain characteristics, aesthetics, or appeal that the target audience identifies with or that fits their current or aspirational lifestyle. Conducting lifestyle marketing is done using psychographic segmentation, where consumers are grouped based on factors such as attitudes, interests, or opinions. This strategy is widely used because people in the same demographic groups often have very different values, attitudes, and lifestyles. How someone looks no longer tells us as much about what they are likely to buy. Rather, how they act tells us so much more.

One psychographic scale that is very useful in lifestyle marketing is the Values and Lifestyles (VALS) typology by Strategic Business Insights (SBI).[51] The VALS framework categorizes consumers into eight personality types (innovators, thinkers, achievers, experiencers, believers, strivers, makers, and survivors) based on a survey measuring not only of consumer values, attitudes, and lifestyles but also demographic and behavioral information. The framework is extremely helpful, as marketers who know the psychographic characteristics of each group can determine what products and services may be desired by people possessing that particular lifestyle. Psychographic and behavioral segmentation and their relation to lifestyle marketing is discussed in greater depth in chapter 5.

Decision-Making Process

The array of factors discussed in this chapter contributes to the difficulty of establishing a standard process by which consumers make decisions about becoming or staying involved with sport products. Nonetheless, such models, even if they are imperfect, can be helpful tools for marketers. We offer one such model, based on a series of five steps generally seen as part of consumer decision making (see figure 3.1).

1. Problem Solving

In the first stage of the decision-making process, the consumer encounters a need or want and must solve the problem of filling that void. For example, if a person decides to try yoga for the first time as a means of getting into better physical and mental shape, she may realize the need for a yoga mat, clothing, and an instructional class. The problem can begin to be solved once information on these items is gathered and evaluated. This leads to the second stage of decision making, which is conducting an information search.

2. Information Search

The consumer may have prior awareness of, or may seek new information about, products that can satisfy aroused needs. Marketers must never underestimate this critical stage. The search process may involve online browsing, shopping in person at retail stores, reading reviews on websites, consulting friends or followers on social media, or utilizing other marketing channels. The search process provides a wealth of opportunities for marketers to get their brands in front of consumers who are in need. Knowing where your customers are going to get information on your product is critical to reaching them and doing so before your competitors. Speaking of the competition, stage three is where consumers evaluate the alternatives.

3. Alternate Evaluation

Consumers make product choices at a number of levels. Philip Kotler distinguished these levels as follows:

- *Product family.* Within the realm of leisure, people make choices between broad families such as competitive sports, outdoor recreation, and hobbies (collecting autographed memorabilia).
- *Product class.* There are many classes of sports, such as motorsports, water sports, field sports, and team sports.
- *Product line.* Within the team sports class are lines of products such as bat and ball sports, ball-only sports, and stick and ball sports.
- *Product type.* Within the ball-only line are product types such as rugby, soccer, and American football.
- *Product brand.* Within the product type of American football are various brands, including the NFL and NCAA brands, and even more specifically the Packers and SEC brands.

Consumers are surrounded by levels of choice as they engage the world around them. They may be steered toward decisions at any of the preceding levels, which may influence their attitudes at other levels. As we move toward an increasingly global marketplace, the amount of competition and number of alternatives grows exponentially.

4. Purchase

Numerous questions demand research concerning the sport consumer's purchase decisions. For instance, to what extent are decisions to purchase a sport experience (with time, money, effort) planned and calculated or unplanned and impulsive? How do price, place or distribution, convenience, and previous experience factor into decision making? Strong marketing considers all these variables and many more when attempting to persuade consumers to buy.

5. Post-Purchase Evaluation

An effective illustration of evaluation is the consumer satisfaction equation:

$$\text{Satisfaction} = \text{Benefits} - \text{Cost}$$

Satisfaction can relate to social experience, self-concept, skill, reliability, or other elements. Benefits relate to characteristics such as quantity and duration. Costs can include money, time, ego, effort, and opportunities to do other things. In the end, benefits must outweigh costs. Marketers attempt to maximize satisfaction through the various elements in the marketing mix. But consumers continue to filter the stimuli around them. They can develop positive or negative attitudes for a host of reasons. One of the most important attitudes is the consumer's assessment of competence, as a player or a fan. Has the experience enhanced the person's sense of competence and self-worth? Has it strengthened the consumer's identity? The answer has a major influence on subsequent behavior.

After evaluating, the consumer has three basic choices:

1. If satisfied, to repeat the experience, and perhaps build a stronger identity or affinity with the activity. Fans of NASCAR reflect high levels of satisfaction, which spill over into brand loyalty to NASCAR sponsors. Satisfied fans typically indicate that they plan to attend more of a team's events in the future—that is, they intend to move up the elevator.

2. If dissatisfied, to reduce or abandon the activity. Some participants and spectators move down or even get off the elevator.

3. If marginally satisfied or dissatisfied, to reevaluate information and decisions about product choices at various levels (family, class, line, type, and brand).

Researchers need to study those who exit the elevator. Customers who leave an organization can be extremely valuable in future product development and marketing strategy. Additionally, data in all forms are readily available on current customers and can explain where and why they are on the elevator and how marketers can keep them on and move them up. The future of sport marketing is data-driven, and the data will paint a picture of consumer behavior that is much more accurate than instinct-driven marketing. What better way to learn about sport consumers than letting their behavior and purchases speak for themselves!

Responses

Throughout this chapter, we have covered the various phases of the black box consumer behavior model. The first phase includes stimuli, or external factors, in the form of the marketing mix and environmental influences. The second phase delves into the black box of the consumer's mind where internal factors, including consumer characteristics and the decision-making process, were examined. The final phase includes two consumer responses: purchase and no purchase. We end the chapter by discussing these two responses and what each outcome means for sport marketers.

Purchase

The goal for most marketers is to fulfill their consumers' wants and needs and persuade consumers to make purchases. Once consumers are on the organization's elevator, building a deep relationship and moving them to higher levels of commitment and loyalty is paramount. However, reaching the ultimate goal of a purchase is contingent upon a variety of factors:

- *Product.* Having the product that consumers want, when they want it, is the first step. Amount of inventory, product selection, and convenience of purchase and delivery of the product are all important to today's consumers. With so many online options at people's fingertips, simply not having the product in stock could cause a potential customer to purchase from another vendor. Retailers like Amazon have made selection, convenience, and swift delivery the cornerstones of their brand.

- *Brand.* For some consumers, making a purchase can be more about having a specific brand than having the product itself. Brand loyalists often choose from their favorite company's product lines without considering the competition or price. Apple is a great example. There are plenty of technology products that work just as well (or even better in some cases) as Apple but having an iPhone or a MacBook is simply the only option for those obsessed with the brand. The same can be said for sport and entertainment brands like Beats headphones, North Face apparel, or Nike sneakers.[52] You will learn much more about how branding affects purchase behavior in chapter 7.

- *Source.* Where purchases are made in the sport industry has changed dramatically since 2010. The secondary ticket market for live games has become the primary market for many people, particularly the millennial generation that grew up with the Internet and mobile device in hand. The secondary ticket market is where fans go when games are sold out, prices are too high, or inventory needs to be sold. The source of the ticket purchase has made the entire experience of going to sports events so much easier, cheaper, and more convenient, and this alternative marketplace drives billions of dollars in consumer purchasing every year. Forbes reported that the total online event ticket market was expected to reach US$68 billion by 2025, and the secondary market would account for US$15.2 billion of that number.[53] So, clearly, sports fans and consumers of all types have demonstrated that *where* they buy is just as important as *what* they buy.

- *Amount.* The amount of product people purchase is a significant determinant in their purchasing behavior. Families or groups of fans who wish to attend a game and need tickets will likely want group discounts or seek out promotional plans. These incentives are effective for bringing in large groups. Loyal purchasers who spend heavily with a brand are often rewarded with frequent buyer programs in order to keep them on the elevator.

- *Method of payment.* Many sport teams and sports events have partnerships with companies like Visa and American Express that give cardholders discounts and exclusive benefits when purchasing with their method of payment. Other forms of payment, like PayPal and Apple Pay, make it easier for consumers to make purchases via mobile, which may lead to more transactions. Making sure to have the preferred method of payment that your target audience is comfortable with is a crucial component for marketers.

No Purchase

In the end, even when strategic marketing is executed successfully, consumers may not purchase. There are countless reasons, which are simply part of the response process, why this happens: no need or desire for the product; insufficient time or funds; preference for the competitor's offerings; and many, many more. However, a shrewd marketer will always want to know why a consumer chose not to purchase.

Market research on nonconsumers and consumers is equally important. The people who are not purchasing hold the key to issues such as innovation, product improvement or development, distribution processes, pricing, branding, and a multitude of other facets in marketing. In the next chapter, you will learn how to conduct market research and use data to make better, more informed, sport business decisions.

Wrap-Up

In this chapter we examined some of the theories that may indicate why people consume sport. Specifically, we considered the literature on sport consumers within the larger context of general consumer behavior. We discussed various factors that help to explain the process whereby people are socialized into involvement in or commitment to sport. We have seen that factors influencing behavior may be either external or internal. External factors are the elements of the marketing mix (product, price, place, promotion, and public relations) and environmental influences (economic, technological, political, cultural, demographic, and situational). Internal factors are consumer characteristics (beliefs/attitudes, values, knowledge, motives, perceptions, and lifestyle) and the decision-making process (problem solving, information search, alternate evaluation, purchase, and post-purchase evaluation).

We have been able to provide only a brief introduction to some of the components in the complex area of consumer behavior. Further research is sorely needed before sport marketers can build effective theories on decision making. In the next chapter, we provide some information on how the marketer should conduct such research.

Activities

1. Define *socialization*, *involvement*, and *commitment* in sport consumer behavior.

2. Describe the most logical indicators of commitment for the following sport consumers: Vegas Golden Knights fans and Peloton users.

3. List and discuss which internal and external factors most influenced your involvement in your favorite sport.

4. Why is it likely that the normal hierarchy of effects (Learn → Feel → Do) is less applicable to sport consumers than to consumers of detergent?

5. Find a social media promoted ad for a sport product or team. Analyze how, in your opinion, the ad is trying to influence consumer perceptions of the product. Is it effective? Why or why not?

6. List the steps in the decision-making process for sport consumers. Reconstruct your most recent decision to attend a major sports event. How did your experience compare with the decision-making model?

7. For an event that you decided *not* to attend, think about the Satisfaction = Benefits - Cost equation, and list all the benefits and costs that were associated with attending. Did the costs outweigh the benefits? Discuss how your final decision was made and how these types of consumer decisions affect sports marketing.

Your Marketing Plan

This chapter outlined many of the factors that influence how people become involved in and committed to sport. As you organize and conduct research on the current and possible consumers for your product, event, or organization, pay close attention to the most prominent environmental and individual factors that influence their behavior. This analysis, in turn, should influence your decisions about product development, pricing, promotion, distribution (place), and public relations.

Go to HK*Propel* to complete the activities for this chapter.

Chapter 4

Market Research and Analytics in the Sport Industry

Melissa Davies

OBJECTIVES

- To become aware of the various sources of data and information available within the sport industry and how businesses go about obtaining or collecting data

- To appreciate all of the ways in which analytics can help inform sport business

- To understand how the sport industry uses market research methodologies in daily business activities through case-study examples

Michael Tureski/Icon Sportswire via Getty Images

The Price Is Right?

Think of all the points of purchase that exist within the sport industry. Sports fans and consumers at any given time may spend money on an array of goods and services. Speaking only of the live game-day experience, attendees may need to pay for tickets, parking, concessions, and merchandise. Beyond game day, fans can lay out cash on TV packages (e.g., NFL Sunday Ticket), apps, merchandise, and more. One lingering question spans all these potential purchases: How much are people willing to pay?

Today, an important business practice of data analytics has been established to help make predictions and informed business decisions. Many sport organizations have hired individual staff members or even entire departments devoted to analytics to help collect and analyze data. Readily available data have empowered stronger decision making in some of these areas. For example, sport teams maintain robust databases of ticket buyers and their spending behavior. By combining this information with data from the secondary market and dynamic pricing algorithms, today's sport industry is more armed than ever to price tickets for maximum profit. Teams are not only setting prices for different games at different rates, but some teams have created variable ticket pricing down to the appropriate price point for an individual row and seat. Years of ticket data can help to build a model that uses many variables (e.g., day of the week, opponent, promotion) to predict the optimal price point for a given ticket.

But the picture is not complete; if a team wants to offer a new ticket package never before sold, it must connect a bunch of dots to form an educated guess on price. Of course, we can figure out what people might pay for things in another way. We could simply ask them.

Due to many psychological traits humans share, simply asking people what they are willing to pay for something has its risks as well. As humans, we have an inclination to seek out the best deal. If asked as part of a survey how much they would be willing to pay for, say, a team jersey, respondents may answer with a number that is in fact lower than what they would pay, hoping to skew the price downward in their favor (should the jersey actually be for sale). On the other hand, respondents may answer with a higher number than they would actually pay if they are trying to impress the person who is asking about price, which is in line with what is called "social desirability bias."

To get around part of this bias, some research methodologies use indirect questioning techniques. One of the stronger methodologies, called Van Westendorp analysis, presents each respondent with a product concept (e.g., a retro away jersey) and asks a battery of four questions:

- At what price would you begin to think that the jersey is too expensive to consider?
- At what price would you begin to think that the jersey is so inexpensive that you would question the quality and not consider it?
- At what price would you begin to think that the jersey is getting expensive, but you still might consider it?
- At what price would you think that the jersey is a bargain—a great buy for the money?

Proper analysis of the resulting data yields (a) an optimal price point and (b) a range of suitable prices. Although an optimal price point provides a clear target number, having a range of suitable prices provides decision makers some flexibility should conditions change, such as having more or less jersey inventory than planned.

- How much money are Team K's season-ticket holders spending on merchandise throughout the season?
- How much of Team Z's brand equity is tied to the head coach and star player?
- In which market should Bank Q invest its sponsorship dollars?
- What out-of-home media platform will create the most impressions for advertising a new ticketing website?

Questions such as these used to be difficult if not impossible to assess accurately. But technological advancements have facilitated opportunities for the sport industry to make more educated business decisions. Not unlike other major business verticals, sport properties and related businesses can tap into numerous sources of consumer data, ranging from terabytes of information stored by credit bureaus to 280-character opinions from Twitter.

The term *market research* means different things to different people. Perhaps the simplest and most direct way to define *market research* is "research on the market." A market researcher's job involves providing insight and wisdom about consumers in the brand's target market. Within the sport industry, *market research* is defined as "the provision of insight and information about sports fans." As referenced earlier, the 21st century has brought us a plethora of data sources from which to derive this insight. We consider those sources of data now.

Sources of Information

Some people in the industry hear the words *market research* and instantly think *survey*. Surveys certainly provide valuable feedback for sport marketers, and these tools will be addressed throughout this chapter. But researchers have many sources of data beyond surveys. Data sources are commonly broken out into two general categories: syndicated data and custom research. We define each category and provide examples of data types as follows.

Syndicated Data

Syndicated data refers to data that have been collected, organized, and repackaged for consumption. Syndicated data suppliers typically monetize their businesses by selling subscriptions to their data sources; the ongoing subscriber fees more than offset the investment required to accumulate and process the data collected. Because multiple clients purchase the data, the supplier can charge a lower price than would be required had the data been compiled for only one client. While the lower costs to acquire the data is a benefit to using syndicated data, buyers of syndicated data do not necessarily receive information that has been customized for their exact needs. The data may answer more broadly about trends but not focus on the market- or organization-specific questions. Many brands will make this tradeoff though, and in some cases, syndicated data provide the only real source of usable information. Consumer packaged-goods manufacturers rely on companies such as NPD, Nielsen, and IRI to sell them retail sales data; without these suppliers, manufacturers would have to spend inordinate amounts of money on consumer studies that would lack sufficient sample size or granularity.

Major syndicated data suppliers are highlighted in this section. Ironically, perhaps the biggest supplier, the U.S. government, provides its information at no cost.

U.S. Census

The U.S. Census offers an often overlooked syndicated data source that provides an abundance of helpful information about the demographic makeup of the U.S. population. Mandated by the U.S. Constitution, the U.S. Census enumerates the U.S. population every 10 years. It identifies trends in the evolving makeup of the U.S. population both for the country as a whole and by state, county, city, and even zip code. The most recent U.S. Census took place in 2020. For the period until 2030, the U.S. Census Bureau will use historical data at its disposal to provide estimates for any related information queries.

A significant advantage of U.S. Census data is that it is available online free of charge. Moreover, in recent years, the U.S. Census Bureau has revamped the data presentation, providing a user-friendly tool for researchers or any other interested party with basic computer skills. The U.S. Census Bureau website provides tables of demographic data that can be compared and sorted through to explore the population around the United States.[1] Table 4.1 provides an example of how a sport organization could explore the

TABLE 4.1 Example of Demographic and Housing Estimates

Race	Houston-The Woodlands-Sugar Land, Texas Metro Area		
	Estimate	Margin of error	Percent
White	2,483,103	+/- 1,289	36.6%
Black or African American	1,143,282	+/- 2,615	16.9%
Hispanic or Latino	2,506,513	-	37.0%
American Indian	12,839	+/- 1,141	0.2%
Asian	514,355	+/- 2,635	7.6%
Native Hawaiian and other Pacific Islander	3,152	+/- 376	0.0%
Some other race (alone)	13,778	+/- 1,661	0.2%
Two or more races	102,082	+/- 4,543	1.5%
Total population	6,779,104	-	100.0%

Data from United State Census Bureau (2018). https://data.census.gov/cedsci/table?q=Houston%20city,%20Texas&g=1600000US4835000 _310M400US26420&hidePreview=true&tid=ACSDP5Y2018.DP05&table=DP05

racial diversity of a given metro area. This might help generate more strategic marketing communication or promotional campaigns relative to the target market.

Demographic Profiling

Despite its robust data supply, the U.S. Census does not fulfill all needs related to syndicated data, nor is the Census positioned only to facilitate businesses in understanding their target markets. Syndicated research companies such as Scarborough and Simmons provide a more detailed overview of the U.S. population than the U.S. Census does, and they tailor their offerings to specific clients by looking at the population as sets of consumers. Scarborough surveys more than 200,000 consumers annually in the nation's 77 most populous designated market areas (DMAs).[2] Scarborough's measurement tactics include phone interviews, survey booklets, television diaries, and Internet surveys that detail its consumer habits across leading product categories, such as automotive, banking, beverage, drug and grocery, health care, lifestyle, restaurant, sport, and many others. Scarborough's insights are conveniently web-based, and the company typically releases two annual data files with information collected in the previous six months. Simmons, on the other hand, offers access to a web-based data bank that provides an array of data fields and segmentation capabilities.

Although both services are well positioned in sport and live entertainment, anecdotal evidence suggests that Scarborough has higher penetration among the properties (or rights holders) in this space. Brand managers and sponsorship sales professionals working for properties mine Scarborough's data to uncover shopping habits and brand preferences within its fan bases. Rights holders often use data like Scarborough's to demonstrate the fit between its property's fan profile and a sponsor's target customers.

The self-proclaimed worldwide leader in sports ESPN offers a subscription to the ESPN Sports Poll, another syndicated research service that profiles sports fans in the United States on their interests, behaviors, and preferences. Other useful resources for sport business professionals are databases and research solutions like Statista or Sport Market Analytics, a service under the Sports Business Research Network (SBRNet). While these platforms are subscription based, these databases offer a wide range of data that can help inform decisions within sport business operations. Many universities have subscriptions to these services so that students can explore these offerings. Statista compiles a wide range of industry data from many outside sources so it can be helpful on several fronts. For example, if you were looking to expand your social media reach among teenagers in the United States and were considering adding a new platform to your official team accounts, you might be interested in investigating the most used social media platforms by age group across the United States. Using the Statista database, you could search for tables that include the most frequently used social networks among 13- to 17-year-olds in the United States or investigate time spent per social media platform per day or per week. You could also get a little more specific with your search by turning to the Sport Market Analytics website and investigate data related to social media usage across your league, where there are tables and charts prepared for a specific sport or within a specific fan market. Table 4.2 shows year-to-year comparisons about how many WBNA games viewers are tuning into over the course of a season.

You might be curious to learn more about who the fans of the WNBA are and how this fan base has evolved in recent years. Table 4.3 highlights the gender breakdown of viewers. League executives could use information like this to better target sponsors who align with the target market or identify opportunities for growth through new promotion or marketing campaigns.

For a broader look at the sport industry, PricewaterhouseCoopers (PwC) has been providing the public with a sport industry report that attempts to highlight trends across the industry, including forecasts and expectations for the upcoming years. The most recent report projected major revenue growth opportunities for the sport industry through 2023.[3] While these reports are syndicated data and open for public viewing online, PwC and other consulting firms also work directly with clients to conduct customized research.

Audience Measurement

In 2017, media rights fees emerged as the most substantial piece of sport properties' revenue pie and are expected to continue growing at a faster rate than other revenues, such as gate revenues, sponsorship, and merchandising.[3] Because this escalation shows no signs of slowing down, all stakeholders will continue to have interest in measuring consumption of sports media. Anyone aspiring to work in the business of sport and live entertainment stands to benefit from having a basic understanding of audience ratings.

A property's TV ratings not only dictate the nationwide and local broadcast rights fees but also play a substantial role in sponsorship rights negotiations. Until recently, Nielsen ratings were the primary source of information for broadcasters to justify rights fees and set ad prices. In each country in which Nielsen operates, the company recruits a large sample of households, representative of all households in that country who own a television. Although some families keep diaries and later report the programming that they watched, most of Nielsen's panel use devices called People Meters. The device is

TABLE 4.2   WNBA TV Viewing: Percent by Frequency of Viewing

Item	2012	2013	2014	2015	2017
1/yr.	26.7	26.3	26.8	29.1	31.1
2-3 times/yr.	36.5	38.4	33.4	34.2	34.5
4+ times/yr.	36.8	35.3	39.8	36.8	34.3
Total	100.0	100.0	100.0	100.0	100.0
Base: Total number of WNBA fans viewing games on TV (add 000)	21,521	18,156	17,585	20,902	16,714

Reprinted by permission from Sports Market Analytics/SMA.

TABLE 4.3   WNBA TV Viewing: Percent by Gender

Item	2012	2013	2014	2015	2017
Male	58.2	55.1	62.6	59.9	53.7
Female	41.8	44.9	37.4	40.1	46.3
Total	100.0	100.0	100.0	100.0	100.0
Base: No. viewing (add 000)	21,521	18,156	17,585	20,902	16,714

Reprinted by permission from Sports Market Analytics/SMA.

attached to the TV sets, and panelists indicate which members of the household watched the respective programming. Results are reported automatically to Nielsen every night. Nielsen monetizes the business through paid subscriptions for its services; these subscriptions provide detailed ratings reports (e.g., ratings breakdown by age group, gender, and geographic location) to clients across all industries concerned with TV viewership. In the sport market in particular, properties want to know how to price advertising slots for sponsors and brands that buy ad space during related programming (e.g., game broadcasts).

Critics of Nielsen ratings have cited challenges in accurately accounting for out-of-home (OOH) viewers (for example, fans watching an NFL game in bars or restaurants), as well as online and mobile viewers. In 2017, Nielsen moved toward a revised reporting system that could measure OOH viewing in real time using a new passive, real-time technology. ESPN was one of the first partners for this new reporting, which helped to better reflect viewership in public places.[4] As consumers transition from linear TV viewing habits, such as watching shows as they are broadcast on a television, and continue to move toward consuming through various streaming and over-the-top (OTT) platforms, Nielsen and other metrics systems are having to further adapt to effectively measure these viewers.

Similar to the television marketplace, the radio marketplace needs to understand listenership metrics. Nielsen Audio (formerly Arbitron) provides similar data in this space, using a methodology that allows for some OOH measurement.

The rise in importance of digital media has created a marketplace for measurement of online behavior. Comscore is an example of a syndicated data provider in this space. Although the company offers several products and services related to online behavior, one area of increasing importance is its Mobile Metrix solution.[5] The module provides usage data across mobile devices and mobile apps for smartphones.

One note here is that although it is considered a competitor to Comscore, Google Analytics does not generally fall under the category of syndicated data. Google Analytics deliverables are generally specific to one client's website, as opposed to being a mineable source of data for multiple clients.

The high-speed evolution of the media landscape has served as a catalyst for introducing service models for summarizing publicly available information, which by itself is also syndicated data. As an example, Critical Mention tracks brand references across news outlets, live event broadcasts, and other various media platforms. It qualifies the direction and tone of the brand-related sentiments mentioned by TV anchors or analysts as well as on blogs and in social media. The company's services allow businesses to keep a pulse on public discourse related to their brand on TV, online, and in social media.[6]

Broadcast Exposure Research

Traditionally, signage and brand exposure have been pillars of sponsorship rights agreements. Sponsor signage within TV camera sightlines—be it on-court signage, static in-venue or rotational signage, or brand marks on athlete uniforms—is typically considered premium inventory. But how can we assign a dollar value for the benefit of seeing Megan Rapinoe drink from a Powerade bottle on the sidelines of the pitch during warm-ups? One widely used methodology counts the minutes (or seconds) of exposure that a brand gets during a game or event broadcast and applies a conversion factor to estimate the advertising equivalent value. In other words, a comparison is made between the cost of buying standard advertising time and the exposure gained through the sponsorship.

As the broadcasting of sport content diversifies to platforms like ESPN+, DAZN, or Twitch, traditional ratings evaluations have had to shift and now include metrics such as number of subscriptions, streaming numbers, social media reach, engagement, and exposure. Companies like GumGum and MVPindex have developed algorithms using artificial intelligence and speech processing technology to help measure various components of media valuation, streaming performance, and sponsor KPIs, often in or close to real time. GumGum, for example, might use its artificial intelligence technology to automate the impressions earned every time a jersey patch is clearly visible on a broadcast or across social media platforms. This can help marketers and rights holders evaluate the value of the sponsorship investment. Meanwhile, MVPindex could offer real time measurement of the number of concurrent viewers on a Twitch esports broadcast.

Melissa Davies

New technology allows organizations, such as those featured on the outfield wall, to measure the value of their advertisement exposure across various platforms.

Custom Research

Although syndicated data offers cost-effective, readily available information, the available sources of syndicated data only sometimes adequately address the needs of a business. GumGum and MVPindex are two companies that offer custom research in the above media exposure research examples. In many situations, only customized market research will satisfactorily resolve open business questions. Customized market research, or, more simply, custom research, refers to any situation in which researchers customize and implement a methodology for obtaining data. Unlike syndicated data suppliers, custom research produces primary data—data not already collected and available for usage.

More often than not, custom market research explores opinions, attitudes, and behaviors among the consumer marketplace. Objectives can vary, of course, dictating different target populations and methodologies.

To explore insights directly from consumers, data generally fall in either quantitative or qual-

itative data. Sometimes researchers will combine both quantitative and qualitative data and form a "mixed methods" approach to answering a set of questions. Quantitative data refer to data types that can be represented numerically. Quantitative data can be nominal (in which order has no significance, such as an area code or a category) or ordinal (in which order does matter, such as weight or dollars). Quantitative data can also be categorized as discrete (meaning countable, such as number of tickets sold to a game) or continuous (meaning uncountable, such as game-time temperature). Quantitative data provide the built-in advantage of bringing into play the many available data analysis techniques, software packages, and graphical representations that allow researchers to identify higher levels of insight. Some questions researchers might ask using quantitative methods include the following:

- What is the relationship between bobble-head giveaways and attendance figures at minor league baseball games across the United States?

- How much would you be willing to pay to purchase a family ticket package, including four tickets, four hot dogs, four sodas, and a popcorn?

Qualitative data, on the other hand, are composed of nonnumerical metrics—text, images, objects, sounds, and so forth. Analysis of qualitative data requires more complex techniques because researchers must explore the meaning and context of the data to identify common themes and patterns. Technology has facilitated advanced techniques of qualitative data analysis. Many companies offer software to aid with the analysis of open text; content analysis is one of the more common techniques to try to generate meaning and synthesize the data.

Qualitative consumer research offers a particular benefit to the sport industry because the evaluation of the effect of emotion and passion between fan and team or sport is better handled through dialogue than through survey. On the downside, projects involving qualitative data collection and analysis generally cost more than similar projects focusing on quantitative techniques. Driven primarily by the cost factor, most market research conducted in the sport industry tends to be quantitative. Without question, finding ways for sport marketers to access less expensive qualitative consumer research will remain an opportunity for the foreseeable future. Some questions researchers might ask and use qualitative data include the following:

- What are the challenges fans face in accessing the stadium?
- How could we improve your experience in the arena?

We now turn our attention to methods of data collection within custom consumer research. (Similar methods will apply to business-to-business [B2B] research, addressed in an upcoming section.) Surveying is overwhelmingly the most common method to obtain custom quantitative research data, although how and where a survey is administered certainly matters. Qualitative research can come from myriad other sources, such as interviews, focus groups, or observation. We will generally focus on the more common methodologies in play today.

Quantitative Research

As mentioned earlier, surveying provides the source of most quantitative custom market research data. Surveys allow people to provide opinions, report behaviors, and identify things that matter to them within a framework that is usually anonymous and confidential. The advent of newer technologies has allowed researchers to personalize the survey experience for respondents, at the disadvantage of removing anonymity. The experiential versus anonymous part of research can be evaluated only on a case-by-case basis.

To get completed surveys, respondents have to know that a survey exists, and they must be invited to complete the survey. Common methods of inviting survey responses are described as follows.

Digital   With Internet connectivity in U.S. households now reaching 90 percent of adults (18 years of age or older), online surveying has become one of the most popular and easiest forms of surveying.[7] Digital surveying can consist of many different forms:

- Sending a survey invitation by email to a database or online panel
- Hosting a survey link on a web page or social media site
- Presenting a survey invitation through a pop-up window on a web page
- Distributing copies of a survey URL by text, hard copy, or SMS
- Sending a push notification through a team app to invite participants to complete a survey through the app

In addition to the large Internet presence within households, the birth of numerous survey software companies has made online surveys easier than in the past. Companies such as Verint, SurveyMonkey, QuestionPro, Confirmit, SurveyGizmo, Qualtrics, and others provide solutions ranging from simple DIY options to full panel-management and data analytic capabilities. Survey software companies help make online surveying one of the fastest ways to receive data. Most software tools offer real-time results, allowing the researcher to see data coming in as soon as a respondent completes a question.

Years ago, when something at your house wasn't functioning correctly, you hired someone to fix it—a plumber, electrician, or other contractor type. If you were one of the few home-owners brave enough to try to fix it on your own, you ventured to your local hardware store in search of replacement parts and perhaps expertise on how to go about the repair.

Fast forward to 1979, when The Home Depot opened its first two stores in metro Atlanta. At that moment, the do-it-yourself (DIY) era commenced. (In all fairness, Lowe's first store dates back to the 1920s, but we defer to The Home Depot's stronger market share and larger number of retail locations.) With the Internet providing nearly infinite resources on how to fix anything from a leaky faucet to a broken lawnmower engine, virtually everyone has some level of DIY skills.

The DIY phenomenon doesn't stop at home repair. In the business world, few, if any, industries have been as affected as much as market research when it comes to the influence of DIY. Just as anyone with a hammer feels empowered to fix something, thousands of marketing, sales, communications, and public relations professionals have been armed with straightforward, inexpensive DIY market research technology. Want to run a survey? Tools such as SurveyMonkey, Google Polls, QuestionPro, Qualtrics, and SurveyGizmo provide users the ability to do simple to moderately complicated research at commoditized prices.

The sport industry has boarded the DIY train, motivated by the low cost and availability of bright, young data analysts who welcome the chance to work in sport. Just as a homeowner taking the DIY approach risks breaking a pipe and having to pay a plumber thousands of dollars, DIY research has its hazards. A poorly written questionnaire renders the resulting response data worthless, even detrimental. Failure to analyze data correctly can easily lead to incorrect business decisions. And tapping the same database for survey respondents repeatedly can alienate an organization's most loyal customers. Furthermore, asking the wrong people to fill out the surveys out of convenience can introduce bias into the findings, minimizing the accuracy of the findings. Say for example, the survey is only handed out to season-ticket holders, and questions are asked about willingness to pay. These season-ticket holders are already some of the most devoted fans, so it's likely that their willingness to pay does not reflect that of the general population. If ticket prices were raised based on findings from this survey, it's possible the casual fan would come to fewer games, thus reducing the effectiveness of the ticket price points and reducing ticket sales.

In truth, data-driven decision making can offer many benefits in the long run; however, it must be conducted with sound research principles. All involved are advised to proceed carefully and with all necessary precautions in place. As any DIYer would agree, one wrong cut of the electrical wire can cause all the good work to go up in flames.

The prevalence and ease of online research has caused ordinary people to become inundated with invitations to complete surveys. This inundation of surveys paired with poorly worded survey items or surveys that are too long lead to a concept called **survey fatigue**. Survey fatigue prompts survey respondents to lose interest in the survey and either stop answering as accurately as they could, or stop answering all together.

Neither outcome is ideal for researchers who are seeking complete and accurate answers to their surveys.

To help make the process of survey completion less burdensome on the respondent, software providers have optimized mobile devices' formatting and adapted features to help respondents avoid survey fatigue (e.g., drag-and-drop question types, pictures, and videos). **Skip logic**

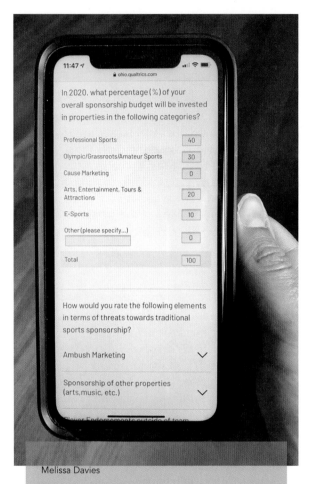

Melissa Davies

Online surveying offers a simple way to obtain information about and feedback from consumers. It can also serve as an expedient tool to gather information from sponsors and other industry partners.

a game or event where respondents are busy rushing to seats, trying to watch the game, and so on).

Although online surveying provides an effective all-around methodology for collecting quantitative research data (and even qualitative, depending on need), it is not always the best choice. Say, for instance, that a venue wants to survey event attendees to measure experiential satisfaction. Any database held by the venue will likely contain email addresses of ticket buyers, people who receive an online newsletter, or other database opt-ins, but that venue likely will not have contact information for walk-up cash buyers or guests of the ticket buyers.

More pitfalls exist within the online surveying world. Survey invitations emailed out to respondents commonly are caught in spam filters. And spam regulations are tougher than ever; researchers and research agencies must ensure permission exists to contact potential respondents or face the wrath of email domains everywhere.

Response rates for emailed surveys (the number of respondents who complete the survey divided by the number of respondents who received the survey) vary based on the type of respondent. Respondents with more investment (financial or emotional) in the brand are more likely to complete a survey. For instance, fans who are signed up to receive a team's email newsletter yield survey response rates of 2 to 5 percent, whereas single-game buyers tend to be at 5 to 15 percent, and season-ticket holders are around 20 to 35 percent. If a survey is posted to a web page, the web page needs to be heavily trafficked. If it is not, the response rate will be low.

Here are some examples of online surveys:

- To determine what influences fans to watch games at home instead of attending in person, the Chicago White Sox use an online survey to reach its TV and online audience. During live game-day broadcasts, the URL is shown on the screen and the broadcasters announce where to complete the survey and the incentive for their participation. TV and online viewers type in the URL on an Internet browser and complete the survey.

- Following the participation in the Yosemite Half-Marathon, Vacation Races sends out an online survey to all participants via email to collect feedback on the event, from

within surveys keeps respondents from having to answer questions that are not applicable to them. For example, the Los Angeles Dodgers send a game-day satisfaction survey after every home game to all individual-game ticket buyers who purchased their tickets online. The respondents are asked whether they bought concessions at the ballpark. If respondents bought concessions, they receive a series of concessions-specific questions; respondents who did not purchase concessions get automatically skipped forward in the survey to more relevant questions or in some cases, sent right to the end of the survey. Because respondents are settled in at their computers or on their mobile devices, online surveys usually can incorporate longer questionnaires (as opposed to surveying at

Chatbots

Advancements in artificial intelligence (AI) have allowed teams to use automated natural language processing and natural language generation to communicate with fans through various applications (e.g., Facebook, WeChat) or text messaging. Natural language processing and generation involves training algorithms so that computers can recognize and produce the human language. Whether you realize it or not, you have encountered this technology. If you click on a website and a dialogue box pops up, it is most likely a trained chatbot—a computer program that is fueled by machine learning and meant to simulate natural human conversation. A human customer service representative can be trained to interact with customers through the onboarding process. Chatbots, on the other hand, are trained to recognize patterns of conversation in a history of chat logs and also through engaging with customers. Has a chatbot asked you, "Did I answer your question correctly?" This is the algorithm's way of continually training. When you answer "yes" or "no," the chatbot adds this repetition to pattern generation. When a chatbot gets asked a question for which it doesn't have an answer, the human operator can step in and help the chatbot recognize a meaningful response for this question in future interactions. Over time then, the chatbot "learns" and improves its efficiency in communicating with the public. Learning in this case means automated and continually precise pattern recognition.

Like a virtual assistant, teams are able to employ chatbots to communicate with fans throughout the sales cycle (targeting, retention, and upsell) as well as to off-load the general consumer helpline. Chatbots help teams answer fan questions, sell tickets and merchandise, and increase engagement with fans. One customer representative can handle one conversation, email, or phone call at a time. Chatbots can handle an unlimited number of chats. Related with market research, the chatbots can be used to engage with fans about a given topic to gather feedback through direct questions about a topic, but more importantly, the questions fans are asking within the chatbot platform can help the team understand what fans are interested in knowing more about. If fans continually ask questions about which concession stands are gluten-free, for example, the team might consider its gluten-free offerings and find a way to either better provide gluten-free options or more clearly communicate where fans can find them. In the past, questions like this about where to find various elements within an arena may have been asked of game-day employees. Fans may have heard a range of answers depending on the knowledge of that single employee, but with the consistent knowledge and responses from the chatbot, fans might receive a more consistent answer. In addition, the teams also learn more about the questions fans have and can in turn resolve or improve operations accordingly.

Beyond AI-related solutions, fans can also give teams plenty of data via engagement on the team or stadium app. The Sacramento Kings call its app the "remote control" to the stadium. At the time that it opened and with its proximity to Silicon Valley, the Golden 1 Center, home of the Sacramento Kings, was the most advanced arena around. The app, which was powered by Xfinity, enabled fans access to real-time and on-demand information regarding every aspect of their experience from the closest and shortest bathroom line to advanced game metrics and exclusive video angles to even controlling the temperature in one of the lower bowl sections by reporting that it's "too cold" or "too hot."[12] In addition to the direct feedback teams could utilize from feedback about the temperature, the engagement on the stadium app also helps again to show teams what fans are interested in within the stadium, from which concessions see the longest lines to the times during the game when app engagement is highest and on which pages and so forth.

ease of access to the event to the quality of the trail to the food selection at the finish line. Participants are also asked about their travel and spending surrounding the event to help provide organizers with a sense for the economic impact in hosting the event at a rural location outside a National Park.

Intercepts   Sometimes the easiest way to locate survey respondents is to go physically to where they are. Intercept surveying consists of interviewing respondents in person, usually with the aid of some type of instrument for data capture. Although modern interviewers surely appreciate the development of iOS and Android devices, pen-and-paper surveys and even voice recorders provide alternative and effective means of recording pertinent information.

Numerous applications of intercept surveying exist. An earlier example in this chapter cited databases being void of contact information for event attendees; surveying onsite ensures access to those people at the event. Winter Park Resort in Colorado really took surveying via intercept to new heights when it sent a team out on its skis with an iPad to approach skiers on the mountain with a satisfaction survey. A team may conduct interviews at a nearby sports bar to assess why fans preferred that environment to the stadium itself.

Intercept surveying can backfire if done inappropriately. Here are some guidelines to conduct intercept surveying most effectively:

- Employ objective, unbiased staff in unbranded attire. Like any other market research, respondents must be allowed to give their true opinion. Staff dressed in team (or sponsor) garb or staff that talks up the company behind the research can sway responses, introducing unwanted bias into the analysis process.

- Keep the questionnaire short. Unless you have a desirable incentive to give out, like a big giveaway or gift certificate, nobody will want to spend a long time completing the survey. As a rule of thumb, don't go over four minutes per survey (about the length of a typical rock 'n' roll song).

- Employ an adequate number of interviewers. Here's a rule of thumb: Assuming that the staff person is administering the survey (as opposed to a self-administered

version) with one device (or clipboard) and no incentives are offered to respondents, expect no more than 40 minutes of surveying during a one-hour period. If you are using a four-minute survey, expect at most 10 surveys per hour per person.

- Have your staff employ a sampling scheme. If your interviewers want to talk only to good-looking respondents or respondents who share their age range, the chance is good that your data will not accurately reflect the opinions of the whole crowd. Staff should be encouraged to select targets to approach randomly or have a scheme that forces them to consider a wide array of people. It is recommended to invite every nth person to take the survey, with n depending on crowd size. (Big crowd? Maybe every fifth person. Smaller? Every third.)

Some sport teams or brands are fortunate to have enough volunteers or interns to administer surveys, but often, paid staff must be brought in, which must be accounted for in the budget. Although the objectives of any research project will determine when surveying should take place, typically interviewing will not be done while the main event is happening (e.g., before the start of a game, between matches at a tournament). If a survey must be conducted during a game or event, asking fans who are waiting in line (e.g., for concessions) provides a good way to reach respondents looking to kill time anyway. Furthermore, as more stadiums and teams launch their own apps, there are increased modes to communicate instantly with consumers.

Telephone   Once one of the more popular methodologies for market research, telephone surveying—the act of calling a respondent by telephone to administer a survey—has fallen off dramatically in recent years. Many factors have contributed to the drop-off in phone surveying, such as the simplicity of Internet research, the obstacles posed by the National Do Not Call Registry (www.donotcall.gov), and the number of U.S. households that have only mobile phones, that is, no landline (57 percent).[9]

Phone surveying certainly is not as popular as online or intercept surveying in the sport and entertainment industries, primarily because of the comparatively expensive nature of telephone interviews. With all the aforementioned caveats, telephone interviewing still provides a viable and handy method of collecting survey data. Telephone surveying can be helpful if a sport team is trying to reach respondents who may not be in the database or easily reached by email. For example, if a team is trying to conduct a survey among DMA residents who have never attended a game, that team will not have a readily available list of people to contact. And purchasing a list of DMA residents from a company such as Acxiom or Full House Solutions will not necessarily provide a full array of email addresses. In this situation, obtaining a list of all phone numbers in the region becomes more straightforward than assembling an email contact list.

Given the abundance of unlisted phone numbers today (mainly cell phones), phone surveying projects often include random digit dialing (RDD). RDD is the process of generating phone numbers within a geographical area based on typical phone numbers given out in that area, not taken from a list. Generating phone numbers using RDD circumvents the obstacles of unlisted numbers and cell phones.[10]

When conducting telephone surveys, computer-assisted telephone interviewing (CATI) is typically used. CATI refers to computer software that helps the interviewer dial the phone number, schedule phone calls for a later time if the call is not answered, place the survey questions on the monitor for the interviewer to read, code data as the interviewer records the response from the respondent on the computer, and apply appropriate skip logic based on the answers provided.[11]

Direct Mail Similar to telephone surveying, direct (U.S.) mail has become less popular within the research industry and among sport and entertainment companies. To survey by direct mail, the company must print and mail surveys (invoking printing and postage costs), include a return envelope with postage, open the returned surveys, and manually enter them into a system to analyze the data. After all that effort, direct mail surveying tends to have lower response rates than online surveys or intercept surveys because more effort is required of the respondent to fill out the survey and mail the envelope back to the company, even though respondents are given the envelope and free postage.

One advantage offered by direct mail research is the assurance of anonymity and confidentiality. Although online and phone surveys offer those benefits, respondents have reason to be skeptical. After all, computer technology makes emails and IP addresses easily traceable, and phone surveying suggests that the interviewer has the person's phone number. But with direct mail, respondents control the location from which they mail the survey and what information they include.

Qualitative Research

Qualitative research can be conducted using many sources of data from interviewing people to examining photos to observing behaviors. A person could walk around the stands at a college football game, read the emotions of the fans, and later report that, "Most people were having fun." Although the example may be silly, that information is in fact qualitative research.

More structured forms of qualitative research exist within the market research industry. We will touch on a few here, focusing on those most relevant for the sport and entertainment industry. For a broader view of qualitative research, you may wish to review Belk's book.[13]

In-Depth Interviews   In-depth interviews, or IDIs, are comprehensive question-and-answer discussions between a respondent and an interviewer (or a moderator). IDIs provide a preferred protocol when the research objective focuses on a person's decision process or reaction to stimuli without interactions from other respondents. As an example, a sport team might want to understand the benefits most appreciated by

premium suite holders. Having multiple suite holders in the same conversation could bias one (or more) respondents because of the demands of another (e.g., "Wow, I never thought to ask for a concierge.").

IDIs offer some additional obvious advantages, such as easier scheduling and absence of bias. Two more subtle but important advantages include the following:

- *Cost efficiency.* You end up using a respondent for 100 percent of the time for which you are compensating him or her. (And at about 30 to 60 minutes per interview, cost can be significant.)[14]

- *Deeper insights.* Qualitative research moderators like to probe respondents, often using a technique referred to as "laddering." Laddering is a question sequence composed of four (or more) questions related to a feature. The questions consist of asking about a feature, and its functional, higher, and finally emotional benefits.[15] When interviewing one person, the moderator can delve deeply into a topic and potential sensitivities without worrying about how the respondent will feel when discussing the topic in front of others.

Focus Groups   A focus group typically includes between 5 and 12 respondents who are recruited

Best Practices for In-Depth Interviews and Focus Groups

- Use a discussion guide document to ensure that the interactions remain in the scope of the research objectives.
- Conduct the research at a location unrelated to the client. Many clients prefer to conduct qualitative research at their office location (e.g., within a stadium or an arena) to save money. In fact, the potential bias introduced by the branded surroundings has the power to render the research useless. All major cities offer professional research facilities equipped to optimize the power of qualitative research, offering amenities, such as recording capabilities, transcription of conversations, and refreshments, for participants.
- Have a third-party moderator lead all discussions. Despite best efforts to be objective, a company employee will naturally allow some subjectivity to slip through during the research process. Bias on the part of the moderator can lead a respondent to either overstate or suppress true feelings on a topic, which renders the research results useless.

based on their relevance to a particular business issue or research topic. A moderator bears responsibility for ensuring that the discussion provides feedback on the outstanding research issues. As with IDIs, moderators typically rely on a discussion guide to enforce the structure of the discussion.

Conducting focus groups allows not only the gathering of insights unlikely to surface in survey research but also clients to target a group of respondents who may not be willing or able to participate in survey research. For example, an NFL team's youth program conducted a focus group in which the respondents were kids aged seven through 14. Conducting this focus group allowed the NFL team to gain insights into its youth program from a kid's perspective, which would be impossible to do by online surveys because of federal laws.

Individual focus groups should be as homogeneous as possible in terms of participants' age, gender, and product usage. Homogeneity promotes group dynamics, which can lead to greater insights. When the demographics of one respondent are not consistent with the other participants, misleading information is often provided. If a client desires to obtain information from a variety of ages, genders, and so on, conducting multiple focus groups is recommended.

Online focus groups have become more popular, correlated with the availability of chat software and virtual meeting platforms (e.g., Zoom). Online focus groups do provide some obvious benefits, such as ability to recruit respondents without geographic restriction. Online focus groups are limiting by nature; live product demonstrations, visuals, and written exercises pertaining to the topic are included more easily in person. Additionally, valuable nonverbal behavior, including body posture, hand gestures, and facial expressions, provide additional insight but get lost in a chat room. For example, mentioning words such as "parking egress" and "public seat license" to NFL season-ticket holders will produce negative facial expressions from some participants.

Ethnography   Yogi Berra famously quipped, "You can observe a lot just by watching." Ironically, the form of market research that most follows this line is hardly ever used in the sport industry. Ethnographic research is the act of observing respondents, be it one person or a group of people, in their real-life environment. This type of research can provide deep insight into consumers' need states, daily habits, and decision-making processes. Have you ever noticed that ketchup and shampoo bottles now stand on their lids? That change came through ethnographic research; consumer goods brands noticed that consumers would typically stand the items upside-down to ensure that they used the entire contents.

Often, ethnography requires the permission of the subject being studied. But simple ethnographic studies can be accomplished in the sport industry without such formal steps. Simply sitting in the stands during a game or walking around a pregame tailgate can reveal a lot about satisfaction with in-seat service and beer consumption respectively. More often than not, ethnographic research takes place at the beginning of a project and generates hypotheses for future study.[16]

Ethnography has its share of potential pitfalls. For one, people don't always act the same when they are being actively observed. The studies can also require a long time to conduct. Subjects must feel as natural and unaffected during the research process as they do when no research is taking place. More so than other forms of qualitative research, ethnographic research requires an experienced practitioner to ensure the study's validity and success.[17]

Other Qualitative Data Sources   Although much qualitative research continues to follow protocols cited in previous sections, newer technologies and social media are providing new ways for properties and brands to collect feedback from consumers:

- *Social media sites.* With respect to market research, data posted on social media platforms (e.g., Facebook, Instagram, Twitter) are fundamentally observational; you read or observe what fans post. But information from these sites can be valuable for sport properties because it both comes from the most invested customers (fans) and also is an opportunity to gauge interest and perceptions in real time. If Nike observes a feed of basketball fans criticizing the durability of a line of shoes, that information can clearly motivate action in Oregon. Fans might also post pictures of red tail lights in front of them as they complain about the two hours it's taking them to leave the parking lot after a game. These are helpful observations that marketers might be able to use to revise the product, place, or the communication with fans to help alleviate problems or improve operations. Teams can also look to the comments, likes, and shares across social media platforms to identify the types of content that resonate best with fans by exploring the number of likes, shares, comments, and follows.

- *Fancam technology.* Using facial recognition technology and computer vision technology, Fancam provides very high pixel photos of fans sitting anywhere in the stadium. Designed originally as a fan engagement tool, where fans could zoom in on their seats and share a picture of themselves in the seat, there are also several business-related opportunities involved. After the COVID-19 global pandemic shut down most of the sport industry in the spring of 2020, Fancam also adjusted to offering teams the opportunity to monitor social distancing and measuring capacity within stadium sections in real time. Beyond periods of social distancing, this kind of technology can provide teams with qualitative data, by providing imagery that can be analyzed for a variety of reasons, including determining which sections of the arena are filled earliest, a scan of where families tend to sit or avoid, whether any trends exist for what food and drink people are holding in one section over another, and so forth. The visual scan is qualitative since it requires the documentation of observations.

- *Market research online community (MROC).* Businesses of all types, including the major U.S. professional sport leagues, commonly employ consumer panels for survey research. An MROC is a dedicated online community created for the purpose of qualitative market research. An MROC can provide respondents for IDIs and focus groups, provide unmoderated conversation between participants, or even be a source for journal and diary entry.[18]

Business-to-Business Research

Market research in the B2B space happens more outside the sport industry than within. The reason for the gap is easy to comprehend—obtaining feedback from business people costs more than getting it from ordinary consumers. Whereas consumers willingly take online surveys just for the opportunity to win a sweepstakes or for a small monetary incentive, getting someone to take time out of a busy business day often requires much higher compensation.

But this is not always the case. Some businesses definitely have a stake in providing feedback to sport marketers. Here are a few examples:

- *Corporate partners.* Corporate partners provide a valuable source of revenue for sport teams. The team needs to ensure that partners are satisfied with the fulfillment of its contractual terms. Objective third-party research can provide a better understanding of where partners are satisfied and where they are not.

- *Vendors.* Teams can just as easily play the role of client. For instance, concessionaires benefit from ensuring satisfaction of their key stakeholders.

- *Premium seat holders.* Many premium seating areas, such as suites or high-level clubs, serve the hospitality needs of business development personnel. If the business developers do not see positive momentum because of using the venue for client or employee entertainment, renewal becomes an iffy proposition. Teams and venues can use research techniques to identify their clients' needs within the premium areas.

Users of Market Research in Sport and Entertainment

We now turn our focus specifically to the sport industry. Except for conducting the occasional project, research has not held a regular role in the typical sport organization. Historically, market research in the sport world has been designed, performed, analyzed, and interpreted by a tenured market researcher sourced from a third-party vendor or partner. These people were likely to have been trained academically on how to collect and interpret data. A person with this skill set was often employed by a professional sport franchise, allowing third-party suppliers to make a living providing these services to sport teams. Examining the historical landscape of larger businesses, such as sponsors, league offices, and agencies, the likelihood grew that a market researcher would be employed in-house.

Sport Data Analytics Jobs

As the proliferation of data and its applications continue to grow in the sport industry, there are opportunities to apply analytics within each and every department:

- Ticket sales and retention can clearly develop and utilize customer relationship management (CRM) databases of information to better understand fans and their buying behaviors.
- Corporate partnerships can develop better algorithms to measure the effectiveness of a sponsorship activation or season-long key performance indicators (KPIs) to retain and grow partnership contracts.
- The digital and social department can utilize engagement data, such as likes, follows, and shares, of specific posts to help identify content that is resonating best with fans.
- Facility managers can identify flow and usage data using heat maps to identify opportunities to improve the design, signage, or staffing throughout the arena.
- Players and their agents have turned to critically assessing player performance data to help effectively valuate players during contract negotiations.

These are just a few of the possible areas where hiring someone with the ability to collect and analyze data can help to improve the efficiency and profitability of any sport organization.

According to ZipRecruiter,[19] as of 2020, the national average annual salary for a sport statistician was US$71,664 per year. That said, while many sport organizations have invested in hiring analysts within the player scouting and in-game analytics departments, fewer analysts have been hired directly within the business side of the front office. Instead, many sport business professionals must develop a basic understanding of data and its uses in addition to their other departmental roles, such as ticket sales or social media.

Tremendous growth has occurred in the use of market research and data analytics to drive day-to-day business decisions in sport. With database marketing and the Internet allowing for ease in data collection and data storage, properties now have valuable data at their fingertips. Interpreting that data and putting the findings into practice is the next big hurdle, and this challenge has spurred many organizations within the sport industry to bring on staff internally to facilitate the wide array of market research needs. No longer is there a typical market researcher or analyst; that title can mean something different to each organization that employs a researcher. In one instance you could have someone who is skilled at managing an influx of syndicated research data from various sources. Another instance may present a person who is well versed in designing a survey questionnaire and performing stable data collection. Yet another orga-nization may have a person who truly analyzes data, hunting for trends and pulling out findings. To complicate matters further, an analyst at one place may have 15 years of experience, whereas an analyst in another organization may be an intern who will be returning to school in three to six months.

Each of the aforementioned skill sets can serve a specific need. Needs for research arise from different places across the sport industry. The following examples show how different organizations use market research services.

Professional Sport Leagues

A market researcher within a professional sport league serves several purposes. Media ratings and broadcast research have high relevance because leagues typically control a portion, if not all, of their television rights. All major sport leagues employ media researchers who mine ratings data to support the rights fees and advertising fees charged. Nielsen and Nielsen Audio are the primary ratings measurement systems that league offices use. Media research also helps to validate contractual obligations that leagues owe to sponsors and advertisers.

A market researcher at a professional sport league often satisfies the internal consumer research needs across multiple departments. Primary consumers of research include the sponsorship, ticketing, and marketing departments. A league office needs to understand consumer behaviors and perceptions as they affect the branding of the league, league partners, and league marks. Consumers may well have different perceptions and intentions toward the Vegas Golden Knights brand, Golden Knights sponsors, and the Golden Knights experience than they do toward the NHL and its respective brand, sponsors, and experience. In this particular example, an NHL market researcher might seek out the

How Much Is Enough?

The question that market researchers get all the time, and hate getting whenever they get it, is: "How many respondents do I need in my sample?"

No one-size-fits-all answer can provide an adequate response to this question. The best answer is, "It depends," which raises the follow-up question, "Depends on what?" When conducting survey research, identification of an appropriate sample size requires consideration of the following issues:

• *What is the size of the population to which your inferences will relate?* Quite often, the size of the population is so large that it may as well be considered boundless (e.g., the U.S. population). But sometimes the population size can be rather small (e.g., season-ticket holders for a class A MiLB team in the Southeastern United States).

• *How precise do you need your estimates (and hence inferences) to be?* Think carefully when evaluating this question. Although many clients express concern about not collecting a sufficient sample, oversampling occurs quite frequently. And although an out-of-pocket cost may not be associated with sampling from a fan or ticket-buyer database, asking your customers to answer too many surveys has a hidden cost. Certain fields require incredible precision, such as spinal surgery and air-traffic control. On the other hand, when estimating the proportion of game attendees who approve of the music selection, plus or minus a few percentage points can certainly be deemed tolerable.

• *What is the budget?* More often than not, larger sample sizes result in higher cost. Even if the sample source does not require out-of-pocket spending, a higher number of respondents results in larger data files, more intricate analyses, and more resources required to compile findings. If onsite research is the methodology of choice, larger sample sizes require more time in field, which usually means higher cost for staffers to administer interviews. Also, online research that uses third-party panels produces a one-to-one correlation between cost and sample size. If your budget does not allow you to collect enough respondents to have solid, trustworthy data, you are probably better off skipping the project or identifying an alternative methodology.

Only after population size, precision, and budget are identified can a researcher adequately address sample size appropriateness. A typical survey project with only one population of interest requires anywhere from 250 to 500 respondents to generate a robust data set.

league's fans for feedback regarding national broadcasts, methods for consuming the NHL, experience at league-facilitated events (the Winter Classic, All-Star Game, and so on), and behaviors relating to NHL sponsors. League offices will analyze this data market by market, region by region, and nationwide. Normal practice is to analyze the data across the various fan segments as well (avid versus casual, attendees versus viewers, young fans versus old fans, and so on).

Finally, a market researcher at a professional sport league often serves in the role of advisor or consultant to its member clubs. Not all teams have access to the same resources in terms of staff and budgets, but a league office doesn't want to look across its member clubs and see a landscape of haves and have-nots. A league office wants to provide as many resources as possible to empower member clubs and support their business operations. No league does this better historically than the NBA through its Team Marketing and Business Operations (TMBO) division. Market researchers within TMBO assist NBA clubs with research in areas such as ticketing, sponsorship, premium seating, impression measurement, and promotional nights. They share best practices of clubs using market research across NBA, WNBA, and NBADL clubs. In other words, teams are working together on a lot of their business practices by learning and sharing from each other's data across the league(s). This is one of the unique characteristics about the sport industry, where teams are competitors on the court but collaborators for the greater good of the league.

Leagues have the ability to perform market research across multiple clubs at much lower pricing than clubs would have to pay if they performed research by themselves. Investing in these efforts ensures that teams are maximizing the margins in good times and minimizing the effect on revenues in bad times.

Professional Sport Properties

The use of market research on a day-to-day basis at the professional sport property level has grown substantially since 2010. Some teams invest heavily across custom and syndicated research, whereas other properties employ no market research in their business operation. At the most basic level, the vast majority of professional sport properties collect fan feedback. Topics frequently covered include event satisfaction (concessions, parking, ushers, etc.), season-ticket holder satisfaction, ticket purchase intent, and fan segment profiling. These studies help an organization keep its finger on the who, what, when, where, why, and how of the fan base. Marketing and ticketing departments use this type of research to create promotions, ticket packages, and at-event features.

Professional sport properties are now engaging in increasingly sophisticated research projects. Specifically, sponsorship measurement and ticket-pricing studies have proved to be highly effective in maximizing revenues within those respective departments. Sponsorship departments are under significant pressure to justify rights fees and measure the effectiveness of a corporate partnership. Brands are being held accountable internally, and they often rely on the property to provide data. Sponsorship departments can collect data respective to specific brands, categories, or perceptions of sponsors in general. These data are analyzed and translated to help convey to the brand how the partnership is moving the needle with the property's fan base.

When internal resources, such as time, money, equipment, or expertise, are insufficient, a growing number of market research companies that exist can help sport organizations better collect and make sense of the data surrounding their business. Navigate is one of those companies that focuses on providing data about the impact and return on investment of sponsorship deals, among other projects. Table 4.4 illustrates the range of projects a company like Navigate can offer the sport industry.

In the ticketing world, all professional sport properties are trying to find the optimal price point to charge for a ticket:

- Which price point will result in unsold tickets?
- Which price point will damage the perceived value of a ticket?
- Which variables should drive the price up or down?

Ticketing departments analyze many sources of data to modify prices. Sales data from the primary and secondary market account for two of the more important sources. Knowing the

TABLE 4.4   Market Research Projects Conducted by Navigate Research

Sport organization	Research conducted	Outcomes
Maple Leaf Sports & Entertainment (MLSE)	Comparison of impact of jersey patch sponsorship between fans versus general population in the local region	Helped club renew sponsorship for a record fee
NFL	Sponsorship category overviews for NFL each season with data on industry trends, competitor overviews, sponsorship spend, and best practices	Helped NFL position themselves in sponsor renewal contract negotiation
The Ohio State University (OSU)	Media rights appraisal, contract projection	OSU teamed up with IMG College for the largest collegiate media rights deal in history
Major League Soccer (MLS)	Fan surveys with more than 6,500 season-ticket holders from 15 MLS clubs to assess season-ticket holders' experiences, behaviors, interests, and purchase barriers	Findings reported to MLS league office and respective clubs to provide individualized and comparative insights, helping teams during season-ticket renewal period
Real Salt Lake (MLS)	Assessment of exposure value for a potential jersey sponsor as well as provide benchmarking information and key insights during acquisition stage of jersey sponsor	Resulted in Real Salt Lake signing one of the largest MLS jersey sponsorship deals (US$30 million over 10 years), despite playing in one of the smallest markets in the league
ESPN	Assessment of a specific sponsor's exposure and effectiveness, using both interviews and real-time app engagement during select MLB broadcasts	Provided unbiased qualitative feedback for sponsor from viewing audience
USA Fencing	Utilization of a proprietary tool, the Sponsorship Navigator, to evaluate and provide recommendations on how to sell sponsorship packages	Provided fair market value and suggested price points for each sponsorship package for USA Fencing to set price points moving forward
Monumental Sports Entertainment and WNBA	Assessment of exposure value for jersey sponsorship in WNBA and provided a three-year recap deck and demographic research	Helped in negotiations for the renewal process or in recruiting and securing new sponsors

Data from Navigate Research. www.navigateresearch.com/navigate-research-case-studies

available inventory, prices already paid for tickets, and advanced purchase information helps with identifying the optimal price point going forward. Some professional sport teams use this data to make pricing recommendations every day of the year, but others perform this analysis less frequently. As the ticketing platforms and servicing continue to move digital, more data become available for sport organizations to gather and analyze insights in the ticketing space. Furthermore, some teams and leagues have developed strategic partnerships with secondary ticket companies like Ticketmaster and StubHub to gain access to even more insights about fan ticket purchase behaviors and optimal price points.

Sponsors

The primary objective of a sport sponsorship is to use the assets (e.g., marks or logos, hospitality, fan reach, event access) of the property to drive the business objectives of the sponsor more effectively than it could without the sponsorship. Generalizing about how sponsors use their sponsorships is difficult. Comparing the use of sponsorship

StubHub Partners With Major League Baseball

MLB has had an agreement with StubHub since 2007 and renewed a contract for another five years in 2017. The MLB-StubHub partnership was an industry-leading relationship that helped pave the way for other ticket resale partnerships throughout the sport industry.[20] This partnership enables StubHub to serve as the exclusive ticketing integration system for MLB.com and the 30 clubs, providing a secure opportunity for fans to purchase and resell tickets. For the MLB and the respective clubs, this partnership not only allows for the gathering of transaction data and insights on the purchase behaviors of their fans in order to help set appropriate ticket prices but also helps make the transaction process seamless for fans. In return, StubHub receives marketing and sponsorship benefits from signage in MLB stadiums as well as the ticket transaction fees from the millions of tickets sold across an MLB season.

by a global company like Coca-Cola to that of NovaCare, a Philadelphia-based rehabilitation company, makes little sense. More broadly, one brand may want to build awareness of a new product to a male audience. A second brand may want to incentivize partners and employees with exclusive hospitality. And a third partner may be sponsoring purely as a defensive measure to keep a competitor from doing so and effectively building market share. Objectives should be clearly identified during any sponsor relationship.

Because each sponsor and sponsorship has different objectives, market research related to sponsorship can vary. Before beginning any activation, a sponsor should put effort into identifying baseline metrics of any KPIs. These KPIs can be associated with goals such as increasing the sponsor's web traffic by 15 percent over the course of the campaign, measuring the use of a hashtag, or evaluating sales numbers in the region where the partnership and activation are taking place. Teams can work with sponsors to design reasonable expectations to be measured over the course of their partnership. All measurements from that point on will be compared with the baseline metrics to show the effectiveness of the activation. Without a baseline measurement, no metric is available against which to base conclusions on the effectiveness of the sponsorship.

Generalizing about the use of market research in regard to sponsorship is challenging. Generally, the sophistication of market research within a sponsor organization exceeds that of a typical professional sport property. Many sponsor brands have a market research department at their disposal to facilitate studies related to all marketing, including the sport sphere.

As in many situations, budget constraints limit sponsorship measurement. Brands have been known to comingle their research, trying to reduce cost by including sponsorship-related questions in broader brand-tracking studies. Doing so masks the differences between typical consumers and sports fans. Brands sometimes divest the measurement process to their agency of record, which is arguably the equivalent of students grading themselves.

Application of Market Research in the Sport Industry

The following section provides case studies of how market research can be used in the sport industry to facilitate data-driven decision making. Research applications span far beyond the case studies in this chapter, although areas such as marketing, ticketing, and sponsorship tend to benefit especially from fan feedback.

Fan Experience: Ole Miss Football

The following information was provided by Paris Buchanan, Associate Director of Marketing and Fan Experience at the University of Mississippi.

SEC football is king in the South. Each year, hundreds of thousands of fans rush into unique college towns and cities to cheer on their favorite team. The city of Oxford, Mississippi, is no exception. This historic southern town located in North Mississippi sees its population nearly triple on a college football weekend. With more and more luxuries offered in consumers' homes, it's important that fan experience is at the forefront of each decision made by the Ole Miss Athletics Department. For the eighth consecutive year, an electronic survey was sent via email to Rebel football season-ticket holders in December, 2018. The survey generated nearly 2,000 total responses, and the data was segmented into three audiences:

1. Fans who sit in general seating areas
2. Fans who sit in premium areas, such as suites or clubs
3. Student fans who sit in the student section

The groundbreaking survey was created at Ole Miss in 2012, and is now uniform across the SEC. Among the highlights in the findings, Ole Miss finished top three in the league in seven of the 11 concessions elements tested in the general seating area, and the Rebels ranked second in all four elements related to connectivity and mobile access.

Key Findings

Ole Miss fans overwhelmingly disapproved of the many on-field presentations that were taking place:

- The band placement was not satisfactory for many in attendance.
- The student attendance was trending down. An extra incentive was needed.
- The concourse inside the stadium needed more stands for concession vendors to sell.
- Parking procedure could use additional, newer technology for better efficiency.
- Season-ticket holders should be rewarded for their loyalty and financial commitment.
- Fans desired a more diverse food offering at concession stands.
- The option of having the ability to purchase alcohol was wanted.

Follow-Up

The Ole Miss Athletics Department announced that through the survey data, the following changes would be implemented to improve the overall fan experience for the 2019 season:

Ole Miss uses fan survey data to improve fan game day experience.
Joe Murphy/Getty Images

- Drastically reduce the number of on-field recognitions and presentations.
- Move band to a more centralized location in student section.
- Add student party section to accommodate up to 2,400 fans with shade, TVs, fans, and charging stations.
- Introduce contactless tickets on mobile devices for students.
- Add 15 new concession points of sale.
- Add new concessions partners.
- Introduce three combo meals exclusively for 2019 season-ticket holders wearing their STH19 lanyard and ticket holder.
- Sell beer and spiked seltzer at many concession locations.
- Add seating option for faculty and staff.
- Partner with Clutch! app for game-day parking sales.
- Enhance Coca-Cola Rebel Fan Fest.

Digital Strategies: Dallas Cowboys

In 2019, the Dallas Cowboys, sometimes dubbed "America's Team," was worth US$5.5 billion, making it the most valuable brand in the NFL for the ninth consecutive year.[21] With millions of followers worldwide, the social and digital teams are constantly having to evolve and deliver content that engages the fan base and best positions the brand. Furthermore, while social followings are strong, the team still wants to drive as much traffic as it can to its own website and app.

The social and digital teams for the Cowboys comprise nearly 50 people. During the 2019 training camp, the teams came together for an internal, incentive-based program that aimed to grow the Cowboys' website page views and video views by more than 15 percent as compared to the 2018 training camp period (Taylor Stern,

personal communication, June 24, 2020). In part, this program was aimed at being more strategic to engage fans in a way that sent them back to the team-owned platforms (i.e., website and app) and to promote a higher preseason following. It also sought to generate buy-in and collaboration from the large digital and social teams from the start of the season, where everyone from content writers and producers to social and website managers could feel as though they were working toward the same measurable goal. The number of page views and video views from each day of the 2018 training camp were paired with the data from the same day of training camp in 2019, and daily email updates were sent to the teams to mark their progress along the way.

During this period, some key strategies from the social and digital teams included the following:

- A higher number of videos produced during the training camp period
- More strategic sharing and distribution of the content across platforms
- Specific integration of YouTube, which had previously been an underutilized platform

Key Findings

The key metrics the social and digital teams were examining during the 2019 training camp period were page views and video views (table 4.5). They surpassed the goal of growing the 2018 metrics by at least 15 percent. The teams really came together and showcased ideas such as including podcasts, social videos, photo galleries, and series-based articles to help increase page views.

Follow-Up

The success from this experiment led to a further investment in certain social and digital strategies, particularly as it pertained to posting more video content across social platforms, including YouTube. The department-wide challenge was also

TABLE 4.5   Cowboys Training Camp Digital Metrics

	2018 (actual)	Goals for 2019	2019 (actual)	% increase
Page views	37,834,101	41,650,000	48,120,269	27.2
Video views	26,745,248	29,400,000	37,962,802	41.9

Data from Taylor Stern, personal communication, June 24, 2020.

Taylor Stern is a content strategist for the Dallas Cowboys (NFL). This means that she is primarily responsible for working with content creators to build and post relevant content across multiple social platforms in order to best engage with fans, while still maintaining the Dallas Cowboys' brand image. In order to know what content to design and post, Stern works closely with data analysts within the Cowboys organization. By exploring key metrics such as likes, shares, and video and page views, Stern is able to identify what content is resonating with fans. She can then further improve the type of content being designed by monitoring what fans are looking for on one platform compared to another and when certain posts are more successful during the day or week. Beyond the analysis of trends within the Cowboys' channels, Stern is also constantly examining the trends going on throughout the NFL, with other professional sport team accounts, and within pop culture, in general. This helps her prepare and capitalize on trends in as close to real time as possible.

In her more than five years working with the Cowboys, first as a social media coordinator and now as content strategist, Stern has watched the shift from marketing and communicating with fans through TV, print, and the team website to a much more substantial focus on social media. Today, social media has become the voice of the organization; the voice of the brand. For a brand like the Cowboys, which has an enormous fan base reaching around the world, the ability to communicate directly with fans in a way that doesn't require fans stepping into the stadium is crucial. This shift has meant that the Cowboys' social and digital teams have had to get smarter and really invest in the analytics of understanding their fans and how they respond to content. Stern emphasizes that social content needs to be accurate and not rushed, and it requires the collaboration of many departments. Conducting periodic research and being able to analyze the data helps to make more strategic decisions and best align the brand with fans.

---

seen as a success in fostering innovation through collaboration and working toward measurable short-term goals.

Performing the Right Research

In the sport industry, a sizeable amount of revenue is converted into salaries for players, coaches, and managers. Still, other money goes to stadium leases, team travel, and other on-field expenditures. Off the playing surface, a sport franchise functions on a lean budget that must pay for marketing, payroll, community outreach, data infrastructure, and all the way down to pens and a cleaning staff after hours. Nowhere is the budget leaner than in market research. In some cases, sport marketers simply don't value research enough to devote

significant money to it. And even in cases in which research brings tremendous value to the organization, funds may be unavailable. The reality is that in all businesses, market research is a cost center whose ROI frequently comes under question.

Thankfully, readers of this book understand that customer feedback has a place in the operation of any sport-related business. The key issue becomes performing research for the right reasons, at the right times, and within appropriate budgetary constraints. The main question becomes how best to use limited research resources and get the optimal bang for the buck out of market research projects.

In other words, what is the right research project?

Of course, that question has no answer. But by abiding by the following set of tips, chances are that the research project at hand will provide the level of insight required to make powerful, informed decisions:

- *Identify the business objective at hand as it pertains to your business.* A business objective pertaining to market research should involve an open question whereby consumer feedback will provide a way to answer that question and move the business forward. For example, a team might ask the following:
    - How can we improve the in-game experience for the attendee?
    - Does our advertising improve brand perception?
    - Is our sponsorship of Team X helping to improve brand recall in market?

- *Let your objective define your methodology, and never vice versa.* As tempting as it might be to use an online survey to answer all business-related problems, there are pros and cons that exist with this and any other method. As alluded to earlier in the chapter, sport and emotion go hand in hand; qualitative research provides a more effective method of understanding the emotional component to avidity and behaviors. Expecting a survey to provide the right type of data to account for the emotional piece is expecting something unfair. Instead of leaning on one method of data collection, teams and researchers should aim to select a methodology that best answers the questions and meets the research objectives.

- *Plan as much as possible.* One study or another will always need to be fielded as soon as possible because of an unforeseen PR nightmare or similar issue. Putting that aside, realize that conducting quality custom research and data analysis takes time. As a simple rule of thumb, assume that writing a comprehensive questionnaire from scratch takes eight to 10 business hours and that creating an insightful research report can easily take from 40 to 80 business hours. Computers facilitate the process to a point, but human thought is required to formulate the story, that is, the findings that address the business objective, and provide actionable recommendations.

- *Have a sense of budget before moving forward.* Identify a cost that the team would willingly spend to solve the business issue at hand. Then explore methodological options that meet that objective. If the project costs significantly exceed budget, chances are that the information from the project will not merit the amount required to do it. That said, an organization should not just abandon a research project without exploring options for reducing the cost. To ensure that research is done efficiently, follow the advice in the next bullet.

- *Search out a research partner, not just a supplier.* Chances are that your sport organization has an ad agency of record, an accounting firm on retainer, a concessions partner, and even a preferred shipping company. Why, then, would you try to shuffle market research companies in and out as if they were interns? Research agencies will provide more insightful information at streamlined cost by having the opportunity to work consistently with individual clients. The firms get to know the business, brand nuances, fans' habits, and successful methodologies. As any market researcher will tell you, knowledge of the client's business is vital to delivering impactful work.

Data Analytics

With all of the sources of market research methodologies just described, front office staff have the potential to be left with an enormous wealth of data to organize and sift through. In order to really make informed decisions from the data, front office staff must analyze it. In essence, data analytics requires reducing large quantities of data into information that is actionable in the workplace. The availability and improvements in technology have certainly aided in data collection and management for sport organizations.

CRM is one of the most widely used tools to support analytics within professional sport organizations, but many sport organizations use some form of this analysis as well from college through minor leagues as well as the professionals. Basically, CRM involves documenting information about consumers in order to acquire, maintain, and develop relationships with these consumers over time. CRM platforms are essentially customer profiles that include as much information about customers (fans) as possible. This includes documenting

- demographics (e.g., age, gender, household income),

- buying history (e.g., how tickets were purchased, when they were purchased, how many tickets, which seats),
- attendance (e.g., how long they've been attending, what games they prefer), and
- client engagement (e.g., notes section from any conversations with sales staff).

With the documentation of all of this information, team staff can be prepared to effectively interact with the consumer and provide a personalized ticket package, send out marketing materials that are most applicable to this consumer, or recommend the appropriate upgrades based on anticipated capacity and interest. Understanding current consumer interests can also help sports executives position themselves to recruit new customers in the future.

Once sports executives have the documentation about individual fans, they can conduct a cluster analysis, which groups fans into segments based on their similar characteristics. To help prioritize engagement with fans within the CRM, teams utilize what's called an RFM model, which stands for recency, frequency, and monetary (table 4.6). By using these metrics to segment fans, ticket associates can generate a grading system that's used for better prioritizing the consumers they should target their attention toward in order to maximize sales.

Several programs exist to help front office staff keep track of all of this data and produce meaningful analyses and output to help inform next steps. Microsoft Dynamics is one of the more pop-ular software at the professional level. Dynamics has the capabilities of both documenting customer information and then sending customized messaging or specific promotions to groups of fans who may be best suited to these promotions based on the data collected about them. Without sophisticated CRM platforms, sport organizations can start with a simple spreadsheet to build out the things they do know about their fans.

Teams can also utilize data analytics to make a variety of other decisions, beyond trying to manage relationships with fans. Collecting and analyzing data can help teams make decisions about promotions, sponsorships, concessions, and more.

Descriptive statistics help to identify visible trends, outline frequencies, and essentially describe the data in a way that summarizes what has been collected. This would look like the average number of fans in attendance or the percentage breakdown of age groups attending a given game. This sort of analysis isn't necessarily trying to make predictions yet, but it is a way of identifying important findings within available data. Common descriptive statistics include looking at the mean, median, mode, and frequencies of occurrences in a data set. How many times did a fan purchase tickets to a game last season? What was the average number of beers sold between the first and second period? What was the highest attended game last season?

Inferential statistics refers to when a researcher takes an observation from a smaller group of people and tries to generalize it to a larger pop-

TABLE 4.6   Recency, Frequency, and Monetary Model

RFM Model	Definition	Examples
Recency	How recent they've purchased	Less than 6 months 6 to 12 months 12 to 18 months 18 to 24 months More than 24 months
Frequency	How often they've purchased	1 event 2 to 3 events 4 to 5 events 6 or more events
Monetary	How much they spent	Less than US$25 US$26 to US$50 US$51 to US$100 US$101 to US$200 More than US$200

ulation. In this case, a researcher could interview several focus groups made up of four to six fans at a time and try to draw conclusions about the sentiments of all fans. Similarly, a researcher could survey 300 fans and try to apply the findings to the thousands of fans in the company's fan base.

Predictive analytics focuses on analyzing previous sets of data or behaviors to understand and predict future behaviors. This kind of analysis can be particularly useful for generating retention models for season-ticket holders or predicting attendance to help hire the right number of concession staff for a given game. With ample access to data to input into the predictive algorithms, sport managers are becoming more savvy and capable of optimizing across all areas of operations.

A common statistical method used to make predictions is called linear regression, also often referred to as "regression." What regression does is allow a person to insert one or more independent variables into a model and try to understand how each variable contributes to a dependent variable. Say, for example, you work in a marketing department for an MiLB team and you want to know what day of the week (independent variable) and type of promotion (independent variable) combination would help you attract the largest audience (dependent variable). You could take data from the last four years and code the days of the week and promotion types into categorical variables to identify their respective contribution to attendance size.

Many other statistical modeling techniques exist that make strong predictions about future behaviors, but in any event, these predictions are only as good as the data involved, so care and attention should be given before throwing variables in a model and making real business decisions from the findings.

Wrap-Up

Successful businesses have come to rely on a multitude of data sources to create a solid understanding of their markets. The sport business works no differently because all types of organizations in the industry employ data-driven decision making to varying degrees. Data may be obtained from syndicated sources, such as Nielsen, Arbitron, and Scarborough, or similar companies. When suitable information is not available through syndicated offerings, researchers turn to customized data-collection methodologies, resulting in qualitative or quantitative data. Typical data-collection methodologies include surveying, individual interviews, and focus groups, just to name a few. Of course, the objectives of an individual project will dictate the correct methodology.

Within the sport industry, the most frequent usage occasions for market research apply to sponsorship, ticketing, and marketing, not surprisingly, given the contributions of these areas to revenue streams. Sponsorship measurement has taken off because of the need for brands to monitor budgets carefully and understand what they get in return. Ticketing research helps ensure the value proposition of ticket packages, and sport marketers have begun seeing the parallels between branding in sport and in more traditional marketing arenas.

Despite the sport industry's increasing investment in research and data analytics, budgets in these areas remain tight. Performing optimal research at the lowest cost involves having a full understanding of objectives and careful planning to ensure that all aspects of a project run smoothly.

Activities

1. Beyond the sources cited in this chapter, identify three syndicated data sources that could have value in helping sport organizations determine optimal sales and marketing strategies.

2. For each of the following scenarios, identify which custom research approach would be of most value. First, specify a quantitative or qualitative approach, and then include any specifics (e.g., quantitative onsite surveying, qualitative focus groups).

   - A minor league hockey team wants to find out how game attendees feel about the at-game experience.

- A brand of baseball gloves and gear, looking to develop a new advertising campaign aimed at parents of little league players, wants to understand what emotional ties kids and their parents have to equipment handed down.
- A motorsports venue is considering offering various ticket packages that include multiday passes, varying food and beverage options, and merchandise offers. The venue needs consumer feedback to identify appropriate pricing and interest in the offers.
- A professional sport league wants to gain an understanding of how avid and casual fans' opinions of the league change when athletes run afoul of the law.
- A major sports drink brand wants to know how its sponsorship of college football is driving purchase behavior among people ages 18 to 25 who are athletically active.

3. What market research topics might cause a respondent to answer dishonestly? What methodologies allow the researcher to obtain data that are honest and objective?

4. Review the promotional schedule and corresponding attendance for the Stockton Ports, the MiLB team. Suppose it had hired you as an outside analytics consultant to garner meaning from this table and provide recommendations.

Date	Weather	Attendance	Promotion
Friday, July 14, 2017	Hot	3,221	Nate Diaz Bobblehead Giveaway
Saturday, July 15, 2017	Very hot, 100+	4,271	Faith Night With Fireworks
Thursday, July 20, 2017	Warm	2,142	Hat Giveaway, Dollar Beer Nights
Friday, July 21, 2017	Hot	2,755	Cape Giveaway, Scout Night
Saturday, July 22, 2017	Very hot, 102+	3,822	Princess/Superhero Night With Fireworks
Sunday, July 23, 2017	Very hot, 100+	2,574	Root Beer Float Day
Monday, July 31, 2017	Hot	2,147	US$3 Buck Monday
Tuesday, August 1, 2017	Very hot, 104+	1,311	Tallboy Tuesdays
Wednesday, August 2, 2017	Very hot, 105+	2,026	Baseball Bingo
Tuesday, August 8, 2017	Nice night	1,471	Tallboy Tuesdays
Wednesday, August 9, 2017	Nice night	2,537	Baseball Bingo
Thursday, August 10, 2017	Nice night	1,909	Hat Giveaway, Dollar Beer Nights
Friday, August 11, 2017	Hot	2,893	Free Shirt Friday
Saturday, August 12, 2017	Hot day, nice night	4,709	Pink Night With Fireworks
Sunday, August 13, 2017	Nice	2,653	Fan Vote Bobblehead

a. Discuss at least three ways this data set could be useful for the Stockton Ports' marketing department.

b. Prepare a descriptive summary of the data presented here for the month of May, including:

- The average attendance for the month from July 14th to August 13th
- The top three best-attended games. What variables do you think contributed to these highest-attended games?
- The top lowest-attended games. What variables do you think contributed to these lowest-attended games?
- Describe one other observation you would describe from this data set.

c. From your descriptive observations above, summarize what your recommendations would be for the Stockton Ports to create a schedule that would maximize attendance. What time of year, day of week, weather conditions, and promotion seem optimal from your initial analysis?

Your Marketing Plan

1. Data-driven decision making is becoming the way of life for the sport business, even on the field. How can you use familiarity with market research to improve your marketing plan?

2. What are the open business questions related to your organization where market research can fill the holes?

 Go to HK*Propel* to complete the activities for this chapter.

Chapter 5

Market Segmentation and Target Marketing

OBJECTIVES

- To appreciate the role of segmentation in the marketing process in identifying specific audiences to whom products may be marketed

- To recognize the standard bases of market segmentation in sport

- To understand the importance of focusing marketing efforts on a finite number of target markets

The Asahi Shimbun via Getty Images

109

The heading is a deliberate use of an oxymoron to make the point that the original foundation of market segmentation was the concept of recognizing different clusters or groups within a market who shared similar characteristics, such as demographics or usage patterns, and then targeting their needs with a similar product (such as an all-inclusive business entertainment ticket and hospitality package or a family ticket package that includes food and drink and a souvenir). The key to accessing the segment relied on having a media vehicle that would permit access to that target segment. Each of the five editions of this text, published since 1993, has witnessed a continued evolution toward marketers having the ability to reach more specific customer audiences, due to technological advances. First, with the advent of the Internet, and more recently, social media, just about every person within the cluster can now be accessed individually by an email, text messaging, social media, and a digital marketing campaign.

The ability to segment a market is made possible by the kind of market research we discussed in chapter 4. In this chapter, we explain segmentation, its centrality to the marketing process, and its feasibility. Next, we look at the common bases for segmenting the sport market: state of being (demographics), state of mind (psychographics), product benefits, and product usage. Finally, we discuss the process of target marketing, whereby segments are evaluated and a determination is made as to which segments to specifically target with marketing initiatives.

What Is Market Segmentation?

Market segmentation is a key concept in this text because it creates the bridge between managerial analysis and managerial action. It provides a conceptual framework on which a sport marketer builds direct marketing and promotional strategies.

In simple terms, market segmentation is the process of dividing a large, heterogeneous market into more homogeneous groups of people who have similar wants, needs, or demographic profiles, to whom a product may be targeted. Ship Sticks is a golf company that ships golf clubs for golfers traveling to and from golf destinations, particularly those who don't want the hassle of hauling their golf bag through airline travel. Ship Sticks doesn't target all golfers, or even all avid golfers. Instead, the company focuses on golfers who travel to play. Such segmentation is basic to most successful marketing efforts throughout the world. Even within the massive global marketing strategies of corporate giants, such as Nike and Coca-Cola, marketers recognize that consumers in Germany are different from consumers in Japan. If technology has made the world smaller, it has not homogenized the world's cultures. Neither has television created a mass mentality within a nation of television viewers, such as the United States. To the contrary, the scores of channels now available on streaming, cable, and satellite systems and the even more diverse media available through the Internet reflect the fragmentation of the general and niche media marketplace.[1]

The sport marketplace is equally segmented. As chapters 3 and 4 indicate, no single profile describes the sport consumer. The consumer profile varies by sport, by place of residence, by life situation, and by a host of other factors. However, one thing is clear: Segmentation rules. Sports television provides clear evidence. From the 1950s to the 1980s, the broadcast networks dominated sports television, and sports fanatics had little choice in their viewing. Then came HBO, TBS, ESPN and others, which significantly widened the choices. ESPN wagered its program schedule (and its corporate life) on the sports fanatics to whom the old networks had appealed a few times per week. From 2000 to 2020, "narrowcasting" spawned even more clearly defined segment strategies, such as the Golf Channel, Tennis Network, and collegiate sports examples, such as the Atlantic Coast Conference (ACC) Network and Longhorn Network.

Given the competitiveness of the sport market and the intangible nature of most sport products, market segmentation is both logical and necessary. A product is nothing more than a bundle of benefits. The deeply committed fan may want special privileges that come with a season ticket (newsletter, special functions with the team), whereas the infrequent fan may need an online ticket-ordering system that reduces anxieties and hassles over ticket purchase. The young executive who uses a fitness health club on a frequent basis may require a club that provides laundry service. Another member may prefer fewer amenities for lower fees. Segmentation, then, is designed to maximize consumer satisfaction, but it is also a marketing tactic to maximize market response. Thus, segmentation should not be carried to the point beyond which it no longer provides meaningful returns. The WNBA's Seattle Storm might wish to maximize attendance by individualizing ticket packages to suit the desires of every individual fan, but that method would not be feasible. The Storm's marketing staff identify and target segments that they can reach by offering a flex plan of 10 ticket coupons that fans can individually redeem as they see fit. The Storm also offer several mini-plans, ranging from four to nine games.

Identifiability, Accessibility, Responsiveness

Several issues are important in choosing whether to segment a market: the identifiability, accessibility, and responsiveness of potential segments.[2]

Until recently, the sport marketer would have to ask, "Can the segment be identified or measured in terms of its size and purchasing power?" The marketer would have to make this determination using the kind of research discussed in chapter 4. Today, the ubiquitous nature of electronic media, the widespread use of social media, and the proliferation of online purchases make the gathering of segmentation data on an individual fan or consumer basis possible. MLB clubs did not spend time in a previous era trying to determine the size or strength of the market for a souvenir pin or bobblehead giveaway promotion. The raging success in other markets was enough for them to go with a gut instinct that the items were hot everywhere, at least for the moment. Precise consumer data is far more prevalent now than ever before.

The second question that the marketer once had to ask was, "Can the marketer access the segment?" With today's digital marketing, this question is less relevant, but an essential question remains: Is it possible to gain access to those groups of consumers individually without upsetting marketing efforts aimed at other segments? Souvenir pin and bobblehead promoters had no problem with this. A few weeks of promotional ads brought out more than enough collectors. It is not so easy, however, for a state high school association trying to promote its championship games, especially in minor sports. The time between playoff rounds is often short, upsets happen with regularity, and fan bases are segmented by community identity. Most state associations cannot feasibly prepare special contingency plans for each team that might advance. Hence, campaigns tend to be broad-based promotions of high school sports and focus heavily on group sales. The same problem exists for minor league teams, the early rounds of the Men's NIT and Women's NCAA Division I basketball tournaments, and even early round CHL or Major Junior Hockey playoffs in Canada.

The final segmentation question that the marketer must ask remains unchanged: Will the segment be responsive? Two questions need to be answered here. The first is whether the product will match the wants of the chosen segment. With customer and lead propensity scoring tools provided by companies like SSB, that point is particularly prevalent in ticket marketing, allowing ticket sellers to become increasingly precise in targeting, less costly, and more effective. The second question concerns the significance of the segment. Is it worthwhile (given segment size and response) to break down product characteristics and promotional efforts sufficiently to reach a segment? The significance question is less relevant in the digital era because the cost of email, web, and social media campaigns is so low that the ROI is still individually beneficial.

The marketer must address all these factors in deciding whether (and to what extent) to pursue segmentation. In professional team and collegiate sport marketing, the consensus has evolved over time that at a minimum, certain segments need to be identified and targeted with a different product menu and unique direct marketing and sales promotional strategy (table 5.1). We will revisit these factors later in the chapter when discussing

TABLE 5.1   Typical Sport and Entertainment Segments for Ticket Marketing

Segment	Product offer
Corporate business	Premium seating location, high-end hospitality, close-in parking
Children	Youth plan—discounted or free ticket with a kid's meal or souvenir
Student (high school and college)	Thursday night ticket and food and drink
Full season-ticket holders	Offer to experience premium seating and hospitality
Partial- and mini-plan holders	Early-bird price offering for buying a plan with more games
Group leaders	Group leader appreciation night with complementary ticket when the leader brings a guest who buys, plus fan experience packages for group attendees
Families	Discounted family pack ticket package offering tickets, concessions, and family-oriented entertainment or amenities

target marketing, which is the process of selecting which segments to specifically focus marketing initiatives on.

Segment or Niche?

You may occasionally hear the term niche strategy; the concept is not quite the same as segmentation. Marketing theorists distinguish segments from niches largely based on size and competition. Segments are large, but they are also prone to competition. Consider, for instance, adult male football fans. Colleges and pro leagues compete for this audience at live gates, on television, and with merchandise. A niche may be smaller, but in the past, larger firms typically ignored a niche. But in today's society of mass customization and individual communication strategies through digital and social media, large companies are much more willing to target smaller niche segments. In sport marketing, niches have also been distinguished from segments based on sport specificity. Niches arise from the sport market; segments are imposed on the sport market. Snowboarding was once a small niche within the skiing industry as a hybrid between skiing and skateboarding. In the 1970s, snowboarding grew dramatically in popularity, allowing skiing to grow beyond its wealthy, middle-aged demographic to attract children and young adults to the ski slopes. By the early 2000s, snowboarding's participation had grown well beyond what would be labeled as just a niche any longer.

The history of many popular sports is a progression from niche to mainstream markets.

And who is to say what the next wave will be? The 2004 feature film *Dodgeball* spurred a spike of adult interest in the game. In a similar era, ESPN television coverage of the World Series of Poker, along with the 1998 release of the movie *Rounders*, brought about a spike in the popularity of poker in the 2000s. Topgolf expanded rapidly in the 2010s as a reimagination of the golf driving range concept incorporating a social experience along with food and drink.

Niches or segments? Much of the distinction is semantic, especially within the sport industry, where many firms exist in a single-sport domain. In both cases, however, the key questions of identification, accessibility, and responsiveness remain.

Four Bases of Segmentation

Because the overwhelming majority of people in the Western world have their own smartphones and tablets, the temptation is to assume that we no longer need to segment. But few businesses (if any) have the resources to mass market to every individual consumer. Even mass retailers, such as Amazon, do not use the same marketing strategies to reach all consumers. Most sport organizations have much more limited marketing resources and must still rely heavily on broader segmentation strategies to target specific groups of consumers with their marketing techniques.

Market segments are formed based on differentials in consumer wants and desires; that is, segments derive from consumer satisfaction. Four bases are commonly used for segmentation, each of which rests on an assumption that homogeneity in one variable may relate to homogeneity in wants and desires:

1. Consumers' state of being (demographics)
2. Consumers' state of mind (psychographics)
3. Product benefits
4. Product usage

Typically, marketers employ cross sections of segments, such as middle-income Hispanic families living within a baseball team's metropolitan market or affluent and active older people who live within 20 minutes of a particular golf and country club. We discuss integrated, or nested, approaches to segmentation and target marketing at the end of this chapter. The following sections, then, must be understood to represent fluid categories.

State-of-Being Segmentation

State-of-being, or demographic, segmentation includes the following dimensions, which are generally easier to measure than state-of-mind or product benefits:

Geography

Age

Income

Education

Gender

Sexual orientation

Marital status and family life cycle

Ethnicity

These dimensions are discussed in the following sections.

Geography

Several clear principles apply to geographic segmentation in sport:

- *First, proximity rules.* A simple survey of participants will typically support the long-recognized relationship between proximity and activity or involvement. The closer people live to a sport facility, the more likely they are to become involved with activities there.

- *Know your clusters.* Good internal marketing data from ticket applications, membership inquiries, and similar sources often reveal especially important geo-demographic clusters of these consumers. Digital and social marketing data provide more precise geographic consumer behavior than ever available previously. Mapping allows the marketer to see whether certain suburbs or neighborhoods are especially prone to a certain product. Those areas can be targeted for specific marketing initiatives, whether through digital and social media, outbound calling, or direct mail channels. With scarce resources for advertising, sport organizations can more efficiently use those resources by promoting products where higher densities of their customers live or work. The Atlanta Braves used geographic segmentation in making the monumental decision to build its new stadium well north of downtown Atlanta, and it opened in 2017 in Cobb County, where its wealthier, predominantly Caucasian fan base resides.[3]

- *Value your outer rims (or secondary market radius).* Some consumer clusters may come from considerable distances. These represent outer-rim markets that can repay extraordinary attention in terms of advertising, promotions, radio, or television networking. The recognition of outer rims in sport date at least as far back as baseball's early radio broadcasts. Midwest major league teams, such as the St. Louis Cardinals, developed fan bases at great distances, nurtured largely by radio. Outer-rim markets (typically defined as more than 50 miles [80 km] from the venue but within a 100-mile, or 160 km, radius in most markets or within a 150-mile, or 240 km, radius in larger geographic markets) are now primarily reached through television, and they represent logical targets for group sales and special events. But in football, which has relatively few home games (the NFL plays mostly on Sunday afternoons, and college football plays mostly on Saturday afternoons), outer rims can mean season tickets.

The Seattle Seahawks have long maintained an outer rim of Alaskan fans, over 1,000 miles (1,600 km) from CenturyLink Field. The Miami Dolphins have looked to develop a wider rim of markets, to both the north and the west, possibly through partnerships with media outlets and corporate sponsors in places such as Naples,

Vero Beach, and Port St. Lucie. State universities have cultivated outer rims by scheduling some "home" games at venues in other parts of their home states.[4]

Some outer rims are what might be called borderlands, in that they rub against the territory of a competing organization. A good example is the central swath of Connecticut, which is the borderland between the Yankee Empire and Red Sox Nation. A 2003 survey showed a clear line of demarcation running through Hartford and Middlesex Counties. The turf is important because it contains the several counties that have the highest per capita income in the country and represents a gold mine in cable TV revenues when winning the ratings war. The Red Sox have been aggressive in courting this borderland. At one Hartford rally, owner Tom Werner announced, "We want to welcome all those Connecticut Yankees who don't want to be in King George's court," a reference to the now-deceased Yankees owner George Steinbrenner. Some of the jousting has been in good fun, but it has been a marketing competition as hot as that on the field.[5] Collegiate sports programs often have geographically overlapping fan bases as well, particularly those located within state borders, including rivalries such as Kentucky–Louisville, Alabama–Auburn, and Michigan–Michigan State.

Age

The old notion of the generation gap contains obvious truth—the young have different tastes and lifestyles from their parents, who in turn diverged from their own parents. Marketers talk about cohorts rather than generations (e.g., the Baby Boomers cohort, the millennials cohort). Musical tastes, approaches to debt and savings, and fashion sense are but a few of the cohort touchstones. In some cases, we may include sporting tastes. For instance, a 2016 poll conducted by media research firm Magna Global studied U.S. television viewers of major sport organizations. The study's results revealed that the PGA golf tour's average viewer was 64 years old, followed closely by ATP tennis at age 61, while MLS and the NBA skewed much younger at ages 40 and 42, respectively.[6]

Youth have been a target of sport promotions since the 1900s, often with the idea of building character through baseball, basketball, or just about any sport. In the early 20th century, the sport curriculum swept gymnastics and calisthenics to the background of the burgeoning physical education programs in U.S. public schools. After World War II, organized youth leagues exploded in the suburbs, first in baseball and then across a broad range of sports. Starting ages drifted downward, so that today, under-eight travel teams are the norm. But registration does not ensure commitment. In fact, American youth appear less committed to mainstream modes of fitness, exercise, and sport, at least as measured in national surveys. Young people are no longer interested in their parents' sports.

Many sport organizations have intentionally sought to reach the youth segment, often through initiatives to actively engage kids rather than expecting them to passively watch a sports event for three or more consecutive hours. In major and minor league baseball, teams got kids more engaged with on-field mass autograph sessions and started letting kids run the bases between innings or after games. The PGA Tour provides free admission for children accompanying a paid adult at all of its tournaments, which it promotes as the best youth policy in professional sports. The PGA Tour also partnered with the LPGA and other golf organizations in 1997 to start the First Tee program to provide opportunities for kids to learn to play golf, particularly in economically disadvantaged locations. Many collegiate and professional sport organizations operate kids' clubs that provide discounted tickets, merchandise, access to programming, and other amenities for children. These types of initiatives typically serve both short-term goals of increasing attendance and fandom, but they also attempt to increase the number of fans and participants for decades into the future.

The senior, or maturity, market is another target for special marketing plans. As Baby Boomers and Gen Xers grow older, they bring their vast cohort into another life or family stage. Data show that in the United States and Europe, the over-50 market is growing far faster than the under-50 market. More research is needed on the sporting attitudes, lifestyles, and subsegments of this maturing market, but the implications are obvious for sport marketers from the major leagues to the local athletics club. In the past, most seniors did not want to attend as many games in person, particularly night games and

- Does the program speak to the possibilities of aging, as opposed to its limitations?
- Does the program have motivated leadership?
- Is the program user friendly?[7]

Income and Education

Education, not surprisingly, is related to income. Like their counterparts in the golf industry, members of the tennis industry target affluent, highly educated consumers (although not exclusively). Among North American sports, fans with higher incomes and education levels are more likely than others to be fans of MLB, the NHL, and college football and basketball. Fans with lower incomes and education levels support NASCAR and MLS at higher rates.[8]

Geo-demographic clustering matches income with residence and, presumably, lifestyle. Although a certain income is no guarantee of a particular lifestyle, it is frequently a central index. The NFL can demand high television-rights fees because it delivers to males with relatively high disposable incomes. Golf does not draw as many fans, but its income profile is even higher, which explains why luxury car companies advertise during golf telecasts. Skiing and polo are other sports closely tied to high-income levels.

Gender

Sport firms have recognized women as a special segment for over a century. For much of that time, however, marketing strategies focused on rather glib visions of the "fair sex"—white, relatively affluent, and limited in capabilities. Bicycle companies made V-shaped women's frames to avoid criticism that cycling forced women into unladylike positions. Golf and tennis firms made smaller clubs and rackets for women. Baseball teams promoted ladies' days to elevate the image of their crowds. This was segmentation, but it was not necessarily formulated in a positive way.

The women's sport market is no longer an afterthought to the market for men. In the 1970s, the passing of Title IX legislation and the impact of pioneers like Billie Jean King ushered in a new era. More than one-half of women consider themselves sports fans, and females comprise nearly one-half of all fans for many sport leagues. Sport entities now have a full line of specifically designed merchandise for women, including

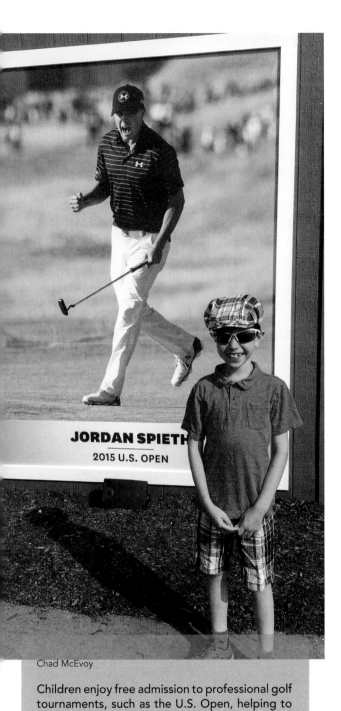

Chad McEvoy

Children enjoy free admission to professional golf tournaments, such as the U.S. Open, helping to build potential lifelong fans of the sport.

games in inclement weather. But the behavior of today's 60-year-olds, in particular their sport participation and spectatorship needs and interests, has been likened to that of their parents in their 40s. So how does this notion affect today's silver-haired generation? Marketers should ask some simple questions about marketing and sales plans proposed for any older segment:

differently sculptured women's authentic game jerseys and golf-style polos with a different cut and look. This merchandise is now prominently featured during game broadcasts and has driven massive increases in the percentage of licensed apparel sold to women and girls.[9]

At the same time, sport marketers must avoid lumping women into an amorphous category. It is important to base segmentation and marketing strategies on sound research and not on intuition or stereotypes. Further, female fans attend sports events or purchase sport products for a variety of different reasons, as is the case with male fans. Marketers should not attempt a "one size fits all" approach in selling to female fans.

It should be noted that these gender marketing issues hold true for both men's and women's sport products. Females comprise 37 percent of LPGA fans, nearly identical in proportion to the 36 percent of PGA fans who are women.[10] Spectators at women's sports events include considerable numbers of both females and males, as is true with men's sports events. The use of market research and segmentation strategies allows sport marketers to understand the needs and wants of both female and male consumers, allowing them to develop marketing approaches to meet those needs and wants.

Sexual Orientation

Historically a taboo market to target within the sport world, gays and lesbians continue to struggle for recognition, opportunity, and understanding. Since 2000, however, clear progress and growth have occurred within sports, as in other aspects of society. Until the early 2000s, and perhaps even more recently than that, marketers were often hesitant to create initiatives targeting a LGBTQ+ audience, fearing that any sales gains would be offset by larger losses amongst upset heterosexual consumers. In 2001, the Minnesota Twins ran a promotion called Out in the Stands, sponsored by *Lavender* magazine, a local publication, targeted to the LGBTQ+ audience. A Twins VP stated emphatically that the organization was open and accessible to any fan. Perhaps the Twins was responding to an incident the year before, when two lesbians were ejected from Dodger Stadium for allegedly kissing in the stands. The Dodgers had to apologize profusely and promise to train its stadium attendants better.

The WNBA's 2014 Pride campaign is recognized as the first league-wide marketing initiative focused on the LGBTQ+ segment, although the league possessed many LGBTQ+ fans from the audience for years prior. Subsequently, scholars Ceyda Mumcu and Nancy Lough studied fans' attitudes and purchase intentions resulting from the campaign. The authors found that while heterosexual consumers did not respond negatively to the campaign and homosexual consumers responded positively, the campaign did not increase purchase intentions.[11] While sales and revenue generation are vital goals for marketers, this campaign could still be judged as a success in affecting consumer attitudes, particularly in light of past treatment of LGBTQ+ issues and people in sports and societally.

Marital Status and Family Life Cycle

Another demographic variable that may be useful for segmentation is whether the consumer is married and, relatedly, at what stage of the family life cycle is the consumer. A 25-year-old single consumer likely has very different needs and wants in potentially attending a sports event than a 45-year-old with multiple kids, or a 65-year-old empty nester. The 25-year-old single fan may attend a game with friends, clients, or with a date. The 45-year-old parent may need to consider factors such as the price of buying tickets and concessions for a large family, having to entertain restless young children, or juggling older kids' own sports and activities. These are issues that likely do not influence the 65-year-old empty nester's purchase decision.

Marketing to families with children is a challenge marketers have faced for decades. Key considerations for the family often include price and game environment. With price, marketers have long used discounting techniques, such as providing free or discounted tickets to youth with paid adults, or the family pack, which typically includes a package of tickets, concessions, and merchandise at a value price. Game environment is another consideration. Families with children may be leery of sitting right next to fans drinking heavily or behaving badly (we note that these fans are often not keen on sitting next to young families either). Dedicating specific seating sections to families is a common tactic used to address concern such as these.

Ethnicity

Ethnicity is used here to refer to segmentation of consumers based upon race, ethnic background, or national origin. American history has been heavily influenced by enduring struggles between natives and immigrants and among races and ethnic groups. The nation's motto—*e pluribus unum* ("out of many, one")—captures part of this ethos. Opinions still diverge on whether the motto represents an achievement or a goal. Battles over bilingual education reflect opposition on the emphasis: Is it the *unum* or the *pluribus*? And minority groups increasingly challenge the right of white European immigrants to control the definitions of the American *unum*. Despite popular beliefs, the United States is less a melting pot and more a mosaic. Its presidential and congressional elections since 2004 have sadly defined the increasing diverseness and animosity among the races. Consequently, ethnic marketing, much like marketing to the alternative lifestyle community, requires sensitivity and communication strategies that use direct methods through predominantly niche channels.

Cultural diversity is both the American strength and the American conundrum. In some ways, the sport world has provided the most vivid theater for this struggle. Jack Johnson, Joe DiMaggio, Eddie Gottlieb, Althea Gibson, Jackie Robinson, and Roberto Clemente are just a few names that represent millions of athletes, promoters, and fans for whom sport has been a touchstone of racial and ethnic pride and tension. Although the dominant leagues, teams, and clubs have gradually opened their doors to qualified athletes of any color, they have been slower to pursue minority fans. That situation is changing, however, in response to the obvious. Americans of African, Asian, Hispanic, and Middle Eastern descent now represent more than one-third of the population, and their numbers are growing rapidly. In some markets, minorities comprise a majority, including the student body at the University of Texas at Austin. By some estimates, minorities will be a national majority in the United States and Europe by 2050, perhaps sooner.[19] Clearly, minorities represent important consumer bases that demand diligent respect, not benign neglect.

Black people have been historically underrepresented as targeted consumers in professional and collegiate sports spectatorship, although they represent 13 percent of the U.S. population. As with other racial and ethnic groups, African Americans as a group are disproportionately higher in their fandom of some sports, and less so with others. According to Nielsen data, African Americans make up almost one-half (45 percent) of NBA television viewers in the United States, a staggeringly high number compared to their representation in the overall U.S. population. Black people represent just 9 percent of MLB viewers, 3 percent of NHL viewers, and 2 percent of NASCAR viewers.[8]

The Hispanic market has been pursued more aggressively than other ethnic markets, perhaps because it is the fastest growing minority segment, projected to represent one-quarter of all Americans by 2050.[19] Latin nights are common in baseball venues, and Spanish radio and television broadcasts are prevalent in MLS and MLB in many markets. Asian Americans represent an untapped segment that has received little attention among sport marketers, despite representing 6 percent of the U.S. population.[8]

As discussed earlier in this chapter with gender segmentation, ethnicity is another area where marketers must be careful. Historical prejudices have existed for centuries in U.S. society in discriminating against people of color. Marketers should make decisions based on comprehensive research data and not stereotypes when using segmentation based on ethnicity.

State-of-Mind Segmentation

State-of-mind, or psychographic, segmentation assumes that consumers may be divided by personality traits; by lifestyle characteristics, such as attitudes, interests, and opinions; and by preferences and perceptions. The most noteworthy approach to state-of-mind segmentation was developed by the Stanford Research Institute (SRI). Called the values and lifestyle (VALS) typology, it assumes that attitudes, opinions, desires, needs, and other psychological dimensions collectively govern daily behavior. VALS identifies eight segments of the adult population, based on resources and primary motivations (ideals, achievement, and self-expression):

Innovators

Thinkers

Achievers

Experiencers

Believers

Strivers

Makers

Survivors

VALS is used extensively in proprietary research. For instance, telecommunications companies have used VALS to identify components that will be attractive to early adopters. We are not aware, however, of recent studies of sport consumers using VALS as a base. The possibilities of state-of-mind segmentation, however, are intriguing. For instance, Discovery Communications, which runs TLC (previously known as The Learning Channel) and Discovery Channel, uncovered eight segments among its viewers. "Machos," who comprised 12 percent of viewers, were 76 percent male; largely blue-collar; average in income; and oriented toward action programming, including sport and war. In contrast, the 15 percent of viewers who were "Scholars" were 54 percent female; urbane; upscale; and favored programming in archaeology, history, and anthropology. Discovery Communications can use the knowledge to create and promote programming for these various segments. We might project similar segments among ice hockey fans—"Rumblers" who revel in aggressive hitting and fighting and "Aesthetes" who focus on skill, craft, and grace.[12]

Research in sport consumer behavior has opened up other prospects for state-of-mind segmentation, particularly in terms of fan or team identification and loyalty. While some authors have put forth various definitions for team or fan identification, the consensus is that it refers to the level of psychological connections fans have with the sport team or product. Highly identified fans have a deep level of connection with their favorite teams. In 2016, some Chicago Cubs fans took phones or radios to cemeteries to share the experience of winning the team's first World Series title in a century with their deceased love ones. Leading scholars in this area include Daniel Wann, Jeffrey James, and Galen Trail. Collectively, their work has shown that different fans have different motives for consuming sport products.[13] We discuss this further in the next section on product benefits segmentation.

While capturing demographic data about who the organization's customers are can be pretty straightforward, learning about their psychographic characteristics, such as attitudes, personalities, and lifestyle characteristics, can be more challenging. Qualitative methods are often used in market research to help marketers understand why consumers behave the way they do. Technological advances have also helped make this information more accessible to marketers. Google Analytics provides organizations with data about website visitors' interests, for example. Social media platforms provide businesses with information about their consumers' interests and what other pages and sites consumers like or follow. This data can assist the marketer in better understanding segments of their consumers and how they think and behave.

Product Benefits Segmentation

Benefits segmentation is closely related to state-of-mind segmentation. After all, the sport product is a bundle of benefits. If those benefits don't exist in the consumer's mind, then they don't exist at all. Sport marketers have adopted benefits segmentation in many ways. The most easily illustrated applications are in the sporting goods industry. Take athletics shoes, for example. The competitive runner who logs over 60 miles (100 km) per week seeks the product benefits of support, shock reduction, and long wear; the intermediate tennis player seeks sound grip and comfort; and the casual sneaker purchaser is just looking for a light and fashionable shoe to use as regular footwear. Each purchaser is looking for different benefits and will be best served by different shoes.

The motivational factors discussed in chapter 3 provide insights into the benefits sought by sport consumers. Affiliation, achievement, status, health, and fitness, in various forms and configurations, are certainly related to benefits that consumers perceive from sport consumption. Team marketers, for instance, know that season-ticket holders expect exclusive benefits, such as access to inside information (often through newsletters); special events (autograph sessions); or participation in on-field, on-court, or on-ice fan experience packages. Large groups, on the other hand, look for scoreboard recognition, on-site liaisons, discounts, and team promotional materials to drum up interest. The most successful sport organizations understand the importance of identifying the core benefits that define their products in their consumers' minds. For example, in the late 1990s, the NFL defined its six core equities (with sample symbols) as follows:

1. Action and power: hitting, circus catches, the NFL shield
2. History and tradition: autumn leaves, NFL legends, tailgating
3. Thrill and release: fans and players laughing and screaming
4. Teamwork and competition: the "steel curtain" defense of the Pittsburgh Steelers Super Bowl champions
5. Authenticity: the pigskin, muddy field, blood
6. Unifying force: groups of fans, teams

These core equities may be viewed as core benefits to be cultivated and promoted in live events, broadcasts, videos, programs, and merchandise.[14]

The steady rise of high-performance, commercialized women's team sports (e.g., college and pro basketball, international soccer, and ice hockey) appears to be a case in alternative benefits more than demographics. To be sure, fan research suggests that women's team sports attract a wider age range than their male counterparts. And the generally lower prices are more attractive to families. But the strong male base—30 percent in the arena and 50 percent on television for the WNBA—belies notions that women's sports are only for female fans. As an NCAA survey revealed, fans of women's basketball, regardless of gender, enjoy a game that in their minds is distinctly different (e.g., "below the rim"), played by athletes who are more articulate, more accessible, and, yes, more appropriate as role models than the men. Women's sports are

Males make up a large percent of fans of women's sports.
Katherine Frey/The Washington Post via Getty Images

evolving rapidly; time will test the margins of these product differences.

Unfortunately, sport managers are often out of touch with the benefits segments in their fan base. In this state of ignorance, they can hardly hope to fashion a strategy that does not alienate one group or another. An investigation of an NHL franchise and its fans found that the team envisioned a strategy that would appeal to both tradition (classic merchandise for the hard-core fan) and dynamism (rock 'n roll music for the casual, especially young, fan). Unfortunately, the team strategy belied an ignorance or avoidance of other key segments revealed in fan research. In particular, the franchise was neglecting social fans who needed special group rates and better fan rituals (like signature songs or cheers) to encourage their attendance. Marketing researchers have found ways to identify segments of benefits in sport consumers' minds. Managers must start to use that research. We look closer at such strategies in chapter 6, when we consider product positioning.[15]

Product Usage Segmentation

We know that product usage segmentation is also significant and that it interacts with consumers' state of mind. Here, marketers have predominantly concentrated on the heavy half, the heavy users of the product. In many markets, the so-called 80-20 rule applies, according to which 80 percent of market consumption comes from only 20 percent of the consumers. Sensitivity to factors of the marketing mix has been shown to vary significantly with product use. In sport, we have long been cognizant of the various usage patterns (e.g., the season-ticket holder versus the individual-game ticket purchaser). This point is true across most sports, for players and fans alike. According to National Golf Foundation data, avid golfers comprise 26 percent of players, but that group accounts for 76 percent of all golf rounds played.[16]

Although heavy users may return greater immediate dividends, the sport marketer must aim to satisfy the needs of each group as much as possible to ensure a steady stream of light, medium, and heavy users, because the light user of today may be the medium user of tomorrow and the heavy user of next year. Chapters 8 and 10 address the need for special promotions for differ-

ent user groups. For instance, special groups may fit into the category of light users, but they have special needs and interests. Many have particular interests in some charitable cause (fundraising), seating in a special area, or special recognition on the scoreboard. The smartest marketers offer a full menu of group benefits and fan experience packages.

Several summary points about usage segmentation demand emphasis:

- Not all consumers consume at the same rate.
- Levels of consumption (e.g., heavy, medium, and light) vary from sport to sport, so the relative importance of usage rates (in terms of total attendance or participation) differs from sport to sport.
- Levels of consumption are likely to vary from age group to age group. Thus, sport spectatorship and consumption show a life cycle pattern. For any given set of consumers, levels of consumption are likely to vary by other variables (e.g., state of being, state of mind, and benefits).
- The sport marketer needs to maintain opportunities for consumers to consume at many usage levels. That is, the marketer should not depend too heavily on season-ticket sales and thus exclude the occasional user. This latter problem is well known to the Baltimore Orioles, who sold out regularly between 1992 and 2000 with the opening of Oriole Park at Camden Yards, competitive teams, and Cal Ripken's chase of Lou Gehrig's record for consecutive games played. Upon Ripken's retirement and the honeymoon effect wearing off with the new stadium, attendance declined significantly without a base of light and medium users.[17]
- An increase in sales volume is much more likely to be generated by increased frequency or a higher consumption rate of existing users than it is from an increase in sales to first-time users.

Sport organizations should also conceptualize (and segment) use in terms of breadth of activities. In this case, the notion of a heavy user should include the number of different activities as well as the frequency of participation. Marketers could then develop a grid to visualize segmentation along the dimensions of breadth and frequency, placing internal marketing data within the grid.

Figure 5.1 provides a sample grid for a hypothetical Boston Bruins fan base. Only three cells are filled in here, but the concept of such a grid is the important point. Specific group names

Four Types of Sports Fans: An Alternative View on Segmentation

Based on extensive research done for many clients by Old Hat Creative, *Winning Is Not a Strategy* author Zac Logsdon segments sports fans into four basic types. The four types primarily align with the product usage segmentation base, but they also incorporate elements of the other bases of segmentation as well:

1. *Die-hard fans.* Die-hard fans are those who support the organization through thick and thin. Their wardrobe consists extensively of fan apparel, they follow the team religiously on social media and sports talk radio, and they can be counted on to purchase season tickets year in and year out. While maintaining a solid relationship is vital, Logsdon argues that die-hard fans don't require much marketing attention because they are purchasing and attending no matter what.

2. *Casual fans.* Casual fans have a connection to the sport organization and attend perhaps a few contests per year, but they don't have the same loyalty the die-hard fans do. Casual fans often may choose to stay home and watch from their couch rather than from 40-yard-line seats at the stadium. Logsdon believes that this segment is one worth investing significant marketing resources on because these people were already fans of the team, and they have room to grow in terms of their purchase behavior, without too much difficulty.

3. *New fans.* As the term implies, new fans are those who haven't purchased from the organization previously. This group includes those who have recently moved to the area. While they may be more difficult than other segments to reach, Logsdon recommends investing resources in marketing to new fans as a way to grow the customer base. He describes that new fans may need to be educated about the product and enticed to purchase the first time, but they provide a growth opportunity.

4. *Fair-weather fans.* Fair-weather fans are supporters of the team, but they are the first to wear the team's sweatshirt when the team wins, and the first to take off the sweatshirt when the team loses. When clouds appear in the sky on a football Saturday, these fans are likely to stay home instead of attending. Quite simply, fair-weather fans lack loyalty as consumers. This is a group Logsdon recommends that marketers ignore. This group's purchase behavior is not connected to good marketing efforts, but rather it is based on the whims of the team's success and other uncontrollable factors.

Winning Is Not a Strategy provides an interesting perspective on market segmentation and target marketing. In using these strategies, marketers should consult their own market research and assessment of their consumers' behavior to determine how Logsdon's perspectives hold true for their organization's marketing efforts.

Frequency / Breadth	High frequency (>10 times/month)	Medium frequency (5-9 times/month)	Low frequency (1-4 times/month)
High breadth (>3 activities)	"Captains": Follow team's social media; attend five games/month; watch all away games on TV		
Medium breadth (2-3 activities)		"Growlers": Share mini-plan; wear Bruins hat; watch some televised games	
Low breadth (1 activity)			"Cubs": Watch big game on TV

FIGURE 5.1   Sample frequency and breadth grid for Bruins fans.

are not crucial, but they are sometimes used as shorthand. For instance, "Captains" are clearly committed in breadth and frequency; they are the hard-core fans. On the opposite end, "Cubs" represent the bottom of the involved fan base. They are highly prone to falling off the escalator and may well turn their attention to another sport before they even attend a game. Such a frequency and breadth grid with all the cells filled in would provide the basis for promotional campaigns. Indeed, a strategy that aims for breadth of activities may provide the club with a buffer to prevent members from becoming bored and burned out and thus from defecting.

In his book *Winning Is Not a Strategy*, author Zac Logsdon, Founder and CEO of Old Hat Creative, a notable sport marketing agency focused primarily on intercollegiate athletics, argues that sport marketers should not watch their attendance and revenues rise and fall with their winning percentage, but instead they must strategically attract consumers to the product and provide them with quality experiences. The book presents a slightly different spin on product usage segmentation in identifying certain types of fans.[18]

Target Marketing

As noted earlier, our divisions of segmentation—state of being, state of mind, benefits, and usage—are simply organizational conveniences. Sport marketers must recognize that successful marketing plans will typically require the integration of these divisions and, ultimately, the selection of certain segments that the organization will focus on reaching with its marketing efforts. This practice is known as target marketing.

Having discussed each of the four bases of segmentation in this chapter, marketers must integrate those bases to better understand specific segments of their customer base. In marketing college sports programs, the college or university's own students are often a segment of interest. In terms of demographics, the college student segment often shares a common age (18 to 25) and (lower) income characteristics, but it may be diverse in terms of gender and ethnicity. College students may also share common lifestyles and interests in the psychographics base, potentially deriving similar product benefits from attending their college's sports events like providing a release from schoolwork and socializing with peers. In terms of product usage, students may vary widely from those uninterested in sports to those heavy users who attend nearly every event. In this regard, it may even be possible to segment the student audience further, such as focusing on freshman students, those involved in Greek Life, or students who frequently attend athletics events.

Market research, as described in the previous chapter, plays a key role in better understanding the makeup of market segments. These data allow marketers to know, rather than guess, how many consumers possess certain characteristics and comprise specific segments. In segmentation analysis, one common and simple data technique used is examining crosstabulations. Crosstabulations, or crosstabs, are used to examine the interaction between two or more variables. For example, if the researcher wanted to see how gender affected product usage, the crosstabulation between these two variables might show that a higher percentage of the organization's female fans were heavy users than male fans. A more sophisticated segmentation data tool is a cluster analysis, which allows for a high number of factors to be examined simultaneously, and the statistical analysis identifies groups, or clusters, of customers that share common factors.

The ultimate goal of the segmentation process is for marketers to identify which specific segments they want to target with their marketing efforts. Near the beginning of this chapter, three issues were provided for examining segments:

1. Identifiability
2. Accessibility
3. Responsiveness

These issues are important in examining which market segments to target. If the segment isn't identifiable in being large enough, it may not be worth the effort to target such a small audience. The segment also needs to be accessible, or reachable, through advertising and other promotional means. Finally, the segment must be responsive to the marketing efforts made to target it. If the Chicago Cubs spend considerable time and effort trying to sell tickets to consumers 300 miles (483 km) south in the St. Louis region, the team may not be successful given the considerable distance, not to mention that many in that region are Cardinals fans rather than Cubs fans.

A question that often arises with target marketing is how many segments should the organization target? This is a difficult question to answer. Imagine you are the marketing director for the Houston Rockets, and you are planning your marketing efforts for just one of the team's 41 regular-season home games. Like other professional sports teams, the Rockets offer a wide range of tickets to its games, from courtside seats that cost hundreds of dollars apiece to seats in the upper deck that cost a tiny fraction of that. The team also sells seats in club sections and luxury suites. Each type of ticket may have a different target market. The segment to which the Rockets target to sell courtside seats is likely quite different than the one targeted for US$20 tickets in the upper deck of the Toyota Center. Ultimately, the number of target markets selected for marketing initiatives is a function of the scope and complexity of the organization's product offerings and its marketing plan.

Wrap-Up

Market segmentation is truly central to the notion of knowing the sport property's consumers because segmentation recognizes that consumers vary along a number of dimensions that the marketer may use to form the basis of specialized strategies. Therefore, the sport property's CRM system should be connected to the notion of segmentation, and research should examine the possible bases for meaningful segmentation of the marketplace. Whether segmentation makes the most sense in terms of psychographics, demographics, usage, benefits, or some combination depends on the marketer's knowledge of and feel for the market. Indeed, it makes sense to pursue a relational approach to segmentation. That is, consumer segments distinguished by benefits sought should be evaluated for any internal homogeneity in demographics, psychographics, or usage. Discoveries of such relationships will provide fruitful insights for improved communications with such target segments. An example of combined segmentation might be the targeting of a fan in a sport property's database who has purchased multiple individual game tickets in the past, has a six-figure income, and lives in a prime zip code for season-ticket purchases. This fan could be sent an offer to purchase a premium club seat or high-end package hospitality offer. In any case, the decision maker must recognize that people can and must be distinguished from one another. Whether the business is pro basketball, high school lacrosse, or public parks and recreation programs, it is hard to consider any plan a marketing plan if it doesn't incorporate market segmentation and target marketing.

Activities

1. Define *segmentation*. Describe the differences among segment identification, segment access, and segment responsiveness. Think of examples in the sport world of segments that might be identifiable but not accessible or responsive.

2. What are the basic components of state-of-being segmentation? Give examples of the state-of-being segments most important to your local college or university's volleyball team.

3. Define *state-of-mind segmentation*. Try to find an ad for a sport product or team that appeals to a state-of-mind segment.

4. Explain why the heavy-user segment is important to sport marketers.

5. How would you relate the notion of benefits segmentation to the discussion of motivation in chapter 3? List and compare the benefits of attending an MLB game and playing golf at the nearest public golf course.

6. How would you set up a segmentation plan for your favorite sport property and match each segment to a unique or customized product or ticket-package offering?

Your Marketing Plan

Can you define the core benefits of your products? Will any of these benefits link to consumer segments defined by demographics, psychographics, or product usage? You should begin to clarify, at the least, the product usage segments in your consumer base. Try to fill in a frequency and breadth grid for your consumer base. Use figure 5.1 as a guide. Then use your answer to question 6 to detail your specific market segmentation plan and match each segment with the most relevant product offering.

 Go to HK*Propel* to complete the activities for this chapter.

Chapter 6
The Sport Product

OBJECTIVES

- To recognize the elements of the sport product that contribute to its uniqueness in the wider marketplace of goods and services

- To learn the process involved in product development as well as its relation to the concept of the product life cycle

- To understand differentiation, product positioning, product image, and product branding, and their roles in successful sport marketing

Budrul Chukrut/SOPA Images/LightRocket via Getty Images

The Reebok brand and products we know today are much different than they were in the 1990s and early 2000s. Reebok, which once had sponsorship deals with major sport properties, such as the NBA, NFL, and NHL, and endorsement deals with elite athletes, such as Peyton Manning and Shaquille O'Neal, has completely changed the focus of the entire brand and product line since 2010. In 2000, Reebok began focusing on developing products for these mainstream sports. While it always made athletic shoes and apparel, Reebok also produced sport equipment. For example, Reebok sold items such as baseball gloves and bats, a full line of hockey equipment (skates, helmets, gloves, pads), football gloves, and basketball hoops to name a few. However, now gone are the days of focusing on mainstream sports and elite professional athletes, and in is a complete focus on Reebok's personal fitness roots, which allowed the brand to gain popularity in the 1980s when it capitalized by creating products geared for the booming interest in group-fitness and aerobics.

The thinking behind this shift in focus was Reebok's realization that shoe and apparel companies had created a spotlight on elite athletes and fandom as opposed to the physical activity of individuals. Reebok President Matt O'Toole, when discussing the focus, stated "We know every athlete, but we don't recognize the athlete in ourselves. So our purpose is getting these people off the couch."[1] Further, O'Toole mentioned that "Our desire is that the brand becomes a beacon for living a fit life and that we're not just promoting sports to create fans for elite athletes. We want to be the brand that says 'life isn't a spectator sport; you've got to get involved.'"[2]

This renewed focus on fitness began with a licensing and sponsorship relationship with CrossFit in 2011. During this agreement, which ended in 2020, Reebok created a whole collection of CrossFit-branded products, endorsed CrossFit athletes, and served as the title sponsorship of the Reebok CrossFit Games. By deciding to focus its attention on the growing CrossFit and personal fitness craze, Reebok was able to differentiate itself and its products from its competition. In addition, Reebok has focused a lot of its marketing efforts and products on millennial consumers who, Reebok notes, want more social experiences incorporated into their fitness lifestyle. At the time, O'Toole was noted as saying, "How we differentiate ourselves—it's all we do, it's what we do. Look at the big brands. They're kind of moonlighting in fitness, and then you have Lululemon or Sweaty Betty—brands like that are really catering to a much older and mature consumer. And the net of it is, we've been able to carve out a very unique identity in tough social fitness in this space."[3]

Reebok also has relationships with the UFC, which was signed in order to reach the 35 million people globally who use mixed martial arts as part of their fitness routine,[1] Les Mills' group fitness programs, and celebrity influencers, such as Ariana Grande and Gal Gadot. A quick look at Reebok's product line now will show its focus on products designed for training, running, walking, combat (mixed martial arts), studio and yoga, and dance.

This example showcases how a major company repositioned itself in a very competitive market. Reebok was able to differentiate its brand and products from its competition, focus on specific target markets, and make changes to its product line to meet a growing consumer need. This chapter will focus on the sport product and strategies sport organizations can execute in order to produce and market the most competitive products which meet consumer demand.

As noted before, any sport product is best understood as a bundle of benefits. Like countless organizations, Reebok was tinkering with its bundle in hopes that it would attract a specific audience and differentiate its products from the competition. In this chapter, we review the elements that make the sport product unique. We discuss the intricacies of developing products, issues in launching new products, and the product life cycle. We also introduce differentiation, positioning, and branding, the most critical parts of contemporary product development. Chapter 7 digs much deeper into branding.

What Is the Sport Product?

The sport product is a complex package of the tangible and intangible attributes of a good or service that combine to meet the needs and wants of sport consumers. When you hear the word *golf,* you think of little dimpled balls and oversized metal "woods" that are, in different ways, standardized. They are tangible elements of the golf product. But the golf experience is hardly standardized: It can be total frustration for the occasional casual golfer and total infatuation for the frequent and more skilled golfer. It is no different in any other sport, because all sports depend on human performance—by the players, the fans, and the marketers. As we discussed in chapter 1, this makes the marketer's job challenging in a number of ways, some of which are noted in the following list as a reminder:

- *The core game or performance is just one element of a larger ensemble.* Players and fans rarely consume the game, event, or contest in isolation. The sport experience includes the atmosphere of the venue, the equipment, the apparel, the music, the concessions, the pre- and postgame festival, and the in-game entertainment (see the later section on game presentation). All these elements extend the sport product beyond the contest itself, for players and fans alike. In some cases, the contest is almost secondary. Television, the Internet, social media, and streaming video with their instantaneous, worldwide reach, have prompted an increase in sports events that exist less for their intrinsic value and more for their ability to deliver unique and engaging entertainment and experiences that keep fans coming back.
- *The marketer typically has little control over the core product, which is inconsistent from consumption to consumption, and consequently must focus efforts on product extensions.* Marketers cannot control the contest, especially the winning and losing. In plenty of instances, teams go to the playoffs one year and miss the playoffs the next, lose a game they are heavily favored to win, or have a big lead only to lose at the end of the game. Every season, game, and day is different in sport.

The emotional nature of fan involvement, the uncertainty and spontaneity of the game, and the mix of sights and sounds all create a unique product experience for each individual consumer.

While this inconsistency is one element of what makes the sport product so unique and exciting, it also makes a sport marketer's job very difficult. Ideally, in marketing, you want your product to be consistent as you know exactly what it is you are trying to market and sell. If you drink a can of Coca-Cola, you know that every time you drink a Coke, it will taste exactly the same. However, in team sports, that consistency does not exist—even the very best teams are going to lose or have a bad game. Despite your marketing of a tangible sport product like equipment, its performance will be inconsistent. A golf club manufacturer may claim that its clubs will allow the golfer to hit the ball further; however, the performance of the person who is actually using the club will determine if that is true or not. While this is challenging for the sport marketer, it also opens up opportunities to be creative with how you market your product, and in sport marketing, that focus cannot be solely on winning or performance. Rather, you must focus on all the other elements of the event that can add to a fan's overall experience. As described later in the chapter, NHL team Vegas Golden Knights has become known for its elaborate pregame shows. Ayron Sequeira, the Golden Knight's senior director of entertainment production, said "We can't control the hockey, but we can control everything else, we can control those 15 minutes before the game."[4] This is the mindset people must have when marketing the team sport product: Create product extensions and such a memorable experience that it does not matter if the team wins or loses.

The Sport Product: Its Core and Extensions

As figure 6.1 suggests, the sport product is both an integrated ensemble and a bunch of components with lives of their own. At the core is the event experience, or the game presentation, composed of six components:

1. Game form (rules and techniques)
2. Players (star power)

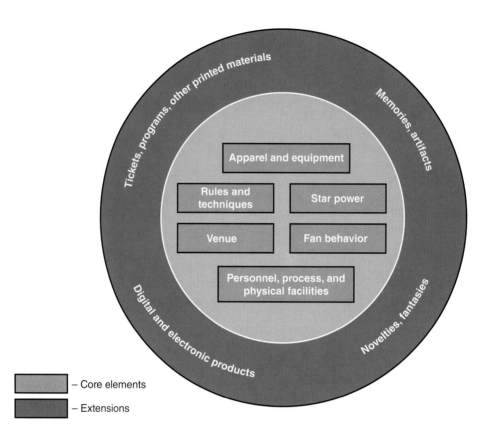

FIGURE 6.1   Core elements of the sport product and a sample of extensions.

3. Fan behavior

4. Equipment and apparel

5. Venue

6. Personnel, process, and physical facilities

Game Presentation: Core Product

Whether we consider a friendly game of three on three on a hot asphalt court or a Brooklyn Nets game in the lush surroundings of the Barclays Center, we will find the common features of game, players, equipment, fan behavior, personnel, and venue. Everything else builds on those components. Take the game of golf: Although the inexperienced or casual golfer has a different experience from the experienced golfer, the particular nature of rules and techniques, equipment, and venue joins the two players and distinguishes golf from tennis. Moreover, it is the playing out of rules and techniques, equipment, and venue that makes sport products distinct from all other products.

As figure 6.1 also suggests, the event experience may include an abundance of extensions.

Several elements move us from the playground to the Barclays Center: tickets, luxury boxes, video, music, memorabilia, and mascots. A **product extension** is simply a product component that enhances the value (and often the price) of an event experience. At the same time, any product component—from the player to the mascot—can also become a product extension, with a life (and sales) beyond an event or even a season of events.

Teams, schools, colleges, clubs, and leagues are the entities that commonly prepare and sell the experience. These entities must determine what fan needs are and package a bundle of benefits to meet those needs above and beyond simply offering a ticket for entrance to an event. What other experiences will be available for the fans?

- Sideline passes?
- An opportunity to run the bases or shoot baskets after the game?
- Meet-and-greets with players or coaches?
- A postgame concert?
- The chance to take a picture with the Stanley Cup?

Bundles must be considered in order to provide a great event experience. For example, one of the desires of fans is to interact with their favorite players or coaches, and teams have created opportunities to do so through items such as autograph sessions and fan festivals. However, in today's digital age, the autograph may not be enough. Photos and selfies that can be shared on social media may be just as important as an autograph to some fans. Some organizations have realized this consumer interest and work this into their fan experience. For instance, after Syracuse University basketball's "midnight madness" event, the organization set up selfie stations where fans could take selfies with players and coaches. More and more facilities are also installing items such as graphic murals, art, and other unique products so people can take pictures with these backdrops and share the pictures on social media.[5] For example, the Tampa Bay Buccaneers created an area outside its stadium called "Bucs Beach." Here, fans are able to gather at tiki huts surrounded by sand, Buccaneers-branded surfboards, and lifeguard stands while enjoying music and other forms of entertainment. One of the goals of Bucs Beach was to provide fans with "shareable" moments on social media. Atul Khosla, chief corporate partnership and brand officer for the Buccaneers, stated that "We knew that a big part of it was trying to design a space that would look good on Instagram."[6]

Game presentation is an art and science of combining and manipulating all elements of a game night in order to create a memorable experience for fans. An analysis determined that the average length of an NFL game is three hours and seven minutes long.[7] However, we know when taking into account commercial time, on-field time-outs and injuries, replay reviews, penalty discussions, team huddles, etc., the amount of actual gameplay and action on the field during an NFL game is significantly less than those three-plus hours. The rest of that nonaction time must also be filled in order to keep fans engaged and entertained. Teams can decide to do this with items such as a halftime show, on-field and in-stadium promotions, music, crowd shots, highlights, and replays on the jumbotron among a host of other activities throughout the entirety of the game. Imagine going to a game without

any of these elements and how it might make you feel as a fan. In 2017, during a New York Knicks versus the Golden State Warriors game in Madison Square Garden, the organization decided to do just that. The first half of the game had no music, promotions, or any form of in-game entertainment that we have come to expect. The decision to do this was an attempt to have a sole focus on the game itself. However, this idea was generally not well received by the players or the fans.[8] Ultimately, it is the team's job to make sure that fans have a great experience at the event. Remember that the sport product is unique because it is inconsistent and you have no control over the outcome of the product (if the team wins or loses). Everything that is done from a game presentation perspective should be designed to counteract this inconsistency and ensure a good fan experience regardless of the outcome of the game.

As previously mentioned, one professional team that has focused a lot of attention on creating a unique game presentation experience is the Vegas Golden Knights. The team produces an entire storyline that takes place on the ice prior to games. The Golden Knights created a live-action character, the Golden Knight, who typically battles the team's opponent in a scripted fight scene that is fit for the city of Las Vegas. While each scene may vary, the Golden Knights has incorporated high-tech on-ice projections, music, sword fights, arrows being shot, a castle perched in the stands, a drum line, and pyrotechnics. For example, during the Golden Knights run to the Stanley Cup Finals, the team faced the San Jose Sharks. Prior to that series, the Golden Knight character squared off against a projection of a shark on the ice. Further, against the Winnipeg Jets, the Golden Knight cut a projected Jet in half that was flying toward him. Each scene was supported with a scripted story that took place on the team's video boards and throughout the arena. The Golden Knights realized it had to enhance its game presentation and product in order to be successful in the competitive Las Vegas market. "Coming to the entertainment capital of the world to serve a fan base that could already see world-class shows forced us to think differently," said Jonny Greco, the Golden Knights' vice president of entertainment production. "We went all in with our storytelling and characters."[9]

The Vegas Golden Knights create a unique pregame presentation.

In addition to the previously mentioned experiences discussed on the game presentation, the core product is made up of the following elements.

Game Form: Rules and Techniques

Each sport has unique special features that may make it especially attractive to certain consumers. For instance, basketball has speed, agility, physical contact, power, and grace. If James Naismith, who invented the game in 1891, could see the Golden State Warriors play today, he would be surprised at the radical changes in his product. Senda Berenson, who quickly adapted Naismith's game for women, would be even more surprised at a WNBA game. Of course, game forms change all the time. Players invent new moves, and rules committees tinker with this or that as they work to balance offense and defense. For example, starting with the 2019 season, the NCAA decided to move the three-point line farther back to match the distance used in international basketball. This was done in order to lessen the amount of three-point shots taken, encourage more dribble-drive plays, and force defenses to cover more area on the court.[10]

We might argue that changes in rules and techniques are comparable with design changes in any consumer product, somewhat like making a tastier, low-fat potato chip or a faster computer chip. Changes are made to satisfy consumer wants and needs. American college football's rules committee first allowed forward passing in 1906, clearly concerned with public opinion about the deadly nature of the "mass" game. Likewise, American League owners approved baseball's designated hitter rule in 1973 in an effort to increase interest and attendance; National League owners, with higher average attendance and more new ballparks, felt no such urgency. More recently, MLB has instituted some changes, and proposed others, in an effort to speed up the pace of play of the game and decrease the total time of the game. For instance, it made a rule that teams can visit the pitcher's mound only five times over the course of a nine-inning game, and have proposed a 20-second pitch clock to begin play in 2022.[11]

Star Power: Players, Coaches, and Owners

The most memorable event experiences build drama from the playing surface outward. Players and coaches are the keys, as all successful promoters have learned. The architects of the golden age of American sport in the 1920s (e.g., Tex Rickard) recognized the need to accentuate the struggles of hero against villain or mind against muscle. Their strategy was simple: star power. Babe Ruth, Satchel Paige, Jack Dempsey, Helen Wills—these

Interview With Shawn Bennett—Executive Producer, Event Presentation for the Golden State Warriors and Chase Center

Shawn Bennett began his career in sport with an internship in MiLB with the Evansville Otters. Since that time, he has enjoyed a career path that has focused on creating exciting and memorable experiences and events with teams and facilities across the United States. Prior to his current position, Shawn held various roles, including the director of entertainment for the Memphis Redbirds, manager of game operations for the Orlando Magic, director of event presentation for the Memphis Grizzlies, and vice president of event presentation for the New York Knicks and New York Liberty with the Madison Square Garden Company.

In his current position as executive producer, event presentation for the Golden State Warriors and Chase Center, Shawn sets the strategy for all aspects of the programming and operations for the game experience. With Chase Center being one of the newest and most technologically advanced facilities in all of sport, we had the unique opportunity to ask him a variety of questions about the importance of enhancing game presentation and the fan experience.

In the early design stages of Chase Center, how much time and effort went into incorporating elements that would enhance the game presentation and fan experience?

A lot. One of our main focuses was to not only enhance the fan experience by going to the new facility but to be one of the most technologically advanced arenas in sport. My main strategy, as far as going into the new facility, was to create a basketball haven for stat fans—fans into advanced statistics—to make sure that we had more readily available, and visible, advanced statistics than any other arena, so we included things like shot charts and graphics that were easily accessible, could be seen, and all the advanced statistics that were being computed on a real-time basis are displayed on the video board.

The scoreboard [which is the largest scoreboard in an NBA arena with the most LED square footage] outputs real-time rendering of graphics, which allows us a lot more flexibility for the shows. It allows for less pre-production and more real-time live production during the show, which keeps our graphics and information updated while still being able to display it in a 3D graphic way.

How does being located in San Francisco and being surrounded by Silicon Valley influence the type of entertainment and elements that you incorporate into your game presentation?

We want to be representative of the area of which we are from. In order to be in the middle of Silicon Valley and the tech-savvy Bay Area, we wanted our presentation to reflect that, and I think that is important for any team to reflect the area in which you are from and to represent it well.

In your 20-plus years in the industry, what are some of the key differences in what fans want to see at games now versus when you first started your career?

Besides the obvious technology advancements, when I started out, the entertainment was a little more skits and slapstick–comedy driven. Since then, the audience has sort of advanced and the people going to games has changed, especially in premium seating areas, there has been a natural sophistication of the presentation that has occurred over the years. We are

> *continued*

competing with the highest level of entertainment—Broadway, Las Vegas shows—so the production value has gone up tremendously and there is more attention to the finer aspects of lighting, sound, and video production. So that has sort of been my philosophy the last 10 to 12 years. Somewhere around 2008 to 2010, things started shifting, and I think there has been a big advancement in game presentation, including the storytelling aspects. You really have to be a little smarter with your programming and make sure you are conveying the right message and the right story that your brand wants to tell.

What do you think the future holds for event presentation in sport? Are there any new design features, technologies, etc. that are likely to change the way we consume and enjoy live events in the future?

I think its technology and customization. I think it's coming up with ways to directly reach each fan and connect with them, whether that's through second screen experiences, virtual reality, mixed reality, or augmented reality—any of these advances in technology that will let fans be immersed in this new world. We have recently seen just how engaging these new technologies are. I feel that is the future and that is where we want to advance and invest in our show as well.

What is your advice for how to create a great game presentation and environment?

It is important to separate yourself and your brand from others through your common purpose and your why. One of my big philosophies over the years has been creating that why statement for everything you are doing, which will then be your north star or your guiding light. What we are about is to bring joy, and fun, and excitement to the games with current, thoughtful, creative, and cutting-edge activations, entertainment programming, and content that break the mold of traditional sport teams. That is my mantra that we have gone after in the past and stuck with me.

Everything you do should be through the filter or lens of these two things: 1) creating a home-court advantage, and 2) entertaining. If any of your elements don't do either one of those things, then it's out in my book. There are many ways to reflect on this especially from a game momentum standpoint and how you can affect the game. I always use the analogy of we don't start the fire, we need the other elements. We are the gasoline. If the players and the momentum of the game are the actual campfire, we are just dousing gasoline on it to create the excitement. We can't get the game going when it is flatlining—it doesn't work. One of the core principles and philosophies is you have to strike when you have the right timing and opportunity in order to create momentum. That's one of the big principles that I like to teach our interns and students—don't try too hard, try to let it breathe, and strike when the opportunity is right.

Also, from a content standpoint, we are always putting things through the filter of appealing to the 3 Hs—head, heart, or humor. And that comes down to everything falling into one of those three categories. As we are starting to program games and look at how to map out our content for the game, we are always looking at the two I talked about [creating a home-court advantage and entertaining], but through that filter of "is it appealing to your head, heart, or humor."

are names many will know and remember nearly 100 years later and associate with that fabulous era.

In some respects, not much has changed: The drama of sport still requires star power. On the other hand, today's players and coaches are extended beyond the event far more than their predecessors were. Players still provide most of the script in sport. They can make or break teams and leagues. There are numerous studies and examples which illustrate the impact that star athletes can have on attendance. For instance, a study that analyzed over 30 years of NBA attendance trends highlighted that attendance increases if either the home team or away team has superstar players, and if there are multiple star players, then attendance will further increase.[12] This impact can be similar in college sports as well. During the 2019 college basketball season, Duke University star Zion Williamson had a major impact on TV viewership and the price of tickets. The top three viewed games on ESPN that season all featured the Zion Williamson–led Duke team, tickets for the team's games had the highest resale value on the secondary market, and ticket prices for Duke road games increased by 194 percent over the average price.[13] This "Zion effect" continued the night he was drafted first overall by the New Orleans Pelicans in the NBA Draft. Pelicans' ticket sales increased 350 percent when compared to draft night the previous year,[14] and the Pelicans

had already sold 3,000 new season tickets less than 24 hours after finding out the team was awarded the first pick in the NBA draft and the right to pick Williamson.[15]

Various measures attempt to quantify the likeability and marketability of professional athletes. The Q score strives to measure the American public's embrace of celebrity figures. As Terry Lefton explained, "Hundreds of millions of dollars worth of advertising and marketing decisions are based" on the annual Q-score reports, one of which is specific to sport.[16] Marketing Evaluations, Inc. annually surveys several thousand people in a national sample, and respondents rate their awareness and likeability of the athletes included in the study. While Q scores are an extremely useful measure that have been around for many years, newer measures have also been developed:

Zion Williamson's unique style of play and star power had a major impact on the 2019 college basketball season.
Streeter Lecka/Getty Images

- Nielsen's N-Score highlights athletes' endorsement potential by measuring their awareness, likeability, and a series of other traits, such as their ability to be a role model and trend setter. In 2017, Serena Williams scored highest on this scale with an N-Score of 83 (out of 100), followed by Venus Williams and LeBron James.[17]

- ESPN produces its "World Fame List" each year, which measures an athlete's popularity. This measure includes a "search score" of how often an athlete's name is typed into Internet search engines, how much money the athlete has earned in endorsements, and how many social media followers are on the athlete's largest social media site.[18] In 2018, Cristiano Ronaldo topped this list, followed by LeBron James, Lionel Messi, Neymar, and Roger Federer.

Coaches and owners can also be stars and fundamental parts of a product. When many people think of NFL coaches, Bill Belichick likely is the first coach that comes to mind. Or perhaps it could be Sean McVay of the Los Angeles Rams who, at the time he was hired, was the youngest head coach in NFL history. His star status certainly rose because of this, but he also instituted an exciting offense and took the Rams to the Super Bowl in only his second year of being a head coach. During head coaching searches, you often hear the media saying that teams are "looking for the next Sean McVay."[19] Then there are the owners. Just think of Pro Football Hall of Fame owner Jerry Jones and the Dallas Cowboys. For three decades, his name and the image of the team have gone hand in hand. While some may consider him to be brash, his large persona and willingness to invest in his team, business, and facilities have positively influenced the Cowboys brand.[20]

Athletes Using Star Power for Social Activism

The star power of athletes and coaches can also be used to bring attention to social issues in an effort to bring about change. Throughout history, athletes have attempted to be the first to accomplish an athletic feat, fought for equal rights, or used their notoriety and platform to spread messages of social activism across a number of different issues. There are numerous famous examples of this:

- During the 1936 Olympic Games in Germany, many athletes decided not to participate as a protest to the ideals being spread by Adolf Hitler's Germany, while others chose to compete in order to prove the worth of other races such as Jesse Owens, who went on to famously win four gold medals during those Games.

- In 1967, women were not allowed to compete in the Boston Marathon. However, that year Kathrine Switzer signed up under the name K. V. Switzer, competed, and finished the race despite a marathon official coming onto the course and trying to forcefully remove Switzer from the race.

- During the Vietnam War, Muhammad Ali refused to be drafted into the war, while Bill Walton was arrested during an anti-war protest.

- In 1989, Georgetown University basketball coach John Thompson walked off the court in protest of an NCAA rule, which denied scholarships to freshman who were not academically eligible to compete. The rule, which Thompson and other coaches believed unfairly targeted African American athletes, was eventually rescinded by the NCAA.

- In 2010, the Phoenix Suns wore jerseys with its team name spelled out in Spanish, "Los Suns," partially in protest of a recent passing of strict immigration laws in Arizona.[21]

- In 2019, the United States Women's National Soccer team began fighting for equal pay to its male counterparts.
- In 2020, after the deaths of George Floyd, Breonna Taylor, and Ahmaud Arbery, numerous athletes from around the world used their star power to bring attention to and support for the Black Lives Matter movement.

Many examples, like those previously mentioned, focus on a variety of different causes and issues, but perhaps one of the most famous, and disputed, recent examples revolves around the controversy of athletes kneeling during the playing of the United States national anthem. Athletes began to do so in an effort to bring awareness to a number of social injustices toward minorities in the United States, and others have engaged in other forms of protest outside of kneeling during the anthem as well. While many athletes have participated, former NFL player Colin Kaepernick not only has been at the forefront but also has received the most media attention.

Outside of potentially bringing light to political issues, when star athletes do this, it is not without controversy. Of course, fans, leagues, media rights holders, or sponsors may agree or disagree with the athlete's stance on an issue, which raises some important marketing implications as well. For example, the response from NFL sponsors to the players kneeling during the national anthem ranged from no comment to support of the country and a person's right to free speech to disagreement and asking the league to intervene.[22] Whether correct or not, some also claimed that the main reason for a decline in television ratings for NFL games was the anthem protests.[23] However, in light of the renewed calls for action in 2020, NFL commissioner Roger Goodell released a statement condemning racism and systematic oppression against Black people, while also encouraging peaceful protests.

Companies that endorse athletes will also need to make decisions in regard to their further use of athletes for promotional purposes. In 2018, Nike unveiled a new advertising campaign featuring Colin Kaepernick, which received a good amount of both positive and negative mainstream feedback. However, following the campaign, Nike sales reported a 10 percent increase and a US$6 billion increase in overall value of the company.[24,25] Regardless of what people feel about a particular issue, there is no doubt that athletes will continue to use their star power in the years to come in order to raise awareness on a number of fronts and attempt to influence change, and this will have a major impact on sport marketing moving forward.

Fan Behavior

Nothing is quite so energizing as sitting among tens of thousands of sports fans who begin to sing in unison some signature song or perform some special movement, such as Wisconsin Badgers football fans who leap to the song "Jump Around" by House of Pain. Live spectators are fundamental to the sport product, just as they are to opera or theater. Their responses are central to the unscripted "script" of action.

Fans are an essential part of any event. They move the core product into the realm of spectacle; they expand the drama. But they can also poison the atmosphere and promote violence. There is nothing new in this. Fan riots occurred in the ancient world. In the 19th century, gangs of troublemakers stormed fields of play with some regularity. With the advent of social media, negative fan activities can reach the masses and spread quickly. A search online will find numerous articles and videos of fan fights in the stands and stadium parking lots, along with other instances of negative fan behavior. The sports media site Bleacher Report even has an article online titled "25 Most Awesome Fan Fights in the Stands," which includes videos of the fights.[26]

But what can be done about it? Because the worst behavior has often been linked to alcohol consumption, people regularly call to prohibit or restrict sales and consumption at or near events. At the professional level, such a policy would eliminate major sources of revenue, so franchises have used technology and staff training to control aggressive fans. Modern venues have infrastructure that allows text-message reporting of unruly behavior. Other policies, such as allowing fans into the facility earlier, may eliminate the length of time fans tailgate in stadium parking lots, and cutting off alcoholic beverage sales at a certain point in time of the game are also commonly implemented across sports. Jorge Costa, Senior Vice President, Ballpark Operations for the San Francisco Giants, explained that its team collects and analyzes data on ballpark incidents to identify potential problem areas prior to a game and properly staff that area with additional security. The Giants have even repurposed areas of its stadium that used to be problem areas into "calmer" spaces. For instance, behind the center field bleachers, the Giants added a garden with flowers, dining tables, a bar, benches, and firepits to set a calmer mood.[27]

Most professional sport leagues have also instituted fan codes of conduct. In 2008, the NFL established a fan code of conduct that banned the following, which could result in "ejection without refund and loss of ticket privileges for future games:"[28]

- Behavior that is unruly, disruptive, or illegal in nature
- Intoxication or other signs of alcohol impairment that result in irresponsible behavior
- Foul or abusive language or obscene gestures
- Interference with the progress of the game (including throwing objects onto the field)
- Failing to follow instructions of stadium personnel
- Verbal or physical harassment of opposing team fans

School and college programs have also developed fan codes. When profanity and taunting reached intolerable levels, the University of Maryland established a special student committee to prepare a code of conduct for fans. Some critics argued that restraints on student behavior would violate First Amendment rights, but State Attorney General John Anderson supported the university's efforts to maintain a civil environment at its sports events.[29] Even with legal cover, however, controlling a student section of fans is

not easy, especially if several hundred chant a profanity in unison. Ejecting one fan causing an issue is one thing but attempting a mass ejection of an entire section is quite another.

Equipment and Apparel

Equipment is part of the core product for any sport consumer. No sport is played today without equipment and uniforms. But equipment, apparel, and merchandise take on a life beyond the core-event experience. Uniform designs and colors have been part of sport events for centuries. Fans in the ancient Roman stadiums cheered for chariot drivers of particular stable colors—red, white, green, and blue. Many of today's teams are known by their colors. If you say, "the Crimson" around Boston, most fans will think of Harvard. If you say, "Crimson Tide," American football fans will think of Nick Saban and Alabama.

Since the 1990s, uniform design has been part of broader strategies that extended the event into everyday apparel. Every major league team expanded its properties division to oversee the careful development and sale of merchandise, including official team jerseys. Among other things, this meant that two basic uniforms—home and away—were no longer enough. Teams developed secondary home and away uniforms. In college football, some teams will wear a new uniform combination every game of the season by creating new combinations of jerseys, pants, and helmets. Teams will often post or tease pictures of their uniform combinations on social media prior to the game and allow fans to vote on which uniform combination to wear. For example, Ball State University allowed fans to vote a uniform combination during its 2019 Family Weekend game,[30] while Baylor University did so for its home opener.[31] In addition to this level of fan engagement, there is potential for this content to be sponsored and generate revenue. When North Carolina State would tweet out pictures announcing its uniform combination for an upcoming game, the tweets were sponsored by Belk, the department store.[32]

Sport-related T-shirts, jackets, and ball caps are badges of personal identity. Even casual research into crowd shots over the years will show a sharp contrast from workaday (and often rather formal) clothing before 1980 to team-branded apparel today. And sport brands are truly global: Manchester United, Real Madrid, and FC Barcelona apparel sell briskly worldwide. We discuss the growth of branded and licensed apparel in the next chapter, but we cannot overstress the high stakes involved in careful development, distribution, and control of a team's, school's, or league's sport marks and logos.

That said, apparel can be used as a promotional tool and to affect the in-arena environment. One such trend is "shirting," a strategy that has become very common in the NBA, particularly during the NBA playoffs. This occurs when teams provide fans throughout an arena with free T-shirts and encourage fans to wear the shirts, thus creating a sense of being in uniform or part of the team while also creating a visually appealing environment filled with team colors. Scott Sonnenberg, former Vice President of Corporate Sales for the Chicago Bulls, noted that "When you come to the game, you want to feel you're a part of it, that you can impact the game. To have those red T-shirts, they feel like they are part of it, like they are impacting the outcome."[33]

Whether it's Cleveland's "Defend the Land," Golden State's "Strength in Numbers," or Toronto's "We the North" T-shirts, they all provide a relatively cheap giveaway that becomes a valuable keepsake for fans. Such giveaways are also valuable for the team because the demand for the shirts are high and people are willing to wear them outside of the arena as well. Ken Sheirr, Senior Vice President of Marketing for the Houston Rockets, said "I go to the gym, and I see every campaign from the last seven years. For a few dollars a shirt, I'm getting somebody to advertise for our brand in perpetuity, or at least for a certain amount of time."[33]

Apparel can also become the focus of special theme nights to create excitement and generate revenue. Each year, Penn State University designates one of its home football games as the "White Out" game. In one of the most anticipated games each year, all fans encouraged to wear white apparel to the game, which creates a unique environment both in the stadium and on TV with 100,000-plus fans all dressed in white Penn State apparel. In addition, each year, the university creates a specially designed shirt specifically for the White Out game, which becomes not only a collectible that fans seek out each year but also a new product that can generate revenue on a yearly basis.

Penn State's "White Out" game creates an exciting and visually appealing environment.
Abby Drey/Centre Daily Times/Tribune News Service via Getty Images

Venue

All sports have a venue, field, or facility as part of the product package. We look more closely at the sport place in chapter 14, but we note here that teams and franchises are closely aligned with their venues, which are cauldrons of powerful memory and community. Historian Bruce Kuklick captured this well in his monograph on Philadelphia's historic Shibe Park, longtime home of the city's major league teams: "Meaning and the items that bear it are fragile. The meanings accrue over time in their visible embodiments, artifacts like Shibe Park. Memories do not exist in the mind's isolation but are connected to objects and stored in them."[34] A fan's identity, particularly in a large city, often resides in the stories or the recollections that link people and events with a place. A place like Shibe Park offered special rituals that made Irish or Italians into Philadelphians. Old Trafford has a similar, but global, effect on Manchester United fans. The same may be true for any venue. Small towns everywhere have sport venues ripe with tradition and collective memory.[34]

Many of today's venues have such broad appeal that they provide significant revenue streams outside normal game days. A place like Fenway Park attracts consumers for much more than baseball. When the owners of the Boston Red Sox looked to reverse the "Curse of the Bambino," they had to find revenue to compete with the Yankees. But ticket prices were already the highest in baseball. And the options for expansion were limited—a few hundred seats atop the Green Monster and a new section in right field were all that could be added. But the Fenway Park calendar had plenty of open dates—some 284 of them. So the Red Sox began to advertise for parties, weddings, and business meetings inside Fenway's friendly confines. Rentals were not cheap: The price was anywhere from US$1,000 to US$100,000, depending on numbers, location, and quality of food. But in baseball-mad New England (a.k.a. Red Sox Nation), everybody wanted to get to Fenway. The Red Sox were not alone in this approach to product extension.[35] For example, Barclays Center in Brooklyn has held the premier for HBO's *Game of Thrones* series, the MTV Video Music Awards, and the Rock & Roll Hall of Fame Induction Ceremony, while the Mercedes Benz Superdome in New Orleans can charge between US$250,000 and US$500,000 to host a dinner on the field for conventions of up to 10,000 people.[36]

Personnel, Process, and Physical Facilities

If the core sport product is a performance or an event, then successful marketing depends on the people who process the product and the environment in which the service is delivered. A.J. Magrath argued persuasively that personnel, process, and physical facilities are additional Ps in the marketing mix:[37]

- Personnel relates to the people whom a customer or fan might interact with and the service they receive.
- Process relates to the way the service is delivered from start to finish.
- Physical facilities are items that help to create an overall atmosphere at the point of interaction.

Think about when you go to a restaurant. The host, wait staff, manager, cooks, etc. (i.e., the personnel) may all have a major influence on your experience and ultimately if you decide to come back to the restaurant. There may have been many instances when your meal was not amazing, but if you had a good experience because of the people you interacted with, there is a good chance that you will return.

The same is true for the process. From the time you enter the restaurant to the time you leave, a number of things will influence your overall experience: how long it takes to order, get your food and drinks, and ultimately pay your bill and leave. Again, you can have a great meal, but if it took a long time to get your food, that may spoil your overall experience.

Finally, the atmosphere of the restaurant likely will have an influence on your experience. The noise level, music, entertainment, and décor are all things that can add to, or subtract from, your experience.

At a sports event, this is no different. That event is trying to provide a great experience in hopes that you will return to future events. The service provided will have a major influence on this, especially if the game is not exciting or your favorite team happens to lose when you are there. Remember, you can't control the outcome of the game, but you can, to some levels, control the experience. Interactions with personnel, such as ushers, guest service staff, security, box office personnel, and maybe even the athletes, could all influence your overall enjoyment of the event. The entire process of all these interactions will have a major influence as well. From how long it takes to get in and out of the parking lots, how long the lines are at the concession stands, how busy the concourse is, to how easy it is to find your seat, the process involved with items such as these may affect your enjoyment of the event. Also, as we previously mentioned, the music, promotions, replays, half-time performances, and all of the other aspects that contribute to the atmosphere of the event, or the physical facilities, will have a major impact on your event experience. Unlike a general product a customer buys off the shelf that can be returned if it does not work, the experience someone has at a sports event cannot be exchanged. You have one chance to deliver this experience, and the personnel, process, and physical facilities will all be linked to the fan's overall evaluation of the product.

Ultimately, it is up to the team, facility, league, and event to understand what is important to their fans and deliver this experience. Studies may help shed some light on this. A study of over 15,000 sports fans determined that attendees have a core set of needs that they want to have met at sports events. Outside of having a good game, the following elements were of highest importance to fans:[38]

- A safe, comfortable, and clean stadium
- An exciting atmosphere in the stadium
- A good view from their seats that matches the price they paid

Outside of these core needs, the study also identified other important factors that influence the fan experience. Fans expect to have good and fairly priced concession options, that the stadium is easily accessible and easy to navigate, and that they can exit the stadium quickly once the event has ended.[38]

A separate study of 10,000 sports fans rated fan satisfaction across nine different stages of what they called the "sporting event journey." This was also compared across seven different sports: NASCAR, the WNBA, NHL, MLB, MLS,

NBA, and NFL. The nine stages below represent a good analysis of the process of a fan's sports event experience:[39]

1. Select and purchase tickets
2. Park
3. Enter arena or stadium
4. Find your seat
5. Use the bathroom
6. Purchase food
7. Purchase souvenir
8. Watch the game
9. Leave arena or stadium

Not surprisingly, watching the game had the highest level of satisfaction (79 percent satisfied) when averaged across the seven sports. However, items such as parking (60 percent), entering (68 percent) and leaving the stadium (66 percent), using the bathroom (66 percent), and purchasing food (65 percent) and souvenirs (66 percent) were all at lower levels.[39] The results of these studies point to the need for sport marketers to provide basic needs for sports event attendees and how important it is to focus on the personnel, process, and physical facilities in order to provide a good event experience.

Product Extensions

The core product—the game experience itself—is supplemented by numerous product extensions that often have a life of their own. Some of those extensions include the following.

Memories

One thing is clear in sport: History captivates and motivates consumers. Arguments about the best player of all time, interest in retro merchandise and apparel, and the proliferation of halls of fame at every level in every sport all testify to the power of the past. Sport memories have spawned different product lines and are often used as promotional tools. For instance, many teams have individual halls of fame into which teams induct former players or retire the numbers of past great players. When this occurs, typically there is some sort of ceremony, often at one of the team's games, and usually a special line of products is created to be sold to fans to help commemorate the event. Sport memories are so

Be Our Guest: What Sport Can Learn From Disney About Customer Service

People who have been to Disney resorts, hotels, or even cruise ships can probably attest to the great service and overall experience they have had in any of the Disney properties. For years, Disney has guided its customer service by seven key principles that are presented to all Disney employees during their training:[40]

1. Make eye contact and smile.
2. Greet and welcome each and every guest.
3. Seek out guest contact.
4. Provide immediate service recovery.
5. Display appropriate body language at all times.
6. Preserve the magical guest experience.
7. Thank each and every guest.

Disney has mastered these principles and become so well known for creating memorable guest experiences that for over 30 years, the Disney Institute has provided companies with leadership, employee, and customer service training. During this time, the institute has worked with companies in the automotive industry, finance, retail, restaurants, healthcare, and sports. Individual teams, leagues, arenas, and governing bodies all have hired the Disney Institute in an effort to improve their overall product offering, train their employees, and have a positive impact on the fan experience.

The NBA was one of the leagues to do so. It partnered with the Disney Institute in order to create a league-wide customer service program in which Disney Institute executives would travel to individual teams in order to customize the program for each team and arena.[41] This program was further specified based on the positions that were being trained. "It will be position specific," said Amy Brooks, President, Team Marketing & Business Operations and Chief Innovation Officer at National Basketball Association (NBA). "There will be behavior guidance for what an usher will do, what a concessionaire will do, or what a ticket taker will do."[41]

The Disney Institute has even consulted on some of the largest sports events in the world. For the 2010 FIFA World Cup, it trained 15,000 hospitality workers in preparation for the event.[42] It also created a customer service and fan engagement program, which was implemented at Super Bowl 46.[43] Numerous other teams, colleges, and venues have also used the Disney Institute services, spending well into six figures for its services. This showcases the importance of your personnel and process in affecting the overall product and experience that fans have at sports events and how sport can incorporate best practices from other industries to ensure a good fan experience.

---

powerful that they perhaps spawned the boom in the sports collectible business. Brandon Steiner, founder and former CEO of Steiner Sports, discussed in his book the moment he realized that he was not just selling collectibles and autographed merchandise, but rather he was selling memories.

In the book, Steiner said that "instead of merely being a collectible, each piece had the potential to be a totem—a magical gateway into the past." In order to capitalize on the strong connection fans had with particular moments from their favorite teams, athletes, and sports, Steiner determined that "We were going to create product lines that revolved around not just players, but players and moments."[44]

Some historical artifacts have reached staggering values. In March 2019, a baseball bat Babe Ruth once used between 1918 and 1922 sold for US$156,000 at auction.[45] In another auction, a series of old baseball cards netted a total of US$2.9 million in sales. During this same auction, one Ty Cobb card sold for US$288,000, while a Mickey Mantle card sold for US$132,000.[46] Sport memorabilia has a long history, and collectors have sought investments for well over a century. Counterfeiters have followed closely behind, so leagues have created or hired authenticators in an attempt to ensure the authenticity of the memorabilia. For example, MLB has authenticators at every home game who collect, authenticate, and put official holograms and unique identifiers on every piece of memorabilia. Ultimately, the memories that swirl around historical data and artifacts are a key component to fan commitment, a phenomenon recognized by the smartest sport organizations that carefully manage a variety of products, from autographed memorabilia to dirt or turf from a stadium, in order to capitalize on the memories of sports fans.

Novelties and Fantasies

Sport toys and novelties go back over a century, but since the 1990s, they have become part of sport organizations' integrated marketing strategies. From athlete and team figurines, commemorative products, team licensed "ugly sweaters," die-cast NASCAR cars, plush toys, pillow pets, and cornhole games to myriad other novelties, teams have continually searched for hot collectibles to drive promotions and fan loyalty. Bobblehead figures continue to be one of the most popular promotional tools. Each year, *Street & Smith's Sports Business Journal* analyzes MLB promotional giveaways. For seven years in a row, Bobbleheads top the list of the giveaway most frequently used by teams, having been distributed at 157 games in 2017. Bobbleheads have become so popular that a Bobblehead Hall of Fame opened in 2019 in Milwaukee, Wisconsin.[47] Teams have even partnered with outside entertainment properties to create one-of-a-kind giveaways and promotional items. Marvel Comics partnered with 10 MLB teams to create player and mascot superhero–themed

bobbleheads, T-shirts, and posters. For example, they created a Noah Syndergaard bobblehead as the cartoon character "Thor" for the New York Mets, while through an MLB agreement with the movie studio 20th Century Fox, 25 teams had promotional giveaways based on the classic baseball movie *The Sandlot*.[48]

Then there are the fan fests and fantasy camps, which have developed for two simple reasons. The first is the meteoric rise in price of tickets, concessions, and parking at big-league events. The standard event in any sport has become less accessible to the majority of potential consumers. If fewer people can afford to get on the consumer elevator, how can they sample the sport product up close and personal? At the same time, even the most committed consumers want to learn, feel, and do more. Fan fests and fantasy camps became the answer. Free or low-cost fests are offered at the entry level, and high-cost camps are available to consumers willing to pay for closer contact with past or present-day players. For example, the Milwaukee Bucks 5th Annual Fan Fest included the following features:[49]

- Fan–player autograph, photo, and connection/experience opportunities
- An open practice
- The chance to shoot free throws on the court
- NBA 2K video game station
- Renderings on display of the new team arena
- Interactive inflatables and games for kids

Fantasy camps take the fan festival to a whole other level in terms of the experience and the cost. Typically, these camps allow people to individually experience what it would be like to be a member of the team. For example, Notre Dame hosts a yearly fantasy camp. For US$5,750, Notre Dame fans can experience what it is like to be a Notre Dame football player. For four days, campers spend time on campus at the athletic facilities, practice, attend team meetings, and play a game at the end of the camp. During this time, they are coached by former Notre Dame players and coaches and get to interact with them in social settings. In addition, all of the campers receive the latest team merchandise and equipment.[50]

Tickets, Programs, and Other Print Materials

Few people realize the full value of a ticket to an event. The obvious uses are to provide a receipt, to guide people to their seats, and to communicate the terms and conditions of purchase. Statements of limited liability are standard these days. But these mundane applications are just the tip of the iceberg in terms of marketing potential. The look and feel of a ticket may vary in ways that represent the different experiences that the ticket symbolizes. Thus, tickets represent a ladder of products that parallel the elevator:

- Premium seating
- Full-season plans, partial plans, mini plans, and subscriptions
- Group ticket sales
- Single-game ticket plans and promotions
- Complementary tickets and sampling programs

Tickets can clearly be used both as a promotional tool and as a source of revenue. Many teams use the ticket as an advertising medium for sponsors. Other organizations have been quick to use it for a promotional tie-in, such as drawings of ticket numbers for prizes or printing redeemable coupons (often for fast food) on the back of the ticket. We discuss these ideas in more detail in chapters that follow. Beyond the game experience, tickets often carry prestige (not to mention a value on the secondary market) that turns them into souvenirs. Tickets to major events like the World Cup and Super Bowl often include an embedded hologram that makes counterfeiting much more difficult. However, as described later, more and more events are now turning to mobile ticketing, with some eliminating paper ticketing altogether and adding additional elements like real-time barcoding to help prevent counterfeiting.

Other print materials can extend the product. Programs are one example. Besides including player, coach, or game profiles and statistics,

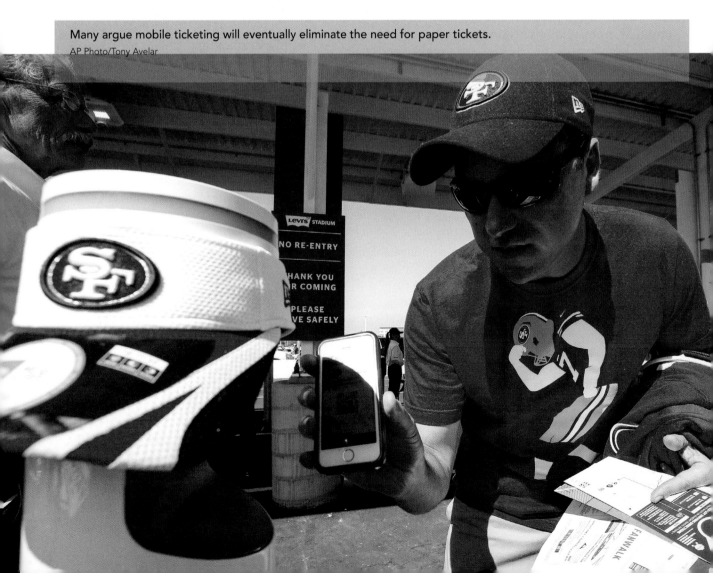

Many argue mobile ticketing will eventually eliminate the need for paper tickets.

AP Photo/Tony Avelar

rules, and records, programs can contain lucky numbers used for special prize drawings. And like tickets, programs can be tailored for big events, with added features that make them collectibles. Teams, clubs, and leagues can also publish magazines and newsletters. Few sport organizations in North America match the reach of Manchester United, whose magazine *Inside United* can be purchased at newsstands all over Britain and shipped worldwide, although many publications now are also going solely digital or ceasing publication altogether. For instance, ESPN announced that *ESPN The Magazine* would publish its final issue in September 2019 after 21 years of publication.[51]

Digital and Electronic Products

In August 2011, one of the Internet's pioneers—Marc Andreessen, who cofounded one of the first web browsers (Netscape)—wrote an article titled "Why Software Is Eating the World." His basic point was that electronic and digital products have changed the way we work, bank, drive a car, read books, take classes, and do just about anything.[52] What he left out of his discussion was how we produce and consume sport. However, we are well aware of the significant impact digital technologies have on sport and vice versa. They have opened new opportunities to extend a fan's involvement with a player, a team, or an event.

One significant development that has changed the way sport organizations engage with their customers and fans is social media. This will be discussed in more depth in chapter 12, but sites such as Twitter, Instagram, YouTube, and Facebook have created new distribution platforms that provide instantaneous ways to communicate, market, build relationships, sell product, and create unique and valued content for fans. Ultimately, social media acts as another touch point between the consumer and the product, and now teams, leagues, events, and athletes can control their own message and create unique content. For example, the rise in popularity of behind-the-scenes television shows like the HBO's *Hard Knocks* has led to sport organizations creating their own versions of this and posting the videos on social media. The Indianapolis Colts and Buffalo Bills are just two teams that developed behind-the-scenes shows that followed team executives and players throughout the off-season, leading up to, and including, picking players during the NFL Draft. These shows were posted for viewing across the teams' social media accounts and websites. Social media has also been used as an outlet to live-stream sports events. Among others, the NFL, NBA, WNBA, PGA Tour, MLB, Champions League, English Premier League, and MLS have all streamed events live via social media. One development to keep an eye on will be the negotiation of exclusive streaming rights for major sport properties. We may not be too far away from a service like Amazon, YouTube, or Facebook having exclusive rights to live-stream a certain league's events.

In addition to social media, most sport organizations have created their own digital platforms, such as mobile apps. While the functionality of these apps varies, they can be used to house accessible content (interviews, highlights, stories, statistics), buy and sell tickets and merchandise, and store digital tickets that can be used for entry. The following is a list of additional examples of what apps can do:

- The NCAA March Madness app lets fans watch live games, access game highlights and recaps, read news and watch features on the games, and play the popular bracket challenge game.

- Apps with game-day functions keep fans engaged throughout the games by having fans answer trivia questions during timeouts and vote on what songs to play during the game. These apps also provide various elements of customer service, such as maps of the stadiums; updates on traffic; parking information; and wait times at the gates, concession stands, and bathrooms.

- Apps can be used as subscription services. For example, in 2018, ESPN launched its ESPN+ streaming service. For US$5.99 per month, sports fans are able to watch live game broadcasts on their digital devices from a large number of sport leagues. Designed to act as a complement to the ESPN linear TV stations, and not a replacement, the service includes other shows, features, and content that are exclusive to ESPN+ and not found on other ESPN platforms. Showcasing the demand fans have for additional sport content, ESPN+ passed 2 million subscribers in its first 10 months and expects to have between 8 and 12 million subscribers by 2024.[53]

Other electronic-based products, such as fantasy sports and sport video games, also play a significant role in the consumption of sport. What started as sports fans gathering together to draft players for a team and calculate scores by hand has turned into a major component of the sport industry with a variety of affiliated products. The Fantasy Sports & Gaming Association estimates that 59.3 million people participated in fantasy sports in the United States and Canada in 2017, and on average, fantasy players spend over US$600 per year on fantasy sports-related fees and products.[54] These fees and products include items such as daily sports participation fees, draft kits, draft prep magazines and other publications, and premium fantasy sports websites and apps. Fantasy sports have become so popular that sports media outlets have created entire shows dedicated solely to fantasy sports, such as ESPN's *Fantasy Football Focus*. Some will even argue that fantasy sports drives significant interest and viewership and has changed the way fans consume the sport by opting to watch individual players and scoring plays as opposed to full games. Sport video games also provide another outlet where millions of fans are continuously exposed to team, league, and athlete brands by playing the game. Popular games, such as EA Sport's FIFA 18 (24,000,000 units sold in one year) and 2K Sports NBA2K 18 (more than 10,000,000 units sold in the year), allow fans to interact and consume the sport any day and time of year.[55,56]

The Organization

Ultimately, all product elements can add value to the individual team, club, league, or association, which is the ultimate objective of a careful marketing strategy. Players, equipment, venues, merchandise, social media, mobile apps, and websites can all combine in the consumer's mind as representations of a particular organization. For that reason, all major leagues have business divisions that include in their names terms like *enterprises* or *properties*. Integrated product strategies yield values through synergy, meaning that the whole is more than just the sum of the parts. Therefore, professional franchise values continue to escalate despite salary pressures and fan antagonism. In the 2019 team valuations by *Forbes*, the Dallas Cowboys topped the list at US$5 billion, followed by the New York Yankees (US$4.6 billion), Real Madrid (US$4.24 billion), Barcelona (US$4.02 bil-

lion), and despite poor performance on the court, the New York Knicks (US$4 billion).[57] Sometimes we also gasp at franchise selling prices—US$2.35 billion for the Brooklyn Nets[58] or US$2.2 billion for the Carolina Panthers.[59] But if we begin to add up all the value associated with the core and extended product elements, those selling prices make more sense.

Key Issues in Sport Product Strategy

As we discussed in chapter 2, strategy is essential. Here we discuss the major issues of sport product strategy: differentiation, product development, product position, brands, and product and brand cycles.

Differentiation

If consumers don't recognize the club, team, player, event, or product as meeting their needs, then marketing becomes a one-way drive to oblivion. Like successful coaches who must tinker with their lineups and strategies, marketers must continuously revise, delete, and add elements to their comprehensive product. Unlike coaches, however, marketers must consider their consumers and competitors simultaneously. Whether the product is new, established, or old, the ever-present challenge is to make the product distinctive and attractive in the consumers' minds. What is it that makes my product unique and worth purchasing over all of the competitors in the market? This is the question marketers must ask and what they must prove to consumers. Philip Kotler formally defined this tactic of **differentiation** as "the act of designing a set of meaningful differences to distinguish the company's offering from competitors' offerings."[60]

As an example, let's think about the sports drink category. Gatorade, Powerade, and Body-Armor are all names you may be familiar with. For the most part, each of the primary products from these brands are sports drinks designed to do the same thing: rehydrate you after working out or competing in some athletic competition. So what is it that makes each of the products different? Why do you buy one as opposed to the other? Why has Gatorade been able to have a staggering 70 percent-plus market share in this product category? The answers to these questions can partially be uncovered in the way these brands differentiate themselves:

- Gatorade was the first product of its kind in this product category, which gives it a major advantage in being able to claim that it is the first and the best. It also tries to back this up with science through the Gatorade Sports Science Institute, with scientific claims that Gatorade will provide you with better results over its competitors.

- Each brand markets itself differently. Each is endorsed by different athletes and sponsors various sports events. Gatorade's major sponsorships include the NFL and NBA, Powerade sponsors the FIFA World Cup, and BodyArmor sponsors the NCAA and UFC.

- A brand can differentiate its products by underscoring the unique features that its products provide or by highlighting

something the brand does better than its competitors. This is the strategy that BodyArmor engaged in. During the 2019 NCAA Basketball Tournament, BodyArmor introduced an advertising campaign claiming that BodyArmor was a healthier alternative to Gatorade and essentially indicating that Gatorade was old and outdated. BodyArmor claimed it is the sports drink of the future and has used the tagline "Thanks Gatorade. We'll take it from here." In taking this approach, according to its founder Mike Repole, BodyArmor aims to "be the number one sports drink in 2025. The dream is to be on every sideline, college, high school, and pro."[61]

- A brand can differentiate itself through taste and flavors, product pricing, packaging and design, and distribution outlets.

Regardless of the strategies a company takes, it must find ways that make its product different from its competitors.

One of the key ways the NLL differentiates itself from other professional lacrosse leagues is that it is played indoors in an arena as opposed to outdoors on a field.
Dave Evans/Sports Studio Photos/Getty Images

Sport leagues must also make an effort to differentiate themselves from each other, particularly if there is a competing league that plays the same sport. For example, the three major professional lacrosse leagues in North America—National Lacrosse League (NLL), Major League Lacrosse (MLL), and the Premier Lacrosse League (PLL)—all play some version of the game, but they also differentiate themselves in a number of ways:

- NLL is played in indoor arenas in what is called box lacrosse. The playing field, nets, rules, and style of play in NLL are much different than MLL and the PLL, which are both played outdoors in the more traditional style of play.

- The season of play across the leagues are different. MLL and the PLL both play at relatively the same time of the year in the summer months, while the NLL season typically runs through the winter and spring.

- The PLL has taken a much different approach to its teams and events. As opposed to teams being assigned to a city or specific market as most professional team sport leagues do, the PLL teams are not market specific. Rather, they travel to different markets and have multiple games in those markets over the course of one to two days.

- Leagues differentiate themselves based on their media distribution. The PLL has games broadcasted on the NBC Sports Network and NBC; MLL has a deal with ESPN+ and other streaming platforms; and NLL has a streaming deal with Bleacher Report Live.

As the sports drink products and professional lacrosse league cases suggest, marketers must constantly evaluate and reevaluate their products, especially as they exist in consumers' minds. Sport products can be differentiated based on any or all of the elements that we have discussed. Ultimately, marketers must use their knowledge and imagination to recognize the ways that their products may be distinct in the consumer's mind.

Product Development

Marketers must continuously develop the product. They may need to delete, revise, or add any one or more of the elements that make up the comprehensive bundle of benefits. Product development includes two standard steps:

1. Generation of ideas
2. Screening and implementation of ideas, which includes refinement of the product concept, market and business analysis, development of the actual product, market testing, and commercialization

To think about product development, we can again use Gatorade as an example. When Gatorade first launched to the public in 1969 (it had previously been used and tested by the University of Florida football team, Florida Gators), it offered Gatorade Thirst Quencher lemon-lime flavor as the only product. The Gatorade we know today offers many more products as the brand has continually evolved in an attempt to meet consumer needs and differentiate itself from its competition. For example, in 2008 Gatorade was offering several varieties and flavors of its famous drink but then faced stiff competition from brands like Powerade. During this time, Gatorade conducted research to determine what athletes wanted and found that athletes needed much more than just hydration during an event: They needed products for before, during, and after their games or events. From these findings, Gatorade created a whole new series of products that athletes can use before an event (energy chews and carbohydrate drinks), during an event (its line of sports drinks for hydration purposes), and then to recover after the event (protein shakes and bars).[62] In essence, Gatorade added products that allowed it to become much more than just a sports drink company; it evolved into a sport nutrition company that offered a variety of products for its target markets. This resulted in a growth from US$4.5 billion in sales in 2009 to US$5.6 billion in 2015, while capturing 78 percent market share and stalling the growth of its main competitor in Powerade.[62]

While the results have been impressive, Gatorade continues to expand its product lines. In 2018, Gatorade launched Gatorade Zero drink, which contains no sugar or carbohydrates, in order to develop products for athletes who are increasingly concerned with their sugar consumption. In 2019, Gatorade introduced Bolt24, a new, low-calorie electrolyte drink that is designed to give hydration to athletes while off the field and keep them in shape 24 hours per day. PepsiCo (Gatorade's parent company) chairman and CEO Ramon Lagurata noted that "We're trying to give them [athletes] a good combination of hydration with lower calories. That's working very well. Now we're adding vitamins and some other positive functionality."[63]

Product innovations and repositioning efforts like the Gatorade examples often walk a fine line between success and failure. In the end, of course, consumers determine the results. Theories of innovation suggest that consumers grapple with five perceptual issues as they decide whether to adopt a product innovation:

1. *Relative advantage of the new product over old preferences.* Gatorade has developed new products designed for modern-day athletes and their needs.

2. *Complexity or difficulty in adoption and use.* Their products are available in a number of supermarkets, convenience stores, health and nutrition stores, and online.

3. *Compatibility with consumer values.* Gatorade has developed products athletes can use during the entire day while also developing healthier products.

4. *Divisibility into smaller trial portions.* Products are available for sale in low quantities to encourage trial.

5. *Communicability of benefits.* Advertising and athlete endorsements are used to highlight the benefits of using Gatorade products.

Product Positioning

The elements in any sport product should contribute to a coherent image; product development should not be pursued haphazardly. Further, the sport organization must get this image across to the consumer. When all elements of the product provide the same message, the image is clear and distinct. In other words, product positioning occurs when an organization attempts to showcase or influence how it wants to be perceived by the public in its marketing activities. As we previously discussed, differentiation is a key product strategy, and is often used when positioning products. Some may also refer to this element of differentiation as a unique selling proposition (USP),

which focuses on unique features, attributes, or benefits of a product that may be seen as being attractive to the organization's target markets. However, a major factor influencing the reception of this image ultimately is consumer perception of the product. As Ed O'Hara, founder of SME Branding, said, "Customers will own a brand's narrative, and the brand's job will be to curate, evolve, and engage that narrative in real time."[64]

One simple way to create this narrative and help position your products is to develop a tagline, which is a brief phrase companies use to create some associations in consumers' minds with the brand. The best taglines can be very simple and relate a strong message to consumers. EA Sports, which produces some of the most popular sport video games in the world, has used the tagline "It's in the game" for many years. In this short four-word phrase, EA Sports is able to portray that if you see it in the actual real-life game, you will see it in the video game. In other words, EA Sports is positioning its products as the most realistic sport video games available and if you want the best, and most true-to-life gaming experience, you should buy its games. In essence, this is EA Sports' USP.

At the same time, a simple tagline is not enough for proper positioning. The tagline must be supported by product development and other marketing efforts. If EA Sports does not continuously work on developing the most realistic sport video games (updating players, stadiums, rules, style of play, etc.), then the image it is attempting to portray will not be consistent. This will lead to consumer frustration and EA Sports' positioning will not be successful. After all, as Ed O'Hara described, consumers ultimately decide what image they have for the products, but it is the brand's job to position the product and try to make consumers believe what it wants them to believe.

The bottom line is the product's positioning in the minds of the target consumers. Marketing campaigns often focus on positioning or repositioning the product in consumers' minds. Positioning strategy, however, is especially tough in the sport industry, where media images are public and often beyond the control of team and league marketers. Here are some examples:

- After a number of reports of the damaging long-term health effects of playing American football, the NFL, NCAA, and USA

Football have all begun making changes in order to position the sport as a much safer version to play than in past years.

- NASCAR has often been publicly criticized for its lack of diversity and is now attempting to address this through a program designed to increase the number of minority and female drivers and crew members.

- The NCAA continues to fight the perception of amateurism despite the millions of dollars college sports generate each year.

This battle for positioning occurs at all levels, in all sports. Mixed martial arts is attempting to hold on to the rising position it once had. Esports is attempting to prove that it is a competitive sport worthy of potential inclusion in the Olympic Games. High school athletes are continually trying to position themselves as the best players at their position to recruiting services and websites in order to earn a higher ranking and be recruited to premier college athletic programs. Regardless of the level of sports, all organizations must manage the perception and image of their products.

Sergio Zyman, longtime marketing whiz of Coca-Cola, described positioning as a matter of managing the five images of any organization or product:[65]

1. *Trademark imagery.* The mark or logo of a team or organization must represent something of interest or value. Think of the Nike swoosh or the New York Yankees "NY."

2. *Product imagery.* Nike shoes and the Yankees' on-field performance have been consistently exceptional in the minds of their many fans.

3. *Associative imagery.* Nike has battled against negative associations (e.g., cheap overseas labor), but it is also associated with top leagues, athletes, and teams.

4. *User imagery.* Nike uses athletes in its advertisements to portray the target users of its products, while Yankees fans conjure different images among Bostonians than they do among New Yorkers.

5. *Usage imagery.* The swoosh on a new, high-tech shoe makes many people think of a more efficient or effective workout,

and Nike's promotional efforts typically highlight its products being used in some athletic setting.

Brands and Branding

Over the years, coaches, writers, and fans have discussed certain "brands" of play—the New England Patriots' brand of football, the Golden State Warriors' brand of basketball, the Brazilian brand of soccer. Branding is both a means and an end to product differentiation. Brands can be created or retained in the names, marks, designs, or images of any one or more of the product elements described in this chapter. Nike successfully built its overall brand (the swoosh) as well as special product brands (the Jordan brand). Phil Knight explained how the ad firm of Wieden+Kennedy helped to build the special image of the Nike brand: "They spend countless hours trying to figure out what the product is, what the message is, what the theme is, what the athletes are all about, what emotion is involved. They try to extract something that's meaningful, an honest message that is true to who we are."[66] Brand building never really ends.

A good example of an organization that has successfully built and leveraged a strong brand in sports is ESPN, whose parent corporation, Disney, pushed the ESPN brand as a major weapon in its marketplace showdown with other major networks. Over the years, ESPN branded products have included the following:

- ESPN flagship network with its *SportsCenter* core
- ESPN2, ESPN News, ESPN Classic, ESPN Deportes, and ESPNU
- ESPNW
- ESPN Radio
- ESPN.com
- ESPN social media accounts (Twitter, Facebook, Instagram, Snapchat, and YouTube)
- ESPN app
- ESPN+
- WatchESPN.com
- ESPN Espy Awards show
- *ESPN The Magazine*
- ESPN Zone restaurants
- ESPN Wide World of Sports Complex

ESPN, like many other organizations, was conscious about building brand equity, a crucial concept for sport marketers. On its face, brand equity is a relatively simple concept. According to David Aaker, a leading expert on branding, brand equity is "a set of assets and liabilities linked to a brand, its name and symbol, that add to or subtract from the value provided by a product or service to a firm and/or that firm's customers."[67] Nike, ESPN, Adidas, and Gatorade are good examples. Put their name or image on a product, and it is worth more than a generic product of similar quality. This is due to the various components that make up an organization's brand equity, which is discussed in more detail in chapter 7:

- Name recognition or awareness
- Strong mental or emotional brand associations
- Perceived brand quality
- Strong customer loyalty

Product and Brand Cycles

Product and brand development has a long history in sport. Figure 6.2 offers an overview of some of this process. Each stage of development, from family to line to type to property and brand, required the work of entrepreneurs who took advantage of new technologies to design rules, equipment, apparel, stories, and images that might win the embrace and loyalty of consumers. We sometimes take for granted the existence of a popular sport like MLB. But its success was not a given in 1850 when North Americans and Europeans played a variety of bat and ball games that might have evolved to become the national pastime of the United States. The same is true with football, a sport with at least five distinct national brands.[68]

Many products seem to have stages, which some theorists have referred to as the product life cycle:

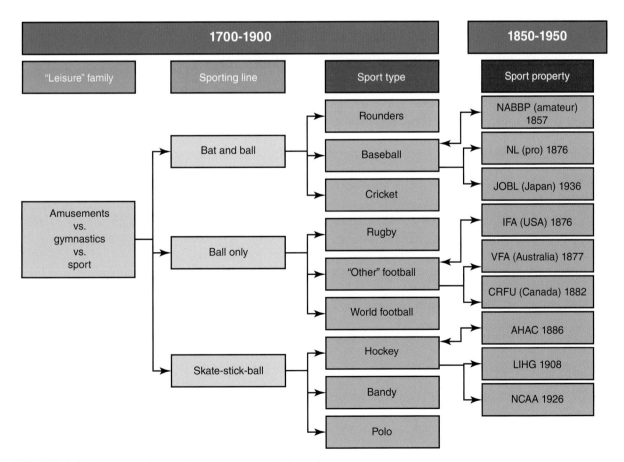

FIGURE 6.2 The tree of sport branding, general chronology.

Copyright Stephen Hardy, used with permission.

- Introduction
- Growth
- Maturity
- Decline

Other theorists have attacked the notion of a standard life cycle as an unsupported concept that, in the worst scenarios, could become a self-fulfilling prophecy whereby managers would reduce support for a product because it had reached its decline stage. Sport products vary in the actual shape of their developmental and life cycles. The following are speculations about sport product life cycles:

- It was once thought that game forms that enjoy any kind of maturity seem to be resistant to decline. That was true for baseball whose popularity hit a low in the 1960s and early 1970s, rebounded in the 1980s, and then had to rebound from the strike of 1994. But MLB is in solid shape. Many people wondered whether the NHL would stagger from lockouts in 2004 to 2005 and in 2012. But it bounced back. However, what about other sports? NASCAR had a long, flat maturity but has since seen some evidence of decline. Will it recover to its previous levels of success? Boxing was once one of the most popular spectator sports but has seen a steady decline in mass interest. Both MLS and the WNBA have moved beyond the introduction stage. What will their growth curves look like? Will they reach maturity? Introduction of new sports and entertainment options may have influenced this change in how we look at growth cycles in sport. For instance, esports is currently in its introduction stage in North America and has captured the attention of a younger demographic. Will it reach the growth stage, become a viable sport and entertainment entity, and potentially affect the life cycles of other sports?

- Teams and franchises have much more volatile and unpredictable cycles than those of their overall sports. Team and franchise cycles are more subject to owner or management whims, economic downturns, and labor issues.
- Equipment cycles appear to be driven by technological advances.
- Apparel cycles blend the more stable trends in game forms with the wide fluctuations of fashion.
- Teams, leagues, and sport organizations that embrace technological and digital innovations will experience greater potential for growth.

For sport marketers, it is important to understand what stage of the product life cycle their organization, sport, or product is in. Doing so will allow them to develop product strategies in order to move on to the next stage in this cycle, or at the very least, grow and mature while minimizing any potential for decline.

Wrap-Up

In this chapter we have begun our investigation of the marketing mix, or the five Ps of sport marketing—product, price, promotion, place, and public relations. We reviewed the features that make the sport product unique and outlined its various components. These include the game or event and its stars, equipment and apparel, novelties and fantasies, the venue, personnel and process, the ticket, digital and electronic products, and finally the organization itself. We also discussed the intricacies of product development, including developing new products, positioning, branding, and the product life cycle. As much as possible, products must be shaped to meet the needs and wants of the consumers targeted in prior research.

Activities

1. Investigate the website of your favorite sport organization. List the various product components (as discussed in this chapter) that you find on the website.
2. Think about a recent sports event you have attended. Discuss how the personnel, process, and physical facilities influenced your experience at the event. For any negative experiences, discuss how they could be improved.
3. Come up with a new product idea that you think will fulfill a need in the sport industry. What is this product? Why do you think it is necessary and will be successful? Who would be this product's competitors, and what would your product do better than them?
4. Recommend two significant rules changes to your favorite sport league that would have a significant impact on the overall product and fan experience of watching or attending the event. Describe why these rules changes are necessary and what impact you believe they will have.

Your Marketing Plan

1. Briefly outline a new digital, virtual, or interactive product for your organization (perhaps to be placed on your website or on an app).
2. Create a comprehensive list of the various ways you will differentiate your organization from the competition.
3. Develop a tagline for your organization that will help position your product and could be used as a unifying theme across all of your marketing activities.

 Go to HK*Propel* to complete the activities for this chapter.

Chapter 7

Managing Sport Brands

OBJECTIVES

- To understand the scope and importance of brand management and branding in the sport setting

- To demonstrate an understanding of how brand equity is developed in a variety of sport settings

- To identify and discuss the sources of brand associations for teams, athletes, agencies, and other sport entities

- To understand how to leverage brand equity in order to generate revenue and diversify product offerings

GEOFFROY VAN DER HASSELT/AFP via Getty Images

Becoming More Than Just a Football Team Brand

Paris Saint-Germain (PSG) Football Club plays in the highest level league of French domestic football, Ligue 1, and regularly competes in the highest levels of inter-country club competition. In recent years, PSG has dominated its domestic league, winning six of the last seven titles as of 2019. However, it has never won what is considered to be the top prize in European soccer, the Union of European Football Associations (UEFA) Champions League. Despite this, PSG has been able to invest significant amounts of money and resources to secure some of the top football talent in the world in players such as Neymar and Zlatan Ibrahimović.

While the organization remains focused on its success on the pitch, and ultimately attempting to capture the elusive UEFA Champions League title, the team has successfully become more than just a football club. According to Forbes, PSG is now the eleventh most valuable football club in the world, valued at US$1.092 billion.[1] So how has PSG accomplished this? It has made strategic decisions that have positioned itself in such a way that football fans and non-fans want to associate with the club. PSG has successfully used its image and assets to build a unique brand image and become a worldwide lifestyle brand.

In an interview, PSG team executive Jérôme de Chaunac noted that "The global objective is to become one of the top sport brands in the world. And we're talking about a brand, not just a team or a club."[2] In order to build a global brand, PSG made a strategic decision that it would need to have a strong presence in the United States. As such, it opened an office in New York City to add to its already existing offices in Paris, Qatar, and Singapore.[2] From these global offices, PSG has been able to capitalize on some of the unique aspects of its brand. One such aspect is its association with Paris. Worldwide, Paris is known as being a city of high fashion, food, and design. Being the only internationally relevant football club in Paris allows PSG to solely associate its brand with the unique associations of the city. It has done so by including an image of the Eiffel Tower in its logo and also by working with fashion designers, musicians, and artists to incorporate the PSG brand into its designs. This has resulted in appearances in fashion shows in New York and Paris, a collaboration with the Rolling Stones, and having PSG-branded product sold in high-end retail stores.[2]

Since the mid-1990s, *branding* has become a popular term in the spectator sport industry. Almost every day, it seems, you can read about a sport organization embarking on some new branding initiative. The fact that branding is a prevalent part of today's discourse is a good sign for the sport industry. Chapter 1 described the sport marketing myopia that has often pervaded the sport industry. This myopia was characterized by a short-term focus on revenue generation, rather than a long-term focus, for developing loyal customers. Sport organizations that look at themselves as brands to be managed are taking an important step away from such myopic tendencies. As you will soon see, branding is vitally important to the long-term health and success of a sport organization.

This chapter begins by answering the question, What is branding? In doing so, it provides an understanding of branding and brand management, with a particular focus on the spectator sport setting. Following the introduction and definitions of concepts, we discuss in depth the development of brand equity. Central to this discussion is a focus on how to build a brand identity and how brand associations are formed by organizations involved with sport. To give a holistic look at the brand management process, the chapter then focuses on how sport organizations can leverage their brand equity while also developing procedures to understand consumer response to their brand and protect the brand from infringement and dilution. Throughout this chapter, we provide examples from the sport setting so that you can see how those concepts are at work in the sport setting.

On the pitch, PSG paired with another lifestyle brand, the Jordan Brand, to produce PSG jerseys. De Chaunac noted that the new jerseys were designed to be "very high end and trendy" with a modern black-and-white design.[2] In addition to the jerseys, the team has offered fashionable Jordan-branded items, such as hoodies and jackets, to appeal to fans and non-fans alike, and both have responded well. The team launched its jersey with a temporary pop-up shop in New York City, and de Chaunac estimated that PSG would sell over one million new jerseys worldwide in 2019.[2] PSG also realizes that in the hands of celebrities and influencers, its jerseys and brand will reach millions of individuals and support its brand associations of trendy and fashionable. As such, while PSG does not pay celebrities to wear its jerseys, it does provide celebrities with apparel and has hosted celebrities at its stadium and matches.[2] As a result, celebrity influencers in and out of sport, such as Justin Timberlake, Beyoncé, LeBron James, and Steph Curry, to name just a few, have either been photographed wearing PSG apparel or have posted pictures of themselves on social media while wearing the jerseys.

Finally, PSG has engaged in more traditional brand building efforts, such as international competition, camps, and academies, while leveraging its unique brand to build a worldwide following on social media. In 2020, it had 41.2 million Facebook followers, 29.1 million Instagram followers, and has Twitter accounts translated into seven different languages. Through each of its platforms, PSG has branded content that is unique to the market.[2] It also benefits from having worldwide superstars who can promote the PSG brand on its social media accounts.

While the ultimate goal for PSG is to win championships, PSG has built a unique brand that will enable the team to sustain its business even if the team on the pitch does not perform as expected. PSG has differentiated its product offerings, created new ways to interact with fans, developed a distinctive image that other teams may not be able to emulate, and generated brand awareness and attention worldwide, across a variety of different platforms. PSG is just one of many examples of how a sport organization can successfully develop and leverage its brand.

What Is Branding?

Branding starts with a brand, which includes the name, logo, and symbols associated with an organization that are used to identify its goods and services and to act as a point of differentiation from its competition.[3] For example:

- The Nike name and the Nike swoosh are both important components of the Nike brand.
- The Seattle Storm name represents the region's propensity for rainy weather, while the iconic Seattle Space Needle is a prominent feature of its brand logo.

Ultimately, the brand name and marks associated with a sport organization provide a point of differentiation from the other sport, leisure, and entertainment-oriented products in the marketplace. For example, imagine three identical pairs of athletic shoes are placed in front of you without any brand names or logos. These shoes are all the same design, color, and size. Now imagine we attach the Nike swoosh to just one pair of those shoes. Immediately that once generic pair of shoes becomes Nike shoes and now carries the image associated with the Nike brand. While each pair of shoes may be exact replicas of one another, the simple act of branding one pair with the Nike swoosh acts as a point of differentiation over the others while also providing the shoes with a distinctive image and competitive advantage over the others.

But thinking of branding as simply the management and manipulation of an organization's marks would be shortsighted. The brand name, logos, marks, and colors of a sport organization serve as a starting point in the brand management process, serving to trigger other feelings and attitudes toward the organization. When a Boston Red Sox fan hears the team's name mentioned, a variety of thoughts may come to mind, including the Red Sox's World Series victories, the fabled "Green Monster" outfield wall at its home field Fenway Park, or great players who have worn a Red Sox uniform, such as Ted Williams, Carlton Fisk, and David Ortiz. The brand is, as author Daryl Travis suggested, "like a badge that lends you a certain identity."[4] Thus, a key point about branding is that it goes much deeper than the names, symbols, and marks of an organization. Branding is really about what customers think and feel when they see the marks of a particular brand.

As they relate to the sport setting, consumers' thoughts and feelings toward a sport-related brand are developed based on experiences that they have when consuming sport (for example, attending a game, watching a game on television or through a digital device, or watching highlights of a game on ESPN's *SportsCenter* or through a team's social media posts). The benefits provided by consuming sport are much more experiential than tangible. You cannot touch or taste a baseball game, whereas you can taste the toothpaste that you put into your mouth. Additionally, what makes the experience of consuming sport unique is the emotion tied to sport. Sport has the ability to trigger emotions that are arguably unlike those activated by other leisure or entertainment products available. Can you think of an experience that triggers your emotions (good or bad) more than watching your favorite team play its rival in a game that has playoff implications? Despite the fact that we live in a time when we regularly record or DVR shows, we are hesitant to do that with sports events because reviewing the event later is just not the same as seeing it, or experiencing it, live.

Being experiential and emotional lends sport organizations some advantage here. As author Marc Gobé stated,

In this hypercompetitive marketplace where goods and services alone are no longer enough to attract a new market or even to maintain existing markets or clients, I believe that it is the *emotional* aspect of products and their distribution systems that will be the key difference between consumers' ultimate choice and the price that they will pay. By emotional, I mean how a brand engages consumers on the level of the senses and emotions; how a brand comes to life for people and forges a deeper, lasting connection.[5]

Think about your favorite team for a minute. Beyond its name and marks, how long does it take you to come up with a memory that has some emotion attached to it? Spectator sports is inimitable in the variety of emotions that are generated and in the level of emotional involvement that consumers have with their favorite sport team or athlete brands. This emotional involvement can be favorably transferred to sponsors of sport. How else can you explain the fact that many NASCAR fans buy only the products of the corporations that sponsor their favorite drivers? Logic goes out the window when brands are able to create such emotional connections.

Therefore, one of the key goals of branding is to create such a strong impression in the consumers' minds that when they see or hear something that includes a brand's name or see its logo, marks, or colors, they experience intense positive feelings. As Jeff Bezos, founder and CEO of Amazon.com, said, "Your brand is what people say about you when you're not in the room."[6] This would suggest that, ultimately, consumers or fans make a final decision on what they think about your brand. As such, it is important to develop marketing activities that create positive feelings about your brand. If a sport brand triggers positive emotions, the sport marketer can more easily engage fans and consumers in that sport brand's products.

While much of what has already been mentioned focuses on brand names and logos, managing an organization's brand requires a much more detailed and strategic approach. One way to think about the brand management process is to incorporate the BLIP model (figure 7.1):[7]

- *Building brands.* The building brands process highlights the need to develop your brand identity by establishing items such as your name, logo, and colors; how you will create your brand image; how you will market your brand; and, ultimately, how you will build your brand equity.

FIGURE 7.1 The BLIP model provides a framework for the management of brands that can be used in sport.

- *Leveraging brands.* Leveraging brands allows an organization to take advantage of its established brand by introducing new branded products.
- *Identifying and measuring brands.* Identifying and measuring brands refers to conducting market research to understand what consumers think of your brand.
- *Protecting brands.* Protecting brands requires an organization to establish guidelines (both legal and internal) in order to protect the brand from any infringement and negative harm.

The remainder of this chapter highlights some of the key elements involved in this framework, specifically as it relates to the sport industry.

Importance of Brand Equity

One of the key elements of building a brand is developing a strong image. When a sport organization is able to achieve this, it realizes brand equity. The formation of strong, positive emotional connections between the fan and a team is an example of the assets to which David Aaker refers in his definition of brand equity (see chapter 6). The New York Yankees' 27 World Series wins have helped create a number of strong

emotional connections with the Yankees' brand that can be seen as assets.

But the sport marketer must also be wary of creating negative feelings toward the sport organization. For example, many high profile arrests have been made of NFL players for violations such as drug charges, DUIs, and domestic disputes.[8] These events have created negative impressions in consumers' minds that could be viewed as liabilities linked to the brand. In order to try and eliminate these types of occurrences, the NFL has developed educational and training programs throughout the league for their players while also increasing the financial penalties and suspensions given to players who are arrested, or even found to have violated NFL policy without an arrest. For example, in 2018, Kansas City Chiefs running back Kareem Hunt was released by the Chiefs after video surfaced of a physical altercation between Hunt and other people. Hunt was eventually signed by the Cleveland Browns and was suspended by the NFL for the first eight games of the 2019 season for violating the league conduct policy.[9] While it is impossible to eliminate such negative occurrences, sport organizations must have strategies in place in an effort to minimize any negative impact on their brands.

Benefits of Brand Equity

When a team, such as Manchester United of the English Premier League, is able to generate a wealth of assets linked to its brand, the team is thought to have high brand equity. This position is the ultimate goal for the sport franchise manager because a number of benefits result from having high brand equity. Perhaps most important, loyalty to the team brand increases when brand equity is high. Take for example the Chicago Cubs, who won its first World Series title in over 100 years in 2016. Despite such a long championship drought, and many years of being dubbed "the lovable losers," the Cubs still regularly sold out its home games in Wrigley Field prior to the 2016 Championship. In contrast, despite winning the World Series in 2015, the Kansas City Royals attendance has steadily declined since that time. The Cubs have a stronger brand because of noteworthy brand assets, such as Wrigley Field, which is located in an appealing Chicago neighborhood about one mile (1.6 km) from Lake Michigan and just a few miles from the downtown business district. Achieving a high level of brand loyalty allows the sport marketer to realize increases in revenue through ticket and merchandise sales. Brand loyalty also typically results in a larger viewing audience for events, which, in turn, allows the sport organization to realize higher broadcast fees for the rights to televise a property's games or events and attract more sponsors looking for widespread television exposure.

The case of the Cubs also underscores the fact that winning is *not* the only important factor in the creation of brand loyalty. Research has documented that factors other than winning are more predictive of brand loyalty for North American professional sport teams.[10] Again, referring back to chapter 1, recall the winning-is-everything mentality as an example of sport marketing myopia. Researchers have documented that winning is *not* everything and that other factors contribute to the realization of ticket sales, corporate sponsorship sales, and other positive revenue outcomes.[10,11] In fact, sport marketers can create equity for their brands in a variety of ways, many of which are discussed later in this chapter. The important point here is that brand equity creates brand loyalty. As chapters 9 and 11 point out, relationship marketing is central to the development of loyal customers. Similarly, building relationships with the customers of a sport organization can enhance the brand.

Less Drastic Revenue Declines When the Team Loses

Because strong brands have high levels of loyalty, they are better able to withstand downturns in fortunes on the field. Although winning is not the only creator of brand equity, teams clearly reap short-term benefits when they win. Few teams, however, are able to compete for championships year in and year out. The myopic sport marketer sees the organization's fortunes tied to the performance of the team on the field. The sport marketer who adopts a longer-term view, however, focuses on other actions to be taken to enhance brand equity so that when the team loses, fortunes do not drastically decline.

Take the Toronto Maple Leafs as an example. Here is a team that has not won a Stanley Cup since 1967, yet it still draws large crowds for its

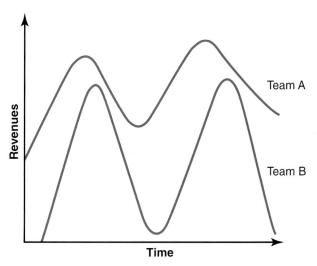

FIGURE 7.2   Revenue fortunes for teams with high and low brand equity.

home games. In fact, from the 2005 to 2006 to the 2018 to 2019 seasons, the Maple Leafs have ranked in the top 10 in NHL attendance every year.[12] However, during this time period, the team has made the playoffs in only four seasons and has advanced past the first round of the playoffs just one time. So, yes, performance may affect attendance, but when a team has high brand equity and high brand loyalty, the drop-offs are much less extreme.

Figure 7.2 depicts the revenues over time of two teams that experience cycles of winning and losing, one with high brand equity and the other with low brand equity. When brand equity is high (Team A), revenue declines are less drastic over time as the team's fortunes change. Meanwhile, when brand equity is lower (Team B), more drastic revenue changes are seen as the team wins and loses.

Ability to Charge Price Premiums

Another potential benefit of high brand equity is the ability to charge price premiums.[3] When branding was defined at the start of this chapter, you were asked to imagine three identical pairs of shoes placed in front of you without any brand names or logos. You were then asked to imagine one pair now had the Nike logo. This example helped illustrate what branding can do (i.e., provide a point of differentiation, give the shoes a unique image, and provide a competitive advantage). This same example can be used to help illustrate how a brand with high brand equity is able to charge a higher price. In this example, most people would likely be willing to pay more for the shoe that has the Nike logo as opposed to those that do not have a logo or maybe even have a logo of a competitor. Despite being very similar, or even identical products, the brand equity that Nike has developed may signify associations, such as quality or an image, that consumers want to affiliate themselves with. As such, Nike is able to charge more for the shoe.

In the sport setting, this benefit of being able to charge higher prices can be particularly important. *Team Marketing Report* annually publishes the *Fan Cost Index,* a report that highlights both the average ticket price for a professional sports event and the average cost of attending for a family of four. Take for example the 2019 NFL FCI:[13]

Most expensive (US$)

- Los Angeles Chargers: $820.56
- Chicago Bears: $647.52
- New England Patriots: $645.14
- Green Bay Packers: $631.62
- Los Angeles Rams: $628.87

Least expensive (US$)

- Cincinnati Bengals: $403.20
- Cleveland Browns: $418.62
- Buffalo Bills: $435.32
- Arizona Cardinals: $445.30
- Jacksonville Jaguars: $453.76

While a number of factors need to be taken into consideration when examining these figures, it can certainly be argued that some of the teams at the top of the list have very high levels of brand equity, making it more likely for fans and consumers to be willing to pay a higher price. Another interesting comparison is the FCIs of the New York Giants (US$577.16) and New York Jets (US$526.57).[13] These teams play in the same market and the same stadium, but the Giants' brand equity allows the team to charge more despite these similarities.

More Corporate Interest

As we later note in chapter 10, corporate sponsorship is an ever-increasing presence in sport today. Although corporations clearly see the benefits in this marketing method, another reason for the increased presence may be sport organizations' efforts to seek new revenue streams. But more events than ever are looking for sponsorships, and sponsors are becoming more discerning about which events they sponsor. One factor that sponsors may consider is the strength of the sport organization's brand. For example, NASCAR sponsors realize that both the governing body (NASCAR) and a number of the individual drivers have high brand equity. One contributing factor to this high brand equity is the emotional connection and commitment that fans have toward the race teams. As a result, sponsors are attracted to NASCAR teams because they know that these brands hold powerful places in the minds of consumers.

Sport organizations with high brand equity increase the price of the sponsorship package to take advantage of the fact that many corporations might be interested in becoming sponsors. Think for a minute: What sport event or organization can charge some of the highest rates for a sponsorship? If you said the Olympic Games and soccer's World Cup, you are correct:

- The International Olympic Committee (which oversees the Olympic Movement and has the responsibility for selling Olympic sponsorships) is estimated to charge US$200 million for Olympic sponsorships for a four-year period.[14]
- FIFA, which oversees the World Cup, is estimated to have earned US$1.65 billion from 2015 to 2018 in sponsorship revenue, with that number projected to increase to US$1.8 billion from 2019 to 2022.[15]

Without question, the equity associated with the Olympic Games and World Cup events creates the opportunity to charge high sponsorship fees for affiliation.

How Brand Equity Is Developed

Now that we have established the important benefits of brand equity (and their relationship to long-term revenue generation), you are probably thinking, OK, how is brand equity developed? That is a good question. According to brand researcher Kevin Keller, two of the components essential to developing brand equity are

The brand equity developed by NASCAR drivers, such as Bubba Wallace, creates high demand for corporate sponsors.

1. the creation of awareness about the brand and

2. the creation of a brand image.[16]

Think about your favorite professional athlete for a minute. First, and most obviously, you are aware that the athlete exists. That is brand awareness. The second step is a little more challenging. What adjectives come to mind when you think of that athlete? Why is that athlete your favorite? Your answer probably has something to do with the way that the person plays the sport or the athlete's personality both in and out of competition. The combination of these elements is what we call the brand image.

Brand Awareness

As brand researcher David Aaker put it, "An unknown brand usually has little chance."[3(p19)] If a potential consumer is not aware that a minor league hockey franchise exists 20 miles (32 km) from her home, then the minor league hockey franchise has no brand awareness. For that reason, brand awareness is often seen as the starting point in developing brand equity. The easiest way to define brand awareness is to refer to it as *the ability of a consumer to recall or recognize the brand when its product category is mentioned.*[3] For example, if we were to ask a resident of Charlotte, North Carolina, to name all the professional sport franchises in the area and he did not name MiLB's Charlotte Knights, then the Knights would not have brand awareness.

The two most important components to building brand equity are brand awareness and brand image, but brand image cannot be developed without brand awareness. Developing brand awareness is typically not an issue for major league sport franchises, such as NBA, WNBA, NFL, NHL, MLB, and MLS teams, but it does become more challenging for events, facilities, and minor league sport franchises. Additionally, a primary challenge for sport agents representing new athletes is to create brand awareness for their clients. Similarly, you may be familiar with "Heisman hype," the publicity campaigns that colleges and universities undertake to promote their star athletes for college football's most outstanding player award. Past efforts to promote athletes have included a number of strategies:

- The University of Oregon put up billboards in New York City's Time Square to promote the team's quarterback Joey Harrington.
- The University of Oklahoma created social media posts for its quarterback Baker Mayfield with the hashtag #Baker4Heisman.[17]
- Clemson University posted quarterback Deshaun Watson's resume on Twitter highlighting all of his accomplishments with the copy "To @HeismanTrophy voters: Attached please find Deshaun Watson's resume."[18]

These are great examples of efforts to develop brand awareness.

The development of brand awareness is also important for corporations that sponsor events. Sponsors pay to be associated with athletes, teams, events, and leagues (often called sport properties). Part of their expectation is that fans of those sport properties will feel better about the corporate sponsor because they are supporting the property. Such a transfer of goodwill cannot happen if the consumer is not aware of a corporation's sponsorship efforts. If you have even the most remote interest in professional golf, you are probably aware that FedEx is the sponsor of the FedExCup, which is awarded each year to the PGA Tour champion. But are you aware of the other PGA Tour sponsors or the individual golfer sponsors? How many of Phil Mickelson's or Rory McIlroy's sponsors can you name? For this reason, sponsorship evaluation usually involves measuring the level of awareness of the sponsorship.

Brand Image

Although the concept of brand awareness is easy to grasp, understanding brand image is more difficult because brand image can be thought of as the combination of a number of different thoughts

a person has about a brand, or more simply put, how the brand is perceived by consumers.[3] Take out a piece of paper and think about your favorite team. Now, time yourself. Spend one minute writing down all the words and phrases that come to mind when you think of that team.

The words and phrases that you have written down are called brand associations, because they represent the thoughts that the mention of a brand name triggers. In other words, as Aaker describes, brand associations are "anything linked in memory to a brand."[3(p109)] If you were thinking of the New York Yankees, you may have been thinking such things as "world champions" because of the many World Series that the Yankees have won. Or you may have been thinking about Monument Park, the area in the outfield of Yankee Stadium where statues of Yankees greats stand. In each case, these thoughts are unique, strong, and favorable, which is the goal in developing a brand image—to develop unique, strong, and favorable brand associations. Sport marketers may have an advantage when it comes to creating unique associations. Where else is the product so packed with drama because of an unknown outcome? Where else is the emotional involvement between the consumer (the fan) and the product (the game or event) so high?

The key is making sure that these brand associations are both strong and favorable. This task is not necessarily easy given that the outcome of the event is unknown. And, as previously noted, the marketer cannot control when a team performs well or when an athlete gets hurt. In an ideal world, we would be able to know when the team we were marketing was going to succeed. That way, we would know that fans would have strong and favorable associations with winning. The team's ability to win in the current or upcoming year, however, is undetermined. Thus, although winning can certainly create a strong, unique, and favorable brand association, sport marketers should focus their energies on nurturing this association in advance of a team's actual performance.

One aspect of winning can serve as a valuable brand association—past success. Think about the teams that have the most championships in the NFL (Pittsburgh Steelers and New England Patriots, six each), NBA (Boston Celtics, 17), NHL (Montreal Canadiens, 24), and MLB (New York

Williams Paul/Icon Sportswire via Getty Images

The continual, and oftentimes dominant, success of the UConn Huskies Women's Basketball team is a strong and unique brand association for the team and the university.

Yankees, 27). Regardless of these teams' current success, they have the added associations that no other franchise can use from a marketing perspective: the most championships in their league. For these teams, and others with a history of success, they can use this association in a variety of ways in an effort to sell tickets during downtimes on the field, use for promotional purposes, or create specialized throwback merchandise. Thus, a *tradition* of past success can be an important brand association. Given the traditions of competing for national championships at schools such as Duke University (men's basketball), the University of Alabama (football), and the University of Connecticut (women's and men's basketball), fans of those schools have strong associations with the past accomplishments of their teams.

Beyond success and tradition, a variety of other sources of brand association exist in sport. We discuss a sampling of these in the following sections.

Sources of Brand Association With Teams

The success of the team is one source of brand association, but other aspects of the team and its marketing, promotion, and publicity efforts can develop strong brand associations. These include, but are not limited to, the following:

- Logo, marks, nickname, and mascot
- Owners
- Players
- Head coaches
- Rivalries
- Entertainment package surrounding the game or event
- Stadium or arena in which a team plays

Although branding is more than just managing the organization's logo, the brand name, logo, marks, and mascot can all create strong, unique, and favorable brand associations. Take team colors as an example. Los Angeles Lakers fans would probably mention the purple and yellow uniform colors; all of the major professional teams in Pittsburgh (i.e., Steelers, Penguins, and Pirates) use the colors of, and associations with, black and yellow; and University of Michigan fans have strong associations with the maize and blue. When creating or changing a logo, teams should take great care to consider the ways in which brand associations can be developed:

- Should the brand name represent a unique feature about the location of the team, as is the case with the Phoenix Suns (referring to the perpetually sunny, warm weather in Phoenix) and the Pittsburgh Steelers (hearkening back to Pittsburgh's history as a steel town)?
- Should the logo contain colors that are modern, fashionable, and attractive (such as the black and white colors previously used by Paris Saint Germain)?
- Should the name be easily translatable into a mascot that can create strong brand associations in the minds of kids (as is the case of Benny the Bull, the mascot of the Chicago Bulls)?

All these things need to be considered when changing the logo or brand name.

Owners of the sport franchise are often the most visible team personnel aside from the head coach and the players. Through their actions, owners can generate positive brand associations:

- When John Henry and Tom Werner purchased the Boston Red Sox of MLB, they publicly stated initiatives geared toward pleasing their fans and making their fans more proud of the team.
- Mark Cuban has responded directly to emails from fans of the Dallas Mavericks of the NBA on a daily basis. By doing this, he creates the impression that he cares about the fans' opinions, thus creating a favorable brand association.
- Now consider the Steinbrenner family, owners of MLB's New York Yankees. Although baseball fans who do not like the Yankees tend to have negative associations with the Steinbrenners, Yankees fans tend to have favorable associations with the family because they are committed to winning championships and do everything in their power to do so.

A more obvious source of brand associations for teams is the players themselves. A variety of associations can be developed in relation to the players. For example, associations can be formed based on how a player actually performs.

- Perhaps the most famous athlete brand association belongs to Michael Jordan. The way Jordan jumped and sailed through the air to dunk the ball was like nothing we had seen before. He was perceived to walk on air, particularly in his early years with the NBA's Chicago Bulls. This association helped lead to the creation of Air Jordan products and ultimately the Jordan brand that we know today.
- P. K. Subban of the New Jersey Devils has become known for his flashy style of play, upbeat personality, and fashion sense.

The player's look or style can also become an association:

- James Harden of the Houston Rockets is known as "The Beard" due to his now famous beard that has become part of his brand.
- The New York Mets' Noah Syndergaard is known as "Thor" due to his resemblance to the comic book character that shares similarly long blonde hair.

Associations can also be formed around a player off the field. JJ Watt has earned a reputation as one of the most dominating defensive players in the NFL, having been named NFL Defensive Player of the Year three times. However, he may be most associated with his charitable work off the field. Watt had been involved in charity work through his JJ Watt Foundation, but when Hurricane Harvey caused significant damage in Houston in 2017, Watt began to fundraise through social media posts with a goal to raise US$200,000. In a little over a year, that goal was far surpassed and Watt helped raised US$41.6 million for Hurricane Harvey relief, making his efforts the largest crowdsourced fundraiser ever.[19] This has helped

Watt not only build brand awareness outside of football but also create the associations of being a charitable and caring individual.

Similarly, the head coach of a team can serve as a significant source of brand associations. If you are a football fan, think about the brand associations that Coach Bill Belichick of the NFL's New England Patriots generates: successful coach, great strategist or game planner, a man players respect, and someone who is often referred to as a "genius" when it comes to football. Similar to players, coaches have the potential for associations that go beyond their performance on the field or court. Given the fact that high-profile college athletes play for their teams for a maximum of four years, head coaches can be a more important source of brand associations on college campuses.

PGA Tour professional Rickie Fowler has become known for his unique fashion choices and bright colors that he wears on the course.

Michael Reaves/Getty Images

For example, Mike Krzyzewski, or Coach K as he is most often called, has generated a number of brand associations during his long tenure as the head coach of the men's basketball team at Duke University. Besides directing the significant success that Duke has experienced on the court, Coach K has developed a variety of associations, such as an academic focus and integrity. Beyond the fact that Coach K has graduated student-athletes at a high percentage and has never experienced a rules violation scandal, he has been a significant benefactor to Duke and its surrounding community. Coach K's name is on an academic leadership center, and his Duke basketball legacy fund has helped create a large community center in downtown Durham, North Carolina.[20]

A word of caution must be offered with respect to players and coaches as sources of brand associations. Player mobility at the professional team sports level is as great as ever; few players remain a member of the same team for their entire careers. Think about the impact LeBron James had on the Cleveland Cavaliers during the years 2003 to 2011. During this time, they were successful, on national television frequently, and near the top of the league in attendance. The majority of the focus on the Cavaliers at that time was due to LeBron James, a great benefit for the Cavaliers. However, when James left to join the Miami Heat as a free agent, all the associations of LeBron James left Cleveland as well, leaving Cleveland with a large marketing and branding void. Despite his return to Cleveland and winning an NBA Championship in 2016, this example is a cautionary tale. Being able to use athlete brand associations to affect a team's brand equity can be a great point of differentiation, but the team must develop its own strong, unique, and favorable associations in order to sustain its brand beyond the players on the team. Further, many high-profile collegiate athletes now stay at their universities for only one or two years before turning professional. For that reason, a team should not focus its brand-building efforts on one player, particularly when that player's contract is nearing an end. Professional and collegiate coaches are also mobile these days. So, although coaches can be tremendous sources of associations, their departure can cause a significant loss of brand associations that ultimately hurts the team's brand. One way to counteract such departures is to understand whether and how the player or coach played a role in building the team brand and then sign players and coaches who either have the potential to build similar associations or have the potential to build their own unique and favorable associations. Does this mean that owners and athletics directors should consider the marketing implication of their coaching decisions? Based on the preceding discussion of how they create brand associations, the answer is yes.

Opponents can create strong brand associations for a team. For example, the Boston Red Sox–New York Yankees rivalry serves as a strong brand association for both MLB teams, while rivalries such as The Celtic Football Club and Rangers Football Club in the Scottish Premiership may have a much deeper meaning to their rivalry rooted in the history of their clubs, country, and varying political ideals. Such rivalries and the crucial games that are played between teams create long-lasting memories that motivate sports fans to follow teams. At the college level, rivalries at all echelons create strong associations not only among sports fans but also alumni. Although they play at the Division III level (the lowest level of college competition in U.S. intercollegiate athletics), the Amherst (Massachusetts) versus Williams (Massachusetts) and DePauw (Indiana) versus Wabash (Indiana) football games are so popular that they are typically televised by regional sports providers. Thus, strong brand associations can be reinforced not only by attending one of these games but also by watching them on television all over the country.

As noted in chapter 8, the effective use of promotional elements can greatly enhance the experience that people have at games. This enhancement of the entertainment package through promotional tactics, such as giveaways and on-court, on-ice, or on-field promotions during time-outs and intermissions, can serve to create strong brand associations. Here are some examples:

- In their inaugural season, the NHL's Vegas Golden Knights surprisingly earned a trip to the 2018 Stanley Cup Finals. However, despite its historic season (first expansion team ever to make the Stanley Cup Finals), the Knights may be best known for its game-day experience. From concerts outside of the arena—a drumline that marches into and around the arena at every game—to high-tech theatrical pregame shows, the Golden Knights has created the brand associations of fun and entertaining. In essence, it has brought the Las Vegas atmosphere to a hockey game.

- The famous Milwaukee Brewers' sausage mascot race in between innings has become so popular that the team has created a website that tracks the total wins of the brat, chorizo, hot dog, Italian sausage, and Polish sausage mascots. The Brewers main mascot "Bernie Brewer" has also become known for going down a massive slide in the outfield after every Brewers home run. These mascots themselves are brand associations for the team and add to the overall enjoyment of the game.

- Where college athletics events attract large and loud student sections (such as at Duke University men's basketball games), the exuberant, youthful crowd can also serve as a source of brand associations. In fact, when asked what would enhance their enjoyment of college athletics events, season-ticket holders (who are not students) often mention larger and louder student sections.

Another way that the entertainment experience can be enhanced is through a focus on the service elements that a consumer experiences when attending a game. Think about all the experiences that you have when attending a game; any of these could theoretically form a brand association. Some facilities offer unique cuisine items at their concession stands, whereas others have special features built into the stadium, such as the lazy river in the outfield of the Frisco RoughRiders minor league stadium or the zip line and climbing wall at SunTrust Park in Atlanta.

Now more than ever, the stadium or arena can serve as a source of brand associations. Strong brand associations are typically formed around two types of arenas:

1. Those with long histories and traditions
2. New facilities that are built with many features to enhance the customer experience

Facilities such as Wimbledon (tennis), the Daytona International Speedway (motorsports), Yankee Stadium (MLB), Fenway Park (MLB),

Patrick S Blood/Icon Sportswire

The Milwaukee Brewers' sausage race not only provides entertainment for fans but also acts as a unique brand association for the team.

Lambeau Field (NFL), Old Trafford (English Premier League), and Notre Dame Stadium (college football) all have long histories of hosting significant sports events. Because of the tradition associated with these venues, consumers may form strong brand associations.

The stadium construction boom that started in the early 1990s focused on building facilities that not only generate more revenue but also have distinctive features that form strong brand associations. This trend is particularly noticeable with baseball stadiums. Since 1992, stadiums such as Oriole Park at Camden Yards (Baltimore), Progressive Field (Cleveland), Coors Field (Denver), T-Mobile Park (Seattle), Citi Field (New York City) have incorporated features that are reminiscent of baseball from a long time ago. Because baseball stadiums have no standardized size, individual features can be tied to the dimension of

the park, such as the hill in center field at Minute Maid Park in Houston. Or, the actual location of the park can create a unique association. At both Oracle Park in San Francisco and PNC Park in Pittsburgh, home runs can land in bodies of water.

Brand Associations Based on the Benefits of Consumption

Beyond the features and aspects of the sport product, brand associations can also be developed based on the consumer needs that are satisfied or the benefits that consumption provides. For example, nostalgic (remembering and perhaps glorifying an experience) memories can serve as a source of brand associations. Whether it is a recollection of following a team with a family member or friend or remembering the elation felt when a team won a championship, nostalgic memories can serve as a strong source of association. For these reasons, a hidden benefit for teams that own or partially control their own cable networks (often called regional sports networks, or RSNs) is the ability to generate programming that will foster these nostalgic memories of team accomplishments. For example, New England Sports Network (NESN) is owned by Fenway Sports Group (the parent company of the Boston Red Sox) and distributed through cable networks to most of New England. That arrangement affords the Red Sox a unique opportunity to create programming (particularly in the winter months) that reminds people of the march to their World Series titles.

Social benefits can also serve as a source for brand associations. Parents could form a strong association to an MiLB team because it provides a platform for them to do something fun with their children. Think about the athletics programs at your college or university. You may have some associations tied to attending games with a large group of friends.

A person's feelings of identification with a team can serve as a source of brand associations as well. Identification with a team entails several things, mostly tied to what it means to be a fan of a particular team. In the case of the Boston Red Sox, being a Red Sox fan means that a person is a member of Red Sox Nation. At heart, *Red Sox Nation* is a term that creates a sense of belonging to a group, or even a special club. Up until the 2004 World Series, membership in this club meant being a part of a group that often suffered when the team failed to win a big game. But with the 2004 World Series championship and the additional titles in 2007, 2013, and 2018, Red Sox Nation celebrated as a group. Just as identification can form with a team, so too can it form with a particular geographic location. In this sense, identification with a city can be exhibited by someone following a sport team. For example, someone from Chicago living in another part of the country could demonstrate to people that he is from Chicago by wearing a Chicago Cubs hat.

Leveraging Brand Equity

After organizations understand how to build brand equity by creating positive and unique brand associations, they can take advantage of, or leverage, their brand by introducing new products to the marketplace. An organization can take a number of approaches to accomplish this.

Line Extension

An organization can create a line extension by producing "a new version of the product within the same product class."[21] That is, a line extension typically will add another similar product to the preexisting products that an organization already produces. Organizations may introduce line extensions for a variety of reasons:

- To diversify their product lines
- To add new products with different price points
- To reach a new target market with similar products that fulfill different customer needs

Regardless of the approach, the company is able to take advantage of its brand name and image to introduce these new products. For example, the well-known golf club manufacturer Callaway is arguably best known for its Big Bertha line of golf clubs, which it still makes today. However, Callaway has established a strong brand that has allowed it to develop and market a variety of different golf club lines that all carry the Callaway brand name, such as the Callaway Epic Flash Driver, X Forged Irons, and Rogue Irons, to name a few. Each of these line extensions is unique in that it includes different technologies, has different price points, and as such is designed for different target markets within the golf industry. Sport leagues have also used a line-extension strategy to create new versions of their sport. For instance, the NBA introduced line extensions when it created the professional women's basketball league (the WNBA) and development league (the G-League).

Brand Extension

Sport organizations with strong brands may decide to develop brand extensions, or to use "a brand name established in one product class to enter another product class."[3(p208)] Brand extensions use the brand name of the parent organization, but they do so to create a product that is not in the same product category as their primary, or original, product. For example, in 2019, the Chicago Bears opened a public fitness center named Bears Fit.[22] This fitness center not only carries the Bears brand name but also includes the Bears logo, colors, imagery, and décor. This new product allowed the Bears to extend its brand from the category of professional football to fitness.

Brand extensions like Bears Fit are popular in professional sports because they provide another potential source of revenue for an organization, and for teams, they also are another way to interact with the organization's fans outside of the core product of the game itself.[23] Other numerous examples like this include teams that have opened team-branded merchandise stores, camps and clinics, television networks, restaurants, and even massive retail and entertainment destinations. For instance, "The Star" in the north Dallas suburb of Frisco, Texas, is a development owned by the Dallas Cowboys. The development includes not only the Cowboys headquarters and practice facility but also a luxury hotel, gym (named Cowboys Fit), private club (Cowboys Club), 12,000-seat facility, and several restaurant and retail locations.

Brand extensions are also a popular strategy at the league or property level. For instance, many leagues have their own merchandise stores (e.g., the NBA Store, NHL store), and most leagues also have their own television networks (e.g., NBA TV, NHL Network).

While brand extensions do offer many potentially positive outcomes, some risks are involved as well:

- Brand extensions are costly to introduce when taking into account all of the product development, research, marketing, and staffing involved with introducing these new products.
- If not executed properly, brand extensions could potentially damage the brand equity that has been developed by the parent brand. If people have a poor opinion of the new product, or they do not understand the fit between the parent brand and the new brand extension, they could then pass these negative attitudes to the parent brand, thereby damaging the positive brand equity of the brand as a whole.[24]

Licensing

For organizations that wish to leverage their brand without as much risk, they could do so by licensing their brand. Licensing occurs when a brand grants an outside company the right to use the brand's intellectual property, such as its brand name, logos, colors, taglines, and even its mascot's image, to produce new products. While this may sound similar to a brand or line extension, the major difference is an outside company is producing the product. For example, companies like Nike, Adidas, and Under Armour enter into licensing agreements with sport teams, leagues, conferences, events, etc. in order to produce officially licensed apparel for these sport organizations. In return, the sport organizations will typically receive a royalty in the form of a negotiated percentage of the sales of the licensed product. In addition to apparel, there are numerous examples of licensed product ranging from bobbleheads, trading cards, video games, blankets, and team flags to dog collars. Chances are, if you own a team-branded item, it is an officially licensed product. This is yet another way for sport organizations to leverage their brand equity, reach their target markets, and generate revenue without the added risk of producing the product themselves as they would with a line or brand extension.

Identifying and Measuring Your Brand

After reading chapter 4, it should go without saying that sport organizations should be conducting research to understand if their desired outcomes are being reached. This research should take place throughout the entire brand management process because the research can answer a variety of questions, such as the following:

- What are my brand's most commonly mentioned brand associations?
- What attitudes do my fans hold toward my brand?
- How are fans responding to my new brand extensions?
- What type of branded merchandise do my fans want?
- What price are fans willing to pay for my products?

Licensing provides another beneficial outlet to influence a sport organization's brand while also generating revenue.

Research to understand these types of brand-related questions can take on a variety of forms:

- In order to measure a team's brand associations, a team could develop a survey to quantitatively measure how representative certain brand characteristics are with the team's brand.
- A team could qualitatively measure team brand associations by asking fans to list the first thoughts that come to mind when they think about the team.
- Interviews and focus groups are another way to understand how fans are responding to a team's branding initiatives. For instance, Syracuse University Athletics created what it calls the 'Cuse Fan Council.[25] Fans who are interested in serving on this focus group panel must fill out an application, and those chosen for the council are invited to focus groups to provide their opinions on a variety of topics affecting the athletic department.

While many research programs are broad in scope like those previously mentioned, brand research can be very simple in nature, too. When the New York Mets minor league AA affiliate Binghamton Mets announced it was going to change its name, it solicited online feedback for suggestions for the new team name and then held an online vote where fans voted for one of six finalists for the team name.[26] This very simple process represents brand research by gathering feedback from fans and then measuring attitudes and opinions toward brand names. After the vote, the team unveiled its new brand identity, the Binghamton Rumble Ponies.

Regardless of the type of research employed, sport organizations must ultimately determine what their goals are with the research, what questions they want to address, and what they feel would be the best method and measures to answer those questions.

Protecting the Brand

Anything that has value is worth protecting, and an organization's brand could be argued to be its most important asset. As such, good sport organizations will institute policies and procedures to make sure that their brand is presented in a consistent and positive way. Without doing so, they may not be able to develop positive brand equity because multiple brand messages, colors, or logos can cause confusion for consumers. Internally, an organization can institute a variety of procedures to protect its brand.

Brand Guidelines

Brand guidelines, or a brand guidelines book, are common and important. These guidelines, which typically are digitally available to everyone in the organization, provide the rules for how the brand should be portrayed. They will depict items such as

- the official/approved fonts to be used,
- primary and secondary logos,
- colors,
- taglines,
- and how these items can and cannot be modified or used on certain types of backgrounds and marketing materials.

Having and following these guidelines will provide a consistent brand image and message across all marketing platforms. In addition, these guidelines are generally provided to any external partners, such as sponsors or licensees, so they are aware of how they should be using the sport organization's brand.

To further protect the brand, sport organizations will assign people to oversee an approval process in which external parties must submit samples for approval if they are going to use the organization's brand. For instance, if Nike is a licensee for a university, any product that it produces with the university's logo will be approved by someone at the university or the agency prior to production of the product. This will ensure that the university's brand is properly represented on all products.

Legal Protection

Sport organizations can legally protect their brand. As discussed in further depth in chapter 14, organizations can legally protect items such as brand names, logos, colors, and taglines by obtaining items such as trademarks and service marks. Doing so allows the organization to pursue legal action against anyone who may be using its intellectual property without having the right to do so.

Additional Brand Management Considerations

Along with understanding the brand management process outlined in this chapter, other important elements of branding should be considered: specifically, rebranding and athlete branding.

Rebranding

While following the brand management process example we provide in this chapter may best set up an organization for success, oftentimes sport organizations need to make changes to their brand. This **rebranding** occurs when an organization makes changes to its name, logo, and colors in order to alter its brand positioning or associations.[27] These changes may range from very small modifications to brand elements, such as a minor change to the logo or colors, to larger changes that may include a complete change to the brand's name.[28] This is a very common practice in professional sports. Some research has indicated that over half of the teams combined in the NBA, NFL, NHL, and MLB have made changes to their brand since 2010.[29]

The reasons why teams decide to make these changes vary:[29]

- Teams may want to establish a connection to their team history or the region where they play.
- Teams may want to modernize their brand or better connect with their target market.
- Major changes could be taking place within the organization that make it necessary or logical to rebrand.
- Fans have asked for a change.

Teams will frequently use a combination of these strategies when rebranding. For example, in 2017, the Detroit Pistons rebranded by intro-

Detroit Pistons Logos History

National Basketball Association Logos · Fort Wayne Pistons (1941/42-1956/57) ► **Detroit Pistons** (1957/58-Pres)

Detroit Pistons Primary Logos History

1957/58 - 1970/71

1971/72 - 1974/75

1975/76 - 1978/79

1979/80 - 1995/96

1996/97 - 2000/01

2001/02 - 2004/05

2005/06 - 2016/17

2017/18 - Pres

The Detroit Pistons has rebranded on numerous occasions but most recently has used elements of modernization and nostalgia to create its current brand logo.

ducing a new logo with a modern approach to colors and the logo the team used from 1979 to 1996, consequently connecting to a time in the team's history when the Pistons won two NBA Championships.[30] Concurrently, the team was also moving into a new arena, so the timing was right to introduce additional changes to the brand to coincide with the move.

Another team that has used various rebranding strategies is the Miami Marlins. When the Florida Marlins became the Miami Marlins in 2012, its name change prompted the team to create a logo with colors that were meant to be representative of the city of Miami.[31] In 2019, the Marlins made yet another change to its logo. The new Marlins Chief Executive Officer Derek Jeter, when discussing the new logo, said that "It differentiates the past, present, and future. I think it's reflective of the Miami culture. We tried to capture the energy of Miami."[32] Specifically the Marlins felt that the colors were more vibrant and representative of Miami's nightlife, skyline, and energy.[32] The Marlins even introduced the

new brand on social media with a video devoid of baseball or team references, instead depicting images of the city, people, music, and food of Miami while also using the hashtag #OurColores (Spanish for Our Colors). This example is representative of a team that rebranded due to a major organizational change (new ownership) while also attempting to connect with the city, region, and target markets.

Regardless of the rebranding strategy an organization uses, it is important for organizations to control the process and have a strong plan in place. Rebranding efforts may positively influence the brand equity, but they also can take a significant amount of time, money, and effort. If not executed correctly, these efforts could have a negative impact on the brand associations. This is the reason why it is important for teams to have a strong plan and clear goals and objectives in place prior to engaging in any element of rebranding. Additionally, teams must make sure that they are the ones to introduce the new brand and highlight the reasons why the changes

Following an off season in 2019, during which the team hired a new head coach and signed a number of high-profile free agents, the New York Jets unveiled its new logo, colors, and uniforms. However, that process was nearly five years in the making. Beginning in 2014, the Jets began trying to figure out how to attract younger fans while also reaching its core customer base.[42]

Like many teams that rebrand, the Jets had to first conduct research. To do so, it conducted a brand audit that included interviews with key people, such as season-ticket holders. This audit, which alone took between eight and 12 months to complete, allowed the Jets to understand what the brand means to its fans and areas that fans thought could be changed. Following this research, it was clear to the team that it wanted to incorporate New York more into its brand identity and that green was a key brand association. Because green was so highly tied to its brand, it took nearly two years to find the perfect shade of the color to represent the team and its new identity. After approval of the new color and logo, league partner Nike then began developing uniform samples that needed to be designed and approved by the team and the league prior to launch.[42]

Following this nearly five-year process, the Jets held an event at Gotham Hall in New York City to officially unveil the team's new logo, colors, and uniforms. The outcome of this rebranding process now includes the words *New York* on both the team's helmet and the front of the jersey. The team's primary color is a lighter and more metallic shade of green that the Jets refer to as "Gotham Green." The Jets also created a bolder white color (Spotlight White) and added black to the color palette (Stealth Black), including a black jersey, to appeal to a younger demographic and make the apparel more modern and fashionable.[42,43] The logo is also a more modernized design that spells out the words *New York* as opposed to using just *NY*, and the helmets changed from white to green.[43] The team's then president Neil Glat noted that "Our new uniforms are inspired by the toughness, grit, and resilience of the entire New York City area. They are clean, bold, and dynamic."[43]

This example highlights the length to which teams will go to ensure their rebrand is a success and the amount of time, consideration, and resources that are used throughout this process. It also demonstrates how important teams feel it is to develop a proper brand identity, one that connects with the fan base and residents of the city or region of the team.

were made. Any unofficial leaks of new names, logos, and colors are detrimental to the success of a rebranding initiative since the team would then lose control of the brand messaging behind the rebrand.

Athlete Branding

While this chapter has primarily focused on teams and other sport organizations, athletes have the ability to create their own brand identity and associations, which can be leveraged on and off the playing field. As brand consultant Jeremy Darlow's book title succinctly suggests, "Athletes are brands, too."[33] In essence, athletes are human brands: well-known athletes who may have unique brand associations that are used to market themselves or their brand.[34] Another way to think of an athlete brand is an athlete whose name, likeness, or attributes have been shown to have some value in the marketplace.[35]

Athletes can take advantage of their value in the marketplace in myriad ways. Of note, athletes have been used for many years to endorse products. Whether it is credit cards, automobiles, soda, athletic apparel, or any number of types of products, some corporations spend millions of dollars a year with athletes in an effort to affiliate their corporate brand name with the athlete's brand, thus connecting with the athlete's unique brand image and associations. This also allows athletes to supplement their revenue, frequently making as much or potentially more off the field than on the field. Every year, *Forbes* publishes its list of the 100 highest-paid athletes. In this list, *Forbes* includes how much athletes are paid for their athletic contract and how much athletes make in endorsements. In 2020, some of the highest-paid (US$) endorsers were as follows:[36]

- Roger Federer: $100 million
- Tiger Woods: $60 million
- LeBron James: $60 million
- Cristiano Ronaldo: $45 million
- Stephen Curry: $44 million

These athletes have built a brand of success not only in their particular sports but also outside of sports. Their unique brand associations and worldwide brand awareness have allowed them to capitalize through endorsements.

Athletes' social media presence is another way to build and showcase their brand associations while providing another outlet for corporations to spread their brand to potentially millions of followers. For example, due to his more than 224 million Instagram followers, Cristiano Ronaldo is able to command US$889,000 from companies for just one promoted Instagram post.[37]

While many athletes have used their brand to endorse other products, athletes may also choose to create their own brand identities and brand extensions. In numerous instances, athletes have used their brand name to open restaurants, athletic training facilities, and car dealerships or to develop all types of products and services. These brand extensions can range from small businesses to major international operations.

Notwithstanding the size and scope of athlete brand extensions, the most successful athletes are likely to capitalize on the unique characteristics of their brand. Here are some examples:

- In 2012, international tennis star Maria Sharapova introduced and created her own candy line called Sugarpova. According to the company website, Sugarpova "is a premium candy line that reflects the fun, fashionable, sweet side of international tennis sensation Maria Sharapova. A long-time candy lover with a surprising sweet tooth, Maria has created her own candy business to offer an accessible bit of luxury interpreting classic candies in her own signature style."[38]

- This brand extension has been very successful for Sharapova and is now sold in retail locations, hotels, and entertainment venues worldwide with an estimated value of US$20 million.[39]

- While Tom Brady may arguably be the best quarterback in NFL history, one of his unique brand characteristics is his sustained success at an age when most players, particularly quarterbacks, have retired. Brady has attributed his longevity to his unique training method, lifestyle, and eating habits and what he calls the TB12 method. He has since turned this TB12 method into its own brand that markets a number of different products and services, such as TB12-branded workout equipment, drinks and supplements, protein bars and snacks, and apparel.[40]

- Tiger Woods has created TGR, a parent company that includes a number of different business and community-based ventures. Under the TGR brand is Woods' philanthropic organization (The Tiger Woods Foundation), a golf course design firm (TGR Design), an organization that manages charitable events (TGR Live), and a sports bar and restaurant (The Woods).[41]

Wrap-Up

Regardless of the sport setting, you likely now recognize that branding entails much more than managing logos and marks. Sport organizations that successfully manage and build their brands create both awareness and a strong image for their products. Organizations that are successful in this endeavor receive a variety of benefits, including increased fan or consumer loyalty, increased revenue, and the ability to leverage

Maria Sharapova showcasing her Sugarpova brand extension.

their brand equity by creating line extensions, brand extensions, and licensed product. When doing so, it is important that the organizations have systems in place to both monitor and measure their brand equity while protecting the brand from any harm or dilution. Ultimately, following this framework will allow for the development of a strong brand that will provide points of differentiation and a competitive advantage in the marketplace.

Activities

1. Manchester United, Real Madrid, and Chelsea are three of the strongest professional soccer (football outside the United States) brands. Visit their websites and Instagram accounts—www.manutd.com and @manchesterunited; www.realmadrid.com and @realmadrid; and www.chelseafc.com and @chelseafc—and identify how the websites and Instagram accounts are used to create, reinforce, and nurture strong, favorable, and unique brand associations.

2. Identify the brand associations with your school's athletics program. A useful way to do this is to ask some friends what comes to mind when they think of your school's

athletics teams. You may want to focus on one team in particular. After you have prepared your list, identify which of these associations are strong, unique, and favorable. Are there negative associations that need to be overcome?

3. Based on your assessment of the strong positive and negative associations with your school's athletics program, develop three strategies either to nurture these brand associations or to overcome the negative brand associations.

4. Let's say that MLB has decided to put an expansion franchise in Portland, Oregon. What would be a good brand name for this new franchise? Why would that be a good team name? (Hint: The answer needs to have something to do with brand associations.)

5. Based on the team name you created for the new MLB expansion franchise in Portland, Oregon, create two brand extensions for this team. What are these extensions, how would you brand and name these extensions, and why do you think they would be successful?

6. Choose one professional sports team that you think should be rebranded. Discuss why you think the team should be rebranded and what you would recommend they do. Should they create new logos, use new colors, change the team name, etc.? What strategies should they incorporate while making these changes?

Your Marketing Plan

1. Analyze the name and logo of your product. Does it trigger positive memories in consumers? If not, should it be changed?

2. Identify the various associations your product creates. Are they positive or negative? Are they unique? Develop strategies to reinforce and nurture the positive associations and brainstorm what must be done to manage the negative associations.

3. Recommend some brand extensions that could be created for your product. Why would these brand extensions be a good fit for your product?

4. What type of market research would you conduct in order to measure your product's brand awareness and brand associations?

 Go to HK*Propel* to complete the activities for this chapter.

Chapter 8

Promotion and Paid Media

Shawn McGee

OBJECTIVES

- To recognize the importance of promotion in the marketing mix to drive brand recognition, affinity, and sales

- To appreciate the importance of both price and non-price promotional strategies and the way in which they are used in the sales process to influence buyer behavior

- To recognize the key characteristics of effective promotional campaigns aimed at expanding existing consumer bases and at increasing frequency of consumption

- To understand how media, both paid and earned, are part of the promotional marketing mix and how media can help, and possibly hurt, the brand affinity and equity

Albert Dickson/Sporting News via Getty Images via Getty Images

Giveaways at sports events have been a staple of the promotional effort by sport teams for decades. Teams learned long ago that one way to entice fans to attend games or matches was to offer promotional items, such as hats, T-shirts, and bobbleheads. MLB has made promotional giveaways a large part of its marketing mix, hosting promotional item giveaways on over 25 percent of its games. Some teams have as many as 12 bobblehead nights and give away as many as 40,000 bobbleheads per game.

However, there has been a movement toward experiences, as opposed to giveaways, with a decrease in the distribution of promotional giveaway items. While partly due to the rising costs of giveaway items, there is also a realization that today's millennials and Gen Z are attracted by experiences as opposed to material items, while Baby Boomers and Gen X are no longer interested in swag items due to age.

In the effort to attract the next generation of fans, while not ignoring the current core fan, marketers are funneling dollars to programs that give lifetime memories for fans. Teams are finding that the experiences themselves create affinity, not cheap gifts. Promotions are focused on opportunities like being on the field during pregame warm-ups, ice-skating on the ice after an NHL game, or having lunch in an NBA locker room. The philosophy is to go deeper and narrower, as opposed to shallow and wide. In doing so, these experiences are usually focused on smaller groups, allowing for a deeper interaction between the organization and the fan.

Make no mistake, the time of promotional giveaways is not going away. Thousands of bobbleheads, T-shirts, and hats will still be given away each year. But experiences such as those previously mentioned are trending and becoming more important to teams as they try to entice people to attend their games and matches.

In addition, changes in the sponsorship world are affecting the promotions that teams are using to promote their games and matches. For a long time, sponsors simply wanted their brand marketed within the stadium, using signage. Then, sponsors were willing to put their logo on the promotional items that teams were giving away, thus paying for the promo items. The promo items were ways for the brand's logo to make it into the fans' homes, or out in the community, on the fronts of T-shirts and hats.

However, sponsors are not valuing branding in the same way as they did in the past. The theory of deeper and narrower has become the norm for many sponsors. The era of sponsors having copious signage around the facility and bringing hundreds of clients and prospects to the games is over. Now, sponsors want more targeted social media and digital content exposure and bring only a handful of clients and prospects to the games. But they give them incredible once-in-a-lifetime experiences, like meeting the players after the game or being on the field during warm-ups. Logos on promo items are no longer as highly valued by sponsors: They are not willing to pay the price they once did to see their logo on the giveaway. That, in turn, forced teams to not only find ways to market to the consumer but also give value to the sponsor—in other words, experiences.

This chapter focuses on promotion, which works in conjunction with media (both paid and earned) and sales to drive consumers to take action and invest in the product via time, money, and emotion. It often takes all three (promotion, media, and sales) to generate enough incentive to cause a consumer to act. In this chapter, after discussing how these basic activities apply to promotion, we consider these activities' potential for attracting consumers and placing them on the frequency elevator.

Promotion: The Driver to Sales

Promotion, another of the Ps in sport marketing, is a catchall category for any of the numerous activities designed to stimulate consumer interest in, awareness of, and purchase of the product. Promotion, first and foremost, is a critical element for positioning a product and its image in the mind of the consumer. Promotion conveys information about product, place, and price, driving the consumer toward the purchase decision.

The marketing term *promotion* includes the following forms of marketing activity:

- *Paid media (advertising)*. Any paid, sponsored message conveyed through media
- *Earned media (publicity)*. Any form of exposure in the media not paid for by the organization or within the control or influence of the organization
- *Sales*. Any presentation in which the seller has an opportunity to have a dialogue with and persuade the consumer, including phone, face-to-face, and social media
- *Sales promotion*. A wide variety of activities aimed to drive purchase of the product; examples include sampling, discounting, couponing, giveaways, premium items, performances, etc.

To be successful, promotional efforts should follow the following steps of the AIDA approach:

A. Increase **a**wareness

I. Attract **i**nterest

D. Arouse **d**esire

A. Initiate **a**ction

All promotions must take into account the following:

1. *The goal of the promotion*. Why are we creating this promotion? What would be considered a success? Is it to create awareness of the product? Is it to drive knowledge of and interest in the product? Is it to get new prospective consumers to try the product?
2. *The resources required for the promotion*. Will there be a cost to the promotion? Is there enough budget to justify the expense? Will the outcome be worth the cost (return on investment [ROI] and return on objectives [ROO])? What other resources are required for the promotion, such as time, staffing, etc.? Can the promotion be funded in another way, for example, by a sponsor?

3. *How the promotion will affect the product's value in the future*. Will a short-term bump in publicity, attendance, or revenue from the promotion have any adverse effect on the long-term?

Paid Media

As with all forms of promotion, the core of paid media, also known as advertising, is effective communication that spurs a desired action. That is, paid media are a communication process and subject to the same problems as any other communication process. A major challenge in advertising is perceptual distortion, which occurs when the receiver of a message interprets it differently from the way the sender intended. This phenomenon can cause misunderstanding of advertising messages, which may prevent consumers from taking the action desired by the marketers. Thus, in terms of advertising and other promotional activities, the sport marketer must operate under the axiom that perception is reality. In other words, the sport marketer must attempt to ensure that the message is targeted, clear, and specific so that the receiver comprehends it. If this doesn't happen, the promotion will not be successful and, even worse, the marketer will have to work twice as hard to undo the damage caused by the confusing messaging.

For many years, it was considered unconscionable to put more than one marketing message out into the community for fear that it might confuse the consumer and not deliver the desired results. Organizations created one universal marketing message, normally with a tagline, that aligned with brand perception. They would create an advertising campaign around that message using one or more channels (i.e., radio, TV, or print), to deliver it. Although there might have been slight variations in the marketing depending on what action the marketing was desiring to drive (e.g., ticket sales vs. viewership), the overall messaging was the same.

However, GEICO changed all that in the early 2000s with the rollout of a lizard, cavemen, a googly-eyed stack of cash, a talking pothole, and a camel. GEICO took a chance by rolling out multiple marketing messages, targeting different demographics with a unifying message that GEICO could save customers 15 percent or

By Jeffry Pilcher, CEO, President, and Founder of The Financial Brand

GEICO uses more branded characters at one time than probably any other company in the history of marketing. Turn on the TV tonight and you could see an ad starring their Gecko, Cavemen, or the googly-eyed pile of Kash. Or all three.

Presently GEICO has no fewer than six—count 'em . . . SIX!—different ad campaigns running, each with their own unique tone, style, flavor, and message.

Ask any brand-builder in the world, and they'll tell you that using a seemingly disjointed and eclectic lineup of ads is the wrong way to create a cohesive, focused brand image. Consistency, they all say, is the key to shaping people's perceptions and getting your messages to stick.

GEICO (pronounced "GUY-co," and short for Government Employees Insurance Company) doesn't just ignore these widely accepted branding "rules." They do everything possible to break them.

1. The Gecko

The gecko first appeared in 1999 during a Screen Actors Guild strike that prevented the use of live actors. In the gecko's first TV debut, he pleads for people confusing "gecko" with "GEICO" to stop phoning him. The gecko speaks with an English (Cockney) accent. Why? Because it would be unexpected, according to GEICO's ad shop, the Martin Agency.

Message: "15 minutes could save you 15% or more on your car insurance."

2. Cavemen

These metrosexual cavemen have somehow eluded extinction while developing a taste for racquet sports, plasma TVs, and "duck with mango salsa." They are insulted by GEICO's ad tagline, "So easy, a caveman can do it."

GEICO and its ad agency tried to capitalize on the success of their Cavemen with a TV series in the fall of 2007. The move made GEICO the first advertiser in recent history to turn a fictional company spokescharacter into the star of a primetime TV show. But the show received overwhelmingly negative critical reaction, and was canceled after only six episodes. It's a clear case of "jumping the shark."

Message: "So easy, a caveman can do it."

3. Kash

Starting in 2008, GEICO has aired a series of TV ads featuring two paper-banded stacks of U.S. bills with a pair of big, buggy eyes on top. Kash, who never says anything, just sits and stares at people (it's intentionally creepy), set to an obnoxious remix of a Rockwell/Michael Jackson song, "Somebody's Watching Me."

Message: "This [stack of cash] is the money you could be saving on your car insurance."

4. Rhetorical Questions

An actor asks the familiar question, "Could switching to GEICO save you 15% or more on car insurance?" He then follows up with a rhetorical question: "Does Charlie Daniels play a mean fiddle?" or "Did The Waltons take way too long to say goodnight?"

Message: "15 minutes could save you 15% or more."

5. Talking Objects

Objects causing damage to people's cars—a pothole, a fire hydrant, and the fender of another car—stumble through feeble apologies.

Message: "Accidents are bad. But GEICO's good, with emergency road service."

6. Motorcycles and Toys

GEICO's division for motorcycles, RVs, and other toys has an entirely different campaign. These ads occasionally feature cameo appearances of the Gecko and Cavemen, but not usually. Most of them are markedly less creative than any of GEICO's other spots.

Message: "You could save with GEICO motorcycle insurance."

But Wait . . . There's More!

There's a multitude of different spots GEICO rolls out every year, and no two campaigns are ever the same.

In 2003, GEICO debuted a campaign called "Good News," featuring ads where one character would break bad news to another, ending with the tagline: "I've got good news! I just saved a bunch of money on my car insurance by switching to GEICO."

In another spot circa 2008, a squirrel causes a car to swerve and crash. The squirrel fist-bumps and high-fives another squirrel. The message: "Accidents can happen anytime. That's why GEICO's here 24 hours a day, every day."

Little Richard, Joan Rivers, Peter Frampton, Don LaFontaine, and James Lipton are among the notable celebrities who spoofed themselves in yet another series of GEICO spots.

The Agency's Rationale

The Martin Agency has given different assignments to multiple creative teams, along with instructions "to tell multiple, distinct narratives that highlight various aspects of the brand."

"Once upon a time, an ad was about a company's unique selling position. But people can now accept more complex brands," Mike Hughes, The Martin Agency's president and creative director explains.

"I thought we might be able to build a deeper relationship if we built on multiple fronts," Hughes told *Fast Company*.

The Martin Agency believes it has found a better way to do branding, perhaps even a new media strategy altogether. The ad shop has since begun rolling out multipronged strategies for a variety of clients including UPS and Walmart.

Reality Check: This strategy is probably not for you. Most marketers have to spend a ton of money just to make one message stick, much less two (or more!). GEICO spends in the neighborhood of $500 million.

Reprinted from The Financial Brand. https://thefinancialbrand.com/9663/geico-gecko-caveman-kash-tv-commercials/

more, in just 15 minutes . . . and it won. GEICO's marketing resonated with consumers, becoming water-cooler talk because people loved the ads.

Not all companies have the budget to create multiple marketing messages, but those that do have followed suit, however not with the success that GEICO has achieved. It takes millions upon millions of dollars to be able to create multiple campaigns and place them on enough platforms to resonate with consumers.

The Goal of Paid Media

An advertising message can create awareness, communicate information about attributes and benefits, develop or change an image or personality, associate a brand with feelings and emotions, create norm groups, and precipitate behavior. At the end of the day, the message should evoke an action, whether that be a new understanding ("now I know something about the product"), a new feeling ("now I like the product or support the product"), or a decision ("now I am going to purchase the product").

Advertising Communication Process

Figure 8.1 shows a basic model of the advertising communication system. Advertising communication always involves a source, message, communication channel, and receiver. (Note that the receiver can also become a source by talking to friends or associates, commonly referred to as word-of-mouth communication.)

• *Source.* The source can be defined as the originator of the message. Several types of sources are used in the context of advertising, especially in sports. For example, Atlanta United's initial marketing campaign when it launched its MLS franchise was all about uniting the community as one team and one family in support of Atlanta United, regardless or one's race, creed, ethnicity, or even sexual orientation. Via the "We Are United" campaign, the team was able to rally a large, incredibly diverse fan base that became truly passionate about the team and led the league in attendance.

• *Message.* The message can be defined as both the content of the message sent and content of the message received. In practice, the message is the actuality of what the receiver of the message has perceived.

• *Media mix channel.* The media, mix channel refers to one or more kinds of media, such as social media, Internet, TV, radio, newspapers, magazines, billboards (Out of Home [also called OOH], both static and LED, and mobile), signage, logo placement (on scoreboards, dasher boards, center ice, race cars, uniforms and apparel, caps, premiums and giveaway items, game programs), virtual signage, point-of-purchase displays, and special events.

• *Receiver.* Receiver commonly refers to the target market for the message, also known as the intended audience. The receivers (or audience), as in the case of any target market, usually share certain demographic, psychographic, or behavioral traits. In the context of sport marketing, these traits may include type of tickets owned (season vs. group vs. individual, for example), zip code, past purchasing history, children in the household, alumni status, demographic segment, and social media history.

Advertising Media for Sport

We have examined the advertising message model and what advertising hopes to accomplish. A sport organization must decide what it wants

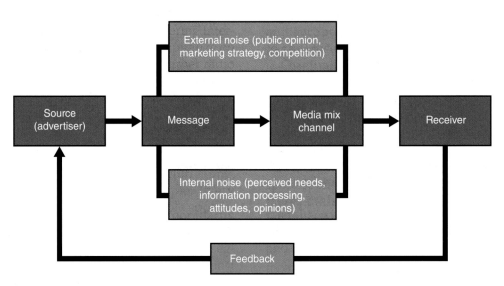

FIGURE 8.1   The advertising communication system.

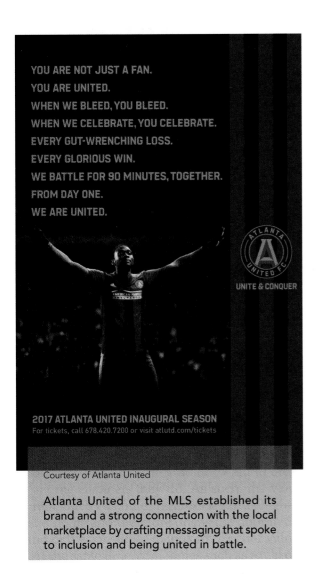

YOU ARE NOT JUST A FAN.
YOU ARE UNITED.
WHEN WE BLEED, YOU BLEED.
WHEN WE CELEBRATE, YOU CELEBRATE.
EVERY GUT-WRENCHING LOSS.
EVERY GLORIOUS WIN.
WE BATTLE FOR 90 MINUTES, TOGETHER.
FROM DAY ONE.
WE ARE UNITED.

UNITE & CONQUER

2017 ATLANTA UNITED INAUGURAL SEASON
For tickets, call 678.420.7200 or visit atlutd.com/tickets

Courtesy of Atlanta United

Atlanta United of the MLS established its brand and a strong connection with the local marketplace by crafting messaging that spoke to inclusion and being united in battle.

to advertise, what message it desires to deliver, which form or forms of media to use to deliver the message, and how much to budget to get the message out to the desired audience. In the following section, we examine the various advertising channels commonly used in sport or unique to sport. Each has its own sets of advantages and disadvantages.

Electronic Media

Electronic media—TV, radio, digital, and social—are the most valuable assets in the marketing mix. TV is the most expensive media, due to the large exposure it offers by reaching massive audiences, as well as the cost to produce a promotional ad. Radio is less expensive but offers a decently sized audience for each ad. However, with both TV and radio, there is no evergreen opportunity, meaning that once the ad runs, it is gone. Of course, there is some possible exposure via someone watching a show or an event that was recorded via DVR.

The newest—and quickly becoming the most valuable—assets are digital and social media. Not only are they the most economically feasible of the media options previously mentioned, but they also

- have the most flexibility in regards to being able to make real-time changes or tweaks to the messaging;
- can be passed on and on and on, thereby stretching the marketing dollar while exposing more potential prospects to messaging;
- allow the message to be of variable lengths, as opposed to being forced into a 15-second, 30-second, or one-minute slot as in TV or radio; and
- allow the message to be evergreen, meaning that people can see the message over and over on social media sites, websites, etc.

Since 2010, brands and sponsors have been moving more of their budget toward social media and digital marketing (see sidebar on the Miami Dolphins). This demand has allowed sport organizations and facilities to charge more for access to their digital and social media channels. In fact, teams have been making large investments on video and audio production so that they can create much or all of the content in-house. For example, many of the teams in NASCAR have built out complete broadcast studios so they can create broadcast quality content for distribution on both social media channels and television. And now, those studios are making ancillary revenue for the teams while they are being asked by sponsors and other organizations to create content.

Signage

Signage creates an impression on the receiver, delivers a marketing message, and hopefully, drives action based on the awareness and feelings of the receiver with regard to the sender. Signage is often measured and valued by the number of impressions it receives. Because of the large amount of clutter (number of advertising

How the Miami Dolphins Became the NFL's Leader in Digital Strategy

Darren Heitner, Founder, Heitner Legal

In 2017, the Dolphins generated over $4 million in new season tickets through leads on Facebook.

In 2016, the NFL's Miami Dolphins decided to completely overhaul their content strategy. In the two years since making this decision, the Dolphins have experienced a 250 percent increase in digital revenue, become the No. 1 NFL franchise in video views, and seen 30 percent of new tickets revenue coming from Facebook lead generation.

I recently spoke with Dolphins president and CEO Tom Garfinkel about why the Dolphins chose to go with a new strategy and how the team accomplished such remarkable results in a short amount of time. Part of the success resulted from shifting away from use of outside agencies and creating all new content in-house.

What was the precursor to the Dolphins deciding to overhaul their content strategy?

Garfinkel had a branding, creative, and sponsorship-marketing background early in his career and recognized the opportunity to do things differently and bring creative and content creation in-house in order to better control the brand aesthetic, storytelling opportunities, and platform creation for revenue growth.

"Technology enabled us to control our own storytelling as well as the distribution, and create platforms that we could measure and sell ourselves," says Garfinkel. "We just needed to build a creative infrastructure to execute a vision of an elegant and simple design aesthetic that was differentiated from other sports teams. We wanted to create content that was unique, behind the scenes, and of the quality of brands we admired, like Nike and Apple."

What specifically influenced the Dolphins in reshaping that strategy?

In his conversations with CEOs and CMOs back in 2013 and 2014, Garfinkel recognized the beginning of a shift of marketing spend away from traditional methods towards more digital and social media platforms.

"I had seen a transition to a more targeted, measurable, and impactful approach," notes Garfinkel. "I wanted to be ahead of the curve and create specific platforms to grow and sell."

What should other NFL teams be taking away from the Dolphins in terms of what to do in order to try to mirror that success?

"Marketers are increasingly less interested in static signage and nonspecific eyeballs," says Garfinkel. "We can now know a lot about who we are reaching, how they are engaging with our brand and the brands that attach themselves to us, and how that engagement drives revenue. The quality and consistency of the content itself is also hugely important to driving that engagement. We generated over $4 million in new season tickets through leads on Facebook, and our digital and social-sponsor revenue is seeing exponential growth—but it's a consequence of an investment in building a creative and data analytics infrastructure. It's not as simple as just hiring a young social-media manager and posting more on Instagram."

What else is the organization currently working on from a business standpoint to be more efficient and productive?

"How we incorporate our NFL and college football business with our international soccer business, concerts, the Miami Open tennis tournament, and now potentially promoting a Formula One race here in Miami," says Garfinkel. "Miami is a curator of culture—art, food, music, sports, fashion—for the rest of the world. We want to build a vehicle for brands to be a part of that in a targeted, measurable way, and monetize the opportunity."

Reprinted by permission from D. Heitner, "How the Miami Dolphins Became the NFL's Leader Digital Strategy," *Inc.*, March 19, 2018. www.inc.com/darren-heitner/how-miami-dolphins-became-nfls-leader-in-digital-strategy.html

messages and impressions) in American (and, for that matter, most of global) society, many messages or impressions are not received because the intended audience has built up an immunity—that is, it has become so accustomed to advertising messages, that they do not stand out.

Due to clutter, companies search for ways to stand out from the crowd. By partnering with a sport team, facility, or league, they can differentiate themselves from other companies in the same industry. It is a way to not only grow brand recognition but also to elevate the brand's status within consumers' minds through their association with the sport team, facility, or event. However, with sponsorship now being so prevalent within sports, companies must find innovative and distinctive ways to stand out among the other sponsors being promoted at games and events.

Once seen as the most important and valuable asset in the marketing mix, signage in totality and static signage, in particular, has certainly diminished in importance. For some companies, signage remains an important asset, but for many others, it has become just a value-add. Most companies with the ability to pay large sums of money for a sponsorship already have high brand recall, so adding another impression via signage has diminishing value when compared to cost to obtain that additional impression.

The value of the signage is based upon the number of impressions, or as it is called in the sport industry, the number of eyeballs. Signage includes electronic or printed messages or logos on any of the following types of materials and media: billboards (fixed—static or digital) or movable (e.g., billboard truck), banners, street-pole banners, scoreboards, dasher boards or rink boards, electronic message boards including digital displays, and posters. Signage also includes impressions such as on-ice and on-field mes-

sages, rotational courtside messages, on-court or on-field logos, and virtual signage (superimposed on blank stadium walls and playing surfaces but visible on the broadcast).

Digital signage, previously known as LED signage, presents moving, changing, dynamic images. Digital signage is a powerful vehicle for market visibility and sponsor recall because people recall motion video messages much better than static ones.[1] With sharper images and brilliant color and motion, digital signage creates the wow factor, which is what facility managers, corporate spokespeople, and game presentation directors aspire to when communicating with their customers. This allows the message to cut through the clutter and resonate with the receiver of the message. While digital signage is an expensive investment for an organization, the ROI makes sense, because digital signage allows the venue, organization, or team to sell advertising based on time, not space, thereby raising more revenue using the same signage footprint. In other words, it allows the organization to charge more for the same sign.

The next evolution in signage is hologram signage. Already being tested in some venues, it is still in its infancy but certainly appears to be the future of signage.[2] Teams have already been testing unique digital hologram and motion video promotion on cell phones via VR codes.[3]

Virtual advertising on broadcasts is made possible by a live video insertion system, or L-VIS, a "proprietary technology that interrupts the broadcast feed and inserts electronic images in real time into any video stream."[4] The tool creates two signage revenue streams—one for those viewing in the arena and one for those watching on the broadcast. For example, a Canadian live audience could be viewing signage for Molson while a U.S. audience in the United States for the same game could be watching virtual signage that converts the image to one for Budweiser.

Logo placement, which is a static logo on the field of play or on a uniform, continues to drive significant revenue for sport teams and facilities. NASCAR has long led the charge of putting sponsor logos all over the race car and on the driver's fire suit and helmet. Other sports have begun to realize the revenue from logo placement. Soccer teams have long had a primary jersey sponsor featured on their uniforms. Golf and tennis players followed suit and began putting sponsor logos on their shirts and bags. The NBA now allows teams to sell a two-inch by two-inch logo patch that can be sewn on players' uniforms. While some suggested that the small patch would never deliver enough value to justify the multi-million dollar–price, companies such as Wish and Rakuten rushed to purchase the opportunity.[5] MLB appears to be falling in line as it was recently announced that MLB teams will be allowed to sell sleeve sponsors.[6] It will be interesting to see if the NFL follows suit any time soon.

In regards to on-field logo placement, European and Central and South American soccer leagues have long placed logos around the field to provide exposure for their sponsors. Originally, a static sign was hung or staked to the ground. Later, digital signage was used. Now, signage is being superimposed for the broadcast. For instance, during the "MLS is Back Tournament," a large Adidas logo was superimposed in the center circle at midfield and league sponsor logos were digitally placed both along the far sideline and behind the end lines. Golf and tennis also superimpose sponsor logos around the field of play during broadcasts.

While some companies pay to sponsor teams in order to see their logo on the team uniform or race car, other companies simply buy the team:

- Red Bull owns New York Red Bull in MLS and FC Red Bull Salzburg in Austria.
- Furniture Row, a large furniture store out of Denver, Colorado, bought a NASCAR race team, as opposed to just sponsoring a team.

Buying a team gives companies complete connection and exposure related to the teams because all of the content related to the team (i.e., game and race footage, social media content, advertising, media coverage, etc.) will feature the company's name and logo. This may be just the tip of the iceberg, and we may see a dramatic rise in the number of corporate-owned teams in the future.

Print Media

Print media is the inclusive term used to refer to newspapers, magazines, brochures, programs, point-of-purchase displays, direct mail pieces, posters, and all other forms of printed collateral. Print media allow the creator to have total control over the messaging and look of the printed piece, while delivering detailed information about the product.

Historically, newspapers and magazines were an obvious choice for where an organization spent its advertising dollars. However, declining subscriber bases, decreasing circulations, and diminishing frequency of printing have made newspapers and magazines less appealing due to their lower ROI. To combat this, many newspapers and magazines are focusing on digital delivery and selling ads across both print and digital platforms:

- Newspaper advertising can be purchased on short notice, placed in multiple sections of the paper (e.g., sports and business, lifestyle, special weekend inserts), and reach a broad distribution on a targeted date.
- Magazine advertising requires more advanced planning for ad purchases because of the infrequent printing, but the high print quality and color reproduction are more appealing to readers.

Posters are also declining in popularity, but they offer a unique advantage—namely, degree of control—because the organization can determine where and when to distribute them. They can also be self-financing, because the sponsoring organization can sell advertising space on the posters to pay for printing and materials. High schools and collegiate athletics programs (and some minor league sport organizations) are likely to use this form of advertising to list team schedules, upcoming promotions, and special events for their various athletics teams. Some teams distribute posters to fans as part of a promotional giveaway or so that fans can get player autographs. Although these forms of promotion can provide sponsor impressions and drive to retail opportunities, the major limitation is that posters are constrained to an immediate area of exposure impact dependent on attraction and flow. In addition, many places that were once available for hanging posters no longer approve of the "clutter" of posters. In fact, some municipalities require a permit to hang posters. Critics might also point out that posters are not green and often contribute to a litter problem.

Posters are often part of a point-of-purchase (POP) promotion—a promotional activity that takes place at the moment of purchase. Retailers have relied for years on POP promotions and must now compete with the Internet for impulse purchases, putting more pressure on the sales environment in their stores and increasing the need for innovative point-of-purchase media, materials, and techniques. For example, a sporting goods store may offer an instant rebate through a couponing activity at the store to encourage the purchase of a particular brand or product, such as athletics footwear, during the customer's visit. POP promotion is often referred to as reminder advertising. Reminder advertising works in several ways. It can enhance the top-of-mind awareness of the brand, thus increasing the probability that the consumer will include the brand on a shopping list or purchase it as an impulse item. Additionally, it can reinforce the key elements of a national advertising campaign at the point of purchase.[7]

Game or event programs, with their photographs, stories, and statistics, promote the organization or event and serve as excellent public relations tools. However, many teams no longer print game programs because of the cost and the fact that patrons do not collect them as they once did. Special events and championship games continue to produce and sell programs due to the collectability and the high price point that such programs can fetch.

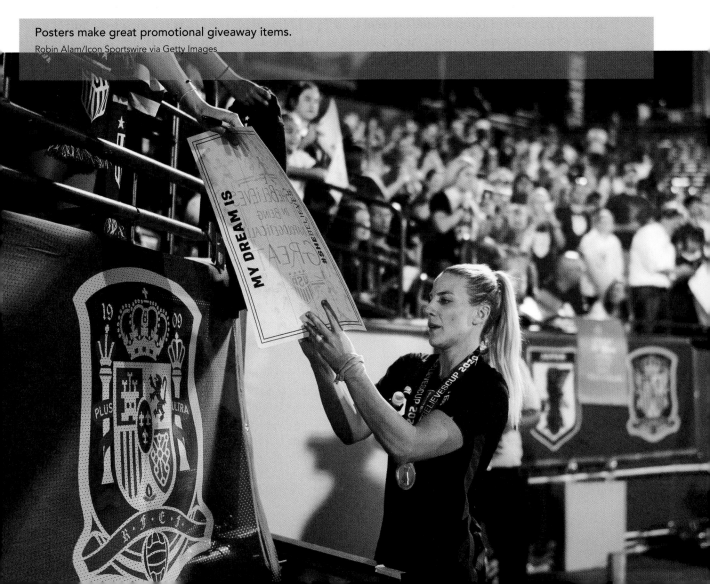

Posters make great promotional giveaway items.
Robin Alam/Icon Sportswire via Getty Images

Pocket schedules, once a key print element for sport teams, have gone the way of game and event programs, too. Many teams are ditching the printed version and instead opting for an app or digital version, as those versions can be changed easily and are more cost effective.

Direct mail advertising allows the organization to minimize spending and maximize efficiency when compared to advertising via other print or electronic media, because the marketing message is received by only those to whom the organization is directing it. Organizations often promote season tickets, mini-plans, group tickets, and single-game tickets through direct mail. Suites and club seats have also been marketed to specific high net-wealth people and companies via high-end, polished direct mail. Sponsorship departments have even used direct mail to solicit new sponsors.

Over the years, the use of direct mail as a marketing and sales tool has decreased due to several factors:

1. The budget to create a direct mail campaign has increased dramatically due to a substantial increase in the price of paper and postage.

2. It is hard to get one's direct mail piece to stand out from all the other items received daily. Direct mail is often seen as "junk mail" and tossed into the recycling bin without having been looked at.

3. It is incredibly difficult to track the effectiveness of a direct mail piece as it relates to sales. Social media and digital marketing allow for tracking each person, from receiving the message, to opening it, to going to a website or social media page, to ultimately purchasing the product.

Despite these limitations, direct mail is having a bit of a resurgence. Because so many companies have moved away from direct mail, there is less clutter to have to cut through. According to the Data & Marketing Association, direct mail achieves a 4.4 percent response rate, which is 10 to 20 times higher than email.[8] If direct mail is personalized to recipients, there is a higher likelihood that they will read it, as opposed to thinking it is "junk mail." This method, as you would expect, is costlier.

Many organizations are using a two-pronged approach, first sending a direct mail piece and then following up with some form of digital or social media inquiry. Of course, this means you must have the target's mailing address and email address or social media address(es).

One common approach in selling tickets is to cultivate leads from credit card purchases of individual game tickets or merchandise and then to develop a direct mail piece to sell those individuals season tickets or a mini-plan. This results in a higher possibility of conversion since this direct piece is targeting an audience that has already demonstrated a familiarity with and interest in the product.

When designing any print materials or, for that matter, e-campaigns, the sport marketer should consider the following guidelines:

- The headline must grab readers' attention immediately and incentivize them to keep reading. This is because most people never read beyond the headline, so the headline and the visual component must complement each other and tell a clear story so that those who look only at the headline and the visual can get the message without having to read a word of the body copy.

- The body copy should be detailed and specific, support the headline, and be readable and interesting. Readers should be able to understand what the offer is, how taking advantage of the offer will benefit them, and what they must do to take advantage of the offer (a call to action).

Research has shown that people recall information better when it is presented both pictorially and verbally, with visuals being recalled more than words.[9] Marketers often want to cram too much information into the marketing piece and use a lot of text to get their message and the information across. However, too much text will lead to disinterest and will cause customers to stop reading. For this reason, sport marketers should use a balanced approach, using carefully designed images to convey their message, with the text to support the images and overall message. A good rule of thumb is to make the message as simple and concise as possible, with just enough information to entice readers to want to try, buy, or learn more about the product. And if more in-depth information is needed, marketers should then direct readers to a website, app, or social media page where they are able to provide it. That way, marketers provide just enough information to get people interested; and if they are, they can get all the information they need to make an informed decision.

Electronic Media

Electronic media include radio; TV; streaming services and podcasts; and in-venue media, such as scoreboards, digital signage (previously discussed), and public address systems. All are critical (along with digital and social media, which are discussed later) for reaching today's consumers, whether they are in the facility or watching or listening at home, in their cars, or accessing broadcasts on computers or mobile devices.

Scoreboards and Digital Signage

While scoreboards and digital signage can represent a significant capital investment, they are low cost in terms of producing messages and can incorporate animation, video, and sound to produce more complete and eye-catching messages. Using scoreboards and digital signage is a cost-effective way of reaching a targeted, captive market that, through its presence in the venue, has demonstrated interest in and ability to purchase the product. Scoreboards and digital signage can perform a variety of functions, including

- making announcements;
- providing advertising messages for corporate partners;
- providing information about upcoming games or other events at the venue, special events, and promotional activities; and
- doing simple things like recognizing groups in attendance.

Radio

Radio provides an audio advertising message that can be powerful and relatively inexpensive when compared to other in-broadcast or in-event advertising. Teams themselves often sell advertisements on their local radio broadcasts to sponsors that cannot afford more expensive sponsorship assets or as part of larger, more encompassing sponsorship packages. In addition, teams often create ancillary programming, such as coaches' shows, which are on throughout the week and offer additional opportunities to sell advertising within.

Radio plays to the imagination and lets us hear the message while letting our minds create a picture that may be based on memories, hopeful expectations, or, perhaps, just wishful thinking. Because each radio station (and format type) has its own audience, sport organizations can choose a format that is compatible with their target market.

In an ethnically diverse country such as the United States, radio permits sport organizations to offer broadcast and advertising opportunities in languages other than English. Many teams provide broadcasts in both English and Spanish, while a few teams broadcast in other languages, such as Korean or Japanese, depending on their fan demographics. Broadcasting in Spanish or other languages will continue to become a best practice as the population of non-native English speakers continues to grow.

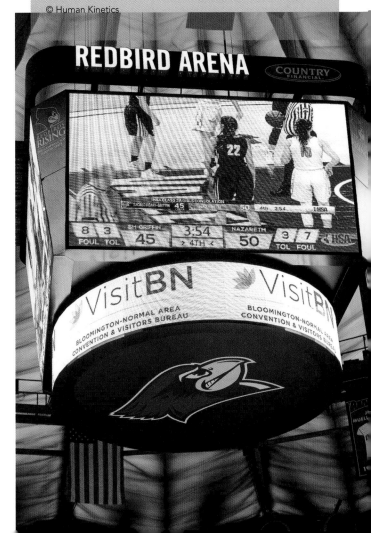

Scoreboards are a cost-effective way to reach a captive audience.

© Human Kinetics

Over-the-air (OTA) radio, sometimes called terrestrial radio, like many other forms of media, has encountered challenges from new competitors in the industry, specifically satellite radio and streaming, causing an overall decline in listenership. Fortunately, sports is destination programming, meaning that the games are of high priority for the listeners, so they make sure to listen during the scheduled time. In effect, this helps mitigate the listenership decline somewhat.

Satellite radio is a subscription-based radio service that delivers commercial-free programming. As this offering has grown in terms of adoption by the general public, the price has decreased, which has, in turn, driven more subscription purchases. SiriusXM offers hundreds of channels, with everything from music to talk shows to comedy. Many leagues and teams have invested in their own channels, which allows them to control the format (talk shows; games, matches, or races; coaches' shows; etc.), as well as receive a portion of the subscription revenue. Some are doing this to supplement their OTA radio distribution efforts, while others have moved all their programming to satellite radio.

Streaming, sometimes known as Internet radio, involves streaming media over the Internet, presenting listeners with a continuous stream of audio. Internet radio is distinct from podcasting, which involves downloading rather than streaming. Originally, streaming was an innovative and inexpensive way for content distribution. It allowed for just about anyone to be able to be a DJ or talk show host. However, as streaming increased in popularity and OTA radio listenership declined, radio stations began offering Internet radio and streaming options to capitalize on the revenue opportunities. Many Internet radio services are associated with a corresponding traditional (OTA) radio station or radio network. Internet-only radio stations are independent of such associations. Most of it is offered as free content that is found in various national (e.g., ESPN) and local (e.g., The Fan family) stations.

Podcasts

Podcasts have seen a meteoric rise in popularity since 2010. Originally subscription-based, episodic series, podcasts were a very narrow segment of the radio or streaming market and most focused on sport or politics. However, with the growth of satellite radio and subscription-based streaming services, podcasts have gained popularity with millions of listeners and viewers. Podcasts now cover just about any topic and most are available for free via Internet streaming. The benefit of being able to listen (or watch) at your convenience (on demand) and on just about any device (such as your phone, tablet, or laptop) has allowed podcasts to become incredibly popular, with some having millions of fans. The majority are in audio form, but the most popular often add video to the offering. In fact, some podcasts are so popular, streaming services, such as Spotify, are paying large sums to secure podcasts with large followings.[10] Podcasts also afford the creator an opportunity to generate revenue from sponsors via sponsor and product integration, sweepstakes, contests, etc.

Television

Although radio has its benefits as compared with television—most notably, cost—nothing rivals television in advertising reach and the ability to convey to a mass audience the attributes of an advertiser's product or service.

Television started out as an over-the-air signal with three national networks (ABC, CBS, and NBC) and the Public Broadcast System (PBS), all of which were broadcast only within the United States. Now, hundreds of highly segmented channels from all over the world are offered via satellite and cable to go along with the major networks. While the major national networks still provide the largest viewership, the cost to advertise on those channels is significant. The segmented channels allow for a more focused audience at a much lower price for those wishing to advertise to specific demos.

Originally, if you wanted to promote your brand to sports fans on television, you bought ads within sports events and sports games on the over-the-air networks. With the birth of ESPN and its 24/7 sport programming, advertisers could target sports fans anytime, both in-game and in-news. Seeing the insatiable appetite for sport-related content, NBA launched its own network, the first sport league to do so. Since then, it has been joined by the NFL, MLB, the Olympic Games, the NCAA and several of its conferences and universities, NHL, MLS, and others.

Television reaches the greatest number of people, yet ratings for most shows have been declining. This is due to several factors, including an overabundance of program offerings, ability for on-demand viewing, and non-broadcast content (e.g., YouTube, gaming, etc.). Viewers' desire to watch what they want—when they want and how they want—has challenged networks, but it has also provided more opportunities to interact with viewers in unique ways and to create new revenue streams. For example, viewers use smart TVs, along with second and third screens (smartphones and tablets) while they are watching television. Thus, networks have been afforded the opportunity to create new revenue streams for sponsors and advertisers via the creation of additional content. In-broadcast messaging drives viewers to go to these websites and social media platforms during the broadcast, or even after the broadcast, to get behind-the-scenes content, interact with the athletes and coaches, and enter contests and sweepstakes. This provides sponsors and advertisers direct interaction with viewers to further promote the brand.

The biggest trend over the past few years is the cord-cutting and growth of OTT (over-the-top) media. Cable and satellite companies bundle their channel offerings into different packages for consumers. In doing that, they force customers to purchase channels they do not want in order to get the channels they do. As such, the value or ROI that a customer receives is not as high as it should be and therefore opens the door in the mind of the consumer to look for a better value.

At the same time, companies such as Amazon, Netflix, YouTube, and iTunes, began offering access to movies and shows via their platforms. They even offered OTA network shows the next day after the shows had premiered. In addition, some companies began creating their own original programming. This on-demand content allowed people to watch what they wanted, whenever they wanted, at a much-reduced price compared to cable and satellite. Millennials and Gen Zers quickly adopted this new style of viewership, followed by Gen Xers and even many Baby Boomers.

There are also some new OTT streaming services that show live sports. Amazon, YouTube, Facebook, and others are not only showing live sports but also bidding on the broadcast rights for leagues and teams. This is a great revenue opportunity for the leagues and teams and also creates new opportunities for sport organizations to find new and creative ways to incorporate their sponsors and generate revenue from them.

Some leagues and teams are also looking to create ancillary programming to promote their brands via OTT.

Sports events are typically immune to such viewership declines because they are appointment television, meaning people put the event on their schedule and make it a point to watch it live. As such, viewership tends to be higher, allowing networks, leagues, and teams to charge more for ad spots.

Obviously, premier sports events and their ability to generate a large, live audience are important as promotional advertising vehicles for corporations and businesses wanting to use sports to achieve their marketing objectives and ultimately sell their products or services. Due to the cost related to advertising during these big events being out of reach for most companies, typically Fortune 100 companies are the ones that can afford to advertise during such events.

TV ads integrate audio and visual elements to elicit emotions and actions on the part of the receiver of the ad. It is the creator's job to craft the message so that the receiver understands it and acts accordingly. The creator can use one or more of the following approaches to accomplish this goal:[11]

- *Story line.* Telling a story. The message has a beginning, middle, and end.
- *Problem and solution.* Presenting the viewer with a problem to be solved. The sponsor's product is presented as the solution to that problem.
- *Chronology.* Delivering the message through a series of related scenes. Facts and events are presented sequentially as they occurred.
- *Special effects.* Achieving memorability. Some kind of striking device, such as an unusual musical sound or pictorial technique, can be used.
- *Testimonial.* Advertising by word of mouth. A well-known figure is often used but could even be an unknown person in the street, who vouches for the value of the product.
- *Satire.* Using sophisticated wit to point out human foibles. This form is generally produced in an exaggerated style, often a parody.

The Big Trends in Sports Broadcasting for 2019

A 2019 blog post on Interxion predicted some over-the-top (OTT) media services trends for the coming year. Though written in the past, those predictions are still very relevant today. OTT is still in a growth phase as teams and leagues look for new ways to deliver content to their fans while raising revenue. Here are those predictions.

Keep an Eye on the Platforms

Large tech platforms, such as Amazon and Facebook, will compete for rights to the most popular sports and sporting events. Amazon has secured ATP World Tour Tennis and Premiere League rights, and Facebook won La Liga rights for India. Platforms will also expand the direct to consumer (D2C) delivery approaches. "Rather than going through traditional broadcasters to get in front of consumers, platforms will distribute digital media directly to consumers through streaming services."

Focus on Latency

Currently, broadcast feeds arrive "tens of seconds before online feeds, which is becoming a greater problem as online streaming continues to grow in popularity." Solving latency issues will be a focus for digital media companies, many of which claim to have a solution.

Chasing the Pirates

In 2018, data revealed "nearly five million illegal streamers during the UEFA Champions League knockout stages before the final in May. Digital media companies are becoming increasingly aware of piracy threats as more viewers turn to online streaming over traditional broadcast, particularly when it comes to sports."

Expect to see active discussions between leagues, content owners, distributors, and content protection technology companies as they explore how to maintain the value of sports content by combatting piracy threats.

Source: Interxion, *The Big Trends in Sports Broadcasting for 2019*, January 9, 2019. www.interxion.com/us/blogs/2019/01/the-big-trends-in-sports-broadcasting-for-2019

- *Spokesperson.* Using an on-camera announcer who attempts to persuade the sell. A personal and intimate approach or perhaps the hard sell can be used.

- *Demonstration.* Using some sort of physical apparatus or experiential element. These help to demonstrate the product's effectiveness, value, and appeal.

- *Suspense.* Telling a story, as with the story-line approach. In this approach, a high level of drama is incorporated into the buildup of curiosity and suspense until the ending.

- *Slice-of-life.* Beginning with a person needing to make a decision or in a situation requiring a solution. This approach then shows how the solution has worked.

- *Analogy.* Instead of presenting a direct message about the product, the message is conveyed through a comparison with something else.

- *Fantasy.* Using caricatures or special effects. This creates fantasy surrounding the product and product use.

- *Personality.* Relying on an actor rather than an announcer to deliver the message. The actor plays a character who talks about the product, reacts to its use, or demonstrates its use or enjoyment.

Out-of-Home Advertising

Out-of-home (OOH) advertising is a term that encompasses those forms of advertising that are out in the public space and includes advertising such as fixed billboards, mobile billboards, and other highly visible message systems. Price varies according to location, the number of impressions, the number of placements, and the length of the agreement, but this form of advertising can be relatively inexpensive compared with other kinds of advertising like television.

Fixed billboards are most often placed along highly traveled roadways and highways and are priced based upon their location and the number of people who pass by them on a daily basis. Most billboards are static, meaning the message does not change. The message is usually printed on vinyl and attached to the fixed billboard, but sometimes is painted. Most billboards are rectangular in shape, but occasionally, the advertiser will build an addition to the billboard, in order to make it unique and stand out from the other billboards in the area. This is called a spectacular.

Static billboards display only one message, and the advertiser pays for that exclusivity.

A current trend in billboards is the digital, or LED, billboard. This lighted billboard attracts more attention because the images are brighter and sharper. These billboards allow for multiple messages to be distributed by way of the billboard's ability to rotate one ad to the next. This means that the owner of the board can generate more revenue by selling to several companies and it affords a more economical opportunity for advertisers that share the billboard's price with other organizations. Another differentiator from static billboards is that the advertising message can be changed when and as needed, due to the fact that it is a digital message, as opposed to a printed message. This is very advantageous for sport organizations since they can change the message day-by-day or game-by-game.

Mobile billboards, which are often much less expensive than static billboards, are "rolling" advertisements on trucks or other vehicles. Originally, the signs were printed on vinyl and then mounted on trailers that were pulled by a truck. Now, most are LED boards on the sides of panel trucks, buses, cars, or even golf carts. They are strategically driven through the marketplace in order to hit certain high-traffic areas at the

The Goodyear blimp is a classic example of OOH advertising.

Adam Lacy/Icon Sportswire via Getty Images

appropriate times and particular areas that may have a specific target demo. Mobile billboards are also commonplace at large special events, such as festivals, all-star games, and college conference championships.

Other OOH forms of billboards include blimps and planes pulling advertising banners. Companies, such as Goodyear, Met Life, and Direct TV, use blimps that travel to sports events and other large gatherings. These bigger-than-life advertising platforms are expensive but garner much sought-after attention for the brand displayed on the side of the blimp, since they receive free logo exposure not only to the fans at the event but also to the millions watching the broadcast. Newer blimps have attached digital signage boards on their sides to deliver more detailed messaging as opposed to just a company's logo. Many sport organizations have incorporated miniature blimps into their game presentation. These sponsored blimps are flown around the facility and drop prizes or coupons to the fans. The sponsor receives not only their logo on the blimp and on the prizes that are given away but also exposure on the videoboards and via PA during the promotion.

Promotional Concepts and Practices

The remainder of this chapter deals with promotional practices and concepts in the sport industry. Some of the greatest promotions in American history involved sport and entertainment activities. P. T. Barnum, Albert Spalding, C. C. Pyle, Tex Rickard, Abe Saperstein, Rube Foster, J. W. Wilkinson, Ned Irish, Bill Veeck, Charlie Finley, Walt Disney, Evel Knievel, Don King, Humpy Wheeler, Vince McMahon, Jerry Jones, Mark Cuban, and Dana White, are just a few of the imaginative minds that sought to promote products (or themselves) in visionary ways.

Major Event

Once called a hallmark event, a major event is a large, one-time or annual event for crowning a champion or showcasing special athletic competition. These events are managed by leagues or sports federations and are often held at neutral locations (as opposed to at the location of one of the teams participating in the event). Examples of major events include the NFL's Super Bowl, MLB's World Series, the Olympic Games, the World Cup, and X-Games.

Major events typically raise more revenue than a regular games or events, due to higher ticket and sponsorship prices and even broadcast revenue. Only the largest companies are capable of affording the rights fees to sponsor these events.

Major events also drive significant economic impact to the community in which they are held, so much so that communities are willing to put forth millions of dollars just for the chance to bid on the event. They even build facilities in which to host the events at the cost of hundreds of millions to billions of dollars. This has led to some corruption in the bidding process for major events like the World Cup, with millions of dollars being paid in bribes for votes for the 2018 and 2022 World Cups in Russia and Qatar, respectively.

Exhibition Games

Many leagues and teams desire to grow their brand beyond the local communities in which they play. As far back as the early 1900s, soccer teams from across the globe have gone on preseason tours, mostly to get their players ready for the upcoming season, but also in the hope of creating new fans. Today, teams are paid millions of dollars by promoters to travel during the off-season to participate in exhibition matches and tournaments. While the money is important to organizations, if done correctly, they garner even more by making lifelong fans of the teams who purchase team merchandise and pay for content.

Leagues like the NBA, NFL, MLB, NHL and MLS have played exhibition games and regular-season games in countries in Europe, Central America, South America, and even Asia. Other leagues, like LaLiga, are working to host actual league games in the United States in order to grow and promote the league within the country. Even college teams are touring other countries to promote their schools and play exhibition games.

These tours and exhibition games not only promote the brand and create fans but also give the teams and leagues an opportunity to find new sponsors. Since the games and tours are outside

Mark Cuban Changed the Game

I (the chapter author) was attending Lamar Hunt's funeral and happened to sit next to Don and Linda Carter, the former owners of the Dallas Mavericks. After sharing stories about what an incredible man and sports entrepreneur Lamar was, we began talking about Don's investment in the Mavericks. He quickly told me that while he loved owning the team, he never would have bought it if it weren't for his wife Linda. She was the one who loved basketball: the fluid play, the fundamentals, the Xs and Os, the incredible athleticism, and the beauty of the game itself.

They had sold the team a few years prior to Mark Cuban taking the reins. He, too, loved the sport of basketball and was among a group of young progressive billionaires who made their money in the new digital world.

Linda liked Mark, but she did not favor the way the focus had shifted away from basketball to entertainment. She felt the game got lost with everything else that was going on.

It got me thinking about how sports was evolving and what Mark was doing that was so different. Most teams planned their game presentation to include certain promotions during time-outs, between periods, or at half-time. But Mark was different: He looked at the event holistically, basically taking the fans on a journey from before tip-off to the time they walked out of the arena.

First and foremost, Mark made a commitment to winning, both on and off the court. His first step was to make the organization a place where players wanted to come to play. He built a new arena, complete with a world-class practice facility, and even put gaming systems into each locker so that players would have a place to chill out. He paid for better players and better coaches.

Mark also understood that sports fans were wanting more than to just watch basketball—they were coming to be entertained. Because he was also in the entertainment business and not just the sport business, he began to focus more on the game presentation. He rebranded the Mavs Dancers to be a provocative dance company, one that wore very revealing uniforms and danced evocatively to newer music. Mark also introduced dance troupes into the presentation, including an all-female company who, disguised as elderly women, would walk out with canes, dressed in housecoats, only to rip them off to expose skimpy outfits and dance to hip-hop. He also provided audiences with the ManiACCs, a dance troupe that featured large and overweight men and the Mavs Band, a drum line and band that played throughout the game.

Mark was always wanting to promote the fact that he had US$5 tickets available, so he held a small number of tickets in the upper deck and sold them day-of-game only. However, in order to be able to purchase those specially priced seats, fans were required to dress up, paint their faces, and stand in line at the box office because the tickets were first come, first served.

Mark made each game an event. There was never a moment of downtime: Each stoppage of play was filled with something to keep fans entertained. The purpose was to have them leave feeling happy and believing they got their money's worth, regardless if the team won or lost.

Mark changed the game, or at least the game presentation. And as Linda told me, "While I appreciate the purity of the sport of basketball and do not like things that take away from the game itself, I appreciate what Mark has done to elevate the fan experience. Sports entertainment had, has, and will continue to evolve . . . for the fans."

Note: This story was long before the #MeToo movement that has led to the elimination of the Mavs Dancers, the ManiACCs, and other controversial game presentation elements. The Mavericks are in the process of revamping all of their game presentation again in an effort to be more inclusive and self-aware of the current climate in our culture.

Alex Trautwig/MLB via Getty Images

Playing an exhibition game in Tokyo, Japan, helps the Seattle Mariners create a global appeal.

the normal marketing territory of the team or league (e.g., the United States), they are able to source sponsors for the tour specifically but also for the territory in which they are playing games. A team might have an exclusive sponsor in the soft drink category for its local territory. However, for the tour to another country, it could go with a competitor from the same territory or find a soft drink company from the territory to which the team is traveling. Some sport organizations have been able to parlay those deals into year-round sponsorship deals. For example, a soccer team may have Miller Lite as its exclusive beer sponsor but could conceivably have Budweiser sponsor its tour to Asia. Or, the team could sell Sapporo Beer for the tour or exhibition game and then designate Sapporo as its official beer for the team in Asia.

Content and Access

Thanks to the growth of social media and digital platforms, fans have been afforded unfettered access to their favorite teams. In the past, the content that was distributed by the team, centered around the games the teams played and the players' stats.

NBC was the first to tell the story of the Olympic Games by reporting the stories of the athletes who were competing. In doing this, viewers became vested in the athletes and the sport in which they competed.

Teams realized that fans want this same content. They wish to feel as if they are a part of the "family." They desire to really know the players—what motivates them, what their daily lives are like, and what it takes to play at the level they do. And, by consuming that content, fans become more attached to the organization, which leads to more investment via the purchase of tickets, merchandise, etc.

The growth of social media and digital marketing allows teams to feed that desire for information in a very easy and inexpensive way. Websites, chat rooms, blogs, vlogs, social media platforms, online fantasy leagues, and even online gambling sites have met and continue to fulfill those needs and at the same time serve as promotional vehicles, providing a content-focused, user-friendly environment that consumers can access at their convenience and manage to fit their needs.

Content creation has become one of the most powerful promotional mechanisms in the marketing toolbox for sport organization. It not only gives your current fans access, creating even stronger bonds, but also promotes the brand globally and creates new fans of the team. The fact that the team is not in one's local community no longer matters because people now can follow teams on the other side of the globe.

Content marketing does not have to be done by the team or the league alone. Anyone with a computer or a smartphone can create content, or at least forward the content created by the team. Consequently, social media and digital platforms promote the organization and the players to millions of people across the world at virtually no cost.

Sales Promotions

Sales promotions, which can take the form of price-oriented or non-price-oriented tactics, are an essential part of the marketing strategy of any sport organization and are used to incentivize non-fans and light user fans to try the product, usually through the purchase of a ticket package for a game or an event. Fans decide to attend a game based on several reasons:

- Whom the team is playing against
- The cost of the ticket
- The date of the game
- How the team is playing
- What the promotion is for at that game

If a promotion does nothing more than entice people to attend one game instead of another, then it is not effective. This pattern indicates that fans are cherry picking—attending games only when a promotion or an incentive is offered to choose a particular game. When cherry picking occurs, the value of a sales promotion is minimal unless someone other than the sport organization sponsors the promotional item or offer. And the perceived value of all tickets, regardless of whether it is part of a promotion or not, can decline in fans' minds, which makes it more difficult to sell regularly priced tickets in the future, which can lead to lower attendance.

Promotion Planning

Sport organizations typically create a season-long promotions plan in advance so that they can manage both the budget and the plan holistically. The first decision they must make is to determine what they wish to accomplish from the overall plan as well as from each promotion:

- Is the promotion's goal to bring in more new fans?
- Is the promotion's goal to promote a team sponsor to a target market?

- Is the promotion's goal to give your best fans a value-ad that then creates more affinity?

The answers to these questions often depend on how well the team is doing attendance-wise. Teams who sell out most or all of their games are not as in need of promotions as those who are in need of driving ticket sales for certain games. Of course, those organizations may still need an avenue to expose their sponsors to the fans in unique ways, so they may still use a promotion.

Timing is another key element in the planning of promotions for sport organizations. The concept of timing includes day of the week, opponent, starting time, and month of the year (sometimes referred to as time of the season). The sport marketer must determine whether a promotion should be scheduled against a better or a weaker draw. A better draw might be defined by a weekend date versus a weekday date, an opponent with a strong tradition of attracting a crowd away from home (e.g., Dallas Cowboys, Los Angeles Lakers, New York Yankees, Toronto Maple Leafs, LAFC), or an opponent with a much talked-about player (e.g., Steph Curry of the Golden State Warriors) who attracts significant media attention and social media buzz.

Sport organizations must determine what is most important to them. Is ensuring that an anticipated sellout actually sells out more paramount than generating higher attendance for games that have no chance of selling out? The answer will differ depending on which organization is asked. Teams often look at their schedule and designate games as A-level, B-level, and C-level, with A-level designated as the best games that will have the highest attendance (e.g., weeknight or weekend games played against well-known opponents), B-level classified as games that will have decent but not great attendance (e.g., weekend games played against team that are not incredibly popular or weeknight games played against popular opponents), and C-level considered as "dog" that are certain to have lower attendance (e.g., weeknight games played against unpopular teams).

The questions are, then:

- Do you create a promotion for an A-level game to ensure that you sell out?

- Do you create a promotion for a B-level game to increase your attendance and maybe sell out?
- Do you create a promotion for a C-level game to try to increase attendance, and thereby turn it into a B-level game?

Once those decisions are made, the team must decide what promotion should be implemented when and how much budget will be put toward it. Of course, the budget must include the cost of the promotion itself, as well as the cost of marketing the promotion to the marketplace.

Price-Oriented Promotions

Price-oriented promotions involve discounts, rebates, special prices, or other financial incentives in relation to the product or service purchased. They can also include other value-added benefits, such as all-you-can-eat packages. Price promotions are used to give selected target markets the opportunity to sample the product with less investment, subsequently mitigating the issue of risk vs. reward in the consumer's mind. The hope is that with the lower price, people will be more willing to give the product a try. A negative effect of a price-based promotion is a traditionally lower attendance for the event immediately following a promotion.

Although research suggests that many fans are attracted to price discounts, price promotions can backfire on a sport organization. Secondary ticket market brokers, such as StubHub and SeatGeek, watch for these sales promotions and purchase a large number of them, then break out the ticket packages (tickets, parking, etc.) to sell individually at a price closer to retail. In this scenario, the organization may sell a ton of promotional packages, but the fan does not realize the benefits that have been carefully put together to drive affinity. The sport organization does not realize the total revenue, and the fan does not really become more attached to the team. As the secondary ticket market becomes the go-to place to purchase tickets for sports fans (basically turning into the primary market), it is becoming even more important for sport organizations to find creative ways to create sales promotions that give extra value to the fan while not being manipulated by the ticket brokers and not upsetting their most loyal fans.

Non-Price Promotions

Non-price promotions include special events or opportunities, such as fireworks or concerts, giveaway items, and other tangible incentives. These promotions not only target non-fans and hopefully entice them to come to a game but also provide current fans, who are already vested in the team via the purchase of season tickets or mini-plans, a value-ad experience or item. However, unless a sponsor pays for the promotion, which is always the hope, non-price promotions involve higher risk because the team has to pay for the event or items regardless of their success.

The late Bill Veeck (see the chapter 1 sidebar, Bill Veeck: Sport Marketing's Foremost Prophet), owner of the Cleveland Indians, St. Louis Browns, and Chicago White Sox (twice), was the master of the non-price promotion. Veeck, who was the originator of bat day, recognized the importance of attracting new fans by implementing special theme days, such as ladies' days and A-student days. Veeck used fireworks, had roving entertainers, gave away orchids and other premiums, and practiced a promotional philosophy that said, "Every day was Mardi Gras and every fan was king [or queen]."[12] He recognized the need to market something other than the core product, realizing that an organization cannot always field a winning team but must provide an entertaining atmosphere every day. Thus, he pioneered non-price promotions in sport to placate fans whose team might not be winning and keep them interested in coming out to the park. This idea of promoting something other than the core product is a key to group sales, which are often composed of as many non-sports fans as sports fans.

A perceived problem with giveaway days is that, depending on the premium item or promotional concept (e.g., dollar dog night), it may hinder merchandise or concession sales. The marketer must attempt to measure how much revenue these giveaways generate versus how much they possibly eliminate. Most sport organizations contract out their merchandise sales and their concession and catering. Teams usually receive a lump sum payment from the merchandise and catering companies, as well as a percentage of sales. The partnership is based upon the opportunity for the merchandise or catering company to generate most to all of the revenue in those areas of the business. Any promotion that gives fans a freebie or a discount can affect sales revenue, so it is vitally important that the merchandise and/or catering partner is involved in the creation of any promotions plan.

The partnership must find creative ways to implement promotions that drive attendance since that is in the best interest for everyone involved: The more fans in the stands, the greater the opportunity is to sell more merchandise and concessions. For instance, a T-shirt giveaway promotion could involve printing a T-shirt that does not resemble anything available for sale at the team store in the stadium, so the merchandiser still has a chance to sell something different to fans. In fact, promotions that involve items that cannot be purchased, such as bobbleheads in baseball, drive the greatest sales without affecting the ability for the merchandiser or concessionaire to make their necessary margins.

In baseball, the "all-you-can-eat" ticket promotion is very popular, but the rising costs of food means that the concession company is taking a big risk by allowing that promotion to take place. While the team pays the concessionaire a portion of the proceeds from the ticket package, this normally does not cover the revenue that the team would have made if it had sold the same amount of food and drink to those fans. And, of course, the team will not realize any other revenue from those package buyers, as their food and drink needs are met through the promotion.

Loyal Fans

Sales promotions are, as the name implies, a promotion to generate sales. In order to be successful, the promotion must be advertised to the general public, or at least to a targeted segment of the community. Being public facing, the promotions have the chance to be seen by many people, including those fans who pay regular price. In doing so, it has the potential to upset the best fans who are often season-ticket holders. Organizations could potentially lose their season-ticket holders for the possibility of making a discounted-price sale.

Loyal fans should receive something comparable with the discount or item featured in the promotion. Organizations must proactively address these groups by communicating that the team is developing and offering special promotions and discounts during the upcoming season in order to grow the fan base; fill the facility on certain nights; or ensure that every fan, regardless of household income or size, has an opportunity to attend a game. In addition, if a giveaway is within the promotion, each loyal fan should receive one as well (something that most teams now do). For example, if the promotion comes with an autographed jersey, then the team would purchase extras for each current account holder in addition to the ones purchased for the promotion. Other teams are offering up a designated credit to fans that can be used during the season for merchandise, concessions, or even more tickets. These approaches serve to not only minimize the number of potential complaints but also create a reservoir of goodwill among season-ticket holders, who can now be ambassadors and spread the word regarding how the organization has treated them.

Promotional Components

The proper way to use sales promotion is to design and orchestrate balanced and creative sales promotional activities. An effective promotional campaign consists of the right type of activities, is conducted at the appropriate time, and appeals to the proper target market.[13] In this section, we briefly describe and give examples of some program activities.

Theme

In developing the theme or creative component, the marketer needs to ask and answer a series of questions to develop an effective strategy. Although innovative strategy development may seem like a function of advertising rather than promotional selling, promotional planning should address this issue annually.

Effective marketing themes should be concise and easily understood. For example, the iconic Nike theme "Just Do It" is short, simple, and certainly comprehensible (yet can mean different things to different people). By purchasing Nike shoes, consumers can do whatever activity they choose, or perhaps do none at all and just make a fashion statement or simply have comfortable shoes. "Just Do It" does not suggest the value of any sport, activity, or even athlete over another. The message emphasizes participation, without

Questions to Ask When Creating a Promotion or Theme

What is the goal of our promotion or theme?
- To obtain new customers and get them to sample the product?
- To get current customers to increase their spend?

Who is our target audience?
- What are their demos?
- What are their values?
- What motivates them take action/purchase?

Do they want or need our product?
- How does our product satisfy their needs/wants?

What elements should be involved in the promotion or theme, and how do we make it unique and memorable?
- Discount?
- Giveaway?
- Experiential opportunity?
- What have our competitors done or are doing?
- What budget do we have to both create and market the promotion or theme?

How do we market the promotion or theme?
- Direct mail?
- Social media?
- Email?
- Radio?
- TV?

How do we measure the success of the promotion or theme?
- What does success look like?
- What data do we need/want from promotion or theme to determine if it is a success?
- What determines our decision to repeat the promotion or theme again in the future or not?

Based on Profitworks, *Good Marketing Questions to Ask for Explosive Sales and Profits.* https://profitworks.ca/blog/281-good-marketing-questions-to-ask

implying serious competition or belittling low-key recreational activity. Consumers choose whatever they wish to do by engaging in something personally meaningful and rewarding.

One important thing to keep in mind when selecting a theme for a promotion is to ensure that the theme cannot be turned against the organization in a negative way. Several teams have used a creative theme that implied some level of positive performance. Although such themes didn't directly promote winning performance, the perception and implicit meaning of a theme such as "We Will" can be easily manipulated, particularly in the realm of social media, which has far fewer restrictions than traditional media forms. For example, we might see such variations as "We will not meet your expectations," "We will not make the playoffs," or even "We will not be worth the price of admission."

Sport organizations must look at any promotion from as many different angles and viewpoints as possible to ensure that no group or segment could be offended. It is better to be ultrasensitive and not use a certain promotional message if it could be perceived as tone-deaf by the marketplace. An example of being safe, rather than sorry, was the Dallas Burn (now FC Dallas) of MLS. In year three, the marketing team considered a tagline of "Shoot to Thrill." The team was an exciting team to watch, scoring many goals. The idea for the tagline was that by scoring (shooting) goals, the team was thrilling the crowd. The tagline was simple, clear, and easy to understand. However, after much discussions and passing it by a few select fans and community leaders, the Burn passed on the potential marketing tagline. For some, the word "shoot" conjured images of gun violence. And with the team playing at the Cotton Bowl in Fair Park (the area of Dallas with the highest crime rate), it was easy to make the connection between the word "shoot" and violence, as opposed to shooting the ball toward the goal. For a team still trying to find its place in the local sport marketplace, such a slip could have caused issues that could affect ticket sales and the team's ability to build a fan base. Needless to say, "Shoot to Thrill" did not see the light of day.

Product Sampling

An effective method for introducing new products and encouraging trial and purchase is to distribute samples to the public. The beauty of product sampling is the lack of risk to the customer and the opportunity for the manufacturer or supplier to put the product in the hands of a prospect. When no charge is involved (except maybe shipping and handling), people will often give new products a try. When combined with couponing (discussed later), sampling can be effective in driving sales and providing a direct ROI or ROO.

For energy drink companies, such as Monster Energy, Red Bull, and Rockstar, sampling is at the core of their marketing strategy. Brand ambassadors, walking around in branded clothing and driving logo-wrapped vehicles, hand out full-sized samples of their product to fans and attendees at sports events, concerts, festivals, etc. While these companies are sponsors of some events, they also are ambush marketers at events for which they are not paying a sponsorship fee.

Open House

An open house is similar to a free trial offered in product sampling but is geared toward attracting an audience to a facility such as a professional or collegiate sport venue. Open houses give fans and potential fans a peek behind the curtain at what happens during a game. The day's activities might include a guided tour of the locker room, a meeting with former or current players, interaction with the mascot and dance team, an opportunity to participate in a basketball clinic or take batting practice, and an opportunity to assess the seating inventory and ticket plans available for the upcoming season. The sale of ticket packages would be promoted at that time.

Digital Couponing

Coupons, vouchers, and discount codes had long been popular and accepted promotional strategies for getting people to both sample and purchase a company's product or service. Now, in the digital age, the vast majority of coupons are delivered directly to smartphones. Coupons are useful for driving sampling and purchase, but they must be appropriate to the image and style of the organization. In some cases, couponing or discount codes may cheapen the organization's image and possibly suggest desperation to generate sales, particularly if the organization has no history of offering coupons or discount codes.

Coupons give the holder some form of discount on a product or service. Printed coupons typically show the store or organization name, the offer or discount, and the expiration date. Users present the coupon at the time of purchase. Most modern coupons are digital coupons, and sport teams deliver many of their price promotions this way. Digital coupons are advantageous to printed coupons because of their ease of use and the ability for the provider to make changes easily and in real time.

Here's an example of how digital coupons work. A ticket buyer purchases the "Family 4-Pack," which contains four tickets, four soft drinks, and four hot dogs (or other concessions item). The normal purchase price for this package, if purchased individually, is US$120. However, the promotion is priced at US$99. The team sends the buyer an email that contains a barcode. The buyer and his family arrive at the stadium and show their smartphone with the barcodes for access into the facility. In addition, the buyer shows the barcode at the concession stand to pick up their drinks and hot dogs. This digital redemption allows the sport organization to kill the barcode upon being scanned so that it cannot be used again. In addition, the organization is able to get an accurate and up-to-the-minute count of redemption, eliminating the need to hand count the coupons and possibly have an erroneous calculation.

Contests and Sweepstakes

Contests and sweepstakes are both useful for engaging the community (both non-fans and fans alike) and a great way to mine data and create leads. Teams often partner with a sponsor to provide the winning item(s), which gives both the team and the sponsor marketing exposure outside of the marketplace. Although there is a slim chance of winning, people are more than willing to enter and give their contact information. A sport organization must follow several rules and laws in order to implement a contest or sweepstakes, and significant costs exist. However, the ability to take the contact information generated by the contest and then market the team's tickets, merchandise, etc., to those people is worth the effort and cost.

Premiums and Giveaways

Organizations use premiums and giveaways to attract new consumers and encourage greater frequency of purchase among existing consumers. *Premiums* and *giveaways*, as terms, are used interchangeably, with a **premium** being something given to fans at the game to entice them to attend that particular game. A premium may be a tangible item that is distributed to fans, like a bobblehead, or it can also be a value-ad experience like a concert or fireworks display. A

giveaway is a tangible item that is given away, like a bobblehead. Sport organizations use a mix of both in their promotional plan.

Although Veeck's bat day is widely accepted as the first example of a premium item giveaway, a promotion created by the Oakland A's in the early 1980s had a significant influence on giveaways. Organizations began to think thematically and about driving attendance to multiple games. The A's created a promotion called "Year of the Uniform," which encouraged consumers to attend multiple (six) games by providing a different clothing item premium (sponsored by Adidas) to members of the target market (those under 14 and their parents or other adults and friends) at each designated game. One game featured a cap, another a jersey, another wristbands, and so on.[14] This promotion was geared to a target market and designed to increase frequency of attendance, an approach related to the frequency elevator described next.

Ultimate Goal of Sport Marketing: Get and Keep Consumers in the Frequency Elevator

The ultimate goal of promotion in sport is to attract nonconsumers, increase their awareness and interest, turn them into consumers, and subsequently raise their consumption of the products or services. When launching a new sport product or offering, marketers have little choice but to expend the majority of their efforts attracting first-time (new) consumers. In such situations, sport marketers must educate nonconsumers about the sport and the benefits of experiencing the sport in the hope that nonconsumers are willing to sample the product. To do this, the organization must market broadly, usually by using mass media to send their message to a broad market base. Of course, social media and digital marketing have allowed for more targeted and cost-effective ways to reach the intended audience.

Data consistently show, however, that the more mature a sport organization is, the lower the effect new consumers have on total attendance or participation figures. This circumstance is true not just in terms of new consumers as a percentage of existing customers but also in terms of attendance frequencies of new consumers versus existing consumers. The effect of new consumers is often minimal and short lived, such as the bandwagon effect that occurs when a team is having a championship season. Although competition for a championship often attracts new fans, the increased attendance of existing consumers or core attendees dictates the long-term viability of the franchise.

The intelligent approach to sport promotion is to attract consumers, get them in the frequency elevator, and then allow them to be at whatever floor or level that best suits them. Customers must be allowed to move up or down in terms of their commitment to the organization, not be forced to move upward in their commitment unless they are ready and it fits their wants and needs.

Obviously, marketers of new products or new organizations or those moving into new markets can face situations that have unique challenges or, in some cases, unique advantages. Beyond this, sophisticated campaigns target both existing and potential consumers, concentrating more heavily on current users. Figure 8.2 shows the promotional progression planning model, a framework for such a campaign.

To be effective, promotions must be arranged and directed. Promotions such as giveaways; all-inclusive one-price nights; discounts; and events such as fireworks shows, concerts, and other forms of entertainment have an audience, but it is a limited audience. Promotional strategies must be developed with the entire range of attendees in mind: first-time attendees, parents who bring children, price-conscious or value-seeking attendees, partial-plan holders and mini-plan buyers, group-ticket buyers, season-ticket holders (personal and corporate accounts), and attendees who are not participating in any plan or package but perhaps are looking for a social or entertainment experience.

Level 1: Nonpattern Attendees, or Light Users

The consumers on this first level may be classified as having no established attendance pattern (first-time attendees, people with free tickets, spontaneous attendees, social media followers, bargain buyers, people wanting to experience the venue [e.g., Fenway Park], and so on). These people are motivated to attend by a variety of factors including the opponent; the weather; the day of the week; giveaways, special events, and discounts; team performance; and the opportunity for social interaction with friends, coworkers, or relatives. Interest in the sport, distance from the stadium, and financial resources may or may not be factors.

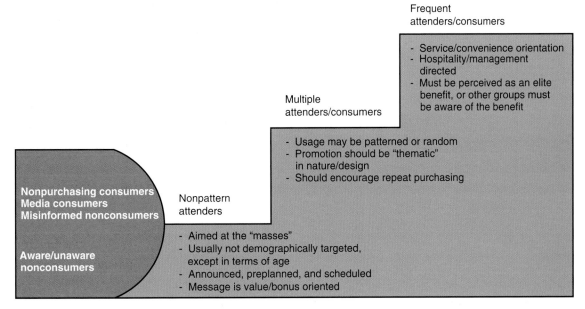

FIGURE 8.2   Promotional progression planning model.

These nonpattern attendees, who for the most part are light users, would appear to be the easiest of all consumers to move up to higher floors on the frequency elevator. Given that light users attend or participate at the lowest frequency level (many attend or participate only one to two times annually), they obviously have the greatest room for improvement on frequency. The experiences of organizations that have applied increased frequency programs show that this is true for most light users, although some consumers, regardless of the offers or effort involved, cannot be moved. Activities that succeed in increasing the frequency of light users are often effective in attracting non-consumers for trial involvement as well.

Level 2: Multiple Attendees, or Medium Users

Multiple attendees can be categorized as consumers who attend between 10 and 30 percent of a team's home games or participate in an activity between 10 and 30 percent of the available dates. Multiple attendees may or may not be purchasers of mini-plans or partial plans. Consumers may have various reasons for not owning a ticket plan, and some may even be unaware that such plans exist. Some may be aware of the plans but lack understanding of the ownership benefits of such plans. Others have time commitments or work schedules that are not conducive to plans with set dates. Still others, because of the availability of seats at the ballpark, the easy access, and the affordability of buying tickets on the secondary market without having to make a commitment, perceive no advantage to owning such a plan.

Plans offered to those consumers to increase their attendance or participation frequencies (or to just keep them in the frequency elevator) should use a menu approach or membership campaign to attract interest, show value and benefits, and overcome reasons for not purchasing. This approach requires offering several options with different benefits at various price points, presenting flexible plans, or establishing exchange policies for purchasers when other commitments prevent them from attending or participating. This is often a good time to introduce a loyalty program (often called an affinity plan), in which the fan is encouraged to continue, or even better, to increase, consumption through new and enhanced benefits offered in exchange for investment of time or money or both.

Level 3: Frequent Attendees, or Heavy Users

Frequent attendees are those fans who are the heaviest users, meaning that they invest significant time and money. They mostly are buyers of full-season and half-season ticket plans, club seats, and premium seats (such as suites). These users generate the largest portion of seat-related revenue for a team and must be treated extremely well, so as to not lose them. Promotional strategies aimed at this level should include benefits that are perceived as exclusive and elite (not available to consumers at lower levels), as well as all incentives offered to lower-level users (both light and medium users). Such strategies emphasize high-level customer service, hospitality, comfort, convenience, location, priority, increased communication, interaction, and, most important, access. Examples of access include invitations to special events exclusively for this group; the ability to purchase tickets to shows and events not included in their plan before the general public; access to players and meet-and-greet events involving players or other officials not generally afforded to the lower levels of consumption; and special content and communications from the coaches, players, and front office. This approach not only persuades medium users to become heavy users but also retains heavy users and reduces reasons for defection (decreasing involvement at one level and dropping to a lower level or getting off the frequency elevator entirely). The benefits of being a heavy user are promoted to both light and medium users so that they understand the value and benefit of moving up the elevator. The organization should convey the fact that light and medium users are missing out on unique benefits and opportunities if they remain at their current levels.

Organizations must give careful attention to developing programs to attract customers to the various levels without cannibalizing consumers from higher levels. It is important that the benefits increase significantly from level to level and that each higher level has a much higher perceived value, so as to both encourage those at the lower level to increase their investment and to ensure that those at the higher level remain at that level (or increase to an even higher level).

Descending the Elevator or Just Getting Off

Regardless of the product or service offered, some consumers decide to decrease their investment or even stop investing all together. Some encounter lifestyle changes that cause them to become unable to commit as much time or money to support the team. These may include getting married, having kids, changing jobs, moving to another city, or experiencing health issues. Others just overbuy or overcommit and then have to reassess their situation and make adjustments. Still others make a determination that their ROI is just not where they want or need it to be. This may be due to team performance, poor customer service or experience at the event, or the easy accessibility of the secondary market at a lower price.

Teams certainly want to keep customers ascending on the frequency elevator, but sometimes they must help customers find something that works for them at a lower level of investment.

Ensuring that customers are at the right level that matches their ability to invest (both time and money) and their expectations (ROO) both is the right thing to do and guarantees that they do not defect and get off the elevator altogether.

While it is said that the price of obtaining a new customer is six to seven times more than retaining a current customer, it is still costly to try to regain a lapsed customer. Our explanation of LAV in chapter 2 suggests that retaining customers at a lower annual spend is better than losing them altogether and trying to recapture them at another time or replacing them entirely.

Putting It All Together: An Integrated Promotional Model

Although ticket sales and revenue are obviously major components of most promotional campaigns, several marketing platforms can boost the value and impact of a fully integrated promotional campaign.

As a marketing platform

- To establish a foundation and brand for future applications

- To create an environment that will build equity or value each year
- To develop a blueprint to emulate in future platforms and campaigns
- To create a market buzz
- To create content and conversation via social media platforms

As a revenue platform

- To develop a sales platform for increased ticket, sponsorship, and broadcast sales; to build attendance, which then affects and increases ancillary revenue streams, such as parking, hospitality, facility rentals, food and beverage sales, and merchandising
- To provide a sales base to cross-promote other venue events or create a series of owned events in which the team is the promoter

As an entertainment platform

- To create a memorable experience that brings fans back
- To deliver new broadcast and social media content opportunities and features
- To strengthen the emotional connection and create a bond between the sport product and the fan

For those reasons, it might be advantageous to consider promotional campaigns as the hub of a wheel. The spokes of the wheel represent the various departmental units of the sport organization that can enhance and build on the promotional concept as well as capitalize on the opportunity through a variety of platforms (figure 8.3). Starting at the center of the wheel, the promotional concept is the focal point. It should have corresponding goals and objectives, primary and secondary strategies and tactics, and, whenever possible, a hook to draw in the intended audience. Addressing each spoke of the wheel provides insight into the successful planning and possibilities of an integrated promotional model.

Wrap-Up

Promotion is a common and widely used term in sport marketing. Broadly, promotion is the

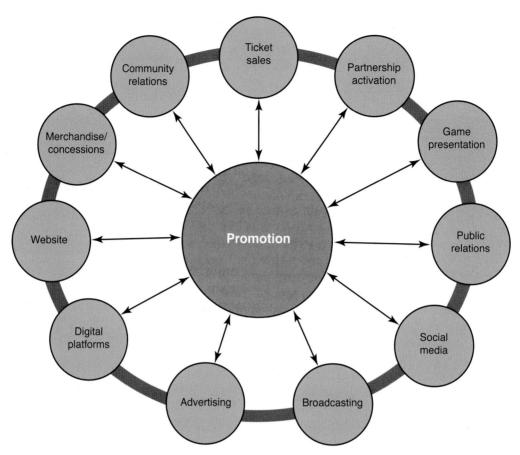

FIGURE 8.3 Promotional wheel.

Original created by Hersh, Mullin, and Sutton (2000); modified by Sutton (2013).

marketing of a company, an event, a product, or a service and includes advertising, personal selling, and publicity. At the core of any and all promotion is communication—the attempt by an organization or entity to reach its audience. To be effective, any promotional activity, using all appropriate communication channels, must be able to cut through the clutter of the marketplace, inform and persuade the targeted recipient of the message, and initiate some type of action on the part of the recipient.

Advertising continues to evolve due to the explosion of social media and digital platforms and because of the ineffectiveness of past practices. Organizations are always looking for new and creative ways to increase reach in a feasible manner while becoming more targeted and individualized in relation to their marketing messages.

Promotional activities are a valuable strategy for attracting new consumers and increasing the frequency (participating, purchasing, attending) of current consumers. In determining how to implement such activities, the reverse planning process—knowing what the organization wants to achieve through the promotion (outcome)—is an essential approach.

Promotional activities, which can take the form of price-oriented efforts, such as discounting and packaging, or non-price efforts, such as giveaways and special events, are an essential part of attracting consumers and increasing their frequency, spend, or volume. The theory of the frequency elevator suggests that the team provide unique promotions and benefits to its different users (light, medium, and heavy) so that they have a reason to stay on the elevator, but also to provide incentive for the fan to move up to a higher level.

Because the repeat user is the lifeblood of the sport organization, overinvesting time and money in an effort to attract one-time, or first-time, patrons is a questionable strategy. Even if a sponsor underwrites the cost of a giveaway, the marketer must consider the resources (staff, time, and advertising) spent on attracting consumers who may be nothing more than cherry pickers. Obviously, any strategy should attempt to attract nonusers, but it should not neglect any groups currently on the elevator, who typically provide the bulk of all product consumption. Ultimately, each organization must determine the ideal balance in its promotional strategy. Tactics include some combination of the elements of paid media advertising, personal selling, public relations, and sales promotions. Successful strategies, however, must recognize the need of consumers to move both up and down the escalator of consumption. The key is to retain them on a "floor" where they are comfortable, so that they do not defect and need to be replaced. Promotional concepts that are integrated and have a variety of connecting points and communication channels have a greater likelihood of attracting an interested audience that is likely to act on the promotional offer.

Paid media, depending on the channel employed, is controllable, targeted, cost effective, and productive. Not all organizations have the resources to use a broad paid media approach to promotion, and they may have to rely on other forms of media, which may not be as controllable, to promote their goals and objectives.

Activities

1. Interview 15 to 20 students at your institution to determine the most effective way of reaching them (i.e., communicating a message). After identifying the best methods, determine how your athletics department should attempt to communicate with students (both on and off campus) with regard to attending athletics events.
2. Using the same audience as in activity 1, determine whether price or non-price promotional activities would be more effective in attracting college students to athletics events.
3. Create a list of promotions that have attracted you to an event. What qualities did these promotions have that made the event attractive?

Your Marketing Plan

Communicating to your target audience about your product or service is an essential part of the marketing mix and usually involves promotion or paid media. Choosing a scenario related to the segment of the sport industry that is important to you in terms of potential future employment (e.g., action sports, professional sport, intercollegiate sport, etc.), select one of the aspects of promotion and paid media (advertising, personal selling, publicity, sales promotion) and develop an action plan to communicate with your target market by drawing attention to the product, event, or activity that will best promote the unique opportunity you are offering to enable you to monetize the opportunity, gain market share, increase attendance, or whatever your primary promotional objective may be.

 Go to HK*Propel* to complete the activities for this chapter.

Chapter 9

Public Relations

Kathy Connors

OBJECTIVES

- To understand public relations and communications outreach and its role in positioning and formulation of the marketing mix

- To recognize the importance of effective community relations, philanthropic and charitable initiatives in product positioning, and effective marketing efforts

- To understand the role, scope, and influence of the news media and how media relations, public relations, and communications efforts can be used in conjunction with community relations programming and digital and social media outreach to alter perceptions and influence public opinion and support

The Pro Football Hall of Fame Produces Must-See TV and Scores a PR Victory

The goal in television is to reach the widest possible audience. The goal of a public relations event or PR announcement is to maximize the reach of the message. Successful television and smart PR activations are ideally designed to make an impression and have an impact.

The Pro Football Hall of Fame scored a huge PR victory kicking off the announcement of the Centennial Class through a pair of made-for-TV moments in January of 2020. Prior to the Tennessee Titans–Baltimore Ravens Divisional Round playoff game, Pro Football Hall of Fame President David Baker walked out on the CBS Sports NFL studio set and informed a stunned Bill Cowher that he had been elected to the Hall of Fame. It was such a surprise, even the voters of the blue-ribbon panel who selected the class were unaware that Baker was going to deliver the news to an unsuspecting Cowher and the live television audience watching the broadcast.[1] A day later, at halftime of the Seattle Seahawks–Green Bay Packers Divisional Round matchup, Baker surprised Jimmy Johnson on the Fox Sports NFL studio set with the news that he, too, would be enshrined in the Hall of Fame. The two Super Bowl–winning coaches were the first two members of the Centennial Slate announced. Johnson had coached the Dallas Cowboys to two Super Bowl titles, while Cowher had led the Pittsburgh Steelers to one Super Bowl victory in his tenure.

These surprise Hall of Fame announcements harnessed the power of live TV and social media buzz. A perfect and potent combination of a captivated TV audience, unscripted drama, emotional reaction shots, and genuine surprise—moments custom-made for television in the digital and social media age. It produced wonderful television, a spontaneous and overwhelming positive reaction on social media, and significant media attention. The success of this PR activation can be measured by the overall impact and positive results—a massive live TV audience, substantial digital media views, and significant traditional and social media impressions. Another way to judge the effectiveness of this PR strategy is how the news had generated much more traction across all media and content platforms than it would have received through the traditional Pro Football Hall of Fame PR announcement.

In addition to being a great way to maximize PR for Cowher and Johnson's selections, it also provided a platform to shine a spotlight on the special class celebrating the NFL's 100th season. It also provided a digital and social media opportunity for the Pro Football Hall of Fame to create and share behind-the-scenes video content on social media that provided fans and viewers unique access and footage of how it was able to pull off the secret announcements.[2] As Rodger Sherman wrote in *The Ringer*, "These were two of the best television moments of the football season."[3]

Public relations, or PR, as it is often called, plays an essential role in promoting the image and ideals of organizations, institutions, brands, sponsors, networks, athletes, or personalities in sport. PR is a critical tool used to amplify a positive message and a strategic, integrated, and diversified marketing communications strategy.

Throughout this text we have discussed a variety of ways in which the sport marketer can use advertising, promotion, and social media to position the organization and its sport products in the marketplace. Unfortunately, these efforts can be undermined and rendered ineffective if the organization does not value the PR function, embrace a proactive PR approach, develop a solid PR and communications strategy, and use creative outreach tactics. In this chapter, we examine the role of PR in the sport context where, historically, it consisted primarily of **media relations** and **community relations** but has expanded to include digital and social media and content creation.

What Is Public Relations?

Public relations is a strategic communications function and media relations and external outreach capability that is an essential part of the global sport industry. The Public Relations Society of America (PRSA) defines public relations as "a strategic communication process that builds mutually beneficial relationships between organizations and their publics."[4] PR practitioners provide valuable counsel, insight, and tactical advice to sport organizations, athletes, leagues, teams, schools, brands, and clients on public relations, marketing and business communications, media relations, and digital and social media. The PR department is the conduit through which many communications functions flow, including serving as the chief liaison with the press. PR professionals direct a wide range of communications tasks and spearhead a broad array of outreach initiatives:

- Award nominations and campaigns
- Biographical and statistical information
- Internal communications
- Media guides
- Media relations
- Media training
- Photography
- Press releases and press kits
- Promotional materials
- Publications
- Social media
- Speechwriting
- Video
- Websites

The combination of internal and external stakeholders that the public relations professional interacts with makes it an all-encompassing job. Public relations has always been an important, dynamic, strategic role, but in the social media age, it has become an even more essential and consequential role in any organization. The breadth of responsibility is magnified by the sheer number of news outlets, media platforms, and volume of content a PR practitioner must be aware of and communicate with on a daily and even hourly basis.

Public relations strategy and engagement can be used to raise awareness, build brands, enhance image, drive television tune-in, direct award campaigns, increase ticket and merchandise sales, develop and build new business, influence public policy, advocate for social causes and breaking down cultural barriers, promote civic issues, spearhead fund-raising efforts, elevate charitable or community relations initiatives, cultivate and expand fan base, promote executive leadership, and recruit talent. PR-savvy athletes and personalities, teams, leagues, organizations, and brands understand how to use publicity as a catalyst to amplify business endeavors, marketing deals, advertising campaigns, sponsoring partnerships, and content creation while also attracting new business ventures.

Public relations is a highly specialized function that requires the acumen of trained professionals. PR is not a subset of marketing; rather, it is a complementary function. PR strategy and tactics should synthesize with marketing, advertising, sales, branding, and digital and social media initiatives. A PR component, application, and extension exists for almost every facet of the sport industry. PR professionals must be well versed in their company's business interests, corporate initiatives, priorities, and mission but also conversant in issues that confront the broader industry.

In the fast-paced information age characterized by the pressure of relentless breaking news cycles, it is imperative that sport organizations and brands value sharp PR instincts, skills, and sensibilities. PR and communications professionals must have command of the comprehensive role and full scope of the responsibilities of the job function. It is also critical that all sport industry professionals understand the role of the PR professional and the daily impact PR and communication strategy and media relations have on their organization and the industry at large. It is vital for any sport industry professional who may serve as a spokesperson to be PR and media savvy. PR professionals and spokespeople must be focused on and committed to message discipline, careful with context, and rigorous about facts. Every public-facing employee in an organization should have media training, know the organization's media policy, and ensure proper channels are followed for media requests.

There unfortunately is a tendency to view and elevate public relations only in times of crisis and view the value of the function through the prism of crisis communications, but the capability should always be a top priority. Sometimes PR problems are PR problems. Sometimes PR problems cause business problems. Sometimes PR problems are caused by business problems. Sometimes PR problems are a direct result of poor executive leadership or bad player or employee decisions or executive malfeasance. It is incumbent upon PR professionals to navigate these circumstances and important to understand the differences and provide good counsel on how to craft an effective strategy and response in the attempt to minimize the PR brand and reputational damage.

PR and media relations outreach efforts also build professional skills that benefit people beyond PR and communications professionals. Effective media management skills for athletes and coaches can lead to lucrative careers in motivational speaking, broadcasting, advertising opportunities, brand spokesperson and ambassador roles, philanthropic endeavors, and other commercial activities. The emergence of roles in television; radio; and podcasts for former team executives, business professionals, and officials provides future career opportunities as well. Media training and interviews are a tremendous way to develop public speaking and effective communication skills.

Role of a PR Professional

Public relations is the function of communicating an organization's message externally, including to the press, and a PR professional is the liaison between those parties. In the modern 24-hour-a-day, 7-day-a-week news cycle world—a culture now fueled by an omnipresent media, blogs, and constant social media conversation—the need for competent public and media relations specialists is expanding. Like their counterparts in other industries, PR professionals in sport need to understand the art of effectively communicating with a wide range of media outlets, external mediums, and contacts as representatives of their organization or clients. The chief role of the public relations professional is to serve as the spokesperson to the media and external constituents on behalf of those they represent. The spokesperson in media interviews or press

opportunities can also be an appropriately identified person—an executive, administrator, a coach, or an athlete.

PR professionals plan and execute media and award campaigns; facilitate interviews for athletes, coaches, and executives; pitch stories to media; respond to media inquiries; and distribute press releases, statistical information, media guides, press kits, photography, and other helpful promotional information and content. PR staffs also determine and schedule media availability sessions with coaches, players, and executives; schedule and facilitate radio and TV media tours; consult on social media and content creation; and host media briefings, press conferences, and events for more formal announcements. The ultimate goal for public relations professionals is to cultivate the most positive image possible for those they serve by proactively seeking and accommodating as many favorable opportunities in the press as possible. PR staffs must also manage the difficult or negative press as effectively and professionally as possible. There are elements and responsibilities of public relations that remain reactive, and reactive public relations is part of the job, but the PR function and PR and communications practitioners must be proactive, forward thinking, and strategic.

The most successful organizations fully integrate their public relations efforts with advertising, marketing, sales, sponsorship, community relations, and digital and social media efforts so that the external messages all reflect the same theme. The synergy among these areas of an organization or individual athlete's management team is vital in presenting a unified image through all external communication.

PR professionals should possess the following attributes: credibility and integrity, commitment to serving media outlets in a timely manner, excellent written and spoken communication skills, and capacity to work on and with deadlines. Good public relations specialists should adopt the following skills in their practice.

Building Relationships

The cornerstone of a successful career in public and media relations is possessing the ability to forge and maintain good working relationships with the press. Even if a reporter or media outlet has done a negative story or is difficult to deal with, the PR professional should seek to manage a working relationship with that reporter or media outlet, always trying to keep the lines of communication open. The need for relationship building should also be important in serving internal organizational constituents and clients as well. Internal colleagues, executives, and clients must be educated to understand the value of publicity and be willing participants in the process. Trust is probably the most important element in building effective working relationships in any realm, including public relations. A skilled public relations person should be a trusted and respected member of the company, organization, or management team and a valued resource for the press.

Communication

Obviously, one of the most important skills in public relations is effective communication. Communications, both internally and externally, should be directed in the most clear, concise, timely, and efficient way. The PR person should produce materials that contain the necessary information in the best and clearest possible way. As mentioned earlier, building and maintaining good interpersonal working relationships is important, but when routine and basic information is being exchanged, the PR professionals need to be efficient and considerate of deadlines by using technology, social media, and email to their advantage. Email is a helpful tool and has become the primary form of communication in business, including between PR professionals and media, but maintaining interpersonal relationships is important as well, so dialogue by phone and occasional in-person conversations are advised. PR spokespeople should keep in mind that in all forms of on-the-record communication, they are speaking as representatives of their organization or clients.

Creating the Public Relations Plan

For a large-scale public relations project, a comprehensive plan should be designed to spell out the strategy to promote that message. The plan should detail a chronological outline of how the objective of the campaign will be achieved and what tactics will be used. When creating the plan, the PR professional should consider the timelines and deadlines of the publications being targeted.

Outlets that make sense for the message should be identified, and adequate time should be set aside to meet deadlines, achieve all objectives, and reach the targeted outlets. For instance, if the goal is to increase exposure for the brand, athlete, league, or organization in a certain segment of the population, the PR professional should build a targeted plan around outlets that the demographic group reads, hears, or views. Managing multiple tasks and story placements simultaneously is critical. Opportunities should be maximized in both major outlets and smaller ones. All placements play a role in the overall strategy, especially now because digital and social media have expanded the potential reach of every content platform, media impression, and story placement.

Have a Balanced and Strategic Approach

While evaluating the hourly, daily, and weekly media requests and the goals and media targets of the PR plan, PR professionals need to use a balanced and strategic approach. They must evaluate the reactive media requests received and be proactive about securing opportunities that are maximally beneficial. A balance should be struck between stories in traditional and digital outlets and the use of social media. Public relations professionals should consider and include outlets across the full spectrum of media platforms—social media, websites, digital, blogs, print newspapers and magazines, TV, radio, and podcasts—and recognize the value of securing a range of international, national, regional, and local opportunities.

Making the Pitches

After creating a plan or identifying a storyline that is a priority, PR professionals have to be proactive and pitch stories. They should always know whom they are pitching to—that they are pitching the right reporters and catering the pitch to the specific publication or outlet. They must be aware of deadlines and editorial calendars and be considerate of the time that will be required to cover the story adequately. PR professionals should avoid pitching a reporter a story idea that makes no sense for either the outlet, the subject matter it covers, or the type of stories it typically does.

Managing the Story

One of the most important skills in media relations is the ability to manage a story while it is being completed. The routine story and placements usually do not require more than basic interview coordination and post-interview follow-up skills. The art of managing a story is a practice generally reserved for in-depth pieces or pieces in major outlets. The tone or spirit of the piece should always be established at the beginning of the process. By keeping a dialogue going with the reporter as she conducts her interviews (a process in which the PR professional should be actively involved) and collects her facts, the PR professional can get an idea of the general direction of the piece. By staying involved in the process, the PR person can correct inaccuracies, make appropriate suggestions, emphasize key points, or learn whether the tone or focus of the story has changed while the piece is being reported.

Managing Expectations

Athletes want to be profiled in publications like *Sports Illustrated*, and executives want to be featured in outlets like *The Wall Street Journal*. The role of the PR professional is to make pitches to those outlets and work diligently to create influential media opportunities. Managing the expectation that those proactive pitches will turn into potential placements is also important. PR professionals cannot control or guarantee the success of the pitches or outcomes of the placements if secured, but they can try to forecast the range of opportunities that may be available to their clients in the media marketplace.

Media Training and Talking Points

Being an effective spokesperson and feeling comfortable dealing with media are invaluable skills. Helping athletes and executives achieve success in this area is an important responsibility of the PR professional. One of the important roles of the PR professional is identifying, cultivating, and mentoring effective spokespeople. Every organization and brand needs credible spokespeople. Media training and mock interviews are helpful exercises in preparing people for media interviews and public question-and-answer forums. The public relations professional can provide instruction, suggestions for improve-

ment, and useful techniques during these media training sessions. Providing ongoing feedback on interview performance after media appearances is also recommended. Talking points are a helpful resource in both media training and the public relations practice to help subjects prepare for interviews. Talking points will help people prepare responses to questions, organize thoughts, and stay on the desired message when speaking to the press. The talking points document should include a carefully crafted and clear response to every conceivable question that could be asked on that particular subject. Talking points are recommended especially when dealing with a difficult or complicated matter because they will help the spokesperson stay on message. Although some criticize PR practitioners as being gatekeepers and critics may deride "PR handlers" or use terms like *spin* to describe the PR professional's work, it is a fundamental role designed to protect the organization or client.

Crisis Management

Not all public relations is positive, and unfortunately, negative media stories are an increasingly frequent reality. Managing bad press is a special skill. Obviously, the response required depends on the nature and scope of the issues involved with the negative story or crisis. The first step in this type of reactive situation is formulating a plan for making a media and public response. A quick, effective response can help minimize the initial damage and ideally will decrease the shelf life of the story—the goal in all crisis, reputation management, or damage control situations. Social media and the ability for media to report quickly on the Internet have made these situations more difficult to handle because the reporting cycle has now become immediate. PR professionals need to recognize the intensity of the media's desire for a response, particularly as reports and rumors reverberate through the social media ecosystem. A PR representative or spokesperson should not release official statements until they are ready with an appropriate, well-thought-out, and strategic response. PR pros must also understand the potential perils of non-response or non-engagement or an indifferent or incorrect response that then needs to be modified and corrected.

Media Relations

In sport, public relations is often perceived to be synonymous with publicity or media relations, which is one of the primary roles of the PR professional. Media relations is a large component of the public relations function and is one of the most important functions because of the volume of media coverage available and the influence that media have on sport and society in general.

The evolution and transformation of the media landscape continues unabated. Sports are covered by a full range of outlets across the media spectrum, including broadcast networks, national and regional cable TV and radio networks, newspapers, magazines, podcasts, websites, blogs, digital platforms, and sports outlets. The ubiquity of social media, omnipresence of media content, and the saturation of breaking news present myriad PR opportunities but also a host of new potential avenues for challenges and problems for PR professionals.

News cycles in the modern media environment move at a blistering speed and social media intensifies the pace. It is imperative for athletes and personalities, organizations, teams, colleges and universities, and brands to understand the media ecosystem. Sports events, athletes and personalities, and storylines are covered by mainstream outlets beyond the sports pages, particularly marquee events like the Super Bowl or Olympic Games. The breadth of news coverage that these types of events attract provides ample opportunity for brands, athletes, sponsors, and advertisers to gain PR traction in the marketplace. PR professionals must continue to be proactive and vigilant in their ability to monitor news, react to trends, and manage the changing media and communications landscape. The size of the audiences and the intensity of the interest are reflected in the scope of media attention and coverage. A highlight, video, photo, or tweet going "viral" can be positive when it is good news but harmful when negative or controversial.

Although there has been contraction in local news and print outlets and some reduction in specific sports reporting beats, there has also been growth in coverage areas, such as sport business, sports television and sports media, sports wagering, sports technology, and analytics, and a wider emphasis on sports in television trade publications and in the public affairs media and political press. The growth in coverage of the insider scoops and blockbuster trades, the eponymous breaking news alert combined with the power of social media and impact of TV is both dynamic and dramatic.

News cycles are national and media coverage extends far beyond the local market, but local sports news is still robust. Hometown coverage is vibrant and consequential, and teams, athletes, organizations, and brands should prioritize local outlets. Maintaining positive relationships and a strong connection to the local community and home market for teams, colleges and universities, organizations, and brands is critical. The hometown connection is also important for athletes and personalities throughout the duration of their careers and into retirement. The hometown feature is a valuable mechanism that achieves both a media relations function and a community relations function. Reinforcing and maintaining the hometown connection is essential, not just for college athletics PR staffers but also for media relations personnel in all facets of sport.

According to a survey by the Pew Research Center, 22 percent of American adults use Twitter. The survey also revealed that 80 percent of the tweets are sent by the top 10 percent of the most active Twitter users. This is an important statistic for perspective because sports PR practitioners and PR pros need to recognize the challenge that this reality presents. It is also important for PR professionals to understand that reporters and media personalities use Twitter, a platform that often drives and determines media coverage. Social media in general, but Twitter in particular, affect the media ecosystem and in some instances play an outsized role in influencing media storylines. Social media content can inform and influence press storylines and public sentiment as well. These factors present challenges and opportunities that PR professionals must be aware of and view with perspective and approach with balance.[5]

Public Relations, Community Relations, and Charitable and Philanthropic Initiatives

The sport industry is a cherished form of entertainment and valuable television content and programming, but sports also have an incredible impact on society. One of the ways that sports extend beyond the games is through community relations outreach, charitable initiatives, and philanthropic efforts. Athletes and sport personalities and organizations can galvanize charitable giving and philanthropic initiatives.

Community relations programs, charitable initiatives, and philanthropic endeavors provide opportunities to make lasting connections between athletes or sport organizations and the communities where they work and compete. These programs also provide potential media opportunities in the marketplace and a chance to showcase athletes and sport organizations as good citizens who make a meaningful impact. Sports attract large and captive audiences, which presents a big platform to promote a powerful message through visible messengers. Sport PR professionals should strive to create media opportunities that amplify an individual or organizational message in the community by using recognizable sport personality messengers.

Athletes are an integral part of community relations initiatives. Almost all community relations programs and most charitable programs have some element of athlete involvement because the presence of athletes and their involvement attract funding to the program through sponsorship, garner media interest and coverage, and attract an audience of participants and observers to the program. One of the great benefits of community relations programs and charitable activities is that they allow fans and the community to see athletes and organizations through a different lens and to interact with them in a personal way. These programs provide the opportunity to humanize athletes and sport personalities. Although fans already have an emotional connection to the teams and athletes whom they support and follow, these community events, charitable initiatives, and outreach programs provide an additional perspective and have the potential to make a beneficial human connection.

When Hurricane Harvey hit the Houston area in 2017, Houston Texans star JJ Watt and his foundation launched an online fundraiser to help victims and aid the recovery effort. Watt's original goal was to raise US$200,000. Watt's gracious social media posts and videos updating the public on the progress of the fundraiser garnered widespread media attention and quickly attracted donors from all around the world who contributed a stunning US$41.6 million to his relief effort.[6] In 2019, Watt provided an update on the foundation's efforts, revealing that his Hurricane Harvey relief fund helped rebuild more than 1,183 homes, rebuilt and recovered more than 971 childcare centers and after school programs in the Houston area (helping more than 108,000 children), and distributed 239 million meals to victims of the hurricane. Watt was co-named "Sportsperson of the Year" by *Sports Illustrated* in 2017 because of his heroic fundraising effort.[7]

The Ice Bucket Challenge, launched in the summer of 2014, was a campaign to raise awareness and encourage donations to fight ALS (amyotrophic lateral sclerosis, also known as Lou Gehrig's disease). The Ice Bucket Challenge, inspired in part by former Boston College baseball player Pete Frates, was an international phenomenon and embraced worldwide by prominent global sport figures and organizations. (Frates died in 2019.) Participants in The Ice Bucket Challenge would record a video of themselves pouring a bucket of ice water over their heads and then nominate and encourage other people to participate and donate to The ALS Association.[8] The Ice Bucket Challenge was a powerful illustration of the combination of the power of sports and social media and the ability to inspire charitable contributions and raise awareness for an important cause. According to The ALS Association, The Ice Bucket Challenge raised US$115 million in donations and "spurred a massive increase in The ALS Association's capacity to invest in promising research, the development of assistive technologies, and increased access to care and services for people with ALS."[9] The Ice Bucket Challenge is another fantastic example of a charitable initiative propelled by social media engagement. In addition to producing interactive and uplifting content, The Ice Bucket Challenge not only raised awareness, inspired a call to action, and earned widespread media attention but also highlighted and showcased the positive impact and nexus between social media engagement, PR efforts, and philanthropic endeavors, earning positive social media impressions and media placements.

Since 2005, NFL Network star Rich Eisen has run a 40-yard (36.6 m) dash at the NFL Scouting Combine dressed in a business suit and custom cleats to raise money for charity. Eisen's Run Rich Run has raised nearly US$1.2 million in the fight against childhood cancer and other

Joe Robbins/Getty Images

Rich Eisen runs the 40-yard dash during his annual Run Rich Run charity campaign at the NFL Scouting Combine.

Rich Eisen Announces 2020 Run Rich Run Campaign, Benefitting St. Jude Children's Research Hospital

MEMPHIS, Tenn., Feb. 24, 2020 /PRNewswire/—NFL Network and DIRECTV AUDIENCE Network personality Rich Eisen has issued a social media challenge to join his 2020 Run Rich Run fundraising campaign for St. Jude Children's Research Hospital to raise critical funds to support its lifesaving mission: Finding cures. Saving children. Eisen also broke the news that Pro Football Hall of Fame wide receiver, Jerry Rice, accepted this challenge and will 'suit up' for the kids of St. Jude.

Since 2005, Eisen has donned his business suit and custom cleats for this cause. His efforts have raised nearly $1.2 million to help the battle against childhood cancer and other life-threatening diseases. The history of Run Rich Run, featured on St. Jude Inspire, showcases how this annual event started and the reason Eisen continues to challenge himself and his fans year-after-year. Last year, Eisen had a strong showing in warm-ups, as he ran neck-and-neck—for the first two steps of his race—with famed sprinter, Usain Bolt.

"I'm still shocked and so humbled that what started out as a lark has grown into a charitable effort that has raised over $1 million for St. Jude Children's Research Hospital," said Rich Eisen. "I'm genuinely excited to know that thanks to Jerry Rice, Marc Lore, Michael Rubin, and the thousands of donations from people throughout the country, 2020 should be the most successful 'Run Rich Run' yet for St. Jude."

> continued

> continued

Jerry Rice has accepted the Run Rich Run challenge, and with the backing of Kynetic CEO, Michael Rubin, he will race against returning supporter Marc Lore, President and CEO, Walmart eCommerce U.S. Rice and Lore have both committed to race for St. Jude by running and asking others to donate. The friendly challenge between Lore and Rubin will result in a guaranteed donation of $250,000 from either party. Lore will make the donation if he loses to Rice, but if Rice loses, Rubin will make that donation on his behalf. Either outcome ends in a win for the children of St. Jude.

St. Jude patient, Von, who currently resides in Indiana, will be on hand to give Eisen a pep talk as he laces up his custom cleats for the main event. Von came to St. Jude in January 2019 after having a recurrence of anaplastic ependymoma, a type of brain cancer. His treatment at St. Jude included surgery to remove the tumor followed by proton therapy treatments. Von is now back home and returns to St. Jude for checkups.

Fans across the nation can share their best 40-yard-dash videos on social media, using #RunRichRun and #StJude. They can also donate now to show their support for this great cause at runrichrun.pledgeit.org. Jerry Rice and Marc Lore have also set up their own donation links, which are available at pledgeit.org/jerry-rice and pledgeit.org/marc-lore.

The NFL is a longtime supporter of St. Jude Children's Research Hospital. Since 2012, the NFL has partnered with St. Jude through NFL PLAY 60, which is the "Official Champion of Play" at St. Jude Children's Research Hospital. The NFL PLAY 60 initiative helps patients and families cope with serious illnesses through play therapy, peer interaction, and other activities. This partnership has provided the opportunity for St. Jude to be a part of the NFL Draft and NFL Network's Run Rich Run campaign during the NFL Scouting Combine. NFL PLAY 60 is the League's national youth health and wellness campaign encouraging youth to get physically active for 60 minutes a day.

"The NFL has once again raised the bar of philanthropic giving by providing this tremendous platform for our friend Rich to share his heartfelt dedication to create awareness and raise funds for St. Jude Children's Research Hospital," said Richard Shadyac Jr., President and CEO of ALSAC, the fundraising and awareness organization for St. Jude Children's Research Hospital. "His purpose is clear. Rich is a role model for standing up for a cause in which he believes, yard-after-yard and year-after-year. The kids and families at St. Jude will be watching closely as Rich runs the 40-yard dash and spreads the message of our founder Danny Thomas that no child should die in the dawn of life."

Tune in to the NFL Network on Sunday, March 1 to find out how Eisen's 40-yard run stacks up against his past records and current NFL Scouting Combine athletes.

St. Jude is leading the way the world understands, treats, and defeats childhood cancer and other life-threatening diseases. Events like this help ensure families never receive a bill from St. Jude for treatment, travel, housing, or food—because all they should worry about is helping their child live.

To learn more about St. Jude, visit stjude.org.

About St. Jude Children's Research Hospital

St. Jude Children's Research Hospital is leading the way the world understands, treats, and defeats childhood cancer and other life-threatening diseases. Its purpose is clear: Finding cures. Saving children. It is the only National Cancer Institute–designated Comprehensive Cancer Center devoted solely to children. Treatments invented at St. Jude have helped push the overall childhood cancer survival rate from 20 percent to more than 80 percent since the hospital opened more than 50 years ago. St. Jude won't stop until no child dies from cancer. St. Jude freely shares the discoveries it makes, and every child saved at St. Jude means doctors and scientists worldwide can use that knowledge to save thousands more children. Families

never receive a bill from St. Jude for treatment, travel, housing, or food—because all a family should worry about is helping their child live. Join the St. Jude mission by visiting stjude. org, sharing stories and videos from St. Jude Inspire, liking St. Jude on Facebook, following St. Jude on Twitter and Instagram, and subscribing to its YouTube channel.
   SOURCE ALSAC/St. Jude Children's Research Hospital

Saying Goodbye and Showing Appreciation—How Communications Connects Players, Teams, Fans, and the Community

Player departures, either by trade or through free agency, are industry transactions that organizations, executives, and players understand are part of the sport business. Despite the fact that these deals are both routine and expected, they still can be difficult experiences for players, teams, and fans, especially when the player has had a significant influence on the organization's success and the community. Although these situations are often emotional and sometimes bitter, handling the athlete's departure in the best way possible is important.

Some athletes have taken the opportunity to place thank-you advertisements in local newspapers to communicate their appreciation and express thanks to the fans for their support during their time with the team and the city. Organizations have also used newspaper ads to extend thanks to players for their contributions to the organization and community during their time with the franchise. These ads are effective from both a public and community relations perspective. The individual player can express a personalized and positive message reflecting and commemorating his or her time with the team and to fans and the city.

Congratulatory ads are also an effective and versatile tool that can be used on a wide variety of occasions, including a career milestone, retirement, historic achievement, or victory. There have also been occasions when fan bases run ads to acknowledge or congratulate other fan bases and host cities and organizations and to thank fans. The messages from teams, organizations, athletes, or brands can appear across the spectrum of content platforms—local newspapers, social media, videos, or commercials—that air digitally or on TV. The benefit of these types of ads are PR, community relations, sponsor activation, and the generating of goodwill.

When New York Giants quarterback Eli Manning retired from the NFL, the New York Jets placed an ad in *The New York Post* to salute the cross-town rival QB.

"CONGRATULATIONS ON AN EXTRAORDINARY CAREER."[11]

The Golden State Warriors provide another example of a gracious congratulatory ad. After the Toronto Raptors captured their historic NBA Championship in 2019, the Warriors took out an ad in *The Toronto Star*.

> *continued*

"THE GOLDEN STATE WARRIORS CONGRATULATE THE TORONTO RAPTORS ON THEIR HISTORIC ACHIEVEMENT AND BRINGING THE 2019 NBA CHAMPIONSHIP TO THE CITY OF TORONTO"[12]

When MLB icon Derek Jeter retired from the New York Yankees, Gatorade, one of Jeter's marketing partners, ran an ad on his behalf thanking New York.

"NEW YORK,

YOU'VE BEEN WITH ME FOR THE PAST 20 YEARS.

YOUR GRIT FUELED MY WILL.

YOUR HISTORY STRENGTHENED MY RESOLVE.

YOUR SCRUTINY EXPOSED MY FLAWS.

YOUR EXPECTATION WAS MY INSPIRATION.

FROM MY FIRST AT BAT UNTIL MY FINAL OUT.

YOU HELPED MAKE ME WHO I AM.

FOR THAT I AM FOREVER THANKFUL

DEREK JETER"[13]

When Tom Brady signed with the Tampa Bay Buccaneers after 20 seasons and six Super Bowl victories with the New England Patriots, the Kraft Family placed an ad in the *Tampa Times*.

"THANK YOU TOM

For 20 amazing years, you gave us everything you had. When you arrived as a sixth-round pick—and the best selection this franchise has ever made—no one imagined all you'd accomplish or how much you'd soon mean to an entire region. You now leave New England after two decades of dominance as the GOAT and forever a part of our family.

Your passion for the game, competitiveness, and constant pursuit of excellence resulted in an unprecedented six Super Bowl victories, nine conference championships, and 17 division titles. You're now recognized as the greatest of all time for what you've accomplished on the field, but you're an even better person. Thank you, Tom, for your countless contributions to the New England Patriots, and we wish you and your beautiful family continued success. There will never be another Tom Brady.

To the Buccaneers fans and Tampa Bay community—take care of him. You got a great one.

With much love and appreciation,

The Kraft Family and the New England Patriots"[14]

Although seeing their favorite players depart for a new team or retire from competition is difficult for fans, players and organizations can make an effort to share a personalized message with the community through traditional or social media platforms to extend well wishes and express feelings of gratitude, appreciation, and farewell.

life-threatening diseases. In addition to raising money for St. Jude Children's Research Hospital, the Run Rich Run initiative combines compelling and entertaining TV content and social media engagement. Fans are encouraged to participate through an interactive element by creating videos running a 40-yard dash and posting them with the hashtags #RunRichRun and #StJude. In addition to the videos being shared on social media, videos have a chance to be aired on NFL Network, during the network's coverage of the NFL Scouting Combine and "Run Rich Run." Fans and viewers are also encouraged to donate to St. Jude Children's Research Hospital. Run Rich Run has created an effective PR platform, raising awareness and money for a worthy cause, driving tune-in for a TV event, creating terrific, interactive social media content, and shining a spotlight on patient stories.[10]

Public Relations in the Sport Marketing Mix

Public relations is a vital part of sport marketing strategy and a critical component of effective sport sponsorship activation plans. One of the objectives of the sport marketing strategy is to develop a brand association between the athlete, team, league, or sport property, and their sponsors. Media exposure is a great way to increase awareness of the sponsorship and showcase the connection between the parties in the marketing partnership. Athletes and teams that are capable of capitalizing on PR opportunities to highlight existing marketing relationships illustrate to the sponsor that they are valuable partners. Marketing and PR personnel should work diligently and collaboratively to develop creative and effective PR and media opportunities for sponsor-driven appearances or events to create and extend awareness of the brand association.

Many sponsors are interested and willing to include a community, charitable, or philanthropic element in their marketing partnerships with athletes and sport organizations. Supporting an individual athlete's foundation or a sport organization's charitable initiatives is a great way for a sponsor to extend its charitable activities and develop a more meaningful partnership. The combination of athletes, teams, sponsors, and charitable, philanthropic, or community-driven initiatives can create unique media opportunities locally and nationally.

How valuable can effective PR and media strategy be to an athlete's marketing portfolio? Tennis star Caroline Wozniacki was profiled in *The Wall Street Journal* after her run to the U.S. Open final in 2014. When talking about corporate sponsors and endorsement prospects with her agents, she was quoted saying that she wanted a chocolate deal. The Godiva CEO read that *WSJ* piece and saw Wozniacki's remarks. A few months later, a deal was struck and Wozniacki became the luxury chocolate brand's first ever athlete endorser.[15] This is an example of an athlete and a brand maximizing a PR opportunity. Wozniacki capitalized on the unique PR and marketing window created by her on-court success at the season's final grand slam event, which is played in the top U.S. media market. While discussing potential business opportunities, she expressed a genuine interest in a marketing category and sponsorship partnership she was looking for to a leading global business publication. Godiva's Wozniacki deal announcement had two compelling elements: The brand's first-ever athlete endorser and the story of how the deal came to be added a newsworthy element to the announcement.[16] This example illustrates how valuable PR and media opportunities can be for athletes and also how important PR placements are to sponsors, brands, and marketing partners.

Sport Public Relations and Content Creation in the Digital and Social Media Age

The 24/7 news cycle and the Internet age forever changed the dynamics of the media ecosystem and drastically expanded the heightened role of the PR professional. The social media age has only intensified the environment, transforming the way that people consume media content. Athletes, teams, leagues, organizations, brands, colleges, and universities are developing their own content, which provides an excellent opportunity to create direct communication mechanisms and content distribution channels with fans. This type of content creation can drive media attention, social media engagement, community relations initiatives, philanthropic endeavors, and ticket and merchandise sales and build new audiences.

Traditional media outlets are still a major source of sports news, but people have increasingly turned to digital and social media platforms for information and news updates. Athletes, leagues, teams, and organizations across the global sport industry have embraced digital and social media platforms, including blogs, websites, and social networking sites, such as Twitter, Facebook, Instagram, and Snapchat, as promotional vehicles to connect with fans and the public. The direct interaction provided on social and digital media platforms is an effective way to stay connected to fans, share information and content, cultivate new followers and fans, and create public interest—an extension of the goals of the PR strategy and job function. Digital and social media have also provided athletes, coaches, teams, leagues, executives, and sponsors their own platforms to break news and a place to share information and opinion, showcase their personalities, describe charitable initiatives, and promote marketing partnerships without having to rely on traditional media outlets to report stories.

Professional lacrosse player Paul Rabil has done a very strong job of building his personal brand by creating an effective PR, marketing, and communications strategy. Rabil built a broad platform through a combination of media and PR outreach, content creation, digital and social media engagement, marketing partnerships, and business ventures. He has very efficiently enhanced his brand by using his PR skills and tech-savvy and robust digital and social media presence to help catapult himself from being the star of a niche sport into a sport industry entrepreneur, investor, and cofounder of the Premier Lacrosse League (PLL).

Rabil has capitalized on effective PR outreach, securing media placements in a wide assortment of publications, including *The New York Times*, *Fast Company*, *Bloomberg*, *Sports Illustrated*, *The Players' Tribune*, *Entrepreneur*, CNBC, and *Recode*. He appears at industry conferences, showcasing his business, tech, and entrepreneurial interests. He hosts a podcast called "Suiting Up," produces videos on his YouTube channel, including a behind-the-scenes series designed to promote the PLL called "The League," and hosts lacrosse camps. He is also the Chairman of The Paul Rabil Foundation, an organization with a mission of helping children with learning differences, by cre-

ating programs and partnerships through sport and scholarship.[17] Rabil has created an enviable platform, which serves as a textbook example for athletes and personalities looking to build an effective brand and stay relevant in the social media and content creation age.

The Los Angeles Chargers capitalized on the podcast trend starting *The Chargers Podcast Network*, which initially started with a single podcast called "Chargers Weekly." The Chargers' podcast network expanded, including a podcast hosted by and for women. Targeting female fans through strategic PR outreach, content, and special events is a smart business decision, considering that female fans are an expanding and vital viewing audience and customer base for the NFL.[18]

Social media have provided enormous communications benefits, but the medium also presents numerous pitfalls. Communications professionals must understand, embrace, and use the upside of the social media universe while also anticipating, comprehending, and communicating the negative impact and real downsides of the phenomenon. PR professionals must help organizations, clients, talent, and brands strike the delicate balance of navigating the positive attributes with the negative realities and trends presented by the social media landscape.

The use of social media as an activation platform in addition to serving as an effective engagement mechanism can also become an additional PR opportunity. Social media practitioners must view all content created and posts through the prism of PR and external impact. Social media managers should have PR training in addition to content creation and digital skills. Social media have provided an unlimited forum for producing compelling and interesting content and providing behind-the-scenes access. The medium is a terrific communications platform and engagement tool, but it is not a panacea and does not exist in a parallel universe. Athletes, personalities, brands, organizations, networks, and schools need to understand that social media are revelations and amplify who people are and what they represent.

During the first round of the 2018 NCAA Men's Basketball Tournament, the University of Maryland, Baltimore County (UMBC) scored a historic upset, defeating the University of Virginia, the tournament's top overall seed, in the first round. The dramatic March Madness victory was not the only headline-grabbing result and trending topic of the game for UMBC, as the athletic department's Twitter feed capitalized on the school's unexpected shining moment. The most unlikely upset thrust the school into the limelight, but UMBC's savvy Twitter account broadened the scope of the story through animated, entertaining, and humorous posts.

The lead in a *New York Times* story by Malika Andrews captured it perfectly.

"Sure, the men's basketball team from the University of Maryland, Baltimore County, pulled off one of the greatest—the greatest?—victories in college sports history late Friday night, toppling Virginia, the NCAA tournament's No. 1 overall seed.

But how about that UMBC athletic department Twitter feed?

As word spread that the Retrievers were doing the unthinkable in a first-round game in Charlotte, N.C., sports fans flocked to their favorite digital bar, Twitter, and found a seat next to a new breed of color commentator: an institutional social media account with sass, verve, and that special ability to burn, burn, burn.

The human behind the triumphal stream was Zach Seidel, 27, the director of multimedia communications and digital for the athletic department. For a couple of hours on Friday night, he was the voice of the ultimate underdogs, the about-to-be-vindicated sports fan who got to revel in something historic—with an audience of millions high-fiving his every remark."[19]

UMBC provided a great example of maximizing the moment in the spotlight and taking full advantage of a Cinderella story and the dream season. The overall benefit for the institution extended well beyond athletics, creating a positive media cycle for UMBC in a story that encapsulates a positive PR story unique to the combination of a marquee sports event and the social media era.

As part of the partnership between the NFL and Twitter, the NFL printed Super Bowl–related fan and player tweets on tens of thousands of pieces of confetti that were used in the Super Bowl LIV postgame celebration at Hard Rock Stadium. The tweet-themed confetti contained tweets sent during the Super Bowl. Included in the Super Bowl confetti tweets was a tweet sent by Super Bowl LIV MVP Patrick Mahomes from when he was a high school senior. It was a creative activation of the partnership, a smart social media–driven audience engagement tool that allowed fans not in attendance but watching the event on TV to take part in the postgame celebration at Hard Rock Stadium. This creative activation also generated media coverage.[20]

Social media activity cannot be viewed in a vacuum. It has a significant PR and business impact, implications that continue to grow as the medium becomes even more important as both a communications platform and a cultural force. Ill-advised social media activity, posts, tweets, content, and interactions have launched countless negative news cycles. In more serious cases, they have impacted employment through suspensions or termination and the loss of sponsors, business partners, and future business in what are now near constant instances of the surfacing of insensitive, inappropriate, offensive tweets. Sponsors, colleges, organizations, and networks must conduct due diligence on all potential employees, signees, and marketing partners. Review of social media history is imperative, but so is the need to educate athletes, executives, talent, and employees of the best, most appropriate, and maximally beneficial way to use the tool of social media and know the boundaries and the consequences of using the platform.

The danger of social media is immediacy and lack of context. Often there is no context given in a swift social media post. PR gaffes or misstatements or even controversies that occur in media interviews can be contextualized or clarified or even corrected in real time. When "send" is pushed on a post, it is a bit more challenging to fix in real time. The sheer volume of social media platforms combined with other digital or online mediums, and the overwhelming level of activity on these platforms, require vigilance in terms of both how they are used for maximum benefit and how they are monitored.

The dawn of the smartphone era ushered in a new age in technological innovation and global communication. Cameras are everywhere. Fans now have ample opportunity to capture personal or behind-the-scenes interactions with athletes and personalities at events or gatherings. Selfies are the new autographs. Photos and videos are posted to social media in an instant. This type of engagement has generally been overwhelmingly positive, particularly the revealing or heartwarming moments that go viral. It is important for athletes, organizations, and fans alike to remember that interactions at events, incidents, or confrontations are all subject to scrutiny via smartphone video, which can be shared instantaneously and become an immediate media storyline and PR challenge.

One of the challenges with posts on social media pages is whether an individual is speaking as a public figure, as a member of an organization, or as an individual on a personal page or in a personal capacity. This can be a particularly thorny issue for those social media accounts that are not directly linked to an organization. Is the executive or TV talent speaking in his capacity as an individual or should he be judged speaking on behalf of or reflecting the views of his employer? These cases are becoming more frequent and are issues that must be considered. The existence of and adherence to social media policy is important for organizations and brands. Violations of social media policy are becoming more frequent and often result in a PR challenge both for the poster and the organization, depending on the visibility of the talent, athlete, executive, broadcaster, the intensity of the discussion, and the potential impact of the news cycle and backlash. What is important from both a business and PR standpoint is consistency of policy and clarity. Social media engagement is both an important and valuable means for expression, but people must be mindful: Every word on social media can be scrutinized, analyzed, discussed, and judged.

The social media age requires an important focus on cybersecurity, and it is critical to safeguard access to social media platforms. Hacks or security breaches present potential PR challenges. Beyond the occurrence of the breach itself, embarrassing posts, offensive content, email leaks, data theft, or hacks of personnel records or customer payment databases are just some of the issues that can arise. On January 28, 2020, 15 NFL teams' social media accounts, including Super Bowl LIV contestants the Kansas City Chiefs and San Francisco 49ers and the league's official account, posted messages that were the product of a hack. This hack underscored the heightened need for vigilance in the area of cybersecurity from both an organizational and institutional standpoint and also from a PR perspective.[21] Being aware of inauthentic activity and combating the spread of disinformation and misinformation on digital and social media platforms are vitally important.

Public Relations, Advocacy, and the Art of Influencing Public Opinion

The sport industry can provide an essential platform to influence public opinion, inspire dialogue, and propel change. PR and communications strategy are important forces in helping raise awareness for civic and societal issues, charitable causes, or public policy initiatives. Persuasion and advocacy are effective tools and important elements of PR and communications strategy in helping sway public opinion.

Sports have had a transformational impact on society and served as a conduit for positive change and social progress. Athletes and sport organizations have been strong advocates of social and political movements, including promoting civil rights, women's rights, and human rights in the United States and internationally. Sport personalities have been among some of the most important champions of gender equality and most powerful activists against racial inequality and injustice by using their celebrity and capitalizing on the media and PR platforms afforded through their fame and sport careers to demand, create, and inspire change.

The willingness of athletes and sport personalities to discuss personal challenges, mental health, bullying, addiction and substance abuse, and political and social issues through both conventional media interviews and first-person accounts either in writing, social media posts, or video and documentaries is increasingly more common. These types of PR campaigns and media placements play an important role in inspiring change, breaking down barriers, facilitating dialogue, encouraging acceptance, and bringing attention to and raising awareness of important issues.

Olympic icon Michael Phelps was named *PRWeek's* 2020 Communicator of the Year in recognition of the work he has done to reduce the stigma of depression and mental health challenges. Phelps, in efforts to raise awareness about mental health issues, has become open and candid about his own struggle with depression

Michael Phelps Named *PRWeek*'s 2020 Communicator of the Year

Olympic swimming legend Michael Phelps is being honored as *PRWeek*'s Communicator of the Year in recognition of his work to reduce stigma around depression and mental health issues.

Phelps is the most decorated Olympian of all time, winning 23 gold medals, 28 in total. His performances made him a global phenomenon and a household name.

But, away from the pool, Phelps struggled with debilitating depression and anxiety, leading to self-described public "explosions" involving drugs and alcohol after victories in 2004, 2008, and 2012. He even considered suicide in 2012 following the London Olympics.

He sought help and got his life back on track, and then embarked on a mission to raise awareness of mental health issues and encourage others to seek help and not suffer in silence.

Phelps introduced stress management into programs offered by his Michael Phelps Foundation. He also worked with the Boys & Girls Clubs of America.

In May 2018, Phelps used his global platform to publicly admit that "it's OK to not be OK." Partnering with online therapy platform Talkspace, he shared his personal experiences in TV ads and YouTube videos, encouraging people to speak openly about mental health and demonstrating the benefits of Talkspace.

Reacting to his award, Phelps said: "I am honored to be recognized by *PRWeek* as their Communicator of the Year and appreciate the opportunity to address the importance of mental health.

"Accepting professional help changed my life. When I fully embraced that it's OK to not be OK, I opened up and discovered there is strength in vulnerability. Ironically, I learned to communicate at 30!

"We are all impacted by mental health and communication is the key to understanding, connection, and meaningful change."

In November 2019, Phelps was named number one on *PRWeek* and sister title *MM&M*'s Health Influencer 50 list for his advocacy around mental health issues.

Phelps joined Talkspace's advisory board and approaches the role with the same zeal he put into his Olympic training. He authentically committed to a cause he was passionate about and leveraged his fame to help others.

A year after launching the Talkspace partnership, Phelps published two tweets from his Twitter handle in May 2019, reigniting a global discussion about mental health awareness.

"Did you know that one in four people around the world experience a mental health issue? I was one of them," he wrote.

"I struggled with anxiety and depression and questioned whether or not I wanted to be alive anymore. It was when I hit this low that I decided to reach out and ask for the help of a licensed therapist. This decision ultimately helped save my life. You don't have to wait for things."

The tweets resulted in hundreds of thousands of likes, retweets, and replies. Talkspace has seen a rise in clientele and Phelps' words have helped save lives.

"Those moments, feelings, and emotions, for me, are light years better than winning the Olympic gold medal," Phelps said.

Sponsored by Johnson & Johnson, the Communicator of the Year category was introduced in 2013 by *PRWeek* and honors the outstanding communicator in the period covered by this year's awards.

> continued

> continued

The individual can come from within or outside the PR industry and previous honorees include March For Our Lives' cofounder David Hogg, #MeToo pioneer Tarana Burke, State Senator Clementa Pinckney (D-SC), ALS campaigner and ice-bucket challenge founder Pete Frates, and schoolgirl human rights activist Malala Yousafzai.

"Michael Phelps is an iconic example of someone who has achieved so much on the world sporting stage but who is now using that platform to communicate effectively around one of the biggest issues in modern society," said Steve Barrett, editorial director of *PRWeek*.

"We are proud to acknowledge his commitment to improving awareness of mental health issues and using smart communications as a core part of that process."

Phelps will accept his honor at the *PRWeek* Awards gala ceremony at Cipriani Wall Street in New York City on Thursday, March 19. Go here for more information and to purchase tickets.

and anxiety. As the most decorated Olympian of all time, he partnered with Talkspace, an online therapy platform in 2018 to discuss "It's OK to not be OK," sharing his personal experiences in videos, social media posts, and ads. Phelps has encouraged others to discuss mental health challenges. He has also included stress management into his Michael Phelps Foundation program.[22] Phelps has done media interviews highlighting his work and mental health advocacy in a wide range of outlets and served as the executive producer, narrator, and featured subject of the HBO documentary *The Weight of Gold*, featuring Olympic athletes and the mental health crisis in sports.[23] A press release discussing *PRWeek*'s recognition is presented in the sidebar.

In June 2020, sport organizations, universities, coaches, and athletes helped play an important role by joining long-standing calls from civil rights activists and Mississippi residents in advocating that the State of Mississippi remove the Confederate battle emblem from the state flag. Greg Sankey, Commissioner of the SEC, released the following statement:

> It is past time for change to be made to the flag of the State of Mississippi. Our students deserve an opportunity to learn and compete in environments that are inclusive and welcoming to all. In the event there is no change, there will be consideration of precluding Southeastern Conference championship events from being conducted in the State of Mississippi until the state flag is changed.[24]

The NCAA released a statement that the NCAA Board of Governors has "expanded the Association's Confederate flag policy to prevent any NCAA Championship events from being played in states where the symbol has a prominent presence"—a change that would exclude Mississippi from hosting any NCAA Championship.[25] Mississippi State running back Kylin Hill tweeted that he would not represent the state until the state changed the flag. As Mississippi was engaged in legislative deliberations, coaches and administrators from Mississippi's public universities traveled to Jackson, the state capitol, to deliver a visible and vocal message advocating that it was time to change the flag. The Mississippi state legislature passed a bill that Mississippi Governor Tate Reeves signed mandating the removal of the state flag and banning the future use of the Confederate emblem.[26]

Proponents of college athletics reform have been vocal advocates for changes, allowing college athletes to benefit from the use of their own name image and likeness (NIL). The public sentiment has moved, shifting in favor of structural changes in the collegiate model for athletes, as a result of a combination of PR advocacy, public pressure, persuasion, media commentary and news coverage, and lawsuits and legislative action. After lawsuits and longstanding resistance to the issue of NIL reform and athlete compensation, college athletics stakeholders have engaged in more open and solutions-based dialogue. In a move toward allowing student-athlete compensation for endorsements and promotions, the NCAA Board of Governors announced in April

Sport Industry Public Relations and Communication During a Global Pandemic

The COVID-19 pandemic illustrates how important communicating externally with fans, media, and the general public is in the face of a natural disaster, national tragedy, or public health crisis, particularly during an unprecedented global event. The global outbreak of the novel coronavirus caused widespread cancellations and postponements due to the significant concern for health and safety and need to prevent the spread of this highly contagious virus. It also showcases the role that sport plays in terms of influencing public awareness and public opinion and providing a powerful messaging platform.

The PGA TOUR cancelled the 2020 THE PLAYERS Championship after the first round as a result of the impact of the outbreak of the coronavirus. PGA TOUR Commissioner Jay Monahan sent the following message to fans, communicating that the TOUR season would be suspended due to the concerns surrounding the impact of the global pandemic.[30]

A note to our fans,

We're incredibly disappointed to suspend the PGA TOUR's season. I've said all along, the health and safety of everyone associated with this organization is our number one priority. We tried to be as thoughtful and measured as possible during this dynamic and challenging time. We took all the steps within our control and felt comfortable proceeding.

I wanted to fight for our players and our fans and for this TOUR to show how golf can unify and inspire. As the situation continued to escalate and there seemed to be more unknowns, it ultimately became a matter of when, and not if, we would need to call it a day.

Our focus now will be on how we use this moment in time to inspire the communities where we won't be playing, continue to inspire once we resume playing, and make sure we use the strength of this organization to do good.

I love this TOUR. I love our players. I love our fans. I love our charities, our volunteers, and our partners. And like we always say, golf is a great unifier and equalizer. We're hard at work ensuring that our sport has a positive impact in this time of need.

Sincerely,

Jay Monahan
PGA TOUR Commissioner

Monahan vowed that THE PLAYERS Championship's commitment to the charitable component of the event would continue despite the event's cancellation. THE PLAYERS Championship and TPC Sawgrass donated 2.8 tons of food, including 7,500 prepared meals to Feeding Northeast Florida and Jacksonville's Sulzbacher Center.[31] The PGA TOUR's charitable initiatives have donated more than US$3 billion, a commitment to charity that dates back to the TOUR's first recorded charitable donation of US$10,000 at the 1938 Palm Beach Invitational.[32]

MLB sent the following message to fans on Twitter after suspending the 2020 Spring Training as a result of the COVID-19 pandemic.[33]

> continued

> continued

To baseball fans worldwide:

Just like you, we miss our game right now. But in these unprecedented times, we need to do what is best for the health and safety of everyone. That means staying home, but it **does not** mean we're alone.

Talk to your friends and family about the players you can't wait to see—and talk to us. We want to hear from you! Watch highlights, share opinions, and start debates.

We're not out on the diamond, but we'll always be right here.

With love,
@mlb

Sport stars also became highly effective in helping educate the public about how to prevent the spread of the virus. Golden State Warriors superstar Steph Curry hosted an Instagram Q&A with Dr. Anthony Fauci, Director of the National Institute of Allergy and Infectious Diseases and member of the White House Coronavirus Task Force. The Q&A was designed to educate the public about symptoms to look for, social distancing, hygiene practices, and other necessary precautions to take while also answering questions and concerns about COVID-19.[34]

In a *USA Today* piece headlined "Stephen Curry's coronavirus interview with Dr. Anthony Fauci is most significant move of his career," writer Mark Medina detailed "The session became as informative as watching C-SPAN. But it was hardly boring. Through it all, Warriors fans and the general public saw a different side of Curry that makes him a beloved teammate and respected leader."[35]

In addition to the live audience, the Steph Curry–Dr. Fauci Q&A was archived on a variety of digital platforms and shared widely on social media channels and through traditional media. It was a great example of an athlete harnessing his platform and social media following to raise awareness for an important cause and assist with critical, potentially life-saving messaging during an unprecedented modern public health crisis. Curry used his celebrity and credibility with sports fans to engage in a vital dialogue with and highlight the expertise of Dr. Fauci, the country's leading infectious disease expert. The Q&A was strategic outreach, smart PR, and a valuable public service in the efforts to mitigate the spread of the virus, designed particularly to reach younger audiences across social media.

2020 that it supported "rule changes to allow student-athletes to receive compensation for third-party endorsements both related to and separate from athletics. It also supports compensation for other student-athlete opportunities such as social media, businesses they have started, and personal appearances within the guiding principles originally outlined by the board." These steps are part of the NCAA's effort to modernize its rules regarding NIL. The new rules are expected by January 2021 and to take effect by the 2021 to 2022 academic year.[27] In early 2020, the NCAA Division I Council also announced that "athletes designated as elite by nationally recognized groups may receive developmental training from the U.S. Olympic and Paralympic Committee or national governing bodies." This rule change also allowed the elite athletes to use elite coaching without it impacting their eligibility.[28]

Global sport organizations and brands have made the environment and sustainability a priority through smart, innovative business practices but also by creating mechanisms to raise awareness surrounding environmental issues and impact. The International Olympic Committee (IOC) has made sustainability a priority, which, in addition to helping the environment, attracts positive PR storylines and media attention. The IOC Sustainability Report in 2018 included the following description of the organization's efforts:

"With the publication of the 'Olympic Agenda 2020—The New Norm,' which, through 118 reforms, reshapes the way the Olympic Games are planned and delivered, sustainability principles are now present throughout the entire life cycle of the Olympic Games—from the earliest stages of the candidature process through to the handover to legacy bodies. The reforms aim to ensure the Games are affordable, beneficial, and sustainable by reducing their cost and complexity, minimizing risks, resource consumption and waste, and—consequently—lowering their environmental impacts and carbon emissions. The goal is to ensure that the Olympic Games act as a catalyst for sustainable development within the host city and region."[29]

Coping With Crisis

One of the most visible roles that a public relations professional performs is coping with crisis and providing damage control. Because most of these cases elicit media interest and often receive intense coverage and scrutiny from the press and the public, the words and actions of the public relations department and its professionals are often in the news and sometimes engender as much interest as the incident that precipitated the crisis. In some cases, the effect of these negative situations is short-term, but a crisis can have substantial long-term effects. The PR personnel involved in handling the crisis must aim to develop a strategic response that maximizes the effectiveness of the response to alleviate the crisis and that minimizes the lasting damage caused by the crisis. During a crisis or damage control situation, PR professionals must work closely and collaboratively with the appropriate team of people (executives, administration, and legal counsel) to coordinate media strategy and public response.

Sport is not immune to problems. A number of crisis or scandal situations have occurred in recent years. The following are some examples:

• *Ray Rice domestic violence scandal.* Baltimore Ravens running back Ray Rice was released by the team and he was suspended indefinitely by the NFL after TMZ released the surveillance video from inside the elevator, revealing the full extent of the domestic violence incident between Rice and his then fiancée (they subsequently married) at an Atlantic City casino in February 2014. TMZ had previously released footage from outside the elevator. After the incident, Rice was arrested, subsequently indicted, pled not guilty to aggravated assault, and applied to and was accepted into a diversionary program for first-time offenders. The NFL initially suspended Rice for two games, a punishment that faces public scrutiny. The public outcry and anger intensified when the second TMZ video revealed the footage from inside the elevator showing the full extent of the brutal incident. Rice was released and suspended indefinitely.[36]

• *Dallas Mavericks' sexual harassment investigation.* Mark Cuban, the owner of the Dallas Mavericks, agreed to pay US$10 million in 2018 to women's leadership and domestic violence organizations in an agreement with the NBA to address sexual harassment and other improper conduct of front office employees.[37] Cuban did not face accusations of misconduct, but the report released by investigators cited "significant errors of judgment" and "institutional failures" on Cuban's part. The accusations against the Mavericks were first reported in *Sports Illustrated* in a report that portrayed a toxic environment for female employees.[38]

• *MLB and Houston Astros sign stealing scandal.* A story published in *The Athletic* in November 2019 revealed the Houston Astros' system for using electronic sign stealing, details of which were provided by former pitcher Mike Fiers. MLB launched an investigation into the matter that led to the suspension and subsequent firing of Astros GM Jeff Luhnow and manager A.J. Hinch. The Astros were also fined US$5 million and lost their next two first- and second-round amateur draft picks. In addition to casting a cloud of suspicion over the Astros' 2017 World Series victory, the scandal rocked MLB.[39] The Boston Red Sox fired manager Alex Cora, and the New York Mets fired Carlos Beltran before he managed a game for the team as part of the fallout from the sign stealing scandal. Cora had been an Astros bench coach and Beltran a player on the 2017 World Series team. As part of the investigation into breaking video rules, the Red Sox were stripped of a second-round draft pick in the 2020

Deflategate: The Anatomy of a Sport and Entertainment PR Crisis

On January 18, 2015, the New England Patriots defeated the Indianapolis Colts 45 to 7 in the AFC Championship Game in a game played in rainy and wet conditions. News broke shortly after the game that the NFL was investigating an accusation that the Patriots had intentionally deflated the footballs to gain an advantage over the Colts. A headline-generating controversy ensnared the NFL, a marquee franchise, and Patriots superstar quarterback Tom Brady in a dramatic episode that eclipsed every other storyline leading up to the Super Bowl XLIX. What became known as "Deflategate" transcended sports and dominated the sports and news media in the United States and throughout the globe. The NFL hired attorney Ted Wells to lead the probe into the alleged misconduct. The Wells Report detailed the league's investigation and findings on the matter. The Patriots organization was fined US$1 million and lost its first-round draft pick for 2016 and fourth-round pick for 2017. Brady was suspended without pay for the first four games on the 2015 regular season. The NFL player's association appealed Brady's suspension, kicking off a series of events that involved appeals, disciplinary hearings, lawsuits, legal suspense, courtroom drama (including the publication of a memorable courtroom sketch of Brady), the nullification of suspension, and subsequent reinstatement of suspension. Brady declined, 544 days into the controversy, to appeal his case to the Supreme Court and served the four-game suspension at the beginning of the 2016 regular season.[44]

Deflategate was an all-consuming story, a PR and legal morass that overshadowed two Super Bowls, two NFL off-seasons, and an entire NFL regular season in between. There are myriad PR lessons to learn from Deflategate. In sports, the integrity of the game is paramount—it must be preserved and safeguarded. Rules must be enforced, and infractions, when proven, should be punished. The process must be fair and transparent and handled in a careful, timely, and swift manner when possible. If legal issues are involved, best practices are to follow the legal process, be transparent, and communicate.

The lasting PR legacy of Deflategate is that an incident that probably could have or should have been limited to an equipment fine and routine disciplinary action turned into a full-blown PR crisis—an entirely avoidable one. One of the enduring PR and business lessons of Deflategate is what happens when the way an organization handles a crisis becomes an actual crisis itself.

As Kevin Seifert wrote on ESPN.com,

> At best, it was a relatively minor rules violation that no rational person would link to the Patriots' victory two weeks later in Super Bowl XLIX. At worst, Deflategate was a retroactive framing of the league's most successful franchise and a future Hall of Fame quarterback, a clumsy and forgettable endeavor, and an unfortunate reminder that the NFL's standard for discipline demands only that an event was "more probable than not" to have occurred. Brady ultimately served a four-game suspension because the NFL believed he was "generally aware" of the scheme.[39]

Deflategate plagued the NFL for an extended period of time, caused endless negative storylines and countless PR headaches, and created a loss of public trust and significant brand damage. It was an embarrassing spectacle and dismal PR chapter for a leading global sport organization and the most powerful sport league in the United States.

amateur draft, the team's replay system operator was suspended without pay through 2021, and Cora was suspended for the 2020 MLB season.[40]

- *PGA of America President Ted Bishop removed for sexist remarks.* In 2014, the PGA of America board voted to remove then-President Ted Bishop from his position one day after Bishop used inappropriate and sexist remarks on social media. Bishop used the phrase "Lil girl" at the end of a tweet, which was directed at and criticizing professional golfer and European Ryder Cup star Ian Poulter. Bishop made an additional sexist comment in a post on Facebook characterizing comments Poulter had made as "sounds like a little school girl squealing during recess." Although Bishop's tenure was set to expire the following month, the board acted swiftly to remove him, citing that Bishop's comments were inconsistent with the association's policies and noting that the organization recognized its leadership responsibility to "make golf both welcoming and inclusive to all who want to experience it."[41]

- *Sportscaster Thom Brennaman suspended for homophobic remark during broadcast.* Thom Brennaman, a longtime Cincinnati Reds broadcaster, was suspended by the organization after uttering a homophobic slur during the telecast of the first game of a Reds–Royals doubleheader in Kansas City on August 19, 2020. Brennaman appeared to be unaware that Fox Sports Ohio had returned from commercial break when he made the offensive remark on the air. During the fifth inning of the second game, he made an on-air apology and left the broadcast booth, replaced by another broadcaster who called the rest of the game. The Reds issued a forceful statement saying their organization was "devastated by the horrific, homophobic remark" made by Brennaman, noted "he was pulled off the air, and effective immediately was suspended from doing Reds broadcasts," and offered "sincerest apologies to the LGBTQ+ community in Cincinnati, Kansas City, all across this country, and beyond." Brennaman, who had been part of Fox Sports NFL coverage, was removed from the network's NFL TV lineup as a result of the incident. Fox Sports issued a strong statement condemning the language used as "abhorrent, unacceptable and not representative of the values of Fox Sports."[42]

Alex Rodriguez: The PR Comeback

Alex Rodriguez is the architect of one of the greatest sport PR comebacks of all time—a textbook case of effective personal brand rehabilitation. The transformation from a disgraced former MLB MVP and PED cheat into a popular, trusted TV personality and valued pitchman is the result of humility and hard work. After a successful guest stint on the Fox Sports MLB postseason studio show while he was still playing for the New York Yankees, Rodriguez joined the network's MLB postseason studio show on a full-time basis after retiring from MLB. Rodriguez's star turn on Fox Sports' Emmy Award–winning MLB postseason studio show turned into additional TV roles, including serving as analyst on ESPN's *Sunday Night Baseball*, ABC's *Shark Tank*, CNBC's *Back in the Game*, and a podcast called *The Corp*. Rodriguez is arguably more popular now than during his playing career, which was often marked by controversy and negative headlines. As the CEO of A-Rod Corp, he has created a substantial business portfolio, including real estate and sports and wellness investments. Rodriguez has emerged as an effective and trusted PR spokesperson for baseball and brands alike and is a force in sports and popular culture. He is tech savvy, engages on social media with compelling content, and is accessible with reporters. He has completed what sports business reporter Darren Rovell calls the "greatest sports image rehab of all time."[45]

• *Houston Rockets GM Daryl Morey Sends Tweet That Ignites a Geopolitical Firestorm.* Houston Rockets General Manager Daryl Morey shared a tweet with an image and message in support of Hong Kong pro-democracy protests against China's crackdown on Hong Kong's freedoms. Morey's tweet—"Fight for Freedom Stand with Hong Kong"—ignited a geopolitical firestorm. Rockets owner Tilman Fertitta attempted to distance the organization from Morey's tweet. The Chinese Basketball Association ceased its cooperation with the Rockets as a result of the tweet, which also drew the ire of Rockets and NBA sponsors, broadcast, and business partners in China, resulting in financial losses, the suspension of deals, and the cancellation of events of the NBA preseason tour in China. The NBA sent out an initial statement about the incident that was roundly criticized. Morey deleted the tweet and attempted to backtrack and provide an explanation. The NBA sent out a second statement clarifying the league's position. The damage from the tweet from a business and PR standpoint has the potential to be lasting for the NBA who had made a huge investment in China. The incident caused a fierce debate about the balance of personal right to freedom of speech and expression, protecting those rights of expression, and the desire to advocate for human and civil rights while maintaining business interests in international markets. The controversy opened up the socially progressive NBA that proudly supports outspoken and politically active players, coaches, and executives to significant criticism for appearing to place business interests ahead of human rights concerns and the individual right to free expression.[43]

Sport, Television, and Entertainment Influence on Sport Public Relations

Television coverage has played a transformational role in the tremendous growth of the modern sport industry. TV has fueled the increased media attention that sport received and has helped propel sport, the athletes who competed, and the broadcasters who televised the events into the entertainment business. The creation of ABC's *Monday Night Football* in 1970 and the groundbreaking launch of ESPN, the first all-sports TV network in 1979, both played significant roles in driving the growth of the sport industry and an increase in media attention for sport. *Monday Night Football* and ESPN both helped provide sport with a new cultural relevance and popularity in society, influencing the continued emergence and evolution of sport as an entertainment vehicle.

Monday Night Football moved NFL games into prime time and helped carry the league to a new level of popularity. ABC Sports President and Executive Producer Roone Arledge believed that the program would be as much entertainment as football. The broadcasts featured more cameras and storytelling and appealed to women and casual fans.[46] As then NBC Sports Chairman Dick Ebersol said about Arledge after Arledge's death in 2002, "Roone was surely the only television executive of his time who would have dared to put sports in prime time." The effect, according to Ebersol, was that the move to prime time helped transform the business of sport: "All of the money the athletes are making, all the big money in sports, none of that would be happening if not for Roone."[47] (*Monday Night Football* aired on ABC from 1970 to 2005; beginning in the 2006 season, it moved to ESPN. Both ABC and ESPN are owned by the Walt Disney Company.)

The combination of the successful and increased presence of sport in the prime-time television lineup and Arledge's hallmark "up close and personal" philosophy, which introduced U.S. television audiences to relatively unknown Olympic athletes and transformed them into household names, had a lasting influence on future media and TV coverage.

In mid-2005, Dick Ebersol, then Chairman of NBC Sports and Olympics, finalized negotiations with the IOC to move the swimming and gymnastics competitions for the 2008 Beijing Games to mornings instead of evenings, thus allowing those sports to be broadcast live during the NBC prime-time telecasts in the United States.[48]

The change in the Beijing Olympic competition schedule was a brilliant strategic negotiation that proved to be "golden" for swimming sensation Michael Phelps and for NBC. The media zoomed in on the storyline of Phelps' second attempt to chase Olympic greatness and match or break Mark Spitz's mark of seven gold medals, which dominated the pre-2008 Beijing Olympics news cycle. NBC's ability to showcase Phelps' nightly swimming feats live in U.S. prime time allowed the network to reach the largest possible audience available, further amplifying the Olympic coverage and the Phelps storyline. Phelps served as the centerpiece of intense Games media attention, commanding the top spot in a rapidly moving multiplatform news cycle during the first week of the Beijing Games, creating watercooler conversations for the public and fueling even greater interest.

In today's fractured TV universe and competitive content environment, live sports event broadcasts command the largest television audiences on broadcast and cable TV. Sports are entertainment television; they are prime-time television. Sport programming has emerged as a coveted and dominant force across the spectrum of content platforms. In an era of expanded entertainment options, niche programming, and time-shifted viewing, live sports events have emerged as dominant and durable programming. Sports events accounted for 88 of the top 100 most-watched broadcasts in 2019. The NFL boasted an impressive 41 of the top 50 and 73 of the top 100.[49] NBC's *Sunday Night Football* is the top show in prime time. Fox Sports' *America's Game of the Week* is the most-watched program on all of television. The Olympic Games telecasts dominate prime time throughout the duration of the event.

How has the television landscape over the years changed for sport programming? The difference in national Nielsen household ratings between the Super Bowl and the top entertainment show in prime time over a 50-year period speaks volumes: In 1969, it was +13 percent; by 2019, it grew to a whopping +414 percent.[50]

The sheer magnitude of content platforms that broadcast sports events, sports news and talk, and ancillary sports programming is overwhelming. The ubiquity and dominance of sport programming is illustrated by 24-hour sports TV and radio networks, regional sports networks (RSNs), sports-specific digital outlets, and the emergence of sports podcasts. Technology companies and social media networks partnering with leagues, teams, athletes, and personalities to produce and broadcast programming reinforce the importance of sport content. Documentaries and reality shows present TV opportunities for sport personalities, including the growing trend of athletes producing content or running production companies, which are also avenues for sport programming.

The large audiences and the sheer tonnage of sport programming present a huge spotlight for the industry while presenting a wide variety of PR and marketing opportunities for athletes, personalities, teams, leagues, and organizations. The combination of the robust ratings and the broad viewership and reach of sport programming creates an optimal brand-building platform for sport personalities as moments are captured and magnified from every angle.

Although attention spans are getting shorter, there are far more outlets for amplification of sport programming. In addition to live events, there is an abundance of studio shows, pregame and postgame shows, news programs, documentaries, and gambling shows. The buildup to sports events and then the competitions themselves are documented from every angle. Moments are captured and instantly put into the highlight and feedback loop on TV and social media platforms to be viewed, discussed, and shared. These clips and trending topics provide ample PR opportunities. Television and sports are at their best when they are shared experiences and social media enhances that concept, providing a connectivity for the audience.

As technology and broadcast innovations have improved the quality of telecasts, so too has the impact of the broadcast talent and sports media personalities. Television made stars out of the athletes, but it also made household names of the sportscasters and sports TV personalities who broadcast the games and host events. TV personalities are as popular and recognizable as the athletes they cover. Fox Sports rules analyst Mike Pereira has distinguished himself, defining the role of TV rules analyst and helping to make the role an essential part of NFL and sports TV. His expert commentary and rules analysis enhance the telecast because rules and replay situations are so crucial and require immediate expert scrutiny. As Kevin Clark wrote in *The Ringer* about Pereira's role "By mastering the NFL's confusing and ever-changing rule book, the Fox Sports analyst has become an essential voice in a complicated time."[51]

Pereira has not only proven to be an asset from a production vantage point but also has provided a significant, strategic benefit from PR standpoint. He has been an invaluable PR resource explaining controversial calls and replay or rules situations during and after games. Pereira is a respected voice who possesses the ability to provide explanations in real time on the air, on video posted to social media, and in media interviews—all of which increase his value as an on-air personality and PR spokesperson. His PR role also underscores how broadcast TV talent helps drive tune-in for the broadcasts and general interest in the sport properties that talent covers through media, PR communications, and social media outreach.

National and local sports cable TV and talk radio provide constant discussion, commentary, opinion, and criticism while their hosts debate current sports headlines and issues. These shows collectively provide an ample range of opportunities for PR personnel to secure interviews for athletes, coaches, executives, and broadcasters to promote their teams, accomplishments, upcoming events, marketing partnerships, and charitable initiatives and to showcase their personalities and gain exposure.

Today's sport entertainment landscape presents a wide array of opportunities and challenges for sport PR professionals because of the interest level generated by sport. Stories featuring athletes and sport appear in the full spectrum of media across all print, electronic, and digital platforms, spanning topics from general news to sport, business, and lifestyle outlets. Topics include business interests and marketing partnerships, philanthropic and community relations initiatives, athletes' opinions on politics and social issues, and details of sport personalities' lives. You are as likely now to see stories about athletes in *People* and on *Entertainment Tonight* as you are to see them in *Sports Illustrated* and on *SportsCenter*. But the exposure can bring additional media scrutiny, which may require attention from PR professionals.

Fans and media want behind-the-scenes access and detailed information—demands now compounded by the immediacy of the volume of information available on the Internet and social media. The media spotlight that has catapulted sport into entertainment—bringing fame, fortune, and celebrity to athletes—has also brought trouble and controversy. Historic and remarkable athletic achievements and success on the field are documented by the press, but so too are the off-field personal issues and shortcomings (e.g., character issues, substance abuse, performance-enhancing drug use, financial problems). Today's media landscape has the ability both to amplify and celebrate the positive news and, on the other end of the spectrum, to expose and magnify the negative stories. The trend toward sensational and negative media storylines and the increased attention paid to off-field topics and personal lives has caused some athletes, organizations, and PR staffs to be more guarded in their approach to dealing with the press and granting media access.

PR professionals play a significant role in providing strategic counsel to help athletes and organizations navigate the diverse media landscape that requires interaction and access to remain relevant; that same media landscape can be harsh in a time of difficulty and crisis. The ultimate goal for the sport PR professional is to balance the expansive range of media opportunities available by striving to create the maximum amount of positive exposure while avoiding potential pitfalls that the intense scrutiny and media coverage in the digital and social media age can present.

Wrap-Up

The modern 24/7 news cycle moves with speed and intensity. Its volume of coverage, rapid rate of reporting, and immediacy of information available make it important for PR professionals to take advantage of opportunities that allow their athletes and organizations to break through and make a meaningful and positive impact. PR personnel must be strong, passionate advocates on behalf of their athletes, organizations, and brands while promoting them, but they also must be able to engage in rapid response in reaction to negative stories, incorrect reporting, and crises. Public relations is an important part of the marketing equation and the primary vehicle through which an organization interacts with the media and various publics. The media landscape continues to change, and technology continues to influence the future evolution of the media industry. Although the mediums and platforms may change, the core responsibilities of the PR department and its practitioners continue to revolve around positioning and promoting a favorable image of the sport entity in the marketplace. For public relations to be effective, the PR specialist must react and respond to requests and situations and actively initiate and develop media relations and community relations efforts in an integrated, proactive methodology. This methodology should focus on both short-term and long-term objectives with attention to building and fostering relationships. These activities and the public relations and communications functions, in general, must play an integral role in both the strategic planning process for the organization and the implementation and management of the strategic plan.

Public relations programs fulfill a variety of roles, including image shaping and enhancement, reputation management, educational efforts, business development, content development, coping with crisis, and community relations.

Finally, although media may be receptive to story pitches and can be influenced to consider different perspectives or opinions, they are never controlled by the PR department. Thus, public relations professionals must build mutually beneficial relationships with the various publics related to their particular sport industry segment. Again, these publics are best served if the public relations program is not only reactive but also proactive, creative, and well-integrated.

Activities

1. Set up an informational interview and visit the media relations entity in the athletics department on your campus or a professional sport franchise in your home market. During your interview, discuss the concepts of reactive, proactive, and integrated media relations and the amount of time that the entity spends on each approach. Identify an example of each function in that media relations setting.

2. Begin a journal that you will keep for 30 days. The focus of the journal is to identify through sports-related media outlets crises or controversies in sport that have required PR response, reputation management, or damage control efforts. Do some issues seem to come up more frequently than others? Do some organizations seem to be more adept than others at dealing with a crisis? Do you think that the strategy used to deal with the crisis was effective, and why?

3. In reading sports-related media outlets, trade publications, and business press, identify an example of a fully integrated PR placement that includes sponsors, advertisers, marketing partners, community relations, or philanthropic storylines. Evaluate the piece and the way in which the marketing, sponsor, or charitable elements are presented. In what type of publication did the piece appear? Did it have a digital or social media or content component?

4. A professional sport franchise is hacked, with the team website, social media accounts, email, and company databases all affected. The breach exposes corporate communications, sensitive personnel and business files, and customers' personal and credit card information. The hack also results in embarrassing messages and content posted across the team's digital and social media accounts and website. Develop the PR and communications strategy in response to the breach.

5. Watch or listen to the weekly media availability; pre-event, postgame, or post-round press conferences; or on-air TV or radio interviews of a head coach, player, or general manager or team executive. How effectively does this person deal with the media? Detail this person's strengths, weaknesses, and areas needed for improvement in press relations.

Your Marketing Plan

In any marketing plan (even those developed primarily for an internal audience), public relations is a critical function. Effective public relations can garner support for your concepts. A solid media relations and communications component can ensure awareness and comprehension of your ideas and intent, and attention to community relations may generate acceptance of your ideas and programs. Review your marketing plan to determine how each of these elements should be addressed to achieve acceptance and support of your objectives internally, externally, or both.

 Go to HK*Propel* to complete the activities for this chapter.

Chapter 10

Sponsorship, Corporate Partnerships, and the Role of Activation

OBJECTIVES

- To illustrate the triangular relationship between the sponsored property, the corporate entity, and the consumer

- To demonstrate the importance of fit and the use of exclusivity between the sponsor and the property

- To develop a comprehension of the motivations and rationale for the use of sponsorship by sport properties and corporate entities

- To convey the importance of activation to engage the target market while simultaneously bringing the brand to life

Andrew Boyers/Pool via Getty Images

Toyota's Olympic Sponsorship and the Future of Mobility

It was a no-brainer for Toyota to join the Olympic movement by becoming the first-ever mobility partner in The Olympic Partner (TOP) Programme in 2015.[1] The Tokyo 2020 Games were quickly approaching, and Asia was going to play host to the Beijing 2022 Games as well. While the decision to become only one of a dozen or so major corporate partners was a relatively easy one for Toyota, the creation of a global marketing campaign and lasting Olympic legacy was the difficult task. The Olympic Movement is about bringing the whole world together not only to celebrate through sports but also to generate lasting, positive change that moves humanity forward. It was that final phrase, *moving humanity forward*, that resonated with Toyota's creative agency. Toyota had already branded itself as "the human movement company," so a sponsorship slogan for the Olympic Games needed to drive home this idea that people, not products, were the focus of the future.[2]

The company felt that every athlete, and every person, has had a dream of accomplishing something in their life that seemed impossible and had trouble gaining the courage to take the first step. Getting started is always the hardest part. If Toyota could help people take that first and most important step toward their dreams, no matter how difficult, then they could truly move the world forward. After several iterations of campaign taglines, "Start Your Impossible" became the theme for Toyota's global marketing efforts.

> Today, "Start Your Impossible" anchors Toyota's first Olympics in the International Olympic Committee's TOP (The Olympic Partner) program, after it had to wait for several country-level car deals to expire after Rio 2016 to claim global rights. The campaign spawned 10 television commercials with versions running in 40 markets, a digital-social campaign, local and regional commercials, and, not insignificantly, the decentralized company's first corporate initiative to touch its approximately 370,000 employees.[2]

Showcased in its commercials and other activations were wearable devices that assist the blind in moving about as well as human support robots designed to care for the elderly. The most unique aspect of the campaign was the total lack of automobiles present, as people were truly at the heart of the message. Toyota's own employees were part of the target market, as the brand looked to imitate what other Olympic sponsors had done in the past with internal marketing. UPS reported spending 60 percent of its budget on improving employee morale, while John Hancock Insurance incentivized its sales staff with Olympic tickets and hospitality leading to US$60 million in increased revenue.[2] Toyota sought to bring its employees in all departments across the globe together to solve the most challenging mobility and transportation problems. According to Toyota's Olympic mission statement, sustainability in transportation is one of its pillars. The company is driven to "provide sustainable mobility solutions for the Games to help with safer, more efficient mobility, including intelligent transport systems, urban traffic systems, and vehicle-to-vehicle communications systems."[1]

The Olympic partnership was not the only piece of the integrated sponsorship puzzle for Toyota. The car manufacturer also signed with the Paralympic Games in 2015, the United States Olympic & Paralympic Committee (USOPC), four U.S. national governing bodies (NGBs), and endorsed 19 Olympic and Paralympic athletes. Toyota believes the Paralympics were even better suited to highlight its advancements in mobility and help athletes with peak performance. As an executive for the automaker described the holistic sponsorship portfolio: "This is not a toe in the water, it's a full-body plunge."[2] Through its sponsorship of the biggest sports event in the world, Toyota has dedicated the next 12 years (and possibly beyond) to supporting athletes, the Olympic Movement, and the betterment of society. While no one knows exactly what the future holds for human mobility, Toyota knows technology and innovation will play major roles in how the world moves forward.

In this chapter, we examine the integrated nature of sponsorship. Sponsorship activities are more integrated than other promotional activities and contain a variety of marketing mix elements. Although a number of marketing mix elements can function as standalones (e.g., an open house, discounts on tickets, community relations programs), a sponsorship usually involves two or more of the elements of the marketing mix to provide sponsors with associations, recognition, value, exposure, and activation opportunities to help them achieve their marketing objectives. The term *sponsorship* includes not only funding agreements between sport organizations and corporate entities but also financial grants and assistance from governmental units and departments as well as foundations and trusts. This chapter focuses primarily on the sponsorship form of corporate partnerships because this is the predominant format globally, and in light of the current global economy, it will continue to occupy that position.

What Is Sponsorship?

Sponsorship is a triangular business relationship in which three stakeholder groups are involved:

1. Sponsored property
2. Corporate entity
3. Consumers

Corporate sponsorship is defined as "an investment in cash or in-kind, in an activity, in return for access to the exploitable commercial potential associated with that activity."[3] Consider the following activities and entities:

- NCAA–Capital One Cup
- PGA Tour–Waste Management Phoenix Open
- NBA Miami Heat–American Airlines Arena
- MLB–New Era headwear
- Emirates–Arsenal US$56 million per year jersey sponsorship[4]

What do all these have in common? They represent the types of promotional licensing agreements that have become commonplace in sport and lifestyle marketing. *Promotional licensing* is an umbrella term that encompasses corporate sponsorship, but *sponsorship*, and in many cases *corporate partnership*, has become the accepted term throughout the world. Therefore, throughout this chapter and the text, we will use the word *sponsorship* to refer to the acquisition of rights to affiliate or directly associate with a product, a person, an organization, a team, a league, or an event (throughout the chapter any or all of these types of entities will be referred to as the *sport or entertainment property*) for the purpose of deriving benefits related to that affiliation or association. The sponsor then uses this relationship to achieve its promotional objectives or to facilitate and support its broader marketing objectives. The rights derived from this relationship may include retail opportunities, purchase of media time, entitlement (inclusion of the sponsor name in the event or facility name, such as FedEx Cup, Staples Center, and Outback Bowl), contests or sweepstakes, endorsements, logo placement on uniforms or apparel, hospitality, website access, or other associations or benefits.

Although sponsorship agreements are customized and specific to the participating parties, the following provisions and benefits are the most common elements of such agreements:

- The right to use a logo, name, trademark, and graphic representation signifying the purchaser's (or supporter's) connection with the sport property, which can be used in advertising, promotion, publicity, or other communication activities employed by the purchaser or supporter
- The right to an exclusive association within a product or service category
- The right of entitlement to an event, a venue, or a facility
- The right to use various designations or phrases in connection with the sport or entertainment property, such as *official sponsor*, *official supplier*, *official product*, or *presented by*
- The right of service (use of the product or exclusive use of the product) or the right to use the sponsor's product or service in conjunction with the performance, event, or facility

- The right to use certain promotional activities, such as contests, advertising campaigns, sales-driven activities, and so forth, in conjunction with the sponsorship agreement
- The rights to the media assets of the sport property—including broadcast and Internet rights and the opportunity to associate digital and social media platforms with those of the sport property

Sponsorship, then, includes a wide array of activities associated with a communications process that is designed to use sport, entertainment, and other forms of lifestyle marketing to send messages to a targeted audience. The amount of money spent on sport and special-event sponsorships, as well as the number of sponsorships, has grown dramatically (table 10.1).

Sponsorship in the Marketing Mix

As previously discussed, the marketing mix comprises variables that fall into five broad categories: product, price, promotions, place (including distribution), and public relations. The marketer's function is to manipulate these variables to meet the target market's needs in a continually changing environment.

As a key component of the marketing mix, promotions are often referred to by theorists as the communications mix (figure 10.1).[5] In comparison with many other promotional activities, which are often stand-alones, sponsorship activities are much more integrated and are composed of a variety of marketing and promotional components.

TABLE 10.1   North American Sponsorship Spending by Property Type

Property type	2016 spending	2017 spending	Increase from 2016	2018 spending (projected)	Increase from 2017 (projected)
Sport	$15.7 billion	$16.26 billion	3.6%	$17.05 billion	4.9%
Entertainment	$2.22 billion	$2.29 billion	3.2%	$2.4 billion	4.8%
Causes	$1.99 billion	$2.05 billion	3.0%	$2.14 billion	4.4%
Arts	$962 million	$993 million	3.2%	$1.03 billion	3.7%
Festivals, fairs, and annual events	$878 million	$903 million	2.8%	$936 million	3.7%
Associations and membership organizations	$604 million	$616 million	2.0%	$635 million	3.1%

Amounts listed are in U.S. dollars.

Reprinted by permission from IEG, *What Sponsors Want & Where Dollars Will Go In 2018.* www.sponsorship.com/IEG/files/f3/f3cfac41-2983-49be-8df6-3546345e27de.pdf

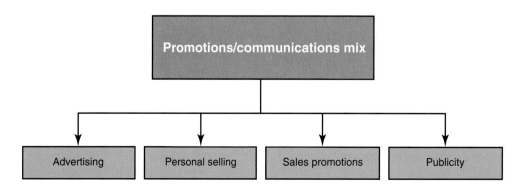

FIGURE 10.1   The traditional promotions or communications mix.

The role of promotions is to inform and persuade consumers and thus influence their purchasing decision. The elements of the promotions or communications mix are traditionally considered to be advertising, personal selling, publicity, sponsorship, and sales promotion. Combinations of some or all of these elements are inherent in sponsorship agreements (figure 10.2).

One sponsorship activity that combines personal selling and promotion is hospitality. Hospitality opportunities are a sponsorship asset or benefit commonly associated with premier events, such as the Olympic Games, World Cup, Super Bowl, NBA All-Star Weekend, Daytona 500, and the concert tours of major performing artists. *Hospitality* can be defined as "the provision made for the sponsor by the sport or entertainment property of tickets in exclusive seating areas, lodging, transportation, on-site special activities, and special events and excursions related to the activity or event." The sponsor can in turn use these assets or benefits to entertain its own clients, reward its best customers for their longtime support or volume of purchases, or court new prospective clients. In this guise, hospitality not only positions the sponsor as a person or entity with influence and access but also acts as a form of personal selling because the sponsor can conduct activities through face-to-face contact with key customers and prospects. This sponsorship also functions as promotion because it is promoting the company to current and potential clients.

Sponsorship benefits and relations could also be used in a combined advertising and sales campaign. For example, Mars Incorporated might use a relationship with NASCAR to conduct a national sales promotion that could include any or all of the following promotional elements and rights or benefits derived from the sponsorship relationship:

- Sweepstakes to win an all-expenses paid trip for two to the Daytona 500
- Promotional presence on the NASCAR website with an enter-to-win offer
- Hospitality including a chance to meet Kyle Busch
- On-track advertising
- Television advertising
- Retail POP displays tagged with the NASCAR logo and Kyle Busch image

Thus, the sponsor has the opportunity to integrate a number of the elements of the promotional or communications mix in any sponsorship relationship with a sport or entertainment property.

The costs that the sponsor incurs to promote or activate its affiliation or association comes in addition to the costs usually referred to as rights fees, particularly when a multimedia rights agreement is incorporated or forms a major element of the sponsorship, that grant the sponsor the relationship and the rights to use that relationship. Activation is commonly thought of as bringing the brand to life by creating a variety of ways for the brand to interact with its target market. According to IEG, activation is "the marketing activities a company conducts to promote its sponsorship. Money spent on activation is over and above the rights fee paid to the sponsored property."[6] Sometimes activation is also known as leverage.

For example, Mountain Dew is a sponsor, actually a corporate partner, of the NBA. Mountain Dew (through its parent company Pepsi) pays an

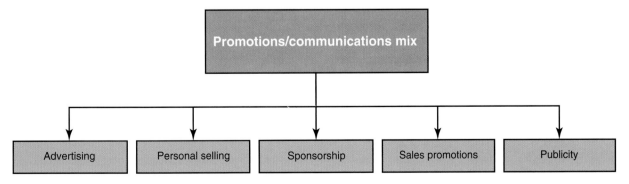

FIGURE 10.2   A broader promotions or communications mix.

annual fee to the NBA in exchange for the affiliation or association with the NBA and receives certain benefits that include, but are not limited to, the following:

- Category exclusivity in the soft-drink category (no direct competitors because Mountain Dew is a corporate partner; therefore, soft-drink products not affiliated with the Pepsi family of products cannot be granted any sponsorship or promotional rights)
- Use of NBA registered trademarks, official product designation ("Mtn Dew 3-Point Contest" and "All-Star Celebrity Game Presented by Ruffles")
- Preferred ticket packages and hospitality opportunities during NBA All-Star Weekend
- The right to conduct in-store and web-based promotions and to create POP displays featuring NBA marks and agreed-upon NBA players
- The right to conduct national promotional activities and events associated with NBA All-Star Weekend, such as Mtn Dew Ice Rising Stars

Thus, when NBA corporate partner Mountain Dew executes its annual Mtn Dew Ice Rising Stars event, Mountain Dew assumes all costs associated with activating this event in addition to paying the licensing fee to the NBA to become a corporate partner.

Growth of Sponsorship

Sports events have attracted sponsors for a long time. Several factors, however, have contributed to an explosive growth of sport sponsorship. The marketing literature shows some agreement that the emergence and growth of sponsorships coincided with the ban on advertising of tobacco and alcoholic beverages.[7] During the 1970s, manufacturers of tobacco and alcoholic beverages were forced to look for ways of promoting their products other than through direct advertising channels. The banning of cigarette ads in 1971 was a triumph for anti-tobacco forces, but as a result, those companies had to redirect their massive advertising clout (and budgets) to sport sponsorships.[8] The *IEG Sponsorship Report* noted

that in 1997, tobacco firms spent US$195 million on sport sponsorships, 95 percent of it in the area of motorsports, making up about 20 percent of the total sponsorship revenue for that sport segment.[9] But the landscape of the tobacco industry has undergone incredible change since the 1980s. R.J. Reynolds Tobacco Company departed NASCAR as the last big tobacco company to be involved with the motorsports venture. The FDA passed new regulations that went into effect in June 2010, preventing cigarette and smokeless tobacco sponsorships in any sports event. Consequently, the tobacco industry has gone from a patron and supporter of sport to being a cancer (literally) and being banned from involvement in sport sponsorships.[10]

Companies with substantial advertising budgets gradually discovered that too much "noise" was present in print and electronic media. The average person is exposed to more than 5,000 selling messages per day, or about 362 ads only per day. That number can quickly increase to 20,000 if you include any type of brand exposure, meaning all logos you see each day at the grocery store, or the mall, or on people's clothing. In terms of ads that actually make an impression or have some form of engagement with the consumer, the number is only 12.[11]

Moreover, advertising costs, especially on television for premier shows and events, continue to rise. Interest in sport-related ad spending in various mediums has been altered dramatically by technology, affordability, and access. Statista listed these numbers as media ad spending growth from 2018 to 2021:[12]

Mobile Internet: US$74.3 billion

Cinema: US$1.7 billion

Outdoor: US$162 million

Radio: US$1.3 billion

Desktop Internet: US$2.6 billion

Magazines: US$5.8 billion

Newspapers: US$8.7 billion

Television: US$9.7 billion

Advertising costs for the NFL's 2002 Super Bowl amounted to US$2.3 million for a 30-second ad spot;[13] a 30-second ad spot for Super Bowl LIII in 2019 cost US$5.25 million. Since 2001, Super Bowl ad prices have increased more than 60 percent. Why is so much spent on Super Bowl advertising? A look inside the numbers for Super Bowl LIII in 2019 makes the case:[14]

- Sixty-seven percent of U.S. households tuned in to the Super Bowl.
- The game attracted 98.2 million TV viewers and 32.3 million social media interactions.
- There was US$382 million spent on in-game ad revenue and US$450 million with pregame and postgame ad revenue included.
- The Pepsi "More Than OK" spot featuring Cardi B and Steve Carell generated more than 23 million YouTube views.

Thus, by developing alternative channels of communication through sport sponsorships, companies found that they could achieve new levels of exposure, in many cases (the Super Bowl excluded) at lower costs than through advertising campaigns.

Table 10.2 shows digital advertising spending by industry, and table 10.3 shows the top 20 sport advertisers by brand.

The 1984 Los Angeles Olympic Games was the first privately organized Games in history and a landmark in the evolution of corporate sponsorship and promotional licensing through sport. The 1984 Olympic sponsors received significant media exposure and, to some extent, positive image building, and the Games generated a profit for the Los Angeles Olympic Organizing Committee (LAOOC). Peter Ueberroth, President of the LAOOC, inaugurated his dream of a corporately subsidized Olympic Games by limiting the number of Olympic sponsors to 30 to avoid clutter and duplication as well as to ensure category exclusivity.[15] In doing so, Ueberroth was able to increase the value of a sponsorship in relation to the increased cost of those same sponsorships. By demonstrating that as cost increased, the value of the subsequent benefit increased, Ueberroth showed that sponsorships actually became partnerships because they were mutually beneficial for both the sport property (the Olympic Games) and the sponsor (the 30 corporations). Experiences such as the 1984 Olympic Games and other mutually beneficial relationships helped give rise to the term *corporate partners*, suggesting that sponsorships could be partnerships whereby corporations hoping to achieve benefits work in harmony with a sport property to create a desirable result.

Following the 1984 Olympic Games, promotional licensing and sponsorship agreements skyrocketed as the public and sport governing bodies increasingly accepted the commercialization of sport. Figure 10.3 shows the use of advertising,

TABLE 10.2   Digital Ad Spending in the United States by Industry From 2016 to 2020 in Billions

Industry	2016	2017	2018	2019	2020
Retail	$15.78	$19.36	$23.78	$28.33	$33.12
Automotive	$9.11	$11.35	$13.74	$15.91	$18.15
Financial services	$8.75	$10.77	$13.21	$15.69	$18.25
Telecom	$7.89	$9.59	$11.57	$13.45	$15.58
CPG and consumer products	$6.24	$7.75	$9.49	$11.12	$12.80
Travel	$5.95	$7.22	$8.95	$10.86	$12.97
Computing products and consumer electronics	$5.45	$6.70	$8.47	$10.35	$12.25
Media	$4.23	$5.11	$6.60	$8.15	$9.85
Entertainment	$3.44	$4.31	$5.52	$6.88	$8.40
Health care and pharma	$2.01	$2.47	$3.01	$3.62	$4.23
Other	$3.09	$3.77	$4.30	$4.99	$5.70
Total	**$71.94**	**$88.40**	**$108.64**	**$129.34**	**$151.29**

Reprinted from R. Benes, "Digital Ad Spending by Industry 2019," *Marketer*, August 1, 2019. www.emarketer.com/content/digital-ad-spending-by-industry-2019

TABLE 10.3   Top U.S. Sponsors by Amount Spent

Rank	Company	Amount
1	PepsiCo, Inc.	$360-$365 million
2	Anheuser-Busch InBev	$350-$355 million
3	The Coca-Cola Co.	$265-$270 million
4	Nike, Inc.	$260-$265 million
5 (tied)	Adidas North America, Inc. AT&T, Inc.	$195-$200 million
7	Ford Motor Co.	$175-$180 million
8	Toyota Motor Sales U.S.A., Inc.	$165-$170 million
9	Verizon Communications, Inc.	$155-$160 million
10	General Motors Co.	$145-$150 million
11	MillerCoors LLC	$120-$125 million
12	FedEx Corp.	$95-$100 million
13	Microsoft Corp.	$90-$95 million
14	Hyundai Motor Co.	$85-$90 million
15 (tied)	Bank of America Corp. Berkshire Hathaway, Inc. The Proctor & Gamble Co.	$75-$80 million
18 (tied)	Citigroup, Inc. Under Armour, Inc.	$70-$75 million
20	The Allstate Corp.	$65-$70 million

Reprinted from IEG, *2016 Top U.S. Sponsors by Spend*, September 18, 2017. www.sponsorship.com/Report/2017/09/18/Number-Of-Companies-In-ESP-s-Top-Sponsor-Rankings-/2016-Top-U-S--Sponsors-by-Spend.aspx

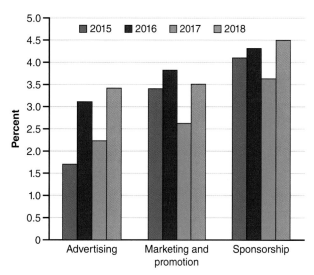

FIGURE 10.3   Annual growth of advertising, sales promotion, and sponsorship.

Data from IEG, *What Sponsors Want & Where Dollars Will Go In 2018*. www.sponsorship.com/IEG/files/f3/f3cfac41-2983-49be-8df6-3546345e27de.pdf

promotions, and sponsorship from 2015 through 2018. Table 10.4 depicts the amount of money spent on sponsorships throughout the world in the period between 2016 and 2018.

Because sponsorship has proved to be effective, sponsorship costs have risen. Additionally, increasing concern about the cost effectiveness of marketing expenditures has made it crucial for managers to be able to justify their marketing investments, including sponsorships.[16] To reign in those costs and exercise greater control, some deep-pocketed companies have created and own their own events. This practice was pioneered during the 1960s and 1970s by Donald Dell and the late Mark McCormack, founders of ProServ and IMG respectively, who sought to create opportunities for their clients. Today, IMG is a global leader in the sport, entertainment, and fashion industries and represents some of the icons in all three areas. The company operates in over 30 countries, stages hundreds of live events and entertainment experiences, and boasts a

TABLE 10.4   Global Sponsorship Spending by Region

Region	2016 spending	2017 spending	Increase from 2016	2018 spending (projected)	Increase from 2017 (projected)
Europe	$16 billion	$16.7 billion	4.5%	$17.6 billion	5.1%
Asia and Pacific	$14.8 billion	$15.7 billion	5.8%	$16.6 billion	5.7%
Central and South America	$4.4 billion	$4.5 billion	3.4%	$4.6 billion	3.3%
All other countries	$2.6 billion	$2.7 billion	3.3%	$2.8 billion	3.5%

Amounts listed are in U.S. dollars.

Reprinted by permission from IEG, *What Sponsors Want & Where Dollars Will Go In 2018*. www.sponsorship.com/IEG/files/f3/f3cfac41-2983-49be-8df6-3546345e27de.pdf

roster of over 800 properties worldwide. IMG owns and operates events in a multitude of international sports such as tennis, golf, cricket, rugby, action sports, motorsports, soccer, and UFC. Owning and executing its own events allows IMG to produce and distribute content-rich experiences for consumers interested in varying lifestyles.

This philosophy of ownership and locus of control was a prime motivator for ESPN to create, produce, and broadcast the first-ever Extreme Games, now X-Games, in 1995 and for the sports network to partner with Capital One to launch ESPN Capital One Bowl Mania each December.[17]

Other factors in the growth of sport sponsorship relate primarily to additional sponsorship opportunities created by new sport offerings, such as the following:

- More television channels devoted to sport programming, especially at the collegiate level as conferences have added their own networks, and the success of regional sports networks and networks created by professional sport leagues, such as NBA TV and the NFL Network
- Technological developments that have led to the portability of sport through cell phones, tablets, and other devices no longer tethered to viewing sport in the traditional way on television or at a specific time
- Emergence of new sport offerings such as esports as well as the importation of programming from other countries, such as English Premier League television packages and cricket matches through satellite

or cable television providers or streaming sources
- Sport-themed video gaming and fantasy sports attracting a broader audience to sport programming and content
- Globalization of sport—that is, importing and exporting sport programming and content from one country to another, including exhibition matches and regular-season competitions outside the home country with the intent to create a following on television and online

What Does Sport Sponsorship Have to Offer?

During the 1970s, marketing through sport often served either the personal interests of top executives or as a vehicle for charitable contributions and support. But beginning in the 1980s, marketing through sport became a practice involving serious research, large investments, and strategic initiatives related to corporate objectives and targets. Today, it is readily apparent that we live in a true global economy and that what happens in one country can have a serious effect on the finances and economic outlook of others. Sponsorship, in terms of structure and spending, has been significantly affected by global economics and the issues that result from those conditions. More than ever, expenditures are scrutinized not just by the companies themselves but also by the media and in certain cases governmental departments.[18] *ROI, ROO,* and *return on experience (ROE)* have been buzz words in terms of the accountability and measurement expected from sponsorship investments. What rationale and benefits can sport or entertainment offer its prospective sponsors in this world of economic uncertainty?

By marketing through sport or entertainment, a company attempts to reach its target consumers through their lifestyles. Lifestyle marketing is a strategy brands use to create products, services, and promotions based on the recurrent patterns of attitudes and activities displayed by a particular group, population, or demographic.[19] Corporate marketing executives, regardless of the size of their companies, have found that linking their messages to leisure pursuits conveys those messages immediately and credibly. The rationale is that leisure is a persuasive environment through which to relate a sales message to targeted consumers. The association of the company or product with the event or activity is also important because sports events have good public acceptance, have a strong fan following, and are newsworthy events for all forms of media coverage. By establishing a link with an event or activity, a company shares the credibility and intentions of the event itself while delivering a message to a consumer who is apt to be more relaxed and potentially more receptive.

In addition, certain events enable the marketer to reach specific segments such as heavy users, shareholders, and investors, or specific groups that have been demographically, psychographically, or geographically segmented and identified as important. L.L. Bean and SWIX became the official suppliers of the U.S. Cross Country Team in a corporate partnership with the U.S. Ski & Snowboard Association. The partnership made sense on multiple levels as L.L. Bean has carried SWIX products in their stores for years and both companies focus on providing high-quality and technologically advanced products that help people live active lifestyles outdoors. The rationale for the sponsorship was to "help the U.S. Cross Country Team achieve athletic excellence."[20]

Another example is Audi, which signed sponsorship agreements in international skiing, international soccer, and MLS. Entertainment also plays a large part in Audi's sponsorship strategy because Audi has signed deals to have its vehicles appear in blockbuster movies like *Iron Man* and *50 Shades of Grey*.[21]

Corporate Objectives

Not every company has the resources and global reach of Nike, Adidas, or Apple. Therefore, every approach to sponsorship or other promotional licensing activities should consider the fact that classifying corporate objectives in a uniform or clear-cut way is difficult. As they develop sponsorship objectives, corporations frequently have a number of objectives that overlap and interact.

The following are traditional objectives that often influence the decision to enter into sport sponsorship agreements:

- Brand awareness
- Image enhancement
- Market segmentation
- Community relations
- Goodwill
- Media benefits
- Showcase products and services
- Sales objectives
- Competitive advantage and exclusivity
- Hospitality and internal marketing
- Entitlement or naming rights
- Athlete endorsement

The objectives that an organization is trying to achieve guide key decision makers in a marketing department to select sponsorship benefits that will best meet those needs. Table 10.5 shows the most important corporate objectives for key decision makers, while table 10.6 displays the most valuable sponsorship benefits.

Each of those objectives can be achieved in multiple ways. The objectives should provide the sponsor with a ROI that would be in monetary form or a ROO or ROE that would be measured against the goal or objective. That is, did the sponsorship accomplish what it was intended to do? In the following section, we illustrate the importance of various objectives by explaining what each objective is and why it is important and by providing examples of how such objectives can be used and achieved in the context of sport sponsorship. The sponsorship paradigm depicted in figure 10.4 illustrates a simple model of what the sponsor and the sport property hope to receive because of their

TABLE 10.5   Corporate Objectives Ranked by Decision Makers in Terms of Importance

Rank	Objective	Percentage rating of importance
1	Create awareness/visibility	50%
2	Increase brand loyalty	46%
3	Change/reinforce image	46%
4	Entertain clients/prospects	33%
5	Stimulate sales/trial/usage	30%
6	Obtain/develop content to use in digital, social, other media	29%
7	Showcase community/social responsibility	29%
8	Capture database/lead generation	28%
9	Sell products/services to sponsored property	26%
10	Access platform for experiential branding	22%

Reprinted by permission from IEG, *What Sponsors Want & Where Dollars Will Go In 2018*. www.sponsorship.com/IEG/files/f3/f3cfac41-2983-49be-8df6-3546345e27de.pdf

TABLE 10.6   Sponsorship Benefits Ranked by Decision Makers in Terms of Importance

Rank	Benefits	Percentage rating of importance
1	Category exclusivity	55%
2	Presence in digital/social/mobile media	42%
3	Tickets and hospitality	38%
4	Rights to property content for digital and other uses	36%
5	Right to property marks and logo	36%
6	On-site signage	32%
7	Right to promote co-branded products/services	21%
8	Spokesperson/access to personalities	21%
9	Access to property's audience/fan data	19%
10	Broadcast ad opportunities	19%

Reprinted by permission from IEG, *What Sponsors Want & Where Dollars Will Go In 2018*. www.sponsorship.com/IEG/files/f3/f3cfac41-2983-49be-8df6-3546345e27de.pdf

partnership. Both parties have obligations for themselves and expectations to be delivered and fulfilled by one another.

Brand Awareness

Sponsorship is often used with the sole aim of increasing brand awareness or educating the public about the capabilities of a company or the benefits of its products or services. Sponsorship is also extremely useful when launching a new product and introducing it to consumers. The widespread exposure that sports events provide, particularly through the variety of media channels associated with these events, affords sponsors a level of awareness they may not be able to purchase otherwise.

Image Enhancement

Sponsorship is powerful because it has the ability to assist a company in crafting a new brand

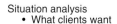

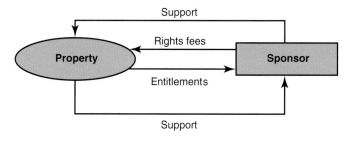

Situation analysis
• What clients want

Support

Rights fees

Property   **Sponsor**

Entitlements

Support

Wants
• Money
• Brand-building support
• Limited interference from sponsor

Wants
• Turn key program
• Positive equity transfer
• Marketing partnership
  with mutually beneficial goals

FIGURE 10.4   The sponsorship paradigm.

image, reinforcing or strengthening an established brand image, or altering or repairing a tarnished or weak brand image. The transfer of the sport or event's image to the company's brand makes sponsorship attractive to businesses as a marketing communications tool. The choice of a sport or an event with particular attributes can help a company achieve a desired image that will reinforce or change consumers' perceptions of the company or its products. Choosing the sport or event becomes less formidable when the company has an actual or logical link to the sport or event. The potential for an effective sponsorship agreement is greatest when an association exists between the target market of the company and the target market of the sport or event, between the desired image of the company and the image of the sport or event, or between the product characteristics promoted and the credibility of the sport entity helping to promote the product. Brands like Mountain Dew, Monster Energy, Taco Bell, and Jeep have used action sports as a platform to promote their products to young, active consumers while reinforcing an image of excitement, high energy, and hipness.

Market Segmentation

Not every sports event has the same type of audience and this is a major benefit to sponsors. Sponsoring companies look to attract a plethora of market segments such as women, youth, ethnic minorities, military, LGBTQ, and others. Selecting a sponsorship agreement with a sport

property that possesses the desired target market has proved beneficial for many sponsors. Professional sport leagues like the WNBA and MLS boast a younger, more diverse, and progressive fan base than the traditional pro leagues, and due to their demographic and psychographic makeup, companies can reach and communicate with niche markets without any waste. Corporate partners of the Olympic Games have always been invested in diversity, and athletes who reach new or unique audiences bring value. For example, Gus Kenworthy, a silver medalist freestyle skier who came out as gay, became one of the most sought-after athlete endorsers when his story captivated Olympic fans in 2018. Kenworthy signed a portfolio of major brands, including Visa, which had a very specific strategy with the Olympian. "'We certainly like individuals who stand for the concept of acceptance, and the concept of diversity,' said Chris Curtin, Chief Brand and Innovation Marketing Officer. 'And not just stand for it themselves, but embrace it in others as well.'"[22]

Community Relations

Sponsorship has demonstrated more potential than any other promotional tool in having direct impact on the community. In this context, sponsorship often takes the form of public or community relations, and its objective is usually to position the company to appear concerned and interested in trying to give back to the community. Companies may target community relations through sport sponsorship to specific communities, regions, or other geographic areas of influence as dictated by corporate objectives. Through licensing or sponsorship activities, the company demonstrates its awareness of local issues to influence potential customers and local social and governmental agencies. In some cases, the corporate partner provides financial or other support to an event that otherwise would not occur or could not continue. For example, many well-known sport sponsors like Nike, Oakley, and Anheuser-Busch stepped up amid the COVID-19 pandemic and offered to create medical supplies that would ease the burden on the overwhelmed health care system that was lacking personal protective equipment (PPE).[23] Giving back to their local communities in a dire time of need created immense positive publicity for companies that joined the effort. These types of community relations strategies benefit brands in the long-run when trying times are over and consumers remember their generosity.

Goodwill

One of the biggest differentiating factors between traditional advertising and sponsorship is the concept of goodwill, the feeling fans develop toward companies connected to their favorite sport or event when those companies support an activity they enjoy. This emotional state is created when consumers believe that brands are not just simply supporting properties for commercial gain but also are providing unique benefits and improving the overall state of the event. In essence, fans want to feel that sponsors care about the team, league, or event as much as they do, and when sponsors provide more than just financial support, this feeling of goodwill intensifies.

Sport provides an excellent environment in which to conduct or influence business on a relaxed, personal basis. The competition for market share among existing customers and for new customers and growth (particularly in

The NBA Get Fit Time Out program helps kids stay in shape and learn about the game of basketball.
Ray Chavez/Media News Group/The Mercury News via Getty Images

international markets) has been intense. Corporations that can deliver unique opportunities, such as entertainment, tickets, and hospitality, for key clients are perceived to be potentially good business partners that will deliver good service. For example, the Masters Golf Tournament has only three official sponsors: Mercedes-Benz, AT&T, and IBM. These three firms alone provide enough financial backing to cover the broadcast fees such that the Masters can be viewed by fans with very little commercial interruption.[24] The golf course also has no signage and minimal advertising. These are major benefits for fans that get to watch more golf and fewer commercials on television, or enjoy a pristine environment while attending the golf major on-site. Additionally, the tournament is an upscale prestigious event that provides a perfect fit for executives from these sponsoring companies to entertain their clients in a plush, relaxing atmosphere.

An excellent example of building goodwill comes from the NBA's partnership with health care sponsor, Kaiser Permanente, to build healthier communities. Kaiser Permanente became the first-ever official health care sponsor for the NBA, WNBA, G-League, and USA Basketball. According to the NBA, "NBA FIT is the league's comprehensive health and wellness platform that encourages physical and mental well-being for fans of all ages. As an official partner of NBA FIT, Kaiser Permanente provides health and wellness consulting with a focus on joint research initiatives, digital content, and year-round grassroots programs that aim to create safe spaces and build healthier communities."[25]

Media Benefits

Media benefits include advertising and publicity related to the promotional efforts surrounding the product or event. Media benefits are usually equated with ROI and measured in the number of impressions generated and the source of those impressions. Impressions are the number of viewers (television), listeners (radio), readers (all print forms), unique and repeat visitors (websites), page views (websites), and members and activity (social media sites) exposed to the advertising or promotional message. The advertising or promotional message may be an actual advertisement, but it is often a logo or sign that appears

during the television coverage or an image on a website. In auto racing, for example, the driver often wears a cap with the name of a sponsor and may switch caps during a press conference, interview, or photo session to provide exposure and impressions for multiple sponsors.

Simply measuring impressions and seeking short-term benefits, however, are no longer sufficient for most sport sponsors. The digital and social benefits that have proliferated in recent years have begun to emerge atop the list of sponsors' priorities. According to IEG, in addition to the traditional advantages sponsorship provides, companies now seek the following benefits in contemporary corporate partnerships:[37]

- *Market intelligence.* Sharing of data and other information relevant to the property's fans, attendees, and other stakeholders that sponsors may not otherwise be able to obtain on their own
- *Product and service development.* Assisting sponsors with creating or improving products, services, or events marketed to their target audience
- *Sales, digital, and other expertise.* Sharing strategies and best practices between properties and brands to assist each other in achieving common business goals
- *Social strength.* Providing sponsors with social metrics beyond follower counts and likes, and generating fan participation, engagement, and ultimately rewards or purchases, through social media
- *Dedicated servicing staff.* Providing specific employees to service major sponsorship accounts full time for the largest events and biggest rights holders
- *Brand value.* Being able to provide tangible evidence of brand equity to sponsors and demonstrating high levels of brand loyalty from fans
- *Flexibility.* Being willing and committed to communicate, altering terms or benefits of the contract, and delivering personalized service

Most sponsorship packages for major sports events include multimedia rights. Depending on their spend, sponsors receive the following types of media benefits:

- Digital signage in the sport venue
- Presence on the team's website and social channels
- Print advertisements in the game program
- Radio spots
- Opportunities to conduct promotions and giveaways in and around the event
- Other media-generating activities

Live streaming sports events is increasingly in demand as more and more consumers cut the cord and quit cable. Streaming sports events on mobile and other devices provides a unique, and often cost-effective, way for sponsors to reach large audiences. Amazon paid the NFL US$65 million per year for the live streaming rights to *Thursday Night Football*. Amazon's strategy was to attract new users to its Prime video and delivery service. Amazon reported 18 million viewers over 11 NFL football games and suggested plans to live stream even more international sports events. [26] Not all live streamed sports have to be professional. In fact, streaming smaller events, like high school sports, has proven to be effective enough to lure brands into using this marketing method. Bleacher Report live streamed three high school football games in order to attract an entirely new, younger audience and do so affordably.[27]

Showcase Products and Services

Increasingly more companies have become sponsors of particular sport properties because of an opportunity to promote unique product features or technological innovations or applications. Sponsorships of this sort have always been common in technologically rich sports, such as NASCAR, but the concept has also gained a foothold in traditional sports, such as hockey, basketball, and golf.

SAP and Apple partnered with the NHL to supply iPads and a custom coaching app, which delivered in-game statistics, to the teams. Real-time data on players, collected and analyzed by SAP, was provided on four Apple iPads to coaches on the bench. The technology was designed to assist coaches in making decisions to enhance team performance and minimize stoppages in play. "It became clear there were certain analytics and data points they wanted to have to complement the video," said David Lehanski, the NHL's Senior Vice President of Business Development and innovation. "And so we set out with Apple and SAP to design and build an app for the coaches that would give them real-time data on the benches."[28]

Sales Objectives

The ultimate objective of marketing is to increase market share, notably by increasing sales volume and, ultimately, profitability. Sponsorship, along with other elements of the communications mix, is usually viewed as an element that can be used to influence the purchasing intention of a prospective buyer. In this sense, sponsorship constitutes an important stimulus within purchasing as a multistage, multi-influence process, but it can also influence sales in a more direct manner. BMW invests heavily in the sponsorship activities that it identifies as appropriate for its upscale audience. From placing its cars in James Bond 007 films to sailing and to fitness-related events, BMW uses sponsorships to achieve its marketing and sales goals.

An excellent example of a sales-driven sponsorship agreement involved the Olympic Games, namely BMW's promotion "Drive for Team USA," which helped the company sell more than 6,000 new cars. The promotion involved a special test drive opportunity, a US$10 donation to the U.S. Olympic Committee for every test drive taken, and a US$1,000 allowance toward the purchase of a new vehicle. The sales promotion generated 26,535 test drives, which BMW converted into 6,633 new car sales, representing a conversion rate into purchases of approximately 25 percent. With an average new car price of US$63,251 BMW's "Drive for Team USA" program generated more than US$150 million.[29]

Anheuser-Busch, one of the biggest investors in sport sponsorship, launched an incentive-based marketing model to encourage teams and leagues it sponsored to consider helping the beer brand drive more sales. This new business model cost A-B a base price for the sponsorship and more fees if the team or league it sponsored hit performance goals, such as greater attendance, increased fan engagement, and playoff appearances. A-B understands that certain metrics mean more beer sales, and the company is willing to measure these metrics and pay more for the sponsorships that are more valuable. In the end, incentive-based sponsorship agreements have the ability to help both sides in the partnership make more money.[30]

Sales objectives can also relate to product use as a benefit of a sponsorship or licensing agreement. A sponsorship or licensing agreement with an entity such as a cruise line or a venue, such as an amusement park or arena, may require the use of a particular product or line of products at all events or functions in the facility. Minute Maid Park, home of the Houston Astros (MLB), is an obvious example. Supermarket sales of soft drinks have long been a battlefield for Coca-Cola and Pepsi, although Coca-Cola has been winning the market share battle by a few percentage points. But when it comes to park and recreation facilities, theaters, cruise ships, and sports events and entertainment venues, Coca-Cola is the clear winner. The strategy of Coca-Cola is to sign sponsorship and licensing agreements that ensure product exclusivity and use whenever possible.

Competitive Advantage and Exclusivity

In some cases, particularly when the sponsorship fee is high or the commitment is long-term, exclusivity of product or category is integral to licensing or sponsorship agreements. Since the economic downturn in 2007, exclusivity has not been as prevalent as it once was, obviously because of cost. The beer industry is one of the notable sport sponsorship groups that have moved away from exclusivity. Beer companies have moved more toward making their beer the prominent beer in the venue by securing highly visible areas for signage or purchasing the naming rights for a highly visible bar area within the venue.

For sponsors that insist on exclusivity, notably those that sell soft drinks, credit cards, banks, and, in some cases, automobiles, exclusivity clauses provide that the sponsor of that particular category will be the only brand present in that category throughout the sport venue or, depending on the terms of the agreement, through any media broadcasts or on the website. Naming-rights deals, such as the Orlando Magic's sponsorship with Amway for Amway Center and the jersey naming-rights deals in the English Premier League, are guaranteed exclu-

sivity because of the scope and magnitude of the sponsorship deal.

As stated previously, the crucial benefit of exclusivity is that this type of sponsorship provides a great opportunity to drive incremental sales while at the same time denying competitors the same opportunity to interact with an audience of potential purchasers. This limitation of competition can improve the ability of the marketing message to increase sales and may affect the profitability of both the sponsor and the competition. The exclusivity, in light of the strong emotional attachment and following that sport inspires, allows the marketer to position brands or products as supporting an event or a particular team (e.g., PNC: Official Bank of the Pittsburgh Pirates) while implying that the competitors' products do not, thereby encouraging consumer response and support where it matters most—at the cash register.

In its corporate partner agreement with the NCAA, Nabisco is guaranteed category exclusivity. As delineated by Nabisco, the category is defined as official cookies, crackers, and biscuits of the NCAA. Thus, Nabisco can promote any or all of these items as it chooses while preventing any of its competitors for any of the aforementioned types of products from doing so in a relationship with the NCAA. For example, during the NCAA Men's Basketball Championship held annually in March and April, Nabisco, as part of its NCAA partnership, offers the March Madness Snack Bracket and highlights Chips Ahoy and Oreo, as well as Triscuit, Ritz, belVita, and Wheat Thins—all cracker varieties. The NCAA and its basketball tournament provide an opportunity for Nabisco to conduct exclusive association and promotions within the cookies and crackers category.

Hospitality and Internal Marketing

Although hospitality and entertainment relate to a number of the other concepts previously described, this function is worthy of examination on its own. Hospitality and entertainment play a critical role in the packaging of sponsorship and promotional licensing programs. These concepts enable the sponsor to construct certain benefits and opportunities that are often unique and unavailable in the general marketplace. Such opportunities may include trips to the Olympic Games, World Cup, Wimbledon, the Super Bowl, NBA All-Star Weekend, and on-site hospitality and special events that are not available to the public. This hospitality, entertainment, and access can be valuable for a sponsor to extend to clients and identified VIPs. According to William Pate, Vice President of Advertising for AT&T (which sponsors the Atlanta Braves, the Atlantic Coast Conference, and a NASCAR Cup team), "Business people are more open to messages when they are at leisure than when they are working."[31]

Hospitality opportunities have become an integral part of sponsorship agreements for college athletics programs, which package hard-to-obtain tickets in prime locations along with tents, catering, and other amenities. Similar hospitality programs are offered on the professional golf and tennis tours, and within NASCAR and professional team sports in the United States and abroad. Such programs often form the basis for the sales of luxury suites and boxes in sport

venues throughout the globe. The key to successful use of hospitality is to ensure that the hospitality is unique, exclusive, and available only as part of a comprehensive sponsorship agreement. Heineken provided one of the most exciting and memorable hospitality areas in professional golf with its Heineken Lounge on the European Tour. In Denmark, all golfers and their caddies had to walk the length of the lounge through the hospitality tent in order to reach the 14th tee. This meant every patron with a pass to the sponsored area got to see the golfers and caddies up close as they played through the venue. No other brand's experience was quite like it, as fans posted pictures and videos to social media all throughout the tournament, which provided Heineken tremendous exposure.[32] Corporate partners use hospitality benefits to reward their own personnel (known as internal marketing); serve as contest or sweepstakes prizes; court potential new clients; or, most frequently, induce their clients to increase product use or consumption, renew agreements, or sign new ones.

Luxury suites can be an important component of hospitality opportunities.
View Pictures/Universal Images Group via Getty Images

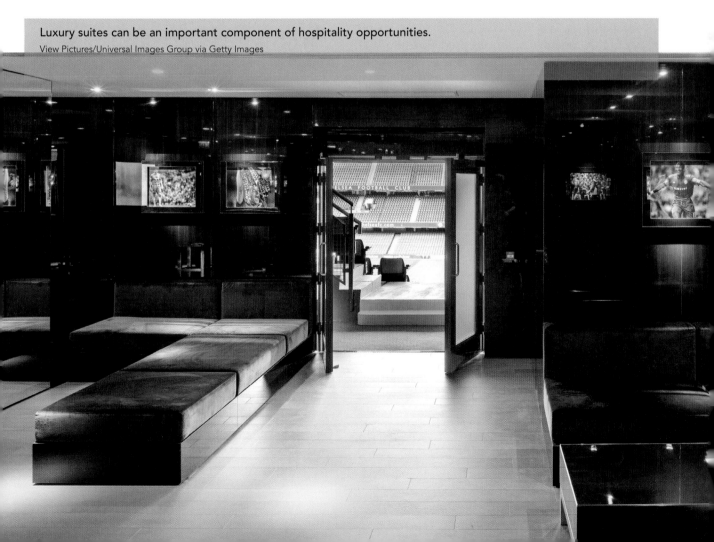

Entitlement or Naming Rights

Corporations interested in purchasing naming rights to venues or events, such as concert tours, marathon and triathlon events, and bowl games, have an agenda in mind when they consider such sponsorship possibilities. This agenda usually consists of the following elements and their value to the company in terms of cost and organizational priority:

- Number of impressions or exposures
- Opportunity for local, regional, national, and international media coverage
- Tax considerations
- Brand exclusivity and brand building
- Public relations and community involvement and support
- Hospitality and related amenities
- Activation platforms—sponsorship and promotional activities

Red Bull, an Austria-based sports and energy drink maker that was looking for a unique sport marketing position in the United States, purchased the then NY–NJ Metro Stars of the rising MLS and renamed them the Red Bulls so that the product name would be present at all times when reference was made to the team. According to Alan Friedman, founder and former editor of *Team Marketing Report*, "Naming rights are the most expensive sport marketing investment in the current marketplace, the best dollar-for-impression sponsorship bargain, and one of the most underutilized promotional assets in a company's marketing arsenal."[33] Corporations electing to become involved in securing naming rights or entitlements must have a strategic plan in place to leverage the opportunity and the financial resources to support that acquisition and activate the brand. One industry that has capitalized on sponsorship deals with naming rights is banking. Banks have led the way in naming-rights deals over the past decade because naming a sport venue not only communicates the impression of success and well-managed investments but also conveys the concept of permanence in that the bank is part of the community for the long-term.[34]

Entitlement and naming rights have a high profile in NASCAR. In stock car racing, the corporations traditionally have a prominent role. If a company sponsors a racing event, the company's name is incorporated into the event name. For example, Ford sponsors the NASCAR championship race each year at the Homestead-Miami Speedway. Hence, the race itself is known as the Ford EcoBoost 400. If a company becomes a sponsor of a racing team, the corporate name or brand is used in conjunction with the team name. For example, Toyota has a racing team and is a prominent participant in NASCAR's Cup Series. Although the Cup Series has had its own title sponsors like Sprint and Monster Energy, Toyota and a number of other automotive manufacturers and businesses seeking exposure sponsor their own racing teams. The corporate or brand name is prominently displayed on the race car. In a study conducted by Zoomph examining brand activity, reach, and value for sponsors involved in the Daytona 500, NASCAR's biggest race of the year, the company found that Toyota reaped the most rewards from their race car drivers. Total social activity around Toyota was 13,823, projected reach was 6.3 million, and impression value earned was over US$76,000.[35]

Athlete Endorsement

Athlete endorsement is the use of celebrity athletes as brand ambassadors to promote products and services in an official capacity for brands. Athlete endorsement is a form of sponsorship where brands sponsor individual athletes, instead of sport properties like teams or leagues, in order to market to that athlete's specific target audience. Individual athlete sponsorship, like event sponsorship, is extremely effective for a number of reasons.

1. Athlete endorsement can be cost effective if brands are seeking to target a specific market that can be reached by partnering with one athlete versus an entire organization.
2. Star athletes have the ability to reach millions of fans through their social platforms, and their follower counts can be greater than the follower counts of the team depending on their popularity. Athletes who are savvy with social media and have high levels of engagement with their fans can perform extremely well for the brands they represent.

3. Today's star athletes have multiple interests outside of sport and these broad interests, such as business, entertainment, and activism, give brands even larger, more diverse audiences in which to communicate.

Depending on the sport the athlete plays (team or individual), endorsement money can play a significant part in the athlete's overall wealth. For individual athletes, such as tennis players and golfers, endorsement money from sponsoring companies can amount to tens or hundreds of millions of dollars and far outweigh what the athlete wins in prize money. Even for team athletes, like baseball and basketball players, endorsements can bring in more earnings than the salary from team contracts. *Forbes* publishes an annual list of the highest-paid celebrity athletes and breaks down their earnings by salary and prize money and endorsements. The numbers make it easy to see why athletes seek sponsorships from brands

Athletes, such as Naomi Osaka, have the ability to reach a large number of fans and increase product sales.

Kyodo News Stills via Getty Images

and are investing their time and efforts to become more effective marketers.[36]

Athlete endorsement works in much the same way theoretically as event sponsorship. The match-up hypothesis states that the more congruence there is between an athlete endorser and a brand, the more effective the endorsement will be.[37] Marketers often refer to this as "fit" in the realm of sponsorship. LeBron James and Nike are seen as having extremely high levels of fit because Nike sells high-performance sport apparel and equipment, and LeBron James is one of the most talented and successful professional athletes of all time. Even when athletes are tasked with endorsing non-sport brands, they can be seen as a good fit if the athletes possess many of the same image characteristics of the brand, often referred to as brand personality. LeBron James could be characterized as cool, exciting, and unique—much like the soft drink Sprite that he endorses. Although Sprite is not a sport brand, there is excellent fit between the product, James as the athlete endorser, and the young target market that watches the NBA and consumes soft drinks.

Three of the most important aspects that companies consider when searching for athlete endorsers to partner with are

1. expertise,
2. credibility, and
3. attractiveness.

Expertise is the level of knowledge the endorsers have on the subject matter in which they are speaking. Professional athletes are fantastic at selling sport products because they have so much knowledge regarding the brands they use to compete every day. Serena Williams is an expert on tennis equipment and is one of Wilson's endorsers for its tennis rackets. It makes sense that the number one player in the world would know the most about which tennis racket a player should use.

Credibility is the degree to which you believe what the endorser is telling you. Athlete endorsers with high levels of credibility have to build trust with consumers by conducting themselves with morality and maintaining trust from their fans over time. Credibility is crucial if athletes are endorsing a non-sport product because they must convince consumers they actually use or would recommend a brand. Stephen Curry endorses

Chase Bank, and although we do not see the basketball star conducting his financial affairs, we trust that if he partners with this brand, he is using the chain for his own personal banking needs.

Attractiveness relates to how much consumers like an endorser based on physical appearance, intellect, or personal appeal. While some athletes like Alex Morgan may be selected to promote beauty products because fans like her physical appearance, other athletes like Phil Mickelson or James Harden may be signed by companies who seek humor and personality in their promotions in order to make an impression.

Sponsor Activation

Activation, often referred to as engagement or experiential marketing, is one of the keys to a successful sponsorship agreement because it brings the brand to life by creating an interactive platform between the target market and the product that the brand is wishing to promote. Activation fees are additional funds set aside by brands after they have paid for rights fees (cost of purchasing an official sponsorship with a sport property) to use for promotional activity of the sponsorship. Every company has a different strategy when it comes to budgeting for activation once they have purchased rights fees. Figure 10.5 shows the ratios that different sponsors use to budget for

rights fees versus activation fees. Corporations search for unique and creative ways to leverage their association with an event or organization, an endeavor commonly referred to as activation. According to Lesa Ukman, Founder of IEG (International Events Group), "Sponsorship can build brand equity, sales, and shareholder value, but it is mostly the activation of sponsorship that does those things."[48] According to Matt Wilkstrom, Senior Vice President at Van Wagner Sports and Entertainment, "Many brands today spend up to two to three times as much on sponsorship activation as they do on rights fees. As with all advertising, sponsorship dollars are intensely scrutinized for ROI. You have to be really creative not only in how you build these partnerships but how you activate them."[49]

The sponsorship activation wheel (figure 10.6) illustrates the variety of platforms that can be used to promote and communicate sponsorship activities. Social media are increasing in importance and spend and will continue to be a highly used platform because of reach, ease of use, and cost. This is evident in figure 10.7, which shows the most frequently used promotional channels by sponsors, with social media being used by 98 percent of sponsoring companies.

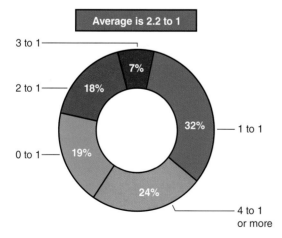

FIGURE 10.5   Ratio of sponsor spending on rights fees versus activation fees.

Reprinted by permission from IEG, *What Sponsors Want & Where Dollars Will Go In 2018*. www.sponsorship.com/IEG/files/f3/f3cfac41-2983-49be-8df6-3546345e27de.pdf

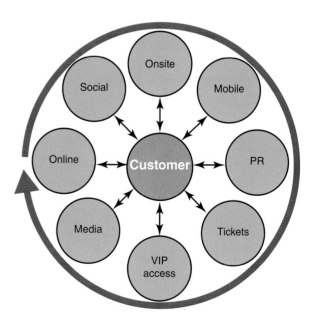

FIGURE 10.6   The sponsorship activation wheel illustrates the variety of platforms where activation can take place.

Reprinted by permission from T. Hughes, "How to Increase Fan Engagement in Sponsorship Activation Through Social Media," *The Migala Report* (2013).

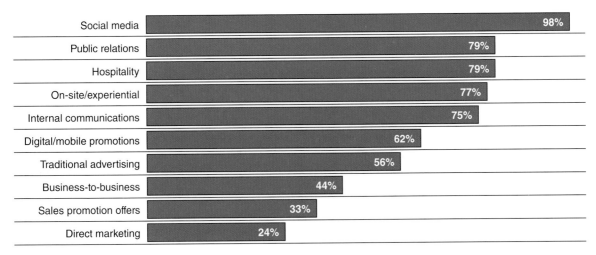

FIGURE 10.7   Most frequently used promotional channels to activate sponsorships.

Reprinted by permission from IEG, *What Sponsors Want & Where Dollars Will Go In 2018.* www.sponsorship.com/IEG/files/f3/f3cfac41-2983-49be-8df6-3546345e27de.pdf

Perhaps one of the more interesting sponsorship activations is the worldwide sponsorship of the Olympic Games by Dow Chemical Company. For years, sponsors of the Olympic Games were more likely to be consumer packaged goods (CPG) companies like Coca-Cola. Dow Chemical, however, is more of a business-to-business (B2B) company. It has approached sponsorship from a practical point of view by featuring its capabilities and products.

In July 2010, Dow Chemical became an official Worldwide Olympic Partner (TOP Programme) and the official chemistry company of the Olympic Movement through 2020. Dow Chemical has more than 5,000 products, which are produced in 37 countries around the world. Observers may not see the fit between a chemical company and the Olympic Games, but the construction of the venues for the Games takes almost a decade, and Dow Chemical is an integral partner in that process. Dow Chemical seeks to provide clean, renewable energy generation and conservation and increased agricultural productivity in the host country throughout the innovation and creation of the Games.

The London 2012 Olympic Games Stadium featured a wrap on the outside of the structure. The wrap was made up of 306 individual panels, each 25 meters high and 2.5 meters wide. The wrap panels were made up of more than 50 colors that represented the official colors of the Games. The panels were produced by Dow Chemical and completed the stadium as the architects had

intended. It became the visual centerpiece of the London 2012 Olympic Games. In an effort to make the Games as sustainable as possible, the wrap was reused four years later in Rio de Janeiro, the site of the 2016 Olympic Games.

Additionally, Dow Chemical products were used widely in the PyeongChang 2018 Winter Olympic Games. "From lightweight composites for more advanced luge sleds to energy-efficient insulation in multiple facilities, Worldwide TOP Partner Dow supports the Olympic Winter Games with dozens of sustainable and high-performance solutions, developed at the intersection of sport and science."[38]

Social Media as Activation

Because of the emphasis on sponsor engagement with the target market, corporations have long viewed sport as an effective way to reach the most avid followers. Signage, however, has become one dimensional, and TV ads have become less effective because of the capabilities of the DVR and because television might not be the primary "screen" for the targeted audience. Marketers, particularly those who use sport as the medium, want to take full advantage of the emotional attachments between fans and the athletes, teams, and leagues that they follow.

Nowhere is this clearer than with social media, which have become the focus of the way in which brands and teams are looking to create fully integrated fan activation. Jeff Weiner, CEO of ESBL

Social Media, a firm specializing in helping clients expand their social media metrics and convert them into revenue, identifies social media, along with the Internet, television, radio, and printing of the first U.S. newspaper in 1721, as one of the five most important aspects of multimedia that have evolved since the 18th century.[39] Facebook pages, Twitter and Instagram feeds, location apps, and mobile platforms seem almost custom-made for the obsessions and chatter of sports fans. These tools give them greater access to the leagues, teams, and athletes whom they follow, while creating virtual camaraderie between far-flung people who share their passion. This passion is what brands want to leverage.

How is this passion being leveraged? Here are the results from the IEG Sponsorship Decision-Makers Survey where brands were asked by IEG what channels they used to leverage their sponsorships:[40]

- Social media: 98 percent
- Public relations: 79 percent
- Hospitality: 79 percent
- On-site/experiential: 77 percent
- Internal communications: 75 percent
- Digital/mobile promotions: 62 percent
- Traditional advertising: 56 percent
- B2B: 44 percent
- Sales promotions: 33 percent
- Direct marketing: 24 percent

It is no surprise that social media have moved into the number one position for sponsorship leverage due to the popularity, reach, and cost efficiency of the medium. Brands have options when it comes to using social media for activation. They can use paid or organic (unpaid) social media to reach their audiences and engage them. The following are ways that sponsors can make the most of organic social media to interact with fans:

- Reply to fan comments when they post on sponsors' social media platforms
- Share testimonials and positive consumer experiences with sponsors' followers
- Strive to achieve positive reviews across social channels
- Comment on and share posts that mention sponsors' brands[41]

Hospitality and on-site or experiential activation also rank highly with sponsors now due to the excitement and lasting impressions these forms of leverage provide. Every year, the U.S. Open professional tennis tournament gets rave reviews from fans on the hospitality and on-site activations of its sponsors. Here are some of the top attractions and promotions at the event:[42]

- *IBM.* The IBM Experience introduced fans to Watson, the AI engine, and the IBM Slamtracker. The technology showcase allowed fans access to thousands of match videos, tournament highlights, player data and analysis, and 12 years worth of match statistics.
- *Chase.* Chase offered fans the opportunity to take pictures with U.S. Open trophies, dispense cash from large tennis ball–branded ATMs, win free prizes from a "Magic ATM," and enjoy food and drinks in the Chase Lounge.
- *Mercedes-Benz.* M-B conducted a social media scavenger hunt where clues on the car maker's Instagram account would lead fans around New York to locate Mercedes-Benz–branded tennis balls and, ultimately, one of its brand new vehicles. Fans who completed the scavenger hunt and found the new car won seats to the ultra-luxurious M-B suite to watch the tennis tournament.

Evaluating and Ensuring Sponsorship Effectiveness

Since the mid-1990s, an increase in corporate accountability and responsibility has been mirrored by growth in sponsorship measurement, growth in business analysis, and more decision making than ever in the sport industry being driven by data. We have moved from the art of marketing (techniques and gut feeling) to the art (experience) and science (data-driven business decisions) of marketing. A declining global economy and corporate misconduct resulting in a lack of public trust have led to a demand for corporate accountability and fiscal responsibility in all business decisions. Before the turn of the century, most sponsor-related research focused on measuring impressions. Although impressions are still a key component of any measurement

Who Measures What, and What Is Important to Measure?

On her blog Power Sponsorship, Kim Skildum-Reid, a sponsorship expert and strategist, answers the age-old question, "What should a rights holder include in a year-end sponsorship ROI report?" The answer? Nothing. Sponsorship is not your job.[44] Skildum-Reid raised an interesting point given that sport properties often feel obligated to demonstrate their partners' success through sponsor fulfillment reports. Fulfillment reports are seen as valuable for several reasons: They provide an opportunity to thank sponsors, showcase deliverables, and begin the renewal process. However, the Power Sponsorship blog makes a very clear distinction between what properties should be responsible for and what sponsors should expect to measure themselves.[45]

Properties should provide the following at the conclusion of the sponsorship:

- Which benefits were promised and the extent to which those benefits were delivered
- Measurable results, such as attendance numbers, exposure, clicks, etc.

Sponsors should follow these steps on their own to ensure they measure what's important:

- Choose the appropriate marketing objectives you wish to achieve.
- Determine previous benchmarks for those objectives.
- Set realistic goals for the sponsorship based on the benchmarks.
- Measure performance throughout the sponsorship cycle.
- Report to impacted stakeholders.

The rights holder and sponsor should work together and communicate openly about what the brand wants to achieve with its sponsorship. Is it exposure? Then access to the team's social media following may be the most important benefit. Is it lead generation? Having a concourse presence to recruit and sign up fans or provide product trials would be critical. Is it image enhancement or increased consumer goodwill? Partnering on a community charitable event could have a positive impact. Whatever the sponsor is trying to accomplish, it should delineate the objectives and benchmarks clearly ahead of time, and the property should provide as many benefits as possible and data related to those benefits. In the end, if you want to create a powerful sponsorship, it is not what you measure that is important (a lot of unimportant things can be measured!), it is important that you measure what matters.

program, they are only part of the assessment. The focus now is on the demographics and psychographics of the audience and its ability to spend; can a particular market segment generate ROI, or at least ROO? Measurement also focuses on what the impression conveys. Is a message being communicated, is that message being communicated effectively and being understood, and ultimately, is that message invoking action?

It is becoming more common in the sport industry to have a strategic and proactive partnership between the sport entity and the sponsor to ensure that objectives are being met, that the agreed-upon platforms are being activated and delivered, and that the opportunity to make adjustments every month or every quarter is available. Effective activation is a key element of effectiveness. For that reason, more sport organizations are creating positions in their corporate partnerships programs that have no new business development (new sales) responsibilities. These activators focus solely on existing clients and their marketing platforms rather than selling signage. Thus, more attention is paid to each of these corporate partners by focusing on creating marketing and promotional activation opportunities that work. The result is greater retention of corporate sponsors, increased spending among existing partners, and more new business growth because sellers are focused solely on creating new business opportunities and activators are focused on delivering on promises and building those relationships. Look for this model to continue to grow throughout the rest of this decade and beyond.

But the motivation to become a sponsor can involve many aspects besides the number of eyeballs, and documenting the reasons to sponsor and realizing those objectives are critical. When measuring this value or ROI, sponsors commonly assess the following practices:[43]

- Sixty-eight percent of the companies surveyed stated that they were considering new sponsorships for the following year.
- Forty-seven percent of the companies surveyed spent 1 percent or less on concurrent or post-event research to measure success, and 31 percent spent nothing at all.

The most common factors considered when measuring sponsorship ROI are the following:[43]

- Attitudes toward brand: 80 percent
- Amount of positive social media activity: 76 percent
- Awareness of products and services/brand: 72 percent
- Awareness of company's/brand's sponsorship: 71 percent
- Product and service sales: 62 percent
- Response to customer and prospect entertainment: 61 percent
- Response to sponsorship-related promotions/content: 58 percent
- Amount of media exposure generated: 57 percent
- TV logo exposure: 42 percent
- Lead generation: 41 percent

Selling Sponsorships

Before beginning the sponsorship process to identify and locate a sponsor for a team, an organization, or an event, the sport entity should develop a strategic planning process about how to conduct the sales campaign. Strategic planning steps should include the following:

- Make a comprehensive list of all assets in the inventory.
- Establish a list price for each item based on the cost per impression (if media are involved) and the cost of implementing activation platforms related to the objectives of the potential sponsor.
- Conduct research with regard to sponsorships sold in the market and in similar markets; identify prospects that would be likely to have an interest based on past behavior.
- Establish packaging prices and, if appropriate, discounting for the more inclusive packages.
- Remember to determine the real cost of the sponsorship, which may include any or all of the following elements: tickets (full face value), promotions (premium items, shipping, fulfillment, and labor costs), print and point-of-sale pieces, web page development, social media campaigns, signage and supporting advertising (including production, design, and layout), and other activation costs that will be borne by the organization. (See the Net/Net Form sidebar.)
- Establish the overall corporate marketing partnership sales strategy. Which, if any, categories will be offered as exclusive? Are there levels, such as founding partners, that need to be sold first? What are the goals for each category? What discounts, if any, will you offer and at which levels—only above a million dollars per year commitment, etc.?
- Initiate the eight-step sales process (see the following section) with the top three product and service categories, followed by the next three, and so on. Sell the best inventory to the biggest marketing partnership categories first.
- The order in which categories and potential sponsors are presented is critical—where a large category is defined by total amount spent first, which means major global or national sponsors first, easy closures first.

Net/Net Form

The NBA's best practices for determining the real cost of the sponsorship is for every sponsorship salesperson to complete and submit a net/net form for every marketing partnership proposal (figure 10.8). The net/net form should be reviewed and then approved by the VP Partnerships and the Chief Revenue Officer (CRO) of the sport property *before* the proposal is submitted to the potential sponsor client. In that net/net form, every element of the proposed partnership must be listed, along with the quantity (e.g., number of regional sports network commercials or spots), the location of that inventory (e.g., center ice dasher board signage on both sides of the rink), frequency and length of rotation, etc., all being included in the proposed package at its "rack rate." If that item is being discounted due to the size of the proposal package, then that discount becomes the first "net" to be deducted. One of the most frequent and egregious practices by sales reps in this respect is to throw preferred location tickets and website and other social media inventory factored at little or no cost to the sponsor. Next, any activation or fulfillment costs are then deducted, such as cost for T-shirt giveaways for a community program, or cost to produce rink (dasher) board or courtside signage. Finally, any agency fees paid for the sponsorship should be discounted to provide the net/net, or true bottom-line, of the partnership to the sport property. Sophisticated CROs and VP partnerships pay only a commission to the sponsorship sales rep based on this true net/net. Otherwise experienced sales reps frequently "sweeten" the pot with activation items that can have considerable fulfillment costs tied to them, which should be the responsibility of the corporate marketing partner, or its agency, rather than the sport property itself.

Gain momentum; use the recognition of name sponsors to attract lesser sponsors and leverage those commitments to secure other relationships.

- Always talk to all major competitors in each category (e.g., carbonation-free beverages, including all beverage subcategories: Coca-Cola and Pepsi; malt-beverage category, including domestic, import, craft, and blended; AB InBev and Molson Coors; and credit card companies, such as Visa, MasterCard, and American Express) simultaneously to ensure a decision within a comparative period. This balancing act to ensure all competing properties are ready to consume the deal at the same stage of the process is the "art" of the marketing partnership business and is essential to the property maximizing revenues and activation leverage. It requires considerable advanced planning to ensure that such large expenditures are contemplated by the potential sponsor partner well in advance, because budget planning for the following

year is pretty well crafted by the third quarter for most major partnership categories.

- Remember that all sponsorship decision makers know each other and often communicate; don't exaggerate and don't make special concessions or side deals.

Eight-Step Sponsorship Process

After an organization has agreed on and implemented the strategic planning process, it can initiate the sales process. The success of the sales process depends on adherence to the principles of the strategic planning process.

1. Research the category and then conduct research on the top prospects within that category. Know the state of their business, number of employees, outlook for the company, last year's financials, and so forth. Research should also include news or web coverage of the company, pro or con.

2. Schedule a meeting with the sponsorship decision maker at the brand within the category that you are targeting. Meet only

Atlanta Spirit Marketing Partnership Net/Net Form (Atlanta Hawks)
(as of 00/00/0000)

PARTNER NAME: Anheuser-Busch (Domestic Malt Beverage Category Exclusivity)

INVENTORY ITEM(S)	#	Rack rate (in US$)	# of broadcasts, games, etc.	Cost at rack rate (in US$)	Cost allocated (in US$)	Actual revenue (in US$)
CATEGORY EXCLUSIVITY:						
Rights		$1,000,000	All season—domestic malt beverage	$1,000,000	$1,000,000	$1,000,000
Subtotal category exclusivity		**$1,000,000**		**$1,000,000**		**$1,000,000**
% discounted from rack rate						0%
MEDIA						
Television advertising & features						
Opening billboards	1	$2,000	80	$16,000	$1,250	$100,000
30 sec spots	4	$2,500	80	$800,000	$1,750	$560,000
15 sec spots	2	$1,500	80	$240,000	$1,000	$160,000
Closing billboards	1	$1,750	80	$140,000	$1,100	$88,000
Features	1	$3,500	80	$280,000	$2,750	$220,000
Subtotal television spend				**$1,620,000**		**$1,128,000**
% discounted from rack rate						30%
Radio advertising & features						
Opening billboards	1	$250	86	$21,500	$10,000	$10,000
30 sec spots	4	$500	86	$172,000	$100,000	$100,000
15 sec spots	0	$300	86	$25,800	$12,000	$12,000
Closing billboards	1	$200	86	$17,200	$10,000	$10,000
Features	1	$750	86	$64,500	$50,000	$50,000
Subtotal radio spend				**$301,000**		**$182,000**
% discounted from rack rate						39%
TOTAL MEDIA				**$1,921,000**		**$1,310,000**
PRINT						
Game program						
Inside back cover	1	$50,000	All season	$50,000	$30,000	$30,000
Regular page ad	1	$20,000	All season	$20,000	$12,000	$12,000
Media guide	1	$10,000	All season	$10,000	$6,000	$6,000
Pocket schedule	1	$20,000	All season	$20,000	$10,000	$10,000
Subtotal print spend				**$10,000**		**$58,000**
% discounted from rack rate						42%
SIGNAGE						
Courtside	1	$250,000	Rotation every 5 min	$250,000	$250,000	$250,000
Mezzanine "halo"	1	$100,000	Rotation every 5 min	$100,000	$100,000	$100,000
Concourse ads	2	$25,000	Prime location near entry	$50,000	$50,000	$50,000
Exterior marquee	1	$200,000	Rotation every 5 min	$200,000	$200,000	$200,000
Subtotal signage				**$600,000**		**$600,000**
% discounted from rack rate						0%

FIGURE 10.8   Net/net form.

INVENTORY ITEM(S)	#	Rack rate (in US$)	# of broadcasts, games, etc.	Cost at rack rate (in US$)	Cost allocated (in US$)	Actual revenue (in US$)
TICKETS & HOSPITALITY						
Private suite	1	$600,000	Suite #524	$600,000	$400,000	$400,000
Club seats	4	$20,000		$80,000	$40,000	$40,000
Season tickets	8	$30,000	Section 101; 4 Row A, 4 Row B	$240,000	$240,000	$240,000
Subtotal tickets & hospitality				**$920,000**		**$680,000**
% discounted from rack rate						26%
PROMOTIONS & GIVEAWAYS						
Baseball cap giveaway	1	$100,000	15,000 caps	$100,000	$80,000	$80,000
Subtotal promotions				**$100,000**		**$80,000**
% discounted from rack rate						50%
WEB PRESENCE & DATABASE USAGE						
Home page banner ad	1	$100,000	100M viewers per annum	$100,000	$75,000	$75,000
Subtotal web & database				**$100,000**		**$75,000**
% discounted from rack rate						25%
COMMUNITY PROGRAMS						
Title sponsorship—Junior Hawks	1	$200,000	50,000 participants	$200,000	$100,000	$100,000
Subtotal community programs				**$200,000**		**$100,000**
% discounted from rack rate						50%
MISCELLANEOUS						
Merchandise		$100,000	Merchandise for suite	$100,000	$60,000	$60,000
Subtotal miscellaneous				**$100,000**		**$60,000**
% discounted from rack rate						40%
GROSS TOTAL				**$5,041,000**		**$3,963,000**
Overall % discount proposed						21%
NET OF AGENCY FEES						
(Less 15%)				$756,150		$594,450
Subtotal (NET of agency)				**$4,284,850**		**$3,368,550**
NET OF ACTIVATION & OTHER COSTS						
TV/radio ad production				0		0
Signage production				$100,000		$100,000
Cost of activation/execution, etc.				$50,000		$50,000
Subtotal activation etc. costs				**$150,000**		**$150,000**
TOTAL (NET/NET to club)				**$4,134,850**		**$3,218,550**
Overall % discount from rack rate						22%

APPROVED TO PROPOSE TO MARKETING PARTNER:

_____   _____   _____
Signature   Date   Name and position title (VP Marketing Partnerships)

_____   _____   _____
Signature   Date   Name and position title (Chief Revenue Officer)

FIGURE 10.8   *(continued)*

if the decision maker is present. Don't accept "no" from someone not empowered to say "yes."

3. At the first meeting, listen 80 percent of the time and sell only when you have to. You are there to observe and learn. Where does the prospective company currently spend its marketing dollars? What is working? What isn't working? What other sport organizations or events does the company sponsor or support? What does the company like or dislike about those relationships? What does the prospect do for client entertainment? For employee benefits and morale building?

4. Close with a statement that you are going back to determine whether you see a fit and to develop a possible solution that you can present next time. Ask for the next meeting before leaving and try to schedule it no more than two weeks following the initial meeting.

5. Create a customized marketing partnership proposal. Give the prospect something unique (creative names, program elements, or ownership). Practice consultative selling. For example, you could say, "Here are some possibilities that may work for you. Let's review them." Then get input from the activation team about time, costs, and other variables.

6. Present the proposal as a draft that you will gladly modify to meet the organization's needs. Custom-tailored proposals are much more likely to succeed than generic proposals. This is not about what you have to sell—inventory; this is about what the customer is interested in buying—a business solution.

7. Negotiate the final deal and get a signed agreement. Close the deal when you have the opportunity; ensure that the final signed deal has agreed-upon deliverables, payment terms, and a mutually agreed-upon timetable.

8. Introduce the client to the activation team and insist that everyone at the sport property treats the new or renewed partnership, *not* as a deal being closed, but as a partnership being *opened*, ideally for life.

Sponsorship and Cross-Promotion

A cross-promotion in a sponsorship agreement is the joining of two or more corporate partners or organizations to capitalize jointly on a sponsorship or licensing agreement. Given the economic climate and the interest in B2B and business-to-consumer (B2C) marketing, cross-promotions are viable in today's marketplace for a variety of reasons. Such agreements do the following:

- Allow companies (or divisions of the same company) to share the total cost of a sponsorship
- Allow the promotion of several product lines or brands (with distinct organizational budgetary lines) within the same corporate structure (PepsiCo and Frito-Lay or Yum Brands)
- Enable corporations to use existing business relationships that make sense (McDonald's and Coca-Cola)
- Enable a newer or smaller corporation with something to offer to leverage the strength and position of a larger or more established corporation to gain the sponsorship and a position of advantage over its competitors
- Allow testing of a relationship when future opportunities are under consideration
- Create a pass-through opportunity, typically involving grocery chains that agree to a sponsorship and pass some or all of the costs (and benefits) to product vendors in their stores

Ethical Issues in Sponsorship

As sponsorship has grown in scope and impact, sport organizations have become highly reliant on sponsorship income to make a profit, secure new facilities, or balance their bottom line. In certain instances, this dependence on revenue has invited scrutiny by outside parties or even regret or second-guessing by one or both of the parties participating in the sponsorship agreement. In the past, we have seen significant repercussions and media coverage surrounding star athletes, including Antonio Brown, Maria Sharapova, Ryan Lochte, Tiger Woods, Michael Phelps, and

Prospecting: The Key Step in Initiating the Sponsorship Sales Process

Jared Schoenfeld, VP, Head of Brand Partnerships at The Players' Tribune

Prospecting is using every available resource to uncover leads and ultimately to create new business partnerships. I learned the value of good prospecting in my first year as a sales consultant with the Phoenix Suns Legacy Partners, LLC. While crossing the street in Phoenix (with the right of way, of course), I was forced to jump to avoid a recklessly driven construction vehicle. Stunned, I jotted down the phone number of the company with the intention of reporting this unsafe driver. After my emotions had cooled and I hadn't called, I realized that what I held in my hand was a lead. Two months later, I had sold the CEO of the construction company a $45,000 premium ticket package. Every time that I saw him and his son at the arena, I was reminded about the importance of having my eyes and ears open at all times and treating everything as a lead.

Before you go out scouting local construction companies, let's review a few principles of prospecting that you should be doing every day to increase business. First, it is import-ant to read newspapers, magazines, and all publications on business and the marketplace. This will keep you informed about people, business, and trends within various industries. Even more crucial, it will allow you to identify who is spending money. A great way to see who is spending money is to subscribe to a publication that showcases who is signing new commercial leases, which means they are expanding their office space and growing (www.therealdeal.com is a good example). Set automatic email notifications and Google alerts about companies you have targeted to stay current on their activity. This will allow you to send touch points when you see their name in the news. Use research to learn more about your current clients as well. The objective is to identify and target other like-minded businesses with hopes of creating a partnership. Note that not all research should take place during the standard business hours of 9 a.m. to 5 p.m., because that is your best opportunity to reach out to potential clients.

Another huge element of prospecting is networking. Conferences, symposiums, and, of course, your own team's games are unbelievable opportunities to expand your network and create leads. Shaking hands is great, but make sure that you get a business card before giving your own and always follow up the next day! Networking sites like LinkedIn have made it incredibly easy not only to follow up but also to learn about people you have met and their companies. LinkedIn allows you to find background information on people, which you can use as talking points to enhance the relationship. Additionally, you're able to find friends and relationships that you have in common with the person you met or are trying to engage in conversation with, which enhance your credibility. When meeting someone, understand that your first impression is everything. The way that you dress, smile, and converse all matters, so prepare!

Referrals are my favorite form of prospecting because they usually reflect a good relation-ship that you have created with the referring client. All referrals begin with this basic rule: You must ask! As with many things in life, if you don't put yourself out there, you will never have the opportunity to reap the rewards. Begin by asking your current clients for referrals; if you have helped them grow their business, they should be happy to introduce you to their contacts because they see the value first hand. Sometimes you will build a great relationship with a company without their becoming a partner. In this situation, you should ask whether

> *continued*

> continued

they know any companies that may be able to capitalize on the opportunities that you have discussed. Then ask whether they can introduce you to them. Always emphasize that you are not trying to sell them anything immediately. Just build a relationship and see whether there happens to be a fit to help grow their business.

Nothing in my sport business or entry-level sales education taught me about jumping out of the way of a construction vehicle and parlaying that into a sale. In devoting time to the aforementioned tactics, you will become more knowledgeable and build your network. But you haven't truly mastered prospecting until you're keeping your eyes and ears open at all times. Treat everything like a lead until you find out that it isn't. Don't be afraid to use unorthodox methods of identifying local businesses that are spending money. And remember, always have confidence that you can create a customized partnership for any company. It's just a matter of finding the leads!

Lance Armstrong, in relation to their roles as brand ambassadors. Tiger Woods' driving mishap and infidelity caused a number of his corporate partners to part ways with the golf superstar. Tag Heuer, Gillette, Gatorade, Accenture, AT&T, and *Golf Digest* all left Woods in 2011, giving rise to the debate about whether athletes have a moral obligation to adhere to a certain code of conduct on and off the field to be compliant with the best interests of their sponsors. Some of Tiger Woods' sponsors later returned, which indicates that athlete image rehabilitation is critical after a negative incident to regain trust and financial support from brands.

Commercial gambling providers (CGPs) have intensified the promotion of their products and services through sport sponsorship. On May 14, 2018, the United States Supreme Court overturned the Professional and Amateur Sports Protection Act (PASPA) and deemed it unconstitutional, allowing states to legalize sports gambling.[46] Consequently, CGPs can sign sponsorship agreements in states that have legalized, and gambling products and services now gain substantial exposure to large audiences through media broadcasts of sport and other promotional channels. Because of the mainstream appeal of some sports, television audiences and fan bases can include youth and at-risk and problem gamblers. These people may be prompted to gamble or increase their gambling because of the alignment of gambling with a healthy activity and the increased normalization of gambling, as well as direct marketing. Therefore, sport sponsorship by CGPs promotes a potentially risky behavior and may exacerbate the public health issue of problem

gambling. Regulatory measures have been implemented by governments and private organizations in relation to sport sponsorship by tobacco companies in recognition of the potential harmful influence of this form of marketing. Subsequently, the involvement of unhealthy products, including alcohol, junk food, and gambling, in sport sponsorship has been publicly questioned. Further regulatory changes that would directly affect the management of sport organizations may be implemented. Few studies have examined these issues, and we have little knowledge of the effects that sport sponsorship arrangements have on society. Research is needed to inform prudent decision making about the appropriate regulation of sport sponsorship.

Wrap-Up

Although ample rationale may support entering into a sponsorship agreement, the key to a successful sponsorship is generating ROI or ROO, which is generally attributed to how the sponsorship agreement has been activated. Simply stated, what did you do with what you bought? Which types of marketing platforms did you create to engage the target market and achieve your marketing objectives? A great sponsorship opportunity can be ineffective if it is not properly activated to engage the target market.

Sponsorships and licensing agreements should always be positioned as partnerships. Partnerships imply a mutually beneficial relationship, often referred to as a win–win relationship, in terms of consideration, negotiation, obligations, benefits, growth, and trust.[47] For example, Nike, often accused of ambush marketing in its practices, is protective of its own agreements and relationships. Nike never uses the word *sponsor* but always *partner*, believing that the term *sponsor* doesn't take into account the importance of partners working together to meet the needs and goals of each other.

To justify the ever-increasing cost of sponsorships, sponsors need to generate a multifaceted ROI, ROO, or ROE. Regardless of the type of return being sought, the return should contain multiple benefits that include one or more of the following: media and exposure, sales opportunities, image enhancement, effective communication with the target market, hospitality opportunities, and brand positioning.

The rationale for entering a sponsorship varies according to the size, mission, vision, geographic scope, target market, and resources of an organization. Regardless of the particulars of the organization, all sponsorship decisions should be based on the fit and potential of the opportunity with the organization and its priorities, as well as how the sponsorship helps achieve overall organizational objectives.

Activities

1. Contact a local sport organization's corporate partnerships department and gather information about one of its corporate accounts. How does the team use various assets to activate its sponsorship?

2. Over the course of 24 hours, track how many selling messages you are exposed to. At the end of the day, which ones do you remember? Why?

3. Give an example of a company involved in sport marketing that has tied goodwill into its sponsorship campaign. Is it successful? Why or why not?

4. Think of a time when you were the recipient of hospitality benefits at a sports or an entertainment event. What did the organization do well? What could it have added or done differently?

5. What are two things that companies should keep in mind when activating through social media?

6. Think of your favorite sport team and list some of its current sponsors. Why are these companies sponsoring the team? What other brands might benefit from partnering in a different category?

7. What is the importance of telling a story in a sponsor's activation strategy?

8. Choose a non-sport related company and create a sport sponsorship activation platform. Use the idea of telling the brand's story throughout your campaign.

Your Marketing Plan

In developing your marketing plan, you have generated a list of objectives, strategies, and tactics. Sponsorship can be instrumental in helping you achieve these elements of a marketing plan by providing the resources (not necessarily just financial) needed to be successful. Integrate one or more of the concepts of sponsorship discussed in this chapter into your marketing plan.

 Go to HK*Propel* to complete the activities for this chapter.

Chapter 11

Social Media in Sports

Karen Freberg

OBJECTIVES

- To define what social media mean to sport marketing

- To examine the types of social media content and tactics commonly used in sport marketing

- To understand the necessity to integrate social media programming and initiatives into the marketing communications mix

- To comprehend the role of traditional marketing concepts such as reach, breadth, segmentation, and impressions as they are applied in a social media context

- To explore the best practices and insights gathered from sport teams into innovative and strategic practices in social media

Koki Nagahama/Getty Images

The Rise of Coco Gauff and Athlete Social Media Marketing

Athletes with personal brands have always been a stronghold for sports, but social media have created more opportunities for athletes to go directly to their audiences through various online platforms. LeBron James, Cristiano Ronaldo, Serena Williams, and Michael Phelps are just a few of such athletes who have built their digital presence to be as large as their offline following. However, other athletes began building their branding empires primarily via social media, so that when they hit big on the courts of their respective sport, they would have a dominant force and following that would support them every step of the way.

Coco Gauff had a breakout year on the tennis court in 2019, becoming the youngest player to win a title at the age of 15 while competing against some of the best players in the sport. By setting standards and new expectations on the court, Gauff helped translate what it means to be an athlete in the modern sport industry. Gauff strategically shares content on her social media profiles. Her posts include not only her competing at Wimbledon matches and other high-profile tournaments but also her opening the window for viewers to see what it is like to be a teenager. The level of transparency, authenticity, and personality that comes from sharing stories and perspectives on social media is in many ways what fans and audiences crave when it comes to team and athlete accounts. This is all part of a marketing strategy that positions Gauff as not only being a talented athlete but also having mastered the equation of promoting, engaging in dialogue (PR), and marketing product (rising Gen Z tennis phenomenon) for her brand. With social media, Gauff has transformed her social media following and tennis success into endorsement opportunities with brands such as Barilla and New Balance.

Having a strong presence on social media allows fans to engage with athletes like Gauff as well as celebrities. From the Wimbledon match Gauff played, which catapulted her to the global stage as the youngest player to make it to the fourth round of the prestigious event, she received congratulations on social media from celebrities such as Jaden Smith, Reese Witherspoon, and Samuel L. Jackson who supported her as she moved forward in the competition. While Gauff did not win Wimbledon, she was able to gain a global following of supporters and enthusiasts who wanted to cheer her on the court, as well as online via social media.

Gauff is an example of a rising trend in the sport marketing and social media fields for a variety of reasons. Gauff is a powerhouse in her sport, with a dominant voice and presence on social media. Historically, athletes were reliant on the media, teams, and athletic associations to promote, engage, and market their work to consumers. However, in today's world, social media allow athletes like Gauff to bypass the traditional gatekeepers to communicate directly with their fans. Having a strong social media following also allows brands to measure the overall impact athletes have online, which provides evidence of their influence and presence on social media platforms. Sponsorship deals are now negotiated with considerations of an athlete's social media following as well as the athlete's impact on the profession. Lastly, social media platforms allow athletes to show a human side of their brand that would not have been shared otherwise.

The sport world will see the strategic application and creative execution of social media efforts among athletes, teams, and organizations not only increase but also evolve and grow as it continues to be a prominent factor in modern marketing practices.

In sports, people often say the battle on the playing surface is just the beginning. They are right because a battle for the most creative, entertaining, and inspiring content to be shared with the masses in the digital sphere exists. Sport leagues, teams, athletes, and brands are all competing for the attention of their fans and customers who spend their time consuming, responding to, and sharing content.

As we move further into the 21st century, social media has permeated all aspects of society with users worldwide. The number of people who use the Internet now tops 4.5 billion, with 3.8 billion people present on social media.[1] The medium has matured since its inception, becoming a staple communication channel in many disciplines and professions, including sport marketing.

The rapid rise of social media has delivered a bounty of fans and followers to sport properties. People proudly declare their fan allegiance and essentially ask their favorite teams to communicate with them directly. This development represents a major shift in communication between teams and fans that may not be obvious to a social native (i.e., one who has grown up with digital and social media). Although sport properties have a relatively easy time attracting fans and followers compared with other brands, building an engaging presence is both an art and a science. Those that had an early presence on the major American-based platforms Facebook and Twitter earned an edge over their competitors. Those that integrate social media into their marketing strategies attract more of a following than those that don't. And those that have a true, dedicated focus on social media are more effective at engaging fans than those that don't.

Unsurprisingly, the big numbers on social media are attracting big attention from both senior management and marketers of all types who would like access to these fans. But a careful balance must be struck. Although social media makes it easy for fans to like, follow, and keep up with their favorite teams, it also makes it easy for them to dislike, unfollow, or perhaps worse, tune out. And social media is still scrutinized in terms of its value and ability to deliver results akin to other digital direct marketing strategies.

Although further research is needed to fully understand the role of social media in the overall marketing mix, social media has proven valuable in sport for many reasons:

- It builds an audience of fans to interact with in real time.
- It engages fans in ways they want to be engaged. Fans get more access, real-time information, breaking news, special offers, and fun stuff. Sport properties and athletes can drive more consumption of brand and content: website page views, video views, articles, photos, sweepstakes, contests, games, and more. Ultimately, it can create more lifetime fans.

- It's viral: Sport teams used to craft strategic plans and incentives to get people to share content with their friends. Now, likes, shares, and comments occur organically within and across platforms.
- It drives behavior that drives business, including tune-in, ticket sales, game attendance, increased brand consumption, merchandise sales, and more interaction with corporate partners.
- People not only want to interact with brands on social media but also want to buy from brands, which is why more and more companies are trying to sell through social.

Table 11.1 displays usage and consumer behavior statistics on the major social media channels.[2] Social media marketing is an evolving discipline that touches all areas of sport business and requires a sophisticated approach. This chapter explores the most effective techniques in social media management and marketing.

What Is Social Media?

Social media are a collective hub of global digital platforms that allow users to engage, discuss, create, and foster relationships in real time. Social media have been at the forefront of bringing both pain and delight to brands, organizations, and PR professionals. Social media have transformed how people are able to consume, disseminate, and engage with news and other forms of information. Evolving communications technology tools allow individual users and organizations to engage with, reach, persuade, and target key audiences more effectively across multiple platforms. Social media provides the ultimate personalized online networked hub of information, dialogue, and relationship management.

What makes social media a powerful entity is the ability to allow users to

- share knowledge,
- engage in digital storytelling through conversations and visual components,
- collaborate with others,
- engage in crowdsourcing tasks and contribute ideas to solve problems,
- conduct strategic monitoring and analytic analysis, and

TABLE 11.1 Social Media Usage and Consumer Behavior

	Facebook	Instagram	Twitter	YouTube
Users	2.5 billion monthly users	More than 1 billion monthly active users	152 million monetizable daily users	More than 2 billion users visiting every month (not including those who aren't logged in)
Reach	1.95 billion can be reached by ads (32% of all people worldwide over age 13)	928.5 million people can be reached by ads	Twitter users linger 24% longer over ads than users on other platforms	People watch 1 billion hours of video on YouTube every day and spend an average of 23 minutes on the site each time they visit
Ranking	World's third most visited website after Google and YouTube	World's seventh most visited website	World's sixth most visited website	World's second most visited website after Google
Consumer behavior	58% of people in the United States say they've become more interested in a brand after seeing it in Facebook Stories (300 million people use Facebook Stories every day)	92% of all Instagram users say they've followed a brand, clicked on their website, or made a purchase after seeing a product or service on Instagram	Twitter users are more likely to prefer "culturally relevant" brands (47% versus 39% of the general U.S. population)	80% of people who watched a YouTube video as part of their buying journey did so early on

- build relationships within a community that shares common interests, investments, and needs.

In many ways, social media platforms serve as gateways where content and conversations are created and ignited between individual users, brands, and organizations. In addition, social media platforms provide first impression management tools for corporations and users to showcase their own brands and reputations.

Although Facebook and Instagram are the most well-known platforms, other channels (YouTube, Twitter, TikTok, Snapchat, Pinterest, LinkedIn, and others) are evolving and new ones are appearing all the time. While the tools and platforms may evolve and change, the overall application of how and why we use these tools does not. Social media are the center of communication and community building, allowing audiences to learn, share, engage, and execute various strategies, experiences, and messaging. For sport professionals and teams, this is a place where agility, creativity, and innovation thrive. In order to be successful, one has to be a student of the platforms that are being implemented.

Social Media and the Marketing Mix

Social media play an integral role in the marketing mix. In this section, we discuss each of the five Ps and how they are important to social media and marketing.

Product

The sport product is any product, service, or experience an organization offers that allows consumers to connect with sports. It includes tangible components, such as tickets, equipment, and apparel, as well as intangible features, such as experiences and memories. The sport product has both core components related to the game-day experience and brand extensions that take place outside the stadium or venue. Sport has many products and services that are used to motivate audiences to support and buy into the sport culture. Social media is a major marketing channel that is now used to showcase the sport product and promote it to fans and consumers around the world. Whether it is getting tickets to a WNBA game or a cricket match, buying your favorite athlete's jersey, or playing fantasy football, these are all examples of the product that is being presented in sport marketing. Personal brands, especially those of athletes, can also be viewed as sport products because both sport organizations and athletes market them.

Social media is often used to showcase the actual on-court or on-field product. Video clips of game highlights, behind-the-scenes content focusing on players and coaches, and in some cases the social media content of the athletes and coaches themselves, are all elements that feature core product or product extensions. With the increasing importance of media content in revenue and marketing, it can be argued that sport businesses are media companies themselves, which makes their media output an intrinsic element of the product. This also allows the sport entity to extend their brand footprint far beyond their geographical footprint. Social media is ultimately why there are tens of thousands of Barcelona and Manchester City fans in the United States, and why the Golden State Warriors were able to grow into a worldwide phenomenon despite a lack of historical franchise success.

Price

Price is a very important factor in sport marketing, and social media greatly affect it. Rising costs related to providing sport products and services have caused price increases for fans and consumers wanting access to virtually all areas of the sport industry. Tickets to events, concession prices, cable and OTT subscriptions, merchandise, and many other products have

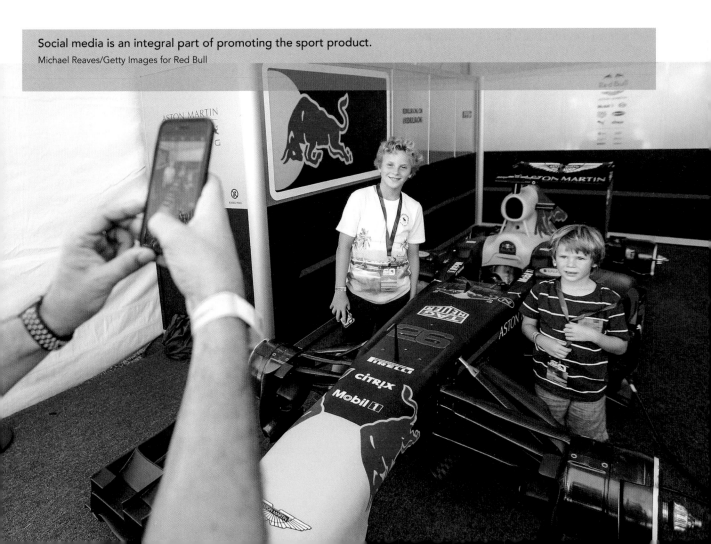

Social media is an integral part of promoting the sport product.

Michael Reaves/Getty Images for Red Bull

become more expensive since 2015. Although access can be somewhat pricey to sport teams and their associated offerings, what is shared on social media (e.g., Instagram Live, Facebook Live, and athletes with their own social media) is free and everyone can access it. Sport marketing departments rely heavily on these no-cost social media platforms to promote all aspects of their business to fans. Sport marketers are constantly creating content and distributing it on the proper social channels to keep fans engaged, while also exploring means to use social media to sell their products. This content can also be promoted or sponsored by corporate partners which generates additional revenue for the organization.

Place

Each designated handle or profile on social media—whether it is via Facebook, Twitter, TikTok, Instagram, YouTube, or others—is prime digital real estate for product distribution to fans and other audiences. Teams use these real-time digital platforms to distribute game scores and updates; share photos, videos, and other player content; promote tickets and merchandise; connect and interact with fans; and continually build their brands through storytelling and experiential marketing. Each social media channel is a distinct avenue for content distribution and brand building that provides access to different consumers with varying demographic, geographic, and psychographic characteristics. Each channel plays a unique and separate role in the strategic marketing of the sport product.

Promotion

The hub of social media is a great place to promote and advertise across the digital network. Each social media platform can be used to sell a product, an experience, an event, or an opportunity for audiences. Some platforms, such as Instagram, have allowed teams and athletes to sell their own products directly through the app. In addition, each team uses specific features on each platform (e.g., Ads Manager for Facebook and Instagram) to focus on directly advertising to specific users based on certain characteristics. Social media have allowed marketing professionals to get very specific in their targeting and segmenting strategies, which leads to more effective campaigns.

But social media is not just about direct sales; it's about indirect sales as well. It is about increasing affinity for players, fostering a sense of online community through interactions, giving fans a channel to cheer online, and showcasing your organization in a way that can be appealing to multiple demographics. It is also about using social media within venues to draw fans closer to the experience, whether that involves using hashtags for displaying content on the big screen, allowing fans to tweet about issues with the crowd, or looking for help in finding concessions.

Public Relations

Public relations is the mutually beneficial relationship between an organization (team, league, brand, etc.) and their audiences (fans, sponsors, etc.), and social media are first and foremost social. They provide the opportunity to build a community, foster a dialogue, and share insights and ideas in real time. The #SMSports community on Twitter, for example, is where sports and social media professionals from all around the world come together to share ideas and perspectives about their work and the industry. Being connected to the community is a powerful way to learn and network as a sport marketing professional. Athletes at all levels also use their favorite forms of social media to harness the power of public relations. Athletes have called for social justice reform through activism efforts on social media and have raised millions of dollars for relief after natural disasters and other tragedies. Athletes use social media to promote their personal foundations and highlight the positive impact they are creating not only in their local communities but also around the world in their respective countries.

Teams are also putting out their own messaging and content, breaking news, and informing fans of issues and activities directly. As sport organizations have begun to use social media more for the purpose of conducting public relations activities, they have become mini media entities, creating and disseminating their own content around the players, coaches, and all other aspects of the organization. To some degree, the team's social media staffs have supplanted traditional PR functions since direct communication with the media is not always necessary. What we have seen is a merging of social media and PR departments as organizations handle many of these responsibilities in-house.

Managing Accounts

Managing accounts is one of the biggest social media challenges for sport teams, organizations, and athletes. Having the keys to the digital front door of the brand is a big responsibility, and it takes substantial planning, coordination, and organization to make things happen. Many aspects to brand management on social media channels must be taken into consideration:

- *Keep personal and official accounts separate.* Many social media management tools enable toggling between multiple accounts, which can lead to staffers making the easy mistake of posting from a personal account instead of the official one. Having training for these platforms is crucial. While there are many certification programs (e.g., Hootsuite, Brandwatch, etc.), having plans in place is necessary in situations when an unintended post goes out.

- *Reserve the right to delete, but do so with caution.* Content or status updates that have already been published can be easily deleted but often not before someone has taken a screenshot and published it elsewhere. As they say, "Google does not forget," and taking a screenshot and sharing it with the world is one of the most consequential actions a person can do.

- *Own your mistakes.* An organization or a person who makes a mistake must address it directly with fans and followers. Denying or even making excuses for a mistake may not go over that well. Simply put, how you craft your response is just as important as what you share on a regular basis.

- *Know who has access to accounts.* In a large organization with a range of platforms, dozens of people may have access to accounts. Having a plan in which you have all of the passwords, protocols, and security measures in place is crucial in case something goes wrong. Develop a crisis communication plan in the event that accounts are hacked and include a decision tree in the plan that designates who in the social media team and athletic organization gets notified and when and how they should be notified.

- *Establish a strong listening and monitoring program.* Listening to and monitoring conversations on social media is key to identifying new opportunities and trends, but it is also essential to preparing for a potential crisis. Having designated search terms for team names, coaches, athletes, and sport accounts are all part of identifying what people are saying online and the tone and context in which they are saying it. Investing in monitoring tools, such as Talkwalker, Sprinklr, and others, allows social media teams to keep their ears to the ground to know what their audiences are saying, feeling, and sharing online.

- *Change passwords frequently and make them complex.* Hacking into accounts is one of the crises most sport professionals need to be prepared to handle. To minimize the possibility of getting hacked, create complex passwords that you change. There are many options to consider here for how to create an effective password. Password generator tools are helpful, but make sure the password is not too noticeable (like 123456). Use a mixture of symbols, a combination of lower- and uppercase letters, and other special characters to make the passwords unique. Two-factor authentication is likely the best method to ensure security.

- *Have clearly written rules on what can and cannot be discussed.* As they say, "Inspect what you expect." Having set guidelines, expectations, and protocols in place will help set up a culture for professional, positive, and ethical behaviors for the social media team. Clear and updated guidelines, including which types of current events can and cannot be commented on and which types of news can and cannot be broken through social media, should be put in writing and posted at the desk of every person who posts content.

Building an Audience

Sport properties organically attract many fans, but they're working hard to acquire others. Winning helps, but it isn't the only way to build an audience. Getting out early on new platforms helps a property gain an advantage over latecomers.

One league that has always been innovative and at the forefront of social media marketing is the NBA. The NBA was the first major professional sports league to surpass one billion likes and followers across all its social media platforms, including league, team, and player accounts.[3] The NBA is extremely active on Facebook, Instagram, and Twitter, as well as its major social platforms in China, Tencent and Sina. According to the NBA, nearly 90 percent of all its players are active on at least one social channel with LeBron James and the Los Angeles Lakers being the most followed player and team. In 2018, the NBA also partnered with the popular video app, TikTok, in order to attract younger fans by providing custom highlights around the world in countries like Brazil, India, and China. Even though the NBA boasts a younger fan base (43 years on average) than most American professional sport leagues, they want to appeal to Gen Z consumers, and more than 60 percent of TikTok's audience is under the age of 30.[4]

Beyond being a popular and winning brand, organizations need to use tried-and-true direct and brand-marketing techniques to build the maximum audience.

In-Game and In-Event

The social media landscape has become an integral part of the game-day experience for sports fans. It is not just about communicating and engaging with others during the event but improving the overall convenience and enjoyment of the activity. Social media can be used in myriad ways to ensure fans have all the information and entertainment they desire.

When the Golden State Warriors built the US$1 billion state-of-the-art Chase Center, the technological upgrades were designed to provide the ultimate interactive fan experience. The team even created the hashtag #Fannovate to ask fans how technology and innovation could improve their fan experience. Some of the results included the ability for fans to take photos and videos and upload them to the jumbotron, as well as access real-time game data and statistics.[5] Advanced mobile connectivity and Wi-Fi allow fans to enjoy social media while also receiving push notifications on the team app about game-day promotions, discounts, seat upgrades, and team content.

Some teams are getting remarkably creative with mobile and social media to incorporate fans into the actual game presentation. At AT&T Stadium, home of the Dallas Cowboys, fans receive a push alert that gives them the option to press a "Unite This House" button. The button causes a "digital wave" by making fans' cell phones vibrate and flash in unison.

In order to create a dynamic and comprehensive experience for fans, sport teams cannot ignore the offline experiences, or those not connected to the World Wide Web. Teams need to be sure to market themselves using traditional means, as well as promote items that allow fans to share, create, and engage on social media platforms during the game and beyond the competition. Prompts around the venue help remind fans to like or follow the property. Teams can use PA reads, LED boards, jumbotrons, signage, ticket backs, and many other assets in the venue to drive more fans and followers to social media. Here are some offline items that enhance the game-day experience while promoting the use of social media platforms:

- *Wi-Fi access.* Wi-Fi is a must-have for many fans to be able to create and share content at a game. Teams want their fans to feel encouraged to check out their fantasy teams, post something on social media, like the team on Facebook, or participate in a TikTok challenge.

- *Branding for social media platforms.* Owning branding online is only part of the equation. An organization's social media profiles need to be part of offline branding, too, so that fans know about those profiles. The following offline promotions are some examples to implement that will help shift more consumers to social media:

  ○ In-game promotion of hashtags and social media handles

  ○ Call-to-action statements for online promotions and contests

- University-wide hashtag for everyone to participate in

  For example, the University of Louisville designated #WeRiseAsOne as their hashtag to be used by fans, coaches, students, and alumni on their social media platforms. Clemson Athletics designated #AllIn for branding on their social media platforms.

- *Charging stations.* Along with Wi-Fi, fans need the ability to charge their devices so they can check scores, upload content, and share experiences with others. This usually involves having designated charging station locations with multiple plugs that allow fans to recharge during intermissions so they can continue to engage in social media during the game.

Increase Fan Engagement

Most everyone loves a mascot, and it is good practice if you can connect mascots and fans via social media. Many teams have created social media accounts specifically for their mascots to enhance branding and experiment with new platforms, techniques, and challenges:

- Gritty, the mascot for the Philadelphia Flyers, is one of the more memorable mascots because he looks and acts quite differently compared to other traditional mascots. Since Gritty was introduced in 2018, he has gone from being an initially unloved mascot to becoming a sport cultural icon. With over 300,000 followers on Twitter alone, Gritty is a critical part of the Flyers marketing strategy, because he has the capacity to reach and engage with a massive part of the Philadelphia fan base.

- The Oregon Duck (otherwise known as Puddles) also has a strong social media presence, thanks to the success of Oregon's football team.[6] Puddles is one of the few mascots that are verified across social media platforms. The content that is created and shared on the various platforms for the Oregon Duck range from supporting efforts for the teams, taking part in viral challenges, and creating content to entertain audiences during the COVID-19 quarantine. These pieces of content are shared across all platforms, but Puddles does particularly well with Twitter.

The Oregon Duck, aka Puddles, entertained audiences with COVID-19 quarantine content by remixing content from one of Taylor Swift's music videos.

Courtesy of University of Oregon Athletics.

Communicate With Fans

Social media provides one of the most direct and unique ways for teams and sport organizations to communicate with their fans. They can talk directly to their audience, in good times and bad, and share all the important information, content, and news in real-time.

One of the most exciting times of the year for sports fans is when the team's schedule is released. This information is also paramount for the organization to communicate as the entire season and business revolves around the upcoming games. Previously, teams would simply announce the schedule and post it on the official website. Social media has now become the preferred medium to announce the exciting news to fans, and teams are getting really creative in their releases. For the 2019 to 2020 NFL season, the Atlanta Falcons adopted a Game of Thrones theme. Their Twitter video with the full schedule titled, "Football is coming," garnered over 3 million views.[7]

Communicating with fans should not always be a one-way street. The beauty and intrigue of social media is that it can be two-way with fans joining the conversation and taking an active role in the organization. Teams and leagues that understand how to communicate *with* their fans

and not just *at* them will have an advantage. Prior to the 2019 season, MLB had each of its teams select an official hashtag that the league would use along with its own emoji on Twitter. The Colorado Rockies saw an opportunity to communicate with their fans and have them actively participate in the development of the official team hashtag. They ran a social media campaign where Rockies fans created four possible hashtags. The team then presented a poll so fans could vote on their favorite one. The poll got more than 3,300 votes, and the social media campaign turned into an opportunity for fans to feel more connected with and a part of the team.

Unexpected crises can cause harm or damage to an organization, a team, or a person, and they happen all the time in society and within the sport community. During a crisis, people often turn to social media for information and direction. They also use social media to see others' reactions to the crisis and come together virtually to cope with a difficult experience.

- *Responding to a tragedy.* After Kobe Bryant's unexpected passing in January 2020, many fans shared their disbelief and shock on social media. The Los Angeles Lakers understood its audience, knowing fans would want a timely response from

Social media provides a unique opportunity to communicate with fans when tragedy strikes, such as the death of Kobe Bryant.

APU GOMES/AFP via Getty Images

the team about the tragedy. The Lakers took a careful approach and used authenticity, transparency, and a commitment to Bryant's legacy in its social media posts.

• *Responding to a crisis.* One crisis that sparked a worldwide response was COVID-19. Once this virus was classified as a global pandemic, it became necessary to close down many businesses and events, including sports functions. Nike, known for its powerful copywriting and creative marketing executions, responded with a simple statement: If you want the opportunity to play for millions in the future, stay at home today. This was a powerful message that allowed the brand to lead with a clear stance on what everyone should do to overcome the crisis.

In-Broadcast

Sport teams can often take advantage of various assets within their game broadcasts to promote team initiatives, including social media participation.

• *During the game.* In-game broadcast reads by the announcer, enter-to-win contests and sweepstakes, and interactive games are the most commonly used in-broadcast tactics to drive fans to engage through social media channels. Teams can drive local broadcast ratings by encouraging fans on social media to tune in to games and providing game times and broadcast information.

• *Postgame.* Postgame press conferences and analysis shows are a great place to encourage conversation about the game on social media. Analysts and announcers can facilitate viewers to follow the team on Facebook, Instagram, and Twitter and use specific hashtags when posting.

Online, Direct, and Digital Marketing

Reminders and calls to action throughout websites and direct marketing, including e-mail newsletters, mobile apps, mobile SMS (short message service) updates, and tags on direct mail pieces, help build social audiences among people who are already within the sport team's or property's database.

Advertising

Paid or mass media advertising can drive a greater audience and more engagement on Facebook, Instagram, and Twitter. Mass advertising can take the form of paid ads on social media timelines, in promoted posts, on external websites, or on outdoor media (e.g., billboards). Mass advertising includes banner ads on the website, courtside signage in-game, broadcast drops, and in-game reads.

Sports teams, especially at the professional level, are finding great success advertising and selling through social, notably on Facebook and Instagram. In 2017-2018, the Miami Heat began investing heavily in Facebook and Instagram ads and continued to increase their investment in that strategy after seeing success. The Heat's digital marketing team used Facebook to target basketball fans and consumers in order to sell more single-game tickets, develop leads for season tickets, increase online commerce, and enhance sales for all arena events. Facebook's automated marketing features and machine-learning algorithms helped the Heat not only identify more well-qualified customers but provide personalized online experiences. After deploying this social media marketing strategy, which emphasized creative testing, advanced audience segmentation, and machine-enabled optimization, the Miami Heat garnered the following results after the 2018 to 2019 season:[8]

• 32 percent lift in return on advertising spend (ROAS) from Instagram and Facebook ads year-over-year

• 12.4x ROAS generated across Instagram and Facebook ad campaigns

• 17 percent of the Heat's online merchandise sales came from Facebook and Instagram ads

• 6,900+ qualified leads generated for season ticket sales

According to Eric Woolworth, Miami Heat President, Business Operations, "It's always a challenge for professional sports teams to generationally turn over their season ticket member base—and we're doing just that. In the last few years, we've doubled down on Facebook and Instagram, and have seen that new members are on average 10 years younger than our existing base.

You can tie that directly into what we're doing on Facebook and Instagram; it's cause and effect."[8]

Share Optimized Content

When great content is shared among friends, a subset of those friends will then like or follow the property. This is the social media version of a long-standing, tried-and-true marketing technique known as word-of-mouth (WOM) marketing. According to Nielsen, a whopping 92 percent of consumers believe recommendations they receive from family and friends over all other forms of advertising![9] For sport marketers, this means your fans could be your most valuable and effective advertisers. According to Forbes, marketers revealed that WOM marketing was the most effective form of marketing. Therefore, getting fans to like and share team or brand content should be an integral part of a sport organization's strategy.

One way to do this is to use what is known as influencer marketing. It can be very effective to work with fans or followers of your team who have large, engaged audiences and have them distribute your content. Influencer marketing has increased dramatically in recent years among sport organizations in order to facilitate the process of content optimization. According to research conducted on amateur and professional sport teams, 65 percent of sport marketers agreed that influencer marketing campaigns are necessary for success in today's digital world. Influencer marketing is extremely important when trying to reach the highly-social Gen Z target. When asked what the top benefits were of influencer marketing, sport marketers responded with the following:[10]

- Drive social media engagement around my product or brand (22 percent)
- Create authentic content about my brand (20.4 percent)
- Reach younger generations who don't trust traditional advertising (13.8 percent)
- Drive online and in-store ticket or merchandise sales (13.2 percent)
- Drive traffic to my website or landing page (12 percent)
- Grow my email database with qualified consumers (10.8 percent)

- Generate authentic, easily discoverable product reviews (6.6 percent)
- Other (1.2 percent)

Identifying, incentivizing, and rewarding influencers among team social followers has gained traction. Not all fans are created equal; a few will have disproportionately large networks of their own. Getting those fans to share content can improve the team's reach exponentially. One way that sport organizations have leveraged influencers is to host events at their home. For example, teams with season tickets to sell have learned that holding small influencer events at a key influencer's (season-ticket holder's name) home can drive tremendous return on investment. Other teams have invited influencers with large followings to sit courtside at games, attend player meet-and-greets, and participate in in-game contests in order to distribute unique content to their personal audiences. According to Matt Diteljan, cofounder at Cascade Influencers, "When compared to organizations similar in size in other industries, sports entertainment companies are much slower to adopt influencer marketing. While other industries have been pouring money into influencer marketing for years, sports entertainment companies are just now starting to jump on the bandwagon."[10]

Segmenting Your Audience

Before you can target social media to your audience, you first need to know who your audience is: What conversations are they having, and where are they having them? Audience segmentation is a strategy companies, agencies, and brands use to collect information to create a profile of an audience with whom they wish to engage. Basic demographic information can be collected (age, gender, household income), but social media users disclose much more additional information. Think about the amount of information Facebook has collected over the years from likes, comments, shares, and videos watched. With insight tools for audience analysis, social media professionals can be very broad in their targeting (prioritizing their audiences and whom they want to reach first), or they can be very specific by identifying particular people to receive their messages and content.

A valid question in the area of social media is whether the organization should have different social media accounts to target different segments of the audience. Some teams have tested this method by creating Facebook pages and Twitter accounts for season-ticket holders only to provide more customized content to special audiences. Targeted accounts can be effective, but they do require extra time, resources, content, access, and interaction. Teams without large staffs should devote their limited resources to their largest audiences on the main platforms.

Engaging Fans

Once you have segmented your audience, you can engage with people in an artful balance. Viral audience growth is directly correlated with how engaged the existing audience is with the content. If fans and followers love what they read, see, and watch, they will share it and come back for more. A carefully calibrated approach that focuses on authenticity and brand voice, listening, learning, optimizing, and delivering is essential.

Authenticity and Brand Voice

The voice of social media should sound like a real person, not a website. The voice should have a conversational tone and some personality, but not too much. A lack of authenticity of voice on social media will cause people to tune out. Different platforms can have different fan bases, each of which expects to hear a unique voice. By surveying fans of different platforms, sport properties can learn quickly what fans expect.

A brand voice is the overall tone, personality, and perspective that is taken into consideration across all content that is shared on a person's or team's social media channels. A brand voice presents an opportunity to add some character to the mix that makes the content entertaining, relatable, and engaging. Many teams and athletes have strong brand voices on social media, such as the Carolina Panthers (NFL), Tampa Bay Rays (MLB), LeBron James (basketball), and Megan Rapinoe (soccer).

Building a strong brand voice on social media is more than pretty creative that is shared across accounts. Social media has to be an integrated communication strategy that involves all levels of the organization. The field of college athletics is one of the most innovative, creative, and strategic applications of brand voice. For example, the creative team at Clemson University Athletics, including student interns, established itself as one of the leading storytellers in the industry. The team uses social media platforms strategically to

Clemson Athletics Vlog highlights the lives of all who are part of their football team from athletes and coaches to staff and more.

Reprinted by permission from Clemson Football.

foster what it is like to be a Clemson Tiger, both academically and athletically, showcasing athletes, coaches, administrators, supporting staff members, and more. Previously, the only brand voices that were showcased from teams on social media were in traditional roles (e.g., coaches, star athletes, etc.). However, Clemson realized it wanted to give voice on social media to all who are part of the Clemson Tiger family. The team developed and shared uniquely different content. For example, new approaches to content, like 360-degree game recaps and team vlogs, gave fans a window into who the Tigers were as a team and the work it was doing on and off the field. The Clemson Tigers marketed themselves in a much more comprehensive way through sharing a compelling brand story.

An investment in digital marketing can lead to more resources and opportunities, such as new team members and new partnerships. The partnership Clemson has with Adobe, for example, has been extremely beneficial for its academic and athletic presence. Clemson and Adobe joined forces to bring the Adobe Creative Cloud suite of applications to the university community and athletics department. The partnership also included the use of Adobe Anywhere, a platform that provides the capability to work on video projects and share content from around the world. The collaboration with Adobe allowed Clemson to have the cutting-edge, creative tools it needed to capture the athletics department's unique team voice in a way that made it stand out. Adobe has been a leader in developing sophisticated digital tools for education and industry, but this was one of the first times when an athletics team used the tools for storytelling and creating content to be consumed, experienced, and shared on social media. In addition, Clemson Athletics was able to be a pilot for new programs, such as Adobe Spark, before any other team, which allowed Clemson's content to stand out from the crowd in its promotional efforts. The partnership between Adobe and Clemson, like others established in the collegiate space, was a digital marketing success for both the university and the global technology company to build and showcase their brands to their audiences.

In addition to investing in technology for creating media, physical investments are also critical to the success of such partnerships. Schools and athletic marketing departments have also made physical investments in smartphones, laptops, lighting kits, and photography and video editing software to help produce the highest-quality content.

Listening

Social media have enabled brands and sport properties to understand brand perception and reactions to events or news in real-time like never before. A multitude of tools is available to organize and aggregate fan and follower sentiment on specific topics. Are people talking about the pending trade? Did they love the game last night? Do they love the food vendors in the arena? Do they hate the beer? Social media listening enables real-time reaction, correction, and amplification. Organizations do not have to wait for the (also valuable) fan surveys to go out midseason to know how people feel about the team, ticket prices, or the experience at the game.

Learning

The real-time nature of social media enables real-time learning of what works and what doesn't. Are 10 status updates a day too many? Does a status update with a photo get more engagement than one without? Does a tweet with a link get more clicks and retweets than one without? By using Facebook Insights, Twitter Analytics, Bit.ly, Hootsuite, and similar tools, teams can learn on a quantitative basis, iterate, and optimize rapidly. Simple, quick surveys of the digital audience will qualitatively answer many of these questions.

Optimizing

Testing is the magic word behind optimization. Many elements can be tested:

- Types of content
- Timing of posts
- Audiences targeted
- Surveys
- Polls
- Questions
- Links

What works in one market, for one sport, for one club, and even for one platform may not necessarily work for all. Testing each of the above elements and tracking interaction and engagement to determine effectiveness will help guide future social media strategy. The dynamism of social media is also important; news feed algorithms change, audiences shift from one platform to another, and content can ebb and flow in sport, further underscoring the need for a rigorous commitment to testing.

Delivering

The most progressive teams in social media not only deliver what their fans want, but also go the extra distance to provide unique experiences and access. The top brands that deliver in social media, whether inside or outside of sport, demonstrate an organizational commitment to it. They recognize the importance of social media, starting at the executive level, invest in people and software tools, are early adopters and pioneers on new platforms, and convert social sentiment into actions that drive brand loyalty.

Twitter seized the moment during the 2019 FIFA Women's World Cup where they had a captive global audience focused on women's soccer. They announced that they would award what they called the #GoldenTweet to Twitter users who were posting the best content around the Women's World Cup. The campaign included multiple award categories such as most retweeted fans, players, brands, journalists, and more.[7] The activation brought tons of attention, sparked conversation around the global tournament, and produced a wealth of content for the platform. Ultimately, they crowned a champion, Mike Magee, who was the father of a young girl who decided to take up soccer after being inspired by the athletes in the World Cup. Mike's tweet read, "I've tried every trick in the book to get my daughter to play soccer. Never pushed her but she simply didn't want to play. She's out kicking a ball against the wall by herself. Not because of me. Because of you @USWNT. Thank you." The video had 797,000 views and the tweet produced 32.8 thousand likes and 2.5 thousand retweets.[7] That same year, the FIFA Fan Zone captured a 360-degree photo at the opening and closing matches of the tournament so fans could tag themselves and share the once-in-a-lifetime experience with others on social.

Social Media Platforms

However present an organization may want to be on all of the social media platforms (discussed in detail in the following sections), it first needs to have a sound strategy and purpose for each platform. Professional and unique content must be provided on each platform while keeping in mind that there are differences to consider when posting from one channel to another. In other words, what works on Instagram may not work on Twitter or TikTok. Each piece of content needs to be evaluated based on the audience or community and the brand, message, and channel. Consideration must be given to the lifespan of the content shared on each platform. New features, channels, algorithm and format changes, and media trends and updates shape the content marketing landscape on a daily basis.

Dozens of social media platforms exist, many of which have been around since the early 2000s, making them mature in scale and a solid presence in the media mix available for sport marketing professionals. Understanding the role these social media platforms play in the sport industry is crucial. Each platform wants to be ranked the best, and they compete for the currency of social media: attention. Society is operating in an attention economy, and the more time and energy that is spent on certain platforms, the more people will engage, share, and consume content and experiences from the teams on these platforms. User numbers, viewership, and engagement numbers all play important roles in determining where to spend resources, time, and energy in the sport marketing industry.

While each platform has its own features, dynamic characteristics, and community attributes, it is also integrated with the organization, brand, or individual's persona online. In addition, platforms are part of the overall communication mix of media channels that can be used to share information, establish communities, and formulate relationships for a brand. Although a variety of platforms are useful to sports and marketing professionals, this chapter focuses on the main platforms that work for strategic social media practices within the sport industry.

Facebook

Facebook, the largest social media platform in the world, is an example of a social networking site. Founded in 2004 by Mark Zuckerberg, who continues to lead the global company, Facebook has grown not only as a social media platform but also as a global powerhouse brand that has bought other platforms and companies, such as Instagram, Oculus, and WhatsApp, to name a few.[11] Facebook has evolved to develop new features to its platform, such as Messenger (direct messages sent to one user or a group), Groups (formulating groups surrounding various topics of interests), Facebook Watch (creation of shows to compete with the likes of YouTube), and Facebook Live (going live for a show or segment, or attending an event).

Because Facebook is the largest social media platform, sport marketers must have a clear strategy to use this major media channel to connect with fans, create excitement and passion, and drive business. Sport marketers can be successful with Facebook in five major ways:[12]

1. Sending an open invite
2. Communicating consistently
3. Providing exclusive content
4. Using player promotion
5. Executing a game plan

Sending an Open Invite

One of the biggest benefits of Facebook is reach, given that so many people around the globe use the platform daily. Sport teams use Facebook to connect with millions of fans all over the world. When fans cannot be at live games, Facebook helps bring thousands of fans together to share their team bond. One example of how Facebook enhances the game-day experience is by providing fans the opportunity to tailgate no matter where they are located. The New England Patriots have hosted online tailgates through their Facebook page with over 200 registered fan clubs that gather virtually to engage and talk Patriots football before games. These online tailgates have live radio broadcasts and chats to make them truly interactive. The Patriots have also used Facebook to host pregame socials during which fans can share photos and videos of how they are preparing for football. Allowing everyone to be a part of the Patriots football family on game days, the most important days of the year, is a critical component to keeping fans everywhere attached to the team even when actual attendance is not possible.

Communicating Consistently

While game days are obviously important, sports fandom occurs daily, making sport marketing a 24/7 job. People check social media around the clock and engage with as much sport content as organizations can provide. Social media marketers using Facebook should post before, during, and after games when traffic on the site is at its peak. However, team marketers have indicated that in the days leading up to games, fans flock to social media during nonbusiness hours to get ready for the events. This is a prime time for team marketers to provide engaging content for fans, including photos, videos, polls, trivia, game stats, behind-the-scenes footage, and other exclusive content.

Providing Exclusive Content

Social media play a special role in helping connect people with the sport organization and allowing for open communication, so it is vital that sport marketers make the messaging special, as well. Facebook pages should feature unique content not found elsewhere on other social channels, like Twitter or YouTube, or the official team website. Even though organizations may offer ticket deals and other items for purchase, their marketers want to make sure this form of media is *social*, and not overstep marketing boundaries. Providing exclusive ticket information, special discount offers only found on Facebook, or other follower-friendly deals is a good way to ensure fans feel the connection is beneficial. The Brooklyn Nets NBA team has used Facebook to create promotions like the "Facebook Fan of the Game," where one follower for each game has the opportunity to create a status update for the team. The Nets also has social media VIP experiences in which followers are selected to meet players, shoot on-court free throws, or join the team high-five line. These special activities, along with answering fan questions, create authentic interactions that make it worthwhile for fans to follow a team's social media and stay involved through liking, sharing, and commenting.

Using Player Promotion

Many sports fans today are more attached to players than to teams. This is due in part to the greater and more intimate access fans have to players through social media. This means that teams should showcase their players as much as possible and provide content that is not necessarily available on the players' own accounts. Some teams have staged Facebook Q&A sessions with players or posted player video messages to fans wishing them happy holidays or inviting them personally to events. These segments often take very little time out of a player's schedule, but they can generate significant interaction with thousands of likes or comments on Facebook.

Executing a Game Plan

Whether it is Facebook or any other social media channel, sport marketers should always have a strategy for their communication. By making posts purposeful, timely, relevant, and authentic, marketers retain and build their audience. Staying on-brand, not feeling obligated to do what everyone else is doing, and experimenting are all ways to capture fans to a team's social media, providing fans the experience—wholly unique to the brand—of joining together with others to enjoy and support the team.

Twitter

Twitter allows individual people and brands to create, curate, and communicate information in real time in a limited number of characters. Twitter also empowers users to push content to their followers that can include textual information, hyperlinks, images, videos, and interactive gifs for entertainment, informational, and conversational purposes. Twitter has evolved by giving users the ability to share not only text but also images and video clips. Users can also participate in chat sessions surrounding particular common interests and topics by following hashtags.

Twitter may not be the most popular or highly used social site, but its unique features make it an extremely valuable tool in the social media marketing toolbox. Twitter has the following characteristics, which prove beneficial to sport marketers:[13]

- *Internationality.* Twitter boasts 79 percent of its 313 million active monthly users located outside the United States. With sport being such a global industry, this helps sport organizations that market on Twitter to reach an international audience. Twitter not only helps reach more fans and grow sports around the globe but also assists

Twitter gives teams and athletes immediacy with their content.

Frank Jansky/Icon Sportswire via Getty Images

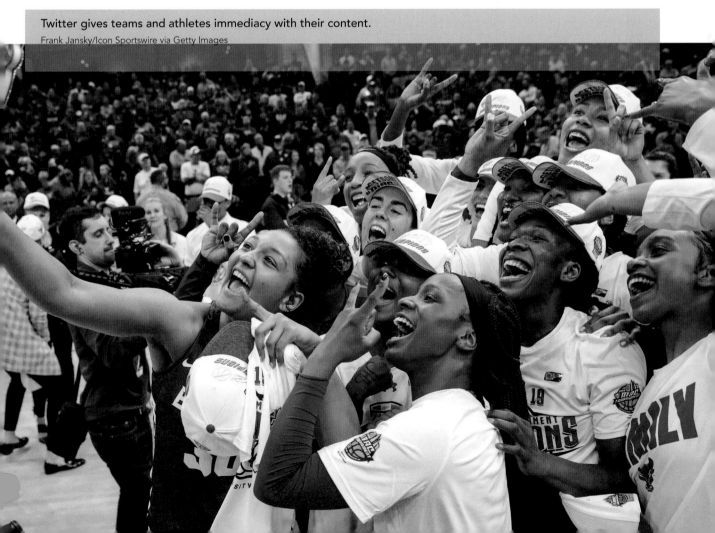

corporate sponsors that want to gain exposure for their brands beyond the domestic segment.

• *Immediacy.* Twitter has become the social platform to use for real-time information, breaking news, and sports scores and highlights as they happen. For this reason, no other social media site works as well for sport teams providing up-to-the-minute content. Fans who follow teams, leagues, and brands on Twitter can get score changes, in-game stats, photos, and videos as they follow along during competition. Fans have real-time conversations and post their reactions as the action unfolds. Twitter has also been used for livestreaming games, such as the NFL's *Thursday Night Football*.

• *Interactivity.* Unlike Facebook, which typically requires a connection to others, Twitter is open to anyone who wants to join the conversation. Fans can like, share, or comment on any type of content because the platform is designed for public interaction. There are no real barriers to users engaging with one another. Topics and trends are constantly updating, displaying content by recency rather than users, so it allows sport organizations to keep communications fresh and relevant. For followers of sports on Twitter, trending topics often include star player performances, major match-ups, highlight-reel plays, breaking sports news, and off-the-field headlines.

There is evidence to suggest that Twitter is highly effective in helping marketers increase fan loyalty.[14] Using a relationship marketing approach, one study examined the determinants of sports fans' loyalty. It was discovered that team attraction, team trust, and team involvement were positively related to team attachment, and team attachment was found to positively influence fan loyalty. When sports fans used Twitter, this behavior significantly reinforced their loyalty. Implications for marketers were that a strategy should be implemented to provide sport-specific Twitter content on non-gamedays and gamedays to promote team attachment and fan loyalty.

• *Non-gamedays:* Loyal sports fans look to athlete and team Twitter accounts to share news and updates, discuss upcoming games, and interact with other fans. They like to talk about drafts, trades, past performances, and future outcomes. Players and teams that react and comment on fan posts help to increase fan loyalty, as fans become more attached to social accounts that are engaging. Twitter has also been shown to increase brand awareness and reputation when organizations communicate directly with fans.

• *Gamedays:* Loyal sports fans who attend games use Twitter to upload photos and videos and show others that they are in attendance. They follow stories surrounding the game as they unfold live on Twitter. Sports fans share their experiences, emotions, and reactions in real-time whether they are in attendance or watching the event from afar. Marketers should consistently communicate with their fans during the event to keep them informed with game updates, related news, exciting content, and visual media. Doing so can drive high levels of awareness and engagement with the event. In 2014, 672 million tweets were sent over the 32 days during the FIFA World Cup in 2014. During the Olympics, tweets about #Rio2016 were viewed 75 billion times and over 187 million tweets were sent when the Games were on.[14]

Instagram

Instagram is the visual social media platform that Facebook bought for US$1 billion in 2012, resulting in one of the biggest and most strategic moves for Facebook in the social media landscape.[15] The platform has evolved over the years, from just showcasing photos to providing an outlet for sport teams, athletes, and others to share videos, create stories through its Stories feature, and create Go Live events with others. Instagram Stories has been so successful in providing a broader range of content that other platforms have created similar versions of this feature.

Instagram, which has quickly become a favorite site for sports fans, allows accounts to showcase photos, videos, and live-streaming content to keep users visually fixated on the sport organizations they follow. Now the third-most used social media site after YouTube and Facebook, Instagram has become a sport marketing must for reaching fans and consumers. Its sheer size and highly interactive nature has made Instagram the primary focus for many sport organizations. It has been estimated that an Instagram post averages 60 times more engagement than a Facebook post and 120 times more engagement than a tweet.[15]

There's also that old saying that, "A picture is worth a thousand words," meaning that people respond much more to visuals than text. As people increasingly seek photos and videos over text, Instagram and other visually centric social media sites like YouTube and TikTok have made creating and sharing this form of content easy and fun. The visual nature of sites like Instagram attracts a younger audience, which has become critical to sport organizations looking to lower the average age of their fan bases. Teams have used Instagram to post photos of players, team performances and championship celebrations, game information and stats, insider content, videos, and live broadcasts.

One way in which Instagram is unique is that, unlike Facebook and Twitter, it was designed as a mobile app. Mobile marketing is rapidly growing, and sport marketers must adapt to this trend. Data on mobile marketing in the United States has indicated that mobile users spend 90 percent of their screen time using apps, and Instagram is one of the top mobile applications.[9] It is not surprising then that teams, leagues, and other sport organizations rely heavily on their Instagram accounts to paint a portrait of their brands for fans.

YouTube

YouTube, the video sharing site that launched in 2005, is the second most popular search engine for the social media community, followed by Google.[16] Google bought the platform in 2006, which was a strategic move for the technology giant in gaining a piece of a growing and powerful platform to host videos and visual experiences for its audiences.

YouTube is a major marketing platform in the sport and social media landscape. Sports are clearly visual in nature, and YouTube works perfectly for the types of content sport organizations and related brands want to share. Fans use YouTube to watch player interviews, game highlights, and sport documentaries and even to learn how to play sports themselves. Brands use YouTube to showcase new products, share ads, and post other unique sport content that helps tell their story in a highly visual way. According to Google, 79 percent of YouTube sports viewers indicated they use the site for sport content they cannot find anywhere else. YouTube has a catalog of more than 8.5 million sport-related videos that have been viewed 280 billion times.

YouTube is a prominent site for sports fans to visit before, during, and after major sports events like the Olympic Games. When a large-scale sports event is taking place, YouTube sports viewers use the video social site in the following ways:[17]

- 57 percent watch related video content BEFORE the sports event.
- 47 percent watch related video content DURING the sports event.
- 60 percent watch related video content AFTER the sports event.

The consumer data suggests that sports fans on YouTube are most active before the event, looking for content while they prepare to watch, and after the event, when recaps and highlights are available. Sport marketers should be keenly aware of when fans are active on certain social sites and what benefits each site provides in order to tailor the content on each platform to fit their consumers' wants and needs.

Snapchat

Snapchat, the camera messaging app that was founded in 2012 by Evan Spiegel, quickly became a popular messaging app for the millennials and the Gen Z cohorts to engage with their friends.[18] The platform has since evolved with its ability to create geo-filters based on certain events, locations, and holidays. While Snapchat's initial idea of stories has also made other platforms take advantage of these features (e.g., Facebook and Instagram), Snapchat still highlights the creativity and innovative application of its augmented reality filters with its 3D images and assets in its platform. Sport organizations have used Snapchat as part of their marketing repertoire, but more recently TikTok, the video sharing app, has replaced Snapchat due to its widespread acceptance and usage particularly with Gen Z sports fans.

TikTok

TikTok is the latest player to the mix of social media platforms. It is the first Chinese-based social media platform to rise to the levels of the other main social media platforms. Originally created as the Music.ly app, TikTok prides itself as a video sharing app that features music and

For years, Leo McCafferty wanted the Pittsburgh Penguins to expand their social media reach to YouTube. As the Penguins' senior director of marketing and content, McCafferty was hoping to see that come to fruition last year when he attended a conference hosted by the Google-owned platform. Heading into the event, McCafferty expected YouTube to talk about how it's a place for people with short attention spans. However, after hearing from executives that a person's average "dwell," or watch time, on the app was over 60 minutes, he instantly thought about how the team could lean into it. Given the Penguins' interest in producing long-form content, McCafferty and his staff began working towards adding YouTube to their social media repertoire. They rolled out the team's first-ever video on July 11 before formally launching a YouTube channel on October 4. That channel features everything from current player content to Stanley Cup documentaries and PensTV archives. "This is a platform that will engage audiences for over an hour—and we produce a lot of long-form content," McCafferty said. "That has been very well received both internally and externally, and it just made too much sense not to have a digital platform or a social channel where we could provide our fans with all of this content that we produce."

Since its inception, the Penguins' YouTube channel has seen rapid growth. As of November 18, they have posted 162 videos on the platform. When the team first posted in July, their first 20 videos averaged only 87 views per video, according to Conviva, which specializes in global streaming and social media intelligence. But over that stretch, the Penguins have amassed nearly 6,450 YouTube subscribers—with roughly 4,700 coming in October alone.

On social media apps like Facebook, Instagram, and Twitter, a person needs to follow an account to immediately receive notifications about recent posts. With YouTube, the beauty of it lies in its ability to bring the latest videos to anyone—even those who aren't subscribers, said McCafferty. Courtesy of YouTube's algorithm, the Penguins can use certain key words to tag their videos in a way that visitors, whether or not they're fans, can see the content. Thus far, the Penguins have not been shy in producing lengthier YouTube videos. On October 2, Pittsburgh released *Pittsburgh is Home—Fifty Years of the Pittsburgh Penguins*. A documentary detailing the Penguins' team history, it has a runtime of two hours and 48 minutes—and can only be successful on a platform like YouTube, said McCafferty.

There are more examples of the Penguins experimenting with longer-form videos. Since joining YouTube, the team has created documentaries remembering each of their five championship years—1991, 1992, 2009, 2016, and 2017. Each video ranges in length from 58 minutes to one hour and 17 minutes. On October 12, the Penguins debuted their ninth season of *In The Room*, which McCafferty describes as a behind-the-scenes look on the hockey team. Since it first aired in 2011, *In The Room* has been honored as the "Best Sports Program Series" at the Mid-Atlantic Regional Emmy Awards for six consecutive years. In 2019, it also picked up an Emmy for the best "Editor-Program." With more than 65,300 video views, Pittsburgh's season premiere of *In The Room* has quickly become its second-most viewed YouTube video. It trails only "Merci Sidney," which followed Sidney Crosby as he traveled to Rimouski, Quebec, to celebrate the retirement of his number 87 from both his former junior team and the entire Quebec Major Junior Hockey League. As of November 20, "Merci Sidney" has over 97,000 views on YouTube. "We still have a few more releases that we're going to put out over the next couple of weeks that will hopefully highlight the channel and bring some more folks onto the channel to subscribe and just check out all the good content that we have there," McCafferty said.

With 63 videos in October, the Penguins were able to garner nearly 3,200 views per video, according to Conviva. Another team that saw similar engagement that month was the Washington Capitals. Despite releasing only 10 videos in October—the third fewest of any NHL team on YouTube—the Capitals totaled 263,840 views, according to Conviva. Of Washington's recent videos, they tended not to feature any game footage or postgame player interviews, focusing more on vlogs, nostalgia, behind-the-scenes, and documentary-type videos. Unlike the Penguins, the Capitals were one of the first NHL teams to join YouTube when it posted its first video on January 25, 2007. As of November 18, it has published 530 videos and accumulated over 34,700 subscribers, according to Conviva.

Similar to the Penguins' approach on YouTube, the Capitals look to get their videos seen by a multitude of audiences, said Capitals senior director of digital media James Heuser. When people type in "Washington Capitals" into the YouTube search bar, he wants to make sure that they have a notable presence to keep them interested in viewing their videos—with the hopes of turning them into subscribers. "We see subscriber platforms being a nice way to share content where stuff shows up on people's computers almost with little to no promotion on other social networks," Heuser said. "We've been on YouTube for a long time. It's a platform we use, and certainly one that we cherish and we focus on making sure that it stays up to date. But we don't necessarily have an outwardly different policy—outside of just making sure that the content is the best of the best."

Over time, McCafferty's main focus is making sure that he and his team are producing quality YouTube content for Penguins fans to see. While he is nonetheless impressed with the 6,400-plus subscribers, that to him is not the biggest indicator of the team's growth on the platform. "We can reach people who aren't coming to us—and this is just another layer to that," McCafferty said. "We are proud of the video content that we put out here, we have done some great stuff over the years, and we have some exciting stuff planned for the future. We think that with the help of our fans and with the help of YouTube and its algorithm, it will just help strengthen our brand and bring our product to more eyeballs—which is the goal," McCafferty added.

Reprinted by permission from Front Office Sports.

other sounds on its platform while its users are able to create dances, challenges, memes, and other entertaining content for their audiences. As of April 2020, there are over 800 million users on TikTok, and it is currently in 39 different languages, which makes it not only a dominant social media platform but a global powerhouse brand.[19] Athletes embraced TikTok immediately, and the app is quickly becoming a powerful weapon in the social media marketing arsenal for sport teams and leagues. However, the issue of Chinese ownership of the app and the discourse surrounding a U.S. ban unless the platform is purchased by an American corporation has given pause to those marketing heavily with TikTok. The following sidebar from Front Office Sports discusses the power of TikTok as a social media marketing tool in professional sports and the growth in followers of the official Golden State Warriors team account.

Leveraging Players and Talent

Social media offers fans an incredible opportunity to hear directly from players and talent. Fans no longer have to wait for official interviews, press conferences, or blog posts. Some players have even more followers on social media than the teams they play for. This circumstance can be both a blessing and a curse for sport teams. If

Golden State Warriors Quickly Find Success on TikTok

The Golden State Warriors have broken many records dating back to their 2015 NBA championship—their first in 40 years. Now playing in its new $1.6 billion Chase Center, Golden State's impact has extended onto TikTok. On November 5, Golden State became the first North American sports franchise to eclipse one million TikTok followers. It caps off a TikTok ascension, which has seen the Warriors grow at least 300,000 followers per month since it launched in April, said Warriors senior vice president of marketing Jen Millet. "I think it's just appealing to this younger audience," Millet said. "I think we have more room to grow because the numbers started lower, but we feel confident in meeting fans where they are on that platform and giving them content that's engaging and is opening us up to new audiences as well."

A distinct feature on TikTok—which is owned by ByteDance Ltd., a Chinese-based Internet technology company—is its sound-on approach to user engagement, said Millet. While Facebook and Instagram content varies between pictures and videos, music is a key component of TikTok's posts. On TikTok, the Warriors have been able to pair two key features: their players with culturally and socially relevant music. On August 1, they posted a TikTok video with Curry kicking a basketball across the practice facility with Fort Minor's "Remember The Name" playing in the background. It reached two team members, with the latter hurling it to Curry, who proceeded to drain a three-pointer from beyond the three-point line.

As of November 6, that post has more than 18 million views, said Warriors vice president of corporate communications Lisa Goodwin. It's also garnered more than 1.4 million likes and nearly 16,000 shares via TikTok. "Sports brands are extremely well positioned to grow significant followings on TikTok if they can get their content right," said Nick Cicero, vice president of strategy at Conviva, which specializes in global streaming and social media intelligence. "The Warriors are the perfect example of this—when you combine quality content, recognizable faces like Steph Curry, and a built-in fan base that spans all ages, you have a recipe for success."

Another popular post from the Warriors' TikTok account did not have Curry in a starring role. Rather, the center of attention was four-year-old Zahara "ZaZa" Bean, whose dance moves made her a viral star on *The Ellen DeGeneres Show* in September. After her *Ellen* appearance, ZaZa performed at the Warriors' Chase Center during their November 4 game against the Portland Trail Blazers. In the two days following her performance, the Warriors' ZaZa–TikTok post became the most viewed in team history, receiving 2.2 million likes and more than 115 million views. Over three days, ZaZa's presence helped Golden State gain 190,000 new TikTok followers. "It demonstrates the power and reach a single piece of content can have on TikTok," Cicero said.

Besides posting content with popular music and recognizable faces, the team's home in California has also been seen as playing a role in developing a TikTok presence. Joe Gagliese, co-founder and CEO of media-marketing agency Viral Nation Inc., sees social-media influencers coming out in bunches across Illinois, New York, Texas, and lastly, California. With the Warriors being located in San Francisco, this helps them resonate more with Bay Area locals—people who Gagliese sees as heavy TikTok users. "If you were going to compare that to Milwaukee or these different places, I think [the Warriors] just have a much higher propensity to get that following than other places do," Gagliese said. "It's also a testament to them being ahead of the curve and posting consistently. A lot of things play into their success, but good for them for kind of engaging in that opportunity—had they not done that, they would have had nothing."

Exceeding one million followers is only the beginning of the Warriors' TikTok presence. Heading into 2020, Millet wants to broaden Golden State's international presence on the platform. With roughly 63% of the Warriors' followers being female, she hopes that TikTok will help provide future insight on how to further diversify and expand its current audience. When it comes to future growth though, it all comes down to content, said Millet. The Warriors have rostered some of the most famous basketball players, and they will inevitably appear on their TikTok profile. But for Millet, there's more to the Golden State franchise that is deserving of attention on the social media platform. "It's about continuing to highlight and showcase our players and their amazing personalities, but also looking for opportunities to extend beyond that and share experiences that are happening throughout the arena," Millet said. "The game around the game, making that content fun and exciting for fans to consume and not having it be about the team or specific players, but opening up to fans that are a part of the experience at every game."

Reprinted by permission from Front Office Sports.

the players are engaged with the team's broader priorities and don't embarrass themselves, their team, or their teammates in social media, they can become tremendous assets in furthering the brand's following. Social media also offers individual athletes the opportunity to further their own brands, make them more appealing to prospective sponsors, and improve their career outlook after their playing days end.

Golden State Warriors' Steph Curry is not only a gifted professional basketball player and social media sensation but also someone who has used his influence to foster partnerships with Under Armour and be part of the MasterClass lineup. After winning multiple NBA titles and growing his social status exponentially, Curry became a much sought-after ambassador with several sponsorships, resulting in social media marketing becoming an industry focus. Curry is the co-founder of Slyce, a platform designed to help athletes and celebrities minimize social media noise while maximizing content production and follower interaction. Slyce uses technology to enhance marketing automation for ambassadors and brand partners, enabling them to streamline content-sharing across multiple social media channels.[20]

Houston Texans' star defensive player JJ Watt has used his massive social media following (4 million and 2.7 million Twitter and Instagram followers, respectively) to generate revenue for others besides himself. In the aftermath of Hurricane Harvey, Watt contributed to the widespread relief efforts by calling on his followers and partners to donate money, with an original goal of US$200,000. The power of his social media presence and popularity produced US$41.6 million in relief funds.[21] This philanthropic example demonstrates the financial power athletes wield when they are social-savvy marketers. According to *Forbes*, Watt is one of the most marketable athletes, ranking in the Top 30 on their Highest Paid Athletes list, with US$7 million annually in endorsements from major brands such as Gatorade, Reebok, Ford Motor Company, H-E-B, NRG Energy, and Verizon Wireless.[22]

These are just some instances of how professional athletes have been able to significantly increase their social media followings through sport performance or community-based initiatives and then monetize their efforts by partnering with major brands.

Personal Branding for Athletes

Personal branding has become one of the core specializations that many sport organizations have invested in for their teams, coaches, and athletes. Athletes especially are interested in personal branding because it allows them to set themselves apart from other athletes, and it can open up opportunities for future collaborations, sponsorships, and financial benefits beyond their time as competitors.

What exactly is a personal brand? A **personal brand** is a collection of a person's various attributes, expertise traits, personality characteristics, and insights that take place both on- and offline. People can create a personal brand for themselves and present it to their personal and professional networks to bring forth new opportunities, relationships, and praise. Personal branding expert and author Jeremy Darlow discussed in his books *Brands Win Championships* and *Athletes Are Brands Too* how athletes can use social media to facilitate personal branding opportunities and make a societal impact.

Many professional athletes have used their personal brands to make an impact beyond their respective sports. NHL hockey player P.K. Subban has used his fierce competitive nature and endearing personality to construct an international brand on and off the ice. He raised US$10 million for the Montreal Children's Hospital, the biggest philanthropic commitment by a sport figure in Canadian history, and started the #CanadaCarols social campaign to encourage his country to sing to hospitalized kids during the holidays.[23,24] His larger-than-life persona and generous spirit resonate on social media and both contribute heavily to his large base of followers and commercial interest from brands. He has amassed a stable of major global sponsors, including Adidas, Gatorade, Samsung, Listerine, and Bridgestone.

Lolo Jones had a successful career as a track and field athlete and Winter Olympian and has used her social media platforms to gain awareness for her personal brand as a dual athlete in bobsledding and track and field. She has produced online strategic communication classes for the learning platform Skillshare to teach others how to build a personal brand; produce unique content; increase follower counts, engagement, and interaction; and use multiple social media channels for promotion. She instructs people on how to create social media marketing success just like Olympic champion athletes.[25] For Instagram, one of the most popular social media sites for athletes, Jones stresses the importance of testing posts to determine appeal, making the most of Instagram stories, editing content, and using analytics tools to track effectiveness. Most importantly, Jones focuses on growing her accounts to secure more brand partners and income over time.

In addition to professional athletes building their personal brands, college student-athletes also need to build and manage their personal brands. This is especially true for student-athletes competing in major revenue-generating sports because there is widespread media exposure around football, basketball, baseball, and softball, and student-athletes can benefit from that national television time. Having an already established online presence and personal brand allows student-athletes to eventually benefit financially through endorsement deals, sponsorship opportunities, and media presence when they turn professional. It is also possible, through the name, image, and likeness (NIL) legislation being considered by the NCAA, that student-athletes may be able to accept money for sponsorships while competing at the college level. If and when this comes to fruition officially, student-athletes with strategically formulated personal brands will be poised to benefit the most, as brand awareness will be just as important as athletic performance (if not more).

Opendorse has led the way for many college teams to have the necessary resources to help their student-athletes manage their personal brands strategically and effectively. The University of Nebraska is one of the first universities to allow their entire athletics department to be powered by Opendorse so that all student-athletes can have the tools to manage their personal brand and control their likeness, messaging, and more.[26] In preparation for the NCAA's decision on whether or not student-athletes can profit from their NIL while in college, there is a trend of more universities investing in personal branding efforts for all of their athletes.

Many agencies, like Opendorse and INFLCR (Influencer), that are hired to consult athletes on crafting personal brands go into great detail on how to curate a specific image on social media. Creating a personal brand requires having to consider many elements, which can be applied to a person as well as a team:

- What unique qualities do you have?
- What life experiences can you showcase?
- What are the personality characteristics that best describe you?

- What are your favorite colors, and which ones are part of your brand?
- Which platforms do you feel most engaged with?
- What types of content resonate with you (e.g., photo, text, video, visual, stories, live video, etc.)?
- What special experiences, stories, interests, and personal connections do you have?
- What perspectives do you have that are unusual?
- How would you describe yourself in your personal, professional, and social circles?

Personal branding for athletes does not happen overnight, and it constantly evolves over time. It takes commitment, energy, resources, and a long-term vision. The first step to move forward with a personal brand is to do an audit of the athletes and ask how they would evaluate their presence online:

- Are they consistently sharing on social media?
- Are they aware of what they are sharing and how it contributes to their brand online?
- What are the first impressions that are made when looking across their social media channels?

The second step is to build a brand kit, which includes the following:

- Brand colors (the three or four colors that best represent the athletes)
- Brand voice (the overall tone used on social media)
- Branding (fonts for images, cover page, etc.)

Tom Brady has engineered a prominent personal brand. He makes sure to use certain images, colors, and content to illustrate and showcase his personal brand to his followers.

The third step is to do an analysis of other athletes to determine what they are doing well on each designated platform. This analysis should also look at personal websites, which allow athletes to control their overall look and presence and serve as a communication gateway to engage, inform, and update audiences. This analysis high-lights potential gaps that can be taken advantage of and allows athletes to differentiate themselves from others.

Steps to Construct a Personal Brand

There are some specific steps that individual people and organizations should take to construct their own personal brands on social media.[27]

Step One: Think About the Story

Each person has a story to tell, and while many may go through similar life experiences with family, careers, hobbies, relationships, struggles, successes, and so on, every person's journey through these aspects is different. Like people, every brand or business has an origin story that relates what it does, and why. How people travel on this journey and the stories they tell along the way are unique to each person. A person or an organization that chronicles the story with a clear lens will intrigue followers. Therefore, the initial step to developing a strong personal brand is to consider what the story will be and how it should be told.

Step Two: Be Focused

There are countless people and organizations to follow on social media, so what makes someone want to follow one over the other? To determine this, one must consider what is to be accomplished by using a brand voice on social media. Whether it is networking and advancing a career, building and promoting a new business, altering or enhancing the image of a brand, entertaining others, or showcasing expertise in a certain field, the person or organization must determine the focus of social media efforts first and then create and share content that communicates that focus.

Step Three: Be Positive

The world and the Internet, in particular, churn out bad news and negativity on a constant basis, so it's essential to keep posts focused on the positive. Providing insights, information, expertise, entertainment, and humor will help grow a personal brand's account. Creating unique content and sharing useful content from others with a similar focus are also positive strategies.

Step Four: Consistency Is Key

While variety is important and enjoyable to followers, consistency is key to building a personal brand and having success on social media. Consistently posting content in focus area(s) will ensure that people know what the person or organization is about. Followers of accounts likely have similar interests to the respective account holders. Social media topics that are consistent in content, voice, and focus not only retain followers but also make followers more likely to share an account's information with others, thereby building interest, follower numbers, and engagement levels.

Step Five: Always Be Authentic

The hardest thing to be is something you are not. A personal brand that tries to keep up an image that is inauthentic is not only exhausting but also ineffective in the long-term. It is important to remember that people seek out unique stories on social media. Brands that try to replicate what others are doing on social media appear both insincere and unoriginal, and this inauthenticity is likely to lead brands down the path to irrelevance and obscurity. However, taking into consideration the best practices of social media and learning from social media experts, who have the highest engagements and largest audiences, what they do well will add fresh perspective to a fledgling personal brand.

Wrap-Up

Social media are firmly established as integral to the sport marketing mix. Social media can influence all aspects of the business—ticket sales, traditional marketing, sponsorship, digital, community relations, game presentation, broadcast operations, and customer service. The sport properties that understand and harness their social media power correctly have an edge over those that don't. People who possess the skills to help sport properties achieve social media fluency are in high demand; their challenge is to translate that fluency into true business results.

Working in Social Media

After reading about all of the components that make up social media and sports, you may find it an attractive field to work in. Here are some factors to consider when applying to work in the sports and social media field.

Experience

Experience is the first thing that employers want to see, so they likely will ask you how many prior internships, projects, work experiences, and clients you have had. Potential employers will have certain expectations of you, such as an online presence or a dossier (online portfolio) showcasing your work virtually for others to see.

Long hours and high levels of productivity can be the expectation in many front offices. While social media is maturing as a field, the expectation for creating wonders and solutions to all sorts of problems and challenges continues to be the norm. The hours working in social media are extensive due to the nature of events taking place primarily on nights and weekends. Covering practices, games, road trips, and producing immediate content across all channels for the team and its athletes are just some of the responsibilities that need to be noted. This is a job that can be 24/7 owing to the engagement that happens around the world and being "on" all the time.

In addition, the list of required and necessary skills for those who are working in sports and social media continues to grow. Some skills now being requested of applicants for social media jobs include being the following: a content creator, a graphic designer with expert skills in Adobe Creative Cloud, both a videographer and an editor (as more content is being driven via video), a copywriter, a paid media manager (to help with ads and understanding changes in the platform algorithms), an analyst (as more jobs are adding listening and monitoring social media to the list), a crisis manager (when things go wrong), and a customer service representative (to help fans and other audiences answer any questions). The skill set will continue to expand as the platforms evolve and change, so professionals who want to work in the field need to be aware of these expectations and plan and train accordingly.

Some unique requirements are not as obvious. For example, working in sports requires not only a strong level of experience in the field but also the ability to network and engage with the sport community on social media. Meeting people—both virtually and face to face—is one of the most important things you can do to advance your career. These meetings do not always have to involve social media. In addition, a willingness to be agile and adaptive to growing changes is crucial. Social media is evolving every day, and new tools, platforms, and ways to create and share stories will become available almost daily. Being adaptive to learning new approaches and gaining experience in a variety of areas will help add to your skill set and résumé. Learning does not end once you graduate or leave the classroom.

Personal Social Media Presence

If you are going to work in social media for a sport team, you need to have a personal presence on social media. The first thing any organization that is looking to hire will do is evaluate an applicant's personal social accounts. But, if you are applying to be a social media manager, your personal channels must showcase your ability to be an effective marketer in this realm. You do not need to have thousands of followers or be an online influencer, but you should be active on social media and portray a positive social presence.

Sports and the Social Media Community

In order to be effective and successful in the sports and social media industry, you have to support what you say or claim with actions. Fellow professionals in the industry need to know who you are, what you stand for, and what you can accomplish for a team or an organization. The social media and sport community (#SMSports) is a vibrant and very engaged audience of professionals, professors, students, and teams. The best way to network and showcase your interests and passions in the field is to be part of the community. This will take time, but engaging with others a little bit each day can help foster some strong relationships. Networking first and foremost starts with a tweet, an update, or a DM.

Networking

Networking is all about relationships that are built on interest and authenticity. Do not go for the hard sell when it comes to networking. If you want to connect with an executive for a sport team just because of the executive's status, you are not doing it right. Reach out to people you respect, admire, and aspire to be as a professional. Ask about their education, qualifications, and experience. In addition, ask for some tips and advice they can offer, such as how to build your skill set or résumé or break into the industry, and see if they can

> continued

> continued

serve as either an official or unofficial mentor to you. Reach out to teams or coordinators of events for volunteer work. The idea is to start small and work to take your talents to the next level. Never assume that just because you are a fan, you will get a job. Instead of telling sport teams why you need them, highlight what experience and expertise you can bring to the organization.

Team Culture and Brand

Culture is one of the most important elements that needs to be taken into consideration. You want to make sure you are in an environment where you can do your best work and have the opportunity to learn, grow, and contribute to the greater good for your clients. Toxic environments (e.g., unhealthy competitive natures, stealing others' work, etc.) are not places you want to be. Assess the level of mentorship in the organization and take a hard look at how the team values or invests in social media. If the team assumes that social media has little or no impact on marketing or sport partnerships, or recruiting, this should be a red flag. In addition, if the team is not willing to invest in the right tools, resources, and continued education for social media practices for the social media team, this is another issue to examine. If a team is not willing to invest in the people who are the frontlines of the brand, this indicates the team does not have the proper level of commitment or respect toward social media marketing best practices.

Skills and Training Investment

In many cases, a sport team may have a small social media staff: It could be a few professionals, or it could be just you. Invest in all of the skills you can in order to create, disseminate, and analyze content. Not only do you need a passion for sports, you need an even greater passion for business and marketing. Be sure to hone the skills that would make you an effective social media marketer in any industry. If you are working for a sport team, reach out to local high schools and universities to see if there are any student volunteers or interns who would like to help out. This can add to your staff, but more importantly, training others enhances your own skills and depth of knowledge.

Quality Versus Quantity

In order to establish a presence in the industry, you have to be able to produce items to showcase your perspective. Content not only allows users to share their personal and professional perspective but also becomes the building blocks in the construction of a long-term brand. Creating content and integrating it into a personal branding strategy has many benefits. The better the content, the better the outcome, so focus on supplying social media followers with quality information and images rather than simply a large amount of it.

Don't Be a Fan Girl or Fan Boy on the Job

The social media manager role is an important one, and being a distraction to fellow colleagues and fans and the team by getting a selfie with a celebrity or sport figure should not be your priority. At the end of the day, you have certain duties and expectations that need to be met, and these cannot be properly executed if you are distracted. As a social media manager, you are on the team now, too, and that should be the most exciting part.

Activities

1. Locate a job posting for a social media manager in sports and answer the following questions: What are the required and recommended qualifications? What are the responsibilities of the job? How is the social media manager positioned to assist the company in its overall strategic marketing?

2. Select a league, a team, an athlete, or a brand and follow them on multiple social media accounts for a month. What differences do you see in how they promote their brands across various social platforms? What strategies work well on certain channels?

3. What non-sport related brand is your favorite to follow on social media? What makes the brand stand out and what could sport-related brands learn and take from your favorite brand to improve their presence on social?

4. Identify three different athletes who you feel have strong personal brands. Make sure the athletes you choose are distinctive by selecting ones from varying categories (male or female, professional or collegiate, individual sport or team sport). What factors have made them successful in establishing their personal brands? What differences do you see in these athletes' social strategies?

Your Marketing Plan

You have been called in for an interview with Dwayne "The Rock" Johnson and his business partner Dany Garcia. They have just purchased the XFL, and they are interested in getting a fresh perspective on social media marketing for the league. This is an opportunity to showcase some new ideas, platforms, and opportunities to better market the sport and its players.

In developing your social media marketing plan, supply a list of objectives, strategies, and tactics. Be sure to integrate an effective use of TikTok to help achieve these objectives, strategies, and tactics.

 Go to HKPropel to complete the activities for this chapter.

Chapter 12

Sales and Service

OBJECTIVES

- To define what sales *is* and what sales *is not*
- To provide an overview of the various sales methodologies used in sport business
- To explore pricing techniques and strategies as they relate to the sport industry
- To examine the influence and role of the secondary market in sport sales
- To explore the concepts of yield management and customer lifetime value (CLV)
- To stress the importance and influence of retention and service activities as they relate to the sales process

Mark Tantrum/Getty Images

Getting professional and amateur sports teams and leagues back up and running has posed a formidable challenge as the industry seeks to come to grips with the global pandemic caused by COVID-19. While much of the media focus has been on the maneuvering and negotiations between athletes and their respective league executives, arguably no department has been affected more in a day-to-day manner than the ticket sales and servicing departments of these teams and leagues.

As the pandemic continues on, ticket sales departments across all sports face a variety of challenges:

- How do we retain season-ticket holders and thus maintain ticket revenues?
- How do we communicate with season-ticket holders and premium seat accounts so that they feel valued?
- How do we keep our fans engaged with the team during the shutdown?
- How do we structure refund policies or otherwise respond with payment plans to fit customers' budgets, especially when many were negatively impacted by the financial recession that accompanied the pandemic?
- When do we restart the ticket sales process once fans are allowed to attend games?

For both professional teams and intercollegiate programs, one of the major challenges is how to structure and effectively communicate their policies on refunds and credits, while trying to balance the need to retain ticket revenue in the face of economic turmoil. Some teams have quietly offered refunds on a case-by-case basis, even with no games yet officially canceled, as a response to particular financial hardships from buyers. To limit potential lost revenue, many teams have developed various ticket credit options including having ticket funds roll over to games next season; attaching food and beverage offers as part of their ticket credits for future games; or offering credits in the form of experiential events, such as behind-the-scenes arena tours and meet-and-greets with players.

The NBA was one of the first of the major pro leagues to react. Soon after its shutdown in March 2020, the league released a statement that said refunds or credits on tickets would be issued should games be canceled or played without fans; NBA teams were also able to work with the league to create their own specific ticket renewal and credit policies. MLS and the NHL gave their teams the flexibility to adopt individual policies around ticketing, refunds, and credits. With the 2020 season not yet begun, the NFL instructed teams to reassure fans they would be given refunds or credits toward future games in the event games were canceled or played without fans.

While the potential of mass refunds poses a major financial concern to teams across all the major sport leagues, arguably no league has faced a heavier burden than MLB, which is especially reliant on ticketing given the sheer number of games played in a typical season. Michelle Price, Director of Client Retention for the Washington Nationals, said the following in June 2020 while MLB and the Players Association negotiated terms for the launch of its season:

> In today's climate with COVID-19, a team's relationship with their fans has never been more important. Nobody knows how long we will all be impacted by COVID-19, but I do know that proactive service teams have the opportunity to be differentiators for their organizations. In a time when budgets are being slashed, unemployment is high, and disposable income is low, being more than just about 'sports tickets' is vital. Service teams are the front line and the main source of information and engagement for fans when there are no games or new/positive news. Whether it's a phone call to see how someone is doing, a personal video message, or sharing favorite memories over a video chat, more than ever, service teams are showing how essential they are to the fan experience and the revenue retention and generation for sports organizations (email, June 10, 2020).

Indeed, responses by ticket sales and service departments have called for teams to get creative. The goal for one MLB team is to get to know the season-ticket account holders on a deeper level by talking about more than just the things associated with its ticket account. This includes having team sales representatives share their experiences working from home; showing photos of their families, homes, and pets; and asking their accounts to do the same. Another MLB team has added programs for season-ticket holders and select groups that include launching a virtual "Lunch and Learn" webinar series where fans can ask questions of team personnel on a variety of subjects ranging from working out at home (presented by their strength and conditioning coaches) to lawn care (hosted by their head groundskeeper).

In addition to the importance of maintaining positive engagement and dialogue with current and prospective clients, the more progressive teams have looked to design more varied and affordable ticket options for the marketplace. "With one in five Americans looking for work—and others balancing child-care, home schooling, and working from home—the sport industry has to be more focused on growing the base and having something for everyone," said Dr. Bill Sutton, longtime ticket sales consultant to major league sport franchises. "Season tickets are still part of the mix, but we need to realize the role that sport can play moving forward. Remember this is the only period in American history since the advent of professional sports where the entire sport industry shut down at the same time. WWII, the Great Depression, the Spanish Influenza pandemic—they never shut down the sport industry" (email, June 10, 2020).

How can teams create more affordable single game purchasing options, especially at a time when over 30 million Americans have lost their jobs and millions of others have experienced salary cuts? One easy way, according to Sutton, would be to institute a "modern" family plan based on a per person cost—instead of an arbitrary number of four—that would better reflect the fact that families come in variety of sizes. "At this critical time, teams should also re-examine Kids Clubs and programming and find something that fits the time and the situation. Let's create a Game of the Month plan—one night per month to provide an affordable option in terms of cost—both financial and time. Rich Luker's research shows that future fan behavior is shaped by attending a game prior to the age of 8—are we facilitating that?" (email correspondence, June 10, 2020).

In addition to ticket sales and service departments facing the practical and financial challenges in navigating the global pandemic, there is also the opportunity to consider what sport—and the fan experience—is to look like in the post–COVID-19 era, and how it may ultimately affect and alter the sales process. These issues have been expanded upon by one of this textbook's original co-authors, Dr. Bernie Mullin (email, June 16, 2020):

Sport business professionals must proceed with the mantra of continuous global search to identify industry "Next Practices" (Future Best Practices); in this case, what happens when sport properties come back to competition, initially without fans, and how and when the introduction of live fans can and should morph back closer to normal.

The rather sterile, no fans and no noise lesson learned from the German Bundesliga, who were the first in the Northern Hemisphere to return, inadvertently led to a near elimination of home-field advantage as objectively measured by the percentage of home wins, away wins, and ties. These figures revealed a very different skew from "Pre COVID Normal." For leagues that started about four or five weeks later, and particularly for U.S. Intercollegiate Athletics that started competition in Fall 2020, the lessons learned were clear. Without straying into offering an unauthentic experience, they had to learn how to pipe in home fan noise, cheerleaders, and the band via the venues' sound systems while less-than-full capacity crowds were in attendance. Tottenham Hotspur of the English Premier League created a "Fan Video Wall" behind the goal with the crowd noise being fed into the stadium's PA system. Similarly, other teams used Zoom or Microsoft Teams video calls to create live fan reaction to gameplay that offered visual and auditory connection for the players to feed off.

> continued

> continued

All in all, COVID-19 provided the sport and entertainment industry professionals with a new creative opportunity to engage fans watching out-of-venue by connecting them to the in-venue experience in a way that positively impacts the home team's performance by generating somewhat of a home advantage. Could this be a new sport product experience that we will be selling for many years in the future to those fans who cannot attend the game in person but want a more immersive experience than TV or live stream because they want their presence and screaming voice to count more and lift up their team?

Clearly, the global pandemic has created unparalleled—even previously unimagined—challenges for professionals in the ticket sales and client servicing business. However, it has also created opportunities to rethink the way business has been done in the past. Despite financial burdens to be felt for years to come by teams and sport consumers alike, the global pandemic has also presented opportunities to get more creative, to reassess the "old" relationship between team and fan, and to reimagine the fan experience that leagues and teams will be selling well into the post–COVID-19 era of sport.

Sales

Sales are the lifeblood of any sport organization. Whether the item is tickets, media rights, corporate partnerships, digital assets, advertising, premium seating, merchandise, or any other component or product of the sales inventory, sales accounts for most, if not all, of the revenue.

"Nothing happens until somebody sells something." The adage, which has been attributed to many executives, aptly captures the importance of selling and the sales process.[1] Unfortunately, the word *sales* or the term *salesperson* too often conjures up images of hucksters—people using guile and persuasion to talk customers into buying products that they might not want or need at prices they sometimes cannot afford. This perception of salesperson and sales organizations has been depicted in such Hollywood films as *Wall Street*, *Boiler Room*, *Tommy Boy*, *Love and Other Drugs*, and perhaps the all-time classic, *Glengarry Glen Ross*.

In this chapter, we seek to alter this perception by exploring the various sales methodologies employed in the sport industry, distinguish between product-oriented and customer-oriented sales, and examine the concept of customer lifetime value (CLV) that has driven the increasing emphasis on client retention and servicing in order to best ensure that the purchase is a win–win situation for both the seller (the sport organization) and the purchaser (the sport consumer). This emphasis on relationship selling (creating and building long-term relationships that grow and increase in value) illustrates the value of the sales process to a sport organization and the professionalism of the sales approaches used in this industry.

As we have discussed earlier in this book, sport marketing differs from other forms of marketing in a variety of ways. One difference is the presence of emotion. This attribute also applies to the sales dimension of sport marketing. In sport, the sales process may involve an emotional element that may be, but is usually not, an element of the majority of sales taking place throughout the world every day. This emotional element can be either an aid or a hindrance, usually depending on the public perception of the sport product at that time. Regardless, the most successful sport and entertainment salespeople know how to turn on the "emotion" in a fan or prospect's mind to maximum effect because sport sales is all about "passion."

Despite the factors that make the sport product unique (including the special place of emotion and passion that fuels consumers of the sport product), today's sport organizations and sales departments face increasing challenges:

- Current and potential consumers have a growing number of alternative ways to spend their discretionary income in the sport realm, due to the creation of increasingly more professional leagues and teams ranging from esports to rugby and every emerging sport in between.
- The legalization of real-time sports gaming will continue to alter the manner and the place in which sports fans consume sport.

- The popularity of fantasy sports, coupled with increasingly "high-def" viewing options and the omnipresence of offerings such as the NFL's "Red Zone," have made the choice of "attending" a sports event from the comfort of one's own living room much more commonplace (not to mention the financial savings).

- The total cost of attending sports events (tickets, parking, and concessions combined), as well as the "opportunity cost" of the time taken to travel to and from the event, continues to escalate, potentially pricing individual attendees and families out of the market.

As the more traditional professional and collegiate sport leagues and teams are facing an increasingly graying (older) demographic, millennials and Gen Zers cannot be counted on to fill future season-ticket rolls. As a result, (detailed later in this chapter) the entire concept of the "season ticket," long the basis of teams' financial foundations, is under assault. In addition, what younger fans want in a sports event has changed. They value experiences and the opportunity to socialize at sports events; hence, many would rather buy a ticket to an open concourse space or a bar area than to an actual seat. The mobile consumption patterns of sports fans, particularly younger fans, continue to alter the sales process, too. Increasingly, what consumers value is convenience, whether that be purchasing tickets on their phones an hour before game time or renewing their season tickets without having to chat with a sales rep. Consequently, salespeople and sales departments, you'll later see, have been forced to embrace social media and technology to better meet the wants and needs of potential customers.

Indeed, the sport landscape has changed and will continue to change for those whose job it is to sell, regardless of whether its tickets, signage, digital advertising, or sponsorship. This chapter addresses the types of sales strategies and tactics most commonly employed in the sport industry, with an eye toward "what's new" as salespeople and sales departments seek to address the many changes and challenges previously described. We illustrate these strategies and tactics through examples and insights from expert practitioners from a number of sport organizations, primarily within the context of tickets and sponsorship sales.

Relationship Between Media, Sponsors, and Fans and the Sales Process

Figure 12.1 depicts a critical relationship among the media (defined to include all forms of social media, the Internet, and traditional print and

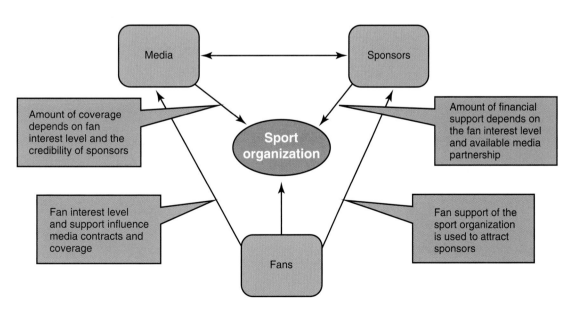

FIGURE 12.1 Relationship among media, sponsors, and fans.

The National Women's Soccer League (NWSL) provides a compelling example of the importance of the symbiotic relationship between fans, the media, and sponsors.

Within days of the USWNT capturing the 2019 World Cup, a familiar refrain arose—one that had been heard immediately following its World Cup titles in 1999 and 2015. Would this victory on the world's biggest stage lead to a wave of fan, media, and corporate support great enough to sustain the NWSL where previous women's professional soccer leagues had failed?

Not surprisingly—and as in previous years—numerous positive signs were emanating from the glow of the USWNT's World Cup victory. When play resumed featuring the USWNT players on their respective NWSL teams, fans came out in droves. In its first game following the World Cup, Sky Blue FC drew a crowd of 5,003—the club's first sellout in four years, and its largest since the 2018 season finale. The Portland Thorns set a club record with 22,329 fans turning out to cheer on the "homecoming" of the Thorns' four USWNT players. Red Stars and USWNT goalie Alyssa Naeher said, "It's great one game is a sellout. But now the challenge is how we continue to have that every weekend. How can we continue to bring people out to the games?"[2]

As Chicago Red Stars owner Arnim Whisler observed, "The goal now is to lock them (fans) in. We've done all the right data capture on not just the people that came, but the people that shopped, the people that considered the ad and didn't buy. And all that marketing starts tonight to get 'em back."[3]

In addition to a wave of record-setting crowds, the buzz around the game in the immediate aftermath of the World Cup victory also quickly led to the signing of a league-wide sponsorship deal with Budweiser and a media arrangement with ESPN to broadcast NWSL games on ESPN2 and ESPNNews. ESPN Executive Burke Magnus said, "We did not want to miss the window of opportunity to seize upon the post–World Cup bounce, to the extent that there is one."[4] As for the Budweiser deal, one reporter noted that while aligning with Budweiser was a big deal for the NWSL, it wouldn't "look as great if the league doesn't bring in more major sponsors."[5] NWSL commissioner Amanda Duffy "gave a less-than-precise answer" when asked if any more deals are coming, saying "There has been a lot of outreach that's happened over the last few weeks, and we feel confident and strong in those opportunities."[6]

So, what of the symbiotic relationship between fans, media, and sponsorship support? Herein lies the rub, as ESPN's Magnus succinctly summed up: "Our (media) piece of it is only one slice of the pie relative to the viability of the league, ultimately. They still have to have appeal in order to get people to purchase tickets and have sponsor support and get venues—the whole 360-degree proposition of making the business work."[7]

electronic media), sponsors, and fans. This relationship is essentially symbiotic because the three elements feed off each other to create the conditions that attract additional fans.

The media, in all its forms, provide coverage and express opinions according to the interest that fans have in sport. The media then are influenced by attendance, website utilization and followers, Twitter content and activity, Instagram likes and activity, and so forth. The media are also influ-

enced by the credibility the sport or organization has with its sponsors: how many sponsors there are, how much they invest, and, of course, who they are. Sponsors make their investment largely in the target markets that are following the sport, whether that following is in venue (attendance), on television or mobile devices (viewership), or online. Having more fans increases opportunities for interactions to occur between the sponsor, the product, the respective media outlets, and the fans (target demos and markets). Fans and their support of the organization are used to attract sponsors, and fans' level of support, interest, and spending influences media interest, coverage, and ultimately, contracts for rights fees.

Baseball Hall of Famer Yogi Berra once said, "Nobody goes there anymore; it's too crowded." In his inimitable style, Yogi captured the goal of any event marketer—to create a crowd because a crowd attracts a crowd. The game or the venue must be the place to be. The crowd is important because it provides credibility to media decision makers and content creators, who then deem the event worthy of coverage and attention. Media coverage and interest function to create value for sponsors, which often rationalize their investments on a per exposure basis. The larger the crowd is, the more exposure and value sponsors receive. In the words of many sport marketers, the goal is to put "meat in the seats." That goal is accomplished through ticket sales.

What Is Sales?

Sales is the revenue-producing element of the marketing process in which goods or services are provided in exchange for money or other valuable consideration. Sales usually involves a questioning process to assess needs and find a product match. The salesperson needs listening skills to gain an understanding of the needs and wants of the prospect and the concerns or objections that the prospect may have. The process typically involves the application of conversational skills that might include persuasive skills and may be supported by print, audio, video, websites, social media, technological aids, and appropriate sampling—all designed and used to promote the brand or product as essential, appropriate, desirable, and worthy of consideration.

In this chapter, we define and explain sales by beginning with the thoughts and ideologies of famed sport marketer Mark McCormack, who founded IMG (now Endeavor) and built it into arguably the world's leading sport marketing and athlete management organization at the time of his death. As McCormack explained, selling consists of

- identifying customers,
- getting through to them,

- increasing their awareness and interest in your product or service, and
- persuading them to act on that interest.[8]

We can also explain sales as customer performance: When customers purchase a product, they perform the act of buying.[9] In sport, four main factors cause customers to perform or fail to perform:

1. *Quality.* How well is the product or service performing? Consider the star power of the recent three-time NBA World Champion Golden State Warriors; the road followers of the Pittsburgh Steelers, Dallas Cowboys, and Green Bay Packers of the NFL; and the 27 World Series Championships of the New York Yankees.

2. *Quantity.* In what quantity is the product sold? Mini-plans, flex plans, and other smaller ticket packages offer the consumer a variety of purchasing options to consider.

3. *Time.* Do consumers have time to consume the product? For example, family obligations, work schedule, hobbies, and other interests and everyday life might dictate that they do not. To make the purchase of a golf membership worthwhile, for example, the potential purchaser probably must be able to play on a weekly basis.

4. *Cost.* Cost relates not only to the overall dollar expense of the sport product or experience but also to such aspects as payment plans and value received for the purchase price. For instance, the "cost" of attending an MLS game includes the cost of the ticket as well as ancillary expenses that are incurred, including parking, concessions, travel, and perhaps even hiring the babysitter.

In many cases, a fifth consideration is social perception: Is it cool? What do my friends and peers think about attending the game? Does it make them think differently about me? Do I achieve "status" by being there? The difficulty here is figuring out how to make things cool, which is the "burning issue of our time."[10] Unfortunately, cool cannot be created and controlled.

Getting the customer to purchase and retaining that customer will dictate how successful a salesperson or sales organization is and how viable the future of the person or the organization will be.

What Makes a Good Salesperson?

Are salespeople born or made? The debate has raged for centuries. In the opinion of experts, the naturally born salesperson is a myth; salespeople are made, not born, although for some it is a much easier development.[11] People usually acquire the skills needed to be successful by developing good listening skills, being comfortable speaking to strangers, and having a competitive attitude in the context of wanting to succeed. These traits are generally learned and developed through experience and modeling; over time they form another critical element in a successful salesperson—confidence. Mark McCormack looked for these qualities in salespeople in his sport marketing agency:[12]

- Belief in the product
- Belief in yourself
- Seeing a lot of people (sales call volume)
- Timing
- Listening to the customer (but realizing what the customer wants is not necessarily what she is telling you)
- A sense of humor
- Knocking on old doors
- Asking everyone to buy
- Following up after the sale with the same aggressiveness that you demonstrated before the sale
- Common sense

Ultimately, the key to success in sport sales is the degree of training that a person gets, as well as the organization's commitment to developing sales talent. In the following sidebars, two highly experienced sales executives pull back the curtain on their approaches to sales training.

What Is a Good Sales-Oriented Organizational Structure?

The organizational structure and style of the organization form a key element in determining the overall success and effect of the sales department's efforts. Organizational structure for sales includes the following:

- The reporting structure within the organization should delineate whom you report to, your immediate supervisor, and so on.

- The relationships between departments that are integral in the sales process. For example, in structuring any organization involved in the sale of tickets, the relationship between the box office manager and the ticket-sales department is critical because of possible offers and incentives and the subsequent redemption of those offers. Similarly, the relationships between ticket sales and marketing, ticket sales and corporate partnerships, and ticket sales and game-day operations are all critical because of messaging, advertising, up-selling opportunities, and implementation issues. Figure 12.2 illustrates a proto-typical organizational chart for ticket-sales and service departments of a professional sport team.

- The organizational style or philosophy with regard to producing support materials for use in the sales process. Examples include brochures, direct mail pieces, e-offers, advertising, in-game announcements, and website page development and design.

- The sales development process within the department. Most sales departments begin their salespeople in entry-level sales positions. In sport, this often involves starting them in outbound phone calling or, as it is often referred to, inside sales, and letting them progress according to performance. The typical sales-development progression begins with an inside sales role and leads to opportunities in group sales or season-ticket sales that may then lead to premium sales or corporate sales, which often involves luxury suites, corporate partnerships, and other high-priced inventory.

- Determining the composition of the sales force and compensation mix for the sales staff. In this process, the organization determines the number of full-time sales staff, the number of part-time sales staff (if any), the use of outside sales services (usually operating an outbound-calling sales center), and the way that sales personnel will be compensated. Compensation is usually a combination of salary and commission (a percentage of the sales revenue generated), and, in some cases, bonuses.

Developing Core Strength

Jeff Ianello, EVP Client Partnerships, SeatGeek

I have always enjoyed hitting the gym. From my high school days through my mid-20s, the majority of my workouts have consisted of lifting, lifting, and more lifting. I would often skip stretching and anything to do with core or cardio. That is, until Father Time caught up with me, when I was swinging a golf club and threw my back out. For about two weeks, I was on the proverbial shelf. After a tip from a friend, I set an appointment with a physical therapist. The prognosis was simple: My lack of core strength and flexibility caused the injury and now nothing else worked. I got by for a while, but eventually the inevitable caught up with me.

As I look back on my leadership stints at the Phoenix Suns and at the NBA league office, and continuously audit my activities at SeatGeek, I couldn't help but pull from the lesson of this experience. With more responsibility comes the pull of identifying new projects as well as trying to improve current ones.

A team or league executive may look at questions such as What types of ticket plans should we have? What events should we host, and what should the creative programming entail? How do we strategically approach emerging categories like sports gambling or cannabis? How do we capitalize on modern digital marketing trends?

These are all important questions that need to be answered, but what is "the main thing"? What is the "core strength"? No silver bullets exist, and what I've observed in my nearly two decades of experience is that most people get easily distracted. When that happens, most people end up doing too many activities at a mediocre level. Does one want to be a great utility player or a gold glove shortstop who had 3,000 hits?

You may say this is great in theory, but how do you execute it in practice? Two ways: (1) Establish a core philosophy and (2) have a day-to-day focus on "the main thing," or as I call them "My Three Rocks." A basic four-pronged actionable philosophy is as follows.

1. Hire great, empower your people, don't act as the smartest person in the room

Everything starts here. If you do not make strong hires, then the training and development program will be ineffective and underapplied. I look for these core attributes when hiring sales people:

- Attitude
- Work ethic
- Coachability
- Leadership
- Commitment to the industry

Diversity hiring practices are vital to driving a variety of ideas and beliefs that are a reflection of the marketplace that one services and sells. Having "smartest person in the room syndrome" is a fatal flaw for many leaders. Ego is the enemy. Establishing ground rules that "I don't know everything and you don't know everything, but that's OK," establishes a no-judgment zone where seeking excellence takes precedence over perceived intellectual muscle flexing.

Finding great people takes work ethic! I always remember this when I think of my first phone interview with Nic Barlage for an entry-level sales position in Phoenix. Nic was surprised that I had reached out because he had applied online for half a dozen other entry-level jobs with teams and never even got an interview. Nic was one of our top producers and is now the President of Business Operations for the Cleveland Cavs—a star in our business.

> continued

2. Invest in training and development

A leader who stops investing in him- or herself is a leader that stops growing. A leader that stops growing will lead to an organization that stops growing. Training and development are probably the last thing[s] that should be cut from any sales and service budget, but inexplicably they are usually the first. Many sport teams have an inexperienced sales force in which three- to five-year tenured reps are the veterans. They need more coaching and learning. Another voice, messaging something that you have attempted to message, can cause a breakthrough. What is it worth to you to increase the productivity in gaining referrals or setting appointments? Do you have data that can track historical conversion rates in these areas? If so, you can measure the success of the training by comparing the month following the training session with that historical record. The increment will be your ROI to validate future investment.

The business world has also seen a breakthrough of new development initiatives like "meditation" and "yoga." Companies like Calm and Headspace are billion-dollar businesses. Studies have shown that those who practice meditation perform better in the workplace. You are also making your employees better people.

Continuing education and other subsidies to support a healthy lifestyle have become the norm and need to stay that way. SeatGeek excels in this area and my introduction to meditation has made me a better husband, father, and human being. Additionally, it has given me the ability to focus on my day-to-day work responsibilities and productively manage the roller coaster of being a sales professional.

3. Coach your people and lead by example

One of the most important turning points in my professional life, while at the Phoenix Suns, was hiring Keith Rosen to deliver his program on sales coaching to the sales managers and me. Rosen, the author of *Coaching Sales People Into Sales Champions*, teaches about how to communicate more effectively with your team by putting them in the driver's seat of their career by creating new possibilities of learning and growth. These teachings have led to great professional success, a healthier sales culture, and more personal happiness. The teachings allow your team to feel individual ownership in projects, which develops increased focus and pride on that piece of the business.

I can't expect my people to be great storytellers unless I'm investing in my own skills. I can't expect them to set appointments unless I have done so or do so. Be with your people throughout the process and allow them to observe you, just as you observe them. At Seat-Geek, I have three people who plug into various roles in the sales process. One is more data focused and the other two are more operational focused. Early on in the sales process, I establish their roles in regards to the prospects we target. When they activate their roles, we practice in advance, where they get feedback from me and others in our group. They also get to observe my role and execution of that role throughout the process. The idea is to continually give them more and more of "my parts" so that they can eventually run their own vertical at the company. This provides them growth and the company is set up for greater success.

Each week I take an audit of my "things to do list" and identify the three most important items that week. I then break those down to "My Three Rocks" for each day. This gives me comfort that I am focusing my time on "the main thing" and creates a pattern of daily success. I adjust my calendar and decline anything that doesn't take up less than 20% of my daily time, not focused on "My Three Rocks."

Much like the human body, if the core of your sales department and leadership philosophy is weak, nothing else can be maximized.

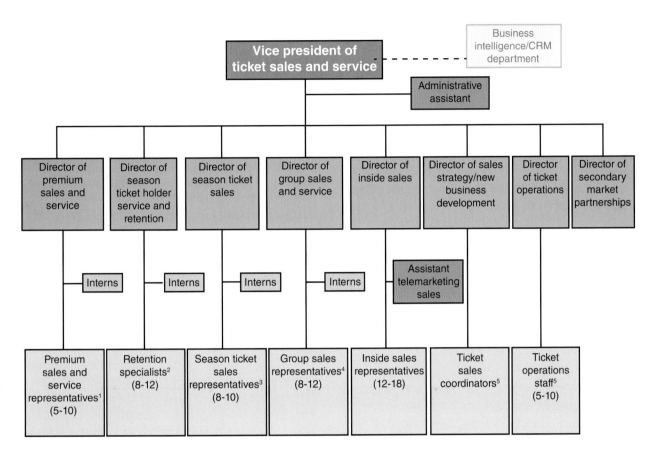

Notes:
1. Representatives typically split evenly between sales and service.
2. One retention specialist per every 500-700 accounts depending on the league and market.
3. One season ticket sales representative per every $500,000 of new season ticket sales revenue to be generated.
4. One group sales representative for every $500,000 of group business (new and renewed).
5. Ticket service coordinators (TSC) are responsible for building season-ticket and group accounts, processing payments, printing tickets, and delivering tickets.

FIGURE 12.2 Sample organizational chart for a typical sales and service team within a major league level professional team sport.

Commission percentages vary according to what the salary-to-commission ratio is, what product is being sold, and whether the sale is a new sale or a renewal.

One of the most important attributes of a high-functioning sales department is the degree of emphasis placed on sales training. Onboarding is often the most critical role that the sales management team can fill, and for the more progressive sport organizations, this important process is taking the form of branded sales training programs.

One of those sport organizations that has taken sales training to the next level is The Aspire Group, as described in more detail in the accompanying sidebar authored by The Aspire Group's Michael Boswell, Vice President of Training.

What Is a Recommended Sales-Oriented Structure?

Figure 12.3 (on page 313) depicts a prototypical organizational structure for a marketing department in a professional sport franchise, and, more specifically, how the ticket-sales and servicing department fits within the context of the overall revenue-generating side of the business.

As we have previously mentioned, the relationship between ticket sales and the box office is essential, but equally so is the relationship between the ticket office and those who manage

The WHOPPPP Way of Sales Training and Personal Brand Building

Michael Boswell, VP Training, The Aspire Group

Training that is provided by any organization, for new hires as well as successful veterans, is vital to the success achieved by each employee. Training reflects the degree of overall support that the organization provides their people. At The Aspire Group, training continues long after the first week of employment.

Speaking to interview candidates, I strongly recommend that they ask the prospective employer about their ongoing training frequency and who in the organization delivers that training.

When we recruit new consultants, regardless of their level of experience, we look for seven specific characteristics more so than experience. We refer to those characteristics as WHOPPPP.

Work ethic

Honesty/integrity/character

Openness to learning

Productivity

Positive attitude

Potential for leadership

Passion

We hire candidates that possess *all* characteristics because our experience shows that they have a higher likelihood to become a superstar.

When employees work hard, for example, good things will generally happen. When employees consistently work hard but also stay focused on their long-term/career goals, great things will happen.

The fundamentals of our onboarding training prioritize how to conduct your business; the sales process; and the activities that lead to success. The "Root" is how we describe the work of targeting the best prospects and building relationships with them. We refer to the sales revenue "production" as the "Fruit."

Onboarding training includes an introduction to our playbook. The first piece of advice given in the playbook is, in the weeks and months ahead, to continually review the playbook and other training notes. We believe this is one of the most underutilized approaches a newly hired employee should take, not only in sales or in the sport and entertainment industry. As any former student-athlete can tell you, a technique cannot be mastered after a few attempts. It is wise to take the time to review the fundamental training that was provided during onboarding.

Information is crammed into our brains during the first week on the job, so it's only natural that ongoing reviews would help anyone retain more information.

As the playbook proceeds, new employees are taught the importance of our company's philosophy and approach to sales and service. We want to improve the connection our ticket-buying fans have with the athletic department or the club/team or sports property—we call this approach "creating fans for life"—which takes more time and requires a lot of genuine caring, but it rewards us with increased revenue on a "lifetime asset value" basis.

Here are a few approaches we believe in and coach our staff to apply.

Relationship-Building Sales

When a prospect says "no," it's not typically because of the product. It happens because people generally do not want to feel like they are being sold. This apprehension is like "having a defensive shield up." To illustrate, depending on the sales consultant's experience or the marketplace, 60-80% of the "no's" we get happen in the first 10-30 seconds of a conversation. That percentage is higher with new consultants because their skills are still being formed.

We help our consultants to create their own outline—a pathway for success—that is based on:

- Knowing the sales progression process (NOT a script, but scripted elements in their own words)
- Having a prepared list of questions and talking points
- Really listening to the customer
- Knowing the best way to respond to what the customer says

We encourage our consultants to use "I/My Statements," an approach that helps the prospect recognize they have something in common with them. This technique, which we refer to as "creating a common ground," has a huge impact on building a relationship with the fan/prospect.

Imagine mingling at a dinner party where you don't know anyone. Naturally, you would have better conversations with people when you find you have something in common with them. Using I/My Statements help show others that we have something in common. It gets their defense shield to come down. It draws people's attention and interest toward us.

Listening

One of the common challenges new consultants have is overthinking. Too much thinking can become a distraction. When we have a conversation, thinking (or "talking to yourself") makes it impossible for us to be fully focused on the other person. A skill in sales that surprises many people during our training sessions is that talking to customers is not as important as listening to customers. In fact, there is a significant difference in passive listening and active listening.

When your sincere intention is "listening to understand," we learn what is important to the other person. Also, the simple approach of asking questions and not interrupting the other person is an effective tactic of earning trust. It's fascinating how much trust we gain from other people by letting them talk. When this approach is used in sales, success rates increase dramatically.

Another example of active listening is "key word listening." Listen for key words the customer uses in the conversation. For example:

- If they mention they are an alum, we can draw the customer in by responding with, "You're an alum—that's great!" Then we can ask a follow-up question, such as "What was your major?"
- If they mention they bring their kids to games, we can continue the topic by responding with, "I'm glad you bring your kids! What do your kids like most about coming to our games?"

People are, of course, most interested in themselves. That's why showing genuine interest in other people is the most successful approach to fan relationship building. Listening for key

> continued

> continued

words and using them in the replies proves to the customer that the consultant cares about what they have to say. When prospects feel the consultant is sincerely interested in them, that creates more opportunities to present the product and to close a sale.

Another way to think about this approach is to make the prospect the sole focal point in the conversations. The prospect's decisions will determine the consultant's success after all. If the prospect's trust is not earned, then lots of sales will be lost completely or diverted to online commerce.

Consistency

Caring about what you say can't possibly be more important than what the customer hears. Be consistent! Following the process completely with consistent phrases and approaches is the best sales and service advice anyone can be given. Think about the all-time greats in sports. One of the reasons they became great is their amazing consistency. Consistency leads to longevity. Once you learn your role, focus on performing consistently well. Sales consultants that say the same things each day make a lot more money and are promoted much more often.

Earning a Promotion

When travelling throughout the country or internationally to train people, a common question we are asked is, "How do I get promoted?" It's a great question. The best way to earn a promotion—in any industry—is to crush the opportunity you have in front of you right now. "Crushing" means far exceeding goals, not meeting or narrowly exceeding expectations.

Think about it logically. If everyone had similar levels of productivity, how would anyone differentiate themselves in order to earn a promotion? The answer—by being noticeably better in your ROOT and FRUIT activity and being an example of best practices to your boss and your team. People that deliver average results don't earn promotions—promotions are earned by top producers that have all of the WHOPPPP characteristics.

Career Motivation

Our company invests a great deal of time and financial resources into the long-term development of our consultants. We find that productivity increases significantly at the 11-month and again around the 20-month of a sales consultant's career. That's an example of success being a marathon, not a sprint.

We value "Potential for Leadership" (from WHOPPPP) and are committed to providing tools to help employees achieve their career aspirations. Career development and a path to promotion is vitally important in our employees becoming future leaders.

Accountability is a decisive factor in achieving success. We recommend to our consultants that they consider the same approach to their profession that a business owner would have to theirs. Own your personal brand. Learn and apply at least one new thing every day so that your personal brand becomes more valuable. Focus on every call and following the process with passion and caring for the prospects. In that way, you will produce superior results every day.

Saying you want a sports business career sounds good, but the question you must ask yourself is "Do I truly approach the sales opportunity with enough commitment every day to earn a career? If peers are working harder than you, then you probably aren't building a career. Words are great, but your actions will always define you.

Aspire's executive development program is called "Raise Your Game" and it is an excellent example of how we help our people develop into future sports-industry leaders.

Over 100 years of sport and entertainment industry experiences are shared in Raise Your Game training, which helps employees improve in their current role as well as gaining a significant advantage for the future.

Once a month, our employees across the country receive a Raise Your Game training designed to grow and enhance their personal brand.

You can't cook a steak in a microwave and expect a good result. We understand the desire to be great that new consultants have. We felt the same way when we began our careers, however in order to be great—at sports and entertainment, business, or anything—the fundamentals must be mastered first. Understand the process. Accept the process. Follow the process. Just like a great golfer can "lose their swing" and need to return to the basics in order to get their swing back, selling well means consistently following the process.

Be patient with success. The career opportunities that come to you are usually better than the ones we look for. Be great at what you do, and great opportunities will find you!

Enjoy the journey and remember the words of the Guinness Book of Records "World's Most Famous Salesman," Zig Ziegler, in his best-selling book *See You at the Top*: "You can get everything you want in life, if you help enough other people get what they want!"

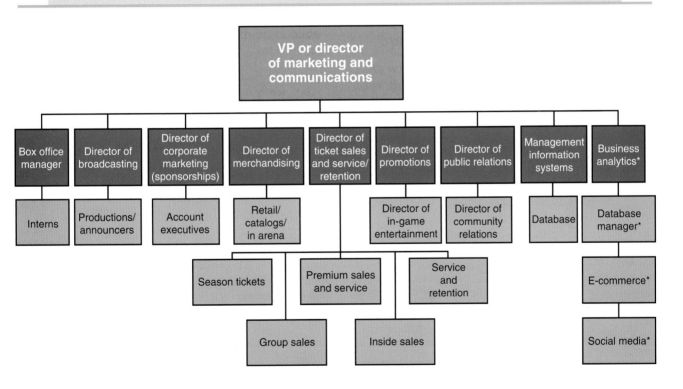

*May also report to the CFO, CRO, or VP of business strategy

FIGURE 12.3 How the ticket sales department fits into sport marketing.

the organization's customer relationship management (CRM) system. Using the CRM system provides the sales department with qualified leads (names of potential consumers who, through some action or activity, have indicated an interest in or ability to purchase the product); the ability to conduct email or direct mail campaigns; and the means to track customer engagement, warehouse data points, and conduct data appends, as applicable, through companies like Axiom. One relatively new technique is to digitally prequalify leads for the sales staff by first sending a text or an email to all leads with an "intelligently targeted" offer, based on knowledge of the prospect's interest and desires. Those who open, click-through, or share and post the offer but do not go online to purchase are passed onto the sales staff as "high-octane" leads.

What Do I Have to Sell?

Sales inventory refers to all the products and services available to the sales staff to market, promote, package, and sell through the sales methodologies described in this chapter. Table 12.1 categorizes the types of inventory available to sellers within the sport marketing industry.

Database Sport Marketing and Sales

According to the Direct & Marketing Association (DMA), the industry trade group for direct marketing, the definition of direct marketing is "an interactive process of addressable communication that uses one or more advertising media to effect, at any location, a measurable sale, lead, retail purchase, or charitable donation, with this activity analyzed on a database for the development of ongoing mutually beneficial relationships between marketers and customers, prospects or donors."[13] Data-based marketing, also known in the industry as "intelligent marketing," has become essentially mandatory for sport organizations in order to drive ticket sales.

Simply stated, database marketing involves the collection of information about past, current, and potential consumers. This information can be generated from membership records, lists of past purchasers, credit card receipts, sweepstakes and contests, and so forth. The organization then cleans the data to improve accuracy and avoid duplicate records and compiles the information into a database or, ideally, a multifaceted CRM system. It can then create campaigns based on past purchasing behavior, demographic segment, or other factors according to organizational intent and the suitability of the target market as it relates to that intent. With the acceptance and growth of sport business

TABLE 12.1   Inventories—What Do I Have to Sell?

Naming rights	Print inventory	Promotions inventory
Arena or stadium	Game program	Premium items
Practice facility	Media guide	On-floor promotions
Team	Newsletters	Video boards (or similar brand)
Electronic inventory	Ticket backs	Contests
Television	Ticket envelopes	Pre- and postgame entertainment
Radio	Scorecards, roster sheets	
Web page	Sponsored text messages, social media posts, etc.	**Community programs**
E-newsletters	**Assets related to ticket sales**	School assemblies
Digital content (i.e., ongoing stories)	Court, ice, field time	Camps, clinics
Signage inventory	Clinics	Awards, banquets
Dasher, score, matrix, message boards, LED signage	Fan tunnels, high-five lines	Kick-off luncheons, dinners
Marquees	Ball boy and ball girl opportunities	Golf tournaments
Floor, field, ice	**Tickets and hospitality inventory**	**Miscellaneous inventory**
Medallions		Fantasy camps
Concourse	VIP parking	Off-season cruises, trips with players
Blimps	Stadium or arena clubs	Road trips
Turnstiles, urinals, etc.	Season tickets	
Patches on uniforms	Club seats, suites, PSLs	
	Group tickets	
	Parties, special events	

Business intelligence is increasingly shaping the ticket sales and service discipline, and numerous companies have emerged to serve the industry. One of the most prominent is KORE Software, which provides the sport industry with a range of software solutions products and services. Its products create solutions for ticket and fan engagement, sponsorship and partner engagement, suites and premium, and analytics and data warehousing, all on a single integrated platform. KORE Software's services are carried out by its consulting and staff augmentation arm that specializes in the field of business intelligence. KORE Software uses business intelligence to positively affect the sport industry through current trends, best practices, and expertise. The consulting arm uses its extensive industry knowledge that comes with its experiences to prepare organizations to use business intelligence and data-driven insights to solve their short-term problems as well as set up an information system that can help them achieve their long-term goals. KORE Software improves the accuracy of data-based decision making by providing organizations with detailed reports and dashboards. It also prepares organizations to understand and adapt a growth mindset when it comes to data collection and utilization since information systems are dynamically evolving in this day and age.

KORE Software's Ticketing & Fan Engagement services assist teams and venues with selling tickets faster and, at the same time, building deeper and more meaningful client interactions.[14] Its software for ticketing and fan engagement collects and analyzes data that gives organizations a more holistic view of their fans and their pipeline. This deep understanding of consumer data allows organizations to spot opportunities, patterns, or trends that can potentially add value to fan experiences and eventually the bottom line. This software can assist strategy and implementation through its insights on activations and customer demographics and, in turn, increase sales team productivity. This software is also able to target revenue more accurately through comprehensively gathering data on the entire pipeline and prioritizing it through various filters. KORE Software's partnerships with Turnkey and Live Analytics give it the ability to identify customer segments to a very specific level. Being able to identify consumers can assist in creating targeted campaigns for sales and marketing. All the abilities of KORE Software's Ticketing & Fan Engagement software are topped by the software's ability to feed ticketing data into various CRM systems like Ticketmaster or AXS. KORE Software's software solutions have truly transformed the productivity of the company's clients.

An example of the usefulness of its software is when the Oklahoma City Dodgers worked with KORE Software.[15] The MiLB team saw a 10 percent increase in retaining season-ticket holders, which added US$300,000 to its bottom line. Additionally, the team grew its group renewals by 150 accounts and more than 10,000 tickets. Through prioritizing efficiency and helping organizations better understand their consumer market, KORE Software is able to creatively approach fan engagement and boost fan retention and ticket sales through its software. KORE Software helped the Oklahoma City Dodgers realize that instead of pushing ticket sales and promoting game attendance, the team should focus on maximizing relationships with fans through channels that create value to consumers. This led to a more specific campaign that focused on family entertainment content like giveaways and group ticket packages. Because of KORE, the team could hyper target its campaigns to meet specific segments of its audience and successively add more value to their experiences.

KORE Software's value can also be seen in its partnership with FC Barcelona through its Sponsorship & Partner Engagement software.[16] The football club partnered with KORE

> continued

> continued

Software to facilitate the transfer of key information and data across its three global offices. FC Barcelona was very strategic about its global expansion and considered its goals, values, and image at every step of its expansion. It made the point to not work in silos and to be very unified from a communications and objectives standpoint. At the same time, it worked at an extremely local level in its different regions to value assets and form a sales pipeline with all the data it collected. It hired KORE Software to find a better solution to help FC Barcelona share data and insights accurately and safely across its three global offices. KORE Software not only assisted FC Barcelona with the transparency of its systems but also increased the number of companies in its CRM system by a factor of 10. KORE Software also made it easier for executives to see what the commercial partnership team does, giving them the ability to view a partnership in terms of assets offered as well as what they get in return for that particular asset. The Sponsorship & Partner Engagement software helped track all assets available globally at their individual values of cost, quantity, and category in real time. The software also provided full transparency to FC Barcelona's sales process and pipeline. KORE Software assisted FC Barcelona's commercial partnerships team to share individual office data across the whole organization to better analyze data and implement insights. The software has raised FC Barcelona's commercial partnerships team to the elite level that the organization relies upon.

analytics and research, the database manager works closely with (and in most cases reports to) the vice president or director of business intelligence. The data is analyzed, targeted, and packaged to assist the sales team in focusing its correspondence and efforts with regard to prospecting and setting up sales calls. Regardless of the sales approach or process that the sport organization uses, some type of database is essential to generate leads.

It has long been considered the best practice for every organization to attempt to secure contact information of everyone who purchases its products or services. Technology that allows paperless tickets and other forms of electronic entry are making this goal much easier to achieve. A product called Flash Seats employs a paperless ticketing system designed to identify and provide the contact information for every person in the venue.

As previously noted, management of the database is also a key element in the sales process. Each group or segment in the database should be tested and its responsiveness to certain appeals measured—ticket plans, telephone solicitation, online offers, emarketing campaigns, and special offers through social media outlets. Responses should be measured to test ROI or ROO and should be documented to increase the targeting and the effectiveness of future efforts.

Lead scoring (identifying the likelihood of potential purchase and spend amount), or in more sophisticated DBM/CRM systems, purchase propensity, is also becoming a highly effective sales management tool. Lead scoring is designed to identify the prospects most likely to buy, and it can also be used to identify the best salesperson to make the solicitation based on the success of that salesperson and the prospect's qualifications.

As analytics, framed more broadly as business intelligence, takes a greater role in the sales and customer management process, numerous companies have emerged to provide their proprietary software and consulting services to sport organizations. One of the most prominent of them is KORE. The accompanying sidebar provides more insights into what KORE does.

Typical Sales Approaches Used in Sport

Keys to successful sales include having a product that everyone wants and can afford and one that considers the amount of time required to consume the product (number of games). Full-menu selling is having something for everyone. A Washington Nationals fan can sit in the bleachers, in a luxury suite, or even in a steakhouse in center field to watch the game. The key is for sport organizations to recognize that demand for the product is present at a variety of price points. Our experience as practitioners and consultants has taught us that full-menu selling is necessary not only because of price but also because of time and the depth and breadth of the fan's level of interest and commitment.

As the ability to pay, the interest in the product or service, and the availability of the product vary, so too must the approaches used to sell those products or services. A successful sport organization will employ a variety of sales approaches. And as the levels and types of products or services offered for sale within a sport organization vary, so should the sales approaches that aim to inform and convince consumers of a product's value to them. Certain approaches are more appropriate and consequently more effective in selling types or volume of the sport product. In this section, we examine the most common sales approaches used in sport.

One of the ongoing challenges for sport teams has become what to do about the traditional notion of the "season ticket." As discussed earlier, the mere cost of purchasing season-ticket packages has become prohibitive for many (although the ease of dispensing with tickets via the secondary marketplace has alleviated some of this concern). Additionally, younger fans want a different experience at the ballpark, one that doesn't confine them to the same seat every game (or even a seat, period!). As a result of these and other market-specific factors, teams are becoming more creative in how they think about the traditional season ticket. An increasing number of sport teams have embraced the "membership" model. Other teams have begun to position season-ticket packages as more akin to Netflix-type subscription models. For instance, in 2019, the Oakland Athletics introduced its so-called Access Plan, with subscriptions starting at US$33 per month. This innovative approach resulted in the sale of 9,535 plans, essentially a full 81-game subscription to general seating at the RingCentral Coliseum. For the 2020 season, all fans with half-season or full-season Access Plans were entitled to add a member for just US$99, and the plan was expanded to be "all-access"—every fan with a membership with access to anywhere in the stadium.[17] The Athletics' Access Plan serves as just one example of how changing demographics, lifestyles, and marketplace realities have forced sport teams to "re-imagine" the season ticket, long the economic bedrock of the sport industry.

Outbound Phone Sales

The entry point for most young college graduates is a seat in the team's "inside sales" department, where they are trained and mentored in outbound sales efforts using the phone. In traditional sales vernacular, this process has been called *telemarketing* (a term that has taken on a negative connotation thanks to robocallers).

Sport organizations are beginning to examine the benefits of expanding incoming phone-line capabilities to provide not only information but also revenue opportunities. To satisfy the desire of fans to stay abreast of team and player information and to increase sponsorship revenues (either in terms of the price the sponsor paid or by revenue sharing in a B2C opportunity), more and more teams are offering 24-hour-a-day interactive phone lines.

Websites have also become an integral part of the sales process in several ways:

- Links on the team web page for visitors to pose questions that someone in the organization will answer
- Links on the web page that immediately connect visitors with someone in the ticket office (i.e., click to chat functions)
- Applications on the website, such as Virtual View and other integrated applications, that help callers visualize seating locations and other opportunities that can be discussed online or over the telephone with a sales representative

The outbound phone sales process can also be two-dimensional, as an outward-oriented vehicle to prospect for customers, follow up leads, research prospects, solicit existing customers for repeat or expanded business volume, or set up appointments to bring the prospect to the stadium or arena to learn more about the product or possibly for an opportunity to sample the product.

Outbound Phone Sales Process

Outbound phone sales involves training sales personnel to follow a script, become effective listeners, identify the objections to the sale (if any), and complete the sales process by countering the objection and selling the original offer or modifying the offer (by up-selling or down-selling) to fit the needs of the consumer better. This process could look like the following:

1. Precall planning
   - Review client information including lead scoring (if available)
   - Plan the objective for the call
   - Psych-up—get in the proper mental frame for the call
2. Approach and positioning
   - Identify who you are and whom you represent
   - Specify the purpose of your call
   - Make an interest-creating statement
   - Build rapport
   - Navigate through the gatekeeper (secretary or receptionist) to the decision maker
3. Data gathering
   - Build on the knowledge obtained from the preplanning investigations and research
   - Move from general to specific questions about practices and interests
   - Identify a personal or business need
4. Solution generation
   - Tailor communication to the specific client need
   - Ask in-depth questions to test the feasibility of the possible solutions
   - Gather data for a cost–benefit analysis
   - Prepare the client for the recommendation or the possibilities that have been identified
5. Solution presentation
   - Get client acknowledgement and agreement on the areas of need
   - Present the recommendations clearly and concisely
   - Describe package benefits to the parties who will benefit from the purchase
6. Close
   - Decide on timing—when to close or, if the call was made to set up an appointment or visit to make the close, set the date and time of that appointment
   - Listen for acceptance or buying signals
   - Handle objections
   - Use closing techniques
7. Wrap-up
   - Discuss next steps, notably implementation issues
   - Thank the client for doing business with you
   - Confirm client commitment
   - Position the follow-up
   - Ask for referrals

Applying the "Outbound Sales" Process

To see how the process works, let's imagine the following scenario. Jane Micelli is an inside sales executive for the Gotham Batmen, a professional baseball team that qualified for postseason play after the 2019 regular season but did not win the championship. Jane has been provided a list of leads, derived from people who used their credit cards to purchase tickets to one or more games during the past season. Jane's goal is to sell partial plans of 40, 20, or 10 games for the 2020 season. For the first time, she has the opportunity to sell a game-of-the-month plan, a six-pack. Here are the steps that Jane follows:

1. *Precall planning.* Jane reviews the file on Mary Stuart, an attorney who bought individual tickets to four games during the past season. Jane notices that Ms. Stuart purchased two tickets for each of the four games and attended once per month in June, July, August, and September. Jane reviews her script and places the call.

2. *Approach and positioning.* "Hello. My name is Jane Micelli, and I am calling from the Midwest Division champion Gotham Batmen. May I please speak to Mary Stuart? Good evening, Ms. Stuart. As I stated, I'm calling from the Gotham Batmen, and we want to thank you for your interest and support of the team during the past season. I hope you enjoyed your experiences, and I would like to take this opportunity to talk to you about the upcoming season. We are excited to have made the postseason last year, but that is just a step on the way to our ultimate goal—winning a cham-

pionship for the people of Gotham. We anticipate tickets being more difficult to obtain for the upcoming season because of our performance last year and the new players we have added to our roster. We would like to make sure that our fans who have supported us in the past have access to better seating locations and options before the tickets go on sale to the general public. Do you have just a few minutes?"

3. *Data gathering.* "According to our records, you purchased tickets to see the Penguins, Riddlers, Jokers, and Cats last season. Is that correct? How did you enjoy your game-day experience? Who do you typically attend games with? What type of things does your law firm typically do to entertain clients and prospective clients?" (Note the use of open-ended questions, versus "yes/no" questions, that are designed to engage the client in a dialogue that will yield valuable insights and information.)

4. *Solution generation.* "We have designed several ticket plans that are less than our traditional full-season plan with people such as you in mind. We have plans ranging from 40 games to as few as six games, and even with our six-game plan, you have priority over the general public to have the opportunity to purchase playoff tickets, and I know that is important to you. We also realize that these games are important to a businessperson such as you to host clients and conduct business meetings in a fun, entertaining setting. Would you be interested in considering a six-game plan for next season?" (The number of games offered is selected based on the previous step.)

5. *Solution presentation.* "The Gotham Batmen have designed a new ticket plan especially for the businessperson. Our game-of-the-month plan offers one game per month located in our premium seating areas, including food and beverage, meeting space, and the opportunity for a dinner seating at three different times. It also guarantees you the option to purchase postseason tickets for at least one game in each of the postseason series in which we are competing. How would that fit your needs?"

6. *Close.* "I am sure that this game-of-the-month plan will meet your needs and be much more convenient and consistent than your current ticket-purchasing options. Can I reserve two Big Game plans for you and schedule a time when we can select your seat location? If it is inconvenient for you to select the seats, we can do that right now using our seat finder, which we can access online. I can assist you with that right now. How does that sound?"

7. *Wrap-up.* "Thanks for taking the time to select your location online. I am sure that you will be happy with your seats. If there is anything that we can do during the season, please contact either me or Thomas Fagan, who will be your account representative. Thomas will contact you in the next 48 hours to provide further explanation of the benefits that we discussed that are part of your account. One last question: Is there anyone else at your firm or anyone in your business circles who you think could benefit from a similar ticket package?"

Outsourcing the Sales Process

Nearly all major college programs outsource the selling of some revenue-generating function, whether it is multimedia and sponsorship rights, trademark and licensing rights, naming rights, and concessions. Outsourcing ticket sales was a logical evolution that was based on

- the success of the previously listed outsourced areas;
- the financial and competitive pressures on colleges and universities to drive incremental revenues;
- the trending attendance declines at major college sports events coupled with an aging season-ticket holder base; and
- the inability or unwillingness of colleges to add employees and implement a compensation system, which are common in sales.

The trend toward outsourcing of ticket sales isn't limited to colleges and universities. Numerous other sports events, ranging from the NFL Pro Bowl to the Formula E races, have turned to the "experts" to take control of the ticket sales process.

Today, well over half of all the schools in the NCAA's Football Bowl Subdivision have hired an outside firm to handle their outbound ticket sales initiatives. Although a number of outside vendors provide such services, the two major players in this space are Atlanta-based The Aspire Group and IMG Learfield Ticket Solutions.

Creating the Successful Outbound Ticket Sales Program for State U

By Rob Clark, PhD, Executive Senior Associate Athletic Director, Long Beach State University

Tickets will not sell themselves. Donations will not automatically come flowing into an athletic department. This is particularly true at institutions that may not be a household name brand or [of] performance in competition [that] has diminished. Revenue generation in these cases is even more critical in order to transform the competitive level and advance the mission of the institution.

Outbound ticket sales and annual giving programs are no longer a luxury; they are a necessity to operate at the Division I level. Not all outbound ticket sales and annual giving models are effective, as institutional, bureaucratic, and cultural factors determine how these outbound efforts are received.

Having worked at all levels of Division I, there are several key factors that I have seen that will determine the success of an outbound sales program:

1. *You must gain complete "buy-in" from university and department leadership.* Guiding university and department leadership to understanding the need for ticket sales and annual giving revenues to offset annual costs (scholarships, operations, etc.) is essential to building an outbound ticket sales and annual giving team that will drive revenues.

2. *You must understand the right outbound sales model fit for your institution.* Namely, can we effectively outsource or build our own sales team? Under the existing regulations of human resources at your university, there might be roadblocks that can prevent hiring sufficient staff or prevent your ability to offer the sales team incentive compensation (i.e., Can you add the positions? Can you pay commissions/bonuses?). If this is the case, outsourcing will most likely be a more effective model for your institution.

3. *Building a mutually beneficial outbound sales partnership.* When outsourcing, the contract terms are critical to the success of the partnership. A strong partnership of trust is built on clear expectations, financial obligations, and goals upon which staff and the outsource third-party can be held accountable. Ensure that the contractual terms are agreeable to university and department business office practices, financial terms are amenable to the scale of revenue generation at your institution, any work within athletics development is in alignment with processes of the university and department, and that there is nothing contractually preventing your sales team from accomplishing the work of generating revenues. Also ensure that the incentive terms for the third-party drive the right kind of behavior, namely the right balance of strong service/retention and aggressive growth in new ticket sales revenues.

4. *A strong director of ticket sales will make or break your outbound program.* It is best practice that all hiring for the ticket sales team must be approved by the institution; without this assurance the partnership is likely to fail. It is crucial to establish clear guidelines for your outsourced partnership including the stipulation that director of ticket sales will be committed for a minimum of two years and not be "promoted" to a bigger school; otherwise, the high staff turnover will likely cause the partnership to fail.

5. *Accountability will lead to success.* With clear expectations and realistic goals, the leadership guiding both the athletic department *and* the outsourcing partner must hold everyone accountable to the revenue targets to be successful. This includes creating an environment where revenue generation is prioritized and internal athletic department roadblocks are removed for the sales team.

Adherence to these guiding principles in our partnership with The Aspire Group has driven record ticket sales at Long Beach State University. We are now implementing the same approach into our annual giving program with the expectation of driving record membership into the Beach Athletic Fund in the coming years.

The Aspire Group's model is based upon the creation of Fan Relations Management Centers (FRMCs) at each of the institutions that it services, and in most cases, Aspire "imbeds" its employees in the respective athletic department so that they are "part of the team" and daily engaged in the athletics department's internal communications process. Just signing a contract with an outside firm is, however, not an instant guarantor of sales success. Rob Clark, Executive Senior Associate Athletic Director at Long Beach State University, shares his insights on the factors that can best ensure a successful association with an outside ticket sales firm.

Direct Mail

We know what your first reaction was when you read the heading: "In this day and age? With social media as prevalent as it is?" The answer is yes. According to Dale Berkebile of Brandwise, direct mail is as effective as ever if you follow one simple rule: Know your target audience.[18] Salesforce.com and other CRM systems should provide you with an excellent up-to-date portrait of your customers or donors, their purchasing or giving history, and their anticipated interests and patterns of behavior.

Like outbound phone calling and other forms of direct marketing, direct mail has distinct characteristics and advantages:

- *Direct mail is targeted.* The appeal is to certain groups of consumers who are measurable, reachable, and sizable enough to ensure meaningful sales (or fundraising) volume.
- *It is personal.* The message can be personalized not only according to the name and other demographic characteristics but also with regard to lifestyle interests and past behaviors (football fan, Cowboys alumnus, merchandise purchaser, fantasy camp attendee, and so on).
- *It is measurable.* Because each message calls for some type of action or response,

the organization mailing the message is able to measure the effectiveness of the marketing effort.
- *It can be tested.* Because the effectiveness is measurable, marketers can devise accurate head-to-head comparisons of offers, formats, prices, terms, and so forth.
- *It is flexible.* There are few constraints (other than cost) with regard to the size, color, timing, shape, and format of the mailing. Also, the marketer determines the mailing date and anticipated arrival of the campaign piece.

As with any approach, direct mail has limitations. Because it does not involve any personal contact (face to face as in personal selling or mouth to ear as in phone sales), no opportunity is available to explain the program and the offer, to counter objections, or even to answer questions. Thus, the sender must clearly communicate the material, including the offer itself, so that the targeted recipient can clearly understand it.

In formulating the direct-mail offer, the sport marketer should consider the following:

- *Differentiating the product to be offered from other products offered.* In other words, in the case of a ticket brochure being mailed to a target audience, is each ticket package option clearly distinguishable from the others? Can the recipient easily assess the benefits of each, make a decision, and act accordingly?

- *Offering options or variations of the product to fit the price considerations, time constraints, and abilities of the marketplace.* One example of this is the flexible season-ticket membership package launched by the Seattle Mariners for the 2020 MLB season. Fans can use an online member portal to choose how many tickets, seat locations, and games they want, at discounts ranging from 10 percent to 50 percent off the single-game price. Flex customers select from six membership levels, each with its own associated discount and benefits.[19]

- *Providing an attractive range of benefits or exclusivity.* Since the 1990s, sport marketers have appealed to consumers to "join them" in various direct-mail membership initiatives. These memberships, such as those offered by the National Baseball Hall of Fame and Museum, the Special Olympics, and others, sometimes entailed various levels that had different fees and a set of benefits, publications, admission privileges, premium items, special access, and special events to join at a particular level.

- *Using discounts, sales, refunds, coupons, premium items, and other incentives to enhance the perceived value of the offer.* Direct mail seeks to cause an action, and the perception of getting a deal in making the purchase is often the catalyst in producing the action. These deals can take many forms. The most popular forms of catalog discounting allows a consumer to receive free shipping or a certain portion off if the order exceeds a certain amount, perhaps an offer of US$10 or US$15 off on an order that exceeds US$100. This offer is prevalent in apparel marketing, but teams often use it with their own merchandise catalogs or stores. Likewise, sport mass merchandisers may offer certain deals to move merchandise or to attract new buyers.

- *Offering flexible payment or deferred payment terms.* Some consumers may be intrigued by the opportunity to purchase merchandise now and pay for it at a more convenient time. This retailing practice is common in the United States, and payment plans have become a fixture in the sport industry, particularly for higher-priced items, such as season tickets. Today, most sport teams allow their season-ticket purchasers to pay for their season tickets over an extended period, often a full 12 months.

Email Marketing

In many ways, email marketing has experienced a healthy metamorphosis into part of a long-promised broader digital marketing arsenal focused on what matters most for most businesses—making money. Marketing automation, cloud-based marketing platforms, digital messaging, and CRM are all ways to deliver email technology platforms designed to persuade customers to buy more often and to turn prospects into customers.[20]

We should also acknowledge that email marketing is also mobile marketing. New content, technology, and savvy testing can accomplish a lot on the mobile front. In addition to understanding the audience and building a game plan with that in mind, the execution of campaigns to a mobile readership is crucial. The right message on the right device can be the difference between a read, a click, and a purchase.

Developing the Email Offer

Many sport franchises have turned to marketing automation firms, such as Oracle Eloqua, Hubspot, and Marketo, which provide a variety of tools and email campaigns designed to assist them in reaching and converting fans into buyers with highly targeted offers, not unlike direct-mail campaigns. For example, Marketo's features include email marketing, landing pages and forms, campaign management, engagement marketing, prediction and scoring, customer life cycle management, CRM integration, social marketing capabilities, mobile marketing capabilities, and marketing analytics that are essential to implementing effective email campaigns.[21]

- Fan profiling and web tracking
- Fan acquisition, append, and cleanse
- Fan segmentation
- Fan (lead) scoring
- One-to-one personalization
- Campaign and conversion metrics
- Segment analysis
- Real-time, multichannel marketing[22]

Email (and Direct Mail) Should Be More Than an Offer

Organizations that use email or direct mail to do nothing more than initiate the sales process through an offer do not understand relationship marketing. As we discuss later in this chapter, the long-term goal of sales efforts is to develop lasting and deep relationships with the consumer. If the only time the consumer hears from the organization is at renewal time or when the aim is to sell more of the product, the relationship will never be strengthened or expanded. Regular communication through these two channels can be used to enhance sales opportunities through several means:

- By providing a regular method of communication to keep the customer informed

February 14, 2019

Dear Robert,

On behalf of the entire Springfield Thunderbirds organization, I would like to thank you for your continued support in year three of the franchise. Our season ticket members are the backbone of our organization. You've come out strong all year long, and it's your support that has helped prove that Springfield is indeed a hockey market. This year has been a fantastic one for us, as we have *risen up* to new heights by hosting the 2019 Lexus AHL All-Star Classic presented by MGM Springfield – a testament to your support, as the spotlight was on us and our city of Springfield. We hope you enjoyed it as much as we did. As we look ahead to year four, I felt it was critical that we maintain our ticket pricing for our most loyal fans – YOU. Again, you are our backbone, and I felt it was necessary to provide each of you the opportunity to keep pricing where it has been since our inception – as a token of continued appreciation. Be sure to renew early as a price increase will go into effect after June 1, 2019.

On the heels of a hugely successful Throwback night yet again this season – one that featured the white/green Springfield Indians jerseys – we have created a line of Indians-inspired gifts again this year just for ticket members. We heard from many of you this year about how much you enjoyed last year's jersey, and we want to provide you, our most loyal fans, the opportunity to receive these exclusive, one-of-a-kind gifts again this season.

In addition, many of your favorite benefits will be returning as well for the 2019-20 season, including discounted concession prices with your T-Birds challenge coin ($3 Beer & $1 soda at every game), the Never Wasted Ticket program, the first Calder Cup playoff game FREE, as well as all of the benefits you've grown accustomed to. As an added incentive, if you pay in full prior to April 13th, you will be entered into a drawing to win a trip for two (2) to see a Panthers game of your choice next season in Florida.

To ensure you retain your seats for next season, you must place your deposit by Saturday, April 13th. Please be sure to mail in your renewal or contact Matt McRobbie at (413) 739-GOAL with any questions or to place your renewal over the phone. It's our goal to always push the envelope and provide the very best customer/in-game experience of any AHL team, and the fourth season of T-Birds hockey will be one you don't want to miss – so RISE UP and renew today!

Sincerest appreciation,

Nathan Costa
President, Springfield Thunderbirds

  /thunderbirdsahl @thunderbirdsahl /thunderbirdsahl @thunderbirdsahl

45 Bruce Landon Way, Springfield, MA 01103 (413) 739-GOAL   Fax: (413) 417-2308   springfieldthunderbirds.com

This letter illustrates the Springfield Thunderbirds' email campaign aimed at renewing current ticket holders.

Reprinted by permission from Todd McDonald, Springfield Thunderbirds.

> continued

> *continued*

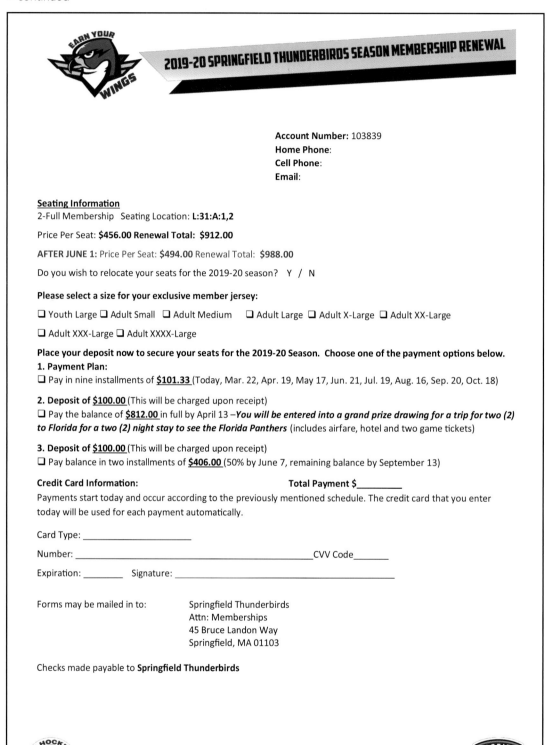

This letter illustrates the Springfield Thunderbirds' email campaign aimed at renewing current ticket holders. *(continued)*

Reprinted by permission from Todd McDonald, Springfield Thunderbirds.

(through letters, newsletters, video blasts, and other ways of sharing content that might be of interest to the recipient and be interesting enough for the recipient to share through social media with a wider audience)

- By soliciting input, opinions, and feedback with questionnaires, surveys, chat rooms, and other ways to create two-way dialogue
- By showing accountability and expanding the knowledge of the consumer with an annual report
- By sending thank-you correspondence that acknowledges the support of the consumer over the past year and asks for continued support
- By delivering invitations to special events and opportunities that may be of interest to the consumer or a member of the consumer's family or organization

Personal Selling

"Selling to customers and potential customers face to face, often in a retail or service environment, requires a particular set of skills. Sales people need to be highly aware of customer needs, able to recognize buying signals, and aware of the competitive advantage their goods or services offer. They also need to be highly skilled communicators; experts in reading body language; and have well-developed questioning, listening, and assertiveness skills."[23]

Although typically more costly than outbound phone calling, direct mail, and email selling techniques, personal selling can be more effective because it enables the seller and the prospect to engage in dialogue. Developing and maintaining a strong sales force can be one of the most expensive elements of the promotional mix, and the management and motivation of this sales force requires an experienced, gifted sales manager with exceptional observational, communicative, and motivational skills. Given that face-to-face selling in sports typically has closing rates in excess of 80 percent, the ROI in the sales force will be well worth the cost if a few simple rules are followed as outlined in table 12.2.

Personal selling involves the integration of data-based marketing, intelligent relationship marketing, and benefit selling to communicate effectively to consumers. Because data-based marketing has been discussed previously in this

TABLE 12.2 Rules for Effective Personal Selling

Rule	Rationale
Use data-based marketing.	Generate leads with a high likelihood of interest and ability to purchase. Score leads whenever possible.
Follow the LIBK rule—*let it be known you are in sales and what you are selling.*[24]	Be proud and enthusiastic about what you do and what you are selling. Carry yourself with the utmost professionalism in your manners and your dress.
Overcome objections and perceived barriers to the sale.	Be familiar with the most common objectives or barriers to the sale and modify the product or provide examples showing that people with the same objection have enjoyed the product.
Manage the conversation by being an effective listener as well as by stating your case.	Consumers want to be heard; they want affirmation to their concerns.
Employ consultative selling.	You are consulting by proposing possible solutions to the various needs and wants of the consumer.
Build your world and your customer's world around the strengths of your product, your service, and yourself.	Customers want to buy from strength; explaining a weakness detracts from their belief in the salesperson.
Match the consumer with the appropriate product.	A good sale fits the needs, budget, and lifestyle of the purchaser.
Always follow up.	Show the same level of interest after the sale as you do during the sale; the sale doesn't end with the first sale.

text, we will examine the other two elements to assess the contribution and importance of each to the personal-selling process.

Relationship Marketing

Futrell defines relationship marketing as "the creation of customer loyalty. Organizations use combinations of products, prices, distribution, promotions, and service to achieve this goal. Relationship marketing is based on the idea that important customers need continuous attention."[25] We believe this performance to be on the part of both the supplier and the customer and believe that besides enhancing performance, the goal is to extend the relationship. A sport organization using relationship marketing "is not seeking simply a sale or a transaction. It has targeted a major customer that it would like to sell to now and in the future."[26] Grönroos, an expert on relationship marketing, identified three main conditions under which relationship marketing is a successful and productive marketing approach:[27]

1. The customer has an ongoing desire for service.
2. The customer of the service controls the selection of the service supplier.
3. Alternative service suppliers are available.

These conditions are present in the sport marketplace, and they provide an excellent application forum for relationship marketing. In general, people who consume sport are highly involved consumers who have a desire for long-term association with a sport team, an event, or a branded product. The extremely competitive sport marketplace includes many providers for each sport product or service (not necessarily in the same sport type, but as a sport entertainment option), enabling the consumer to select from many providers.[28] Therefore, building a relationship with a customer is essential to retaining that person as a repeat customer.

Benefit Selling

Benefit selling involves matching the product or the delivery of product with the customer's preferences, thereby enhancing their experience. For example, for consumers who state that they cannot commit to a ticket plan because they don't know where they will be or what their schedule will look like several months in advance, benefit selling may be the answer. The concept of benefit selling has been responsible for the creation of many new products in the sport industry, one of the most popular of which has become Flex Books, or Flex Plans. These types of plans enable purchasers to use the tickets in any way that they choose—all at once, or in any combination adding up to the number of coupons purchased. Consumers benefit because they are not restricted to particular dates, and in some cases, they receive an extra coupon for a game to choose as an incentive to purchase the Flex Book or Flex Plan. The incentive for the organization is that the tickets are presold, so filling the seats does not depend on team performance, weather, or any other factors. The only limitation is that the coupon does not guarantee admission; redemption is based on availability and on whether the game is a premium game, such as opening day and concert dates.

For example, the State College (Pennsylvania) Spikes, a minor league affiliate of the St. Louis Cardinals, promotes its Flex Book as follows:[29]

- Each book contains 12 undated vouchers for the price of 10. Vouchers can be redeemed for tickets to any State College Spikes regular-season home game, based on availability.
- The plan is affordable and makes a great gift.
- It offers great flexibility. You can use all 12 vouchers at one game or come to 12 different games.
- Vouchers can be redeemed in person at the Medlar Field at Lubrano Park Box Office in advance or on the day of the game.
- Each voucher includes a money-saving coupon to be used at any State College or Milesburg McDonald's location (12 coupons per book).
- Each Flex Book also includes one coupon for either 10 free ball launch balls or five free "Closest to the Pin" golf balls to be used after any 2020 Spikes home game.

Taking the Sales Process to the Next Level

When these three approaches—data-based marketing, relationship marketing, and benefit selling—are integrated into the formulation of a personal-selling campaign and fine-tuned into a sales style involving the personality and experience of the salesperson, the results can be highly effective.

When combined with concepts such as sampling, trial usage, and open houses, personal selling can be even more effective, especially in certain segments of the sport industry, such as fitness clubs, sporting goods sales, and the sale of high-end professional sport seating options, such as club seats, loge boxes, and luxury and party suites. Sampling, trial usage, and open houses are designed to let the consumer experience the product.

Personal selling complements the experience by educating consumers about what they are experiencing and the benefits they are receiving. The fitness industry, for example, is a proponent of trial visits with professional instruction and attention. A sales presentation in the form of an interview between the salesperson and the prospective member usually follows the trial workout. The topics of the interview usually include patterns of physical activity, health and fitness goals, and the importance of wellness and regular physical activity, all in relationship to the

facility, equipment, and staff that the prospect has just experienced.

It has become common practice for both professional and college teams to use the open house concept, sometimes branding it as a select-a-seat event. The open house type of event usually occurs in the preseason (making weather a distinct factor for baseball teams in northern climates) and can include stadium tours; anthem singer auditions; and entertainment activities, such as mascots, clinics, and autographs. Most important, as potential consumers, attendees have the opportunity to sit in the seats available for sale. Balloons or flyers often designate available seats so that potential customers can identify the existing inventory and check out the view. After they are scated (indicating at least some level of interest), sales staff introduce themselves and, usually armed with a special offer that expires that day, initiate the personal-selling process.

Personal selling is especially effective for some types of ticket sales, such as group sales, but it is most important when used in the sale of premium seating options, such as suites, loge boxes, and courtside seats with club amenities—all products with significant hospitality and entertainment benefits to consider and sample in addition to

Athlete–fan interactions are a great way to take sales to the next level.

Ira L. Black/Corbis via Getty Images

the seating location. In regard to these particular products, personal selling becomes experiential selling because a visit-and-trial methodology is an important aspect of the sale and because the sales process usually begins with an invitation to sample by attending a game. The visit to the game usually includes some type of orientation, tour, and education for the buyer along with sampling the other benefits, such as food and club access. In a similar vein, corporate partnership sales and their related visits are best suited for personal selling.

Innovative Promotional Approaches for Selling Sport Products and Services

The unique nature of sport allows us to become highly imaginative in the sale of the sport product. Here are some additional reminders:

- *Education can sell the fan base.* Albert G. Spalding discovered more than 150 years ago that if people understood what his products were (at that point, baseball equipment) and how to use them and benefit from them, they would be more likely to play the game and have a need for his products.[30] Professional team sports, in particular football and hockey, have taken a similar approach and created courses such as Football 101 and Hockey 101 to educate fans on the rules, strategies, nuances, and complexities of the game by simplifying and explaining the terminology. Teams have also been known to offer clinics and demonstrations to help accomplish this educational process.

- *Remember your packaging.* Promotional activities and offers (discussed in chapter 8) can be effective in driving sales for a specific game, event, or period. One such promotion by the NBA's Minnesota Timberwolves is their "Birthday Club" promotion, which offered fans two free tickets on their birthday during the 2019 to 2020 season. The strategy, which resulted in over 20,000 sign-ups, is designed to attract new fans to the Timberwolves' newly renovated Target Center while providing the team with invaluable customer data and tens of thousands of new leads in the drive to boost attendance.[31]

- *Remember that fun is good.* The film *Field of Dreams* made famous the quotation "If you build it, they will come." This quotation now epitomizes the emphasis and dependence on building new stadiums and arenas not only to generate new revenue streams but also to provide an experience and a level of entertainment that is essential to the live experience of attending a sports event. Beginning in the 1940s with Bill Veeck's giveaways and promotions and continuing today with his son Mike and his MiLB franchises, the rally cry has been "If it's fun, they will come." The Veecks believed, and rightly so, that to attract fans, teams can't just sell their win-loss record. Teams have to sell the experience of a good time and the possibility of winning. Through promotional flair, understanding of hospitality management (cleanliness and comfort), and their commitment to fun, the Veecks established attendance records at all levels. Veeck staples, such as giveaway days with items like bats, fireworks nights, and special theme nights and concerts, have become commonplace not only in baseball but also in professional sports at all levels.[32]

- *Couponing is not just for groceries and fast food.* One of the most common complaints about attending a sports event is cost, particularly for families. Creative packaging can answer the need for affordable family entertainment options. Many sport organizations in both professional (major and minor league) and amateur sports (including those at colleges and universities) have developed and implemented one-price tickets for families. The package is usually based on four admissions, parking, and refreshments. Given that in today's world the traditional family of four is less prevalent than it was when this packaging began 20 to 30 years ago, it might make more sense to offer the pricing on an individual basis by pricing packages as low as US$11 per person or whatever makes up 25 percent of the price of the traditional family four-pack. In this manner, larger families will feel more welcome and single-parent households will recognize that this promotion is targeted to them as well. Inclusivity should result in increased sales. Some organizations elect to provide a souvenir (e.g., a cap, T-shirt, or other team novelty item), whereas others may elect to provide a voucher for a sponsor's product. Some organizations use a restaurant or pizza chain to provide the food items instead of providing them at the ballpark.

This arrangement is a good traffic driver to the sponsor's place of business.

- *Remember the profitability and effect of group sales.* As discussed earlier in this book, sport consumers usually do not attend sports events alone. Research has shown that fewer than 2 percent of fans attend games by themselves. We also noted that for some fans, the social interaction defines their enjoyment of the event and that for others, the social component may be their sole reason for attending. For these reasons, sport organizations should make every attempt to attract and sell tickets to large groups (25 or more). Depending on the size of the group and the retail ticket price, discounted ticket packages, as well as special seating sections and dining options (from catered sit-down dinners to picnics), are all effective means to attract a group to a sports event. Typical groups include youth sports teams and leagues, scouting organizations, church choirs, company employees, military units, and college students—any collective that meets or exceeds the franchise's minimum size for a group outing.

Use Your Assets to Sell, Part I

One of the most successful sales campaigns in the history of the New Jersey Nets (now the Brooklyn Nets) was the Influencer Program implemented before the 2005 to 2006 season. The signature marketing tool of former Nets' CEO Brett Yormark generated over US$1 million in new season-ticket sales in its first year and has since become a "best practice" emulated by many professional teams in various leagues.[33] The program is built on connectivity, hospitality, star power, face-to-face selling, and, of course, the perceived and actual influencing ability of the host. The program begins by having a current season-ticket holder host 30 or so friends and business connections not already season-ticket holders at his or her home or at another setting, such a business or country club. At this point, the team sales executives take over, providing hospitality and catering services as well as entertainment (mascot, dance teams) and a representative from the coaching staff or a current or retired player. The business side is usually represented by the senior level team executive who provides a state-of-the-team overview before asking for the sale.

This form of influencer marketing, novel at the time, initially was related to celebrity and athlete endorsement and is now a large part of social media because trust, experience, nonaffiliation, and firsthand knowledge by previous consumers or users can dictate the financial fortunes of restaurants, music, film, apparel, equipment, and almost anything you can imagine. Influencer marketing is an updated approach to marketing and public relations in which marketers target the people to whom prospects turn for information. These influencers help generate awareness and sway the purchase decisions of those who seek out and value their expertise, read their blogs, converse with them in discussion forums, attend their presentations at industry events, and so on.[34] In sport, other season-ticket holders, corporate partners, suite owners, and the like are considered influencers. Their opinions, whether positive or negative, can sway prospects who are involved in the decision-making process.

Use Your Assets to Sell, Part II

The goal of every sport marketer in the repeat attendance business is to provide consumers with an enjoyable experience and a lasting, positive memory that will encourage them not only to attend again but also to become customer evangelists by spreading the word to their friends and associates. One of the best ways to do this is to give them some personal connection to the event that anchors their experience. Group sales (previously discussed in this chapter) provide an ideal target for the selling of assets to create a memory and a story that both can be shared and retold. Assets come in many forms—honorary captains, ball kids, anthem singers, halftime performers, and a variety of others. For instance, many professional sport teams offer dance clinics conducted by the team's dance team as part of a group ticket package. The ticket price usually includes a clinic with the dancers during the day when the participants are taught a routine that they will perform with the dance team during halftime of that night's game, which is the asset. Another option used by baseball, hockey, and basketball teams to sell group tickets is offering the opportunity for local youth teams to play a game on the field, ice, or court of the professional team. This event is usually called Field of Dreams, Court of Dreams, or Arena of Dreams, depending on the sport. Last, but certainly not least, many teams provide fundraising opportunities for organizations in their communities to raise funds.

Online Sales

Websites can be used as stand-alone sales tools or as part of an interactive sales approach that brings the website to life through other technological aids or pairs it with a telemarketer to assist in the sales process. The trend in developing websites as sales tools is to make the process as simple as possible by using technology and interactive video components to enable the visitor to see all available seating options, compare them, price them, and purchase them online. Several teams have added a live chat button in case the visitor has questions or issues and wants to speak to someone on the sales staff. Even teams and organizations that employ a variety of pricing techniques have been able to create web pages that explain the process clearly and enable visitors to purchase tickets.

One of the best examples of an interactive web sales approach that sport teams use works as follows. The current or potential customer first receives an email with a link to the team website. Once on the website, the customer or prospect is asked to enter a favorite jersey number and telephone number. After entering the information, the customer watches a video of the team's coach and GM talking about how important the customer is to the franchise. At the conclusion of the video, the customer's phone rings: The caller is a representative from one of the team's sales representatives who offers the opportunity to purchase a ticket plan. This approach integrates email, the team website, and outbound phone calling to capture the customer's attention and induce the prospect to act and possibly forward the email to friends and associates because of the coolness factor alone. This viral referral process then identifies additional prospects for the team.

Total Inventory Plan: The Ticket Sales Sandwich

What type of full menu should a sport franchise offer in order to have a balanced ticket-sales inventory? Executives of the NBA's Team Marketing and Business Operations (so-called "TEAMBO") were the first to illustrate their recommendations in the form of a "ticket-sales sandwich" (figure 12.4). The intent of the club

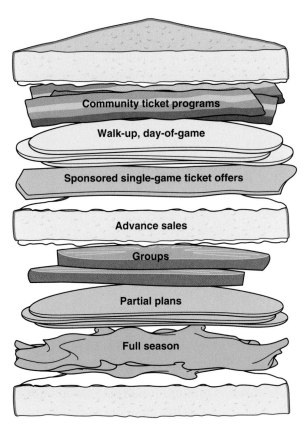

FIGURE 12.4 The "ticket-sales sandwich" components of an effective ticket-sales plan.

sandwich model is to ensure balance and thus minimize dependence on any one ticket-purchasing segment.

In our ticket-sales sandwich model, the "meat" (our apologies to vegetarians and vegans!), or main course, is the full and partial season-ticket holders. Because this group attends the highest percentage of games, it is the most important ingredient in the sandwich. However, as with any good sandwich, it needs to be complemented by a variety of other ingredients. Group-ticket sales, involving a large volume of tickets, are the next most important ingredient in our sandwich. Our final stage of sandwich construction consists of the "condiments" ingredients, selected according to individual preference. A sport organization may prefer to use more than one condiment or to rely heavily on one condiment because the proverbial refrigerator is bare. Condiments include advance ticket sales (sold by in-house phone sales, web sales, and social media sales, including Groupon, Facebook, and Twitter offers), walk-up and day-of-game sales, and complimentary tickets disbursed through community relations programs and activities. Because the flavor of the sandwich will change with the type and amount of ingredients added or the combination of those ingredients, so too will organizational profit margins (e.g., if there are too few season-ticket holders and too many groups or walk-ups). We recommend ingredients in the following proportions for a good-tasting and profitable ticket-sales sandwich:

- Full and partial season tickets: 80 percent
- Groups: 10 percent
- Individual game tickets, community program and sponsored single-game tickets: 10 percent

Because team performance can have a significant influence on the construction of your club sandwich, we have identified certain activities in terms of sales and retention to undertake depending on team performance. Table 12.3 illustrates situational selling factors as they relate to team performance.

The sidebar on the next page taps into the experience and insights of noted NBA sales consultant Dr. Bill Sutton on full-menu selling.

Pricing Basics

Knowing the basics of pricing, whether it's for tickets, merchandise, or luxury suites, is critical for a sport organization. For example, knowing how to price each part of the club sandwich is important because the people consuming each part of the sandwich have different wants and needs.

Marketers must recognize the vast range of product elements that require pricing. In the sport world, these elements include the following:

TABLE 12.3 Situational Selling Factors Related to Team Performance

Declining or losing team	Improving team	Successful team
Adds staff to sell inventory	Adds staff to capitalize on perception and move inventory	Lays off new sales staff because of lack of inventory, but team converts them to service and retention consultants instead
Adds discounts to attract buyers	Uses discounts to create up-selling opportunities	Eliminates discounts but keeps stepped-up pricing so it costs more per ticket to buy a partial plan than a full plan, and it costs more to buy a single game ticket at the gate in advance
Adds ticket plan options—a plan for every fan	Offers a variety of ticket-plan options, but teams push higher-cost plans	Offers few plans, possibly only full- and half-season options
Emphasizes group sales to create a few sellouts, offers a variety of discounts	Uses groups to sell out, leverages attractions by forcing purchase of a lesser game, offers limited discounts	Limits group inventory, has no discounting
Heavily emphasizes sales training and sales contests	Heavily emphasizes sales training and sales contests	Focuses sales training or sales contests on increasing account value
Offers payment plans	Offers payment plans	Offers incentives for payment in full
Adds promotional nights and giveaways	Uses promotional nights as peak on peak to sell out targeted games	Uses premium giveaways for sponsor activation purposes rather than to attract attendance

Full-Menu Selling and Other Thoughts for Ticket-Sales Success

Bill Sutton, Principal of Bill Sutton and Associates

I have long been a believer in full-menu selling. I know this is contrary to what some of my industry friends and even my clients believe and practice, but today I really don't see an alternative—and, in fact, I think it is a best practice. The Internet and, in particular, the secondary market have made sure that potential consumers have a variety of options to consider prior to making a purchase. So let me make my case.

Selling only full-season tickets in many cases is forcing buyers to purchase more than they need or more than they want. I understand why many teams prefer to operate this way. Once a full seat is sold, it is sold. A half season requires two sales and a partial plan, depending upon the number of games in the season and in the plan, can require as many as eight people to buy that same seat. However, everyone that buys a full-season ticket and doesn't use the full amount of tickets in the plan in effect becomes a broker selling those tickets through the team website or on a variety of ticket reselling sites. I have recently begun making the argument that the teams themselves are responsible for the creation of the secondary market, because the unwanted tickets that the purchasers are now selling constitute a large portion of the inventory that makes the secondary market a viable business.

In a related issue, the team is often selling against itself as its own season-ticket holders are selling their unwanted inventory, which, in some cases, can be better than that being offered by the team. In addition to the location possibly being better than what remains in the team inventory, the sellers might be motivated to sell those tickets below what they have originally paid for the ticket, making what they have a "bargain" and driving more bargain hunters to shop the secondary market.

If buyers feel they were forced to buy something they didn't want and had difficulty selling the excess inventory, they are less likely to renew that plan the following season, thus losing a customer and the lifetime value that could have been. Research shows that unused tickets are one of the top reasons for nonrenewals.

By not selling the full menu simultaneously and telling the interested buyer that those plans aren't available for sale, the team runs the risk that the interested buyer who is ready to make the commitment to a smaller plan might find something else to do with those funds while waiting to be contacted at a later date. Car expenses, braces, unexpected expenses, and even buying tickets to another sport are all possible outcomes when the team says that the product the consumer is willing to buy is unavailable. Why would you not take the money when it is offered?

There is a fear that by selling the full menu simultaneously, that sales people will take the easy sale without asking for the bigger sale—the full-season ticket. There is probably some truth to this concern as sales people get paid on sales and if they can make the sale, some people will be happy with any amount rather than ending the conversation without a sale.

Finally, organizations place a higher emphasis on the full-season ticket, and at league and annual meetings, teams are rewarded for the number of full-season tickets sold, not FSEs (full-season equivalencies or total ticket revenue). This causes sales training and day-to-day emphasis to be much heavier on the full-season sales.

Now that I have criticized this approach, I will offer what I think is a fair response. This situation addresses my concerns while providing a way for teams to continue to emphasize the sale of full-season tickets without missing other revenue.

Begin selling the full menu next season with the following parameters:

- Begin the sales conversation as you have been instructed and trained in the past.
- If the customer is not interested in the full-season ticket, ask how many games they might be interested in attending.
- Based upon that response, explain that the seating locations are set based upon the number of games purchased—the larger the plan, the better the seats.
- Go through the full menu, and try to close the plan that best fits what the consumer is most interested in.
- Take payment in full or at least a deposit.
- Explain to the buyer that you won't be assigning a specific seating location until the game plans for the full-season ticket buyers (and the halves if you are selling a partial plan) have been assigned. At this point, you should have a general idea of where the seats will be assigned because of the price associated with that ticket plan.
- Create an in-person event for all of the non-full-season ticket buyers in order to select their seats.
- At the event, the sales team has another chance to show partial-plan buyers other locations for larger game plans in case seeing the actual locations might influence their decision and willingness to buy more games for a better location.
- You may now formally close the sale knowing that buyers are satisfied (at least initially) with what they have purchased and that the sales team has exhausted every opportunity to sell a larger plan.

Years ago, my colleagues Bernie Mullin, Steve Hardy, and I conceived of a model called the escalator in our textbook *Sport Marketing*. The key was getting a consumer on the escalator and endeavoring to move them up by increasing their frequency of attendance. I have come to believe that the model in 2018 is an elevator, because I feel it is acceptable if the frequency remains constant over a period of years and may actually fluctuate with performance and other factors. My essential premise is to get them in the building and retain them—focusing on lifetime value.

Reprinted by permission from B. Sutton, "Full Menu Selling and Other Thoughts for Ticket Sales Success," *Sports Business Journal*, May 21, 2019.

- Hard or soft goods (equipment or apparel)
- Tickets
- Memberships
- Daily usage fees (court times, tee times, lift tickets, and so on)
- Concessions (food and novelties)
- Content (social media, apps, streaming, cable, satellite TV, videos, magazines, and so on)
- Access for corporate entities (entitlement space, signage, naming rights, activation platforms, banner ads, and web links)
- Image (logo, photo, and LED signage)
- Hospitality
- Premium seating
- Exclusive association
- Commercial time and exposure

These elements are priced according to a range of variables including location, time, uniqueness, demand, quality, quantity, and desirability.

Price is a critical element in the marketing mix for several reasons:

1. Prices can be readily changed.
2. In certain market conditions (specifically, where demand is elastic), price is one of the most effective tools.

3. Price is highly visible; therefore, changes are easily communicated, resulting in possible changes in consumer perceptions.

4. Price is never far from the consumer's mind and is often a key determinant in the decision of whether to buy.

The core issues in any pricing situation are cost, value, and objectives. Customer satisfaction can be expressed as

$$\text{Satisfaction} = \text{Benefit} - \text{Cost}$$

Cost is the most visible and often the most compelling part of the equation. For the consumer attending a sports event, the ticket price does not represent the real cost of attendance, which would include travel, parking or public transportation, concessions, and possibly souvenirs of the experience. The ticket price might also contain a service charge or handling fees, depending on how it was purchased.

Yield Management and Pricing Strategies

An effective sales organization employs a variety of pricing strategies from time to time to ensure that the product, particularly tickets, can be purchased by the broadest range of potential buyers. This overall concept, often referred to as yield management, includes both pricing and packaging of tickets to ensure the highest yield on the sale of the product. The following sidebar focuses on yield management as it relates to pure pricing initiatives. Later, we explore yield management in terms of packaging and promotional activities.

Yield Management for Sport Organizations

Lou DePaoli, Former EVP/CRO, New York Mets

For over 40 years, the concepts of "yield management" and "revenue management" have been prevalent in most industries as a way to strategically grow revenues. In its simplest form, yield management is the process of understanding the supply-and-demand curve specific to your inventory and knowing how to find the right price for your product in order to sell it to the right customer at the right time in order to maximize revenues preferably without sacrificing units sold. The most well-known example of this concept in action would be the airlines. As an example, two people sitting next to each other on a flight from New York to Chicago might pay very different prices for their flights. Why? The airlines have implemented complex algorithms based on many variables, predominantly supply and demand, to determine how to price their product at that moment in order to maximize revenues and have full flights in order to cover the costs associated with operating each flight.

Similar to the airline industry, effective yield management is very important for sport organizations and has become more commonplace as teams and leagues are implementing this strategy in an effort to increase revenues and fill ballparks/arenas/stadiums while also managing to remain an affordable live entertainment option. Unlike the airline industry, sports fans have multiple options to engage with their favorite sport teams without actually attending a game (i.e., watching from their couch on a giant 4K HDTV, streaming via their mobile device or team sports app, or listening on radio); thus, teams and leagues have become even more cognizant of maintaining the proper balance between available inventory and pricing of that inventory in order to manage brand perception. Charge too much, and you potentially have empty seats that damage the perception of demand and curbs future sales. Charge too little, and you potentially cannot generate enough revenue to cover your costs, which then leads to reductions in payroll and eventually a reduction in sales. Thus, finding the proper balance of pricing and inventory is so critical for sport organizations.

Here are my recommended steps to ensure successful yield management for sport organizations:

- *Organizational buy-in.* The entire organization needs to understand that their supply, demand, and perception of demand are all in constant state of change and that the organization needs to be nimble enough to adapt with the changing market conditions. What worked for you in the past in terms of pricing decisions is almost certainly not the right strategy going forward, as the marketplace and technology are constantly evolving. For decades pricing decisions in sports were decided by a small group within an organization and usually not very data driven. Typically, someone would suggest the prices increase by +$X per ticket or by +X% as they were trying to back into a revenue target based on an assumed attendance goal. Since 2010, organizations have started to understand that poor yield management as it relates to your ticketing inventory can have disastrous consequences for years to come.

- *Understand YOUR marketplace.* What may work in one market or sport might not work in yours. Just because a team in your league, or in your market, is handling yield management a certain way doesn't mean it is the correct strategy for you. You can learn a lot from peers and by what is happening in your market, but you need to be cognizant of how these decisions might impact your brand. Successful yield management is definitely *not* a one-size-fits-all approach. That said, you need to look at your peers within your league, other teams in your market, general costs for other forms of entertainment, etc. in helping to provide context, however.

- *Data, data, and more data.* One of my favorite sayings is "You can never have too much data," especially as it relates to yield management. Gather as much data as possible from your primary and secondary market sales down to the individual seat level, and look at the sell-through, yield, retention rate, the timing of when the seat was sold via which channel the seat was sold, demographics of who purchased the seat, and so on. This data will provide a snapshot of the supply, demand, and pricing on a per-seat level that can be turned into a heat map of your market sales.

- *Understand the secondary market.* The secondary, or resale, market has been around forever, but it was something of an underground business that many teams and fans didn't necessarily want to admit existed or partake in. Advances in technology have made it much easier for fans and resellers/brokers to buy and sell tickets. Accessing the same sell-through information from the secondary market as the primary market is another valuable data point that should be added to your seat-by-seat sell-through analysis. The secondary market data can be very helpful in improving ticket pricing, but careful analysis is crucial. Proper analysis of secondary market data in conjunction with primary market analysis will generate better pricing strategies for sport organizations.

- *Understand the implications.* One item on effective yield management for sport organizations is to understand that, many times, the supply and demand affects your pricing in ways that are outside of theoretical expectations. There are times when demand is so high that pricing skyrockets as fans become willing to pay "whatever it takes" to attend a specific game or event (World Series, Super Bowl, The Masters, etc.). In the case of that happening for a team or league, it is a case of second-guessing: "Did we leave money on the table by pricing too low?" That is what some would describe as a "good problem to have." The flip side, however, is not.

When demand drops significantly, yield management models will show that the price of the tickets should go down dramatically as well. It is at that point an organization

> *continued*

> continued

needs to look at the impact of having prices drop and how they want to address the major issues related to reducing pricing. For example, if a team's pricing drops by 20% below the expected level, then they need to generate 25% more sales volume in order to be even in terms of expected revenue. Generally, that doesn't occur because once demand falls significantly enough, the demand for tickets is nil until the price is almost zero.

• *Remember the fans.* Yield management and other strategies are all theoretical; remember that you need to get your fans to engage with and embrace the strategies, which is not always an easy task. Remember that the goal of effective yield management is to find the proper balance between pricing and sales volume to increase volume and revenues. If that balance gets upset in either direction, the impact of yield management will in all likelihood be greatly diminished and will potentially have a negative impact on your brand as a whole. Proper messaging containing clear and concise wording along with key data points are recommended when rolling out price changes.

As sport organizations have begun to look closer at yield management, three distinct pricing strategies have emerged: premium pricing, variable pricing, and dynamic pricing. None of these concepts is new, but they are now becoming more widely utilized by organizations and accepted by fans. Below is a brief synopsis of how each impacts yield management:

• *Premium pricing:* Take a game that comes with inherently high demand (opening day for most MLB clubs, a rivalry game in college football, etc.) that will sell out immediately and increase the prices based on that demand. The pricing is higher than the other games on the schedule, but it is based on the theory that this specific game has much higher demand. If something changes during the season to negatively or positively impact demand, the prices for these games are locked in.

• *Variable pricing:* Applying different price scales based on different factors, such as opponent, event, time of season, day of week, etc. As an example, a team might have three different tiers of pricing for games in an MLB season: "Gold" games would feature the highest prices and could include opening day, rival matchups, the final weekend, and marquee interleague matchups. "Silver" games would have the next highest prices for games of above-average demand, such as specific weekend games between June and August. "Bronze" games would have the lowest demand games of the season, typically weekday games early in the season, and would be the lowest price tier. As with premium pricing, if something changes during the season to negatively or positively impact demand, the prices for these games are locked in.

• *Dynamic pricing:* Dynamic pricing allows for the ticket prices to change on a specified basis (i.e., in real time, hourly, daily, etc., depending on your technology and business rules) based on the demand for that game. This is exactly how the secondary market operates and is something more and more organizations are implementing because it allows teams to raise and lower prices as the season goes along in real time, depending on the change in demand. So if a team is on a hot streak and demand increases, the prices will climb too, which generates more revenue on a real-time basis. The risk is that the opposite can also occur; demand drops sharply, and the pricing would then adjust with it, potentially generating less revenue than anticipated. Dynamic pricing is something sport organizations need to be very careful with implementing and executing as it has the potential to drive incremental revenue when demand is stable or increasing, but it could severely hurt revenue if demand is decreasing. Thus, there are currently many different dynamic pricing models in play across the sport industry.

The bottom line is, organizations that understand and maximize yield management will perform better than their peers, all things being equal.

Secondary Ticket Market

One of the biggest challenges to sport organizations is the availability of tickets in the secondary market and the ease of purchasing them in that way, often at prices below the current asking price of the team producing the event. Arguably, today's secondary market, which includes major players, such as SeatGeek, StubHub, Ticketmaster, and VividSeats, has become the primary ticket market for consumers and properties. In many cases, the sport property itself has now effectively become the primary and secondary market seller. By partnering with traditional secondary market vendors and brokers and by seamlessly offering the best tickets available on the property's own website (regardless of whether the inventory has never been sold, or it is "returned" inventory from the secondary market), the fan buys the best seat available directly from the property with full authentication and assurance that the ticket can be transferred electronically for others to use.

Why is this the case? To state the matter simply, for a price-based, the secondary ticket market offers a variety of prices, all of which, except for the marquee opponent games, are usually less than the team offers because the team has a higher cost of doing business. The team or organization must pay the talent, produce the game, and maintain the stadium and the costs related to the fan experience. The secondary market has none of those costs because resellers purchase inventory from consumers (and, in some cases, knowingly or unknowingly directly from the team itself) who have previously purchased from the team and are not planning to attend the games.

The secondary market has always existed. In the past, it was referenced under the collective term *scalper*. The original role of scalpers was to buy low and sell high for high-demand games and special events. Now their role is to buy and sell at a profit, regardless of whether the game is sold out or is a high-demand game. What has changed is that the primary market, and the sport leagues in general, have legitimized the idea of buying tickets from a source other than the team itself by signing sponsorship agreements with these secondary market sources, particularly StubHub (whose parent company is eBay Inc.). In effect, sport organizations have granted them the only thing they lacked—recognition as a

credible, trustworthy source for purchasing tickets. We might argue that the sponsorship deals offered the leagues and their teams a way to benefit financially from at least one aftermarket source because the fans were already routinely buying and selling their tickets offline and online anyway.

But the issue is much more complicated than just the fact that the secondary market sells tickets. Many season-ticket holders purchase their tickets from the team knowing that they will not be attending all the games in their plan. Thus, the opportunity to resell their tickets to offset the costs and, in some cases, to resell them at a higher price than they paid for them can be a critical factor in the decision to purchase the season tickets in the first place. All Ticketmaster teams and organizations offer their season-ticket holders a special web page or an app where they can sell their tickets online. The money is first credited to their season-ticket account. The team encourages the sellers to apply the funds to the next year's season tickets, but they can also request a payment from those funds at the end of the season. Thus, ticket-reselling options are a real benefit to the season-ticket holder.

Secondary markets also offer benefits to non-season ticket holders, a market that is growing as younger fans shy away from the rigidity of season-ticket packages.[36]

Secondary market sellers have the ability to offer packages containing games or events from every team or entertainment venue in the same market, allowing the consumer to enjoy a variety of sport and entertainment experiences without owning multiple ticket plans. This is also becoming more common with regard to suites and other premium seating options. Package flexibility has also emerged. Although some innovative sport organizations are allowing a flex spending approach to ticket buying where the buyer agrees to spend a certain amount of revenue, electing to purchase different types of seating options at prices and locations based upon the buyer's needs throughout the season, secondary sellers have offered this option for years, and it has been very successful.

Consider this comparison: Everyone knows that if you go to a pizza shop, it is always less expensive to purchase the whole pie rather than a number of slices customized to the buyer's preference. Yet, in our current marketplace, customization, and as Burger King would say "having it my way," appears to be king.

The NBA and Ticketmaster have created a centralized online portal for fans, designed to serve as one-stop shopping for all NBA tickets, because it consolidates the teams' primary and secondary ticket-selling options in one place. Users are directed to a page containing all available ticket options for each team, including secondary ticket listings.

In 2018, MLB attendance declined for the fifth time in six seasons and at a faster rate than prior years. Among the contributing factors is consumer confusion during ticket purchasing. Oakland A's president Dave Kaval argues that "It's become too complicated and confusing for fans in a lot of cases, and there are a lot of competing offers out there."[37] Both clubs and StubHub recognize a need for greater coordination in customer outreach and sales.

Firms like Eventellect and Dynasty Sports & Entertainment have emerged to address that very issue. With more marketplaces, it is more critical than ever for properties to manage and strategically deploy their inventory. These firms leverage data insights to specifically target and sell tickets on both primary and secondary markets. These platforms, like most marketplaces, also have the potential to track a ticket's life cycle, giving properties a better understanding of who holds the ticket as well as when and for how long a customer holds it. This data has potential benefits for understanding ticket sales and consumer behaviors, even extending to in-event marketing and better understanding of customer needs.[38]

Customer Lifetime Value, Service, and Retention

The best way to understand the importance of your relationship with a new customer is through the concept of customer lifetime value (CLV). CLV is "the total worth to a business of a customer over the whole period of their relationship. It's an important metric as it costs less to keep existing customers than it does to acquire new ones, so increasing the value of your existing customers is a great way to drive growth."[39] CLV is a formula that helps a marketing manager arrive at the dollar value associated with the long-term rela-

tionship with any given customer, revealing both the cost and the net worth of that relationship over time. Thus, for example, in terms of value, we should look at a season-ticket holder not as a US$4,000 annual spend but as someone who, depending on current age, could spend at least that amount every year, and in addition, pay for price increases, parking, and per capita spending on concessions, parking, merchandise, and other possible spending options each year, possibly exceeding US$100,000 over a 20-year period.

Acknowledgement of the CLV concept has resulted in a paradigm shift in sales departments, as client servicing and retention has become as valued, if not more so, than making 100 outbound calls a day to try and land new customers. Remember the old sales adage: 80 percent of your sales will come from 20 percent of your customers. Teams have invested a great deal more resources in the creation and success of their client service and retention departments, and now they are also adopting new tactics for retaining valued customers. Hence, we have seen more and more teams implement loyalty and rewards programs (not unlike airlines, hotels, and restaurants) that offer their current season-ticket holders with additional perks (e.g., experiential opportunities, limited-edition team merchandise) tied to everything from number of games attended to number of team-related retweets and posts. Teams are also turning from calling their customers season-ticket holders to referring to them as members. This not only has psychic benefits for loyal fans but also (akin to country club and gym memberships) conveys membership status throughout the entire year, complete with year-round team-related events and communications. Finally, teams are engaging technology via both their websites and smartphones, enabling their members to automatically renew their ticket plans without even needing to speak with the team's ticket sales department!

Obviously, customers have different values to an organization, depending on the types of customer (sponsor, corporate buyer, personal buyer), the amount of revenue they contribute in relationship to the cost of servicing them, and the estimated time that they are projected to be with the organization. The more valuable the customer is, the more effort the staff must expend to retain that customer. Figure 12.5 illustrates how a customer's value can be moderated.

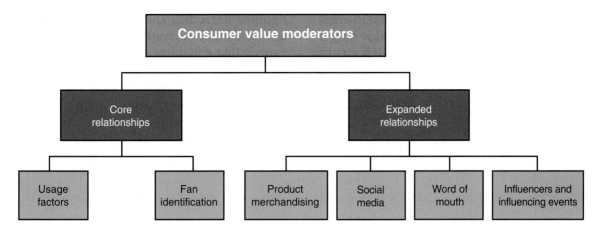

FIGURE 12.5   An organization can increase a customer's value in a variety of ways.

Given the potential CLV, it is clear that certain activities and efforts must follow completion of the sale to ensure that the customer renews and continues an ongoing relationship or becomes a repeat buyer.

Sport organizations should develop customer service and retention programs that encompass at least the following:

- Offering ongoing personalized customer contact and treatment
- Conducting regular customer satisfaction surveys or audits, both via email and in-person focus groups
- Creating and sponsoring special events and activities for preferred customers
- Maintaining a database of current customers and defectors
- Creating a website with special content and features for preferred customers
- Producing a newsletter and distributing that content on a regular basis
- Offering frequency incentive programs (customer loyalty programs)
- Conducting stakeholder meetings or luncheons to gather feedback
- Creating exclusive-access events for preferred customers to demonstrate and show appreciation
- Providing special access to players and other organizational assets that are not available to the public

No matter how successful an organization is at servicing its clientele, some customers will discontinue their purchasing and thus end their relationship for one reason or another. Customers who leave an organization are often referred to as defectors because, in effect, they defect to another product or brand. Defectors are costly to an organization, not only because the organization loses their potential lifetime value but also because replacing them is expensive in terms of time and resources. According to some estimates, replacing a customer costs up to five times more than servicing an existing customer.[40] To prevent defection and, at the same time, attract new customers, increasingly more professional sport teams and other organizations have begun to refer to their season-ticket and premium-seating customers as members and develop benefits accordingly. Michelle Price, Director of Client Retention for the Washington Nationals, shares her insights on best practices as well as what she looks for in hiring salespeople for her department.

Maybe everyone can't be a member, but in the words of Blanchard and Bowles, everyone can be a "raving fan"—those consumers who are so excited and pleased with the product that they not only remain loyal but also help attract new customers through word of mouth and now through social media, by blogging, tweeting, and sharing content and experiences.[41]

How can sport consumers become raving fans? Given the emotional nature of sport, sport consumers are already more emotional about their product compared to other consumers. Sport consumers have stronger feelings that elicit higher highs and lower lows. Because sport marketers don't control product composition or

Michelle Price, Director of Client Retention, Washington Nationals

In my role, I'm responsible for the service and retention of season-ticket holders. At first glance, service and retention seem to go together like hot dogs and peanuts at a baseball game. Makes sense, right? We service accounts to retain them. But when you really stop to think about it, they are different. *Service* is made up of the things that we do. We hear it all of the time to "be of service": It refers to an action. It's the events, discounts, access, friendly and helpful staff, or rewards that we provide our clients. *Retention*, or loyalty, is a behavior that we are consistently trying to evoke. It's actually a goal that we're trying to accomplish. To be responsible for both the journey and the destination of clients is a huge responsibility that accounts for the largest piece of revenue for organizations, and that's why there is more of a focus on service and retention than ever before.

Any organization in the sport industry is focused on growing revenue. If you view "revenue" as water, the goal would be to hold as much water as possible and then be able to increase the amount of water you can hold year after year. Service and retention play the part of the vessel in which you're holding the water. If the vessel is like a colander with water just draining out, then an organization would be in big trouble. The stronger the vessel, and the less water that drips out each year, then the stronger the organization's ability to grow revenue.

When I was coming up the ranks with the Boston Celtics, the natural progression in ticket sales was to start as an inside sales representative and move up to account executive. It was a very general position—and because the position was very general, the account executives did everything. They sold new season tickets, renewed accounts, booked group tickets and suite nights, and handled all of the day-to-day interactions with their clients. It wasn't until about the late 2000s that teams began to realize the value of having specific teams specializing in specific roles and goals. It makes perfect sense now, although at the time, it was somewhat of a paradigm shift in how professional sports teams constructed their sales departments.

So when teams moved to having dedicated service and retention teams, everything was great, right? Well, things improved, but all of a sudden, teams had to compete with secondary markets and other outlets to purchasing tickets. In an effort to differentiate, teams loaded up on the exclusive benefits that only season-ticket holders could receive.

That's how we got to where we are today with many teams (the Washington Nationals included) moving to a so-called "membership model" for season tickets. Season tickets have historically been about the location of seats and the price. Today, it's about so much more. We live—and sell—in a society with apps, on-demand TV, no commercial breaks, chat-bots, one-click purchasing, and day-of delivery for everything. Convenience, entertainment options, and buying options are endless, so teams and organizations need to adapt to compete. It's now about providing our "members" with year-round engagement through access to exclusive events, unique assets and benefits, special rewards, and personalized service that's tailored to meet the needs of each client.

Now, let me clarify something: Nobody *needs* season tickets. Even our die-hard fans. It's a product that falls into the "*want*" category more often than not. So, with retention in mind, we gear our services to increase the value proposition. If we can get our season-ticket accounts to feel like they get more in return for the price they pay, then we're able to renew and retain them. Remember, we service so we can sell and retain.

Key Things That We Do as a Service and Retention Team

- *Exclusive events.* Autograph sessions, field/court time, meet and greets, photo opportunities, Q&As with coaches and players, etc.

- *Rewards.* Loyalty rewards programs, gifts, autographed items, upgraded seats, parking, concierge programs, access to unique events based on tenure, etc.
- *Discounts.* Savings on merchandise and concessions; special pricing on concerts, play-offs, and additional tickets
- *Convenience.* Digital ticketing, ticket exchange programs, dedicated entry and concession lines
- *Touch points.* Handwritten notes, birthdays and anniversary celebrations, phone calls, out-of-office appointments, tutorial/educational sessions, seat visits, and more

Requirements for Being on a Service and Retention Team

- *Superior service.* You have to genuinely like to work with people, get to know them, and want to make their experience the best one possible. That requires friendliness, willingness to help, being proactive, patience, listening, positivity, and so much more. Sometimes the relationship that an account has with their service representative is the difference maker when it comes to their renewal.
- *Build relationships and be curious.* The more we know about our accounts, the better we can service them. If I don't know who your favorite player is, how will I know to invite you to a meet and greet opportunity with that player, should one present itself?
- *You have to want to sell and make suggestions.* We aren't a sales team, but we all sell, just in a different way. Arguably, we are better sellers because we sell accounts on coming back year after year. It's impossible to not be revenue minded when we oversee the largest portion of revenue for an organization.
- *Be a task master.* Expectations of my team are: 150+ calls per week and 10 hours of weekly talk time. We have a lot of accounts and responsibilities, so organizing and blocking out time is vital.
- *Control what you can control.* We can't control wins and losses, the traffic coming to the stadium, the lines at concessions, the weather, or the moves our GM makes. But we can control our attitude, our efforts, and [our] actions.

No matter the sport, league, or city you're in, these skill sets and mindsets all translate. Whether I was servicing a group account with the Boston Celtics, renewing a season-ticket holder with the New York Mets, or, as these days, servicing a "member" of the Washington Nationals, the goal is always to add value to every interaction, exceed what's expected, and represent the brand to the best of my ability. As service and retention professionals, if we continually strive to find new ways to delight our customers, then we can adapt to any situation and retain our fans year after year.

performance, they must aggressively strive to ensure customer satisfaction as it relates to product extensions and the experience itself, which usually involve high levels of interaction and service. All sport organizations should develop a customer service and retention program in the hopes of retaining current customers, growing relationships with those customers, and attracting new customers through their overall service quality and their demonstrated interest in the well-being of their customers. The integral aspects of retention are satisfaction, utilization,

and enjoyment of what the customer has purchased. Although that might seem simple (and in many ways, it is), the subjectivity of customers with regard to the sometimes-emotional purchase of a sport-related product may complicate the decision to renew or buy again. Thus, the overall approach to this problem is to improve the fan experience.

As noted at the outset of this chapter, sport organizations are increasingly facing challenges to their efforts to generate ticket sales that result in "fannies in seats." Among other factors, tech-

Should I Sell a Mobile Pass or Take a Pass? Pros and Cons

Bill Sutton

Attendance at movie theaters fell 6 percent in 2017, and the majority of baseball games were played to less than 70 percent of capacity, indicating a significant number of empty seats. As sport and entertainment venues try to capitalize on the attention and wallets of millennials, the monthly pass has become en vogue for both entertainment and sports—primarily baseball. While it looks like some easy return on empty seats, that might not tell the entire story.

Both movie theaters and baseball stadiums are trying to fill a lot of inventory: 365 dates for movie theaters and 81 dates for baseball teams—thus, selling a monthly pass enabling the buyer to attend all or a significant portion of the monthly dates. Most baseball teams do not include opening day or some key series that usually sell out. The teams (and theaters) are subscribing to the adage that the most expensive seat in the house is an empty seat—a position I have long advocated—but, the pass concept has made me reconsider my position. In part, the pass programs rely on traditional subscription economics: More people pay than actually attend, thus there is money commonly referred to as "breakage." There are little to no costs associated with breakage (not attending), the profit for the games not attended is 100 percent, and that looks pretty good considering it was an empty seat.

Why will it work? Because millennials are familiar with subscription services through Netflix, Hulu, Amazon Prime, and so forth. This concept for both baseball and the movies is right in line with that. The pass program doesn't guarantee a seat location or, in some cases, even a seat. The St. Louis Cardinals pass is standing room only, but "the Cardinals Ballpark Pass gives our fans another flexible and affordable option to take in a Cardinals game at their leisure," said Joe Strohm, Vice President of Ticket Sales. "We believe this ticket subscription service is a perfect fit for millennials and young professionals that may be a bit more spontaneous in planning their visits to Busch Stadium."

What are the objectives in offering such a subscription plan?

- Moving the millennials from the couch to the venue and experiencing the event live and with other people. Also, being exposed to the technology and entertainment aspects of the venues—and did I mention food and beverage? Those sales alone could make the pass an excellent investment in both baseball stadiums and theaters such as Studio Movie Grill, which offers in-seat dining services.

- Spontaneity (not having to plan) can go as the spirit or friends or whatever moves them. In reality, the plan is the ultimate flex plan, without having to choose games or price categories.

- Create repeat attenders. It is hoped that the consumer finds the experience worth repeating and worth sharing with others and worth recommending on social media.

I see several risks to this approach for the baseball teams and very few for the movie theaters. Movie theaters don't offer a variety of pricing options on seats, so the goal is merely to increase frequency of attending and hopefully spending more on food and beverage. The same could be true for baseball, except that there are seating locations that are part of ticket plans and are significantly more expensive than the games offered through the mobile pass program. So much so that you can actually be selling against yourself and alienating your current traditional subscription base, especially if pass holders are moving around to various locations not comparable to what they paid.

For example, last year the Oakland A's offered a mobile pass for $19.99 per month for games June through September. In June, there were 15 games, making the actual cost per game $1.33. A visit to the Oakland A's website would tell you that the monthly pass is usually cheaper than one single-game ticket. If I'm not guaranteed a specific seat, but I'm only paying $1.33 for the same game that everyone else is watching, it might be difficult to convince me that I need a guaranteed seat. I know that isn't the case in the A's current home, and hopefully it will be the case in a new ballpark at some point in the future.

With the movie theater pass, the seat is guaranteed while with baseball it isn't, but the size of the baseball stadium makes the likelihood of having a seat almost a certainty. The movie theater takes something that you are probably already doing in the comfort of your home and encourages you do it in a theater with upscale food and beverage and technological advances in sight and sound as well as the size of the picture. If two people, each having the pass, attend one movie in a month, the net effect is a BOGO: The more they attend, the better the deal. Perhaps they are coming and bringing others with them. The value in the opportunity to collect user profiles and behavioral data can never be underestimated and is at the core of these offerings as well.

But let's get back to baseball, which can also take advantage of the food and beverage sales and the database-building opportunities. I like the Cardinals' model because they have very high attendance to begin with, the ticket is SRO, and it is also being used to promote auxiliary entertainment spaces as well. I am supportive of the A's concept but not at $1.33 per game, even in their overly large ballpark. So my advice would be that if you are selling a monthly pass and hoping at some point to move these new buyers into some type of guaranteed seats ticket plan, the gap between the average cost per game and the lowest available guaranteed seat location can't resemble the Grand Canyon. Perhaps an adjustment is made in the monthly cost, or there is a limit placed on the number of games—maybe up to 10 games per month for $39—or less than $4 per game.

On the other hand, maybe it isn't seats we should be focusing on, but space.

Reprinted by permission from B. Sutton, "Should I Sell a Mobile Pass or Take a Pass? Pros and Cons," *Sports Business Journal* 20 (2019).

nologies that continue to enhance the at-home viewing experience; the next generation of Augmented Reality TV; and subscription services through vendors, such as DirecTV, that offer all the games of every team for a fee significantly lower than the typical season-ticket package, will continue to create challenges for ticket-sales executives. However, many technologies can be turned into valuable tools to create the avidity that will keep fans coming to sport venues and consuming the live sport product: from massive in-stadium LED video boards and FanVision (an in-venue handheld device providing access to TV programming) to mobile ticketing and automatic ticket renewal apps to apps that provide real-time stats, fantasy and *real* gaming information, game-day travel tips, and the like. It is up to creative sales and marketing executives to maximize these tools of convenience and engagement to incentivize sales and enhance the in-venue experience for fans.

One of these tactics is the mobile pass, especially as a means to engage young fans and meet other fans where they are (on their phones!) while also making the ticket purchasing a more convenient process. One such example is the University of Buffalo Football Bull's "MoBull" ticket pass, which has seen great success since its introduction for the 2018 season. The world of sport ticketing promises to look much different in 10 years, but we end this chapter by sharing Dr. Bill Sutton's insight and expertise on the pros and cons of this subscription-based model of sport ticket sales. Is it the wave of the future?

Wrap-Up

A sale is the revenue-producing element of the marketing process. Marketing is communication, and as such, the sales process involves a high level of two-way communication; a salesperson must be able to listen and assess as well as talk. Most organizations have developed to the point where members of their sales staff function as experts who sell a specific type of product. But in smaller organizations, salespeople must function as sales generalists and be able to sell all types of inventory. Regardless of the size of the sales team, sales training and the development of the sales personnel may be the most critical aspects of sales success.

Pricing is a vital component of the sales process. Because of the wide array of sport and entertainment products for sale in any market at any given time, consumers who think that the price is too high or the package is too large will seek out their own purchasing solutions. They may buy from the secondary market, find the product online at a discount, or purchase what they want in a size that they find suitable from another source, perhaps by joining others to share ownership of a product and consume it as a group.

Because of the effort and time involved in the sales process, as well as the shifting preferences and demands of today's sport consumers, sport organizations must create programs and benefits to retain current customers over time. This customer lifetime value, or CLV, is a critical consideration for every customer. It involves expanding and extending the relationship between the seller and buyer by offering specialized benefits and more fan-related dimensions. In previous editions of this text, we have always addressed the importance of placing buyers on the escalator and moving them up in terms of frequency. The expansion of sport and entertainment options, competition for the entertainment dollar, and the growing importance of technology in the sales process have made us recognize that retaining customers on the escalator at a point where they are comfortable and less likely to decrease frequency or terminate the relationship is as important as moving them up, especially as it relates to CLV.

Activities

1. Identify someone you recognize as a leader in the area of sport sales. Obtain the person's bio or profile (usually available on the corporate or organizational website or through LinkedIn). How does the person's current position or past activities reflect sales experience?

2. Interview someone with sport sales responsibilities in an athletics department, fitness facility, or pro sport organization and ask about the person's duties. Ask what percentage of the person's time is devoted to sales activities. Which methodologies does the person employ? How does this person train the sales staff? How did the person begin in the business?

3. Assess your career plans. Does the job you envision have a sales component? What will you need to do to attain this position? Begin compiling a roster of people in similar positions. You can use this roster to gather information and advice as you initiate your job search.

4. Visit with a small business, athletics department, or minor league team in your area. Offer to help calculate the customer lifetime value of a season-ticket holder based on average per capita spending and the prices associated with the various ticket plans offered by the organization.

Your Marketing Plan

In the successful implementation of a marketing plan, objectives must be identified and achieved. Sales, in terms of a revenue-production target goal, are usually accounted for in formulating the objectives leading to a goal. Sales are also viewed as strategies or tactics that are integral in achieving objectives and, ultimately, in reaching goals. In reviewing your marketing plan, how do you see sales fitting in? Do you have an objective that might be stated in sales terms relating to increasing organizational revenue? For example, an objective such as "Increase attendance (membership, if you are interested in the fitness industry or other membership-based industry segments, such as golf or tennis clubs) over last year's levels by 12 percent" implies that some sales strategies and tactics are necessary to achieve the objective. Review your objectives and select sales methodologies and approaches that will help you reach your objectives.

 Go to HK*Propel* to complete the activities for this chapter.

Chapter 13

Delivering and Distributing Core Products and Extensions

Jim Rogash/Getty Images

OBJECTIVES

- To understand distribution as it relates to the marketing process and the place application of the five Ps

- To understand the theory of place as it relates to sport

- To recognize the importance of the venue and facility in sport marketing

- To understand the elements of marketing channels and their application to tickets and retail products

The NHL Winter Classic Brings Hockey Outdoors and to Unique Settings

The NHL Winter Classic has become one of the most important events on the NHL calendar. The first in this series of outdoor games was played in 2008 in Buffalo, New York, at the Bills Stadium. This game, which was played in part during a snowstorm, was a major success, drawing 71,217 fans and 3.75 million television viewers while capturing the attention of hockey and non-hockey fans alike. Since that time, the NHL has taken this yearly event to a variety of unique locations. Other nontraditional venues, and even some non-NHL cities, have included famous college venues, such as Notre Dame Stadium in Indiana and Michigan Stadium in Ann Arbor, and numerous professional football and baseball stadiums, such as the famed Wrigley Field in Chicago and Fenway Park in Boston, Massachusetts. The game at Michigan Stadium in 2014 between the Detroit Red Wings and Toronto Maple Leafs was played before a record 105,491 fans.[1]

While most of the Winter Classic games have been played in traditional cold weather hockey markets such as Buffalo, Chicago, and Boston, the 2020 game played at the Cotton Bowl in Dallas, Texas, between the Dallas Stars and the Nashville Predators was the southern-most outdoor NHL game played in history.[2] The goal of this game was not only to have the game played in a new market but also to reach the largest number of fans possible through a variety of different distribution methods. For the local fans, there was of course the game itself, which was attended by 85,630 people—the second-largest attended NHL game in history.[3] However, in addition to the game, a fan fest also takes place surrounding the Winter Classic. For example, during the game that took place at Notre Dame Stadium, a three-day festival was held in nearby Chicago and included player appearances, the chance to take a picture with the Stanley Cup, live music, and games.[4]

The game, fan fest, and ticket sales are just part of the distribution strategy for the Winter Classic. Ultimately, the NHL is experimenting with distributing this product to the market across unique venues and through different media outlets. The annual game takes place on New Year's Day, is broadcast nationally in the United States on NBC, and is livestreamed on NBC Sports streaming service and the NBC Sports app. While viewership has declined in recent years due to a variety of factors, the NHL Winter Classic remains as one the most-watched NHL games every year, often even beating the viewership for some Stanley Cup Final games. In addition to the game itself, the NHL produces *The Road to the Winter Classic*, a television series that provides a behind-the-scenes look at the two teams as they prepare to play in the Winter Classic. The series airs on the NBC Sports Network; NHL Network; and on the NHL's YouTube, Facebook, and Instagram accounts.

As evidenced by the Winter Classic, distributing the sport product to fans can take on a variety of different forms. For just one event or product, several distribution outlets and strategies need to be considered. The NHL's goal with the Winter Classic and other events is to bring the league's unique content to as many fans as possible, and the NHL has done so by taking its product outdoors into uncommon venues, creating ancillary events surrounding the Winter Classic, and distributing the product through different media outlets. As Steve Mayer, Chief Content Officer for the NHL, has said, "The mission is to create memorable content, events, and moments that our avid fans appreciate, but that also grab the attention of the casual fan. It's a cluttered world out there, and if we can do something that makes someone say, 'Oh wow, check that out,' or get hockey more into the mainstream, that's the goal."[5]

Chapters 8, 9, and 11 examined the use of print, broadcast, social media, and digital platforms as key elements in marketing strategy. In this chapter, we discuss some other facets related to the effective distribution of the sport product—both the core event and its extensions. We begin with a look at the facility and its location, layout, and image. Next, we consider other types of distribution channels related to sport, including retail distribution of merchandise and apparel. Finally, after outlining some features of effective ticket distribution, we discuss some elements for the analysis of product distribution.

Placing Core Products and Their Extensions

The opening vignette shows how the NHL is engaging in a strategy that should be elementary to any sport organization, at any level. The NHL is expanding the distribution of its product or brand to as many outlets as practical and effective, through as many channels as possible. This is not just limited to major sport properties. The director of a youth football club or a high school athletics program must think along the same lines, whether it means running clinics and camps in elementary schools, developing social media content, or using local media outlets to convey information about team tryouts. Effective marketing requires a careful and deliberate strategy for distribution.

In many respects, place (or distribution) decisions may be the most important choices a marketer makes because they have long-range implications and are often harder to change than product, price, promotion, and public relations decisions. Think briefly about the range of product elements that require distribution by a typical sport team:

- The live event itself
- Players and coaches through personal appearances
- Tickets to the live event
- Coaches' radio and TV shows
- Concessions
- Digital content
- Podcasts

- Merchandise and apparel
- Memorabilia

These elements, and more, require an integrated strategy and long-term commitments of assets. Take the game form itself: In a competitive marketplace, most sport governing bodies, like the NHL, are looking to grow their game by introducing it into new markets. But such strategies are not limited to big-time leagues and big-time budgets. High schools, small colleges, and clubs can also use the following tactics. Any sound marketing plan considers the careful distribution of all critical components of the sport product, from basic game knowledge to specialized team merchandise.

Scheduling Competitions in New Markets

MLB, the NFL, the NHL, and the NBA have scheduled international exhibitions and tours for years. The English Premier League (EPL) and other world football teams have also toured North America with regularity. For example, Chelsea FC of the EPL has held previous U.S.-based tours, but in 2020, it announced that it specifically plans on touring the United States to capitalize on its signing of U.S.-born player Christian Pulisic. Some have even questioned whether the Pulisic signing was due in part to his popularity in the United States and the ability for Chelsea FC to market its brand in the United States due to the attention Pulisic will bring.[6]

While international tours and friendlies of top soccer or football clubs are common, one top league, LaLiga, initially made strides in an attempt to play regular season games in the United States. Despite its efforts, LaLiga was unable to gain approval from the Royal Spanish Football Federation and other governing bodies, such as FIFA.[7] Despite this failed attempt, the interest in hosting regular season matches in the United States may be an indication that the country is not too far away from having a major European soccer league's regular season games on its soil similar to how the NFL, MLB, the NHL, and the NBA have all held regular-season contests outside of North America. For instance, one of sport's greatest rivalries, the New York Yankees and Boston Red Sox, played two games in London, England, at London Stadium in 2019. These two games drew 118,718 fans (70 percent of whom were residents of the United Kingdom) and broke MLB's one-day merchandise sales records.[8]

These types of competitions are not just limited to professional sport. The University of Notre Dame Fighting Irish football team played traditional rival the U.S. Naval Academy's Navy Midshipmen in Dublin, Ireland, in 2012, and while the game had to be moved back to the United States due to the coronavirus pandemic, the teams were scheduled to return to Dublin in 2020 for another game at Aviva Stadium in the Aer Lingus College Football Classic.[9] Other universities, such as Boston College, Penn State, Georgia Tech, and the University of Central Florida, have also participated in the event. As part of this event, U.S. high school football teams are also invited to play in Dublin the day before the college football matchup.

Creating Personal Interactions With Fans

In an age of instant global images and data sets, most sport action and information can be con-sumed just about anywhere. But nothing sells like a real human being. Tours of star players have spurred fan frenzy for at least 150 years. In the 19th century, boxers, cricket clubs, and baseball teams made well-publicized circuits on rail and steamer, taking their skills to distant markets. And new markets need not be distant. Many teams have run off-season or preseason "caravans" of players, coaches, and other staff in circuits that extend to a radius of a few hundred miles. What sets apart these market-making tours is the extra touch of special appearances, clinics, or autograph sessions, where heroes can mingle with their audience. It is one thing to watch a star; it is another to shake a star's hand, go home with a personalized autograph, or take a selfie with a favorite athlete and create a "shareable" moment. A number of professional teams have staged fan conventions. What were once small, one-day events with a few autograph signings have become elaborate multiday functions with a variety of events taking place. Take the Chicago Cubs for example. Its three-day fan festival sold all 10,000 tickets and was so popular that a secondary market was created for the resale of the tickets. In addition to traditional meet and greets and autograph signings, the Cubs used its fan fest

The New York Yankees and Boston Red Sox held two games in London, England, in 2019.
Billie Weiss/Boston Red Sox/Getty Images

to communicate the team's strategic vision and to get feedback from the fans in an open forum.[10]

Theory of Sport and Place

We could argue that sport is no different from fast food and retail—it's all location, location, location. Because the core sport product is a game form that is simultaneously produced and consumed, the venue of that game form should maximize exposure. When thinking of beach volleyball, New York City probably does not come to mind. However, each year, the Association of Volleyball Professionals (AVP) holds its New York City Open event in Hudson Park. With the New York City skyline as the setting, an estimated 40,000 people attended the event in 2019.[11] Or think about NASCAR cars doing burnouts on one of Nashville's famous streets. As part of its 2019 Champions Week, NASCAR had all 16 of its playoff drivers participate in "Burnouts on Broadway," which provided a unique setting for the drivers to perform burnouts under the lights of the famous strip. These examples make clear how location maximizes exposure. Setting up a beach volleyball court in Manhattan or allowing NASCAR cars to do burnouts in downtown Nashville took some work, but the effort paid off. Many sports, however, require less controllable topographic or geographic factors, such as a mountain or white-water river, where high levels of exposure cannot be guaranteed. Corporations like McDonald's and Walmart do not operate under such constraints. As we discussed in chapter 6, however, the core experience of the game or the event can be extended in many creative ways, through media distribution, streaming video, merchandise, and apparel—which is exactly the approach that the AVP and other properties are taking to grow their games.

Location is critical to the experience of every sport consumer, whether participant or spectator. At Syracuse University, the famous Carrier Dome is located in the heart of campus making it easy for students and others to walk to the basketball, football, and lacrosse events held there. However, other facilities for teams, such as softball, soccer, ice hockey, and field hockey are located more than a mile (nearly 2 km) away from the main campus. Despite some very competitive teams, the locations of those facilities likely affect attendance.

But the difference goes beyond sheer proximity to the campus center. Being on campus brings the advantage of providing areas to gather near the Carrier Dome for tailgating on campus or take short walks to local restaurants, bars, and shops, while the facilities that house the other sports are not surrounded by any options such as these. The Carrier Dome also provides the comfort of an indoor facility during the winter months while the other facilities remain outdoors.

The notion of the *place ensemble*—a term developed by geographers—is important for sport marketers who work with core events. They must recognize the elements that enhance or diminish the attractiveness of their venue and surroundings. Take Boston's historic Fenway Park, one of the few North American sport venues that are truly cherished. Fenway's ensemble includes the following elements:

- *Landscape.* Fenway Park's surrounding landscape includes both the urban rhythm of Kenmore Square and the rural serenity of the nearby Back Bay Fens, the first park in Frederick Law Olmsted's Emerald Necklace Conservancy.

- *Artifacts.* Fenway Park enjoys two noteworthy artifacts: the Green Monster (the left-field wall) inside the park and the giant neon CITGO sign outside.

- *History and memories.* A statue of Ted Williams welcomes fans to the park, one of many such figures at MLB parks. Although Fenway Park is full of memories like Ted Williams' .406 batting average in 1941, none may stand out more than Carlton Fisk's game-winning home run in the 1975 World Series or the Red Sox's recent World Series victories.

- *Ideologies.* Fenway Park may not conjure up serious political or social ideologies, but it does evoke notions (true or not) that baseball was somehow a better game when ballparks were simple and quaint, like Fenway.

- *Experiences.* Anyone who has attended a baseball game can attest to experiences: the sounds of "Take me out to the ballgame" or the crack of the bat, the sights of the great plays made in the field, the smell of hotdogs and popcorn.

- *Aesthetics.* Besides the Green Monster, Fenway Park has irregular dimensions around the outfield. The various nooks and crannies not only look interesting but also create havoc for visiting fielders and delight the home fans.
- *Problems.* Fenway has plenty of problems, including traffic jams, limited and expensive parking, and all too many seats with views obstructed by support columns.

Facility

The facility is the central element of any sport place ensemble. An essential part of the marketing mix, it includes a multitude of factors that influence the attractiveness of the events held within—from accessibility and other transportation-related issues to design and layout, amenities, and personnel.

External Accessibility and Drawing Radius

Most sport marketers and consultants believe in the "location, location, location" school of thought. For the majority of sport products, the high level of visibility gained through media coverage can often overcome a less accessible site as long as the product is in demand and is getting good media coverage. Nonetheless, a high percentage of a sport facility's customers can be expected to live within an hour's traveling time. This drive-time number will go up as the frequency of events goes down. Football and NASCAR fans have higher drive-time expectations than do baseball season-ticket holders who have 81 games on the menu. Along these lines, venue placement on the periphery of a market area leaves the door open for competition and results in inconvenience for the consumer.

Accessibility influences the size of a facility's drawing radius, which marks and visualizes distances away from a central point (e.g., a sport facility) that can then be used to help make marketing decisions (e.g., to determine target markets, to determine which geographic areas to market to, etc.). Facility directors in the past simply drew concentric circles to define the drawing radius, usually at 5-mile (8 km) intervals, as if distance alone dictated a market. However,

with advances in technology and visualization programs, drawing radii can be based on drive or traveling time, and the drawing radii change markedly for different events.

Although the specific dynamics of the sport drawing radius demand much more rigorous consumer research, the following factors appear to be critical:

- *Demographics.* Discretionary time varies with income, occupation, and stage in the life cycle.
- *Duration and frequency of the event.* As noted earlier, most people will travel much longer for an infrequent event (a concert by a favorite artist) than they will for a multi-week activity (MLB home games).
- *Emotional commitment.* Those with higher levels of identification are more likely to travel farther to watch their favorite teams as opposed to those with lower levels of identification.
- *Perception of quality.* The big game or the big star will typically expand the drawing radius.

When locating a new facility, organizations will often perform a market feasibility study, or a detailed analysis of a project (i.e., a sport facility), that may include items such as an overview of the facility site, the financials of the facility project, demographics of potential customers, and an overall analysis of the viability of the project and its location. For example, included in these studies will be an assessment of facility drawing power in the various market segments. When the Atlanta Braves announced its intention to leave Turner Field and build a new stadium, one of the major driving factors was the desire to be in a location that would allow more convenient travel for the team's fans. Turner Field was located in downtown Atlanta where Mike Plant, Braves Executive Vice President of Business Operations, stated that "it [Turner Field] doesn't match up with where the majority of our fans come from."[12] Plant also noted that traffic in downtown Atlanta and getting to Turner Field was the number one reason why fans would not come to the games. With this in mind, the Braves chose a stadium site north of Atlanta in Cobb County, which resides at the intersection of major highways and is "near the geographic center" of its fan base.[13]

Inter Miami's Search for a Home

While Inter Miami began their first MLS season in 2020, the road to finding a permanent home has been anything but smooth. In 2014, international soccer superstar David Beckham announced his intentions of bringing an MLS team to Miami. From that point, there have been many hurdles to making this team a reality, one of which was deciding where the best location for Inter Miami's stadium would be and securing the land to build the soccer-specific stadium.

On a number of occasions, Beckham and the ownership group were denied the opportunity to purchase land. The first attempt to secure land was at the Port of Miami, but fears over heavy traffic due to nearby Miami Heat games and cruise ship departures were some of the concerns with that location. Similar concerns were held with a potential plot of land next to American Airlines Arena where the Miami Heat play. The group also attempted to purchase land across from Marlins Park in the Little Havana neighborhood of Miami. However, private landowners demanding too much money for their land, among other concerns, derailed that option. Eventually, the team did get approval to purchase land in a neighborhood just north of downtown Miami. Finally, after four years of attempts, Beckham and the ownership group were approved by the city to purchase a US$9 million piece of land in the Overtown neighborhood of Miami, in addition to paying US$19 million to purchase nearby land from private landowners. However, when new people were brought into the team's ownership group, questions were raised about whether the Overtown site would be best for the new stadium.[14,15]

Now with its sights set on a fifth potential site in as many years, Inter Miami appears to have finally found a place to call home and construct its stadium. The US$1 billion stadium project dubbed Miami's Freedom Park is planned for a 160-acre plot of land on a city-owned golf course near Miami International Airport.[16] The plan calls for the construction of a 25,000-seat stadium in addition to a public park, restaurants and retail locations, and soccer fields for the community. Yet, hurdles remain. In the summer of 2019, the potential site was closed by the city of Miami because the soil was found to be highly toxic.[17] In addition, the potential lease with the city of Miami would still need to be approved by vote of the city commissioners—a vote that has been delayed on multiple occasions.

Only time will tell if the location will be cleaned up, approved, and ultimately successful. In the meantime, the team plans on playing at least its first and second seasons in Fort Lauderdale at a smaller renovated stadium that will become home of the team's training complex. Regardless of the team's final stadium location, this example illustrates that finding the proper stadium location is often difficult and filled with numerous challenges.

By analyzing how drawing radii change for various events offered at a multipurpose facility, marketers can make adjustments in the event mix to satisfy all market segments. They can also segment the promotional media and marketing activities in direct response to the drawing radii. That means the marketing approaches may be very different for fans within 10 miles (16 km) of the stadium versus fans who live 50 or more miles (80 km) away. For instance, marketers might consider offering more incentive to the fans who live at a greater distance to get them to show up for events.

The analysis of drawing radii will change when events are scheduled at different times and on different days. Many sport marketers have scheduled their events at the same time every day. When setting starting times, however, a facility manager should account for traveling lead time. Is the market composed primarily of suburbanites who work in the city and stay in town up to the starting time? Or do these people attempt to commute home and then return to the event? Is the market primarily city dwellers? Or is it a mix of the two?

Parking

Parking is one of the most vexing aspects of the fan experience. It is important that the facility not only offers ample parking but also ensures that it is easy to get in and out of the parking lots. As mentioned in chapter 6, this is an element of the process that can influence a fan's overall enjoyment at an event. Think about having a great time at a game, but then it takes an hour or more to leave the parking lot. Regardless of how great the game was, this is the last impression you will have about your experience at the event. One national survey of sports fans measured satisfaction of the live-event experience across a variety of factors, such as purchasing food and merchandise, finding the assigned seat, selecting and purchasing tickets, and among others, parking. Of all the factors measured, parking was given the lowest level of satisfaction among fans.[18]

The industry has responded in several ways in an effort to improve the parking and entry and exit experience for fans:

- Partnerships with both rideshare programs like Uber and Lyft with venues offering dedicated pick-up and drop-off points for these companies
- The reduction of lot congestion at the end of games; for example, the New England Patriots' experiment with giving free parking to fans if they wait 75 minutes after the game before leaving

Parking and traffic can be one of the most frustrating elements of the fan experience.
David Eulitt/Getty Images

- Prepaid parking sold during the ticket purchasing process
- The Miami Dolphins' construction of pedestrian bridges and tunnels around Hard Rock Stadium so cars can get in and out of the lots without having to wait for pedestrian traffic
- The use of digital parking reservation systems like the ParkMobile app, which allow fans to reserve specific lots prior to an event
- The offering of a bike valet for cyclists and a ticket to the game, which acts as a full-day pass on San Francisco's city transit system, by the Chase Center, home of the Golden State Warriors
- Wayfinding signage to assist patrons from lots to the venue itself
- Branded parking lots, such as the Lexus lot at the BB&T Center, home of the Florida Panthers, which has spots reserved solely for Lexus owners[19,20]

Surrounding Area

A facility links to its surroundings in several ways beyond parking.

Design

New or renovated facilities must fit with local landscape aesthetics. With its opening in 2019, the US$1.6 billion Chase Center in San Francisco is one facility that embraced the culture of its city—including its waterfront location—and was designed to be much more than just a sport arena. The arena is surrounded by an arts and entertainment district as well as 3.2 acres of plazas and public spaces, and a future waterfront park across the street from the arena. Murals painted by local artists and public art installations sit just outside of the arena, while the indoor space was designed to resemble a museum or theater more so than a sport arena. As one of the architects of the arena explained, "We mostly drew inspiration from high-tech sailboats that are often in the Bay, and from the digital backstory that is San Francisco . . . You can see the way the white sort of swoops around the building, sort of dynamic and always in motion, and that's how the sailboats are as they're carving through the Bay."[21]

Politics

Sport facilities have never been welcomed by everyone, especially nearby residents, who care less about their own easy access to games than they do about the regular infusion of hordes of fans, their cars, and their often unruly behavior. No sport organization should develop its venue without clear dialogue with its neighbors. For example, the Barclays Center in Brooklyn was not built without controversy—some of which still exists today in the surrounding neighborhoods of the arena. Controversies regarding eminent domain; subsidies and tax breaks; and concerns over parking, traffic, and rowdy crowds were all featured in the 2011 documentary *Battle for Brooklyn*. Today, as the project expands beyond the Barclays Center to the mixed use project known as Pacific Park, neighbors still share many of the same concerns about construction, safety, traffic, and debris. [22,23]

Sense of Safety

The immediate environment surrounding a sport facility is an extremely important factor in determining attendance frequency. When a facility is located in an area that customers believe is unsafe, sales will suffer. The environment can also determine the pattern of attendance.

Design and Layout

Design and layout are crucial to consumer satisfaction. Several aspects of facility design are important.

Ease of Access, Exit, and Flow

As noted earlier about parking, few things upset today's consumers more than waiting in long lines, especially if their intent had been to get away from it all. What's worse than waiting to park and then waiting to get into a facility? Maybe it's a long line to get through! In all venues, a key objective is to minimize bottlenecks and maximize crowd flow. Research on queuing (waiting in lines) suggests that people, on average, inflate their actual time in line by one-third.[24] The best designs consider consumer flow from the point where fans arrive (and even their travel to the venue) to the point where they depart and head safely home. A good design has good flow for humans as well as cars.

At a sports event, this is particularly important. Have you ever been in line for concessions and missed a key play in the game? Fans spend money to watch the game, and missing it because they are waiting in line can be frustrating. An easy solution to this is to have TVs around the concourse so fans can at least see the game. Many new and renovated facilities are designed with open concourse areas so fans can still see the action while waiting in line. Others have incorporated food delivery to audience seats or have created apps that allow event goers to order food for quick pickup and even tell them the wait times at concessions and bathroom areas.

Access for Spectators With Disabilities

Providing access for spectators with disabilities includes conforming to legal requirements, such as the Americans with Disabilities Act (ADA). Some of the key applications of the ADA in stadium design include the following:

- Half of all entrances must be wheelchair accessible.
- One percent of total seating must be for wheelchairs; accessible seating must be integrated and not isolated; companion seats must be provided.
- One percent of wheelchair seats must be aisle seats without armrests.
- All concessions, restaurants, and merchandise stands must be accessible.
- Lines of sight must be comparable to those of surrounding seats.[25]

Sport facilities must adhere to the requirements set forth by the ADA for legal and financial purposes as well as to serve the needs of their entire fan base. In new facility construction, this is often easier to accomplish from the start, but older facilities undergoing renovations must also carefully plan for these requirements. In 2016, the University of Nevada at Reno's Mackay Stadium underwent a US$14 million renovation, part of

The Chase Center was designed to fit with the local San Francisco architecture and landscapes.
Ezra Shaw/Getty Images

which was to ensure the 50-year-old stadium would be ADA compliant. However, after the renovation, it was found that the placement of the wheelchair-accessible seats did not have proper sight lines, leaving fans in wheelchairs unable to see the field. In 2017, the university spent nearly US$700,000 in order to address the issue and add wheelchair lifts to different parts of the stadium. However, those lifts failed, and an additional 167 areas of concern were found at the stadium, including issues with parking, restrooms, and entrance ramps. After additional issues were uncovered, the university hired a new architect and invested nearly US$2 million to address the problems at the stadium, with the renovations completed in 2019 and 2020.[26]

Flexible Versus Dedicated Usage

Professional sport teams have moved away from multipurpose venues toward single-use facilities. A main reason has been to maximize sight lines and intimacy for fans. Many people believe that baseball simply doesn't "play" well in a cavernous stadium meant for 70,000 football fans. The same point applies to soccer. When MLS began play in 1996, most teams played in shared facilities—often the local NFL team's stadium. However, MLS has pushed for the development of soccer-specific stadiums and oftentimes has used the call as a deciding factor when determining where to award expansion franchises. The thinking behind this strategy is that a soccer-specific stadium offers a much smaller seating capacity (between 18,000 and 30,000), thus creating a more intimate fan experience and atmosphere. As of 2019, 17 of the 24 MLS franchises play in soccer-specific facilities, with additional soccer-specific stadiums scheduled for construction for the expanding Miami and Nashville franchises. MLS commissioner Don Garber has even suggested that developing soccer-specific stadiums has been one of the key reasons for the growth of the MLS.[27] While professional teams and leagues may have the financial ability to construct such dedicated facilities, few schools or colleges can afford to do so; flexibility is dictated by budgets and often by space. Further, such facilities must anticipate changes in consumer interest.

Aesthetics

As with any piece of architecture, the sport facility design requires an appealing blend of form, scale, color, and light. The media focus attention on the multimillion-dollar venues such as San Francisco's Chase Center. In many cases, sponsors are pouring millions into the creation of attractive and interactive "entitlement zones." But even small-budget venues can enhance their attractiveness with concepts used at prominent venues. Have you ever simply put a new color or coat of paint on a room in your house, hung new décor, or put down a new rug and it instantly felt like a new room? The same concept can apply at sport facilities, just on a much larger scale. For instance, a number of schools and colleges have been imaginative with the use of colorful new logos, marks, and murals in otherwise drab entrances, concourses, and gymnasiums. Or, for example, even changing the design of the court, field, ice, or any playing surface can have a major impact. A relatively small investment can drastically change the aesthetic experience not only for fans but also, and more importantly, for the athletes and coaches who call the place home. Marketers should keep abreast of the facility design literature at all levels by tracking the Architectural Showcase and Facilities of Merit Awards presented annually by *Athletic Business*, one of the industry's most widely read trade magazines.

Game, Spectacle, and Festival: Framing the Steak and the Sizzle

For as far back as historical sources take us, humans have tended to frame sporting contests with layers of spectacle and festival. People have been motivated to watch sporting contests throughout history. In boxing, they formed a ring around the combatants—hence, the term *boxing ring*. Formal venues defined in wood, stone, or concrete created the threshold that separated the game from the spectacle. But more than just watching always occurred. A festival frame developed outside the layer of spectators. At ancient venues such as Olympia, people mingled, ate, enjoyed musical performances, and listened to poets—all outside the spectacle frame. Ultimately, these elements of the game, spectacle, and festival all combine to create a unique cultural performance.[28] Modern venues reflect these ancient practices in the forms of special tailgating areas, large concourses, and atriums where vendors hawk their wares. In some arenas, the concourse and festival frame lie outside the frame of seats.

In Boston's TD Garden, fans who have milled around between periods buying concessions and mingling in groups must reenter the spectacle through tunnels. In other venues, concourses offer direct sight lines to the action. Camden Yards is a case in point. Similarly, Hadlock Field in Portland, Maine, offers a group picnic area along the right-field line. Here, festival and spectacle are combined inside the park.

Designers have worked hard to create concourse areas that merge spectacle and festival. One of the more unique areas was developed during the renovations of Madison Square Garden. A set of skybridges on the north and south sides of the arena are suspended from the arena ceiling, designed to resemble the suspension bridges common throughout New York City. The skybridges have a 430-seat capacity, concourse areas for fans to walk and congregate, and fabulous sight lines down on the rink or court, which literally put fans on top of the playing surface. In fact, despite being suspended from the ceiling, the seats are only 94 feet to the floor, a similar distance from a front row seat.[29]

American football has a long tradition of fusing the three frames into a single experience. As early as the 1890s, Manhattan hosted "big games" between Yale and Princeton, closely covered in national magazines by feature writers like Richard Harding Davis. Manhattan Field would be packed with 30,000 spectators singing songs and chanting cheers in ways now largely lost in North America (but alive in the world's great soccer venues). The bigger show, however, was before the game, outside the field, in the long parade of partisans marching and riding down Fifth Avenue hours before game time, in what Davis called a "circus procession many miles long"— coaches festooned in yellow or blue, filled with young men and women "smothered in furs; and the flags, as they jerk them about, fill the air with color," cheered on by crowds four deep along the sidewalks. As Davis concluded, "Today, the sporting character of the event has been overwhelmed by the social interest."[30] Nowhere is this notion more alive than at the University of Mississippi in the pregame tailgating on the Grove—among the magnolias, tents of red and blue, mint juleps in silver mugs, and elegantly dressed fans of all ages. As they say in Oxford: "Ole Miss may not win the game, but we will always win the party."[31] Some Seattleites feel the same way about Husky

Harbor, where tailgaters arrive on boats of all kinds in a flotilla that docks on the shore of Lake Washington, at the edge of Husky Stadium.

More than a century ago, Davis captured a phenomenon that is now an essential part of marketing: managing the three frames and balancing the sizzle with the steak, along with the festival and the spectacle with the game itself. Doing this is not always easy. People want food and drink—festival elements—in the spectacle frame. But they don't want vendors blocking their view. And they don't want unruly fans ruining their experience. Leagues want to enhance spectacle, but they don't want players running into the stands, and some leagues limit celebrations that detract from the game.

Sometimes, however, it makes sense to scramble the frames. For example, at AT&T Stadium, the Dallas Cowboys installed an augmented reality photo booth in its concourse. At this "Pose with the Pro" photo booth, fans can choose from a series of Cowboys players on a touch screen to take a realistic virtual photo with. Once fans choose their virtual players, the fans stand on a designated spot and the players then digitally join the fans for their photo on screen. Fans can then enter their information on the screen to receive their image and also share it on social media.[32]

Pulling fans away from the live action is always a gamble, but this scrambling of the frames makes sense because it is all about enhancing the overall experience. Mo Katibeh, Chief Marketing Officer of AT&T Business, stated "We're combining the physical and digital worlds to create a world class experience for fans . . . We're paving the way for how immersive fan experiences could be built in venues across the country as our 5G network continues to grow."[32] There are many other examples of effective frame management at sports events. For instance, giant scoreboards now provide separate spectacles during breaks in live-game action with highlights, promotions, unique video features, a showcasing of fans dancing in the stands, interactive games for the fans, and more.

Amenities: Convergence Toward the Sports Mall

When the Miami Marlins ballpark opened in 2012, *Sports Illustrated* writer Tom Verducci wrote of its two "bulletproof, polycarbonate aquariums," lime 'n' lobster rolls, retractable lid, and its "$2.5 million neon-colored, fish-and-flamingo-studded piece of performance art beyond the center-field wall." It was, he claimed, a long way from the simplicity that opened a century earlier in Boston. "Fenway's architects didn't sweat amusements," he claimed. "The game was enough in 1912. Not so today. The ballpark is a theme park, an art gallery, a TV studio, a shopping mall, a small city unto itself."[33]

It is not just professional or top-level college programs that have felt the urgency to build newer, bigger, and more fan-friendly facilities. In 2017, the Katy Independent School District outside of Houston, Texas, opened a US$70 million high school football stadium. This stadium, which at the time was the most expensive high school stadium ever built in the United States, seats 12,000 fans, has two concessions areas, a 1,500-square-foot (1,394 m²) video scoreboard, color LED lighting system, event space, and suites.[34,35]

Of course, venues change with the times and the needs and wants of fans. Today's sport consumers, many of which pay hundreds of dollars to attend one event with their families, expect a range of amenities that enhance their spectacle and festival experience. Bench seats, boiled hot dogs, a mimeographed program, and a scoreboard that displays only the score—none of this will do. So, the big-time venues have responded with a range of amenities, many of which are designed to provide what is called technological wow.

Connectivity

Millennials, now entering prime years as breadwinners and as fans, have grown up alongside breakthroughs in communications technology. They expect to see the latest connectivity in hotels, resorts, and sport venues. At one time, the next rage was going to be smart seats wired with small computer screens from which fans (for a premium price) could request replays from various camera

Wireless connectivity in stadiums and arenas is important in order to provide a good fan experience.
simonkr/E+/Getty Images

angles, check a rule, call up stats, and order food or merchandise. Now, all fans have the ability to do these things right from their smartphones, and the need for fans to be connected is greater than ever. Think of what you do while at a sports event: checking your fantasy scores, texting, taking pictures to post on social media, checking scores and highlights from other games. You do this and more all from the palm of your hand. Many teams also engage with their fans during the game through their smartphones by encouraging social media posts, text-to-win promotions, team-branded apps, or augmented reality items. In addition, with the heightened use of digital ticketing, it becomes even more important to be connected to simply access your game tickets.

For most facility renovations and new constructions, connectivity is one of the primary areas of focus. The new home of the Las Vegas Raiders, Allegiant Stadium, has been promoted as being one of the most connected stadiums in the world. The stadium was built with 1,700 WiFi access points and 40-gigabit optical connections designed to provide high-speed Internet access to 65,000 fans. In addition, the stadium includes a selfie station with the famous Las Vegas Strip in the background and a virtual reality station where fans will get to virtually interact with their favorite players. Matthew Pasco, Raiders Vice President of Technology, highlighted the importance of providing this service to fans: "Connectivity is like a public utility, it's a requirement . . . It's paramount for fan experience and fan experience is paramount for us."[36]

Big Screens, Electronic Message Centers, and Sound Systems

When arena managers think about fan comfort these days, their concerns go well beyond the older notions of sight lines and seat backs. Now, it's about making the stadium viewing experience better than the at-home viewing experience, which includes bigger and better scoreboards that provide unparalleled views of the action on the field. Los Angeles' Sofi Stadium center-hung scoreboard is one example. The 70,000-square-foot (6,503 m²), double-sided 4K oculus display board provides prime viewing from any seat in the stadium. The display board is so big that the 76-foot-tall (23 m) cable net that holds the board weighs in at 3.6 million pounds (1.6 kg), while the oculus itself weighs 2 million pounds (907,000 kg).[37]

Upscale Food and Drink

Luxury-suite patrons have been munching on shrimp and caviar for years. Suite patrons pay over four times what the typical fan pays per game on food and beverages; in arena jargon, this is the per cap. But if the suite holders demand more high-end food options, that doesn't mean that the other fans in attendance will settle for the same old stale hot dogs. Around the U.S. market, stadiums and arenas are typically expanding their offerings at stands, kiosks, and food courts to include items unheard of less than a generation ago—Philly cheesesteak, sushi, jalapeño poppers, pierogies, chef salads, chicken fajitas, North Carolina–style barbecue, low-calorie wraps, microbrews, sweet tea, Krispy Kreme donuts, and hand-dipped ice cream. Teams and facilities have also started to institute more specialty items, such as gluten-free and vegan options and the new trend of meatless meat.

Of course, after paying the concession bill, some fans might prefer to go back to the old days. That's why some teams still offer more traditional fare while also having started to sell these concession items at reduced prices in an effort to lower the overall cost of attendance for fans.

- The Atlanta Falcons and Mercedes Benz Stadium offer their "fan first" menu, which includes hot dogs, a refillable Coca-Cola cup, pretzels, and popcorn for just US$2, with other items ranging from US$3 to US$6.[38]
- The Miami Marlins have their "$3o$5" menu, playing off the South Florida 305 area code, where ballpark favorites, such as hotdogs, nachos, pretzels, and more, are either US$3 or US$5.[39]

These days, fans don't even have to wait in line to get their food at some stadiums. Through a deal with Postmates, fans at Dodgers Stadium can order concessions through the Postmates app, receive notification of when it is ready to pick up, and go to a dedicated pickup location within the stadium to get their food.[40]

Other Amenities

While greatly enhancing the fan experience, technology and upscale amenities cannot solve all problems; in fact, those same amenities may cause problems for fans, especially for fans who have special needs. All fans want to enjoy the live sport experience, but fans with autism, Down Syndrome, or other conditions may have sensitivity to large crowds or noises. Many teams and facilities have started to serve the needs of this fan base through a variety of different programs by creating sensory safe zones or rooms within the facility that offer a reprieve from the crowds and noise. At Quicken Loans Arena in Cleveland, a meeting room was retrofitted to become a sensory room. Other teams are creating similar spaces and distributing sensory kits or bags that include items such as earplugs, headphones, and other calming devices.[41]

Reconfigurations: From Suites to Inclusive Club Seats to Special Zones

In the 1990s, club seats became a standard component of big venues. The club-seat concept was clearly designed to offer the upscale consumer something between the luxury suite and the best box- or loge-season seat. Like the loges, club seats were both segregated from the crowd and stand-alone; you could buy just one seat for the season. Like the suites, they offered exclusive amenities, such as the following:

- Special parking privileges
- Membership in a club that included a restaurant
- Wait service during a game with better food and drink options
- Invitations to special events
- Comfortable seating areas
- Heated seating options in cold-weather climates and indoor air-conditioned options in warm weather
- Updated restrooms and other facilities

Today, venues have even merged the suites with the club seats. In many markets, luxury suites and their long-term leases lost their 1980s luster when the U.S. economy experienced recession in the early 2000s. Rather than agonize over empty suites, some teams and venues became creative. The Chase Center, which was discussed earlier in this chapter, provides a club for every seat in the arena. Whether sitting in the lower bowl or the upper deck, each section of the stadium offers access to a branded club with areas for fans to congregate and, in some instances, still see the court from the club.[19] This is in line with the trend of providing open areas for fans to gather and socialize as opposed to being stuck to their seats.

The days of going to a game with a group of people and just sitting in seats, oftentimes only being able to talk to the person directly next to you, are not gone; however, teams do realize that they need to provide more areas for fans to gather as a group and socialize. After all, sport is and should be a social experience. In order to accomplish this, some facilities have begun to take out physical seats in favor of creating more open gathering places. At State Farm Arena, home of the NBA's Atlanta Hawks, the team removed seats directly behind the basket and created a courtside club equipped with a bar in the shape of the Hawks logo where fans can congregate and have access to a club with food and drink included.[42]

The trend of social gathering spaces at facilities has led to some very creative and unique offerings:

- Homestead-Miami Speedway in Florida created the first-ever beach in the infield of a racetrack. For US$40, race fans can gain access to the 20,000-square-foot (1,858 m²) beach to not only enjoy the race from this unique location but also to have a live DJ, be able to kayak or paddle board on the water, and have access to different food and beverage options that are unavailable in other parts of the facility.[43]

- If you do not want to watch a race from a beach, how about watching a football game with your dog? Pet Paradise Dog Park at TIAA Bank Stadium in Jacksonville is the first-ever dog park built at an NFL stadium. The park provides space for 250 dogs to play or even to swim in the paw-shaped pool, while their owners can watch the game from the nearby patio or go to their seats and pick their dog up after the game.[44]

Whether it is unique spaces such as these or simply creating an area for fans to congregate with tabletops while still being able to see the game, social areas are a key element of facility renovation and construction moving forward. In fact, in a poll of sports executives taken in 2020 by Turnkey Intelligence, spaces for social interaction were noted as the top area of focus when developing new facilities. Sixty-five percent of those surveyed noted social interaction to be the most important item to consider followed by cellular and WiFi networks (41 percent), which we also previously discussed as a key aspect of facility design and the fan experience.[45]

Personnel

The people who work in a facility may be the major force in projecting a facility's image and its ultimate success. The attitudes of operations personnel directly affect consumer satisfaction because these workers are the primary (and in many cases, only) personnel whom consumers contact. Yet such non-management personnel are often the least trained among a facility's staff. Event staff are almost all part-timers. How often do patrons face an uncaring or even surly usher? Too often. All this is unnecessary, especially when professional trade associations, such as the International Association of Venue Managers (IAVM), offer training programs—in class, online, and in video—on a range of topics including crowd management, food services, and emergency management. Clubs, schools, colleges, and youth programs all run events in venues. Some of the events draw tens of thousands of patrons. Staff training for such events is no longer a luxury; it is a necessity. At U.S. Bank Stadium in Minneapolis, guest services staff undergo a variety of training seminars ranging from new employee orientations, stadium culture, service expectations, effective alcohol management, leadership, and staff management. In addition, staff members are provided with a 64-page guest experience handbook, and they must sign a document indicating that they have read and understand the items outlined in the handbook.[46]

Marketing Channels

Although the facility is the primary element in distributing the core sport product, the concept of place includes other aspects involving the various channels by which marketers can deliver the product—in this case, beyond the facility. Market-ing channels are simply sets or configurations of organizations linked together to deliver a product to consumers. Channel systems often vary by product line or sales territory within a company's distribution network. Channel systems can be complex; they may shift and share functions, as is often the case in sport marketing. Standard product channels have included the following:

- *Manufacturers (M).* The organization that manufactures, produces, or offers the product or service
- *Wholesalers (W) and jobbers (J).* A company that may purchase items directly from a manufacturer and then sell those items to retailers
- *Retailers (R).* Oftentimes where a product can be purchased, whether that be in a physical retail location, online, or in some other format
- *Consumers (C).* The end users or purchasers

A traditional channel for hard goods looks like this:

$$M \rightarrow W \rightarrow J \rightarrow R \rightarrow C$$

The Internet and digital technologies have reconstructed traditional channels of sport products such as equipment and apparel sales. Consumers can go online to find manufacturers' sites, check the online catalog, and order directly from the manufacturer, all without using wholesalers or retailers. In the increasingly complex world of sport marketing channels, the two types of systems often operate in parallel, sometimes to reach the same consumer. Take a professional sport team. It has a traditional channel of on-site or online box offices for event tickets:

$$M \leftrightarrow C$$

But it also may televise the event and distribute it by television or a streaming service to a wider audience, so that the channel looks like this:

$$M \leftrightarrow C = Event \rightarrow Media \rightarrow C$$

If the on-site consumer recorded the game on a home DVR, she would be part of both the beginning and the end of the channel! As teams use websites, social media, apps, and wireless connectivity for the redistribution of broadcast highlights and for direct sale of team merchandise and tickets, the channel loops become more complicated.

The secondary ticket market also has disrupted traditional marketing channels. Buying a ticket that has already been sold by the team to a fan, and now from a fan to another fan through Stub-Hub or SeatGeek might look something like this:

$$M \rightarrow C \rightarrow C$$

As any sport organization considers channels for product distribution, it must weigh at least four factors in tandem:

1. Expertise
2. Cost
3. Control
4. Adaptability

Marketers must continually monitor the value of their marketing channels. For instance, e-commerce could be a double-edged sword. Although online sales certainly offer consumers more access and control, retailers are realizing that cost savings are not always as high as expected. Although the Internet may reduce the payroll for a sales force, it also forces a retailer to expand distribution warehouses (with all the associated labor costs). The same can be true for running your own merchandise operation in-house and selling directly to the consumer versus outsourcing that function. As an organization, you have to determine if you have the expertise and financial ability to properly manage such a function or if it is worth giving up some control to an outside company that will take on these added costs and risks. Ultimately, determining the best marketing channels requires constant evaluation to determine the pros and cons of the different channels.

Retail Operations

Traditional retail outlets remain important elements for sport marketing channels. Specialized outlets for sport products grew rapidly in the 19th century as entrepreneurs recognized, and promoted, an interest in fishing, baseball, hunting, and other activities among urban populations that could support their businesses.[47] Today's big-box firms, such as Dick's Sporting Goods, have a long list of forerunners that include hardware

The NBA Store offers an NBA-themed shopping experience.
Noam Galai/Getty Images

stores and retail chains, such as Sears and Montgomery Ward. But today's sport market has seen some new twists as well, especially the channel movement by teams, clubs, and governing bodies into the retail business.

Professional teams had long operated pro shops in arena lobbies, but the presence of these outlets was often not part of a broader branding and distribution strategy. That has changed with the integration of team or league stores into the broader retail distribution and branding strategies of sport organizations. For instance, the NBA Store on Fifth Avenue in Manhattan is designed to be more than a place to buy NBA goods. The store is an interactive, branded shopping experience that includes a video wall with NBA highlights and NBA-related social media posts, video game consoles, pop-a-shot games, and TVs playing live NBA games.[48] The NBA Store was clearly part of a broad distribution strategy that included branded television shows, branded merchandise, and branded fan experiences.

Some organizations have taken this retail and branding concept to a much larger scale. Patriot Place is a 1.3 million-acre (5,261 km^2) shopping and entertainment venue situated next to Gillette Stadium. Besides the retail stores and restaurants that would be expected at a high-end mall or gallery, Patriot Place houses two hotels, a Trader Joe's grocery store, an outdoor ice rink, an esports facility, a movie theater, a health care facility, a CBS Scene, a restaurant–sports bar–nightclub, and the Hall at Patriot Place, a combination hall of fame and retail outlet.[49] The latter two establishments are located closest to the stadium, following the long tradition of building frames that flow from festival to spectacle to the game itself. While Patriot Place may have been the first to envision this concept, others have now followed: Titletown in Green Bay, outside of Lambeau Field; District Detroit near Little Caesars Arena; the Star in Frisco, Texas; the Ice District near Rogers Place in Edmonton; along with other similar, smaller developments with certainly more to come.

The brilliance of these sport, retail, and entertainment complexes is the fusion of branded and licensed goods with the fan experience of a big game. When all goes well, the consumer does not simply buy a shirt, a cap, or a pair of shoes or eat a nice meal. The consumer learns more about the team or the league, sees a game, and returns home following a great overall experience that may have nothing to do with the game itself but may lead to greater commitment and involvement.

In the past, teams or leagues themselves often managed physical retail spaces, such as the NBA Store, and e-commerce team shops. Some of these retail spaces still are today; however, with the explosion of the sport apparel and merchandise industry came the desire, and necessity, for outside companies to manage the manufacturing, distribution, and sales of licensed sport products. Fanatics is one company that has been immensely successful in acting as manufacturers and wholesalers of licensed sport goods, along with managing team and league retail stores and e-commerce sites. As of 2020, Fanatics had partnerships with leagues such as NASCAR, MLB, MLS, NBA, NFL, NHL, and PGA Tour and with hundreds of teams, and the company has even entered the esports space with a deal with Overwatch League. In these partnerships, Fanatics offers a wide variety of services as evidenced by its relationship with MLB. In 2015, Fanatics signed a 17-year deal with MLB to operate all of MLB's online merchandise business. Prior to 2015, Fanatics worked with MLB to fulfill all online orders, but this new deal allowed Fanatics to run all aspects of MLB's online licensing business, including manufacturing, wholesaling and marketing products to retail partners, and managing online shops.[50,51]

Fanatics has used this model in agreements with other leagues with the addition of also running physical team and league stores. For instance, in 2019, Fanatics entered into a partnership with the Golden State Warriors to manage the Warriors 10,000-square-foot (929 m^2) team shop outside of their arena, another 4,000 square feet (372 m^2) of retail space within the arena, three local fan shops in the San Francisco area, and the Warriors online shop.[52] All told, Fanatics now has the capabilities of running online stores, mobile apps, merchandise operations at stadiums, and team stores while also designing, manufacturing, and distributing licensed products. This shift in the way the licensing and distribution of sport products is managed has allowed Fanatics to grow to a US$4.5 billion company with an estimated 50 million sport products sold in 2019.[50]

With advances in technology, and the use of analytics, distribution at retail outlets has also become more of a science. We no longer have to assume what type of product is selling best or where certain products sell better than others. Now, we can have that information at our fingertips to allow us to determine the best retail merchandising and distribution strategies. Years ago, the Collegiate Licensing Company (CLC), part of Learfield IMG College, used to provide monthly licensed product sales reports to the colleges and universities it worked with. These reports would simply outline sales figures based on the type of product sold—apparel or non-apparel items. Now, the CLC uses analytics to determine what specific products are selling best, which retail partners are selling the most, and what percentage of sales are attributed to which products based on locations, and they can ultimately select the best retail partners and licensees for the schools based on sales. Catherine Gammon, CLC's Senior Vice President of Brand Development, noted, "What it's [their analytics software] helped us do is identify the retailers that were doing a good job and had some momentum behind selling licensed products . . . It also helped us identify where the [untapped inventory] was to really increase distribution and grow that business."[53]

In one case, the CLC was able to determine that there was high demand for youth, toddler, and infant clothes, yet most of its retailers were not carrying these items. For the University of Florida, CLC also determined that the university did not have enough lines of licensed women's apparel, and it had too many licensees producing product that was not selling. This led the university to sign a licensing deal with Victoria's Secret's Pink Collection to fill the gap in the university's women's apparel while, at the same time, also eliminating many of its other licensees that were not performing well.[53]

Ticket Distribution

Ticket distribution is a good example of the fast-changing environment of sport marketing channels. While the traditional box office is still an important distribution point for tickets, consumers have been moving away from buying tickets at the gate for some time. Since 2010, new technologies expanded the possibilities of ticket distribution largely because digital ticketing helped address the problems of duplicate tickets, excess stock, and limited choice—all of which had plagued earlier efforts to go beyond the single box office. Since 2000, as ticketing technology

and distribution methods were advancing, there were concerns about servicing fans who were unfamiliar with the online ticket ordering process, fans who did not have smartphones to participate in mobile ticketing, or fans who preferred to purchase tickets with more traditional methods.[54] The industry responded by slowly transitioning to online ticketing with the plan for some distributors to eventually fully transition to digital tickets. However, it was still important to meet the needs of more traditional consumers with the box office, phone ordering, partnerships with other retail outlets to sell tickets, home delivery, and self-service ticket kiosks, as well as trying to transition the more traditional ticket buyer to, at the very least, order online and print tickets on a home computer.

Many of these concerns do not exist anymore because online and smartphone adoption and use cross many demographics. Now, most consumers can have a virtual box office with their smartphone. Consequently, this has led to a push toward digital as the primary ticket distribution channel and the creation of new programs to meet the demands of the changing sports fan. However, as with any decision on marketing channels, a balance needs to be struck among the factors of cost, adaptability, expertise, and control. What follows is a brief overview of some modern ticket distribution strategies.

Partnerships With Primary and Secondary Ticket Firms

For years, leagues have used companies like Ticketmaster (which dominates the market), Live Nation (which merged with Ticketmaster in 2010), Tickets.com, Paciolan, and similar firms to operate their online ticketing and distribution functions. Now, leagues have begun to also partner with secondary ticket providers like StubHub and SeatGeek to become official secondary ticket providers. In 2010, these secondary outlets may have been seen as major, and oftentimes contemptuous, competitors for the more traditional online services. However, the secondary market is now a viable and needed distribution outlet for tickets.

Chapter 12 describes secondary market sales in detail, but here we remind readers that managing secondary sales is a crucial function for any sport property that has controlled gates, venues with reserved seats, and full-season or partial-season ticket plans. The stakes are high at the big time. For a variety of reasons, some people with tickets want or need to unload them, and leagues are now providing official outlets for fans to do so. For example, in 2018, the NFL signed a five-year extension with Ticketmaster as the league's primary ticket partner, but the category of its secondary ticket partner was left unknown. Shortly after, the NFL announced that StubHub would become an authorized secondary ticketing partner of the league, while SeatGeek soon followed as another official secondary ticketing partner of the NFL.[55] This new partnership was based on the desire to provide fans with as many distribution outlets as possible where they could buy tickets to games and to also provide different options for how they could buy tickets. However, some concerns have been raised about the level of control that teams have over their ticket inventory and if the addition of the official secondary outlets would discourage fans from buying season tickets or minimize the amount of single game tickets that are purchased in advance of the game.[56] Outside of these concerns raised by NFL teams, some events, while limited in numbers, may further attempt to discourage secondary ticket sales. For example, the Masters Tournament (golf) punishes ticket holders for selling their tickets on the secondary market. In order to get tickets to the Masters, a fan has to enter and win a lottery for the right to purchase tickets to the event. In the past, if the Masters determined that ticket holders attempted to sell their tickets on a secondary site, the organization would then invalidate those tickets and remove the ticket holders' names from any future ticket lotteries.[57]

Regardless of any concerns with secondary ticket providers, we have seen a significant increase in these types of deals. SeatGeek partnered with properties such as the NFL and MLS, StubHub had agreements with the NFL and MLB, Vivid Seats had partnerships with the UFC and WWE, and each also have individual partnerships with numerous teams and other properties not mentioned.[58-60]

Mobile Ticketing

For the majority of major sport leagues and teams, mobile ticketing is becoming a primary distribution method, if not the exclusive method for distribution. For instance, in the NFL, 67 percent of fans who entered stadiums in 2019 used mobile entry, which was up from 49 percent in 2018.[61] The NHL has also seen growth of mobile ticket usage at its major events. During the 2018 and 2019 NHL All Star Games, the league had an 85 percent and 88 percent growth in mobile ticket usage, respectively.[62] Numerous teams across all of the major leagues are either encouraging the use of mobile ticketing or even transitioning exclusively to mobile tickets, while some college athletics programs have noted that mobile ticketing may be a good way to increase student attendance.[63] This trend is not just limited to the "big leagues." In 2017, MiLB, which oversees 160 teams, signed a deal with Tickets.com to be its Official Ticketing Provider. One of the main elements of this deal was the integration of a mobile ticketing platform.[64]

The transition to mobile ticketing has taken place for a variety of reasons:

- Combating fraudulent tickets
- Providing an easier and safer method to transfer tickets
- Meeting the needs of digital sport consumers who use their smartphone for daily functions and transactions
- Capturing fan information

In order to receive and use most mobile tickets, fans have to set up an online account or sign up for the team or ticket company's mobile app. In doing so, each fan is then added to the team's database. Previously, a team may have known who the original purchaser of the ticket was and had that person's information in its database, but if that original buyer sold the ticket, the team would not have the information of the person who actually came to the game. That has changed now. For example, with the advent of league-wide mobile ticketing in the NFL, 819,000 new fans were added to team databases.[61] Of course, having their names in a database provides a great opportunity to further market to these people. Now, teams can reach out to their ticket buyers with special promotions, to promote upcoming events, or to sell other team-related products, such as merchandise or apparel.

Even major events, whose tickets have long been collectible items, are using mobile tickets. The majority of the 2020 College Football Playoffs tickets were mobile tickets, and during the 2020 Super Bowl, the NFL anticipated that 10,000 fans would use their phone as their ticket. There is some speculation that the Super Bowl may soon move fully to mobile ticketing, but this does not mean that fans would pay thousands of dollars to attend a Super Bowl and not get a commemorative ticket. A quote from NFL senior vice president of club business development Bobby Gallo should ease the minds of those fans: "If and when we fully go mobile, part of our plan is still to provide the fans who attended the game with a commemorative ticket of their seats."[65]

However, mobile ticketing still has some kinks that need to be worked out. For many fans, particularly those not as comfortable with mobile phones and apps, this new ticketing process can cause confusion in regard to what accounts are needed, what apps to download, and where and how to store the digital ticket. Additionally, poor WiFi connections at stadiums can also lead to accessibility issues with the apps and tickets. Even a simple sun glare may make it difficult to scan the bar code. All of this leads to longer lines at the gates, potentially creating an unpleasant experience for fans, and even worse, causing them to miss part of the game.

Thankfully, most of these problems can be addressed with time and proper education of the fans, training of the stadium staff, and investment in better WiFi capabilities (a more expensive fix). Some organizations have taken a different approach and eliminated the need for bar codes by using tap-and-go technology. Think about using a key fob to open a car door, tapping a hotel room key on the door, or tapping your credit card on a reader to pay for groceries (as opposed to inserting the key or card). Ticketing and technology company Paciolan has created a similar system for tickets to sports events. In partnerships with 11 college programs, fans (primarily student-ticket holders) receive an email or text with their tickets. They can then save these tickets to their Google or Apple wallet. Once at the stadium, the fans simply hold their phone under a reader, which then detects the ticket without having to scan a bar code. Fans can even use their smartwatch to access their tickets.[66]

Authenticity of Tickets and the Sales Process

The introduction of online ticket purchasing has presented problems. Have you ever tried to purchase tickets to an event just to have that event sell out within a matter of minutes? Ticket brokers are able to create automated software programs, often called ticket bots, that can purchase large groups of tickets at once. This could leave fans without the ability to purchase tickets at face value when tickets go on sale and with only one expensive resort—to go to the secondary market where prices will be high for events that are in demand.

Ticket sales and distribution companies have tried for years to combat this problem. One technology created by Ticketmaster, Verified Fan, was developed in an attempt to give actual fans the chance to buy tickets before ticket brokers purchased them in bulk. In order to purchase tickets to an event that is using Ticketmaster's Verified Fan, fans must register online with their Ticketmaster account to indicate their interest in that particular event. Ticketmaster then uses this to verify their individual account and provides them with a unique code to use for purchasing tickets once they go on sale. In essence, fans are receiving an invitation with this code to purchase tickets. While this system does not guarantee that someone will get tickets—after all, major events are going to sell out—it does give more fans the ability to purchase tickets as opposed to tickets being purchased in bulk by ticket bots. In the early stages of this program, Ticketmaster indicated that it has been able to block 90 percent of purchase attempts by suspected ticket bots.[67]

In addition to issues with ticket bots, there are instances when someone has purchased a ticket from a secondary source, received a PDF of the ticket to print out or a screenshot of a mobile ticket, only to find out at the gate that the ticket was either fake or had an invalid bar code. Many fans unfortunately have fallen victim to unscrupulous scammers who sell these counterfeit tickets on the secondary market. As previously discussed, one of the reasons many teams, leagues, and events are pushing to go entirely mobile is to counteract fraudulent tickets. With mobile tickets, unique bar codes can be provided for each ticket and updated each time the ticket is accessed. For instance, Ticketmaster's SafeTix technology links each ticket to a person's Ticketmaster account, but more importantly, it provides a unique bar code that refreshes every few seconds.[68] This not only eliminates the need for printed tickets but also ensures that a screenshot of a mobile ticket would not work for entry. However, with these new technologies, it is important for teams to educate their fans on the types of tickets that will or will not be accepted at the gate so fans do not fall victim to the sale of fraudulent tickets.

Staying Creative

As the previous examples suggest, marketers must use creativity in planning and implementing new channels of distribution. Keeping abreast of the latest technologies and keeping an open mind are critical to success. For instance, as ticket distribution methods evolve, so do the types of ticket packages that are offered. For example, subscription plans are designed to reach a younger demographic that prefers a more flexible schedule and experience, and fans pay a monthly or flat fee and get access to discounted tickets. Depending on the program and the availability of tickets for the particular game, these tickets could be located anywhere within the stadium. Some subscription plans also offer access to special gathering spaces in the stadium or to discounted concession items. Generally, these types of plans are available only on a mobile platform, and sometimes tickets are not distributed until the day of the game.

In the past, implementing a plan and distribution system such as this may never have been a consideration. However, we think of this system as the Netflix or Hulu of sport tickets: fans pay a monthly fee and get to choose the content (e.g., attending the game) when and how they want it. While many different teams in a variety of leagues have implemented these subscription programs, these programs have become especially popular in MLB, where they were first launched in 2016. In the first year of the program, 150,000 tickets were sold, but just two years later, over one million tickets were sold through subscription plans. During the 2019 season, 17 MLB teams offered a subscription ticketing plan.[69]

Advances in technology also allow marketers to be creative in how they can distribute the broadcast of a game. With the introduction of virtual reality and augmented reality, leagues are experimenting with how to bring fans closer to the action. Imagine sitting courtside at a Lakers game all from the comfort of your couch through virtual reality or being able to select certain players and pull up their statistics, heart rate, and personal information while watching the game.

Some may think of this only as something once seen in a futuristic sci-fi movie. However, technology has advanced to the point where these types of applications are becoming increasingly possible. In 2019, the NBA launched an app in partnership with Magic Leap, the tech company that creates products that incorporate augmented reality into the user's current environment. With the app and the Magic Leap headgear, NBA fans can watch a game on a series of three different virtual screens with three-dimensional images and visualizations. For instance, while sitting in their living room, fans can see the game as they would on TV; pull up an image of the court, which shows shooting percentages from certain areas of the floor; or select a player, which then shows all of that player's information from the game in a separate screen or panel.[70]

Regardless of the product being distributed, the following are some simple questions that marketers need to ponder continually:

- Who are my consumers and what are their needs?
- Where are my consumers?
- What are my products and their extensions?
- What vehicles, especially using new technologies, are available for distribution?

Product-Place Matrix

Ultimately, marketers want to ensure effective and efficient use of all available distribution channels. New technologies are not restricted to top-tier professional teams and leagues. New media, wireless, and digital products create opportunities at all levels. Big-leagues organizations need not be the only ones that expand distribution in the digital and wireless age. Of course, not many teams have the draw and power of the Red Sox, Lakers, or Manchester United. But anyone can be thoughtful and imaginative. A valuable analytical tool is the product-place matrix (table 13.1), which helps conceptualize both the array of products offered by a sport organization and the various distribution channels used or available. A simple start to a matrix for a collegiate sport program might look like this. Each row represents a product element (event, players, coach), and

TABLE 13.1 Product-Place Matrix

Product	Place				
	Stadium, arena, fields	Old media	New media	Retail outlets	Outer markets
Events	Games	TV, radio	Apps, streaming services, social media	Game highlights at retail locations, watch parties	Home game scheduled in different market, watch parties
Players, coaches	Autograph sessions, meet and greets	Coaches' radio or TV shows, Internet blog	Podcasts, YouTube or Twitch channels, social media	Clinics, autograph sessions	Community outreach, clinics, coach caravan tours
Tickets	Box office	TV and radio giveaways, Internet	Social media promotions, mobile tickets through app	Kiosks at the mall, schedule cards and posters, giveaways or sales at retail outlets	Group sales, alumni groups in other markets
Merchandise	Stands in the concourse, team store	Direct mail, email marketing, online pro shop	Social media, apps	Licensed outlets	Licensed outlets

each column represents a distribution outlet (venues, media).

The matrix simply provides a graphic representation of current or planned product distribution. In this example, merchandise is distributed in many ways, each with its own unique opportunities and challenges. The facility itself will have stands throughout the stadium and potentially even outside of the stadium. For those who are not able to attend the games in person, they have the opportunity to purchase merchandise through the online shop, perhaps having received an email with a promotion code, which drove them to the site. Or fans may purchase merchandise through the team app or any number of retail outlets that sell licensed team product. It is up to marketers to consider how best to fill each part of such a grid, using their ingenuity while taking into account the needs and wants of their fans and any unique marketplace factors that will influence distribution.

Wrap-Up

Although the place function in sport marketing bears remote resemblance to the distribution function in consumer product marketing, its importance among the five Ps of sport marketing should not be minimized. The place in sport begins with the ensemble of elements, comprising the venue or facility and its surroundings. The facility location is critical to the success of most sport businesses. Of equal importance are the facility image and operation, which are influenced by physical design, amenities, and the attitudes of facility personnel. The core event and its extensions must then be distributed by way of marketing channels that include retail outlets and the media. The marketing channels for sport products are limited only by budgets and imaginations, but the possibilities can be graphically illustrated by use of a product-place matrix.

Activities

1. Apply the theory of place to your favorite sport venue, as we did to Fenway Park. What are the most important elements of the ensemble? What elements of the place ensemble could be accentuated in the design or in promotions?

2. Analyze a local facility in terms of its accessibility, flow, drawing radius, parking, aesthetics, staffing, security, surroundings, design and layout, and amenities. How would you improve these areas?

3. Analyze the ticket purchasing outlets of your favorite team. What are the pros and cons of using each outlet as a consumer?

4. Think about a recent purchase experience of team merchandise. How and where did you purchase the product (online, at the team shop, at a big box retail location)? Why did you use this particular outlet to purchase the merchandise? Were you happy with the shopping experience through this distribution point? In what ways could it be improved?

Your Marketing Plan

1. Outline a ticket distribution plan for your organization that makes use of some new technologies mentioned in this chapter.

2. Review a team's online pro shop to determine what type of merchandise your organization should offer. Determine if your organization should manage this function in-house or outsource it to a company like Fanatics, which was discussed in this chapter.

3. Create a product-place matrix for your organization. Think carefully about alternative channels for distributing your various products.

 Go to HK*Propel* to complete the activities for this chapter.

Chapter 14

Legal Aspects of Sport Marketing

John Grady

OBJECTIVES

- To introduce the key legal concepts and issues that affect the marketing of the sport product

- To inform sport marketers about the need, and the methods used, to protect intellectual property associated with the creation of a sport product or sports event, or with ideas developed out of sport sponsorship and licensing programs

- To examine the legal limits of sport marketing and promotion so that sport marketers can better manage risks and avoid legal liability

Andy Lyons/Getty Images

The USA Track & Field (USATF) Olympic Trials were held in late June 2016 in advance of the Rio 2016 Summer Olympic Games. Because of the restrictions in place surrounding Rule 40 of the Olympic Charter, discussed in depth later in this chapter, all advertising by non-Olympic sponsors had to have been pre-approved by United States Olympic & Paralympic Committee (USOPC).[1] At the USATF Olympic Trials, women's athletic brand Oiselle congratulated Olympic medal favorite Kate Grace, who is sponsored by Oiselle, on making the Olympic team with an Instagram post captioned "She's heading to Rio" along with a picture of Grace wearing her Oiselle race top while competing at the Trials.

The congratulatory post on Instagram was immediately met with a demand by USOPC to cease all "Olympic-related advertising." USOPC sent the following to nonsponsor companies: "Commercial entities may not post about the Trials or Games on their corporate social media accounts . . . This restriction includes the use of USO[P]C's trademarks in hashtags such as #Rio2016 or #TeamUSA." This was the first time USOPC asserted ownership when its trademarks were used specifically as hashtags.

USOPC advanced its legal position one step further by asserting that, other than traditional media companies, no business could reference Olympic results, share or repost anything from the official Olympic social media account, or use any pictures taken at the Olympic Games. This extreme prohibition likely excluded official Olympic sponsors, without explicitly stating it.

Oiselle responded to USOPC's legal threats by changing references to the Olympic Games to generic phrases like "The Big Event in the Southern Hemisphere." Oiselle also agreed it would alter or remove inappropriate references or photos on its website, social media posts, and blog as well to address USOPC's concerns.

This example demonstrates the extraordinary steps USOPC and other sport properties take to enforce their trademarks in an increasingly social and digital marketing space. Not unlike other brands, Team USA vigorously enforces its intellectual property rights against those who are not official "partners" of the Olympic Movement within the United States.

This chapter addresses the issues that arise at the intersection of sport marketing and the law. Without a working knowledge of the legal aspects of sport marketing, those who market the sport product (ranging from teams to players to events), as well as corporations that market their products and services through sport, risk a host of legal consequences. Hence, this chapter provides an overview of the general concepts and practical issues that are most relevant to sport marketers, including intellectual property law, right of publicity law, promotions law, and ambush marketing. At the outset, one must recognize that these legal issues are complex and often require assistance from sport lawyers who increasingly specialize in these areas. It is also important to acknowledge that the legal landscape within sport marketing is constantly evolving as courts decide new legal cases and sport organizations update their rules and regulations based on these

decisions. For instance, the introductory scenario about Rule 40 illuminates some of the practical legal issues that have arisen from the International Olympic Committee's (IOC) decision in June 2019 to ease restrictions on Olympic athlete and non-official sponsor advertising in advance of the 2020 Summer Olympic Games in Tokyo by allowing each National Governing Body (NGB) to set its own Rule 40 policy and prcedures.[1]

Intellectual Property

After many decades, Dylan B. Fan's favorite hometown team, the Aces, has finally reached the World Series. As both a die-hard fan and an entrepreneur, Dylan is eager to put to use all the marketing ideas that she has been dreaming up to take advantage of this momentous event. For instance, she has come up with a catchy slogan to emblazon on T-shirts, above a logo that is remarkably similar to that of the Aces, and she plans to sell the shirts outside the stadium. She's also developed her own special logo to commemorate the event: two interlocking baseballs that prominently feature the colors of her hometown team, with the words *World Champs* superimposed across the baseballs. She has already created the Twitter handle @WorldChampAces and Instagram Business Account WorldChampAces where she plans to post regularly about her love for her hometown team, linking features on Aces players that include their photographs, and sell her wares. She can't wait to begin cashing in.

The primary goal of intellectual property law is to reward invention, ingenuity, and creativity to maintain an open and competitive marketplace. To encourage this type of progress in science and the arts, the framers of the U.S. Constitution delegated to Congress the power to protect the intellectual property rights of artists, authors, and inventors by granting them "the exclusive right to their writings and discoveries."[2] Thus, property rights are granted to protect the "fruits of their labor, even when the labors are intellectual."[3] If Dylan B. Fan has a unique idea, she should be entitled to capitalize on it—as long as she is not infringing on the prior rights of others. Although people often see the symbols identifying intellectual property rights (© [copyright], ™ [trademark]), most do not realize the exact nature of the legal protection provided to a trademark, copyright, or patent owner. The first section of this chapter focuses primary attention on the area of trademark law, the area of greatest relevance to sport marketers. Copyright and patent law, as well as a form of intellectual property recognized as the right of publicity, is also discussed in terms of its relevance to sport marketers.

To decide the type of legal protection that people should use to protect new ideas or products, we must first examine the character of the intellectual property. For example, trademarks protect unique words, names, symbols, and slogans; copyrights protect original works of authorship; and patents protect inventions (new designs and novel processes). Ownership rights to trademarks may last forever, whereas rights to copyrights and patents have time limits. A trademark, copyright, or patent owner may grant permission for a work's use to others for a fee, an arrangement known as *licensing.* When another

person does not have permission or licensed rights to use the copyright, trademark, or patent, that person is said to be infringing on the intellectual property owner's rights.

A single product can conceivably receive intellectual property protection across all three intellectual property categories. Take, for example, Spalding's line of Infusion basketballs. The manufacturer has a patent on the technology that enables consumers to inflate the ball with a micropump that is built into the ball, a copyright on the information conveyed on the packaging, and a trademark for the unique name of the product ("Infusion").

Overview of Trademark Law

Trademarks serve five important purposes. A consumer's decision to purchase a T-shirt featuring the logo of a favorite team, the Blue Sox (a fictional sport team), provides a good illustration:

1. Trademarks serve to *identify the source or origin* of the product (or service) and to distinguish it from others. Based on the logo on the T-shirt, the consumer knows that the Blue Sox team is the source of this product.

2. Trademarks *protect consumers* from confusion and deception. In other words, the law allows the Blue Sox to sue any other person (individual or company) who seeks to confuse or deceive the consumer into believing that the Blue Sox was the source of the product purchased, when it wasn't.

3. A trademark is used to *designate a consistent level of quality* of a product (or service). Thus, the consumer knows that when she buys a T-shirt with the Blue Sox logo, the product has been confirmed for quality and won't fall apart in the washer.

4. A trademark *represents the goodwill* of the owner's products (or services). In other words, the consumer has chosen to buy a Blue Sox T-shirt because she has good feelings about the Blue Sox.

5. Trademarks *signify a substantial advertising investment.* The Blue Sox has invested tremendous time and financial resources in building the value and goodwill of its name and trademarks, and the law is

designed to discourage other companies from trading off this goodwill or diminishing this value by using similar marks on their competitive products (or services).

Trademarks are protected on the national level by the Federal Trademark Act of 1946, commonly referred to as the Lanham Act.[4] The Lanham Act, which has become increasingly important for sport marketers involved in the marketing of sport products, teams, players, and events, protects three primary types of marks: trademarks, service marks, and collective marks.

- A **trademark** is a word, name, symbol, or device used by a person—generally a manufacturer or merchant—to identify and distinguish its goods from those manufactured and sold by others, and to indicate the source of the goods. This section also includes trade dress, a particular type of trademark that provides protection for the packaging of a product. In the sport setting, it typically involves the product's shape, color, or color scheme, a concept that will be discussed later in this chapter.

- A **service mark** is a word, name, symbol, or device used to identify and distinguish a company's services, including a unique service, from those of another service provider. Service marks are typically used in the sale or advertising of an intangible service, such as the entertainment value of a sports event. For example, the *World Series* and the *NCAA Final Four* are service marks, in that they are events (services provided to fans), as opposed to tangible products. (You can't go out and buy a World Series, although some fans would argue otherwise!)

- A **collective mark** is defined in the Lanham Act as a trademark or service mark used by the members of a cooperative, an association, or other group or organization, and

Trademarks protect the GEICO, Nike, and Washington Mystics logos (on the uniform) and the Spalding logo (on the ball).
G Fiume/Getty Images

serves to indicate membership in a union, an association, or other organization. Good examples of collective marks are the logos used by the players associations in the professional sport industry, as well as the logos of the leagues themselves.

To gain national trademark protection under the Lanham Act, the trademark must be registered with the United States Patent and Trademark Office (USPTO), which also resolves any disputes related to trademark registration. For the trademarks of local, community-based sports events and properties, in which federal trademark protection may be deemed not necessary, protection is still afforded under various state statutes that provide their own protections similar to those provided by the Lanham Act but which typically fall under the theory of unfair competition (discussed later). Although federal registration of a mark is not required to establish ownership rights in a mark, it does provide several important benefits, including the following:

- The ability of the trademark owner to sue in federal court
- The ability to obtain trademark registration in foreign countries
- The opportunity to file the trademark with the U.S. Customs Service to prevent the importation of infringing foreign goods
- The acknowledgment and protection of the goodwill of the trademark holder
- The provision of public notice throughout the nation of trademark ownership, thus creating an easier burden of proof in trademark infringement lawsuits[5]

Ownership of a trademark generally requires the holder to appropriate the mark and to use it for commercial purposes.[6] Since 1988, however, the Lanham Act has allowed an individual person to apply for registration to the USPTO if the applicant can establish "a bona fide intention" to use a trademark in commerce within a reasonable period.[7] For example, in 2019, New England Patriots quarterback Tom Brady filed an application to register the phrase "Tom Terrific" for use on product lines for clothing and collectable trading cards.[8] However, after protests from baseball fans and others that the nickname "Tom Terrific" is widely used to refer to baseball great Tom Seaver, Brady clarified his "intent to use" in registering the mark was actually to prevent others from using it because he dislikes the phrase being associated with him.[9] Unlike copyrights and patents, which have expirations, trademarks can last indefinitely as long as the trademark owner continues to use the trademark in commerce.[10] When creating a new trademark, sport marketers are advised to hire intellectual property counsel to conduct a trademark search to determine whether any conflicting marks already exist, which can typically be done for several hundred dollars. Furthermore, although the USPTO does not conduct searches for the public, it does provide a public library of marks as well as a searchable electronic database.

What Marks Can Be Protected?

The USPTO classifies marks on different levels. Simply put, the more distinctive the mark is, the more likely it is that it will be considered for federal registration and thus afforded protection under the Lanham Act. The issue of distinctiveness will typically come up during the registration process, raised either by the USPTO or by a competitor seeking to challenge the registration of a proposed mark. (Legal counsel for sport properties regularly review trademark application lists to ensure that a person is not seeking to register a mark that the sport property would find objectionable.)

Trademarks that are inherently distinctive and completely distinguishable are characterized as *fanciful* or *arbitrary*.[11] Sport marketers challenged with creating a trademark (for instance, the name of a team, an event, or a product) should endeavor to create a mark that is fanciful or arbitrary. Such marks are invented for the sole purpose of functioning as a trademark. MiLB teams have led the way in creating fanciful names, such as the Wisconsin Timber Rattlers, the Cedar Rapids Kernels, and the West Tennessee Diamond Jaxx. (Such fanciful names and corresponding logos have also proven a boon to merchandise sales.) Other common examples of fanciful trade names within the sport world include Speedo and event names such as MotoX and X Games.

Arbitrary marks, although not as distinctive as fanciful marks, are words, names, symbols, or devices that are commonly known words that have become associated with a particular product or service through the advertising and marketing efforts of the owner. Examples in the sport world include the Gravity Games, Field Turf, and the now-defunct Arena Football League (AFL).

The last category of inherently distinctive marks is *suggestive* marks. Although weaker than fanciful or arbitrary marks, a suggestive mark subtly connotes something about the product or service, but it does not actually describe any specific ingredient, quality, or characteristic of the product or service. With suggestive marks, consumers must use their imagination to draw an association. The more suggestive the mark, the more consumer imagination is required to make the association. Examples include Powerade, a word that suggests certain characteristics that the isotonic beverage provides to sweating consumers, and Nike (a Greek goddess who is the personification of victory).

On the opposite end of the spectrum are trademarks that, on their face, do not distin-guish one product or service from another and typically use common words in their ordinary spelling and meanings. Such marks are referred to in trademark law as being either *descriptive*, which are difficult, although not impossible, to protect and *generic*, which are never entitled to trademark protection. Thus, sport marketers are advised to refrain from creating marks that would be deemed either descriptive or generic. A good example of a descriptive mark widely used by sport marketers today is sport-themed hashtags, such as those that refer to a major sports event like the Super Bowl. Because hashtags often serve simply to aggregate or categorize multiple sources of conversation about a particular topic, hashtagged words and phrases can be denied protection as trademarks if they are deemed to not serve the trademark function, which is to identify a single source of origin.[12] This is not to say, however, that a word or words contained in the hashtag do not serve the trademark function.

Some sport organizations now assert trademark protection for their event-related marks when those trademarks are used as hashtags.

Thus, #SB53 may be considered descriptive, whereas the hashtag #SuperBowlLIII meets the requirements for trademark protection since *Super Bowl* is a federally-registered trademark.

Secondary Meaning

Descriptive logos and marks can gain trademark protection if they are deemed by the courts to have acquired secondary meaning, defined as "a mental recognition in buyers' and potential buyers' minds that products connected with the symbol or device emanate from or are associated with the same source."[13] One of the most hotly contested areas of sport litigation has focused on whether color schemes of college and professional teams are subject to trademark protection. This determination is based on the extent to which the team color schemes have acquired secondary meaning. One of the earliest such cases involved a lawsuit filed by the Seattle Seahawks against an apparel manufacturer who was producing football-style jerseys in Seahawks colors, albeit without the Seahawks logo. The court held that the Seahawks' color scheme on a football jersey had acquired secondary meaning, entitling the Seahawks to trademark protection over this particular use of its color scheme on football jerseys.[13]

The collegiate sport industry has provided a legal forum for debating the concept of secondary meaning with regard to school color schemes. In *Board of Supervisors of LSU v. Smack Apparel, Inc.*, the defendant sold apparel using Louisiana State University's team colors (purple and gold), although without any other official university logos or insignias.[14] The apparel contained expressions that obliquely referred to the university and that were calculated to appeal to LSU fans. For example, one T-shirt bearing the phrase "Sweet as Sugar!" was sold after LSU won the Sugar Bowl. The university claimed trademark rights in the team colors. The court, although acknowledging that colors were not inherently distinctive, held that the secondary meaning requirement was met because consumers identified the colors with LSU and were likely to associate the goods with the university. Note that this particular case also turned on the First Amendment free speech rights of the defendant Smack Apparel. Although the court ruled in favor of the university with regard to apparel that included team colors with laudatory phrases, it held in favor of Smack Apparel on the majority of T-shirts that, although using team colors, included disparaging phrases and imagery that were deemed to fall into the category of parody, a type of speech afforded the highest level of First Amendment protection.

Trademark Infringement

The licensing of trademarks has become a billion-dollar business across both professional and collegiate sports. To preserve these revenue streams, sport marketers have become increasingly vigilant in protecting against trademark infringement, sometimes even at the risk of generating negative public relations. For instance, MLB has, in the past, threatened legal action against teams in the Cape Cod League, a college baseball summer league, for using team names trademarked by MLB.[15] Major college football teams have also threatened legal action against high schools using their marks.[16] The Lanham Act provides three primary legal claims that are often jointly incorporated into a lawsuit:[17]

1. *Trademark infringement*, which protects against uses of a trademark that are likely to cause confusion or mistake, or to deceive
2. *False designation of origin*, which is designed to prevent uses of another's trademark that cause confusion as to affiliation or sponsorship (also referred to as a "false endorsement" claim in the context of right of publicity cases)
3. *Dilution*, which protects against the reduction in value of a famous mark's distinctive quality

The burden of proving these Lanham Act violations is on the trademark owner.

Traditional Trademark Infringement

The Lanham Act defines infringement as "any reproduction, counterfeit, copy, or colorable imitation of a registered mark in connection with the sale, offering for sale, distribution, or advertising of any goods or services on or in connection with which such use is likely to cause confusion, or to cause mistake, or to deceive" without the consent of the trademark holder.[18]

Remember that the purpose of trademark law is, first and foremost, to protect consumers. Hence, the linchpin of a trademark infringement case is the likelihood of consumer confusion, which plaintiffs typically attempt to prove with consumer surveys. The factors used by the courts in determining likelihood of confusion were first developed in the seminal case *Polaroid Corp. v. Polarad, Inc.*[19] Although other federal courts have enunciated their own "likelihood of confusion" factor test, they all generally adhere to the eight factors initially set forth in the so-called Polaroid Test.[20]

Assume that the Aces sue Dylan B. Fan, alleging that creating and selling her T-shirts (sporting her catchy slogan above a logo remarkably similar to that of the Aces) constitutes trademark infringement. The Aces' ability to prove likelihood of confusion will be based on the court's evaluation of the following eight factors, or a combination of them:

1. *The strength of the Aces' trademark.* (Is the Aces' trademark fanciful, arbitrary, suggestive, descriptive with secondary meaning, or generic?)
2. *The degree of similarity.* (To what extent are the Aces' trademark and Dylan B. Fan's alleged infringing trademark similar?)
3. *The similarity of the products involved.* (How similar are the slogan and logo?)
4. *The market channels involved.* (Do the Aces offer its product to a group of consumers who are similar to that which Dylan B. Fan seeks to target?)
5. *The distribution channels involved.* (Do the Aces sell its product in the same places as Dylan is offering her product?)
6. *The intent of the defendant in adopting the trademark.* (Does evidence show that Dylan is trying to confuse consumers into believing that her product is somehow sponsored by or affiliated with the Aces?)
7. *The sophistication of the potential consumers.* (Are buying consumers sophisticated enough to understand that the Aces are not the source of Dylan's product?)
8. *The evidence of actual confusion.* (Can the Aces provide evidence, typically through consumer surveys, that consumers are confused about the source of Dylan's product?)

False Designation of Origin

A second claim under which a trademark owner may sue is termed *false designation of origin*. The Lanham Act protects trademark owners by prohibiting a competitor's false designation of origin when it "is likely to cause confusion . . . or to deceive as to the affiliation, connection, or association of such person with another person, or as to the origin, sponsorship, or approval of his or her goods, services, or commercial activities by another person."[21]

Under this theory, the owner of the trademark must establish that the public recognizes that the trademark identifies the owner's goods and services and distinguishes its goods or services from others. After such public recognition is established, the plaintiff must then prove that the defendant's use of the trademark is likely to confuse or deceive the public into thinking that the plaintiff was the origin or source of the product or service. Oftentimes, this is discussed as the alleged infringer confusing the public that it has a sponsorship affiliation with the organization that owns the trademark.

One of the leading sport-related cases is *Dallas Cowboys Cheerleaders, Inc. v. Pussycat Cinema, Ltd.*[22] In this case, the defendant owned and operated an X-rated cinema in which it showed a pornographic film titled *Debbie Does Dallas*. In the film, an actor was shown wearing a uniform strikingly similar to that of the Dallas Cowboys Cheerleaders. The marquee posters advertising the film depicted the woman in a Dallas Cowboys Cheerleader uniform and referred to Dallas and the Dallas Cowboys Cheerleaders. The court, in ruling for the Cowboys cheerleaders and barring distribution of the film, ruled that the plaintiff had a valid trademark (based on the concept of secondary meaning) in its uniform's white boots, white shorts, blue blouse, and star-studded white vest and belt. The court found it likely that the public would associate the Cowboys cheerleaders with the movie and would be confused into believing that the plaintiff had sponsored the movie. Although the defendant argued that no reasonable person would ever believe that the Cowboys Cheerleaders would be associated with an X-rated film, the court challenged such a reading of consumer confusion as too narrow. Instead, the court stated that to evoke consumer confusion, the uniform depicted in the film need only bring to mind the Dallas Cowboys Cheerleaders, which the court stated it unquestionably did.

Dilution

A third potential claim is for dilution of a famous trademark through what is known as blurring or tarnishment. Dilution claims are governed by the Federal Trademark Dilution Act (FTDA) of 1995.[23] Dilution claims are typically brought in conjunction with trademark infringement and unfair competition claims and can occur by blurring (whereby the defendant's use of an identical or similar mark or trade name impairs the distinctiveness of the plaintiff's famous mark) or by tarnishment (whereby the defendant's use of a similar mark or trade name harms the reputation of the plaintiff's famous mark).[24] The 2006 Dilution Amendments established that the plaintiff need only show that the defendant's mark is likely to cause dilution by blurring or tarnishment, regardless of the presence or absence of actual or likely confusion, of competition, or of actual economic injury. The 2006 Dilution Amendments also included a reconfiguration of the factors used to determine whether a mark is famous for dilution purposes and stated that dilution claims were not applicable to trademarks that had acquired only "niche fame."

To state a claim under the 2006 Dilution Amendments, a plaintiff must show the following:

1. The plaintiff owns a famous mark that is distinctive.
2. The defendant has commenced using a mark in commerce that allegedly is diluting the famous mark.
3. A similarity between the defendant's mark and the famous mark gives rise to an association between the marks.
4. The association is likely to impair the distinctiveness of the famous mark or likely to harm the reputation of the famous mark.

The crux of a dilution claim is the premise that the trademark is famous. Perhaps the most significant clarification of the 2006 Dilution Amendments is the requirement that the mark "be widely recognized by the general consuming public of the United States as a designation of source of the goods or services of the mark's owner."[25]

To conclude our examination of trademark rights, it is worth noting that many trademark-based lawsuits often include a variety of claims. A case illustrating how multiple claims are brought together in one legal action is *NCAA v. Kizzang LLC.*[26] The NCAA sued Kizzang to prevent the company from registering the trademarks "April Madness" and "Final 3" in connection with online fantasy sports games. These terms were confusingly similar to the NCAA's registered marks "March Madness" and "Final Four." The NCAA argued that Kizzang's proposed marks not only infringed the NCAA's registered marks but also unfairly competed with and diluted the NCAA's registered trademarks.[27] The court ruled in the NCAA's favor and ordered any merchandise or advertising containing the contested marks be recalled.

Taking Action Against Alleged Infringers

What should a sport property or manufacturer do when it discovers a case of alleged trademark infringement? The property owner typically drafts a letter to the alleged infringer asking the person to cease and desist (i.e., stop) the alleged infringing activity. If the alleged infringer refuses to cooperate, the Lanham Act (as well as applicable state laws) entitles the trademark owner to bring suit for injunctive relief—a court order to stop the infringing activities before and during the trial. To be granted an injunction, the intellectual property owner has to demonstrate three elements to the court:

1. The trademark owner will be irreparably harmed by the infringing activities.
2. The trademark owner will be more harmed if the injunction is not granted than the defendant will be harmed if the injunction is granted.
3. The trademark owner can demonstrate a strong likelihood of winning the infringement case.

After the injunction is granted, the owner seeks a trial on the merits of the case to receive a financial remedy for the infringement.

Defenses to Trademark Infringement

When a trademark infringement claim is brought, the defendant may raise a number of defenses, including, among others, abandonment, fair use, and the claim that the trademark is or has become generic.

Abandonment

Unlike copyrights and patents, which expire, trademarks can last indefinitely, provided the holder continues to use the trademark in commerce. Under the Lanham Act, however, a trademark can be deemed abandoned when the trademark owner discontinues its use *and* does not intend to resume using the mark within a reasonable length of time.[4] Thus, when a sport property changes its name or logo, but it wishes to retain ownership of previous marks, the property must take precautionary steps to prevent abandonment of these marks. Typically, these steps include maintaining the marks' registration at the appropriate renewal periods and periodically using the old marks in some manner. Sport marketers should note that marks can also be deemed to be abandoned as a result of excessive licensing, lack of supervision over other parties' licensed use of the marks, or both.

Because trademarks are valuable, courts do require substantial proof of abandonment.[28] One interesting case, *Abdul-Jabbar v. General Motors Corp.*, raised the issue of abandonment of a birth name.[29] During the time leading up to the 1993 NCAA Men's Final Four, General Motors (GM) ran an advertisement that used trivia regarding Kareem Abdul-Jabbar's UCLA and NCAA records. When Abdul-Jabbar had set the records, his name was Lew Alcindor. Besides citing the trivia question, Abdul-Jabbar alleged that the advertisement compared the car to him. GM responded that when he converted to Islam, he abandoned the name Lew Alcindor and thus infringement did not occur. In finding for Abdul-Jabbar, the judge stated, "One's birth name is an integral part of one's identity . . . it is not 'kept alive' through commercial use. . . . An individual's decision to use a name other than the birth name . . . does not therefore imply intent to set aside the birth name, or the identity associated with that name."[29]

Fair Use Defense

Trademark rights are not absolute, and the law allows the use of another's trademarks on or in connection with the sale of one's own goods or services as long as the use is not deceptive.[30] Thus, a fair use defense allows, for instance, a company such as Adidas to use the Nike trademark in its ads to compare the two products. The fair use defense has been successfully used by a company that sold refurbished discounted golf balls manufactured by another company.[31] The fair use defense has also been found applicable under the constitutional protections of commercial speech. For example, in a case involving the United States Olympic Committee (USOC), a court found that a publisher who produced a magazine titled *OLYMPICS USA* did not infringe on the USOC's rights to the word *Olympics*.[32] The court held that to restrict a publisher's use of the word *Olympics* would raise serious issues regarding the First Amendment protection afforded news media organizations.

Genericness

As discussed earlier, one cannot obtain trademark protection for generic terms, even through the acquisition of secondary meaning. Thus, an alleged infringer can argue that the trademark in question is generic. Because of this, leagues cannot claim to own terms such as *championships* or *the big game*. Moreover, a well-known trademark can become generic over time if it is not aggressively protected by the trademark holder. Familiar examples include aspirin, cellophane, and trampoline, all of which were at one time registered trademarks and have since fallen into the public domain. The possibility that a trademark will become generic points out the need for companies to protect and promote their trademarks aggressively.

Additional Trademark Protection Issues

Legal issues for sport marketers continue to emerge from the use of the Internet for commerce, communication, public relations, and advertising. The ubiquity of the Internet has led to a wild, wild, west of trademark issues, most notably cybersquatting, whereby individuals registered domain names solely for the purposes of trying to sell the names back to the rightful trademark owners. Both the courts and the U.S. legislature have addressed this earliest form of trademark infringement on the Internet. Numerous cases have held that use of another's trademark in a domain name can constitute trademark infringement in violation of the Lanham Act.[33] Before 1999, a trademark owner's sole remedy for the use of its trademark in a domain name was limited under the Lanham Act to infringement or dilution claims. But, in 1999, Congress passed the Anticybersquatting Consumer Protection Act (ACPA).[34] Under the ACPA, a person is liable if that person "has a bad faith intent to profit from that mark" and registers, traffics in, or uses a domain name that "in the case of a mark that is distinctive at the time of registration of the domain name, is identical or confusingly similar to that mark" or "in the case of a famous mark that is famous at the time of registration of the domain name, is identical or confusingly similar to or dilutive of that mark."[35] Under the ACPA, several remedies are available, including forfeiture or cancellation of the domain name, transfer of the domain name, and recovery of monetary damages. Practitioners need to remain diligent in the registration of new team names and slogans that are used in domain names.

With the sport industry having become part of the global economy where more information is carried on the Internet and more commerce is transacted through the Internet, owners of intellectual property must consider registering copyrights, trademarks, and patents in foreign countries. To provide better protection to trademark owners operating in international commerce, the Madrid Protocol went into effect in 2003. Under the protocol, a U.S. trademark applicant is now able to file a single application with the USPTO to obtain protection in all protocol member countries. Over 60 countries are signatories to the protocol. Thus, U.S. trademark applicants no longer need to endure the costly and time-consuming process of filing separate registrations in each country in which they seek protection. After an application is filed in the United States, the USPTO forwards it to the International Register of the World Intellectual Property Organization (WIPO) for processing.

The sale of licensed products and the staging of sports events in foreign countries have become increasingly important revenue streams for U.S.-based sport properties. Furthermore, tremendous growth is occurring in sport industries in China, Korea, and the nations of Europe, particularly for sports such as baseball, basketball, American football, and action sports. U.S.-based sport marketers need to be cognizant of the importance of ensuring that the trademarks that identify their products, services, and events are protected in these countries. In China, for example, Michael Jordan initiated a lawsuit to stop Chinese domestic brand Qiaodan Sports from selling shoes and apparel using the direct Chinese translation of Jordan's name "Qiaodan."[36] Jordan challenged this use by the sport apparel brand when represented as Chinese characters as well as its use of his iconic jersey number 23 in selling Qiaodan Sports products. Jordan claimed this use misled Chinese consumers to believe he was behind the brand. Initial rulings gave Jordan a partial victory in the Chinese court system, forcing Qiaodan Sports to give up its trademark rights to the use of Jordan's name when represented by Chinese characters.[37]

Copyright Law and Sport Marketing

In her excitement over the Aces' pending World Series victory, Dylan B. Fan has written a clever song titled "The Aces Clear the Bases" that she intends to market. Using her entrepreneurial spirit, she also plans to record the World Series games, edit the clips herself, and sell copies of the video, called *The Road to the Title*, through her various social media accounts.

An understanding of copyright law is also important for sport marketers. Copyrights, for instance, protect the music that is played during games and require sport marketers to seek approval through American Society of Composers, Authors, and Publishers (ASCAP), which protects musicians' copyrights of their works. Sport marketers who are responsible for creating advertising or promotional campaigns that use written works, music, pictures or graphic designs, or audiovisual works, including broadcasts of sports events, need to be aware of copyright laws.

At the outset, an important point to understand is that, in the context of copyright law, a person cannot copyright a mere *idea.* This concept was illustrated in the case of *Hoopla Sports and Entertainment, Inc. v. Nike, Inc.,* in which the plaintiff unsuccessfully sued Nike for allegedly stealing its idea for a high school basketball all-star game.[38] Although the plaintiff alleged copyright infringement, the court, in granting Nike's motion to dismiss, held that the idea for the game was not copyrightable.

Copyright law is primarily governed by the Copyright Act of 1976, which protects original works of authorship appearing in any tangible medium of expression.[39] In addition, the Digital Millennium Copyright Act (DMCA) provides copyright laws regarding digital creations and the Internet.[40]

A copyright can be for something currently in existence or something to be developed later; but the work must be something that can be perceived, reproduced, or otherwise communicated. Works of authorship include the following:[41]

- Literary works, such as books and stories
- Musical works, including any accompanying words
- Dramatic works, including any accompanying music
- Pantomimes and choreographic works
- Pictorial, graphic, and sculptural works
- Motion pictures and other audiovisual works
- Sound recordings
- Architectural works

Because of the large number of advances in technology, these protected works are defined in broad terms. Copyright protection for an original work of authorship, however, does not extend to any idea, procedure, process, system, method of operation, concept, principle, or discovery, regardless of the form in which it is described, explained, or illustrated.[41]

The Copyright Act grants a copyright owner the right to do the following:[42]

- Reproduce or distribute copies or sound recordings of the copyrighted work to the public by sale, rental, lease, or lending
- Prepare derivative works based on the copyrighted work

- Perform the copyrighted work publicly (literary, musical, dramatic, and choreographic works; pantomimes; motion pictures; and the like)
- Display the copyrighted work publicly (literary, musical, dramatic, and choreographic works; pantomimes; and pictorial, graphic, or sculptural works, including individual images of a motion picture or other audiovisual work)
- Perform the copyrighted work publicly by means of digital audio transmission (sound recordings)

Under common law, copyright protection begins at the time that the work originates and is fixed in a tangible form. But registering a copyright with the U.S. Copyright Office, like registering a trademark, provides several benefits to the copyright owner in the event of its unauthorized use. For instance, registration allows the copyright owner to sue immediately for infringement; otherwise, if the copyright is infringed, the owner must first register the copyright. Also, if a copyright is not registered before alleged infringement, the amount of recoverable damages is limited. In the event that a person does not choose to register her work with the U.S. Copyright Office, she should at least be sure to keep excellent records of her work as she is creating it and place a copyright symbol, or write out the word *copyright,* along with the origination date and her name, on the work. Another good idea is to notarize the ideas expressed to prove that the date listed on the copyrighted work has been accurately reported.

The U.S. Copyright Office also accepts registration for online works. Again, the key factor in determining if the online site is copyrightable is whether or not it possesses original authorship.[43] Copyright protection for works created on or after January 1, 1978, exists for a term consisting of the life of the author and 70 years after the author's death, after which time, the work of authorship falls into the public domain.[44] If the work was created by more than one person, the protection endures for the term consisting of the life of the last surviving author and another 70 years after the last surviving author's death. An employer holds the copyright on works created for an employer. For works made for an employer, the duration of the employer's copyright protection is 95 years from the time of publication or 120 years from the time of creation, whichever expires first.[45]

Copyright Infringement

Copyright infringement occurs when someone makes an unauthorized use of a copyrighted work. Courts consider four factors when determining if copyright infringement has occurred:[46]

1. The purpose of the use, including whether such use is of a commercial nature or is for nonprofit educational purposes
2. The nature (character) of the copyrighted work
3. The amount and substantiality of the portion used in relation to the copyrighted work as a whole
4. The effect of the use on the potential market for, or value of, the copyrighted work

Defenses to Copyright Infringement

In a copyright infringement case, a defendant may challenge the authenticity of the copyright. However, as is more commonly the case, a defendant may claim the defense of the fair use doctrine, which was originally created by the courts as a means of ensuring that creativity was not stifled through rigid enforcement of copyright law. The fair use doctrine, as first enunciated by the courts, has since been incorporated into the Copyright Act.[46] As such, it allows for the fair use of a copyrighted work when the use is "for purposes such as criticism, comment, news reporting, teaching (including multiple copies for classroom use), scholarship, or research."[46] The courts use the four factors stated earlier to determine whether the use made of the work falls within the fair use defense.

In a leading sport-related case, film clips of Muhammad Ali fights appeared in the documentary *When We Were Kings* despite an attempted preliminary injunction by the copyright owner of the clips to bar their use.[47] The court found that the defendant was likely to succeed on the fair use defense, thus allowing the film clips (between nine and 14 clips, amounting to a total duration of 41 seconds to two minutes) to be used. The key factors appeared to be that the work was a documentary and, although clearly commercial, was a combination of comment, criticism, scholarship, and research. In addition, public interest favored the production of Ali's biography; the use was quantitatively small; the clips were not the focus of the work; and use of the clips would have little or no effect on the market for the plaintiff's copyrighted fights.

Copyrights and Sports Events

You hear it during every game and no doubt know it by heart: "This telecast is a copyright of the National Football League. Any rebroadcast, retransmission, or any other use or description or accounts of this telecast without the express written consent of the National Football League is prohibited." But what does it really mean?

The question of whether sports events are copyrightable has yet to be fully answered. Currently, only broadcast or cable transmissions of sports events are copyrightable.[48] In 1976, Congress amended the Copyright Act expressly to ensure that simultaneously recorded broadcasts of live performances and sports events would be protected by copyright law.[49] Congress found authorship in the creative labor of the camera operators, director, and producer. On the other hand, it would appear that the actual sports events are not copyrightable because no authorship exists. In an event-related case, *Prod. Contractors, Inc. v. WGN Continental Broad. Co.,* the District Court for the Northern District of Illinois determined that a Christmas parade was not a work of authorship entitled to copyright protection.[50]

As technology has progressed, the issue of who owns what intellectual property has expanded. A seminal case in determining ownership of statistics and scores of games while in progress arose in 1996 when the NBA sued Motorola and STATS, Inc. for copyright infringement.[48] Motorola's SportsTrax pager system displayed the information on NBA games in progress including the running play by play, the team in possession of the ball, whether the team was in the free-throw bonus, the quarter of the game, and the time remaining. The information was updated every

Jamie Squire/Getty Images

Although the actual broadcast of the Super Bowl is protected by copyright law, news organizations that photograph the game own the copyright to their photographs.

two to three minutes, and more frequent updates were made near the end of the first half and the end of the game. A lag of approximately two to three minutes occurred between events in the game and the appearance of the information on the pager screen. SportsTrax's operation relied on a data feed supplied by STATS reporters, who watched games on television or listened to them on the radio. Using personal computers, the reporters keyed in changes in the score and other information, such as successful and missed shots, fouls, and clock updates. The information was then relayed by modem to STATS' host computer, which compiled, analyzed, and formatted the data for retransmission. The information was then sent to various FM radio networks that, in turn, emitted a signal received by the individual SportsTrax pagers. STATS also provided slightly more comprehensive and detailed real-time game information on its website. There, game scores were updated at 15-second to one-minute inter-

vals, and player and team statistics were updated each minute.

In deciding whether the NBA owned the statistics and scores of its games while they were in progress, the court determined that Congress intended to protect the league's interest only in the recorded broadcasts of games, not in the real-time data (scores, key plays, and so on) acquired by Motorola's employees and then broadcast on Motorola pagers. Thus, the court found that Motorola and STATS did not unlawfully misappropriate NBA's property by transmitting near-real-time NBA game scores and statistics taken from television and radio broadcasts of games in progress.

Although the athletics competition itself may not be copyrightable, event organizers can take steps to protect their proprietary interest in an event.[51] For instance, ESPN used a trademark symbol for the name *Extreme Games* and for the X symbol in securing trademark protection. A copyright notice was also affixed on all of ESPN's X Games promotional materials. Although these steps cannot protect ESPN and other event organizers from competitors that hold an event similar to the X Games (e.g., the subsequent emergence of the Gravity Games, Dew Tour, and Street-Games), it does protect ESPN from another's use of the name *Extreme Games* and the X symbol.[52] Choosing a distinctive trademark, establishing long-term contracts with participants, and prohibiting sponsors from creating or sponsoring similar competitive events can further protect event ideas.

Technological advancements in broadcasting over the Internet continue to raise challenging intellectual property issues for sports events and sport properties, many of which have involved the application of copyright law. In the early days of these emerging technologies, the distribution of near-real-time scores to consumers with special devices (such as pagers) was upheld by the court under First Amendment principles. The most notable sport case was *NBA v. Motorola*, which held that although the NBA owned the copyright in the broadcast itself, it did not have ownership of the facts of the game after they were in the public domain. Of particular significance in this case was the fact that the defendant Motorola did all the work to obtain and transmit the game scores. This case was distinguished by a subsequent sport case, *Morris Communication Corp v. PGA Tour, Inc.*, in which a U.S. Circuit Court of Appeals found that the PGA Tour was justified in denying Morris Communication, a Georgia publisher of print and electronic newspapers, the right to sell real-time tournament data that had been collected and produced by the PGA Tour through a system called ShotLink.[53] Although the case was brought and decided strictly on antitrust grounds (and not a copyright claim), the court's decision was swayed by its reasoning that compiling scores in golf is more difficult than in other sports because of the simultaneous action of numerous players, and that the PGA Tour had spent millions of dollars building the only system that does it.

A 2015 lawsuit applying core principles of copyright law was brought by a photographer over his 1984 iconic photo of Michael Jordan that he claimed served as inspiration for creating Nike's "Jumpman" logo.[54] The photographer created the staged picture of Jordan flying toward a basket in a ballet-style grand jeté pose for *Life Magazine* in 1984. He claimed Nike staged another photo of Jordan, changing some details but not his image's core layout, creative choices, and purpose. This version became the Nike silhouette of the Jumpman logo, which the photographer claimed was essentially stealing his creation in violation of copyright law. The court initially dismissed the photographer's case, finding the two images were not substantially similar when considering only the protectable elements of both photos—Jordan's pose, positioning, and angle. The appellate court ruled his creative work in the photograph deserved the broadest form of protection possible, but it considered additional elements of both photos to determine infringement, ultimately finding Nike's creative changes were sufficient enough to not infringe the photographer's original work.

Yet another emerging legal issue at the nexus of copyright law and social media is the legal rights of consumers in their user-generated content, and the laws regarding the re-publication (re-posting) of previously publicly disseminated photographs. "Embedding" or "in-line linking" to outside content is a common practice for websites or blogs. One lawsuit involved a civilian photographer who posted to his personal Snapchat account a candid group photograph showing Tom Brady and Kevin Durant, among others, strolling a sidewalk in The Hamptons, a tony section of Long Island.[55] The photograph, feeding into a news story about how Brady was perhaps attempting to recruit Durant for his hometown Boston Celtics team, quickly went viral, moving from Snapchat to Reddit to Twitter, where it was uploaded and tweeted out by several users without the plaintiff's permission. Eventually, the tweets containing the image made their way onto the websites of various news publishers and media websites, which embedded the tweets containing the photo into several articles about the developing sports story. None of the defendant websites copied and saved the photo onto their own servers; rather, they made the photo visible via Twitter's embed tool.

The photographer, stating he never publicly licensed his photograph or posted it to Twitter, filed a lawsuit against several websites, claiming a violation of his exclusive display right under the Copyright Act. In March 2018, a New York district court held that the online news publishers and media websites that embedded the tweets containing the plaintiff's copyrighted photo had violated his exclusive display right, despite the fact that the image at issue was hosted on a server owned and operated by an unrelated third party (i.e., Twitter). The court declined to adopt the Ninth Circuit's so-called "server test" first espoused in 2007 in the case of *Perfect 10, Inc. v. Amazon.com, Inc.* ("Perfect 10"), which held that the infringement of the public display right in a photographic image depends, in part, on where the image was hosted.[56]

Under the "server test," only a server that actually stored the photographs and "serves that electronic information directly to the user … could infringe the copyright holder's rights."[57] In its ruling, the *Goldman* court granted the plaintiff's motion for partial summary judgment, and determined that the reasoning of the Perfect 10 decision, which applied to a search engine's image search function and display of thumbnails to a user, was not applicable to the embedding practices the media sites engaged in.

This New York court decision created a new uncertainty for companies and organizations—including, but not limited to, sport leagues and teams—that, in posting content to their websites, have operated under the assumption that the "server test" is the law of the land. Hence, they believed they "enjoyed near-free reign to in-line link to user posts and display outside content on their own websites without fear of liability, as long as they used the source platform's embed tool and didn't host such content on their own servers."[57]

Under the current reasoning of *Goldman*, "anyone displaying photos from Twitter, videos from YouTube or articles from Facebook, is committing prima facie copyright infringement. This decision, if upheld and adopted by other courts, potentially open the floodgates for copyright litigation and abuse by copyright trolls."[58] However, the copyright law in this area of ownership of consumer-generated content and its dissemination on social media platforms is continually evolving. Hence, sport marketers need to stay abreast of the current laws in order to avoid copyright lawsuits by overzealous and litigious fans whose social media photos are embedded on sport organization websites.

Patents

Dylan B. Fan is also exploring, through an overseas manufacturer, the production of what she believes is a novel contraption—a plastic baseball that, with the push of a button, releases a banner that reads "World Series Champs" and plays "Take Me Out to the Ballgame." (Dylan has, to her credit, researched and determined that the copyright to this song has expired.) She has been advised to procure a patent on this product, which she intends to promote on her various social media accounts. Again, she can't wait to cash in.

Sport marketers will typically have the least involvement with the area of patent law. For those involved in the manufacturing side of the sport industry, however, an understanding of patent law is especially important. Companies invest tremendous amounts of money in developing new technologies for everything from athletics shoes and playing products (e.g., the Spalding Infusion micropump technology discussed earlier) to novel scoring apparatuses and technological enhancements, such as the yellow first-down line that is commonly used in football telecasts. The ability of inventors to profit from their ingenuity is grounded in the protections under patent law.

A **patent** may be granted to anyone who invents or discovers any new and useful process, machine, manufacture, or composition of matter, or any new and useful improvement.[59] A patent cannot be granted for a mere idea; it can be granted only for the actual invention or a complete description of it. Like a copyright, a patent has a limited duration. Currently, its duration is 20 years from the date on which the application was filed with the USPTO.[59] During those 20 years, a patent owner must not violate antitrust laws by virtue of having a patent, such as by unreasonably limiting the licensing of the patent or by using the patent to fix prices or restrain trade. After the 20 years expire, anyone may make, use, sell, or import the invention without the permission of the patent owner.

New methods or processes for playing sport have also been deemed patentable. For example, AFL and its parent company, Gridiron Enterprises, Inc., have been issued patents in the United States and Mexico for Arena Football's game system and method of play.[60] Debate, primarily academic in nature, has also arisen as to whether athletes can patent their moves (as processes).[61] For instance, could U.S. Olympian Nathan Chen create and subsequently patent a revolutionary figure-skating jump that would stifle his competitors? Although some have argued persuasively that such athletic moves fall squarely within the definitions of what is patentable, courts and commentators have suggested that, from a practical standpoint, the enforcement of such patent rights, as well as the chilling effect it would have on competition, make this a moot point. But perhaps it's only a matter of time.

In summary, patent law is the most complex of the three areas of intellectual property. As a result, this area is the one in which people or organizations will most likely need legal guidance for the registration process and protection.

Sport Marketing Communications Issues

The process of communicating marketing messages to sport consumers raises a number of legal issues for marketers of sport organizations, teams, and product manufacturers. Although relatively few cases involving the sport industry have been litigated, sport marketers need to be careful not to run afoul of federal laws against false advertising and deceptive consumer practices, as well as the state laws (adopted by all 50 states) enacted for the protection of consumers and businesses from unfair, false, or deceptive advertising and consumer practices.

Commercial communications typically implicate the First Amendment guarantee of free speech because commercial speech is entitled to some level of constitutional protection from governmental restraints. A balancing act is required between the sport organization's constitutional right to engage in commercial speech and the government's interest in protecting consumers from fraudulent or deceptive business practices. Commercial speech, of which advertising is the most common form, is defined as speech that does not do more than propose a commercial transaction. Furthermore, non-sport cases have held that speech does not lose its First Amendment protection "because money is spent to project it."[62]

The seminal 1980 Supreme Court case, *Central Hudson Gas & Electric Corp. v. New York Public Service Commission*, provided a four-factor test to determine whether a state's (government's) restrictions on commercial speech are constitutional:[63]

1. The commercial speech must concern a lawful activity and not be misleading.
2. The state must have a substantial interest in the restriction of the speech.
3. The regulation must directly advance the state's interest.
4. The regulation must be no more extensive than necessary to meet the state's interest.

Put another way, the governmental purpose or objective of the rule or regulation that prohibits the speech must be sufficiently important to allow a governmental entity to restrict a person's First Amendment rights, and the restrictions must be directly connected to achieving the government's stated objectives.

One notable sport case involved an effort by the Kentucky Racing Commission (a governmental entity) to enforce rules prohibiting jockeys from wearing advertising (commercial speech) on their uniforms during a race, in particular the 2003 Kentucky Derby.[64] As the 2004 Kentucky Derby approached, a number of jockeys filed a lawsuit to prevent enforcement of the commission's advertising ban. The commission argued that the rule was in place to protect the integrity of horse racing; the restriction on sponsor logos would ensure an unobstructed view of the jockey if misconduct was alleged and would foster confidence in the betting public by preventing collusion among jockeys sponsored by the same advertiser. The court found that although the commission's objectives were laudable, the ban on commercial speech was not directly connected to achieving the commission's objectives.

Occasionally, the issue of whether commercial speech is present is not clear. The *Nike, Inc. v. Kasky* case, decided in 2002, provides a key lesson for the public relations department in any sport organization.[65] To determine whether speech is commercial or noncommercial, the court will look at three elements: the speaker, the intended audience, and the content of the message. The Nike case revolved around whether statements made by Nike as part of a public relations campaign rose to the level of commercial speech. Nike had sent written statements to newspapers and letters to university presidents and athletics directors defending itself against allegations of violating human rights in its treatment of workers in Asian countries. The plaintiff, consumer activist Marc Kasky, sued Nike on behalf of the public under California business laws alleging that Nike's statements were false and misleading. The court had to determine whether Nike's statements, made as part of a public relations campaign, were commercial or noncommercial speech. The court held that Nike's allegedly false and misleading statements were properly characterized as commercial speech. The distinction is important in the context of sport marketers because most states' statutes dealing with deceptive trade practices, such as false advertising, apply only to commercial speech. Sport organizations must

therefore be cognizant that even in distributing communications by press releases and letters to stakeholders, such as season-ticket holders and the media, courts are likely to deem these communications to be a form of commercial speech and thus susceptible to claims of deceptive business practices.

Ambush Marketing

One of the largest sources of revenue for sport properties comes from the sale of "official sponsor" rights. Corporations often invest significant amounts of money to secure the rights, typically exclusive within a product or service category, to use the sport property's trademarks in their advertising and promotional campaigns as a means of associating with the sport property's positive goodwill. Marketers working on the

The clever advertising campaign conducted by online gambling company Paddy Power during the 2012 London Olympic Games illustrates the many challenges of trying to stop the practice of ambush marketing.

Zuma Press/Icon Sportswire

property side of the sport industry, however, face challenges from a method of marketing called ambush marketing. Ambush marketing occurs when a company capitalizes on the goodwill of a sports event by using a variety of advertising and promotional tactics to *imply* an official association with that sports event. The ambusher's tactics weaken a competitor's official association with the event acquired through the payment of sponsorship monies.[66]

Perceptions of and perspectives on ambush marketing have evolved as a result of dialogue among both scholars and practitioners. From the earliest definitions of *ambush marketing* as a pejorative term, which described it as an "immoral" practice, has emerged not only an acknowledgment of the considerable vagueness that surrounds the concept but also a conceptual framework of ambush marketing that more accurately reflects the balancing of sponsors' contractual rights against the rights of nonsponsors to maintain a market presence during an event through legal and competitive business activities.[67] Hence, although at one extreme end of the ambush marketing conceptual debate is what the Olympic Movement publicly refers to as "parasite marketing,"[68] at the other end are much more neutral terms such as "parallel marketing."[69]

Historically, the term *ambush marketing* has been defined from the perspective of the sport property. The review of the academic literature illustrates the challenges in conceptualizing *ambush marketing*, the term that was coined during the 1984 Los Angeles Olympic Games to describe the marketing activities of nonsponsors such as Kodak, which used a variety of tactics to "ambush" official sponsor Fuji.[70] The earliest definitions implied that ambush marketing was a kind of unethical business conduct laden with evil intent (thus supporting the perspective of event organizers and official sponsors). For instance, the term was initially defined as "a company's intentional efforts to weaken—or ambush—its competitor's 'official sponsorship.' It does this by engaging in promotions and advertising that trade off the event or property's goodwill and reputation, and that seek to confuse the buying public as to which companies really hold official sponsorship rights."[66]

Townley, Harrington, and Couchman later stressed the concept of unauthorized association in defining ambush marketing, stating that the practice "consists in the sports context of the unauthorized association by businesses of their names, brands, products, or services with a sports event or competition through any one of a wide range of marketing activities; unauthorized in the sense that the controller of the commercial rights in such events, usually the relevant governing body, has neither sanctioned nor licensed the association, either itself or through commercial agents."[71]

In this context, ambush marketing has been viewed as not only those activities aimed specifically at undermining a competitor's official sponsorship of an event but also those activities that seek to associate a nonsponsor with the sports event itself. Additional literature on ambush marketing has suggested that, in contrast to the pejorative definition, ambush marketing can be more broadly defined to describe "a whole variety of wholly legitimate and morally correct methods of intruding upon public consciousness surrounding an event."[70] Although the practice of ambush marketing has been widely debated, the answer as to whether it is an "immoral or imaginative practice . . . may well lie in the eye of the beholder."[73] For instance, event organizers and their official sponsors typically denounce as ambush marketing any activity by a nonsponsor that wittingly or unwittingly intrudes on the property's or official sponsors' rights, thus potentially detracting from the sponsor's exclusive association with the sport property. Using this definition, for instance, even a company that purchases advertising within the telecast of a sports event could be construed by the event organizer and official sponsor as an ambush marketer regardless of that company's business motives, ethical perspective, or legal rights. On the other hand, such activity engaged in by nonsponsors can also be perceived and defended as nothing more than a part of the normal "cut and thrust" of business activity based on a strong economic justification.[73] Further illustrating the ambiguities surrounding the concept of ambush marketing, researchers have argued that it is unrealistic to expect nonsponsors to make decisions regarding sponsorship differently than they would with regard to other promotional techniques designed to compete in the marketplace.[73] Perspectives on and attitudes toward the practice of ambush marketing are largely influenced by the marketer's role in the sponsorship equation. Sport properties and official sponsors will typically hold a viewpoint far different from that of nonsponsors. Although unilaterally labeling ambush marketing as illegal, immoral, or unethical is improper, we should recognize that sport properties may have legitimate concerns if they are unable to prevent unfettered ambush marketing.

Companies may engage in ambush marketing for a variety of reasons:

- The company may view the official sponsorship rights as being too expensive.
- The company may be excluded from becoming an official sponsor because of a sport organization's restrictions on the number of sponsors or specific product or service categories.
- The company may be blocked from becoming an official sponsor because of a sport organization's preexisting exclusive deal with a competing company.

Event organizers and official sponsors typically consider such tactics unethical, without acknowledging that they are not illegal.

The following ambush marketing tactics, provided in the context of marathon running, are by no means exhaustive, but they serve to illuminate the wide range of tactics typically used in combination by ambush marketers.[74]

- *Use of generic phrases.* Although event organizers have become increasingly vigilant in protecting their intellectual property through the registration of marks and symbols associated with their events, ambush marketers often create generic phrases that refer to the event. For example, although the New York Road Runners Club owns the phrase *New York City Marathon* and other phrases related to the event, ambush marketers can create generic phrases such as *The Big Race* or *The Race Through the Boroughs*, which, when accompanied by relevant artwork (such as a drawing of the New York City skyline or a map of the five boroughs), can create an implied association between the ambush marketer and the event.

- *Purchase of advertising time within the event broadcast.* The purchase of advertising within a sports event telecast is one of the most common and popular tactics of ambush marketing. Because the New York Road Runners organization sells its broadcast rights to a third-party broadcaster, it relinquishes a certain measure of control over the advertisers. Although event organizers typically negotiate contractual language that provides their official sponsors with the right of first refusal to purchase advertising within the event telecast, they are rarely in a bargaining position to prohibit their broadcast rights holders from selling advertising to nonsponsors or even competitors of official sponsors. Hence, nonsponsors can purchase advertising within the event telecast that even features creative elements tied to a running theme.

- *Presence in and around the event venue.* In the early days of ambush marketing, companies employed blimps and airplanes with trailing banners to ambush a major sports event. Although event organizers have closed this ambush opportunity by working closely with the FAA and with host cities to enact air traffic restrictions during such events, clever ambush marketers have continued to use other tactics for on-site presence, including strategically placed billboards, tents and inflatables in high-traffic locations, distribution of literature and samples to consumers attending the event, and temporary spray painting of corporate logos along the course route. Ambush marketers of marathon events have even resorted to paying college students to distribute temporary forehead tattoos, as Reebok did at the 2003 Boston Marathon as a means of ambushing Adidas.[75]

- *Conducting consumer promotions.* Such promotions typically are offered at retail locations and are supported by POP displays that feature visuals themed to the particular sports event and words that refer generically to the sports event. For instance, a company intent on associating itself with the New York City Marathon might, in the weeks leading up to the marathon, conduct an in-store running-themed promotion offering consumers discounts on the purchase of running shoes in exchange for proofs of purchase. Or, a company could conduct a sweepstakes that offers winners the chance to meet the marathon champions (assuming that the ambush marketing company could arrange this). Although purposely avoiding the use of any registered trademarks, such promotions are intended to lure consumers through an implied association with the marathon.

- *Congratulatory messages.* Companies often create advertisements offering congratulations to winning teams or athletes. For instance, the day after the New York City Marathon, a non-sponsor could run an advertisement in the local newspaper congratulating the winners by name. Such a tactic is typically legal under the First Amendment, particularly as long as the advertiser refrains from using the ad to convey explicit selling messages or sales offers.[76]

The more popular and global the event is, the more often ambush marketing arises. Historically, one of the most fertile grounds has been the Olympic Games.[77] Generally, the United States Olympic & Paralympic Committee (now referred to as USOPC),[78] when confronted with alleged ambush marketing activity, has been successful in negotiating business settlements with infringers who, more often than not, are simply unaware that their activities are in violation of the USOPC's broad trademark rights afforded through the Ted Stevens Olympic and Amateur Sports Act (OASA) of 1998.[79]

However, when alleged ambush marketers are not amenable to settlement, the formerly named United States Olympic Committee (USOC) has been vigilant in resorting to the courts. For example, a federal judge granted the USOC's request for a permanent injunction preventing a camp organizer from producing a children's summer camp called Camp Olympik.[79] The USOC also threatened to sue to halt an event called the Redneck Olympics, claiming trademark infringement, unfair competition, and trademark dilution.[80]

Although ambush marketing is difficult to eradicate, sport properties can limit its occurrence in several ways. For instance, to prevent non-sponsors from purchasing advertising within the broadcast of an event, a sport property typically negotiates a clause in its agreement that requires its broadcast rights holders to provide official sponsors the right of first refusal to purchase advertising within the broadcasts, as well as a clause requiring the rights holders to monitor potential trademark infringements by nonsponsors. Sport properties can also negotiate with host cities to ban marketing activity that competes directly with official sponsors. For instance, the NFL now requires the host city to create a "clean zone" during its annual Super Bowl week, imposing a ban on nonsponsor advertising and promotional activities, as well as street trading in the area surrounding the facility that hosts the event.[81]

A sport property seeking to protect itself against ambush marketers must be proactive. The property should consider using advertising to explain potential negative effects of ambush marketing to consumers and the media. When faced with ambush marketing activity, the property might also consider launching a public relations campaign accusing the ambusher of unfair business tactics (typically called a name-and-shame campaign). Sport properties remain reticent, however, to bring lawsuits involving ambush marketing, in part for fear of an adverse court decision. As a result, settled case law on the specific issue of ambush marketing is limited. In one of the only decided North American cases specifically addressing ambush marketing, a Canadian court upheld Pepsi-Cola Canada's ambush marketing activities, much to the chagrin of the NHL and its official soft drink sponsor Coca-Cola.[82]

Right of Publicity and Invasion of Privacy

Dylan B. Fan has decided that, during the World Series games, she is going to stand outside the stadium and sell a poster bearing illustrations of a few Aces players. She has asked her friend from art school to provide drawings of the players. The poster is going to read "Good Luck Aces Stars." She has secured a local hardware store to underwrite the printing costs of the posters in exchange for displaying the store logo on the posters. This scenario triggers another form of intellectual property referred to as the right of publicity.

Those employed as marketers for sport teams, sporting goods manufacturers, or individual athletes need to be aware of the intersection of right of publicity and invasion of privacy. Although these claims fall within the area of tort law rather than intellectual property law, these areas at the intersection of sport marketing and the law are extremely important.

The right of publicity was originally intertwined with invasion of privacy, but courts have since separated the right to be let alone from the commercial right to control the use of one's likeness or identity.[83] Invasion of privacy arises out of the common law of torts or state statutes. Among other things, the right of privacy protects against intrusion on a person's seclusion, the misappropriation of a person's name or likeness, unreasonable publicity, and placing a person in a false light. One of the landmark sport-related cases dealing with invasion of privacy was *Spahn v. Julian Messner, Inc.*, in which Hall of Fame pitcher Warren Spahn sued the publishers of an unauthorized fictional biography *The Warren Spahn Story*.[84] The book, the whole tenor of which projected a false intimacy with Spahn, was fraught with inaccuracies and fabricated events dealing with Spahn's marriage, family life, and relationship with his father, among other things. Although the book was laudatory of Spahn, the court held that "the offending characteristics of the book comprehend a nonfactual novelization of plaintiff's alleged life story and an unauthorized intrusion into the private realms of the baseball pitcher's life—all to Spahn's humiliation and mental anguish."[84]

The right of publicity, on the other hand, prevents the unauthorized commercial use of a person's name, likeness, or other recognizable aspects one's persona. It gives people the exclusive right to license the use of their identity for commercial purposes. More than half of all jurisdictions in the United States recognize the right of publicity, although nine states, including New York and Illinois, have rejected the right of publicity after death. In a legal action arising from the unauthorized misappropriation of a person's name or likeness for a product, an advertisement, or any other commercial use, a plaintiff may choose to sue claiming an invasion of privacy, a violation of the plaintiff's right of publicity, or as a trademark law-based false endorsement claim under the Lanham Act (often, the plaintiff will include all three).

Cases often arise when sport figures attempt to stop the misappropriation of their name or likeness or both. Athletes have discovered the commercial value in their names and likenesses, and thus enforcing the right of publicity is crucial in this age of the branding of athletes. The first such case in sport, *Haelan Laboratories v. Topps Chewing Gum*, involved a dispute over the right to market trading cards of professional baseball players.[85] In that case, the court established a property right in a person's identity, naming it the right of publicity. The court recognized the players' right to grant a license (or exclusive privilege) to merchandisers to use their likenesses

for the manufacture and sale of the cards. This case opened the door for athletes and celebrities to enforce a right of publicity against those misappropriating their names and likenesses. In a similar case, *Uhlaender v. Henricksen*, a court enjoined the maker of a table game from using MLB players' names without their consent because the players had a proprietary interest in their names, likenesses, and accomplishments.[86]

Because of the strength of the First Amendment protection of free speech or expression, permission is not needed to use a celebrity's name or likeness in a book, newspaper, magazine, television news show or documentary, or other news media outlet. Courts have also upheld the use of the name or likeness of an athlete to advertise or promote media publications in which the athlete or entertainer once appeared. In both *Namath v. Sports Illustrated*[87] and *Montana v. San Jose Mercury News, Inc.*,[88] courts allowed media entities to use the plaintiffs' photos from prior editions of their publications in advertisements to sell their publications. The courts held that the photographs represented newsworthy events and that a newspaper had a constitutional right to promote itself by reproducing its news stories. These cases differ from the previously discussed *Abdul-Jabbar v. General Motors*, in which Alcindor's name and likeness were misappropriated in an advertisement for the Olds 88 automobile. Although Alcindor's record is in fact newsworthy, its use was to advertise an Oldsmobile and thus was not protected by the First Amendment.[89]

A case considering the legal boundaries of the "newsworthiness" exception found in the Indiana right of publicity statute is *Daniels v. FanDuel*.[90] The case was brought in 2016 by former Northern Illinois University football players Akeem Daniels and Cameron Stingily, and former Indiana University football player Nicholas Stoner as a class-action lawsuit against FanDuel and DraftKings based on their use of college athletes' names, images, and statistics. The Indiana right of publicity statute allows people to limit the use of their name and likenesses by others but includes an exception for items that have "newsworthy value" or a "topic of general or public interest."[91] In considering whether this exception applied, the Indiana Supreme Court rejected the notion that the newsworthiness exception does not apply in the context of commercial use, such as the fantasy sports games at issue. Furthermore, the Court

Do Michael Jordan's Shoes Make the Man?

Companies often run advertisements congratulating the achievements of players and teams. Typically, the players and teams saluted in these one-time advertisements appreciate the positive publicity. Occasionally, however, subjects of the congratulatory message can take offense, believing that the use of their likeness stretches beyond the bounds of the First Amendment and is instead an unauthorized commercial use.

Such was the case for NBA legend Michael Jordan. To celebrate Jordan's induction into the Basketball Hall of Fame in September 2009, *Sports Illustrated* published a commemorative issue to acknowledge Jordan's contribution to the game. One of the advertisers that appeared in the commemorative issue was Jewel–Osco Food Stores, which, at the time, operated about 175 grocery stores in the greater Chicago area. Jewel–Osco's advertisement featured a pair of basketball shoes spotlighted on the hardwood floor of a basketball court. The number 23 (Jordan's longtime uniform number) appeared on the tongue of each shoe, and the following message was positioned above the photo of the shoes:

> A Shoe In! After six NBA championships, scores of rewritten record books, and numerous buzzer beaters, Michael Jordan's elevation in the Basketball Hall of Fame was never in doubt! Jewel–Osco salutes #23 on his many accomplishments as we honor a fellow Chicagoan who was "just around the corner" for so many years.

Beneath this message was Jewel–Osco's trademark logo with the slogan "Good things are just around the corner."

Jordan sued the grocery store for using his image and likeness in the advertisement without his permission, claiming a violation of his right of publicity.[132]

A district court judge in Illinois was faced with deciding whether Jewel–Osco made commercial use of Jordan's identity for a profit without his permission. These types of claims often turn on whether the advertiser is engaged in commercial speech. In simplest terms, if Jewel–Osco's advertisement was deemed not commercial in nature, then the company would not be liable. The district court judge concluded that Jewel–Osco's advertisement was noncommercial speech entitled to full First Amendment protection. The judge held that the advertisement did not propose any kind of commercial transaction, because readers would be at a loss to explain what they have been invited to buy. The judge reasoned that the advertisement was a "tribute by an established Chicago business to Chicago's most accomplished athlete."[100] Finally, the judge ruled that Jewel–Osco had no profit motive to exploit the Jordan brand commercially because Jewel–Osco was not compensated for having created the ad, giving Jewel–Osco the early victory.

On appeal, however, the Seventh Circuit provided a different, and precedent-setting, analysis of the advertisement congratulating Jordan.[100] The court used three questions to guide its decision:

1. Whether the speech is an advertisement
2. Whether the speech refers to a specific product
3. Whether the speaker has an economic motivation for the speech

The Seventh Circuit held that not all are necessary components of a finding of commercial speech and that "[i]f the literal import of the words were all that mattered, this celebratory tribute would be noncommercial."[100]

> *continued*

> continued

However, the court continued that Jewel–Osco's ad served two functions: (1) congratulating Jordan, and (2) enhancing Jewel–Osco's brand by associating itself with Jordan in the minds of basketball fans and Chicago consumers. The Seventh Circuit, therefore, held for Jordan, essentially finding that however sincere its congratulations, Jewel–Osco still "had something to gain" from the ad.[101] As a result of the Seventh Circuit's decision, Jordan was awarded US$8.9 million in damages.[102] This decision provides valuable guidance for companies who seek to use athletes in congratulatory advertising; namely, to make sure that its advertising does not include any messaging that could be construed by the court as overly commercial in nature.

rejected the argument that the exception was only available to news broadcasters and media companies. Ultimately, the Indiana Supreme Court ruled that uses of college athletes' names, likenesses, and statistical data in online fantasy sports contests are of "newsworthy value" under Indiana's right of publicity statute. The *FanDuel* decision sets forth a broad interpretation of the newsworthiness exception to Indiana's right of publicity statute that will have ramifications far beyond this case.[92]

Courts have also recognized a right of publicity and trademark protection for nicknames. In *Hirsch v. S.C. Johnson & Son, Inc.*, the plaintiff, Elroy "Crazylegs" Hirsch, alleged that the nickname belonged to him, that it had commercial value, and that knowing this, the defendants marketed a shaving gel for women called Crazylegs.[93] In an action against S.C. Johnson & Son, Inc., Hirsch sought a remedy under two legal theories. Hirsch argued that the defendant violated his right to privacy by misappropriating his name and likeness for commercial use and infringed on his trademark rights to the nickname "*Crazylegs.*" The court determined that a celebrity's nickname had value and that Johnson could not use the name "*Crazylegs*" without permission from or payment to Hirsch for its use. The court found that all that is required to protect a nickname is that the nickname clearly identifies the wronged person.

Debate continues as to where to draw the lines between athletes' right of publicity and First Amendment freedoms.[94] One of the seminal sport cases involved Tiger Woods. In *ETW Corp. v. Jireh Publishing*, noted sport artist Rick Rush created and distributed prints titled *The Masters of Augusta* that prominently featured Woods.[95] Notwithstanding the fact that Rush profited by selling lithographs of his artwork, the U.S. Court of Appeals held in favor of the artist, ruling that such creative works of art are protected under the First Amendment and thus trump an athlete's right of publicity. Interestingly, the court reasoned, among other things, that Woods was earning more than enough money from his tournament winnings and other commercial endorsement deals. Subsequent cases, such as the Missouri court decision upholding a US$15-million-judgment for former NHL player Tony Twist for the unauthorized use of his name and likeness in a comic book series and the athletes' cases against EA Sports (see "Emerging Issues" later in this chapter), have served only to blur the legal lines between the right of publicity and the First Amendment.[96]

Legal debate has also been waged over who owns player statistics and the corresponding player names in the context of online fantasy sports games.[97] In 2006 a federal court held that although the Major League Baseball Players Association (MLBPA) and its players had a valid claim under right of publicity law, the protections afforded the dissemination of public information under the First Amendment outweighed the players' right of publicity.[98] This decision spurred a similar lawsuit in which CBS Interactive claimed it should not have to pay licensing fees to the NFLPA and Players Inc. in exchange for operating its fantasy football games.[99] Because of these decisions, companies selling online fantasy sport leagues are free to do so without obtaining licenses from the appropriate sport leagues. Many online fantasy sports game providers, however, continue to secure league licenses because of the "official" status, authenticity, and incremental marketing benefits that the respective league can provide as a point of differentiation from nonlicensed online fantasy sports games.

Contractual Issues Involving Consumers

Given the increasing levels of financial commitment involving tickets to sports events, both sport organizations and fans today often resort to the courts. Most of these cases are decided using contract law. For instance, the Washington Football Team and New England Patriots are among professional sport teams that have sued season-ticket holders who were in default on their payments.[103] The practice of teams suing their own season-ticket holders has been criticized because it is unclear whether the teams have sustained any damages because of the season-ticket holders' breach of contract. A party to a contract has a general duty to mitigate damages.

But both the Washington Football Team's and Patriots' season-ticket agreements included a liquidated damages clause arguably giving the teams a right to payment for every year of the multiyear agreement regardless of whether or when they resold the tickets. The liquidated damages clause in the Patriots' personal seat license (PSL) agreement was upheld by a Massachusetts court in the 2008 case of *NPS, LLC. v. Minihane*,[104] although the court struck down an accelerated payment provision as "grossly disproportionate to a reasonable estimate of actual damages made at the time of contract formation." Although teams reserve the right to include such liquidated damages clauses in their agreements, and the law supports the right to enter into contracts, teams should be careful of the negative publicity that arises in the process of suing season-ticket holders.

Season-ticket holders have also sued teams for a variety of reasons. For instance, a group of St. Louis Rams personal seat license (PSL) owners sued the owner of the team, seeking the rights to purchase tickets for the team's games or to receive refunds when the team relocated to Los Angeles.[105] Specifically, one group of PSL owners who bought their seat licenses directly from the team used the terms of the contract to argue that they were entitled to have the opportunity to purchase season tickets at the new stadium, to which the court agreed. Close to 50,000 people had bought the PSLs, which were good for a 30-year term, matching the length of the Rams' lease for The Dome at America's Center in St. Louis. After protracted, back-and-forth litigation about the monetary damages season-ticket holders were owed, a federal judge approved a settlement of US$24 million for the class of PSL holders.[106]

Sport marketers also need to be careful in how they package and sell season tickets. For instance, in 2012, a group of University of Pittsburgh basketball season-ticket holders filed a class-action lawsuit against the university seeking to overturn the university's new season-ticket plan for the men's basketball team.[107] The plaintiffs alleged that Pitt's new ticket plan was a breach of an expressed guarantee that Pitt had made with its season-ticket holders. Before the opening of the Petersen Events Center in 2002, Pitt created and promoted a season-ticket plan that promised in writing that season-ticket holders would be able to keep their same seats every year if they maintained or increased their contributions to the Department of Athletics' fundraising program Team Pittsburgh (currently called the Panther Club). Pitt subsequently announced a new plan that reassigned nonclub season-ticket seats every year based on a number of factors, including the size of contributions to the Department of Athletics' new fundraising drive. The lawsuit alleged that Pitt was in breach of contract and had violated consumer protection laws. The class-action lawsuit was eventually settled, and the affected season-ticket holders were allowed to retain their seats for the next five seasons if they met specified donor levels.[108] Similarly, in 2012, a class-action lawsuit was brought against Comcast Spectacor, owner of the Philadelphia Flyers, alleging that the team had excluded the 2012 Winter Classic regular-season game against the New York Rangers from the season-ticket package only after season-ticket holders had prepaid for each of the 44 preseason and regular-season games for the Flyers' 2011 to 2012 season.[109] Comcast Spectacor then offered to resell the Winter Classic tickets back to the season-ticket holders, but only if they also paid for tickets to two unrelated games—an exhibition featuring Flyers and Rangers alumni and a minor league hockey game. The lawsuit claimed that Comcast Spectacor also charged season-ticket holders, who already paid a US$10 processing fee for the original season tickets, excessive and unearned processing charges for all three tickets. Although these lawsuits were eventually dismissed or settled, they illustrate the types of issues that sport marketers need to be cognizant of in their relationships with customers in seeking to avoid not only unnecessary litigation costs but also the negative publicity that results from such customer relations practices.

Promotion Law Issues

Sweepstakes and contests are popular tactics for sport organizations and corporations to engage consumers and generate brand awareness and sales. If handled improperly, however, they can have expensive and embarrassing consequences, including negative publicity and legal liability. Hence, sport marketers need to understand the distinction between sweepstakes, contests, and lotteries.

Lotteries are promotions in which the elements of prize, chance, and consideration are present. Technically, lotteries also include raffle promotions in which the consumer pays for a raffle ticket (although in practice, local raffle promotions are common and rarely investigated by authorities). As a rule, only states themselves have the legal right to conduct lotteries. By eliminating any one element (i.e., the prize, the chance, or the consideration), an organization can legally sponsor a promotional game without violating state lottery laws.[110]

Sweepstakes and instant-win games are popular promotional tactics designed to encourage product or service sales. In order to eliminate the consideration element, their rules must clearly state that no purchase is necessary. This requirement is most commonly achieved by providing an alternative method of entry (AMOE). Although the consideration element is most often in the form of a payment for a purchase, the consideration element may also be found in nonmonetary methods of entry if the participant is required to exert substantial effort, such as completing a lengthy survey, making multiple trips to a retail location, referring a friend, or otherwise devoting substantial time to participate in the sweepstakes.[110] Conversely, requiring participants to use the Internet (a paid service) or a 900-number phone service to enter the sweepstakes has been deemed, through Congressional bills and settled lawsuits, not to constitute the consideration element.[110] Regardless of whether the sweepstakes entry comes by purchase of a product or service or the AMOE, each method of entry must be given equal treatment, and a sponsor of the sweepstakes

may not directly or indirectly encourage participants to enter by the purchase-based method.

Contests are typically structured to eliminate the element of chance by requiring some level of skill or expertise. Typical examples include coloring contests, create-an-ad contests, and competitions to throw a ball through a target. Most states use the dominant element test to evaluate whether skill or chance dominates in determining the contest winner.[110] In other words, in a consumer promotion based on skill, the participants' skills or effort must govern the result and not be just part of a larger scheme. Hence, for example, a marketer can't have consumers enter a coloring contest and then ultimately select the winner at random. This requirement necessitates a careful enunciation of the rules of the contest and the judging criteria on which the winners will be selected. Most courts have held that contests that require participants to predict winners of events do not rise to the level of skill required to make the promotion legally a contest (legally, these would be deemed to be sweepstakes).

Promotional games often involve an issue as to whether they represent some form of illegal gambling. Courts generally distinguish between bona fide entry fees (which typically include proof of product purchase) and bets or wagers. Generally, entry fees do not constitute bets or wagers when they are paid unconditionally for the privilege of participating in a sweepstakes or contest and the prize is for a specified amount that is guaranteed to be awarded to one of the participants. When the entry fees and prizes are unconditional and guaranteed, the element of risk necessary to constitute betting or wagering is absent.

Gambling, on the other hand, represents an activity in which parties voluntarily make a bet or wager. The legality of online fantasy sports contests was upheld in 2007 in the case of *Humphreys v. Viacom*.[111] The plaintiff challenged the industry as a form of illegal gambling under New Jersey law. The district court, however, dismissed the case and stated that courts throughout the country have long recognized that it would be "patently absurd" to hold that "the combination of an entry fee and a prize equals gambling."[111] The court reasoned that to decide otherwise would result in countless popular contests being construed as illegal gambling, including everything from golf tournaments to essay competitions. The court interpreted the fee paid by online fantasy sports gamers as part of a contractual agreement between the online provider and the participant, not a wager or bet.

One popular form of promotional games is insured-prize promotions tied to specific performances of a team. Typically, these promotions require a consumer to make a purchase before the start of the season. Then, if a particular event occurs (e.g., the team wins the World Series), the consumer's cost of the purchase is reimbursed. This scenario was the subject of litigation in 2007 when the Massachusetts attorney general sued Jordan's Furniture claiming that its Monster Deal promotion constituted an illegal gambling scheme.[112] This promotion enticed consumers to purchase furniture before the start of the 2007 season on the condition that if the Red Sox won the 2007 World Series, the furniture would be free. The court determined that this promotion did not constitute an illegal lottery because it could not determine whether consumers were buying furniture purely for the purposes of entering the promotion or simply because they needed or wanted furniture.[113] Ultimately, to eliminate any legal issues, Jordan's Furniture, in its similar future promotions, provided all participants with a rebate on future furniture purchases (regardless of whether the Red Sox won the World Series), to eliminate the chance element. Notwithstanding this court decision, sport marketers need to make sure that similar insured-prize promotions conditioned on some future event meet legal muster.

For sport marketers, the most important advice with regard to promotion law is that each state has its own set of laws and regulations defining the elements of prizing, chance, and consideration. Hence, sport marketers seeking to conduct a sweepstakes or a contest must consult promotion law experts in the planning stages.

Emerging Issues

In this section, we consider several emerging issues at the intersection of the law and sport marketing.

Increasing Regulations Concerning Athletes' Use of Social Media

Social media regulations targeting athletes' tweets and social media posts started largely around the time of the 2012 Summer Olympic Games, often dubbed the "Twitter Games."[114] In 2012, Nike became the first company in the United Kingdom to have a Twitter campaign banned after the UK's Advertising Standards Authority (ASA) decided that Nike's use of the personal accounts of soccer star Wayne Rooney violated rules for clearly communicating to the public that his tweets were advertisements.[115] Nike, which had an endorsement deal with Rooney, ran the Twitter campaign as part of its wider Make It Count advertising campaign. Rooney's tweet, which went out to his 4.37 million followers, said, "My resolution—to start the year as a champion, and finish it as a champion . . . #makeitcount gonike.me/make it count." As stated by the ASA, "We considered that the Nike reference was not prominent and could be missed. We considered there was nothing obvious in the tweets to indicate they were Nike marketing communications."[115]

For sport marketers, ranging from sport organizations to athlete representation firms to sponsors, the regulations that govern the commercial use of social media are an area of growing concern. The Rooney example illustrates the effect of the UK's ASA. The corresponding authority in the United States is the Federal Trade Commission (FTC), and it too has focused increasing attention on the issue of athletes' use of social media when used to promote endorsement deals.

In 2010, the FTC published guidelines for companies and athletes seeking to leverage social media to promote products and services with the enactment of its *Guides Concerning the Use of Endorsements and Testimonials in Advertising*.[116] The *Guides* clarify that celebrities, including athletes, have a duty to disclose their relationships with companies when making endorsements outside the context of traditional advertising in which the audience would not otherwise reasonably expect that a financial connection exists between the athlete and the advertiser. As examples, the *Guides* include (illustrated here in the context of athletes) whether the athlete is compensated, whether the company provided the product or service to the athlete for free, the length of the relationship between the company and the athlete, the extent of the athlete's previous receipt of products or services from the company or the likelihood of future receipt of such products or services, and the value of the items or services received by the athlete.

The *Guides* also offer additional guidance by listing nine hypothetical examples. The third hypothetical presented in the *Guides* is relevant to sport figures because it discusses an appearance by a well-known professional tennis player on a television talk show. In the hypothetical example, the show host compliments the player on her recent solid play. The player responds by crediting her improved play to her improved vision, the result of laser vision correction surgery done at a clinic that she identifies by name. The player raves about the simplicity of the procedure, the kindness of the eye doctor, and other benefits, such as the ease of driving at night. The player does not reveal that she has a contractual relationship with the eye doctor to speak positively about the eye company in public settings, but she does not appear in any broadcast commercials for the company. This hypothetical states that the weight and credibility of the player's endorsement is adversely affected because consumers are unaware of the contractual relationship that the player has with the eye doctor. The *Guides* thus direct that an athlete in this situation must disclose the relationship.

The hypothetical continues, but it alters the facts to analyze the player's discussion of the eye doctor on a social media site. Assume that instead of speaking about the clinic in a television interview, the tennis player touts the results of her surgery and mentions the clinic by name on a social networking site, which allows her fans to read in real time what is happening in her life. Given the nature of the medium in which her endorsement is disseminated, consumers might not realize that she is a paid endorser. Because that information might affect the weight that consumers give to her endorsement, her relationship with the clinic should be disclosed.[116]

Companies using athletes as an endorsement vehicle need to remember the underlying rationale of the *Guides*—that consumers have a right to know when they are being subjected to a sales pitch. This is particularly relevant as more profes-

Celebrity athletes must follow FTC guidelines when endorsing brands and products on social media.
TONY ASHBY/AFP via Getty Images

sional athletes are now considered social media "influencers." Historically the realm of celebrity entertainers, sport celebrities have increasingly generated large numbers of followers on social media platforms and need to be cognizant of their legal obligations. In 2017, the FTC sent letters to influencers and marketers reminding them that influencers should clearly and conspicuously disclose any material connections between the influencer and the companies or brands they are promoting or endorsing through social media.[117] The guidance was in response to a sample of Instagram posts making endorsements or referencing brands and marked the first time the FTC had reached out directly to social media influencers, rather than the companies they help to promote, to educate them about their legal responsibilities.

Although the *Guides* do not address every potential scenario involving companies' use of athletes, endorsements, and social media, they do provide a framework for recommendations that these companies, as well as sport organizations, athletes, and their agents, should be aware of before engaging in marketing campaigns via social media. Among other measures, companies should provide training and guidance to their athlete endorsers about how to use social media in a manner that adheres to the *Guides* as well as the 2017 guidance for social media influencers. Such measures will best address any liability both parties may incur under the act. For instance, on Instagram, while it has been recommended that influencers include "clear and conspicuous" disclosures—depending on the situation, #ad, #sponsored, or #promotion—so as to inform consumers truthfully, these disclosures must be prominently visible to consumers, especially when multiple links or hashtags may appear in a long string that customers might be likely to skip over.[117]

Athletes Trademarking Names and Slogans

A trend among professional and high-profile amateur (Olympic) athletes is seeking trademark protection of their names, slogans, or catch phrases associated with them.[117,118] Players use the benefits of trademark law not only to assert ownership and control over their trademarked names and slogans but also to generate ancillary revenues by licensing the use of these marks on all types of commercial products and services. Noted examples include Johnny Manziel registering a trademark in his famous nickname "Johnny Football," and the NFL's Marshawn Lynch trademarking his famous phrase "Beast Mode," while football player Robert Griffin III sought to protect his nickname as both "RGIII" and "RG3" as trademarks for use in merchandise sales.[119] Lawyers who handle intellectual property matters for athletes say that the practice of trademarking names and phrases has accelerated recently as athletes seek to extend their brands into the entertainment world.[120,131] Furthermore, with the explosive growth of social media, trademarking an athlete's name gives athletes and their legal team greater ability to control how the trademark is used and on what products or services, as well as monitor for unauthorized uses, ultimately enhancing the overall value of the athletes' brand.

Use of Current and Former Student-Athletes' Likenesses in Video Games

One of the most litigated issues facing marketers of college sports, the NCAA, and the manufacturers of sport video games has been the uncompensated use of likenesses of current and former student-athletes, notably in EA Sports video games, which the athletes have credibly alleged is a violation of their right of publicity. In 2009, Sam Keller, a former student-athlete and quarterback for Arizona State University and the University of Nebraska, filed a class-action lawsuit against Electronic Arts, the NCAA, and the Collegiate Licensing Company (CLC) in the United States District Court, Northern District of California. He sued EA for using his likeness without his consent and the NCAA and CLC for facilitating that use.[121] Keller also claimed that the use of his likeness and the likenesses of other student-athletes violated NCAA bylaw 12.5, which prohibits the commercial licensing of the "name, picture or likeness" of athletes at NCAA-member institutions.[121] Keller's proposed class action consisted of all student-athletes whose likenesses had been used without their consent in the *NCAA Football* and *NCAA Basketball* video games. The complaint alleged that EA's unauthorized use of his likeness deprived the college football athletes of their statutory and

Protecting the 12th Man

No collegiate institution has been more persistent in vigorously enforcing its distinctive team phrase *12th Man* than Texas A&M University. The school trademarked the iconic phrase, which is used to refer to the Aggies fan base, in 1990. Texas A&M claims that it has fought over 550 infringement issues over the mark. The 12th Man mark was the subject of trademark litigation initiated against the Seattle Seahawks in 2006, against a Buffalo Bills fan group in 2014, and against the Indianapolis Colts in 2015 for unauthorized use of the phrase. The Seahawks and Buffalo Bills cases resolved through agreements with the university. More recently, the Colts had been using "the 12th Man" in marketing materials, as the name of an award given to fans during games, and in its stadium as part of the Ring of Honor to recognize fans.[127] The Colts used the trademark to help sell tickets and merchandise, including an ad urging fans to "Join the 12th Man" and sold a "12th Man" blanket online.[128] The crux of Texas A&M's legal claim is that the 12th Man mark identifies the team to the public and distinguishes the university in events and merchandise. In its lawsuit, Texas A&M argued that use of the mark by the Indianapolis Colts would likely cause confusion, imply an affiliation between the teams that does not exist, and dilute the distinctiveness of Texas A&M's trademark.[127]

In resolving the three legal complaints discussed, all resulted in settlements with the university, demonstrating how trademark litigation often gets resolved when there is a registered trademark owner with clear ownership rights and a history of enforcing those rights. Texas A&M said the Colts agreed informally in 2006 not to use "12th Man" outside the RCA Dome. For the latest dispute in 2015, the Colts agreed to stop using the mark for the Ring of Honor, with the Colts' Chief Operating Officer stating the phrase was more important to Texas A&M than to the Colts.[128] The Buffalo Bills fan group agreed to have its domain name and social media pages with 12thManThunder.com revert back to the university's control and recognized that Texas A&M owns the 12th Man trademark.[129] The Seahawks took a more creative approach to resolving the legal matter and entered into a licensing deal with Texas A&M, which permits the team to use the mark only in the Pacific Northwest. The multiyear agreement was in exchange for a royalty fee and an annual donation to the school to help fight to protect the trademark.[130] Under terms of the renewal, the Seahawks no longer use "12th Man" on its Ring of Honor or on team social media, and it has never been permitted to put "12th Man" on merchandise. The team has shifted to using "12" and "12s" instead, which the Seahawks has sought to trademark itself.

common law right of publicity.[122] In December 2010, the Keller class action was consolidated with another class action brought against EA and the NCAA by former UCLA student-athlete and basketball player Ed O'Bannon.[123] The O'Bannon complaint, distinguishable from *Keller* in asserting the legal rights of former collegiate players, included antitrust claims against the NCAA that were dismissed, but Keller's right of publicity claims against EA survived. EA has argued that it does not use student-athlete likeness or, alternatively, that any use of athlete likenesses is protected expression under the First Amendment. In September 2013, EA Sports agreed to pay a reported US$40 million to settle the O'Bannon and Keller right-of-publicity lawsuit.[124] The settlement was undoubtedly spurred by an earlier 3rd Circuit Court of Appeals decision in the *Hart v. Electronic Arts Sports* case, which was seen as a victory for athletes and entertainers.[125] Hart involved the virtual depictions of a class of college athletes like himself in EA's *NCAA Football* video game series. Hart successfully argued that the inclusion of his virtual likeness in the form of a digital avatar without his permission violated his right of publicity. In 2014, U.S. District Judge Claudia Wilken found for O'Bannon, holding that the NCAA's long-standing rules and bylaws of barring payments to athletes operate as an unreasonable restraint of trade, in violation of antitrust law.[126]

Wrap-Up

Intellectual property law is not only complex but also, as seen in the areas discussed earlier, in flux. Rapid advancements in technology have significantly altered the legal landscape, and as new technologies engage sport consumers in novel ways, legal questions such as what constitutes an athlete's persona will continue to emerge. As sport marketers seek to protect their own creativity and avoid infringing on the creativity of others, they would do well to have a basic understanding of copyright, trademark, and patent law, as well as invasion of privacy and the right of publicity. When complex legal issues confront sport marketers, a good rule of thumb is to rely on legal counsel with specific expertise to advise the best course of action.

Activities

1. The introduction of this chapter presents a fictional fan (Dylan B. Fan) who is preparing to capitalize on her favorite team's trip to the World Series. Applying the trademark law concepts discussed in this chapter, do you think that she will be on the right side of the law with regard to the T-shirt logos that she is creating? Why or why not? If you were deciding the issue of likelihood of confusion in this case, what additional information might you need? With regard to the social media platforms that she envisions, do you think that she will be able to retain the platform names? Why or why not? Finally, advise Dylan on the right of publicity issues that she needs to be aware of regarding her plans to post about the Aces players and use their photos in her social media posts.

2. You are the in-house legal counsel for a energy drink start-up. You have been asked to review the plans for a marketing campaign timed to coincide with the start of the Y Games, an extreme sports competition. The energy drink company not an official sponsor of the Y Games, but it is a well-known official sponsor in the energy drink category. The company wants to use imagery with an action sports theme, including snowboarding, and it plans to activate the campaign primarily using social media. The company does not plan to use any of the Y Games' registered trademarks. However, it does plan to have a well-known snowboarder, who will be competing in this year's Y Games, serve as a brand ambassador and contribute unique content, including an Instagram takeover on the company's page. Discuss how you will approach determining the legal issues raised by the campaign as well as the possible threat of legal action over ambush marketing. Then, based on the examples and cases discussed throughout the chapter, suggest alternatives that could be used in the campaign to resolve the legal issues that you have identified.

3. Watch or attend a major sports event and identify all aspects of the event that could be protected using the various intellectual property laws discussed in this chapter. How would you use these laws to create a comprehensive plan for protecting the event's intellectual property? Discuss who owns each type of intellectual property that you have identified.

Your Marketing Plan

Assume that you are the chief marketing officer for Kredit-Kard, a national credit card company. Your leading competitor is the official sponsor of the upcoming MLB World Series. Devise an ambush marketing plan that outlines the tactics that you will recommend your company use to capitalize on the excitement of this upcoming event—without violating trademark laws.

 Go to HK*Propel* to complete the activities for this chapter.

Chapter 15

The Evolving Nature of Sport Marketing

OBJECTIVES

- To be able to compare and contrast the interaction and effect of the five Ps on one another
- To recognize the need to control the marketing function in order to ensure success of the marketing plan
- To understand the importance of examining future trends that will affect sport marketing
- To contemplate how future trends may affect a marketing plan

October 21, 2015: We know this as the day that Marty McFly and Doc Brown traveled into the future in the 1989 film *Back to the Future Part II*. This futuristic movie—for 1989 at least—featured many products and technologies that seemed outlandish at the time. We now know that some of these technologies have yet to see the light of day (e.g., flying cars). But a surprising number of the film's sci-fi technologies, once considered laughable, are now commonplace: personal drones, tablets, mobile payments, fingerprint-scanning technology, hands-free video gaming, wearable technology, video calls and conferencing, virtual reality, and VR glasses, to name just a few.[1,2] And, although the producers' vision may have been off by a year, *Back to the Future Part II* even predicted a Chicago Cubs World Series win!

So what knowledge can we gain about sport marketing from this movie franchise? Surprisingly, the *Back to the Future* films offer a constructive lesson for present-day marketers. Today's smartphones, social media, streaming video, apps, virtual signage, augmented and virtual reality, and esports, among many others, are all having a significant impact on sport marketing. However, like those in *Back to the Future Part II*, many of the technologies we know and use today would have been perceived as being bizarre when the first edition of this textbook was published in 1993. In fact, most of the aforementioned technologies were considerably less advanced when the last version of this book was published in 2014. Due to the rapidly changing nature of the sport industry, it is extremely important for sport marketers to stay on top of industry trends, and, in some sense, try to predict the industry's future. The sport industry will not remain stagnant, and smart sport marketers will stay ahead of the trends as opposed to playing catch-up. Geoffrey Colon, senior product marketing manager at Microsoft, highlighted this mindset when he stated, "What we think is the natural order of behavior today will be altered due to changes in technology, economics, social status, the environment and new products being created, combined and transformed on a weekly basis."[3]

Because staying on top of industry trends is so important, we conclude this chapter and textbook with some predictions that we believe will have a major influence on sport marketing throughout the early to mid-2020s. We purposefully limit coverage with the intention to get readers thinking critically about the future of the industry and making your own predictions. If you were to write a *Back to the Future* movie for the sport industry, what kinds of predictions would you make that may seem outlandish now but may actually shape this industry for years to come?

As we noted in chapter 2, strategic marketing management, with its integration of product, price, place, promotion, and public relations, must be managed in a way that moves the organization toward its overall objectives. In this chapter, we briefly examine the range of cross-effects among the five Ps and the sport marketing mix, and reiterate the importance of effectively controlling these elements. To conclude the textbook, we contemplate something that is important for all sport marketers to consider—planning for the future in sport marketing. In doing so, we outline some current trends we believe all sport marketers should consider in order to properly prepare their organization for long-term success.

Cross-Effects Among the Five Ps

So far, we have treated each element of the marketing mix mainly in an isolated fashion, yet, clearly these elements have a simultaneous cross-effect on the consumer. A potential buyer of a sport product does not view the price of a product in isolation from the promotional mix, the place function (the venue), or the nature of the product and product extensions. This effect can be assessed using a cross-effect matrix (figure 15.1). The following is an examination of how each of these functions may interact with each other. However, each sport product is unique and will

	Product	Price	Place	Promotion	Public relations
Product		Price = quality and value	Distribution point influences image	Product positioning	Consumer receptivity
Price			Pay more for better facility or convenience	Choice of media and promotional outlets	Sincerity of public relations
Place				Promote unique aspects of venue	Proper communication of venue information
Promotion					Completely independent
Public relations					

FIGURE 15.1   Cross-effect matrix for the five Ps of sport marketing.

influence these effects in different ways. As such, as outlined in chapter 2, it is important for sport marketers to consider these interaction effects during their planning process with a full understanding that these effects will evolve throughout the implementation of the marketing plan.

- *Product and Price.* Price, as we have previously discussed, is the most visible and most readily communicable variable of the marketing mix. Price influences perceptions of quality and value, and thereby directly affects product image. Consumers will weigh the benefits of the product with the perceived value of the price when making purchasing decisions.

- *Product and Place.* Perceptions of the product image will be influenced by the distribution point. For example, a new facility may influence the image of the team, while a product distributed in a high-end retail location may be perceived as being high in quality.

- *Product and Promotion.* The type of product will dictate the appropriate outlets used for promotional purposes and how the product is positioned. For instance, it is unlikely to find top-brand golf equipment and apparel advertised in a local newspaper. Rather, businesses will focus their promotional campaigns with targeted efforts in golf-specific media outlets to support their desired positioning.

- *Product and Public Relations.* Public relations efforts will have a direct effect on product image, positioning, and, ultimately, consumer acceptance of the product. The messaging delivered to the consumer by the media, or directly from an organization, will help in framing what consumers believe about the product.

- *Price and Place.* This interaction has two major effects. First, sport consumers expect to pay higher prices at better facilities with more amenities and at high-end retail outlets. Second, consumers will pay more for convenience while shopping (e.g., you may be comfortable paying online fees and shipping to avoid the hassle of going to purchase items at physical retail locations).

- *Price and Promotion.* The price of the product will influence the market being targeted, and as such, the media and promotional outlets needed to reach that target market. For example, the target markets for fans who buy general seating to a sports event are very different than those who may purchase high-priced club or luxury seating. Therefore, the strategies used to reach these different, yet both important, markets will vary.

• *Price and Public Relations.* Pricing strategies can have a strong effect on public relations. For example, raising ticket prices after a string of losing seasons may create a public relations nightmare for a team—particularly with how easy it is for consumers to now voice opinions through social media and other outlets.

• *Place and Promotion.* Sport organizations can promote unique components of their venue whether they be unique seating options, social gathering locations, promotions, or fan engagement opportunities.

• *Place and Public Relations.* Any messages about changes, policies, upgrades, etc., at a sport venue will need to be carefully delivered to the media and the public in order to maintain or enhance the image of an organization.

• *Promotion and Public Relations.* Publicity is one of the four elements traditionally identified under the promotion umbrella; therefore, the two are independent.

Controlling the Marketing Function

We have seen that each element of the marketing mix is interdependent, some to a larger extent than others. Because each could influence the others, the only way to ensure marketing effectiveness is to control all parts of the marketing effort. In chapter 4, we outlined a comprehensive plan for measuring the appropriate analytics to ensure that the return on objectives (ROO) and return on investment (ROI) are where they should be. Only with these accountability measures in place can marketing and managerial control be effective. This plan has as its ultimate goal as ensuring the creation and delivery of products that satisfy consumer wants and needs.

A sound control system can nurture and preserve the credibility of the image that consumers hold of both the product and the organization. The notion of control spans all levels of the industry—from the NFL dictating specifications on player uniforms to a local YMCA training its staff to react courteously to member complaints. Control is a central feature in successful marketing. Even the smallest item can create negative images that seriously undermine the overall organizational image. A small flaw may not affect all consumers or publics that interact with an organization, its personnel, products, services, or facilities, but it can affect enough people to cause damage. For instance, coaches who repeatedly violate NCAA recruiting rules send a subtle but powerful message that their other promises cannot be believed. Maintaining consistency is important in a marketer's ability to communicate a clear and precise position. Inconsistencies blur images and project incoherent product positions.

As was noted in chapter 2 when the marketing management process (MMP) was first introduced, the key to controlling the marketing mix lies in setting a clear direction for all units and personnel and ensuring that all functions work from the same playbook. In marketing, it is extremely important that the departments within an organization do not operate in silos but rather work together as one cohesive organization to drive the mission of the organization while striving to meet the same objectives. For example, in college sports, marketing, ticket sales, the outsourced media rights partner, athletics development (fundraising), and the box office (ticket service) all need to be on the same page. Employees need a road map to tell them where to go and how to get there. They need to know how they will be evaluated and how their efforts relate to those of other departments or functions in the organization. This synergistic approach will ensure the marketing mix is properly coordinated toward the same target markets while incorporating optimal marketing and promotional strategies. As the ticket marketing, sales, and service (TiMSS) plan discussed in chapter 2 stressed, having an effective, and coordinated, strategic plan in place will allow an organization to retain, grow, and acquire consumers. Ultimately, an effective marketing control system, then, must be part of an ongoing planning system that has at least four components:

1. Preestablished mission statements and objectives should reflect the current market position regarding a desired position and

also link strategic planning with the tactics that will move an organization toward its objectives. In other words, every piece of the marketing mix should be framed within a broader strategic vision.

2. The organizational structure should marshal resources to meet objectives by aligning organizational goals and policies and ensuring that personnel and their duties complement one another.

3. Employee performance standards and criteria logically link performance to specific marketing and sales objectives.

4. Methods are designed to adjust strategy, structure, and personnel in light of performance.

In short, marketing control must be incorporated into an overall strategic plan in order to ensure success and influence the overall strategic direction of an organization.[4]

The Shape of Things to Come

With understanding the interaction effects among the five Ps and having proper control systems in place, sport marketers are best equipped for setting up their marketing plan for success. However, marketers cannot exclusively live in the present when considering their marketing plan. One important aspect of sport marketing is trying to understand what trends are going to influence the organization in both the short- and long-terms. Unfortunately, as we know, perfectly predicting the future is not possible. Yet, perceptive marketers still have the ability to analyze industry trends in an effort to make better, more accurate assumptions about certain factors that may affect the industry within the next five to 10 years and beyond. Honing their skill set and planning the marketing mix accordingly helps to set these marketers ahead of their competition. After all, it is much better to be prepared for the next big thing than it is to be reactionary and behind the proverbial eight ball. A "that's how we have always done it" mindset simply does not work in sport marketing. Sport marketers must always be evolving and determining how to best prepare for the future. What follows is certainly not an exhaustive list, and we don't claim the ability to predict everything precisely; it is merely our attempt to do what every sport marketer should do—think about the future of the industry. The following are several key trends that we predict will have a major impact on sport marketing as we move through the early to mid-2020s. We encourage you to review these predictions, think critically about whether or not you agree them, and, ultimately, come up with some more predictions that we may have missed.

Gen Z

For years, the sport industry has rightfully been concerned with how to engage with millennials. While that is still important to consider, and depending on which generation definition you use, the oldest millennial was born in 1980 (41 years old in 2021), and the youngest millennial was born in 1994 (27 years old in 2021). While millennials and other generations are still important targets, we believe it will become imperative to devote more marketing time and resources to the next youngest generation, Gen Z. These people were generally born between the years of 1995 (26 years old in 2021) and 2010 (11 years old in 2021).

Like most generations that have come before them, Gen Z consumes sport differently than their counterparts. As one report indicated, "Generation Z has high expectations for entertainment experiences, and it is a mistake to believe they will automatically grow to love the same sports as their parents and grandparents."[5] Outside of being interested in different sports, several other unique facets characterize this group:

- Gen Z tends to connect more with individual athletes than it does with teams. As such, the use of athletes as influencers will continue to gain importance, and teams must also market their star power in more engaging ways to influence this group.

- Gen Z's interest in music, video games, social media, fashion, and celebrities is higher than previous generations, which provides opportunities to create more unique and engaging experiences at events and collaborations with other industries.

- This group has embraced technology in sport with higher levels of interest in online gaming, esports, virtual and augmented reality gaming, and drone racing.

- This generation is also more likely to consume sports through video streaming, social media, and apps than previous generations.[5]

The sport organizations that best market to this generation and make changes to their product delivery in order to do so will be most likely to build their fan or customer base.

Sports Gambling

The continued legalization of sports gambling in the United States may be the most important trend that will influence the sport industry for years to come. One estimate suggests that in 2021, two-thirds of the states in the country will have legalized sports gambling.[6] However, we are still in the early stages of widespread legalized sports gambling, and as a result, every sport property has taken a different approach, with some being more cautious than others. We predict that the industry will become more receptive over the next few years, and, therefore, we will see increased integration of gambling into sports viewing experiences. As one report noted, legalized sports gambling will likely affect the sport experience at home, at the game, and in other locations where people consume sport.[6]

Sports gambling will have a major impact on, and will change, our at-home viewing experience. We have already seen major media networks that have embraced this by providing gambling-related content. For instance, Fox Sports' *LOCK IT IN* is a daily, one-hour show that discusses the daily betting options, wagers, props, and gambling analytics. We anticipate that more programs such as this will be developed. In addition, we may see more in-game analysis during game broadcasts on how gameplay could affect the gambling outcomes for the games. After all, for many fans, this is why they watch some games. Highly identified fans will continue to watch their favorite teams and players, whether they bet on them or not, but casual fans will consume more

Legalized sport gambling at casino sportsbooks, such as the one shown here, and through other outlets will undoubtedly grow and influence the sport industry.

AP Photo/Wayne Parry

games and related content as the ability to bet on games continues to increase.

As we have discussed in this textbook, the at-home viewing experience of sports events will continue to improve. As it does, it becomes imperative that sport organizations improve their stadium experience in order to get fans off their couch and to the stadium. Incorporating some aspects of gambling into the stadium experience is one area that will be used in the future in order to achieve this. While there are conflicting opinions on the incorporation of sportsbooks or areas to place bets into sport facilities, it is a distinct possibility that this will become the new norm at sports events in the not-too-distant future. At the very least, we will see the increase of gambling-related sponsorships and the integration of their sponsorship activations at stadiums. For instance, in 2020, the NFL announced that it would allow teams to have sponsored betting lounges in its stadiums, which can include official sportsbook sponsor signage and monitors showing the game odds, but they would not have actual betting windows where bets would be placed at the games.[7]

Finally, the legalization of sports gambling may also affect other ways in which people consume sport. Certainly, there will be an increase in gaming apps, social media, and streaming content dedicated to gambling. Even sports bars and restaurants are already considering how to incorporate gambling into their customer experience as well. For instance, in 2019, Buffalo Wild Wings and MGM Resorts International entered into a partnership. As part of this deal, point spreads and game odds will appear on TV screens at Buffalo Wild Wings restaurants and a mobile game, which uses sports gambling concepts without having money be exchanged, will be developed so that restaurant customers can play for the chance to win prizes.[8]

Growth of Esports

The esports industry has exploded globally. It was projected that the global esports market would eclipse US$1 billion in revenue in 2019 for the first time, with sponsorship accounting for US$456.7 million of that figure. The expectations are that this total revenue figure will grow to US$1.79 billion by 2022. The future projections for esports

viewership are also extremely positive. In 2019, it was estimated that the global esports fan base was 453.8 million people, which included 201.2 million esports "enthusiasts" and 252.6 million casual viewers. This fan base is expected to reach 645 million people by 2022.[9]

One predicted outcome of this growth is that companies that are trying to reach a younger demographic, like Generation Z, will begin to shift some sponsorship and advertising dollars away from traditional sports and to esports. Sport leagues that have not fully embraced esports by this point will do so by creating their own leagues, like the NBA 2K League, or developing cross-promotions with existing esports games, leagues, and athletes. For instance, some will follow in the footsteps of the NFL, which partnered with the popular video game Fortnite. In the game, players were able to purchase NFL-themed uniform skins (i.e., what players outfit their characters with). Prior to Super Bowl 54, the NFL was also part of the "Twitch Rivals: Streamer Bowl Featuring Fortnite," which paired NFL stars with esports athletes in a live-streamed Fortnite battle for charity.[10] We also anticipate that we will begin to see more esports content on major television networks, and more esports athletes will become mainstream celebrities like the popular esports athlete Ninja has.

Growth of the Influence of Women's Sports

While there is no doubt that inequities exist in relation to the marketing of women's sports and athletes, we remain optimistic that the 2020s can represent a time for growth and a renewed call for additional media coverage and spending on women's sports. We have seen some positive signs of growth in media coverage, interest, and viewership in recent years, particularly with basketball. In 2019, the NCAA Women's Basketball Tournament had its highest attendance in 15 years,[11] and at one point during the 2019 season, WNBA television ratings were up 64 percent over the previous year with ESPN also broadcasting more WNBA games than in past years.[12] This media momentum for women's sports continued in 2020 when the NWSL signed a deal with CBS to provide the league with enhanced visibility on CBS and the CBS Sports Network.[13]

Esports have had a major impact on how traditional sport leagues and sponsors attempt to reach their fans and customers.

Data also indicate that sponsorship of women's sports can provide a good return on investment for the brands involved. For example, according to a study by rEvolution, fans feel more connected with, and appreciative of, sponsors of women's soccer than other prominent men's professional sports. Specifically, the results suggest that fans understand that sponsors are vital to the success in the sport: 63 percent of those surveyed believed that women's soccer could fail without the support of its sponsors.[14] Consequently, women's soccer fans are more likely to support the sponsors of the sport because they want to support the organizations that are investing in a sport they love. We anticipate a growth in sponsor spending on women's sports and athletes as more findings such as this highlight the positive benefits of partnering with women's sports properties. While there is some concern of how much focus will be on women's sports following the coronavirus pandemic,[15] we expect that more sponsorship spending will also be earmarked for women's sports with the continued cultivation of leagues like the NWSL and up-and-coming, high-profile athletes, such as Sabrina Ionescu, Naomi Osaka, and Coco Gauff.

College Athletes' Name, Image, and Likeness

In 2019, the ongoing argument of whether college student-athletes should be paid reached a potential tipping point. That year, California was the first state to pass a law to allow college student-athletes to benefit financially from their NIL. California's passing of this law, which is scheduled to go into effect in 2023, would essentially permit these athletes to be paid by outside companies (i.e., not by the colleges and universities) for the use of their NIL. Theoretically, this would allow college student-athletes to be paid to be in commercials, on billboards, through social media posts, etc. Since 2019, several other states have introduced similar bills with varying degrees of stipulations, and the NCAA issued a carefully worded statement indicating that college student-athletes could potentially "benefit" from their NIL.

While there are still numerous legal and logistical hurdles to overcome with these legislations, we anticipate that college student-athletes will be able to financially benefit in some way from the use of their NIL. This will create an entirely new potential market for companies to market through college sports and the student-athletes. With that said, we do not expect that most college student-athletes will "get rich" off their NIL. We predict that the biggest impact will likely be with local companies that wish to use student-athletes from surrounding colleges to promote their businesses. For example, in a place like Columbus, Ohio, many of the Ohio State University student-athletes may benefit from working with local businesses in the area. However, a small number of elite, well-known college student-athletes may be able to be used from a national perspective with major brands, and earn more money (in the six figures), if legislation is passed on a national level. In addition, college student-athletes with large social media following will benefit more as companies look to them to promote brands to their followers.

Growth of Jersey Sponsorships in North American Sports

It was only a matter of time before a major North American sport league incorporated some element of sponsorships onto their jerseys. The potential revenue provided by this valuable piece of sponsorship inventory was too great to ignore. While this practice is common in other sports around the world, most major North American sport leagues had been resistant to using their jerseys as advertising space outside of their licensing deals. As you likely know, some leagues, like the WNBA, had experimented with placing corporate logos on their jerseys, while other leagues, like the NHL, allowed for corporate brands to be placed on their practice jerseys.

However, when the NBA started allowing teams to sell jersey sponsorships beginning with the 2017 to 2018 season, it changed the future of this sport marketing practice in North America. During the 2019 to 2020 season, all 30 NBA teams had a corporate ad patch on their jerseys. It's estimated that these 2 ½-inch by 2-½ inch ad patches generated US$150 million in new sponsorship revenue. While many of these deals expire in the 2020 or 2021 seasons, the NBA is expecting a 30 percent increase in this figure.[16]

We anticipate more leagues to follow what the NBA has done, and predict that in the future, MLB, the NHL, and the NFL will all have jersey sponsorships in some form. In fact, MLB has already indicated that it is exploring the possibility of allowing jersey sponsorships. In 2019, it appeared that this was not necessarily going to take place immediately but that it was likely inevitable that we would see corporate patches on MLB uniforms in the future.[17]

Globalization of Sport Marketing

It is safe to say we are not going out on a limb to predict that the sport industry, and as such, sport marketing will continue to expand globally. The ease of access to digital content will continue to allow sport brands to extend their reach well beyond their borders. We expect the number of international competitions for sport leagues and teams will increase (similar to MLB in London, European soccer team tours of the United States, the NFL in Mexico City, etc.), while at the same, the competitions reach out to new and emerging markets where they have not been before. This will lead to an increasing number of leagues and teams opening global offices in an attempt to extend their brands beyond traditional borders, allowing them better interaction with and growth of their international fan base.

Perhaps the biggest potential element of global expansion would be placing a North American franchise abroad. To this point, the NFL has been the most public about its potential interest in having a franchise outside of the United States. While 2022 had been discussed as a potential target date to have an NFL franchise in London,[18] this date may not be realistic due to time and logistical constraints. However, now that the NFL-ready Tottenham Hotspur stadium is complete, we do predict, at a minimum, discussions related to this will intensify, and it is likely that some definitive steps could take place in an effort to make this a reality.

Enhanced Stadium Experiences and Amenities

In order to encourage attendance and meet the changing needs of sports fans, we anticipate that sport facilities will increasingly focus on bringing the "living-room experience" to the live event. With so many entertainment options literally at the fingertips of fans, it becomes more crucial to make the stadium experience unique and to provide all the comforts of home, and more, at sport facilities. In chapter 13, we discussed why facilities

Dylan Buell/Getty Images

The success of NBA jersey sponsorships will likely lead to other major North American sport leagues adopting this practice.

need to provide items such as good wireless connectivity, new seating options, enhanced food and beverage choices above and beyond the standard stadium fare, and, ultimately, a better game-day experience. Integration of new technologies will become increasingly beneficial in enhancing the game-day experience for fans. We will see a rise in the use of in-stadium apps to create a personalized experience at events, while more organizations will incorporate virtual and augmented reality integrations throughout their facilities.

In chapter 13, we also provided some examples of how facilities are creating more areas for social interaction among fans. Sport is a social experience, and many fans want to attend games with family and friends without being confined to their specific seat and section of the stadium. In future facility renovations and construction, we will see more dedicated social interaction areas and unique gathering places where fans can congregate, mingle, and still watch the game. To accommodate this trend, it will become common for sport organizations to remove physical seats in certain parts of the facility and, ultimately,

decrease seating capacities in order to create room for these types of social interaction spaces.

Changing Landscape of Media Rights

From now until the year 2025, the landscape of how and where we consume sport through media is going to change. During this time frame, all or some of the media rights for many of the major sport leagues in North America will be up for negotiation—MLB and the NFL beginning in 2021, the NHL in 2022, and the NBA in 2025.[19]

While the leagues will certainly sign media rights deals with networks such as CBS, Fox, NBC, Turner, and ESPN on ABC, we predict that the battle for streaming rights will reach far beyond these cable networks. Companies such as Amazon, Apple, Facebook, YouTube TV, Netflix, and DAZN will be major players in these negotiations, and many of these companies will certainly be awarded streaming rights to certain content from the leagues. However, as cord cutting continues to increase and all generations become more comfortable with technology, there will likely become a time when a sport property will move all its content exclusively to a streaming service. While we do not anticipate this during the negotiations that take place in the early to mid-2020s, these negotiations will set the tone for the possibility of this in subsequent discussions that will likely take place in the next decade. It may seem like a long time from now, but the potential impact on the industry would be so disruptive that it is important to at least be considering this possibility.

Unforeseen Global Catastrophes

As we were writing this textbook, the world was in the midst of the COVID-19 pandemic. Lives and businesses across the world had been disrupted and, in some instances, in only a matter of days. The sport world was not spared, with leagues and events around the world either being cancelled or postponed. To name just a few: The NCAA Men's and Women's Basketball Tournaments were cancelled; MLB and the NBA put their seasons on hold; several Formula 1 races were either cancelled or postponed; the Masters moved its tournament date from the traditional April date; EURO 2020 was postponed for a full year; the Indy 500 was not held on Memorial Day weekend for the first time since 1946; and the biggest of them all, the 2020 Tokyo Olympic Games did not take place as scheduled in July and August of 2020.

It is not an enjoyable exercise to plan for a potential disruption to your business and marketing activities due to something like a natural disaster, pandemic, or war, but the COVID-19 outbreak is a stark reminder that sport organizations need to have contingency plans. Leagues, events, athletes, media partners, facilities, and sponsors should all have plans in place, both contractually and hypothetically, which allow them to react quickly during an unexpected disruption.

However, to the extent that is reasonable and acceptable given the situation, it is also important to continue marketing during a crisis. There were numerous instances of sport organizations still engaging in creative and appropriate marketing activities during the early months of the COVID-19 pandemic, allowing fans and consumers continuous engagement with their brands, offering fans and consumers emotional and financial support, and simply providing fans and consumers

an escape and distraction from the psychological distress caused by the pandemic:

- Many media outlets aired classic games on TV in the time slots when current games were supposed to be taking place.
- NASCAR had their drivers compete in simulated NASCAR races through the iRacing esports racing platform and broadcast these simulations on Fox Sports.
- Social media have been the primary tool for organizations to provide content, with many showing old highlights, providing contests for their fans, and engaging with fans and other teams in creative ways.
- Many athletes used social media during the pandemic to provide words of support or by showcasing their personality and giving a glimpse of their home life to fans.
- Several teams, sport organizations, athletes, and corporations donated money to various organizations or stadium workers who are now out of work due to the cancellation and postponement of events. For instance, Anheuser-Busch shifted US$5 million of its sport and entertainment sponsorship budget to relief efforts, while Nike perhaps offered one of the simplest, yet powerful statements during this time. On Twitter, Nike urged people to stay home and help stop the spread of the virus by tweeting, "If you ever dreamed of playing for millions around the world, now is your chance. Play inside, play for the world."[20]

As you are reading this, you will have experienced and seen more of how the COVID-19 pandemic impacted sport than we can currently report. However, after the first few months of the pandemic, the sport industry gradually started to return to business and their respective fields of play, albeit under much different circumstances.

- The NBA, NHL, and WNBA all returned to play and completed their seasons in what became known as "bubbles" in Orlando, Florida (NBA), Edmonton, Alberta, and Toronto, Ontario (NHL), and Bradenton, Florida (WNBA). These bubbles allowed players to be quarantined in select locations in order to limit exposure and any spread of the coronavirus.

- MLB and the NFL started their seasons while incorporating some pauses in competition for teams that had positive COVID-19 cases.

- Italian soccer league Serie A, one of the first professional sport leagues to stop play during the pandemic in March 2020, returned to play in June 2020.

- Most sports events initially took place with no fans in attendance, but gradually some sports facilities allowed fans at a significantly reduced capacity to allow for social distancing. Some events even had virtual fans, while others sold cardboard cut outs of fans with their pictures on them and placed them throughout the stadium.

- Leagues such as the NHL, NFL, and WNBA held their player drafts virtually.

- Prominent sports licensees and leagues began to sell branded face masks and other face coverings, with some donating a portion of sales to charities. For instance, FoCo, who produces officially licensed sport products, estimates that they may sell close to US$100 million in sport licensed face coverings, and that by September 2020 they had donated nearly US$5.9 million to charities due to the sale of these new licensed products.[21]

- Many sponsorship activations shifted to a virtual environment, and the industry had to be creative to offer goods for sponsors who could not activate at events. For example, some leagues and teams offered their sponsors new signage locations with corporate brands placed on tarps that were placed over sections in the facilities where fans typically sit.

These are just some examples of how the sport industry returned and how marketing continued despite the COVID-19 pandemic. However, while each situation is different, and sport organizations need to be sensitive to their current environment, it is safe to say that the sport industry, like many other industries, was caught off guard by the COVID-19 pandemic. It took a massive undertaking by sport properties, athletes, media, and corporate partners to accomplish what the industry did from a competition perspective during this time. However, this also provided a reminder that it is important for sport organizations to plan and think ahead to how they would operate and market their brands due to unforeseen cancellations or postponements.

Wrap-Up

As we have illustrated with countless examples throughout this textbook, the sport industry is evolving rapidly. Going forward, the pressures will only escalate to develop effective, innovative, and creative sport marketing techniques. The market is more crowded, and consumers are more complex. In today's digitally connected world, the successful sport marketer will need to have a firm grasp of technology, social media, content creation, mobile applications, streaming capabilities, analytics and data-driven decision making, strategic brand management, experiential marketing, and the rapidity with which tastes and attention change. Whatever the game, the technique will be the same. A comprehensive, controlled, and well-built marketing effort as outlined in this textbook, coupled with listening and observing skills, creative ideas, and the ability to foresee and adapt to potential changes in the industry, will be the winning formula.

Activities

1. As a simple review, find at least two examples of each cross-effect among the five Ps, either in this book or in some other resource.

2. Using an example from a current sport organization, illustrate the effects of price on the remaining four Ps. Describe scenarios that demonstrate both positive and negative effects.

3. In your estimation, does one of the five Ps have greater cross-effect than the others? Price perhaps? Provide examples to defend your position.

4. Describe which of the future predictions outlined in this chapter you either agree or disagree with, and then make your own predictions. What did we miss? What are some of the most important trends you believe will affect sport marketing in the next five to 10 years?

Your Marketing Plan

Develop a cross-effect matrix for your organization taking into account how your product, place, promotion, price, and public relations decisions may influence each other.

 Go to HK*Propel* to complete the activities for this chapter.

Glossary

80-20 rule—A general pattern across industries showing that approximately 80 percent of market consumption comes from only 20 percent of the consumers.

activation—The marketing activities a company conducts to promote its sponsorship.

affective involvement—The attitudes, feelings, and emotions that a consumer has toward an activity.

ambush marketing—A company's attempt to be carried on the goodwill or popularity of a sports event; ambush marketing involves creating an association between the company itself and the event, without getting consent from the relevant organization and without providing payment to the organization to become an official sponsor of the sports event.

athlete endorsement—The use of celebrity athletes as brand ambassadors to promote products and services in an official capacity for brands.

audience segmentation—The ability to identify different ways to group audiences into specific categories to understand their unique qualities, needs, and expectations for a marketing plan.

behavioral involvement—The act of doing or purchasing.

benefit selling—A method of selling whereby a salesperson relates a product's benefits to the customer's needs using the product's features and advantages as support.

benefits segmentation—The process of dividing the consumer market into smaller categories based on the value consumers are likely to derive from the product or service.

BIRG—Basking in reflected glory.

brand—The name, logo, and other symbols connected to a sport organization that are used to identify its products and distinguish it from competitors.

brand associations—The thoughts and ideas that people hold in their memory about a particular brand, which ultimately forms their brand image.

brand awareness—The familiarity consumers have with a brand's existence and distinctive qualities.

brand equity—The intrinsic value added to or subtracted from a brand which is influenced by factors such as the strength and uniqueness of the brand's name and logo, awareness, and image.

brand extensions—New products that use the brand name of an existing brand but exist in a different product category than the brand's initial or primary product.

brand image—Consumers' perception of a brand.

brand voice—The distinctive personality and image that is created through communication on social media

business cycle—The fluctuations in economic activity over time and contains six stages: expansion, peak, recession, depression, trough, and recovery.

chatbot—A computer program that provides text or talk-to-speech, which is fueled by machine learning and meant to mimic human conversation.

cluster analysis—The forming of groups or segments of people within the data based on similar characteristics.

cognitive involvement—The acquisition of information and knowledge about a topic.

collective mark—A trademark or service mark that a group uses to either to identify its products or services or to denote membership in the group.

commitment—The frequency, duration, and intensity of involvement in a sport or an activity.

communications mix—Advertising, personal selling, publicity, sponsorship, and sales promotion.

community relations—The lasting connections between athletes or sport organizations and the communities where they work and compete.

competitive parity—The same level of performance as others in the market.

contextual commerce—The cross-selling of products and services based on what people see or do with their smartphones.

copyright infringement—The act of infringing a copyright owner's sole rights afforded by the Federal Copyright Act.

CORF—Cutting off reflected failure.

crisis communication—The way an organization is able to proactively communicate during a crisis.

cross-promotion—The joining of two or more corporate partners or organizations to capitalize jointly on a sponsorship or licensing agreement.

crosstabulations—A statistical analysis marketers use to examine the interaction between two or more variables.

culture—A shared set of values, conventions, or social practices associated with a particular field, activity, or social group.

custom research—Research that is customized on a client-by-client basis based on unique goals and questions.

customer lifetime value (CLV)—The total worth to a business of a customer over the whole period of their relationship based on the premise that it costs less to keep existing customers than it does to acquire new ones.

customer relationship management (CRM)—Technology for managing customer relationships and interactions with current and potential customers.

cybersquatting—The act of reserving a domain name (especially one that is associated with a company's trademark) on the Internet, and then trying to profit by selling or licensing the name to a company that has an interest in being associated with that name.

data analytics—The science of analyzing data in order to draw conclusions about the information provided.

data appends—A process that involves adding new data elements to an existing database to enhance a company's existing customer files. Companies often collect basic information on their clients, such as phone numbers, emails, or addresses. A data append takes the information they have and matches it against a larger database of business data, allowing the desired missing data fields to be added.

database marketing—The collection, analysis, and interpretation of customer data in order to drive more relevant customer experiences. Database marketing involves the collection of data from a range of sources, including customer email correspondence, CRM system customer info, data warehouses, and, increasingly, external sources like social media.

demographic segmentation—See *state-of-being segmentation*.

descriptive statistics—The measures of central tendency (mean, median, mode) and frequencies or patterns that describe the data.

differentiation—Focusing on the unique attributes or benefits of your product in order to highlight a distinct difference or advantage over your competition.

digital signage—Previously known as LED signage, a lighted display that portrays graphical images or even video. Digital signage is becoming very popular in sport facilities due to its ability to rotate images and play videos, as well as the high recall from those who view it.

dilution—The diminishment of a well-known trademark's strength, effectiveness, or exclusivity by using the mark on an unrelated product, often by blurring or denigrating the trademark's unique character.

direct mail—The distribution of a printed promotional or advertising piece that is sent to people via mail.

direct marketing—A form of communicating an offer, where organizations communicate directly to a preselected customer and supply a method for a direct response. Among practitioners, it is also known as direct response marketing. By contrast, advertising is of a mass-message nature.

drawing radius—The process of marking and visualizing distances away from a central point (e.g., a sport facility), which can then be used to help make marketing decisions, such as determining target markets or which geographic areas to market to.

economic impact studies—Use data to quantitatively estimate the economic benefits of particular events or activities on a region and have three different levels of impact: direct, indirect, and induced.

economics—The study of how societies use limited resources. It is concerned with the production, distribution, and consumption of goods and services.

electronic media—Any video or audio form of mass communication, often delivered via TV, radio, or Internet.

exclusivity—When the sponsor of a particular category will be the only brand present in that category throughout the sponsorship depending on the terms of the agreement.

exhibition games—Sports events that are played or contested for sport and entertainment and are not counted in league or championship standings.

external factors—Product, price, place, promotion, public relations, as well as economic, technological, political, cultural, demographic, and situational.

false designation of origin—A mark, design, or similar detail that generates a misleading or inaccurate impression of a good or product's source.

full-menu selling—Concurrently selling a variety of options in terms of ticket packages (i.e., full- or half-season plans and 10-game plans).

game presentation—The act of combining and manipulating all elements of a game night in order to create a memorable experience for fans.

gate revenues—The primary market for ticket sales for live sports events.

geo-demographic clustering—The process of dividing consumers into small groups based on their geographic residence; as residents of a neighborhood, they may possess similar income levels and lifestyle characteristics.

goodwill—The feeling fans develop toward companies connected to their favorite sport or event when those companies support an activity that fans enjoy.

Gross Domestic Product (GDP)—The total value of all goods and services produced by a country over a period of time and is considered to be a broad measure of a country's economic health.

hospitality—The provision made for the sponsor by the sport or entertainment property of tickets in exclusive seating areas, lodging, transportation, on-site special activities, and special events and excursions related to the activity or event.

inferential statistics—The inferences made about the larger population when a researcher uses a smaller data set or group of people.

influencer marketing—Working with fans or followers of your team who have large, engaged audiences and having them distribute your content.

injunction—A court order that demands or prevents an action.

intercept surveying—Finding respondents to complete a survey by approaching them in person.

internal factors—Beliefs/attitudes, values, knowledge, motives, perceptions, lifestyle, as well as problem solving, information search, alternate evaluation, purchase, and post-purchase evaluation.

invasion of privacy—The unjustified misuse of someone's personality or intrusion into people's personal activities; it is actionable under tort law as well as constitutional law.

lead scoring—A shared sales and marketing methodology for ranking leads in order to determine their sales-readiness. Scoring leads is based on the interest potential customers show in your business, their current place in the buying cycle, and their fit in regards to your business. This methodology can also be used to identify the best salesperson to make the solicitation, based on the success of that salesperson and the qualifications of the prospect.

licensing—Granting an outside company the right to use a brand's intellectual property (e.g., name, logos, colors, taglines, mascots) to produce new products.

lifestyle marketing—A strategy in which a brand or product is marketed so that it is perceived to possess certain characteristics, aesthetics, or appeal that the target audience identifies with or that fits their current or aspirational lifestyle.

line extension—The new versions of a branded product that exist in the same product category as the brand's initial or primary product.

linear regression—A statistical model used to determine the relationship between one dependent variable and one or more explanatory (independent) variables.

macroeconomics—The branch of economics that studies the overall working of a national economy.

major event—Any sports event, or even series of events, that carries historical significance for the sport or league; often a championship game or a special event. Examples include the Super Bowl, MLS Cup, and World Series.

market feasibility study—A detailed analysis of a project (e.g., a sport facility) that may include items such as an overview of the facility site, the financials of the facility project, demographics of potential customers, and an overall analysis of the viability of the project and its location.

market research—Conducting research about the behaviors and insights of the market.

market segmentation—The process of dividing a large, heterogeneous market into more homogeneous groups of people who have similar wants, needs, or demographic profiles, to whom a product may be targeted.

marketing automation—A category of technology that allows companies to streamline, automate, and measure marketing tasks and workflows, so they can increase operational efficiency and grow revenue faster.

marketing channels—Sets or configurations of organizations linked together to deliver a product to consumers.

marketing mix—Factors controlled by a company that are used to get the customer to act.

marketing myopia—A lack of foresight in marketing ventures.

media relations—The act of soliciting publicity for a client or an organization and addressing journalists' queries about the client or organization. Media relations are mutually beneficial for PR personnel and journalists because they reach an audience with content of interest.

media rights—Fees paid to broadcast sports events.

merchandising—The sale of licensed products with team and league logos, player likenesses, and other intellectual property.

microeconomics—The branch of economics that studies how households and businesses reach decisions about purchasing, savings, setting prices, competition in business, etc.

mission—A statement that describes how goals will be achieved.

models—Processes used to frame collected data.

niche strategy—Marketing to a unique subset of the population.

organizational culture—The consistent, observable patterns of behavior found within organizations.

out of home (OOH) advertising—Any form of advertising to people when they are out of their homes. The term is normally associated with billboard or street signage advertising.

outsourcing—The business practice of hiring a party outside a company to perform services and create goods that traditionally were performed in-house by the company's own employees and staff.

paid media—Any form of marketing messaging that is placed by an organization in external media and for which that promotion is paid, as opposed to being obtained for free. Often known as advertising.

patent—The individual right to the profits of an invention or enhancement that is granted by the U.S. Patent Office, for a certain period of time, on the basis that it is original, "non-obvious," and valuable.

perception—The process of scanning, gathering, assessing, and interpreting information in the environment.

personal brand—A collection of a person's (or an organization's) various attributes, expertise traits, personality characteristics, and insights that take place both on- and offline.

place ensemble—Elements that enhance or diminish the attractiveness of a venue and its surroundings.

point-of-purchase (POP) promotion—Some form of sales promotion that is placed next to the area of payment to either promote a brand or to elicit an impulse buy.

predictive analytics—A focus on previous data to try to make predictions about the future.

premium giveaway—An item that a team distributes to fans who attend a game. Also known as swag, the item is designed to be collectible and to drive purchase for a particular game.

print media—Any written form of mass communication, such as magazines and newspapers.

product extension—A product component that enhances the value (and often the price) of an event experience.

product-place matrix—A tool that helps conceptualize both the array of products offered by a sport organization and the various distribution channels used or available.

product positioning—An organization's attempt to showcase or influence how it wants to be perceived by the public in its marketing activities.

product sampling—The act of allowing prospective consumers to try the product or service either at a discount or for free in order to hopefully entice them to purchase the product or service outright in the future.

product usage segmentation—The process of dividing the consumer market into smaller categories based on the amount or frequency of product consumption.

promotion—An activity that supports or provides active encouragement for the furtherance of a cause, venture, or aim. The publicization of a product, an organization, or a venture in order to increase sales or public awareness.

psychographic segmentation—See *state-of-mind segmentation*.

public relations—Managing, promoting, enhancing, and protecting a personal, brand, corporate, organizational, or institutional image and reputation by communicating with a variety of external constituents and entities.

publicity—Newsworthy information from an outside source promoted and shared by news organizations.

qualitative data—Data that are reflected using nonnumerical metrics, such as text, images, objects, and sounds.

quantitative data—Data that are reflected using numbers.

reactive public relations—The act of defensively responding to media inquiries or crises rather than initiating programs.

rebranding—Changing the name, logo, colors, etc. of an organization in an effort to shift consumer attitudes and opinions about their brand and products, or highlight a new direction for their brand positioning.

relationship marketing—The creation of customer loyalty. Sport organizations use combinations of products, prices, distribution, promotions, and service to achieve this goal.

reputation management—The systematic act of putting out messaging that is designed to influence the ways people in key publics think about an organization.

right of publicity—People's right to control the use of their name, image, or likeness (NIL) to prevent others from using a person's NIL for commercial benefit without that person's permission.

sales inventory—All of the available products and services available to the sales staff to market, promote, package, and sell through their various sales methodologies.

sales promotions—Organized efforts to market a product or service to prospective customers. Usually short-term, sales promotions are an attempt to get the prospective customer to sample the product or service, often at a discounted rate.

second screen experience—The gaining of knowledge by utilizing more than one device while consuming a sports event.

secondary meaning—A special denotation that a trademark or trade name for a company has acquired regardless if the trademark or trade name was originally merely descriptive and therefore not safeguarded.

segmentation—The division of consumers into groups based on characteristics.

service mark—A name, phrase, or other apparatus that identifies and distinguishes a specific provider's services.

situational marketing—A strategy that targets consumers' individual wants and needs, often by communicating with them in real time, versus advertising to the masses.

skip logic—A tool in many online surveys that allows respondents to skip ahead to the most relevant questions and avoid being presented with questions that don't pertain to them.

social media—A collective hub of global digital platforms that allow users to engage, discuss, create, and foster relationships in real time.

social networking—Making connections in a designated platform with other users.

socialization—The process by which people assimilate and develop the skills, knowledge, attitudes, and other "equipment" necessary to perform various social roles.

sponsorship—An investment, in cash or in-kind, in an activity, in return for access to the exploitable commercial potential associated with that activity.

sport marketing—All activities designed to meet the needs and wants of sport consumers through exchange processes.

sport product—A complex package of the tangible and intangible attributes of a good or service, which combine to meet the needs and wants of sport consumers.

state-of-being segmentation—The process of dividing the consumer market into smaller categories based on common demographic factors, such as age, gender, or ethnicity.

state-of-mind segmentation—The process of dividing the consumer market by personality traits; by lifestyle characteristics, such as attitudes, interests, and opinions; and by preferences and perceptions.

strategy—Any action taken to outperform competitors.

survey fatigue—A fatigue felt by survey respondents when either being asked too many questions or by having to ask questions that are difficult or confusing to answer, resulting in less accurate responses or survey dropout.

syndicated data—Data that have already been collected, organized, and repackaged for consumption.

tagline—A brief phrase used by a company to create some associations in consumers' minds with the brand.

target marketing—The process of dividing a consumer market into segments and then focusing marketing efforts on a small number of key segments consisting of the customers whose needs and wants closely match the organization's product or service.

ticket bots—Automated software programs designed to purchase large groups of tickets.

trademark—A producer or seller's word, phrase, logo, or other sensory symbol that differentiates its products or services from those of others.

trademark infringement—The unlicensed usage of a trademark in ways that are likely to cause confusion or deception about the original source of the trademark.

values—Standards that describe how the company will behave and act while operating.

vision—A statement explaining what the company wants to do.

wearable tech—Technology that collects participant data, analyzes it, and provides information related to performance.

yield management—The process of understanding the supply-and-demand curve specific to a company's inventory, and knowing how to find the right price for its product in order to sell it to the right customer at the right time in order to maximize revenues, preferably without sacrificing units sold.

References

Chapter 1

1. Bassam T. Women's World Cup 2019: the full review. *SportsPro Media* blog. Posted online July 15, 2019. Accessed June 1, 2020. www.sportspromedia.com/analysis/womens-world-cup-2019-rapinoe-uswnt-viewing-figures-marketing

2. Dillinger J. Biggest stadiums in the world by capacity. World Atlas. October 21, 2019. Accessed June 1, 2020. www.worldatlas.com/articles/50-largest-stadiums-in-the-world.html

3. Carruthers J. Timeline of sports marketing. *FastSigns* blog. Posted online September 25, 2014. Accessed June 1, 2020. www.fastsigns.com/blog/detail/2014/09/25/sport-events-advertising-through-the-years

4. Eby D. The history of athlete endorsements: Part one. *Opendorse* blog. Posted online November 18, 2013. Accessed June 1, 2020. https://opendorse.com/blog/athlete-endorsement-history

5. Broughton D. Top naming-rights deals. *Street & Smith's Sports Business Journal.* Accessed June 1, 2020. www.sportsbusinessdaily.com/Journal/Issues/2018/04/30/Marketing-and-Sponsorship/Naming-rights-deals.aspx

6. League History. AAGPBL. Accessed June 1, 2020. www.aagpbl.org/history/league-history

7. Fact Sheet. ESPN Press Room. Accessed June 1, 2020. https://espnpressroom.com/us/espn-inc-fact-sheet

8. Kesler L. Man created ads in sport's own image. *Advertising Age.* August 27, 1979: 5-10.

9. Meyer J. History of Nike: Timeline and facts. *TheStreet.* August 14, 2019. Accessed June 1, 2020. www.thestreet.com/lifestyle/history-of-nike-15057083

10. At the gate and beyond. Price Waterhouse Cooper. 2019. October, 2019. Accessed June 1, 2020. www.pwc.com/us/en/industries/tmt/assets/pwc-sports-outlook-2019.pdf

11. CBC. NBA TV deal: How the new $24B contract stacks up against other leagues. October 7, 2014. Updated October 7, 2014. Accessed June 1, 2020. www.cbc.ca/sports/basketball/nba/nba-tv-deal-how-the-new-24b-contract-stacks-up-against-other-leagues-1.2790143

12. Thomas I. MLB ticketing revenue expected to increase in 2019, amid another attendance drop. Front Office Sports. July 11, 2019. Accessed June 1, 2020. https://frntofficesport.com/mlb-attendance-2019

13. Levitt T. Marketing myopia. *Harvard Business Review.* 1960;August-July:45-56.

14. Smith M. Reimagining the experience. *Street & Smith's Sports Business Journal.* August 20, 2018. Accessed June 1, 2020. www.sportsbusinessdaily.com/Journal/Issues/2018/08/20/In-Depth/Experience.aspx

15. Keating P. Fans vote Lightning best in sports in Ultimate Standings. *ESPN.* October 21, 2016. Accessed June 1, 2020. www.espn.com/nhl/story/_/id/17816834/tampa-bay-lightning-no-1-franchise-sports-ultimate-standings

16. Broughton D, McClung B. 2018 MLB game-day giveaways. *Street & Smith's Sports Business Journal.* December 10, 2018. Accessed June 1, 2020. www.sportsbusinessdaily.com/Journal/Issues/2018/12/10/Research-and-Ratings/MLB-giveaways.aspx

17. Carson D. The Atlanta Hawks' Tinder night was a strange and beautiful success. Bleacher Report. January 8, 2015. Accessed June 1, 2020. https://bleacherreport.com/articles/2323194-the-atlanta-hawks-tinder-night-was-a-strange-and-beautiful-success

18. Armstrong A. Hawks' "Swipe Right Night" couple to tie knot at Philips Arena. NBA. February 14, 2018. Accessed June 1, 2020.

www.nba.com/hawks/news/hawks-swipe-right-night-couple-tie-knot-philips-arena

19. Rishe P. Atlanta Falcons' 'Fans-First Pricing' model yields numerous unforeseen benefits. *Forbes*. June 26, 2018. Accessed June 1, 2020. www.forbes.com/sites/prishe/2018/06/26/the-atlanta-falcons-fan-first-pricing-model-yields-numerous-additional-unforeseen-benefits/ - 137d2a363998

20. Spanberg E. Data tells the story. *Street & Smith's Sports Business Journal*. May 13, 2019. Accessed June 1, 2020. www.sportsbusinessdaily.com/Journal/Issues/2019/05/13/In-Depth/Main.aspx

21. Reed K. Why does the U.S. continue to permit unregulated sports leagues? *Huffpost*. July 11, 2017. Accessed June 1, 2020. www.huffpost.com/entry/why-does-the-us-continue-to-permit-unregulated-sports_b_5965465fe4b0911162fc2f9c

22. Miller S. USTA uses Fan Week to build excitement around the sport. *Street & Smith's Sports Business Journal*. August 26, 2019. Accessed June 1, 2020. www.sportsbusinessdaily.com/Journal/Issues/2019/08/26/In-Depth/Fan-Week.aspx

23. Loy J. The nature of sport. *Quest*. 1968;10:1-15.

24. Foer F. *How Soccer Explains the World: An Unlikely Theory of Globalization*. HarperCollins; 2004.

25. McGee N. How much money does the NCAA make from March Madness? *MSN Money*. February 6, 2020. Accessed June 1, 2020. www.msn.com/en-us/money/markets/how-much-money-does-the-ncaa-make-from-march-madness/ar-BBZIYDV

26. Weber S. The top 100 athletes on social media: 2019-1. *Opendorse* blog. Posted online January 28, 2020. Updated July 14, 2020. Accessed June 1, 2020. https://opendorse.com/blog/the-top-100-athletes-on-social-media-2019

27. Wigmore T. How are Cristiano Ronaldo and Lionel Messi staying out of jail? Bleacher Report. August 3, 2017. Accessed June 1, 2020. https://bleacherreport.com/articles/2725161-how-are-cristiano-ronaldo-and-lionel-messi-staying-out-of-jail

28. Saracevic A. LeBron James' comments on China an embarrassment to himself and NBA. *San Francisco Chronicle*. October 15, 2019. Updated October 15, 2019. Accessed June 1, 2020. www.sfchronicle.com/warriors/article/LeBron-James-comments-on-China-an-14535304.php

29. Veeck B., Linn E. *The Hustler's Handbook*. New York: Fireside Books; 1989.

30. Edgett S., Parkinson S. Marketing for Service Industries. *Service Industries Journal*. 13(3) (July 1993): 19–39.

Chapter 2

1. Neal Gulkis, oral communication, June 2020.

2. Rothaermel FT. *Strategic Management, 4e*. McGraw-Hill Education; 2018.

3. Smith M. SEC schools retool stadiums based on results of broad survey. *Street & Smith's Sports Business Journal*. September 29, 2014. Accessed May 20, 2020. www.sportsbusinessdaily.com/Journal/Issues/2014/09/29/Colleges/SEC-fans.aspx

4. Southeastern Conference Sports. 2019-2020 Southeastern Conference constitution & bylaws. Published May 1990. Accessed May 20, 2020. http://a.espncdn.com/sec/media/2019/Bylaws.pdf

5. Ole Miss athletics department mission statement. Ole Miss Sports. July 30, 2007. Accessed May 18, 2020. https://olemisssports.com/news/2007/7/30/Ole_Miss_Athletics_Department_Mission_Statement.aspx

6. Ole Miss mission statement. Ole Miss Sports. Accessed May 18, 2020. https://olemisssports.com/sports/2018/7/20/school-bio-ole-mission-statement-html.aspx

7. Ole Miss athletics operating budget for fiscal year 2019-2020. Ole Miss Sports. Accessed May 18, 2020. https://olemisssports.com/documents/2019/10/14/FY_2020.pdf

8. College athletics financial information database. Knight Commission. Accessed May 18, 2020. http://cafidatabase.knightcommission.org/fbs/sec

9. Kotler P. *Marketing Management, Ninth Edition*. Prentice Hall; 1997.

10. Sutton WA. Developing an initial marketing plan for intercollegiate athletic programs. *Journal of Sport Management*. 1987;1:146-158.

11. Reese S. The very model of a modern marketing plan. *Marketing Tools*. 1996;January-February:56-65.

12. Carter DM. *Keeping Score: An Inside Look at Sports Marketing*. Oasis Press; 1996.

13. Thompson A, Strickland AJ. *Strategic*

Management: Concepts and Cases, Thirteenth Edition. McGraw-Hill; 2003.

14. Porter ME. The five competitive forces that shape strategy," *Harvard Business Review.* 2008;January:25-40.

15. Hayina. League of Legends generated $1.5 billion revenue in 2019. Dotesports. January 3, 2020. Accessed May 18, 2020. https://dotesports.com

16. Diversity, inclusion, & culture. Riot Games. Accessed May 12, 2020. www.riotgames.com/en/diversity-inclusion-and-culture

17. David Higdon. Guest speaker at the University of Miami Sport Industry Conference; January, 2020.

18. Shani D. A framework for implementing relationship marketing in the sport industry. *SMQ.* 1997;6:9-15.

19. Consumer Brand Analytics. Retrieved on June 15, 2020. https://www.consumerbrandanalytics.com/About.aspx

20. Ries A, Trout J. *Positioning: The Battle for Your Mind.* Warner Books; 1982.

21. Nash L. Ethics without the sermon. *Harvard Business Review.* 1981;November:79-90.

22. Laczniak GB, Murphy P. Sports marketing ethics in today's marketplace. *SMQ. 1999;8:* 43-53.

23. Spindel C. *Dancing at Halftime: Sport and the Controversy Over American Indian Mascots* New York University Press; 2000.

24. Staurowsky E. Privilege at play: on the legal and social fictions that sustain American Indian sport imagery. *Journal of Sport and Social Issues.* 2004;28:11-29.

25. Benjamin A. Sense and sensitivity. *Boston Globe.* June 21, 2005:F-1,F-7.

26. Smith S. NCAA: mascot ruling. *Boston Globe.* August 6, 2005:D-1,D-2.

27. Brown G. Policy applies core principles to mascot issue. *NCAA News.* August 15, 2005:1,19.

28. Henderson B. The product portfolio. Boston Consulting Group. January 1, 1970. Accessed May 15, 2020. www.bcg.com/publications/1970/strategy-the-product-portfolio.aspx

29. Dawar N, Bagga CK. A better way to map brand strategy," *Harvard Business Review.* June 2015. Accessed May 15, 2020. https://hbr.org/2015/06/a-better-way-to-map-brand-strategy

30. Shaw R, Stone M. *Database Marketing.* John Wiley & Sons; 1988.

31. Ansoff I. Strategies for diversification. *Harvard Business Review.* 1957;35(5):113-124.

32. Martilla JA, James JC. Importance-performance analysis, *Journal of Marketing.* 1957;41(1):77-79.

33. Raphel M, Raphel N. *Up the Loyalty Ladder.* Harperbusiness; 1995.

34. Porter ME. The five competitive forces that shape strategy. *Harvard Business Review.* 2008; January:25-40.

35. Rink DR, Swan JE. Product life cycle research: a literature review. *Journal of Business Research*, 1979;7(3);219-242.

36. Moutinho L. Segmentation, targeting, positioning and strategic marketing. In: Moutinho L., ed. *Strategic Management in Tourism.* CABI Publishing; 2000:121-166.

37. Phadermrod B, Crowder RM, Willis GB. Importance-performance analysis based SWOT analysis. *Elsevier*, 2019;44:194-203.

38. Dickons G. How to identify your unique selling points. *Journal of Aesthetic Nursing.* Published online May 7, 2019. doi/abs/10.12968/joan.2019.8.4.201

39. Fontanella C. How to calculate customer lifetime value. *Hubspot* blog. Posted online November 11, 2019. Updated March 13, 2020. Accessed March 13, 2020. https://blog.hubspot.com/service/how-to-calculate-customer-lifetime-value

40. Sutton W. Escalating your fan base. *Athletic Management.* February-March 1997, 4-5.

41. Boyd, K. Homestead-Miami speedway has $301M annual impact on county. *Miami's Community Newspaper.* November 5, 2015.

42. NCAA Finances. Accessed September 10, 2020. sports.usatoday.com/ncaa/finances

43. 2019-2020 Southeastern Conference Constitution and ByLaws. Accessed September 1, 2020. http://a.espncdn.com/sec/media/2019/Bylaws.pdf

44. Ole Miss Athletics. Ole Miss Athletics Department Mission Statement. Accessed September 1, 2020. olemisssports.com/news/2007/7/30/Ole_Miss_Athletics_Mission_Statement

Chapter 3

1. Mizrahi I. The minority-majority shift. Two decades that will change America. For sports marketing, it's game

on! *Forbes*. January 16, 2020. Accessed June 3, 2020. www.forbes.com/sites/isaacmizrahi/2020/01/16/the-minority-majority-shift-two-decades-that-will-change-america-for-sports-marketing-its-game-on/#54247ca015b8

2. Consumer behaviour models. *BBA | Mantra*. Accessed June 3, 2020. https://bbamantra.com/consumer-behaviour-models/

3. Impey S. Study: more fans streaming sport than paying for TV packages. *SportsPro Media* blog. Posted online November 12, 2019. Accessed June 3, 2020. www.sportspromedia.com/news/dazn-facebook-youtube-sports-fans-tv-streaming-study

4. Sutton B. On my elevator: a new way to think about fan consumption. *Street & Smith's Sports Business Journal*. April 13, 2015. Accessed June 3, 2020. www.sportsbusinessdaily.com/Journal/Issues/2015/04/13/Opinion/Sutton-Impact.aspx

5. The more fans "belong" to their favorite teams, the more they engage. *SSRS*. Accessed June 3, 2020. https://ssrs.com/the-more-fans-belong-to-their-team-the-more-they-engage/

6. Holmes R. We now see 5,000 ads a day . . . and it's getting worse. *LinkedIn* blog. Posted online February 19, 2019. Accessed June 3, 2020. www.linkedin.com/pulse/have-we-reached-peak-ad-social-media-ryan-holmes

7. Minor League Baseball posts attendance increase of over one million fans in 2019. *Minor League Baseball*. September 11, 2019. Accessed June 3, 2020. www.milb.com/news/minor-league-baseball-posts-attendance-increase-over-one-million-fans--310659524

8. Fan cost index. *Team Marketing Report*. Accessed June 3, 2020. https://teammarketing.com/fancostindex/

9. Schilling P. Why Minor League Baseball is so appealing to fans. Samford University. June 22, 2018. Accessed June 3, 2020. www.samford.edu/sports-analytics/fans/2018/Why-Minor-League-Baseball-is-so-Appealing-to-Fans

10. Hill B. Top promotions battle for MiLBY. Minor League Baseball. September 23, 2011. Accessed June 3, 2020. www.milb.com/milb/news/top-promotions-battle-for-milby/c-25003636

11. What is economics? - Definition, history, timeline, & importance. *Study.com*. Accessed June 3, 2020. Study.com. https://study.com/academy/lesson/what-is-economics-definition-history-timeline-importance.html

12. Achuthan L. Business cycle. *Investopedia*. Updated June 1, 2020. Accessed June 3, 2020. www.investopedia.com/terms/b/businesscycle.asp

13. Sandomir R, Belson K. In economic downturn, corporate ties put bind on sports. *New York Times*. March 21, 2009. Accessed June 3, 2020. www.nytimes.com/2009/03/22/sports/22economy.html

14. Sudden vanishing of sports due to coronavirus will cost at least $12 billion, analysis says. *ESPN*. May 1, 2020. Accessed June 5, 2020. www.espn.com/espn/otl/story/_/id/29110487/sudden-vanishing-sports-due-coronavirus-cost-least-12-billion-analysis-says

15. Gough C. North American sports market size from 2009 to 2023 (in billion U.S. dollars). Statista. December 10, 2019. Accessed June 3, 2020. www.statista.com/statistics/214960/revenue-of-the-north-american-sports-market/

16. North American industry classification system. United States Census Bureau. Accessed June 3, 2020. www.census.gov/cgi-bin/sssd/naics/naicsrch?chart_code=71&search=2017 NAICS Search

17. Newton D. Charlotte gets MLS' 30th franchise for record $325 million. *ESPN*. December 17, 2019. Accessed June 3, 2020. www.espn.com/soccer/major-league-soccer/story/4015203/charlotte-gets-mls-30th-franchise-for-record-$325-million

18. Stynes DJ. Economic impacts of tourism. Accessed June 3, 2020. https://msu.edu/course/prr/840/econimpact/pdf/ecimpvol1.pdf

19. Schenke J. The Super Bowl cost Atlanta $46M. Was it worth it? *BISNOW*. February 7, 2019. Accessed June 3, 2020. www.bisnow.com/atlanta/news/economic-development/not-all-the-benefits-of-hosting-a-super-bowl-are-quantifiable-experts-say-97409

20. Most innovative companies: Lululemon. *Fast Company*. Accessed June 3, 2020. www.fastcompany.com/company/lululemon

21. 3 new trends in sporting good technology and equipment. *Winmark* blog. Posted online April 16, 2018. Accessed June 3, 2020. www.winmarkfranchises.com/blog/2018/april/3-new-trends-in-sporting-good-technology-and-equ/

22. Wyshynski G. NHL to feature puck, player tracking next season. *ESPN*. January 25, 2019. Accessed June 3, 2020. www.espn.com/nhl/story/_/id/25850905/nhl-feature-puck-player-tracking-next-season

23. Lee BY. How this new football helmet is designed to protect the brain. *Forbes*. September 3, 2018. Accessed June 3, 2020. www.forbes.com/sites/brucelee/2018/09/03/how-this-new-football-helmet-is-designed-to-protect-the-brain/#785201d64a1e

24. Bode K. ESPN has lost 14 million viewers in 7 years thanks to cord cutting. *Techdirt*. November 29, 2018. Accessed June 3, 2020. www.techdirt.com/articles/20181126/09313541105/espn-has-lost-14-million-viewers-7-years-thanks-to-cord-cutting.shtml

25. Badenhausen K. NFL extends Amazon Thursday Night Football streaming deal for three more years. *Forbes*. April 29, 2020. Accessed June 5, 2020. www.forbes.com/sites/kurtbadenhausen/2020/04/29/nfl-extends-amazon-thursday-night-football-streaming-deal-for-three-years/#2c4492448211

26. Kaufman K. Will Facebook become the preferred way for fans to watch sports? *Forbes*. June 15, 2018. Accessed June 3, 2020. www.forbes.com/sites/karlkaufman/2018/06/15/will-facebook-become-the-preferred-way-for-fans-to-watch-sports/#3ac57662746f

27. Ganguly Zacks A. Facebook-ESPN partnership intensifies sports streaming battle. *Yahoo! Finance*. September 24, 2019. Accessed June 3, 2020. https://finance.yahoo.com/news/facebook-espn-partnership-intensifies-sports-150003911.html

28. Williams R. Ticketmaster brings digital ticketing to all 32 NFL teams. *Mobile Marketer*. August 6, 2018. Accessed June 3, 2020. www.mobilemarketer.com/news/ticketmaster-brings-digital-ticketing-to-all-32-nfl-teams/529415

29. Fisher E. Technologies that have revolutionized the sport industry. *Street & Smith's Sports Business Journal*. April 30, 2018. Accessed June 3, 2020. www.sportsbusinessdaily.com/Journal/Issues/2018/04/30/Technology/Tech-milestones.aspx

30. McCleary M. Politics and sports: a long and complicated relationship. *Northeastern University Political Review*. February 26, 2019. Accessed June 3, 2020. www.nupoliticalreview.com/2019/02/26/politics-and-sports-a-long-and-complicated-relationship/

31. Daniels T. Premier League to replace player names on kits with 'Black Lives Matter'. Bleacher Report. June 12, 2020. Accessed June 29, 2020. https://bleacherreport.com/articles/2895940-premier-league-to-replace-player-names-on-kits-with-black-lives-matter

32. Depta L. 15 ways sports and politics have collided. Bleacher Report. November 3, 2015. Accessed June 3, 2020. https://bleacherreport.com/articles/2585640-15-ways-sports-and-politics-have-collided#slide3

33. Kredell M. One year after PASPA repeal, sports betting legislation appears in more than 75% of US. Legal Sports Report. May 14, 2019. Accessed June 3, 2020. www.legalsportsreport.com/32440/sports-betting-legislation-after-paspa/

34. Parry W. 1 year, $3.2 billion later, New Jersey sports betting soars. *AP News*. July 12, 2019. Accessed June 3, 2020. https://apnews.com/bd16882c051941778d48d9381aaf6327

35. Pope S.W. *Patriotic Games: Sporting Traditions in the American Imagination, 1876–1926*. New York: Oxford University Press; 1997.

36. Dyreson M. *Inventing the Sporting Republic: American Sport, Political Culture, and the Olympic Experience, 1877–1919*. University of Illinois Press; 1997.

37. Watkins MD. What is organizational culture? And why should we care? *Harvard Business Review*. May 15, 2013. Accessed June 3, 2020. https://hbr.org/2013/05/what-is-organizational-culture

38. Schawbel D. 10 New findings about the millennial consumer. *Forbes*. January 20, 2015. Accessed June 3, 2020. www.forbes.com/sites/danschawbel/2015/01/20/10-new-findings-about-the-millennial-consumer/#2afc1ef06c8f

39. The changing customer: how to cater to Gen-Z. *Digital Marketing Institute* blog. Accessed June 3, 2020. https://digitalmarketinginstitute.com/en-us/blog/the-changing-customer-how-to-cater-to-gen-z

40. Elflein J. Participation in leisure-time aerobic and muscle strengthening activities in the U.S. from 1999 to 2017, by gender. Statista. November 7, 2019. Accessed June 3, 2020. www.statista.com/statistics/186926/participation-in-sports-activities-in-the-us-by-gender-since-1999/

41. Gough C. Share of sports fans in the United States as of August 2020, by gender. Statista. Accessed August 31, 2020. www.statista.com/statistics/1018814/sports-fans-usa-gender/

42. Gough C. Share of sports fans in the United States as of August 2020, by ethnicity. Statista. Accessed August 31, 2020. https://www.statista.com/statistics/1018817/sports-fans-usa-ethnicity/

43. WNBA becomes first US league to market to LGBT community. *Guardian*. May 21, 2014. Accessed June 3, 2020. www.theguardian.com/sport/2014/may/21/wnba-market-lgbt-community-campaign

44. Green J. Pro sports leagues fly the rainbow flag. *Bloomberg Businessweek*. September 27, 2016. Accessed June 3, 2020. www.bloomberg.com/news/articles/2016-09-27/pro-sports-leagues-fly-the-rainbow-flag

45. Pro sports teams show increased support for LGBTQ with Pride Nights. *Street & Smith's Sports Business Journal*. September 28, 2016. Accessed June 3, 2020. www.sportsbusinessdaily.com/Daily/Issues/2016/09/28/Sports-in-Society/LGBT.aspx

46. Patel M. Situational marketing: the rise of the hyper-personal experience. *MarketingTech*. October 14, 2015. Accessed June 3, 2020. www.marketingtechnews.net/news/2015/oct/14/situational-marketing-rise-hyper-personal-experience/

47. US digital ad spending will surpass traditional in 2019. eMarketer. February 19, 2019. Accessed June 3, 2020. www.emarketer.com/content/us-digital-ad-spending-will-surpass-traditional-in-2019

48. 7 great (and not so great) sports marketing campaigns. *Bannerflow* blog. Accessed June 3, 2020. https://blog.bannerflow.com/7-great-sports-marketing-campaigns/

49. Wann D, Royalty J, Rochelle A. Using motivation and team identification to predict sport fans' emotional responses to team performance. *Journal of Sport Behavior.*2002;25(2);207-216.

50. Ware A, Kowalski GS. Sex identification and the love of sports: BIRGing and CORFing among sports fans. *Journal of Sport Behavior.* 2012;35(2):223-237.

51. Values, Attitudes, and Lifestyles. Strategic Business Insights. Accessed June 3, 2020. www.strategicbusinessinsights.com/vals

52. Danziger P. How Foot Locker, Nike, North Face, and Starbucks created a culture of customer loyalty. *Forbes.* October 29, 2018. Accessed June 3, 2020. www.forbes.com/sites/pamdanziger/2018/10/29/how-foot-locker-nike-the-north-face-and-starbucks-created-a-customer-loyalty-culture/#744776666269

53. Lunny O. Battle for $15.19 billion secondary ticket market heats up with first Europe-wide anti touting law. *Forbes.* June 24, 2019. Accessed June 3, 2020. www.forbes.com/sites/oisinlunny/2019/06/24/the-battle-for-15-19b-secondary-ticket-market-heats-up-with-first-europe-wide-anti-touting-law/#78bdffb62e02

54. Attendance for Minor League Baseball up 2.6% in 2019. September 10, 2019. Accessed August 31, 2020. https://www.alabamanews.net/2019/09/10/attendance-for-minor-league-baseball-up-2-6-in-2019/#:~:text=Nine%20teams%20set%20single%2Dgame,%2C%20Augusta%2C%20Fayetteville%2C%20Hartford%2C

Chapter 4

1. ACS Demographic and housing estimates. U.S. Census. Accessed April 1, 2020. https://data.census.gov/cedsci/.

2. *Scarborough methodology.* Scarborough. Accessed March 19, 2020. http://en-us.nielsen.com/sitelets/cls/documents/scarborough/Scarborough-Methodology-2012.pdf

3. At the gate and beyond. Price Waterhouse Cooper. 2019. October, 2019. Accessed June 1, 2020. www.pwc.com/us/en/industries/tmt/assets/pwc-sports-outlook-2019.pdf

4. Nielsen announces launch of national television out-of-home measurement service. Nielsen. October 24, 2016. www.nielsen.com/us/en/press-releases/2016/nielsen-announces-launch-of-national-television-out-of-home-measurement

5. *Digital/mobile measurement*. Comscore. www.comscore.com/Products/Digital/Mobile-Measurement

6. Home page. Critical Mention. Accessed April 4, 2020. www.criticalmention.com

7. Internet/broadband fact sheet. Pew Research Center. June 12, 2019. Accessed June, 2020. www.pewresearch.org/internet/fact-sheet/internet-broadband

8. Home page. Happy or Not. Accessed March 14, 2020. www.happy-or-not.com

9. Blumberg SJ, PhD, Luke J. *Wireless substitution*: early release of estimates from the national health interview survey, July-December 2018. Centers for Disease Control. June 2019. Accessed May 2020. www.cdc.gov/nchs/data/nhis/earlyrelease/wireless201906.pdf

10. Sampling. Pew Research Center. Accessed March 30, 2020. www.pewresearch.org/methods/u-s-survey-research/sampling/#random-digit-dialing

11. *Computer assisted telephone interviewing (CATI)*. United Nations Economic and Social Commission. October 2019. Accessed March 30, 2020. www.unescap.org/stat/pop-it/pop-guide/capture_ch04.pdf

12. Sacramento Kings launch new app to serve as "remote control" for world's most advanced arena. National Basketball Association. September 19, 2016. Accessed April 7, 2020. www.nba.com/kings/news/kings-launch-new-app

13. Belk R. *Handbook of Qualitative Research Methods in Marketing*. Elgar; 2006.

14. Azzara C. Qualitatively speaking: the focus group vs. in-depth interview debate. *Quirk's*. June 2010:16.

15. *How to use laddering in qualitative market research*. FocusGroupsTips. Accessed March 30, 2020. www.focusgrouptips.com/laddering.html

16. *When and how to use ethnographic research*. Spotless Interactive. Accessed March 30, 2020. www.spotlessinteractive.com/articles/usability-research/ethnography-when-and-how-to-use.php

17. Brogdon T. Qualitative techniques that go beyond the focus group room. *Quirk's*. February 2011:50.

18. Henning J. *MROC = market-research online community*. *Vovici* blog. Posted online October 24, 2008. Accessed April 1, 2020. http://blog.vovici.com/blog/bid/17991/MROC-Market-Research-Online-Community

19. Sports statistician salary. ZipRecruiter. June 11, 2020. Accessed June, 20, 2020. www.ziprecruiter.com/Salaries/Sports-Statistician-Salary

20. Fisher E. StubHub, Major League Baseball close to another renewal of secondary ticketing partnership. *Street & Smith's Sports-Business Journal*. October, 30, 2017. Accessed April 16, 2020. www.sportsbusinessdaily.com/Journal/Issues/2017/10/30/Leagues-and-Governing-Bodies/MLB-StubHub.aspx

21. Dallas Cowboys. Forbes. September 2019. Accessed June 2020. https://www.forbes.com/teams/dallas-cowboys/#2808550b1426

Chapter 5

1. On the notion of global marketing, see: Levitt T. *The Marketing Imagination*. Free Press; 1984.

2. For a general discussion, see: Kotler P, Keller K. *Marketing Management*. 12th ed. Prentice Hall; 2005.

3. Wilson R. Why the Braves are leaving Atlanta, in one map. *Washington Post* blog. Posted online November 11, 2013. Accessed March 14, 2020. www.washingtonpost.com/blogs/govbeat/wp/2013/11/11/why-the-braves-are-leaving-atlanta-in-one-map/

4. Seahawks rule! Alaska NFL fans choose Seattle as their favorite team, again. *Anchorage Daily News*. November 22, 2015.

5. Kerber R. Sox, Yanks Fight for Conn. Viewers. *Boston Globe*. August 6, 2003:A-1,B-8.

6. Lombardo J, Boughton D. Going gray: sports TV viewers skew older. June 5, 2017. Accessed March 13, 2020. *Street & Smith's Sports Business Daily*. www.sportsbusinessdaily.com/Journal/Issues/2017/06/05/Research-and-Ratings/Viewership-trends

7. J. Rude, "Making the Mature Decision," *Athletic Business*, January 1998, 31–37.

8. Thompson D. Which sports have the whitest/richest/oldest fans? *Atlantic*. February 10, 2014. Accessed March 14, 2020. www.theatlantic.com/business/archive/2014/02/which-sports-have-the-whitest-richest-oldest-fans/283626

9. Jones J. As industry grows, percentage of U.S. sports fans steady. *Gallup*. June 17,

2015. Accessed April 5, 2020. https://news.gallup.com/poll/183689/industry-grows-percentage-sports-fans-steady.aspx

10. Fans Of PGA, LPGA Tours continue to skew older, have high incomes. *Street & Smith's Sport Business Daily.* July 28, 2011. Accessed March 14, 2020. www.sportsbusinessdaily.com/Daily/Issues/2011/07/28/Research-and-Ratings/Golf-demos.aspx

11. Mumcu C, Lough NL. Are fans proud of the WNBA's pride campaign? *Sport Marketing Quarterly.* 2017;26(1):42-54.

12. For information on discovery segmentation, see R. Piirto, "Cable TV," *American Demographics,* June 1995, 40–47.

13. Wann DL, James JD. *Sports Fans: The Psychology and Social Impact of Fandom.* 2nd ed. Routledge; 2019.

14. Seabrook J. Tackling the competition. *New Yorker.* 1997;18:42-51.

15. Richelieu A, Pons F. Reconciling managers' strategic vision with fans' expectations. *International Journal of Sports Marketing and Sponsorship.* 2005;6(3);150-163.

16. Stachura M. The NGF's annual golf participation report uncovers favorable trends for the game's future. *Golfworld.* April 22, 2017. Accessed April 1, 2020. https://www.golfdigest.com/story/the-ngf-annual-golf-participation-report-uncovers-favorable-trends-for-the-games-future

17. Shonk D. Baltimore Orioles. In: Swayne L, Dodds M. *Encyclopedia of Sports Management and Marketing.* Sage Publishing: 2011:113-115.

18. Logsdon Z. *Winning is Not a Strategy: A Game-Changing Approach to Driving Attendance.* Black Lake Publishing; 2018.

19. Frey W. The US will become 'minority white' in 2045, Census projects. Brookings. March 14, 2018. Accessed April 4, 2020. https://www.brookings.edu/blog/the-avenue/2018/03/14/the-us-will-become-minority-white-in-2045-census-projects/

Chapter 6

1. O'Toole M. The sit-down: Matt O'Toole, Reebok. *Street & Smith's Sports Business Journal.* September 21, 2015. Accessed July 30, 2019. www.sportsbusinessdaily.com/Journal/Issues/2015/09/21/People-and-Pop-Culture/Sit-Down.aspx

2. Reidy C. Adidas: Reebok will sharpen its focus as a fitness brand. Boston.com. September 21, 2012. Accessed July 30, 2019. www.boston.com/uncategorized/noprimarytagmatch/2012/09/21/adidas-reebok-will-sharpen-its-focus-as-a-fitness-brand

3. Schlossberg M. CrossFit is leading to a huge revival for a once-disappearing brand. *Business Insider.* July 27, 2016. Accessed July 30, 2019. www.businessinsider.com/crossfit-is-helping-to-save-reebok-2016-7

4. Markazi A. Golden openings: behind the scenes with the Vegas' pregame show. ESPN.com. May 28, 2018. Accessed July 30, 2019. www.espn.com/nhl/story/_/id/23632654/2018-stanley-cup-final-scenes-vegas-golden-knights-pregame-show-wizard-nhl

5. Sunnucks M. Facilities: listening to what women want. *Street & Smith's Sports Business Journal.* December 10, 2018. Accessed August 10, 2019. www.sportsbusinessdaily.com/Journal/Issues/2018/12/10/In-Depth/Female-fans.aspx?hl=selfies&sc=0

6. White A. Bucs Beach showcases the importance of Instagram. *Front Office Sports.* September 27, 2018. Accessed August 10, 2019. https://frntofficesport.com/bucs-beach-importance-instagram/

7. Caldwell D. What will fans do with those 26 extra seconds the NFL has given them? *Forbes.* October 25, 2017. Accessed August 10, 2019. www.forbes.com/sites/davecaldwell/2017/10/25/the-nfl-has-trimmed-the-length-of-its-games-well-a-little-bit/#3337967b48cc

8. Hadley G. For one half, an NBA game had no music, giveaways or gimmicks. The players hated it. *The Charlotte Observer.* March 5, 2017. Updated March 6, 2017. Accessed July 30, 2019. www.charlotteobserver.com/news/nation-world/national/article136644218.html

9. Madkour A. Forum: Golden Knights' approach to storytelling a plot to follow. *Street & Smith's Sports Business Journal.* February 18, 2019. Accessed July 30, 2019. www.sportsbusinessdaily.com/Journal/Issues/2019/02/18/Opinion/FORUM.aspx?hl=golden+knights+storytelling&sc=0

10. Kostka A. College basketball's three-point shot moving back to international dis-

tance. *USA Today.* June 5, 2019. Accessed July 30, 2019. www.usatoday.com/story/sports/ncaab/2019/06/05/college-basketball-three-point-line-moving-back-international-distance/1357922001/

11. Bogage J. MLB reportedly offers to postpone pitch clock until 2022. *Washington Post.* February 27, 2019. Accessed July 30, 2019. www.washingtonpost.com/sports/2019/02/27/mlb-reportedly-offers-postpone-pitch-clock-until/

12. Humphreys B, Johnson C. The effect of superstar players on game attendance: evidence from the NBA. SSRN. July 31, 2017. Published online August 2, 2017. Accessed August 10, 2019. https://papers.ssrn.com/sol3/papers.cfm?abstract_id=3004137

13. Smith M. The business of Zion. *Street & Smith's Sports Business Journal.* March 11, 2019. Accessed August 10, 2019. www.sportsbusinessdaily.com/Journal/Issues/2019/03/11/In-Depth/The-Zion-Effect.aspx

14. Prather S. The Zion impact, Pelicans season ticket sales surge in one night. ESPN1420.com. May 15, 2019. Accessed August 10, 2019. https://espn1420.com/the-zion-impact-pelicans-season-ticket-sales-surge-in-one-night/

15. Wells A. Report: Pelicans sold 3,000 season tickets after winning lottery amid Zion hype. BleacherReport. May 15, 2019. Accessed August 27, 2019. https://bleacherreport.com/articles/2836454-report-pelicans-sold-3000-season-tickets-after-winning-lottery-amid-zion-hype

16. Lefton T. Penalty drop: Tiger Woods plummets on Sports Q Scores list. *Street & Smith's Sports Business Journal. June 7, 2010.* Accessed August 27, 2019. www.sportsbusinessdaily.com/Journal/Issues/2010/06/07/Marketingsponsorship/Penalty-Drop-Tiger-Woods-Plummets-On-Sports-Q-Scores-List.aspx

17. Nielsen. Tops of 2017: Pro athlete marketability. December 21, 2017. Accessed August 10, 2019. www.nielsen.com/us/en/insights/article/2017/tops-of-2017-pro-athlete-marketability/

18. Dawson A. The 18 most famous athletes in the world in 2018. *Business Insider.* May 24, 2018. Accessed August 28, 2019. www.businessinsider.com/most-famous-athletes-in-the-world-2018-5

19. Williams E. Finding the next Sean McVay: head coaches who call offensive plays. *ESPN.com.* blog. Posted online July 12, 2018. Accessed August 10, 2019. www.espn.com/blog/los-angeles-chargers/post/_/id/24331/finding-the-next-sean-mcvay-head-coaches-who-call-offensive-plays

20. Madkour A. Brand, culture and legacy of Jerry Jones is one thing: big. *Street & Smith's Sports Business Journal.* May 22, 2017. Accessed August 10, 2019. www.sportsbusinessdaily.com/Journal/Issues/2017/05/22/Opinion/From-The-Executive-Editor.aspx?hl=jerry+jones&sc=0

21. Wulf S. Athletes and activism: the long, defiant history of sports protests. *The Undefeated.* January 30, 2019. Accessed August 19, 2019. https://theundefeated.com/features/athletes-and-activism-the-long-defiant-history-of-sports-protests/

22. Taylor K, Green D. Here's how all of the NFL's sponsors have responded to backlash over players' national anthem protests. *Business Insider.* November 7, 2017. Accessed August 19, 2019. www.businessinsider.com/nfl-protests-how-brands-have-responded-2017-11

23. Richardson V. Survey: main reason for NFL's ratings slide was player take-a-knee protests. *Washington Times.* February 6, 2018. Accessed August 19, 2019. www.washingtontimes.com/news/2018/feb/6/nfl-ratings-down-due-anthem-protests-survey/

24. Abad-Santos A. Nike's Colin Kaepernick ad sparked a boycott—and earned $6 billion for Nike. Vox. September 24, 2018. Accessed August 19, 2019. www.vox.com/2018/9/24/17895704/nike-colin-kaepernick-boycott-6-billion

25. Youn S. Nike sales booming after Colin Kaepernick ad, invalidating critics. *ABC News.* December 21, 2018. Accessed August 19, 2019. https://abcnews.go.com/Business/nike-sales-booming-kaepernick-ad-invalidating-critics/story?id=59957137

26. Lee A. 25 most awesome fan fights in the stands. Bleacher Report. July 25, 2012. Accessed August 11, 2019. https://bleacherreport.com/articles/1272302-25-most-awesome-fan-fights-in-the-stands

27. Van Milligen D. How to prevent fan violence at sporting events. *Athletic Business.* February, 2015. Accessed August 11, 2019. www.athleticbusiness.com/stadium-arena-security/how-to-prevent-fan-violence-at-sporting-events.html

28. NFL.com. NFL teams implement fan code of conduct. August 5, 2008. Accessed August 11, 2019. www.nfl.com/news/story/09000d5d809c28f9/article/nfl-teams-implement-fan-code-of-conduct

29. Hyman M. Maryland concocting a code to kick the !@#$% out of its arena. *Street & Smith's Sports Business Journal.* May 10, 2004. Accessed August 28, 2019. www.sportsbusinessdaily.com/Journal/Issues/2004/05/10/This-Weeks-Issue/Maryland-Concocting-A-Code-To-Kick-The-$-Out-Of-Its-Arena.aspx?hl=maryland+code+of+conduct&sc=0

30. Ball State University. Help us pick the uniform combination for family weekend. April 30, 2019. Accessed August 11, 2019. https://ballstatesports.com/news/2019/4/30/help-us-pick-the-football-uniform-combination-for-family-weekend.aspx

31. Doughty A. Baylor football fans can vote on uniforms for Bears' season opener. Herosports.com. August 19, 2016. Accessed August 11, 2019. https://herosports.com/news/ncaa-fbs-mens-football/baylor-football-bears-vote-uniforms-northwestern-state

32. Smith M. Colleges find revenue stream in social media. *Street & Smith's Sports Business Journal.* October 12, 2015. Accessed August 11, 2019. www.sportsbusinessdaily.com/Journal/Issues/2015/10/12/Colleges/College-social-media.aspx

33. Branch J. Fans' uniform look is a team effort. *New York Times.* May 18, 2015. Accessed July 30, 2019. www.nytimes.com/2015/05/19/sports/basketball/in-sea-of-t-shirts-nba-hits-all-of-its-marketing-notes.html

34. Kuklick B. *To Everything a Season: Shibe Park and Urban Philadelphia, 1909-1976.* Princeton University Press; 1991.

35. Aoki N. Red Sox owners fielding more nongame revenue. *Boston Globe.* October 16, 2004. Accessed August 28, 2019. http://archive.boston.com/business/articles/2004/10/16/red_sox_owners_fielding_more_nongame_revenue

36. Muret D. Variety pays off as venues fill event dates. *Street & Smith's Sports Business Journal.* July 21, 2014. Accessed August 11, 2019. www.sportsbusinessdaily.com/Journal/Issues/2014/07/21/In-Depth/Events.aspx

37. Magrath AJ. When marketing services, 4 Ps are not enough. *Business Horizons.* 1986;29(3):44-50.

38. Deloitte Consulting LLP. The stadium experience: keeping sports fans engaged—and loyal. Accessed August 11, 2019. www2.deloitte.com/us/en/pages/technology-media-and-telecommunications/articles/stadium-experience-fan-satisfaction-survey.html

39. Temkin B, Lucas A. Fan experience benchmark: U.S. professional sports. Qulatrics XM Institute. April 2018. Accessed August 11, 2019. www.qualtrics.com/xm-institute/fan-experience-benchmark-u-s-professional-sports/

40. Cockerell L. Seven service guidelines. Leecockerell.com. April 16, 2011. Accessed August 28, 2019. www.leecockerell.com/seven-service-guidelines/

41. Lombardo J. Disney Institute, NBA align. *Street & Smith's Sports Business Journal.* November 4, 2013. Accessed July 30, 2019. www.sportsbusinessdaily.com/Journal/Issues/2013/11/04/Leagues-and-Governing-Bodies/NBA-Disney.aspx

42. FIFA training helped 15,000 workers get organized and prepare for World Cup visitors. Disney Institute. Accessed August 28, 2019. www.disneyinstitute.com/about/case-studies/sports-venues/fifa-training-helped-15000-workers/

43. The NFL's fan initiative scored big in customer service and engagement at Super Bowl XLVI. Disney Institute. Accessed August 28, 2019. www.disneyinstitute.com/about/case-studies/sports-venues/the-nfls-fan-initiative/

44. Steiner B. *You Gotta Have Balls: How a Kid From Brooklyn Started From Scratch, Bought Yankee Stadium, and Created a Sports Empire.* John Wiley & Sons; 2012.

45. Kovatch B. Babe Ruth bat sells at auction for $156,000. *Boston Globe.* March 25, 2019. Accessed August 28, 2019. www.bostonglobe.com/metro/2019/03/25/babe-ruth-bat-sells-auction-for/5Xdvn40kgcW8v6zIdvkR3H/story.html

46. Mueller R. Cobb T206 green portrait, Mantle rookie top $2.9 million memory lane sale.

Sports Collectors Daily. August 12, 2019. Accessed August 15, 2019. www.sportscollectorsdaily.com/cobb-cards-ruth-items-among-top-sellers-in-memory-lane-sale/

47. Broughton D. Closing shot: nod of approval. *Street & Smith's Sports Business Journal.* February 4, 2019. Accessed August 15, 2019. www.sportsbusinessdaily.com/Journal/Issues/2019/02/04/People-and-Pop-Culture/Closing-Shot.aspx

48. Broughton D. MLB giveaways: who can save attendance? *Street & Smith's Sports Business Journal.* December 10, 2018. Accessed August 15, 2019. www.sportsbusinessdaily.com/Journal/Issues/2018/12/10/Research-and-Ratings/MLB-attendance.aspx

49. Bucks 5th annual fan fest presented by Pick 'n Save. NBA.com/Bucks. 2018. Accessed August 15, 2019. www.nba.com/bucks/fanfest

50. Football fantasy camp information. Und. com. Accessed August 15, 2019. https://und.com/2018-notre-dame-football-fantasy-camp-information/

51. Schad T. ESPN The Magazine to cease regular publication in September after 21-year run. *USA Today.* April 30, 2019. Accessed August 15, 2019. www.usatoday.com/story/sports/media/2019/04/30/espn-magazine-cease-publication-after-septembers-body-issue/3626602002/

52. Andreessen M. Why Software Is Eating The World. *Wall Street Journal.* August 20, 2011. Accessed August 28, 2019. www.wsj.com/articles/SB10001424053111903480904576512250915629460

53. Impey S. Disney projecting up to 12m ESPN+ subscribers by 2024. SportsPro Media. April 15, 2019. Accessed August 16, 2019. www.sportspromedia.com/news/disney-espn-streaming-subscribers-2024

54. Industry demographics. Fantasy Sports & Gaming Association. Accessed August 16, 2019. https://thefsga.org/industry-demographics/

55. Valentine R. FIFA 18 sells over 24 million copies. GamesIndustry.biz. September 5, 2018. Accessed August 16, 2019. www.gamesindustry.biz/articles/2018-09-05-fifa-18-sells-over-24-million-copies

56. NBA2K 18 hits franchise sales record. *Businesswire.* August 2, 2018. Accessed August 16, 2019. www.businesswire.com/news/home/20180802005110/en/NBA-2K18-Hits-Franchise-Sales-Record

57. Badenhausen K. The world's 50 most valuable sports teams 2019. *Forbes.* July 22, 2019. Accessed August 16, 2019. www.forbes.com/sites/kurtbadenhausen/2019/07/22/the-worlds-50-most-valuable-sports-teams-2019/#2e0a5ec7283d

58. Higgins L. Alibaba's Joseph Tsai to buy rest of Brooklyn Nets. *Wall Street Journal.* August 14, 2019. Accessed August 16, 2019. www.wsj.com/articles/alibabas-joseph-tsai-to-buy-rest-of-brooklyn-nets-11565811497

59. Belson K. Carolina Panthers will be sold for $2.2 billion to David Tepper. *New York Times.* May 15, 2018. Accessed August 16, 2019. www.nytimes.com/2018/05/15/sports/football/carolina-panthers-sold-jerry-richardson-david-tepper.html

60. Kotler P. *Marketing Management: Analysis, Planning, Implementation, and Control.* Prentice Hall; 1997.

61. Badenhausen K. BodyArmor taps March Madness in quest to topple Gatorade. *Forbes.* March 20, 2019. Accessed August 21, 2019. www.forbes.com/sites/kurtbadenhausen/2019/03/20/bodyarmor-taps-march-madness-in-quest-to-topple-gatorade/#63d8b215fd74

62. Robertson D. How Gatorade invented new products by revisiting old ones. *Harvard Business Review.* August 17, 2017. Accessed August 24, 2019. https://hbr.org/2017/08/how-gatorade-invented-new-products-by-revisiting-old-ones

63. Schroeder E. PepsiCo to roll out new Gatorade platform. *Food Business News.* July 11, 2019. Accessed August 24, 2019. www.foodbusinessnews.net/articles/14098-pepsico-to-roll-out-new-gatorade-platform

64. Lefton T. Thinking back, looking ahead: Ed O'Hara. *Street & Smith's Sports Business Journal.* January 7, 2019. Accessed July 30, 2019. www.sportsbusinessdaily.com/Journal/Issues/2019/01/07/Marketing-and-Sponsorship/Ed-OHara.aspx

65. Zyman S. *The End of Marketing as We Know It.* Harper Business; 1999.

66. Willigan G. High-performance marketing: an interview with Nike's Phil Knight. *Harvard Business Review. July-August* 1992.

Accessed August 29, 2019. https://hbr.org/1992/07/high-performance-marketing-an-interview-with-nikes-phil-knight

67. Aaker DA. *Managing Brand Equity: Capitalizing the Value of a Brand Name.* The Free Press; 1991.

68. Hardy S, Norman B, Sceery S. Toward a history of sport branding. *Journal of Historical Research in Marketing.* 2012;4(4):482-509.

Chapter 7

1. The Business of Soccer. *Forbes.* Accessed May 9, 2019. www.forbes.com/soccer-valuations/list/#tab:overall

2. Nudd T. Inside PSG's grand plan to become the world's coolest sports brand: our interview with the French soccer club's U.S. chief. *Muse by Clio.* April 14, 2019. Accessed April 18, 2019. http://musebycl.io/sports/inside-psgs-grand-plan-become-worlds-coolest-sports-brand

3. *Aaker DA. Managing Brand Equity: Capitalizing on the Value of a Brand Name. The Free Press; 1991.*

4. Travis D. *Emotional Branding: How Successful Brands Gain the Irrational Edge.* Prima Venture; 2000.

5. Gobé M. *Emotional Branding: The New Paradigm for Connecting Brands to People.* Allworth Press; 2001.

6. Arruda W. The most damaging myth about branding. *Forbes.* September 6, 2016. Accessed April 18, 2019. www.forbes.com/sites/williamarruda/2016/09/06/the-most-damaging-myth-about-branding/#310ffd145c4f

7. Roedder John D, Torelli CJ. *Strategic Brand Management: Lessons for winning brands in globalized markets.* New York, NY: Oxford University Press; 2017.

8. NFL player arrests. *USA Today.* Accessed May 23, 2019. www.usatoday.com/sports/nfl/arrests/

9. Schad T. Kareem Hunt suspended 8 games by NFL for violating conduct policy. *USA Today.* March 15, 2019. Accessed May 23, 2019. www.usatoday.com/story/sports/nfl/browns/2019/03/15/kareem-hunt-suspended-cleveland-browns-nfl/3172956002/

10. Gladden JM, Funk DC. Understanding brand loyalty in professional sport: examining the link between brand associations and brand loyalty. *International Journal of Sports Marketing and Sponsorship.* 2001;3(1):54-81.

11. Gladden JM, Milne GR. Examining the importance of brand equity in professional sport. *Sport Marketing Quarterly.* 1999;8(1):21-29.

12. NHL attendance report. ESPN.com. Accessed May 23, 2019. www.espn.com/nhl/attendance

13. Fan Cost Index of National Football League teams in 2019 (in U.S. Dollars). Statista. Accessed September 25, 2020. www.statista.com/statistics/202584/nfl--fan-cost-index

14. Boudway I. Olympic sponsorships are about to get more expensive. *Bloomberg.* September 28, 2017. Accessed May 23, 2019. www.bloomberg.com/news/articles/2017-09-28/olympic-sponsorships-are-about-to-get-a-lot-more-expensive

15. Badenhausen K. FIFA World Cup 2018: the money behind the biggest event in sports. *Forbes.* June 14, 2018. Accessed May 23, 2019. www.forbes.com/sites/kurtbadenhausen/2018/06/14/world-cup-2018-the-money-behind-the-biggest-event-in-sports/#4c6879b96973

16. Keller KL. *Strategic Brand Management: Building, Measuring and Managing Brand Equity.* 4th ed. Pearson; 2013.

17. Kirshner A. The best and weirdest school Heisman Trophy campaigns: cardboard ties, ugly websites, billboards thousands of miles away, toy race cars, and more! *SB Nation* blog. Posted online August 15, 2018. Accessed May 21, 2019. www.sbnation.com/college-football/2018/8/3/17625796/heisman-trophy-campaigns-best

18. Macklin O. Clemson football's Twitter account provides Deshaun Watson's résumé to Heisman voters. *Washington Post.* December 3, 2015. Accessed May 21, 2019. www.washingtonpost.com/news/early-lead/wp/2015/12/03/clemson-footballs-twitter-account-provides-deshaun-watsons-resume-to-heisman-voters/?utm_term=.c4fa97ea9314

19. Patra K. J.J. Watt: $41.6 million in Hurricane Harvey relief shared. NFL.com. August 27, 2018. Accessed May 21, 2019. www.nfl.com/news/story/0ap3000000951756/article/jj-watt-416m-in-hurricane-harvey-relief-shared

20. Sokolove M. Follow Me. *New York Times.* February 5, 2006. Accessed May 21, 2019. www.nytimes.com/2006/02/05/magazine/follow-me.html

21. *Aaker DA. Building Strong Brands. The Free Press; 1996: 275.*

22. Thompson P. Bears stretch their marketing muscle with 1st Bears Fit Gym in Vernon Hills. Is a downtown location next? *Chicago Tribune.* May 1, 2019. Accessed May 9, 2019. www.chicagotribune.com/sports/bears/ct-spt-bears-fit-gym-20190501-story.html

23. Walsh P, Ross SD. Examining brand extensions and their potential to dilute team brand associations. *Sport Marketing Quarterly.* 2010;19(4):196-206.

24. Walsh P, Lee S. Development of a brand extension decision-making model for professional sport teams. *Sport Marketing Quarterly.* 2012;21(4):232-242.

25. Carlson C. Syracuse athletics announces creation of fan council to discuss fan experience, ticket sales. Syracuse.com. October 21, 2015. March 22, 2019. Accessed May 15, 2019. www.syracuse.com/orangesports/2015/10/syracuse_athletics_announces_creation_of_fan_council_to_discuss_fan_experience_t.html

26. Mather V. Will the Binghamton Mets become the Stud Muffins? The Internet will decide. *New York Times.* May 20, 2016. Accessed May 15, 2019. www.nytimes.com/2016/05/21/sports/baseball/will-binghamton-mets-become-binghamton-stud-muffins-the-internet-will-decide.html

27. Muzellec L, Doogan D, Lambkin M. Corporate rebranding: an exploratory review. *Irish Marketing Review.* 2003;16(2):31-40.

28. Stuart H, Muzellec L. Corporate makeovers: can a hyena be rebranded? *Brand Management.* 2004;11(6):472-482.

29. Walsh P, Clavio G, Ross SD, Blaszka M. Why teams rebrand: uncovering the motives and process of team rebranding initiatives. *Journal of Applied Sport Management.* 2018;10(4):12-21.

30. Ellis V. New—but old? Detroit Pistons unveil their next logo. *Detroit Free Press.* May 16, 2017. May 15, 2019. www.freep.com/story/sports/nba/pistons/2017/05/16/detroit-pistons-logo/324953001/

31. Lefton T. Loria's eye for art key to logo:

development took 28 months but it's a commercial hit. *Street & Smith's Sports Business Journal.* April 9, 2012. Accessed May 15, 2019. www.sportsbusinessdaily.com/Journal/Issues/2012/04/09/Franchises/Marlins-logo.aspx

32. Spencer C. Jeter's group unveils new-look Marlins logo and colors following marketing campaign. *Miami Herald.* November 15, 2018. November 16, 2018. Accessed May 15, 2019. www.miamiherald.com/sports/mlb/miami-marlins/article221574040.html

33. Darlow J. *Athletes Are Brands Too: How Brand Marketing Can Save Today's Athlete.* Jack and June Publishing; 2017.

34. Thomson M. Human brands: investigating antecedents to consumers' strong attachments to celebrities. *Journal of Marketing.* 2006;70(3):104-119.

35. Arai A, Ko Y, Ross S. Branding athletes: exploration and conceptualization of athlete brand image. *Sport Management Review.* 2014;17(2):97-106.

36. The world's highest-paid athletes: 2020 ranking. *Forbes.* Accessed September 25, 2020. www.forbes.com/athletes/list/

37. Instagram rich list 2020. *Hopper HQ* blog. Accessed August 5, 2020. www.hopperhq.com/blog/instagram-rich-list/niche/sport/

38. Sugarpova. Sugarpova website. https://sugarpova.com/pages/about. Accessed May 15, 2019.

39. Rossingh D. Maria Sharapova's candy brand nets deals with Hudson News, Sbe Hotels. *Forbes.* August 16, 2018. Accessed May 15, 2019. www.forbes.com/sites/daniellerossingh/2018/08/16/maria-sharapovas-candy-brand-nets-deals-with-hudson-news-sbe-hotels/#169e3aec90d5

40. TB12. TB12sports.com. Accessed May 15, 2019. https://tb12sports.com

41. TGR Tiger Woods Ventures. Tigerwoods.com. Accessed February 26, 2020. https://tgr.tigerwoods.com

42. Lefton T. J-E-T-S, new Jets, new Jets, new Jets! NFL team spends 5 years to craft rebrand. *Street & Smith's Sports Business Journal.* April 8, 2019. Accessed May 9, 2019. www.sportsbusinessdaily.com/Journal/Issues/2019/04/08/Marketing-and-Sponsorship/Marketing-and-Sponsorship.aspx

43. Weinstein A. New York Jets unveil new uniforms in glitzy NYC event. *The Sporting News*. April 4, 2019. Accessed May 9, 2019. www.sportingnews.com/us/nfl/news/new-york-jets-unveil-new-uniforms-glitzy-nyc-event/1qumz2k7uo54ezn347uph31xa

Chapter 8

1. Wright L. The 7 most important benefits of digital signage. *Promotion Technology Group* blog. Posted online November 30, 2018. Accessed March 18, 2020. www.promotion.tech/blog/7benefitsofdigitalsignage#:~:text=When%20the%20display%20utilizes%20video,over%20the%20past%2030%20days

2. *What can we expect from hologram technology in the future?* Clean-rooms.org. June 6, 2018. Accessed 11 July 2020. www.clean-rooms.org/what-can-we-expect-from-hologram-technology-in-the-future/

3. Ratna S. QR Code Marketing: QR code marketing: QR code use cases for proximity marketing in 2020. *Beaconstac* blog. Updated July 1, 2020. Accessed 11 July 2020. https://blog.beaconstac.com/2019/01/qr-code-use-cases-for-proximity-marketing-in-2019/#Here-is-a-list-of-things-businesses-can-do-with-QR-codes

4. Johnson, C. Virtual reality is here and it;s a huge opportunity. *Forbes.* November 17, 2017. Accessed on July 3, 2020. https://www.forbes.com/sites/forbescommunicationscouncil/2017/11/15/virtual-reality-is-here-and-its-a-huge-opportunity/#1d362bf37f41

5. Bain M. It's finally happened: The NBA is allowing teams to sell ad space on uniforms. Quartz. April 12, 2016. Accessed July 11, 2020. https://qz.com/663005/its-finally-happened-the-nba-is-allowing-teams-to-sell-ad-space-on-uniforms

6. Bassam T. Report: MLB to allow jersey patch sponsors. *SportsPro Media* blog. Posted online June 22, 2020. Accessed July 11, 2020. www.sportspromedia.com/news/mlb-jersey-patch-sleeve-sponsors-nba

7. Ravenshoe Group. CPG innovation: why your point-of-purchase displays are your secret weapon. March 13, 2019. Accessed July 11, 2020. www.ravenshoegroup.com/blog/why-point-of-purchase-displays-are-your-secret-weapon?

8. Pulcinella S. Why direct mail marketing is far from dead. August 30, 2017. Accessed July 11, 2020. www.forbes.com/sites/forbescommunicationscouncil/2017/08/30/why-direct-mail-marketing-is-far-from-dead/#7d3729cd311d

9. The effectiveness of pictures and words on memory recall. *UKEssays*. January 1, 1970. Published online November 2018. Accessed July 11, 2020. www.ukessays.com/essays/psychology/the-effectiveness-of-pictures-and-words-on-memory-recall-psychology-essay.php?vref=1

10. Koetsier J. Joe Rogan takes $100 Million to move podcast to Spotify, drops Apple, YouTube. May 19, 2020. Updated May 20, 2020. Accessed July 11, 2020. www.forbes.com/sites/johnkoetsier/2020/05/19/joe-rogan-moves-podcast-with-286-million-fans-to-spotify-drops-apple-youtube-other-platforms/#362bca4d2a23

11. Foster P. Storytelling and advertising: how to bring the two together. **The Next Ad** blog. Posted online January 16, 2019. Accessed July 11, 2020. www.thenextad.com/blog/storytelling-and-advertising-how-to-bring-the-two-together/

12. Veeck B, Linn E. *Veeck as in Wreck.* Putnam's; 1962.

13. Ziccardi D. *Masterminding the Store.* Wiley; 1997.

14. Berling-Manual L. Family fun comes to the forefront. *Ad Age.* 1984;2:11.

Chapter 9

1. Breer A. Inside the process of electing the Pro Football Hall of Fame's centennial class. *SI.com*. January 13, 2020. Accessed September 16, 2020. https://www.si.com/nfl/2020/01/13/bill-cowher-jimmy-johnson-nfl-hall-of-fame-kevin-stefanski-browns-nfl-news-notes?utm_medium=social&utm_campaign=themmqb&utm_source=twitter.com

2. Matas A. How David Baker surprised Bill Cowher, Jimmy Johnson on live TV. *CantonRep.com*. January 14, 2020. Accessed September 14, 2020. www.cantonrep.com/news/20200114/how-david-baker-surprised-bill-cowher-jimmy-johnson-on-live-tv

3. Sherman R. The Most Interesting Person of the Divisional Round: The Hall of Fame Guy. *TheRinger..com*. Jan 13, 2020. Accessed

June 28, 2020. www.theringer.com/nfl-play-offs/2020/1/13/21063295/david-baker-hall-of-fame-bill-cowher-jimmy-johnson

4. *Public relations defined: A modern definition for the new era of public relations.* Public Relations Society of America. April 11, 2012. Accessed June 28, 2020. http://prdefinition.prsa.org

5. Wojcik S, Hughes A. Sizing up Twitter users. Pew Research Center. April 24, 2019. Accessed September 15, 2020. www.pewresearch.org/internet/2019/04/24/sizing-up-twitter-users/

6. JJ Watt Foundation. Accessed September 15, 2020. http://jjwfoundation.org/the-foundation/hurricane-harvey-relief-efforts/

7. Caron E. JJ Watt's Hurricane Harvey relief funds has built more than 1,100 homes. *SI.com.* August 29, 2019. Accessed September 14, 2020. www.si.com/nfl/2019/08/29/texans-jj-watt-hurricane-harvey-funds-homes-built-meals-houston

8. Trejos A. Ice Bucket Challenge: 5 things you should know. *USA Today.* July 3, 2017. Accessed September 16, 2020. www.usatoday.com/story/news/2017/07/03/ice-bucket-challenge-5-things-you-should-know/448006001/

9. ALS Association. ALS Ice Bucket Challenge Commitments. Accessed September 17, 2020. www.alsa.org/fight-als/ice-bucket-challenge-spending.html

10. ALSAC/St. Jude Children's Research Hospital. Rich Eisen announces 2020 Run Rich Run campaign, benefitting St. Jude Children's Research Hospital. *Cision PR Newswire.* February 24, 2020. Accessed September 14, 2020. www.prnewswire.com/news-releases/rich-eisen-announces-2020-run-rich-run-campaign-benefitting-st-jude-childrens-research-hospital-301009780.html

11. @AndrewMarchand.Classy and nice gesture by the Jets, taking out an ad in The Post. January 25, 2020. Accessed January 25, 2020. https://twitter.com/AndrewMarchand/status/1221060874317848576/photo/1

12. Srinivasan A. Warriors take out full-page ad in newspaper to congratulate Raptors. *Yahoo!finance.* June 17, 2019. Accessed September 16, 2020. https://finance.yahoo.com/news/warriors-take-out-fullpage-ad-in-toronto-star-to-congratulate-raptors-parade-nba-finals-142912934.html

13. McCarthy M. Ad of the day: Gatorade's epic farewell to Derek Jeter will be tough to beat. *Adweek.* September 18, 2014. Accessed June 2, 2020. www.adweek.com/brand-marketing/ad-day-gatorades-epic-farewell-derek-jeter-will-be-tough-beat-160202/

14. @MikeReiss. On page A3 of today's @ TampaTimes . . . .March 22, 2020. Accessed March 22, 2020. https://twitter.com/MikeReiss/status/1241675256231796736

15. Wozniacki Becomes Godiva's First-Ever Athlete Endorser After Quote in Wall Street Journal. *Street & Smith's Sports Business Daily.* February 11, 2015. Accessed September 16, 2020. www.sportsbusinessdaily.com/Daily/Issues/2015/02/11/Marketing-and-Sponsorship/Wozniacki

16. Rovell D. Godiva brings on Caroline Wozniacki. *ESPN.com.* February 11, 2015. Accessed September 16, 2020. www.espn.com/tennis/story/_/id/12309182/caroline-wozniacki-signs-deal-godiva

17. Paul Rabil. Accessed September 17, 2020. www.paulrabil.com/

18. McCarthy M. 'Let's bring women in:' Chargers lean into podcast for female fans. *Front Office Sports.* November 26, 2019. Accessed September 16, 2020. https://frntofficesport.com/chargers-podcasts-female

19. Andrews M. Man Behind U.M.B.C. Twitter Account Also Takes a Victory Lap. *New York Times.com.* March 17, 2018. Accessed September 14, 2020. www.nytimes.com/2018/03/17/sports/ncaabasketball/umbc-twitter.html

20. Santana D. NFL and Twitter Drop Super Bowl Tweet Confetti With Eye on April's Draft. *Front Office Sports.* February 4, 2020. Accessed September 16, 2020. https://frntofficesport.com/nfl-twitter-super-bowl

21. Moran E. Amid high profile hacks, teams strengthen cybersecurity efforts. *Front Office Sports.* February 5, 2020. Accessed September 16, 2020. https://frntofficesport.com/cybersecurity-pro-sports

22. Michael Phelps named PRWeek's 2020 Communicator of the Year. *PRWeek.* February 25, 2020. Accessed September 14, 2020. www.prweek.com/article/1675133/michael-phelps-named-prweeks-2020-communicator-year

23. Bjornson G. Michael Phelps' 'The Weight of

Gold' Mental Health Doc Heads to HBO. *Decider.com*. June 29, 2020. Accessed July 3, 2020. https://decider.com/2020/06/29/hbo-acquires-michael-phelps-weight-of-gold-documentary/

24. @SEC. Statement from @SEC Commissioner @GregSankey on State of Mississippi flag. Jun 18, 2020. Accessed June 18, 2020. https://twitter.com/SEC/status/1273759965329731585/photo/1

25. NCAA Board of Governors expands Confederate flag policy to all championships. NCAA. June 19, 2020. Accessed July 6, 2020. www.ncaa.org/about/resources/media-center/news/ncaa-board-governors-expands-confederate-flag-policy-all-championships

26. Suss N. Opinion: Athletes and coaches played a huge role in changing Mississippi's state flag. *IndyStar*. June 30.2020. Updated July 1, 2020. Accessed July 1, 2020. www.indystar.com/story/sports/ncaaf/2020/06/30/mississippi-athletes-help-state-flag-change/5352904002

27. Board of Governors moves toward allowing student-athlete compensation for endorsements and promotions. NCAA. April 29, 2020. Accessed September 14, 2020. www.ncaa.org/about/resources/media-center/news/board-governors-moves-toward-allowing-student-athlete-compensation-endorsements-and-promotions

28. Brutlag Hosick M. DI Council adopts Olympic legislation. NCAA. January 22, 2020. Accessed September 15, 2020. www.ncaa.org/about/resources/media-center/news/di-council-adopts-olympics-legislation

29. IOC publishes sustainability report. IOC. October 8, 2018. Accessed September 14, 2020. www.olympic.org/news/ioc-publishes-sustainability-report

30. @PGATOUR. A letter from Commissioner Jay Monahan. March 13, 2020. Accessed March 13, 2020. https://twitter.com/PGATOUR/status/1238489234178220038/photo/1

31. Smits G. Coronavirus: 'day one' of Jay Monahan's vow to hold PGA Tour accountable to help community begins at Sulzbacher Center. *Jacksonville.com*. March 14, 2020. Accessed September 14, 2020. www.jacksonville.com/sports/20200314/coronavirus-lsquoday-onersquo-of-jay-monahanrsquos-vow-to-hold-pga-tour-accountable-to-help-community-begins-at-sulzbacher-center

32. Smits G. PGA Tour's charitable contributions reach $3 Billion. *Jacksonville.com*. January 28, 2020. Accessed September 16, 2020. https://www.jacksonville.com/story/sports/pga/2020/01/28/pga-tourrsquos-charitable-contributions-reach-3-billion/112222690/

33. @MLB. Heart and soccer emojis. March 18, 2020. Accessed March 18, 2020. https://twitter.com/MLB/status/1240301363029999616/photo/1

34. Sprunt B. Fauci interviewed by NBA star Stephen Curry on Instagram. *NPR.org*. March 26, 2020. Accessed September 16, 2020. www.npr.org/sections/coronavirus-live-updates/2020/03/26/822049565/fauci-interviewed-by-nba-star-stephen-curry-on-instagram

35. Medina M. Opinion: Stephen Curry's coronavirus interview with Dr. Anthony Fauci is most significant move of his career. *USA Today*. March 26, 2020. Updated March 27, 2020. Accessed July 3, 2020. www.usatoday.com/story/sports/nba/columnist/mark-medina/2020/03/26/stephen-curry-coronavirus-interview-anthony-fauci-most-significant-move/2922652001/

36. Key events in the Ray Rice story. *CNN.com*. September 16, 2014. Accessed September 17, 2020. https://www.cnn.com/2014/09/09/us/ray-rice-timeline/index.html

37. Cacciola S. Mavericks and Mark Cuban Sanctioned by N.B.A. Over Handling of Sexual Harassment. *New York Times.com*. September 19, 2018. Accessed September 16, 2020. www.nytimes.com/2018/09/19/sports/mark-cuban-mavericks-nba.html

38. Townsend B. 'This isn't just about three bad actors': The key points of the Mavs sexual harassment investigation and what happens now. *Dallas Morning News*. October 5, 2018. Accessed September 16, 2020. www.dallasnews.com/sports/mavericks/2018/10/05/this-isn-t-just-about-three-bad-actors-the-key-points-of-the-mavs-sexual-harassment-investigation-and-what-happens-now/

39. Seifert K. What really happened during Deflategate? Five years later, the NFL's

'scandal' aged poorly. *ESPN.com* January 18, 2020. Accessed September 14, 2020. www.espn.com/nfl/story/_/id/28502507/what-really-happened-deflategate-five-years-later-nfl-scandal-aged-poorly

40. Blum R, Golen J. Red Sox lose draft pick, Cora banned in sign-stealing scams. *Associated Press*. April 23, 2020. Accessed September 16, 2020. https://apnews.com/b0ad44d-1a136f97aacd0b0c3f130a00b

41. Associated Press. Ted Bishop out as PGA president. *USA Today.com*. October 24, 2014. Accessed September 16, 2020. www.usatoday.com/story/sports/golf/2014/10/24/ted-bishop-out-as-pga-president/17858909/

42. Bieler D, Boren C, and Bonesteel M. Thom Brennaman suspended by Reds and Fox Sports for homophobic slur. *WashingtonPost.com*. August 20, 2020. Accessed September 10, 2020. https://www.washingtonpost.com/sports/2020/08/19/reds-broadcaster-thom-brennaman-apologizes-making-homophobic-slur-air/

43. Greer D. The Daryl Morey controversy, explained: How a tweet created a costly rift between the NBA and China. *SportingNews.com*. October 23, 2019. Accessed September 10, 2020. https://www.sportingnews.com/us/nba/news/daryl-morey-tweet-controversy-nba-china-explained/togzszxh-37fi1mpw177p9bqwi

44. Deflategate timeline: after 544 days, Tom Brady gives in. *ESPN.com* blog. Posted July 15, 2016. Accessed September 16, 2020. www.espn.com/blog/new-england-patriots/post/_/id/4782561/timeline-of-events-for-deflategate-tom-brady

45. @darrenrovell. The comeback continues. Greatest sports image rehab of all time. January 23, 2020. Accessed January 23, 2020. https://twitter.com/darrenrovell/status/1220517528713166848

46. Bechtel M. Man caves and football wives. Black hats and creepie-peepies. *SI.com*. September 11, 2020. Accessed September 16, 2020.https://www.si.com/nfl/2020/09/11/monday-night-football-turns-50-daily-cover

47. Carter B. Roone Arledge, 71, a force in TV sports and news, dies. *New York Times*. December 6, 2002. Accessed September 16, 2020. www.nytimes.com/2002/12/06/business/roone-arledge-71-a-force-in-tv-sports-and-news-dies.html?pagewanted=all&src=pm

48. Carter B. On TV, timing is everything at the Olympics. *New York Times*. August 24, 2008. Accessed September 16, 2020. www.nytimes.com/2008/08/25/sports/olympics/25nbc.html

49. Crupi A. NFL games account for nearly three-quarters of the year's top 100 broadcasts. *AdAge.com*. January 8, 2020. Accessed January 8, 2020. https://adage.com/article/media/nfl-games-account-nearly-three-quarters-years-top-100-broadcasts/2225851

50. Clark K. How Mike Pereira changed the way we watch football forever. *TheRinger.com*. November 7, 2018. Accessed September 16, 2020. https://www.theringer.com/nfl/2018/11/7/18069164/mike-pereira-dean-blandino-explain-nfl-rules

51. @mulvihill79. Difference in national Nielsen household rating between the Super Bowl and the #1 entertainment show in primetime. January 27, 2020. Accessed January 27, 2020. https://twitter.com/mulvihill79/status/1221910874744475648

Chapter 10

1. Toyota is the first ever mobility partner of the Olympic movement. IOC. Accessed June 4, 2020. www.olympic.org/sponsors/toyota

2. Fischer B. Toyota's Olympic quest: the inside story of using Pyeongchang to rebrand as a mobility company. *Street & Smith's Sports Business Journal*. January 22, 2018. Accessed June 2, 2020. www.sportsbusinessdaily.com/Journal/Issues/2018/01/22/In-Depth/Toyota.aspx

3. Meenaghan T. The role of sponsorship in the marketing communications mix. *International Journal of Advertising*. 1991;10(1):35-47.

4. Fleming C. The 10 most expensive jersey sponsorship deals in world football. The18. January 8, 2019. Accessed June 4, 2020. https://the18.com/soccer-entertainment/most-expensive-shirt-sponsorship-deals-2019

5. Meehaghan J. *Commercial Sponsorship*. MCB University Press; 1984.

6. IEG's Guide to Sponsorship. IEG. 2017. Accessed June 4, 2020. www.sponsorship.com/ieg/files/59/59ada496-cd2c-4ac2-9382-060d86fcbdc4.pdf

7. Meehaghan J. *Commercial Sponsorship*. MCB University Press; 1984.

8. Wichmann SA, Martin DR. Sport and tobacco—the smoke has yet to clear. *Physician and Sports Medicine*. 1991;19(11):125-131.

9. Meyers N, Clarke L. No trouble foreseen in finding sponsors. *USA Today*. June 23, 1997.

10. http://sportsbusinessdigest.com/2010/06/ending-an-era-tobacco-sponsorship-in-nascar/

11. Johnson S. New research sheds light on daily ad exposures. *SJInsights* blog. Posted online September 29, 2014. Accessed June 4, 2020. https://sjinsights.net/2014/09/29/new-research-sheds-light-on-daily-ad-exposures/

12. Change in global advertising spending between 2020 and 2022, in million U.S. dollars. Statista. Accessed June 4, 2020. www.statista.com/statistics/269977/global-advertising-expenditure-by-medium/h

13. The rising cost of Super Bowl commercials: by the numbers. *The Week*. January 4, 2012. Accessed June 4, 2020. http://theweek.com/article/index/222982/the-rising-cost-of-super-bowl-commercials-by-the-numbers

14. Russ H. Super Bowl audience down five percent from last year, early data show. *Reuters*. February 4, 2019. Accessed June 4, 2020. www.reuters.com/article/us-football-nfl-superbowl-ratings/super-bowl-audience-down-five-percent-from-last-year-early-data-show-idUSKCN1PT1LK

15. Ueberroth P. *Made in America*. Morrow; 1985.

16. Verhoef PC, Leeflang PSH. Understanding the marketing department's influence within the firm. *Journal of Marketing*. 2009;73(2);14-37.

17. History of X Games. X Games. Accessed June 4, 2020. www.xgamesmediakit.com/read-me

18. Sutton WA. Sutton impact: proposed legislation has sports business in crosshairs. *Street & Smith's Sports Business Journal*. 2012;August 2-6.

19. Franklin R. *Making Waves: Contesting the Lifestyle Marketing and Sponsorship of Female Surfers*. Dissertation. Griffith University; 2012.

20. SWIX. L.L. Bean and Swix announce partnership with cross country team. Fasterskier.com. October 1, 2018. Accessed June 4, 2020. https://fasterskier.com/fsarticle/l-l-bean-and-swix-announce-partnership-with-cross-country-team/

21. Inside Audi's sponsorship strategy. IEG. May 15, 2017. Accessed June 4, 2020. http://www.sponsorship.com/iegsr/2017/05/15/Inside-Audi-s-Sponsorship-Strategy.aspx

22. Fischer B. After coming out, Kenworthy finds more interest from sponsors. *Street & Smith's Sports Business Journal. October 9, 2017*. Accessed June 4, 2020. www.sportsbusinessdaily.com/Journal/Issues/2017/10/09/Olympics/Kenworthy.aspx

23. Simon M. Anheuser-Busch donates sport and entertainment budget to coronavirus relief efforts. *Hill*. March 25, 2020. Accessed June 4, 2020. https://thehill.com/changing-america/well-being/prevention-cures/489490-anheuser-busch-donates-sports-and-entertainment

24. Novy-Williams E. How the Masters leaves millions on the table. *Bloomberg*. April 11, 2019. Accessed June 4, 2020. www.bloomberg.com/news/articles/2019-04-11/masters-leaves-cash-on-table-by-putting-its-brand-over-sponsors

25. NBA Fit Mission. NBA Cares. Accessed June 4, 2020. https://fit.nba.com/nba-fit-mission/

26. Dastin J, Paul A. Amazon, NFL reach $130 million streaming deal for Thursday night games: source. *Reuters*. April 26, 2018. Accessed June 4, 2020. www.reuters.com/article/us-nfl-amazon-com/amazon-nfl-reach-130-million-streaming-deal-for-thursday-night-games-source-idUSKBN1HX3EP

27. Patel S. Bleacher Report to broadcast live sports using Facebook Live. *Digiday*. October 13, 2016. Accessed June 4, 2020. https://digiday.com/media/bleacher-report-tackle-live-sports-using-facebook-live/

28. Booton J. NHL adds on-bench analytics to iPads in new SAP deal. *Sporttechie*. January 17, 2019. Accessed June 4, 2020. www.sporttechie.com/nhl-adds-on-bench-analytics-to-ipads-in-new-sap-deal

29. Mickle T. BMW: USOC deal drives strong sales. *Street & Smith's Sports Business Journal*. 2012;November:19-25.

30. Badenhausen K. Anheuser-Busch launches

revolutionary incentive-based sponsorship model. *Forbes*. April 2, 2018. Accessed June 4, 2020. www.forbes.com/sites/kurtbadenhausen/2018/04/02/anheuser-busch-launches-revolutionary-incentive-based-sponsorship-model//#337372ce3d5f

31. Lainson S. Client entertainment. *Sports News You Can Use*. 1997;12:1-3.

32. Marksbury J. At this week's Euro Tour stop, players must walk through Heineken tent to reach tee. *GOLF*. May 22, 2019. Accessed June 4, 2020. www.golf.com/news/2019/05/22/players-must-walk-heineken-tent-reach-tee-euro-tour/

33. Friedman A. Naming rights may be bargain for companies going national. *Street & Smith's Sports Business Journal*. 1998;1(3):8.

34. Lieberman N. Banking on sports: Industry aims to score big with the consumers. *Street & Smith's Sports Business Journal*. 2004;November:22-28.

35. Blosat G. NASCAR sponsors on social—top 10 brands from Daytona 500. *Zoomph* blog. Posted online February 12, 2019. Accessed June 4, 2020. https://zoomph.com/blog/nascar-sponsors-on-social-top-10-brands-from-the-daytona-500/

36. The World's Highest-Paid Athletes. *Forbes*. Accessed September 23, 2020. https://www.forbes.com/athletes/#5d4ea76255ae

37. Till B, Busler M. The match-up hypothesis: physical attractiveness, expertise, and the role of fit on brand attitude, purchase intent, and brand beliefs. *Journal of Advertising*. 2000;29(3):1-13.

38. The science behind sport: how Dow is helping make PyeongChang 2018 highly advanced and sustainable. Olympic Games. February 23, 2018. Accessed June 4, 2020. https://www.olympic.org/news/the-science-behind-sport-how-dow-is-helping-make-pyeongchang-2018-highly-advanced-and-sustainable

39. Weiner J. Organizations dismiss social media as fad at their own risk. *Street & Smith's Sports Business Journal*. 2012;July:16-22.

40. IEG's Guide to Sponsorship. IEG. 2017. Accessed June 4, 2020. www.sponsorship.com/ieg/files/59/59ada496-cd2c-4ac2-9382-060d86fcbdc4.pdf\

41. Welsh TJ. 19 tips to help leverage paid and organic social media throughout the customer journey. *SocialMediaToday*. November 20, 2018. Accessed June 4, 2020. www.socialmediatoday.com/news/19-tips-to-help-leverage-organic-and-paid-social-media-throughout-the-custo/542507/

42. Shea K. Inside the US Open: five brands that scored with tennis fans. Eventmarketer. September 12, 2018. Accessed June 4, 2020. www.eventmarketer.com/article/us-open-five-brands-scored-tennis-fans

43. IEG's Guide to Sponsorship. IEG. 2017. Accessed June 4, 2020. www.sponsorship.com/ieg/files/59/59ada496-cd2c-4ac2-9382-060d86fcbdc4.pdf

44. Skildum-Reid K. What should a rightsholder include in a year-end sponsorship ROI report? Power Sponsorship. Accessed June 4, 2020. https://powersponsorship.com/year-end-roi-report/

45. Skildum-Reid K. Sponsorship measurement: how to measure what's important. *Power Sponsorship*. Accessed June 4, 2020. https://powersponsorship.com/sponsorship-measurement-measure-whats-important/

46. Supreme Court strikes down PASPA, opens door to sports gambling. *Street & Smith's Sports Business Journal*. May 14, 2018. Accessed June 4, 2020. www.sportsbusinessdaily.com/Daily/Issues/2018/05/14/Sports-in-Society/Supreme-Court-Ruling.aspx

47. Sutton WA, McDonald MA. Building a partnership. *Athletic Management*, 1998;10(4):16-19.

48. www.sponsorship.com/About-IEG/Sponsorship-Blogs/Lesa-Ukman/july-2011/Sponsorship -Success-Depends-on-Activation.aspx

49. S. Feil, "The Social Side of Sponsorship: Sports Marketers Take Aim at Activating Fan Engagement," www.adweek.com/sa-article/social-side-sponsorship-137844.

Chapter 11

1. Kemp S. Digital 2020: 3.8 billion people use social media. *We Are Social*. January 30, 2020. Accessed April 12, 2020. https://wearesocial.com/blog/2020/01/digital-2020-3-8-billion-people-use-social-media

2. 140+ social media statistics that matter to marketers in 2020. *Hootsuite*. February 20,

2020. Accessed October 5, 2020. https://blog.hootsuite.com/social-media-statistics-for-social-media-managers/

3. NBA surpasses one billion likes and followers on social media. *NBA Communications*. February 12, 2016. Accessed October 8, 2020. https://pr.nba.com/nba-one-billion-social-media/#:~:text=TORONTO%20%E2%80%93%20The%20National%20Basketball%20Association,social%20media%20likes%20and%20followers.

4. Badenhausen K. NBA cracks the TikTok code as U.S. takes aim at world's hottest media app. *Forbes*. September 10, 2020. Accessed October 8, 2020. https://www.forbes.com/sites/kurtbadenhausen/2020/09/10/nba-cracks-the-tiktok-code-as-us-takes-aim-at-worlds-hottest-media-app/#700376662a54

5. Gandra A. How technology is improving the game-day experience. *Ostmodern Stories* blog. Posted online December 3, 2018. Accessed August 17, 2020. https://medium.com/ostmodern/how-technology-is-improving-the-game-day-experience-8912f24db795

6. Hickman C. The most social media savvy mascots. Business 2 Community. September 13, 2015. Accessed April 11, 2020. www.business2community.com/social-media/the-most-social-media-savvy-mascots-01323406

7. Westendorf J. Top 10 sports social media activations for the first half of 2019. *FANTHREESIXTY*. July 30, 2019. Accessed October 16, 2020. https://www.fanthreesixty.com/blog/winning-off-of-the-field-with-fan-engagement

8. The Miami HEAT scale up and score big with Facebook ads. *Facebook for Media*. January 2, 2020. Accessed October 12, 2020. https://www.facebook.com/facebookmedia/success-stories/the-miami-heat-scale-up-and-score-big-with-facebook-ads

9. Whitler K. Why word of mouth marketing is the most important social media. *Forbes*. July 17, 2014. Accessed October 16, 2020. https://www.forbes.com/sites/kimberlywhitler/2014/07/17/why-word-of-mouth-marketing-is-the-most-important-social-media/#4919a3ad54a8

10. Carufel R. Sports influencer marketing is taking off – here's the play-by-play. *Agility PR Solutions*. April 9, 2019. Accessed October 16, 2020. https://www.agilitypr.com/pr-news/public-relations/sports-influencer-marketing-is-taking-off-heres-whats-happening/

11. About Facebook. Facebook. Accessed April 12, 2020. https://about.fb.com/company-info/

12. Drell L. 5 Tips for marketing to sports fans on Facebook. Mashable. November 28, 2011. Accessed August 7, 2020. https://mashable.com/2011/11/28/facebook-sports-marketing/

13. Schäferhoff N. How to use Twitter to market and promote your sports team. *Themeboy* blog. Posted online August 18, 2016. Accessed August 7, 2020. www.themeboy.com/blog/twitter-sports-team-marketing-promotion/

14. Parker R. Use Twitter to increase sports fan loyalty. *Human Kinetics*. June 22, 2017. Accessed October 19, 2020. https://humankinetics.me/2017/06/22/use-twitter-to-increase-sports-fan-loyalty/

15. Schäferhoff N. How to use Instagram for your sports team marketing. *Themeboy* blog. May 12, 2016. Accessed August 7, 2020. www.themeboy.com/blog/instagram-sports-team-marketing/

16. Press. YouTube. Accessed April 12, 2020. www.youtube.com/about/press/

17. Gross N. How fans tune in to sports on YouTube. Think with Google. June 2016. Accessed August 10, 2020. www.thinkwithgoogle.com/consumer-insights/sports-content-on-youtube/

18. Bernazzani S. A Brief History of Snapchat. *Hubspot* blog. Accessed April 12, 2020. https://blog.hubspot.com/marketing/history-of-snapchat

19. 50 TikTok statistics that will blow your mind in 2020 [+INFOGRAPHIC]. Influencer Marketing Hub. January 11, 2019. Accessed October 19, 2020. https://influencermarketinghub.com/tiktok-statistics/

20. Soper T. How Steph Curry helped his digital marketing startup pivot and land a cameo in HBO's 'Ballers'. *GeekWire*. August 4, 2017. Accessed August 2, 2020.

21. Barshop S. A year after Harvey, $41.6 million raised by J.J. Watt is changing lives. *ESPN* blog. Posted online August 25, 2018.

Accessed August 2, 2020. www.espn.com/blog/houston-texans/post/_/id/22516/a-year-after-harvey-41-million-raised-by-j-j-watt-is-still-changing-lives

22. 2015 the world's highest-paid athletes earnings. *Forbes*. June 10, 2015. Accessed August 2, 2020. www.forbes.com/profile/jj-watt/#-6c70113a587f

23. P.K. Subban commits to raising $10 million to Montreal Children's Hospital. *CBC*. September 16, 2015. Updated June 29, 2016. Accessed August 13, 2020. www.cbc.ca/news/canada/montreal/p-k-subban-montreal-canadiens-children-s-hospital-1.3230086

24. Murphy D. What professional hockey players can teach you about personal branding. *CBC*. February 22, 2016. Accessed August 13, 2020. www.cbc.ca/dragonsden/m_blog/what-professional-hockey-players-can-teach-you-about-personal-branding

25. Social media stardom: how to make the most of Instagram. *Skillshare*. n.d. Accessed August 2, 2020. www.skillshare.com/classes/Social-Media-Stardom-Making-the-Most-of-Instagram/1716976994

26. Sherman M. Building their brands: the next step in how college athletes will profit off NIL. *Athletic*. March 13, 2020. Accessed April 10, 2020. https://theathletic.com/1673378/2020/03/13/nebraska-huskers-name-image-likeness-ncaa-legislation-opendorse-brand-building/

27. Chan G. 10 golden rules of personal branding. *Forbes*. November 8, 2018. Accessed August 12, 2020. www.forbes.com/sites/goldiechan/2018/11/08/10-golden-rules-personal-branding/

Chapter 12

1. Burdett, E. "Nothing happens until someone sells something." *PeakSalesRecruiting* blog. Posted online January 31, 2008. Accessed June 20, 2020. www.peaksalesrecruiting.com/blog/nothing-happens-until-someone-sells-something-2/

2. Higgins L. Women's professional soccer tries to seize the moment, again. *Wall Street Journal.* July 23, 2019. Accessed June 24, 2020. www.wsj.com/articles/womens-professional-soccer-tries-to-seize-the-moment-again-11563893693

3. Spain S. USWNT players draw sellout NWSL crowd to Chicago Red Stars game. ESPN.com. July 22, 2019. Accessed June 20, 2020. www.espn.com/soccer/fifa-womens-world-cup/story/3902668/uswnt-players-draw-sellout-nwsl-crowd-to-chicago-red-stars-game

4. Ourand J. ESPN gets NWSL rights, aiming to ride World Cup wave. *Street & Smith's Sports Business Journal.* July 15, 2019. Accessed June 20, 2020. www.sportsbusinessdaily.com/Journal/Issues/2019/07/15/Media/ESPN-NWSL.aspx

5. Tannenwald J. Can the USWNT's World Cup title push the NWSL to a long-waited breakthrough? *Philadelphia Inquirer.* July 23, 2019. Accessed June 20, 2020. www.inquirer.com/soccer/budweiser-nwsl-expansiona-amanda-duffy-merritt-paulson-portland-thorns-womens-soccer-20190723.html

6. Ibid

7. Ourand, J. ESPN gets NWSL rights, aiming to ride World Cup wave. *Street & Smith's Sports Business Journal.* 2019;July 15:12.

8. McCormack M. *On Selling.* Dove Books; 1996.

9. Honebein P. *Strategies for Effective Customer Education.* NTC Business Books; 1997.

10. Kerner N, Pressman G. *Chasing Cool.* Atria; 2007.

11. Peak Performance Management. Sales myth #3: sales people are born not made. *Sandler Training* blog. Posted online April 8, 2019. Accessed June 25, 2020. www.peakperformance.sandler.com/blog/salespeople_are_born_not_made#:~:text=Rarely%20is%20there%20a%20person,Salespeople%20are%20made%20not%20born

12. McCormack M. *On Selling.* Dove Books; 1996.

13. Feigenbaum E. What is the definition of consumer direct marketing? *Houston Chronicle* Accessed June 25, 2020. http://smallbusiness.chron.com/definition-consumer-direct-marketing-3477.html

14. KORESoftware. Accessed June 25, 2020. https://koresoftware.com/ticketing-fan-engagement/

15. KORESoftware. Case study: how the Oklahoma City Dodgers are driving major league efficiencies in Minor League Baseball. Accessed June 25, 2020. https://info.koresoftware.com/case-study-oklahoma-city-dodgers

16. KORESoftware. Case study: FC Barcelona takes their global brand across the world with KORE Software. Accessed June 25, 2020. https://info.koresoftware.com/case-study-fcb

17. Lombardo J. Ticketing: the laws of attraction. *Street & Smith's Sports Business Journal.* June 17, 2019. Accessed June 25, 2020. www.sportsbusinessdaily.com/Journal/Issues/2019/06/17/In-Depth/Tickets.aspx

18. Berkebile D. Branding tips to increase sales: does direct mail still work in a digital age? *Brandwise* blog. Posted online March 1, 2011. Accessed June 10. 2020. www.getbrandwise.com/branding-blog/bid/54291/Does-Direct-Mail-still-work-in-a-digital-age

19. Fisher E. Mariners introduce new Flex Membership model for season tickets. *Sportbusiness.* November 4, 2019. Accessed June 10, 2020. www.sportbusiness.com/news/mariners-introduce-new-flex-membership-model-for-season-tickets/

20. Jenkins S. Why your brand needs email smarts now more than ever in 2013. Clickz. January 10, 2013. Accessed June 25, 2020. www.clickz.com/clickz/column/2235299/why-your-brand-needs-email-smarts-more-than-ever-in-2013

21. Marketo. Accessed June 10, 2020. www.marketo.com/marketing-automation/

22. Oracle. Accessed June 10, 2020. www.oracle.com/marketingcloud/products/marketing-automation/

23. Brown-Wilson D. Face to face sales training. Bizfluent. September 26, 2017. Accessed June 10, 2020. https://bizfluent.com/about-6662197-face-face-sales-training.html

24. Spoelstra J. *Ice to the Eskimos: How to Market a Product Nobody Wants.* HarperCollins Publishers; 1997.

25. Futrell C.M. *Fundamentals of Selling, 12th Edition.* McGraw-Hill Irvin; 2011.

26. Futrell C.M. *Fundamentals of Selling, 12th Edition.* McGraw-Hill Irvin; 2011.

27. Grönroos C. *Service Management and Marketing: Managing the Moments of Truth in Service Competition.* Lexington Books; 1990.

28. Shani D. A framework for implementing relationship marketing in the sport industry. *Sports Marketing Quarterly.* 1997;6(2):9-15.

29. Minor League Baseball. Accessed June 25, 2020. www.milb.com/state-college/tickets/flexbook s

30. Levine P. *A.G. Spalding and the Rise of Baseball.* Oxford Press; 1985.

31. Lombardo J. Timberwolves say "happy birthday" with free tickets in data-driven promotion. *Street & Smith's Sports Business Journal.* September 16, 2019. Accessed June 25, 2020. www.sportsbusinessdaily.com/Journal/Issues/2019/09/16/Franchises/TWolves.aspx

32. For an enjoyable read and examples of how to sell, see: Veeck B, Linn E. *Veeck As in Wreck.* Putnam; 1962. Mike Veeck's successful exploits with the St. Paul Saints is chronicled in: Perlstein S. *Rebel Baseball: The Summer the Game was Returned to the Fans.* Holt; 1994. Mike Veeck has also written a book about his philosophy: Veeck M, Williams, M. *Fun Is Good.* Rodale Books; 2005.

33. Boeck G. Winning friends and influencing ticket buyers. *USA Today.* September 13, 2005:3C.

34. Maksymiw A. Influencer marketing defined. Open View Partners. January 7, 2011. Accessed June 10, 2020. http://labs.openviewpartners.com/influencer-marketing-defined/

35. Sutton B. Full Menu Selling and Other Thoughts for Ticket Sales Success. *Street & Smith's Sports Business Journal.* May 21, 2018; 23.

36. Fisher E. MLB ticketing in focus. *Street & Smith's Sports Business Journal.* October 8, 2018. Accessed June 25, 2020. www.sportsbusinessdaily.com/Journal/Issues/2018/10/08/Leagues-and-Governing-Bodies/MLB-Attendance.aspx

37. Fisher E. MLB ticketing in focus. *Street & Smith's Sports Business Journal.* October 8, 2018. Accessed June 25, 2020. www.sportsbusinessdaily.com/Journal/Issues/2018/10/08/Leagues-and-Governing-Bodies/MLB-Attendance.aspx?hl=secondary market&sc=0\

38. Fisher E. How teams benefit from tracking ticket's life cycle. *Street & Smith's Sports Business Journal.* August 7, 2017. Accessed June 25, 2020. www.sportsbusinessdaily.com/Journal/Issues/2017/08/07/In-Depth/Tracking-tickets.aspx?hl=secondary market&sc=0

39. Qualtics. What is customer lifetime value (CLV) and how do you measure it? Accessed June 20, 2020. www.qualtrics.com/experience-management/customer/customer-lifetime-value

40. Preiss S. The true cost of losing a customer. Customerthink. Jan. 9, 2019. Accessed June 24, 2020. https://customerthink.com/the-true-cost-of-losing-a-customer

41. Blanchard K, Bowles S. *Raving Fans: A Revolutionary Approach to Customer Service.* (Morrow; 1993.

Chapter 13

1. Ricker J. Is the NHL Winter Classic on the verge of irrelevance? *Sports Daily.* January 3, 2019. Accessed November 27, 2019. https://thesportsdaily.com/2019/01/03/is-the-nhl-winter-classic-on-the-verge-of-irrelevance

2. DeFranks M. What to expect for the Winter Classic: live animals, musical acts and a re-opened State Fair Midway. *Dallas Morning News.* November 22, 2019. Accessed November 27, 2019. www.dallasnews.com/sports/stars/2019/11/22/what-to-expect-for-the-winter-classic-live-animals-musical-acts-and-a-re-opened-state-fair-midway

3. Leslie M. 85,630 in attendance for Dallas Stars win at Winter Classic in the Cotton Bowl. *WFAA.* January 1, 2020. Accessed February 4, 2020. www.wfaa.com/article/sports/85630-attend-dallas-stars-win-winter-classic-in-cotton-bowl/287-41a5141c-9a26-4486-9076-f9fd15ace303

4. Thomas I. NHL plans a Classic fan fest for Chicago. *Street & Smith's Sports Business Journal.* December 24, 2018. Accessed November 27, 2019. www.sportsbusinessdaily.com/Journal/Issues/2018/12/24/Events-and-Attractions/NHL-fanfest.aspx?hl=Winter+Classic&sc=0

5. Thomas I. NHL's Mayer takes events to the next level. *Street & Smith's Sports Business Journal.* April 9, 2018. Accessed November 27, 2019. www.sportsbusinessdaily.com/Journal/Issues/2018/04/09/Leagues-and-Governing-Bodies/Mayer.aspx?hl=Winter+Classic&sc=0

6. Mendola N. Chelsea, Pulisic may tour U.S. in 2020. *NBC Sports.* April 18, 2019. Accessed November 27, 2019. https://soccer.nbcsports.com/2019/04/18/chelsea-pulisic-may-tour-u-s-in-2020

7. Karell D. Spanish FA once again opposes La Liga match in U.S. *NBC Sports.* October 17, 2019. Accessed November 27, 2019. https://soccer.nbcsports.com/2019/10/17/spanish-fa-once-again-opposes-la-liga-match-in-u-s

8. Field Level Media. MLB reports record merchandise sales in London. *Yes Network.* July 3, 2019. Accessed November 27, 2019. http://web.yesnetwork.com/news/article.jsp?ymd=20190703&content_id=308734740&fext=.jsp&vkey=news_milb

9. Dublin's Aviva Stadium to host the 2020 Navy-Notre Dame Game. University of Notre Dame. October 25, 2018. Accessed November 27, 2019. https://und.com/football-dublins-aviva-stadium-to-host-the-2020-navy-notre-dame-game

10. Fisher E. MLB teams use conventions to stay connected. *Street & Smith's Sports Business Journal.* January 30, 2017. Accessed November 27, 2019. www.sportsbusinessdaily.com/Journal/Issues/2017/01/30/Events-and-Attractions/MLB-conventions.aspx

11. Leinonen J. South Bay AVP pros win titles at tournament in New York City. *Beach Reporter.* Jun 12, 2019. Accessed November 27, 2019. http://tbrnews.com/sports/south-bay-avp-pros-win-titles-at-tournament-in-new/article_fbc81798-8d36-11e9-ac25-c72797618a4f.html

12. Galloway J. Watching the Falcons stadium debate, the Braves pursue something different. *Atlanta Journal-Constitution* blog. Posted online November 14, 2012. Accessed November 27, 2019. https://web.archive.org/web/20131111180508/http://blogs.ajc.com/political-insider-jim-galloway/2012/11/14/watching-the-falcons-stadium-debate-the-braves-pursue-something-different

13. Tucker T. Braves plan to build new stadium in Cobb. *Atlanta Journal-Constitution.* September 28, 2016. Accessed November 27, 2019. www.ajc.com/sports/baseball/braves-plan-build-new-stadium-cobb/g4N4VC7nuSPUX62DykwQ9K

14. Iannelli J. Here are all the places David Beckham almost brought his MLS team. *Miami New Times.* August 6, 2017. Accessed November 27, 2019. www.miaminewtimes.com/news/here-is-a-timeline-of-the-david-beckham-miami-mls-soccer-team-deal-9552137

15. Elfrink T. Miami-Dade approves $9 million land sale to David Beckham for stadium. *Miami New Times*. June 6, 2017. Accessed November 27, 2019. www.miaminewtimes.com/news/david-beckham-wins-miami-dade-county-approval-to-buy-9-million-land-for-new-stadium-9399711

16. Brenner S. For David Beckham and Miami, a bumpy road enters the homestretch. *New York Times*. February 22, 2019. Accessed November 27, 2019. www.nytimes.com/2019/02/22/sports/soccer/david-beckham-miami-mls.html

17. Reed A. David Beckham's Miami stadium site is 'contaminated' and closed until further notice. *CNBC*. August 21, 2019. Accessed November 27, 2019. www.cnbc.com/2019/08/21/david-beckhams-mls-miami-stadium-site-highly-contaminated-with-arsenic.html

18. Temkin B, Lucas A. Fan experience benchmark: U.S. professional sports. *Qulatrics XM Institute*. April 1, 2018. Accessed August 11, 2019. www.qualtrics.com/xm-institute/fan-experience-benchmark-u-s-professional-sports

19. Lombardo J. Chase Center: bayside bonanza. *Street & Smith's Sports Business Journal*. October 14, 2019. Accessed December 6, 2019. www.sportsbusinessdaily.com/Journal/Issues/2019/10/14/Facilities/Chase-Center.aspx

20. Fischer B. The more fun league: NFL aims for better fan experience. *Street & Smith's Sports Business Journal*. August 19, 2019. Accessed December 6, 2019. www.sportsbusinessdaily.com/Journal/Issues/2019/08/19/Leagues-and-Governing-Bodies/NFL-fan-experience.aspx?hl=parking&sc=0.

21. Dhingra K. Arena intends to be about more than games—it can be a spot to play or reflect. October 12, 2019. Accessed September 2, 2020. *Street & Smith's Sports Business Journal*. www.sportsbusinessdaily.com/Journal/Issues/2019/10/14/Facilities/Amenities.aspx

22. Oder N. Fears of a tight fit for Brooklyn's arena. *Bloomberg Citylab*. June 8, 2012. Accessed January 8, 2020. www.citylab.com/design/2012/06/fears-tight-fit-brooklyns-arena/2213

23. O'Keeffe M. A living nightmare: neighbors say life next to Atlantic Yards is like living in 'shark tank'. *New York Daily News*. April 11, 2016. Accessed January 8, 2020. www.nydailynews.com/sports/i-team/life-atlantic-yards-living-nightmare-neighbors-article-1.2597149

24. Stone A. Why waiting is torture. *New York Times*. August 19, 2012:SR12.

25. U.S. Department of Justice Civil Rights Division. Accessible Stadiums. Americans With Disabilities Act. Accessed December 6, 2019. www.ada.gov/stadium.txt

26. McAndrew S. UNR will spend $2 million to fix ADA mistakes from its Mackay Stadium renovation. *Reno Gazette Journal*. October 16, 2018. Updated October 17, 2018. Accessed December 6, 2019. www.rgj.com/story/news/education/2018/10/16/university-nevada-reno-mackay-stadium-make-ada-compliant/1597721002

27. Bruning J. Soccer-specific stadiums: key to MLS past and future. *Soccer Stadium Digest*. December 19, 2017. https://soccerstadiumdigest.com/2017/12/soccer-specific-stadiums-key-to-mls-past-and-future

28. MacAloon J. Olympic Games and the theory of spectacle in modern societies. In: MacAloon JJ, ed. *Rite, Drama, Festival, Spectacle: Rehearsals Toward a Theory of Cultural Performance*. Institute for the Study of Human Issues; 1984:241-280.

29. Gould J. First peek at MSG sky bridge suites. *New York Post*. October 14, 2013. Accessed January 14, 2020. https://nypost.com/2013/10/14/first-peek-at-msg-sky-bridge-seats

30. Harding Davis R. The Thanksgiving Day game. In: Reiss S, ed. *Major Problems in American Sport History*. Houghton Mifflin; 1997:116-118.

31. Garner D. Of parties, prose, and football. *New York Times*. October 16, 2011:TR1.

32. Melnick K. Dallas Cowboys AR photo booth lets you strike a pose with your favorite players. *VR Scout*. September 11, 2019. Accessed January 31, 2020. https://vrscout.com/news/dallas-cowboys-ar-photo-booth/

33. Verducci T. The age of aquariums. *Sports Illustrated*. April 9, 2012:58-59.

34. ABC 13. The crown jewel: all eyes on Katy

ISD's $70M stadium. *Abc13*. August 17, 2017. Accessed January 14, 2020. https://abc13.com/2319218

35. Para J. Photos: Katy ISD's new $70M football stadium ready for prime time. *Houston Business Journal*. August 17, 2017. Access January 14, 2020. www.bizjournals.com/houston/news/2017/08/17/photos-katy-isds-new-70m-football-stadium-ready.html

36. Evans P. Allegiant Stadium technology critical to fan experience. Front Office Sports. January 9, 2020. Accessed January 14, 2020. https://frntofficesport.com/allegiant-stadium-cox/

37. Jackson S. How the "sheer size" of SoFi Stadium sets itself apart. *The Rams*. October 11, 2019. Accessed February 4, 2020. www.therams.com/news/how-the-sheer-size-of-sofi-stadium-sets-itself-apart

38. Breech J. Atlanta Falcons' absurdly cheap food and beer prices just got even cheaper. *CBSSports.com*. August 24, 2018. Accessed January 19, 2020. www.cbssports.com/nfl/news/the-atlanta-falcons-absurdly-cheap-food-and-beer-prices-just-got-even-cheaper/

39. Chesterton E. The Marlins paid homage to Miami with a new '3-o-5' menu with ballpark favorites. *Cut 4 by mlb.com*. December 17, 2018. Accessed January 19, 2020. www.mlb.com/cut4/miami-marlins-introduce-a-new-3-o-5-food-menu-c301919276

40. Dhingra K. Postmates signs on for delivery at Dodger Stadium this season. *Street &Smith's Sports Business Journal*. August 7, 2019. Accessed January 19, 2020. www.sportsbusinessdaily.com/Daily/Issues/2019/08/07/Facilities/Dodgers-Postmates.aspx

41. Muret D. Welcoming fans with sensory issues: teams address special needs with more autism-friendly rooms. *Street & Smith's Sports Business Journal*. April 10, 2017. Accessed January 19, 2020. www.sportsbusinessdaily.com/Journal/Issues/2017/04/10/Facilities/Sensory-rooms.aspx?hl=autism&sc=0

42. Sunnucks M. Arena tour: Hawks nest. *Street & Smith's Sports Business Journal*. November 5, 2018. Accessed January 20, 2020. www.sportsbusinessdaily.com/Journal/Issues/2018/11/05/Facilities/Hawks.aspx

43. Infield party at Ally Beach passes now available for Ford Championship Weekend. Homestead Miami Speedway. October 1, 2019. Accessed January 20, 2020. www.homesteadmiamispeedway.com/Articles/2019/10/Infield-Beach-Party.aspx

44. Jaguars and Pet Paradise announce new details on NFL's first in-stadium dog park. *Jaguars*. June 28, 2018. Accessed January 20, 2020. www.jaguars.com/news/jaguars-and-pet-paradise-announce-new-details-on-nfl-s-first-in-stadium-dog-park

45. January TSP: SportsBiz execs look at the challenges sports leagues face as they try to engage the fan of the future. Turnkey Intelligence. January 7, 2020. Accessed January 20, 2020. https://turnkeyintel.com/january-tsp-sportsbiz-execs-look-at-the-challenges-sports-leagues-face-as-they-try-to-engage-in-fans-of-the-future

46. U.S. Bank Stadium guest experience team member employee handbook. US Bank Stadium. August 22, 2017. Accessed January 20, 2020. www.usbankstadium.com/assets/doc/FINAL-Guest-Experience-Handbook-8.22.17-843963ee29.pdf

47. Hardy S. Adopted by all the leading clubs: sporting goods and the shaping of leisure, 1800-1900. In: Butsch R, ed. *For Fun and Profit*. Temple University Press; 1990:71-101.

48. NBA Store NYC. Store NBA. Accessed January 20, 2020. https://store.nba.com/nyc-store/x-265968+z-785787-1605852944

49. About Patriot Place. Patriot Place. Accessed January 20, 2020. https://www.patriot-place.com/about/

50. Lefton T. New business model of the decade: Fanatics. *Street & Smith's Sports Business Journal*. December 16, 2019. Accessed January 23, 2020. www.sportsbusinessdaily.com/Journal/Issues/2019/12/16/Decade-Awards/Business-Model.aspx?hl=fanatics&sc=0

51. Lefton T. Fanatics signs unprecedented 17-year deal to run MLB's online licensed-product business. *Street & Smith's Sports Business Daily*. June 16, 2015. Accessed January 23, 2020. www.sportsbusinessdaily.com/Daily/Issues/2015/06/16/Marketing-and-Sponsorship/MLB-Fanatics.aspx

52. Lefton T. Fanatics gets Warrior's merchandising rights. *Street & Smith's Sports Business*

Journal. July 22, 2019. Accessed January 23, 2020. www.sportsbusinessdaily.com/Journal/Issues/2019/07/22/Franchises/Fanatics-Warriors.aspx?hl=fanatics&sc=0

53. Muret D. Colleges gain insights on merchandise sales. *Street & Smith's Sports Business Journal.* October 12, 2015. Accessed January 23, 2020. www.sportsbusinessdaily.com/Journal/Issues/2015/10/12/In-Depth/Merchandise.aspx?hl=merchandise+trends&sc=0

54. Weiner J. Walk-up sales stumble as technology advances. *Street & Smith's Sports Business Journal.* June 18, 2007. Accessed January 28, 2020. www.sportsbusinessdaily.com/Journal/Issues/2007/06/18/SBJ-In-Depth/Walk-Up-Sales-Stumble-As-Technology-Advances.aspx

55. Fisher E. 10 stories that will define the future of ticketing: 1. The NFL's new ticketing deals with Ticketmaster and StubHub. *Street & Smith's Sports Business Journal.* January 15, 2018. Accessed January 27, 2020. www.sportsbusinessdaily.com/Journal/Issues/2018/01/15/In-Depth/NFL-deals.aspx

56. Kaplan D, Fisher E. SeatGeek adds NFL, Cowboys deals. *Street & Smith's Sports Business Journal.* March 5, 2018. Accessed January 27, 2020. www.sportsbusinessdaily.com/Journal/Issues/2018/03/05/Marketing-and-Sponsorship/SeatGeek.aspx?hl=seatgeek+adds+nfl+cowboys&sc=0

57. Schupak A. Looking to buy or sell pre-owned Masters tickets? Buyers and sellers, beware! *Golf.* March 27, 2018. Accessed June 8, 2020. https://golf.com/news/tournaments/looking-to-buy-or-sell-pre-owned-masters-tickets-buyers-and-sellers-beware

58. Fisher E. 10 stories that will define the future of ticketing: 2. SeatGeek enters the big four leagues with deals with the New Orleans Saints and Pelicans. Is there more to come? *Street & Smith's Sports Business Journal.* January 15, 2018. Accessed January 27, 2020. www.sportsbusinessdaily.com/Journal/Issues/2018/01/15/In-Depth/SeatGeek.aspx

59. Fisher E. 10 stories that will define the future of ticketing: 4. Who will be the new StubHub president? *Street & Smith's Sports Business Journal.* January 15, 2018. Accessed January 27, 2020. www.sportsbusinessdaily.com/Journal/Issues/2018/01/15/In-Depth/StubHub-president.aspx

60. Fisher E. 10 stories that will define the future of ticketing: 3. Vivid Seats' active dealmaking. *Street & Smith's Sports Business Journal.* January 15, 2018. Accessed January 27, 2020. www.sportsbusinessdaily.com/Journal/Issues/2018/01/15/In-Depth/Vivid-Seats.aspx

61. Dhingra K, Fischer B. NFL mobile ticketing a work in progress. *Street & Smith's Sports Business Journal.* October 14, 2019. Accessed January 27, 2020. www.sportsbusinessdaily.com/Journal/Issues/2019/10/14/Leagues-and-Governing-Bodies/NFL-tickets.aspx?hl=venue+staff+training&sc=0

62. Impey S. NHL takes ticketless path with Ticketmaster extension. *SportsPro Media* blog. Posted online May 28, 2019. Accessed January 30, 2020. www.sportspromedia.com/news/nhl-ice-hockey-ticketmaster-ticketless-mobile-technology

63. Smith M. Schools go exclusively mobile to draw students. *Street & Smith's Sports Business Journal.* November 5, 2018. Accessed January 28, 2020. www.sportsbusinessdaily.com/Journal/Issues/2018/11/05/Colleges/Mobile-ticketing.aspx?hl=mobile+ticketing&sc=0

64. Fisher E. 10 stories that will define the future of ticketing: 8. Maturation of minor league sports ticketing. *Street & Smith's Sports Business Journal.* January 15, 2018. Accessed January 27, 2020. www.sportsbusinessdaily.com/Journal/Issues/2018/01/15/In-Depth/Minor-league-ticketing.aspx

65. Kaplan D. Miami Super Bowl could be the last with paper tickets as NFL rushes into mobile ticketing. *Athletic.* January 8, 2020. Accessed January 28, 2020. https://theathletic.com/1517182/2020/01/08/miami-super-bowl-could-be-the-last-with-paper-tickets-as-nfl-rushes-into-mobile-ticketing

66. Smith M. Paciolan's approach to mobile ticketing attracts colleges. *Street & Smith's Sports Business Journal.* September 30, 2019. Accessed January 28, 2020. www.sportsbusinessdaily.com/Journal/Issues/2019/09/30/Colleges/Paciolan.aspx?hl=mobile+ticketing&sc=0

67. Fisher E. 10 stories that will define the fu-

ture of ticketing: 7. Arrival of Ticketmaster's Verified Fan to sports. *Street & Smith's Sports Business Journal.* January 15, 2018. Accessed January 27, 2020. www.sportsbusinessdaily. com/Journal/Issues/2018/01/15/In-Depth/Verified-Fan.aspx

68. Ticketmaster's SafeTix™ encrypted tickets protect fans and provide artists with greater visibility into event attendees. *Ticketmaster.* October 7, 2019. Accessed January 28, 2020. https://business.ticketmaster.com/blog/ticketmasters-safetix-encrypted-tickets-protect-fans-and-provide-artists-with-greater-visibility-into-event-attendees

69. Lombardo J. Ticketing: the laws of attraction. *Street & Smith's Sports Business Journal.* June 17, 2019. Accessed January 27, 2020. www.sportsbusinessdaily.com/Journal/Issues/2019/06/17/In-Depth/Tickets.aspx

70. The new NBA app on Magic Leap is a game changer. Magic Leap. March 25, 2019. Accessed February 4, 2020. www.magicleap.com/news/product-updates/nba-app-launch

Chapter 14

1. Epstein A. The ambush at Rio. *The John Marshall Review of Intellectual Property Law.* 2017. Accessed June 23, 2019. https://repository.jmls.edu/cgi/viewcontent.cgi?article=1415&context=ripl

2. U.S. Constitution, art. 1, § 8, states, "Congress shall have the power to promote the progress of science and useful arts, by securing for limited times to authors and inventors the exclusive right to their own writings and discoveries."

3. Baird DG. Common law intellectual property and the legacy of international news service v. Associated Press. *University of Chicago Law Review.* 1983. Accessed June 23, 2019. https://cyber.harvard.edu/IPCoop/83bair.html

4. 15 U.S.C. §§ 1051-1127 (2009).

5. United States Patent and Trademark Office. Basic facts about trademarks. February 2020. Accessed June 23, 2019. www.uspto.gov/trademarks/basics/BasicFacts.pdf

6. *Blue Bell, Inc. v Farah Manufacturing Co. Inc.,* 508 F. 2d 1260 (5th Cir. 1975), citing *United Drug Co. v Theodore Rectanus Co.,* 248 U.S. 90 (1918).

7. 15 U.S.C. § 1051 (b) (1) (2009).

8. Baker TA Despite having priority over Seaver, Brady may want to pass on "Tom Terrific" trademark. *Forbes* June 6, 2019. Accessed October 12, 2020. https://www.forbes.com/sites/thomasbaker/2019/06/06/brady-seaver-tom-terrific-trademark/#5e8e9386e6b7

9. McElroy J. Tom Brady dislikes 'Tom Terrific' nickname, clarifies trademark filing." *Patriots Wire.* June 6, 2019. Accessed June 23, 2019. patriotswire.usatoday.com/2019/06/06/tom-brady-dislikes-tom-terrific-nickname-clarifies-trademark-filing/

10. Securing trademark rights: wwnership and federal registration. Digital Media Law Project. Accessed June 24, 2020. www.dmlp.org/legal-guide/securing-trademark-rights-ownership-and-federal-registration

11. *AMF, Inc. v Sleekcraft Boats,* 599 F. 2d 341, 349 (9th Cir. 1979).

12. McKelvey S, Grady J. Join the conversation: the evolving legal landscape of using hashtags in sport. *Journal of Legal Aspects of Sport.* 2017; 27:209-226.

13. *National Football League Properties, Inc. v Wichita Falls Sportswear, Inc.,* 532 F. Supp. 651, 658 (1982), citing *Levi Strauss & Co. v Blue Bell, Inc.,* 632 F. 2d 817 (9th Cir. 1980).

14. *Board of Supervisors for La. State University, et al. v Smack Apparel Co.,* 550 F. 3d 465 (5th Cir. 2008), *cert. denied,* 556 U.S. 1268; 129 S. Ct. 2759 (2009).

15. Duca R. Major League Baseball plays hardball with Cape League. *Cape Cod Times.* March 7, 2008. Accessed June 23, 2019. www.capecodtimes.com/article/20080307/News/803070339

16. Chinwah L. Colleges to high schools: stop using our logos. *Daily Herald.* November 30, 2010. Accessed June 23, 2019. www.dailyherald.com/article/20101130/news/712019831/

17. Trademark Dilution Act of 1995, 15 U.S.C. § 1125 (c) (amended Oct. 6, 2006).

18. 15 U.S.C. § 1114 (1) (2009).

19. 319 F. 2d 830 (7th Cir. 1963).

20. Kirkpatrick R. "Likelihood of confusion issues: the Federal Circuit's standard of

review. *American University Law Review.* 1990; 40:1221-1236.

21. 15 U.S.C. 1125 (2009).

22. 604 F. Supp. 2d 200 (2d Cir. 1979).

23. Trademark Dilution Revision Act of 2006, Public Law 109-312 (109th Cong.).

24. 15 U.S.C. § 1125 (c) (1) (2009).

25. 15 U.S.C. § 1125 (c) (2) (A).

26. *NCAA v Kizzang LLC*, 304 F.Supp.3d 800 (S.D. Indiana 2018).

27. Hanna J. NCAA wins another trademark infringement suit re "March Madness" and "Final Four". *Law in Sport.* Jan. 30, 2018. Accessed June 23, 2019. www.lawinsport. com/sports-law-news/item/ncaa-wins-another-trademark-infringement-suit

28. *Indianapolis Colts, Inc. v Metropolitan Baltimore Football Club, L.P.*, 34 F. 3d 410 (7th Cir. 1994).

29. 85 F. 3d 407 (9th Cir. 1996).

30. 15 U.S.C. § 1127 (2004).

31. *Nitro Leisure Products, L.L.C. v Acushnet Co.*, 341 F.3d 1356; 2003 U.S. App. LEXIS 17822 (2003).

32. *United States Olympic Committee v American Media, Inc.*, 156 F. Supp. 2d 1200 (D. Colo. 2001).

33. Protecting your trademark on the Internet: courts limit free riding on the information superhighway. *Newsletter, Intellectual Property Law Section of the ABA.* 2(3):1-12.

34. 15 U.S.C. § 1125 (d) (2009).

35. 15 U.S.C. § 1125 (d) (1) (A) (2009).

36. Brachmann S. Michael Jordan prevails in trademark case, earns right to use Chinese character mark for his name on merchandise. *IP Watchdog.* Jan. 9, 2017. Accessed June 23, 2019. www.ipwatchdog. com/2017/01/09/michael-jordan-prevails-trademark-case-chinese-character/id=76192/

37. Huang Z. Michael Jordan finally won the rights to his own name in China. *Quartz.* December 7, 2016. Accessed June 23, 2019. qz.com/857812/michael-jordan-won-the-rights-to-his-chinese-name-乔丹-qiaodan-in-china-after-supreme-peoples-court-ruling/

38. 947 F. Supp. 347 (N.D. Ill. 1996).

39. 17 U.S.C. §§ 101 et. seq. (2009).

40. 17 U.S.C. §1201-1205 (2009).

41. 17 U.S.C. § 102 (2009).

42. 17 U.S.C. § 106 (2009).

43. U.S. Copyright Office. *Copyrightable Authorship.* September 29, 2017. Accessed June 23, 2019. www.copyright.gov/comp3/chap300/ch300-copyrightable-authorship.pdf

44. University of Michigan Library. Copyright basics. 2018. Accessed June 17, 2020 https://guides.lib.umich.edu/copyrightbasics/copyrightability

45. 17 U.S.C. § 107 (2009).

46. *Monster Communications, Inc. v Turner Broadcasting System, Inc.*, 935 F. Supp. 490 (S.D.N.Y. 1996).

47. *National Basketball Ass'n. v Motorola, Inc.*, 105 F.3d 841 (2nd Cir. 1997).

48. 17 U.S.C. § 101 et. seq. (2009).

49. 622 F. Supp. 1500 (N.D. Ill. 1985).

50. Townley S. Intellectual property and the specificity of sports. *WIPO Magazine.* April 2019. Accessed June 23, 2019. www.wipo. int/wipo_magazine/en/2019/02/article_0008.html

51. Wall AM Sports marketing and the law: protecting proprietary interests in sports entertainment events. *Marquette Sports Law Journal.* 1996;7:77.

52. 364 F. 3d 1288 (2004).

53. Jahner K. Nike 'Jumpman' logo takes center court in photo copyright fight. *Bloomberg Law.* Dec. 17, 2018. Accessed June 23, 2019. news.bloomberglaw.com/ip-law/nike-jumpman-logo-takes-center-court-in-photo-copyright-fight

54. *Goldman v Breitbart News Network, LLC*, No. 17-CV-3144 (KBF), 218 WL 911340 (S.D.N.Y. Feb. 15, 2018).

55. 508 F.3d 1146 (9th Cir. 2007).

56. Reynolds A. New York court rebuffs Ninth Circuit's copyright "server test," finds embedded tweet displaying copyrighted image to be infringement. *Lexology* blog. Posted online March 2, 2018. Accessed June 23, 2019. www.lexology.com/library/detail.aspx?g=926a5241-f277-45df-8057-fec9319168e8

57. Crittenden J, Levine L, Willsey P. Bloggers beware: New York Federal Court holds inline linking may be copyright infringement. Lexology. March 5, 2018. Accessed June 23, 2019. www.lexology.com/library/detail.aspx?g=2d51dfae-5aa8-4b0c-a12c-afa0a5c8480f

58. 35 U.S.C. § 101 (2009).

59. 35 U.S.C. § 154 (a) (2) (2009).

60. Mullen L. Arena football asks court to crack back on rival. *Street & Smiths' Sports Business Journal*. 1998;1(7):13.

61. Smith JA. It's your move—no it's not! The application of patent law to sports moves. *University of Colorado Law Review*. 1999;70:1051-1065.

62. *Virginia State Board of Pharmacy v Virginia Citizens Consumer Council*, 425 U.S. 748 (1976): 761.

63. 447 U.S. 557, 100 S. Ct. 2343 (1980).

64. *Bailey v Kentucky Racing Commission*, 496 F. Supp. 2d 795 (W.D Ky. 2004).

65. Cal. 4th 939, 45 P.3d 24 (Cal. 2004).

66. McKelvey S. Atlanta '96: Olympic countdown to ambush Armageddon?" *Seton Hall Journal of Sport Law*. 1994;4(2):397-445.

67. Crow DD, Hoek J. Ambush marketing: a critical review and some practical advice. *Marketing Bulletin*. 2003;14(1):1-14.

68. Payne M. Ambush marketing: the undeserved advantage. *Psychology and Marketing*. 1998;14(4):323-331.

69. Glengarry J. *Let's Not Ambush Civil Rights*. Buddle Findlay; 2007.

70. Sandler D, Shani D. Olympic sponsorship vs. ambush marketing: who gets the gold? *Journal of Advertising Research*. 1989;29:9-14.

71. Townley S, Harrington D, Couchman N. The legal and practical prevention of ambush marketing in sports. *Psychology and Marketing*. 1998;15(4):333-348.

72. Meenaghan T. Point of view: ambush marketing: immoral or imaginative practice? *Journal of Advertising Research*. 1994;38(1):77-88.

73. Shani D, Sandler D. Ambush marketing: is confusion to blame for the flickering of the flame? *Psychology and Marketing*. 1998;4(1/2):62-84.

74. McKelvey S, Sandler D, Snyder K. Sport participant attitudes toward ambush marketing: an exploratory study of ING New York City marathon runners. *Street & Smith's Sport Marketing Quarterly*. 2011;21(2):7-18.

75. Liberman N. Marathon ambush a real head-scratcher. *Street & Smith's Sports Business Journal* April 28 2003;4.

76. McKelvey S, Grady J. Sponsorship program protection strategies for special sport events: are event organizers outmaneuvering ambush marketers? *Journal of Sport Management*. 2008;22(5):397-445.

77. Maese R. U.S. Olympic Committee changes name to recognize paralympians. *Washington Post*. June 20, 2019;98.

78. 36 U.S.C. § 220501 et. seq. (2000).

79. *United States Olympic Committee v Tobyhanna Camp Corporation d/b/a Camp Olympik, et al.*; M.D. Pa.; Civil Action No. 3:10-CV-162, 2010 U.S. Dist. LEXIS 117650; 11/4/10.

80. Brooks M. Redneck Olympics under fire from U.S. Olympic Committee. *Washington Post blog*. Posted online August 10, 2011. Accessed June 23, 2019. www.washingtonpost.com/blogs/early-lead/post/redneck-olympics-under-fire-from-us-olympic-committee/2011/08/10/gIQAnfS16I_blog.html

81. Maldonado C. The evolution of the Super Bowl clean zone. *Gambit*. Jan. 29, 2013. Updated November 20, 2019. Accessed June 23, 2019. www.theadvocate.com/gambit/new_orleans/news/the_latest/article_d846cebd-bae2-5c22-971c-985d8473a9cc.html

82. 42 C.P.R. 3d 390 (B.C. 1992).

83. *Cardtoons v Major League Baseball Players Association*, 95 F.3d 959, 967 (10th Cir. 1996), citing Vol. 1, McCarthy, J.T., The Rights of Publicity and Privacy, § 1.1[A] [1] (1996).

84. 43 Misc. 2d 219, 250 N.Y.S. 2d 529 (1964).

85. 202 F.2d 866 (2d Cir. 1953), cert. denied, 346 U.S. 816 (1953).

86. 316 F. Supp 1277 (D. Minn. 1970).

87. 363 N.Y.S. 2d 276 (1975).

88. 34 Cal. App. 4th 790, 40 Cal. Rptr.2d 639 (1995).

89. 85 F. 3d 407 (9th Cir. 1996).

90. *Daniels v FanDuel, Inc.*, No. 18S-CQ-00134, 2018 WL 5275775 (Ind. Oct. 24, 2018).

91. Indiana Code Title 32. Property § 32-36-1-1.

92. Gershengorn IH, Doroshow, Bhabbha IK, Sullivan AG. The Indiana Supreme Court's decision in Daniels v. FanDuel, Inc.: what it means for right of publicity law and the future of online sports betting. *Sports Litigation Alert*. 2018;15(21). Accessed October 12, 2020. http://www.sportslitigationalert.com/archive/2018_11_09.php

93. 280 N.W. 2d 129 (1979).

94. Wanat DE. Entertainment law: an analysis of judicial decision-making in case where a celebrity's publicity right is in conflict with a user's First Amendment right. *Albany Law Review*. 2003;67(1):251-277.

95. 332 F.3d 915 (6th Cir. 2003).

96. *Doe, a/k/a Tony Twist v TCI Communications, et al.*, 2002, Mo. App. LEXIS 1577 (Mo. Ct. App., July 23, 2002), aff'd in part, rev'd in part & remanded, 110 S.W.3d 363 (Mo. 2003), cert. denied, 2004 U.S. LEXIS 76 (U.S. 2004).

97. Baldas T. Pro sports: technology changes rules of the game. *National Law Journal* 2005 www.law.com/jsp/article.jsp?id=1109128216973

98. *C.B.C. Distributing and Marketing, Inc. v Major League Baseball Advanced Media*, 505 F.3d 818 (8th Cir. 2007). Cert. denied, 128 S. Ct. 2872, 171 L. Ed. 2d 831 (2008).

99. *CBS Interactive Inc. v National Football League Players Association, Inc. and National Football League Players Inc.*; D. Minn.; Civil No. 08-5097 ADM/SRN, 2009 U.S. Dist. LEXIS 368; 4/298/09.

100. *Jordan v Jewel Food Stores, Inc.*, 743 F.3d 509 (7th Cir. 2014).

101. Foley & Lardner. Michael Jordan v. Jewel Food Stores: the Seventh Circuit explores the boundaries of commercial speech. Lexisnexis. March 19, 2014. Accessed June 23, 2019. www.lexisnexis.com/legalnewsroom/constitution/b/constitutional-civil-rights/posts/michael-jordan-v-jewel-food-stores-the-seventh-circuit-explores-the-boundaries-of-commercial-speech

102. Janssen K. Michael Jordan's $8.9M verdict offers valuable lesson for firms, athletes. *Chicago Tribune*. August 22, 2015. Accessed June 23, 2019. www.chicagotribune.com/business/ct-michael-jordan-dominicks-analysis-0823-biz-20150822-story.html

103. Grimaldi JV. Washington Redskins react to fans' tough luck with tough love. *Washington Post*. September 3, 2009. Accessed June 23, 2019. www.washingtonpost.com/wp-dyn/content/article/2009/09/02/AR2009090203887.html.

104. 451 Mass. 417 (2008).

105. *McAllister v The St. Louis Rams LLC*, E.D. Mo.; Case No. 4:16-cv-00172.

106. Barrabi T. NFL's Rams to refund $24M to St. Louis fans who bought personal seat licenses. *FOX Business*. June 25, 2019. Accessed June 23, 2019. www.foxbusiness.com/features/nfl-rams-fans-st-louis-lawsuit-settlement

107. Pitt season ticket holders file class action suit against university. March 29, 2005. Accessed June 23, 2019. www.prnewswire.com/news-releases/pitt-season-ticket-holders-file-class-action-suit-against-university-54367592.html

108. Heart P. Accord reached in athletic ticket suit. *University of Pittsburgh Times*. June 9, 2005. Accessed June 23, 2019. www.utimes.pitt.edu/?p=944

109. Associated Press. Flyers sued over classic tickets. *ESPN*. May 7, 2012. Accessed June 23, 2019. http://espn.go.com/nhl/story/_/id/7901813/fans-sue-philadelphia-flyers-winter-classic-ticket-policy

110. Lord T, Miller L. Playing the game by the rules: a practical guide to sweepstakes and contest promotions. *Franchise Law Journal*. 2009;29:3-8.

111. *Humphrey v Viacom Inc., et al.*, Case No. 06-2768 (D.N.J. 2007).

112. Bortman E. The Jordan's furniture 'monster deal': illegal gambling? Taxable income? *Business Law Review*. 2008;41:31-43.

113. Burke A. Salem lawyer takes a swing at Jordan's 'Monster Sweep'. *Gloucester (MA) Times*. November 6, 2008. Accessed June 23, 2019. www.gloucestertimes.com/local/x645313948/Salem-lawyer-takes-a-swing-at-Jordans-Monster-Sweep

114. Rowley T. London 2012 Olympics: the first Twitter Games opens debate of athletes using social media. *Telegraph*. July 31, 2012. Accessed June 23, 2019. www.telegraph.co.uk/sport/olympics/diving/9442461/London-2012-Olympics-the-first-Twitter-Games-opens-debate-of-athletes-using-social-media.html

115. Furness H. Wayne Rooney reprimanded for advertising Nike on Twitter. June 20, 2012. Accessed June 23, 2019. www.telegraph.co.uk/technology/twitter/9343349/Wayne-Rooney-reprimanded-for-advertising-Nike-on-Twitter.html

116. *Guides Concerning the Use of Endorsements and Testimonials in Advertising*, 16 C. F. R. § 255.0 to § 255.5 (2010).

117. FTC staff reminds influencers and brands to clearly disclose relationship. Federal Trade Commission. Apr. 19, 2017. Accessed June 23, 2019. www.ftc.gov/news-events/press-releases/2017/04/ftc-staff-reminds-influencers-brands-clearly-disclose

118. Rexrode C. Twitter changes business of celebrity endorsements. *Afro News*. November 5, 2011. Accessed June 23, 2019. https://afro.com/twitter-changes-business-of-celebrity-endorsements/

119. Wildes JJ, Blum KS. Mark my words: protection of athletes' names & catchphrases in the U.S. *LawInSport*. May 7, 2015. Accessed June 23, 2019. www.lawinsport.com/topics/item/mark-my-words-protection-of-athletes-nicknames-catchphrases-in-the-u-s

120. Williams D. Athletes trademarking the phrase that pays. *ESPN* blog. Posted online July 13, 2012. Accessed June 23, 2019. http://espn.go.com/blog/playbook/fandom/post/_/id/6108/athlete-trademarks-becoming-commonplace

121. *Keller v Electronic Arts, Inc.*, 2010 U.S. Dist. LEXIS 10719 (N.D. Cal., 2010).

122. Baker, TA, Grady, J, and Rappole, J. Consent theory as a possible cure for unconscionable terms in student-athlete contracts. *Marquette Sports Law Review*. 2012; 22:, 619- 650.

123. *In re Student-Athlete Name & Likeness Licensing Litigation*, 2010 U.S. Dist. LEXIS 139724 (N.D. Cal. 2010).

124. Players to receive $40 Million. *ESPN*. September 27, 2013. Accessed June 23, 2019. http://espn.go.com/college-football/story/_/id/9731696/ea-sports-clc-settle-lawsuits-40-million-source

125. Edelman M. Appellate court decision in Hart v. Electronic Arts is a win for athletes and entertainers everywhere. *Forbes*. May 22, 2013. Accessed June 23, 2019. www.forbes.com/sites/marcedelman/2013/05/22/appellate-court-decision-in-hart-v-electronic-arts-is-a-win-for-athletes-and-entertainers-everywhere/#3e621f1d2576

126. *O'Bannon v NCAA*, (N.D. Cal., Aug. 8, 2014).

127. Mandour and Associates. Texas A&M sues Indianapolis Colts over "12th Man" trademark. *California Intellectual Property* blog. Accessed June 23, 2019. www.mandourlaw.com/blog/texas-am-sues-indianapolis-colts-over-12th-man-trademark/

128. Alesia M. Indianapolis Colts agree to stop using '12th Man' in settlement with Texas A&M. *Indy Star*. February 18, 2016. Accessed June 23, 2019. www.indystar.com/story/sports/2016/02/18/indianapolis-colts-jim-irsay-12th-man-texas-am/80564736/

129. Dosh K, Travis C. Bills fans settle with Texas A&M over 12th Man trademark use. July 30, 2014. Accessed June 23, 2019. www.outkickthecoverage.com/Bills-Fans-Settle-with-Texas-a-m-over-12th-Man-Trademark-Use-073014/

130. Rovell D. Seahawks reach 5-year licensing deal with Texas A&M. *ESPN*. August 11, 2016. Accessed June 23, 2019. www.espn.com/college-football/story/_/id/17274864/texas-aggies-lends-12th-man-trademark-seattle-seahawks-5-year-deal

131. Murray R. Lochte trademarks 'Jeah!'—his odd, vague, made-up catchphrase. *New York Daily News*. August 17, 2012. Accessed June 23, 2019. www.nydailynews.com/entertainment/gossip/olympic-gold-medal-swimmer-ryan-lochte-trademarks-jeah-odd-vague-made-up-catchphrase-article-1.1138569

132. *Jordan v. Jewel Food Stores, Inc.*, 2012 WL 512584 at 1 (N.D. Ill. Feb. 15, 2012)

Chapter 15

1. Poppick S. 10 Back to the Future predictions that came true. Money. October 20, 2015. Accessed June 9, 2020. https://money.com/back-to-the-future-day-predictions-accuracy

2. Robehmed N. Five things 'Back to the Future Part II' got right about 2015 technology. *Forbes*. October 21, 2015. Accessed June 9, 2020. www.forbes.com/sites/natalierobehmed/2015/10/21/five-things-back-to-the-future-part-ii-got-right/#2e394e8e20d2

3. Patel S. How to predict the future success of possible marketing channels. *Forbes*. April 8, 2017. Accessed June 9, 2020. www.forbes.com/sites/sujanpatel/2017/04/08/how-to-predict-the-future-success-of-possible-marketing-channels/#552b61856f13

4. Slack T, Byers T, Thurston A. *Understanding Sport Organizations: Applications for Sport Managers*. 3rd ed. Human Kinetics; 2021.

5. Game changer: rethinking sports experiences for Generation Z. *Neilsen*. December 19, 2019. Accessed March 6, 2020. www.

nielsen.com/us/en/insights/report/2019/game-changer

6. At the gate and beyond: outlook for the sports market in North America through 2023. PwC. Accessed March 6, 2020. www.pwc.com/us/en/industries/tmt/library/sports-outlook-north-america.html

7. Roberts D. NFL further warms to gambling by allowing stadium betting lounges. *Yahoo Finance*. February 25, 2020. Accessed March 30, 2020. https://finance.yahoo.com/news/nfl-further-warms-to-gambling-by-allowing-stadium-betting-lounges-164519139.html

8. Purdum D. Buffalo Wild Wings, MGM partner on sports betting. *ESPN*. September 5, 2019. Accessed March 30, 2020. www.espn.com/chalk/story/_/id/27540471/buffalo-wild-wings-mgm-partner-sports-betting

9. Pannekeet J. Newzoo: Global esports economy will top $1 billion for the first time in 2019. *Newzoo*. February 12, 2019. Accessed March 31, 2020. https://newzoo.com/insights/articles/newzoo-global-esports-economy-will-top-1-billion-for-the-first-time-in-2019

10. The Fortnite Team. The NFL returns to Fortnite. Epic Games. January 29, 2020. Accessed March 30, 2020. www.epicgames.com/fortnite/en-US/news/the-big-game

11. Paine N. Women's basketball was building momentum. Then all the games stopped. *FiveThirtyEight*. March 24, 2020. Accessed June 10, 2020. https://fivethirtyeight.com/features/womens-basketball-was-building-momentum-then-all-the-games-stopped/

12. Mora R. WNBA's TV ratings are rising fast in 2019. *New York Daily News*. June 12, 2019. Accessed June 10, 2020. www.nydailynews.com/sports/ny-tv-ratings-wnba-games-higher-last-year-20190612-ppzovay3gjhbxedlee74ofk3sy-story.html

13. Megdal H. Takeaways from the new NWSL TV deal with CBS. *Forbes*. March 11, 2020. Accessed June 10, 2020. www.forbes.com/sites/howardmegdal/2020/03/11/womens-soccer-news-takeaways-from-new-nwsl-tv-deal/#80f3107a6324

14. Broughton D. NFL offers top value, women's soccer most connection in sponsor rankings. *Street & Smith's Sports Business Journal*. May 11, 2020. Accessed June 10, 2020. www.sportsbusinessdaily.com/Journal/Issues/2020/05/11/Ratings-and-Research/rEvolution.aspx?hl=women&sc=0

15. Springer S. Women's sports can, and must be, part of our recovery plan. *Street &Smith's Sports Business Journal*. March 30, 2020. Accessed June 10, 2020. www.sportsbusinessdaily.com/Journal/Issues/2020/03/30/Opinion/Springer.aspx?hl=women&sc=0

16. Lefton T, Lombardo J. Study shows strong recognition rates for NBA jersey patch sponsors as new deals near. *Street & Smith's Sports Business Journal*. February 24, 2020. Accessed March 31, 2020. www.sportsbusinessdaily.com/Journal/Issues/2020/02/24/Marketing-and-Sponsorship/NBA-patch.aspx?hl=jersey+sponsorships&sc=0

17. Brown M. Why MLB seems primed to add sponsor patches on jerseys for 2022. *Forbes*. September 17, 2019. Accessed March 31, 2010. www.forbes.com/sites/maurybrown/2019/09/17/why-sponsor-patches-on-mlb-jerseys-seem-prime-for-2022/#2b9a79b919a6

18. Hamilton T. How close is London to getting an NFL franchise? *ABC News*. October 30, 2018. Accessed April 2, 2020. https://abcnews.go.com/Sports/close-london-nfl-franchise/story?id=58849499

19. Nash D. Why 2021 will be a massive year for the future of sports media. *The Sports Daily*. March 2, 2019. Accessed April 2, 2020. https://thesportsdaily.com/2019/03/02/why-2021-will-be-a-massive-year-for-the-future-of-sports-media

20. @Nike. Now more than ever, we are one team. #playinside #playfortheworld. March 21, 2020. Accessed April 7, 2020. https://twitter.com/Nike/status/1241364220555354113

21. Lefton T. Masking the problem: Face coverings have been the savior of the sports licensing industry. *Street & Smith's Sports Business Journal*. September 21, 2020. Accessed October 9, 2020. https://www.sportsbusinessdaily.com/Journal/Issues/2020/09/21/Marketing-and-Sponsorship/Masks.aspx?hl=masks&sc=0

Index

Note: The italicized *f* and *t* following page numbers refer to figures and tables, respectively.

About the Authors

Windy Dees, PhD, is an associate professor of sport administration in the School of Education and Human Development at the University of Miami. Her research expertise is in corporate sponsorship effectiveness and event marketing strategies, and how sport organizations can use these forms of marketing communication to enhance live events and generate revenue. Dees' research has examined a multitude of variables, including brand awareness, brand and event personality, image transfer, sponsorship effectiveness, purchase behaviors, and a multitude of event marketing and management factors. Her research has been published in *Sport Marketing Quarterly*, *International Journal of Sport Management*, *International Journal of Sports Marketing and Sponsorship*, *Journal of Sponsorship*, and *Sport Management Education Journal*.

Dees serves as the graduate program director for sport administration at the University of Miami. She has served as president of the Sport Marketing Association, executive editor of the *Global Sport Business Journal*, editorial board member for *Sport Marketing Quarterly*, and guest reviewer for many other sport management academic journals. Prior to entering academia, she was an account executive for Synergy Sports Marketing in Orlando, Florida, selling and servicing corporate sponsorships in professional golf.

Dees earned her bachelor's degree in psychology and communications from Rollins College in Winter Park, Florida; her master's degree in exercise and sport sciences from the University of Florida in Gainesville, Florida; and her doctorate in sport management from Texas A&M University in College Station, Texas. She is frequently invited to be a sport business expert in publica-

tions such as *Forbes*, *Bleacher Report*, *Variety*, and *Dallas Morning News* and has been a guest on ESPN Radio. Photo courtesy of University Miami.

Patrick Walsh, PhD, is an associate professor of sport management in the David B. Falk College of Sport and Human Dynamics at Syracuse University. He previously held faculty positions at Indiana University and the University of Miami. His research focuses on the brand management practices of sport organizations and how they can best harness the power of their brand to further their business objectives. He has examined topics such as the effectiveness of brand extensions in sports, the rebranding of sport organizations, and the use of new media forums—specifically sport video games and social media outlets—as marketing and branding tools. His research has been published in journals such as *Sport Marketing Quarterly*, *Journal of Sport Management*, *Sport Management Review*, *International Journal of Sports Marketing and Sponsorship*, and *Journal of Consumer Marketing*. Walsh has also served on the editorial boards of *Sport Marketing Quarterly*, *International Journal of Sport Management*, and *Journal of Global Sport Management*, and he was an executive board member of the Sport Marketing Association. In 2016, he was named a research fellow of the Sport Marketing Association, which honors individual accomplishments and excellence in sport marketing research.

Prior to entering academia, Walsh worked in marketing with the National Football League's Buffalo Bills and was an associate with Velocity Sports and Entertainment (now MKTG), where he developed and executed strategic marketing plans for a number of today's top sponsors of professional and collegiate sport properties. Walsh earned a bachelor's degree in marketing and entrepreneurship and emerging enterprises from Syracuse University, a master's degree in sport administration from Canisius College, and a doctorate in kinesiology with an emphasis in sport management from the University of Minnesota. Photo courtesy of Steve Sartori, Syracuse University.

Chad McEvoy, EdD, is vice provost for faculty affairs at Northern Illinois University, having previously served as a faculty member at Illinois State University and Syracuse University. McEvoy previously served as chair of the department of kinesiology and physical education at Northern Illinois University from 2015 to 2019.

McEvoy has coauthored three textbooks in the sport management discipline, and his research has been featured in more than 100 media outlets, such as the *New York Times*, *Wall Street Journal*, *The Chronicle of Higher Education*, *PBS Newshour* with Jim Lehrer, and *USA Today*. In June 2008, he served as a panelist before the prestigious Knight Commission on Intercollegiate Athletics in a discussion on the effectiveness of NCAA penalties for rule violations. McEvoy's research has also been published in leading sport management academic journals such as the *Journal of Sport Management*, *Sport Management Review*, and *Sport Marketing Quarterly*.

McEvoy served as president of the Sport Marketing Association and has previously held the roles of founding editor of *Case Studies in Sport Management* and coeditor of the *Journal of Issues in Intercollegiate Athletics*. McEvoy was the 2015 recipient of the prestigious Sutton Award, awarded by the Sport Marketing Association each year to an educator best exemplifying the organization's mission to expand the body of knowledge in sport marketing through close connection to the sport industry. Photo courtesy of Northern Illinois University.

Stephen McKelvey, JD, joined the Mark H. McCormack Department of Sport Management at

University of Massachusetts–Amherst in 2002, after spending 15 years in the sport industry in New York City.

His sport marketing, sponsorship, and sales experience includes six years in the corporate sponsorship division of Major League Baseball, where he served a pivotal role in the creation of the league's corporate sponsorship program and was instrumental in the generation of over $50 million in corporate sponsorship revenues. He subsequently spent six years building a profitable in-house sport marketing agency within one of the country's leading sport magazine publishers, developing and implementing sales promotions for clients like Wise Snacks, Beck's Beer, Century 21 Real Estate, U.S. Postal Service, and Suzuki.

Prior to joining the University of Massachusetts faculty, he taught as an adjunct professor of sport law at the Seton Hall School of Law. He has authored articles on sport marketing, licensing, and the law for publications such as *American Business Law Journal*, *Virginia Sports and Entertainment Law Journal*, *Seton Hall Journal of Sport Law*, *Entertainment and Sports Lawyer*, *Journal of Legal Aspects of Sport*, *Journal of Sport Management*, *Sport Management Review*, *Sports Business Journal*, and *Brandweek*.

McKelvey holds a bachelor's degree in American studies from Amherst College, a master's degree from the University of Massachusetts sport management program, and a juris doctorate from Seton Hall School of Law. He was admitted to the New York State Bar in 1993. Photo courtesy of University of Massachusetts.

Bernard J. Mullin, PhD, is chairman and CEO of The Aspire Group, a leading global management and marketing consulting business focusing on the sport and entertainment industry. He previously served as president and chief executive officer of Atlanta Spirit LLC, where he was

responsible for overseeing all team and business operations for the NBA's Hawks and NHL's Thrashers and management of the world-class Philips Arena.

Mullin's more than 30 years of experience in the sport management industry has involved executive positions with professional teams and leagues, where he specializes in start-ups and turnarounds, breaking numerous all-time league ticket sales and attendance records. In addition to his position in Atlanta, Mullin served as the NBA's senior vice president of marketing and team business operations, president and general manager of the IHL's Denver Grizzlies, senior vice president of business operations for the Colorado Rockies, and senior vice president of business for the Pittsburgh Pirates. He has also acted as the owner's representative on major design and construction projects, including Coors Field and University of Denver's award-winning athletic facilities.

Before and during his career in professional sports, Mullin spent several years in intercollegiate athletics and higher education. He served as vice chancellor of athletics for the University of Denver and as professor of sport management at the University of Massachusetts. Mullin holds a doctorate in business, an MBA, and a master's degree in marketing from the University of Kansas, where he coached the varsity soccer program. He holds a bachelor's degree in business studies from Coventry University in England, where he played soccer semiprofessionally for the Oxford City Football Club.

Stephen Hardy, PhD, was a professor of kinesiology and affiliate professor of history at the University of New Hampshire (UNH) until his retirement in 2014. In 2003 through 2004, he served as interim vice provost for undergraduate studies. Hardy has also taught at the University of Massachusetts (where he earned his doctorate), the University of Washington, Robert Morris College, and Carnegie Mellon University. Over three decades, he taught courses in sport marketing, athletic administration, and sport history as well as a popular introduction to the sport industry.

Besides *Sport Marketing*, his publications include *How Boston Played* (1982, 2003) and numerous articles, book chapters, and reviews in academic presses. He is completing a coauthored history of ice hockey. His reviews and opinions have appeared in popular outlets such as the *Boston Globe*, *New York Times*, and *Sports Business Journal*. From 1995 to 1999, he was coeditor of *Sport Marketing Quarterly*. In 1997, he was elected a fellow of the American Academy of Kinesiology and Physical Education. He has won college and university awards for excellence in research and teaching.

Hardy also has extensive experience in college athletics. He played hockey for Bowdoin College in the late 1960s and cocaptained the 1969-1970 team with his twin brother, Earl. After coaching stints at Vermont Academy and Amherst College, he joined the Eastern College Athletic Conference in 1976, where he served as assistant commissioner and hockey supervisor until 1979. During that time, he supervised collegiate championships in venues such as the Boston Garden and Madison Square Garden, and he worked closely with the NCAA Ice Hockey Committee and its affiliated championships. He served on the board of directors of the America East Athletic Conference from 2000 to 2002. In 2003, he was selected by the Hockey East Association as one of 20 special friends to celebrate the league's 20th anniversary. At UNH he served as faculty representative to the NCAA and chaired the president's athletics advisory committee from 1996 to 2011. He is a founder of the Charles E. Holt Archives of American Hockey, located at UNH's Dimond Library. He lives with his wife, Donna, in Durham, New Hampshire.

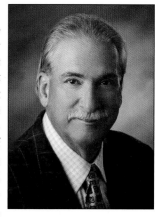

William A. Sutton, EdD, was the founding director and a professor in the sport and entertainment business management graduate program in the management department at the University of South Florida. He is the founder and principal of Bill Sutton & Associates, a consulting firm specializing in strategic marketing and revenue enhancement. Sutton has gained national recognition for his ability to meld practical experience in professional sports with academic analysis and interpretation.

His consulting clients cover a who's who of professional athletics: the NBA, WNBA, NHL, Orlando Magic, Phoenix Suns, MSG Sports, and New York Mets. Sutton frequently serves as an expert on the sport business industry. His insights and commentary have appeared in a variety of media outlets: *USA Today*, *New York Times*, CNBC. com, *Washington Times*, Fox Business, *Orlando Sentinel*, *South Florida Sun-Sentinel*, *Advertising Age*, and *Brandweek*. On the international front, Sutton is a contributor to the Italian publications *Basketball Gigante* and *FIBA Assist*.

Sutton served as vice president of team marketing and business operations for the National Basketball Association. In addition to working at the NBA, Sutton was past president of the North American Society for Sport Management (NASSM), a founding member and past president of the Sport Marketing Association (SMA), president of the Southern Sport Management Association, a special events coordinator for the city of Pittsburgh, a YMCA director, vice president of information services for an international sport marketing firm, and commissioner of the Mid Ohio Athletic Conference. He was inducted into the College of Education Hall of Fame at Oklahoma State University (2003) and was an inaugural member of the Robert Morris University Sport Management Hall of Fame (2006). He has received lifetime achievement awards from the Southern Sport Management Association (2012) and the Sport Entertainment & Venues Tomorrow conference at the University of South Carolina. He lives with his wife, Sharon, in Tampa and Clearwater Beach, Florida.

Contributors

Kathy Connors, MS
  Principal and Founder
  KMC Consulting

Melissa Davies, PhD
  Assistant Professor
  Ohio University

Karen Freberg, PhD
  Associate Professor
  University of Louisville

John Grady, JD, PhD
  Professor
  University of South Carolina

Shawn McGee, BBA Marketing
  Senior Director of Development
  University of Miami Health System

Warren A. Whisenant, PhD
  Professor
  University of Miami